WORLD TRADE ORGANIZATION

Dispute Settlement Reports

2000
Volume VIII

Pages 3539-4090

CAMBRIDGE
UNIVERSITY PRESS

PUBLISHED BY THE PRESS SYNDICATE OF THE UNIVERSITY OF CAMBRIDGE
The Pitt Building, Trumpington Street, Cambridge, United Kingdom

CAMBRIDGE UNIVERSITY PRESS
The Edinburgh Building, Cambridge CB2 2RU, UK
40 West 20th Street, New York, NY 10011–4211, USA
477 Williamstown Road, Port Melbourne, VIC 3207, Australia
Ruiz de Alarcón 13, 28014 Madrid, Spain
Dock House, The Waterfront, Cape Town 8001, South Africa

http://www.cambridge.org

Printed in the United Kingdom at the University Press, Cambridge

French edition and Spanish edition paperbacks of this title are both available directly from WTO Publications, World Trade Organization, Centre William Rappard, 154 rue de Lausanne, CH-1211 Geneva 21, Switzerland http://www.wto.org

ISBN 0 521 82854 6 hardback

THE WTO DISPUTE SETTLEMENT REPORTS

The *Dispute Settlement Reports* of the World Trade Organization (the "WTO") include panel and Appellate Body reports, as well as arbitration awards, in disputes concerning the rights and obligations of WTO Members under the provisions of the *Marrakesh Agreement Establishing the World Trade Organization*. The *Dispute Settlement Reports* are available in English, French and Spanish. Starting with 1999, the first volume of each year contains a cumulative index of published disputes.

This volume may be cited as DSR 2000:VIII

TABLE OF CONTENTS

KOREA - MEASURES AFFECTING GOVERNMENT PROCUREMENT

Report of the Panel

WT/DS163/R

Adopted by the Dispute Settlement Body on 19 June 2000

TABLE OF CONTENTS

I. PROCEDURAL BACKGROUND

1.1 On 16 February 1999, the United States requested Korea to hold consultations pursuant to Article 4 of the Understanding on Rules and Procedures Governing the Settlement of Disputes ("DSU") and Article XXII of the Agreement on Government Procurement (WT/DS163/1 and GPA/D4/1) regarding certain procurement practices of entities concerned with the procurement of airport construction for Inchon International Airport ("IIA") in Korea. The European Communities requested to join in the consultations on 8 March 1999 (WT/DS163/2) and Japan made the same request on 9 March 1999 (WT/DS163/3). Korea accepted neither of these requests.

1.2 A mutually satisfactory solution was not reached during the consultations held between the United States and Korea on 17 March 1999. In a communication dated 11 May 1999, the United States requested the Dispute Settlement Body (DSB) to establish a panel to examine the matter.[1]

1.3 At its meeting on 16 June 1999, the Dispute Settlement Body agreed to establish a panel in accordance with the provisions of Article 6 of the DSU and Article XXII of the GPA, with the following standard terms of reference pursuant to Article XXII:4 GPA:

> "To examine, in the light of the relevant provisions of the Agreement on Government Procurement, the matter referred to the DSB by the United States in document WT/DS163/4, and to make such findings as will assist the DSB in making the recommendations or in giving the rulings provided for in that Agreement."[2]

1.4 The European Communities and Japan reserved third party rights.

---

1 WT/DS163/4 reproduced in Annex 1 to this report.

2 WT/DSB/M/64.

1.5 The Panel was composed on 30 August 1999 (WT/DS163/5). The composition of the Panel was as follows:

Chairman: Mr. Michael D. Cartland

Panelists: Ms. Marie-Gabrielle Ineichen-Fleisch

Mr. Peter-Armin Trepte

1.6 The Panel heard the parties to the dispute on 19 October 1999 and 11 November 1999. The interim report was issued to the parties on 3 March 2000.

II. FACTUAL ASPECTS[3]

A. Introduction

2.1 This dispute relates to the Inchon International Airport (IIA) project, which is being constructed in the Republic of Korea. At issue is whether the entities that have had procurement responsibility for the project since its inception are "covered entities" under the Agreement on Government Procurement. The United States also raised the issue of whether the procurement practices of these entities are or have been inconsistent with Korea's obligations under the Agreement on Government Procurement and whether they nullify or impair benefits accruing to the United States under that Agreement.

B. The Agreement on Government Procurement

1. Uruguay Round Negotiations of the GPA

2.2 The original Agreement on Government Procurement was negotiated during the Tokyo Round of trade negotiations and was done in Geneva on 12 April 1979 ("Tokyo Round Agreement"). This Agreement was amended following negotiations in pursuance of Article IX:6(b) through a Protocol which entered into force on 14 February 1988. During the Uruguay Round of Trade Negotiations, Parties to the Tokyo Round Agreement held further negotiations in the context of an Informal Working Group[4], which involved the broadening of entity coverage, expansion of the coverage to services and construction services and further improvements of the text of the Agreement.

2.3 Coverage negotiations were initiated through a bilateral request/offer process in September 1990. These negotiations involved the tabling of offers and the submission of requests by interested Parties to their trading partners.

2.4 Following the bilateral negotiations for improvement and the finalization of specific offers which occurred in 1993, the final text of the Agreement with the attached draft schedule of parties was issued on 15 December 1993. On that date, the Informal Working Group adopted a Decision concluding negotiations and agreeing that the text entitled Agreement on Government Procurement, together with Annexes

---

[3] All Korean legislation referred to in this report was translated into English by the Government of the Republic of Korea.

[4] The Informal Working Group on Negotiations was originally established in May 1985 to improve the text of the Tokyo Round Agreement.

1-5 of Appendix I of each of the participants embodied the results of their negotiations as at that date.[5] The Decision further specified procedures relating to outstanding work to be completed prior to the entry into force of the Agreement.[6]

2.5 Further, a decision of the Informal Working Group on negotiations, dated 17 January 1994, entitled "Modifications of the Annexes to Appendix I to the Agreement on Government Procurement before its Entry into Force on 1 January 1996", set out procedures for the incorporation into the Agreement of modifications expanding coverage that were agreed and resulted from negotiations between the date of signature of the Agreement and the date of its entry into force.

2.6 The Agreement on Government Procurement (1994) (the GPA) was signed in Marrakesh on 15 April 1994. The GPA entered into force on 1 January 1996.

2. *Overview of the Scope and Coverage of the GPA*

2.7 The GPA establishes an agreed framework of rights and obligations among its Parties with respect to their national laws, regulations, procedures and practices in the area of government procurement.

2.8 The obligations under the Agreement apply to procurement:

(a) by procuring entities that each Party has listed in Annexes 1 to 3 of Appendix I relating respectively to "central government entities," "sub-central government entities" and "other entities";

(b) of all products; and

(c) of services and construction services that are specified in lists found respectively in Annexes 4 and 5 of Appendix I.

2.9 Furthermore, GPA coverage under each of the Annexes is contingent upon certain threshold values being exceeded. These threshold values are expressed in terms of Special Drawing Rights (SDRs). GPA coverage under each of the Annexes is also contingent upon the various notes found in the Annexes.

---

5 GPR/SPEC/77.

6 Specifically, para. 4 of the Decision stated:

> Participants will submit to the Secretariat by 31 January 1994 the texts of their Annexes in final form for circulation to all participants. Those Annexes will be considered accepted by participants as corresponding to what had been negotiated and agreed, unless the Secretariat is notified to the contrary prior to 28 February 1994. In the event of problems, consultations will be held to resolve the matter.

Further, para. 6 of the Decision stated:

> Proposed modifications of the Annexes to Appendix I of participants that expand the coverage of the Agreement and that result from further negotiations between now and the date of signature of the Agreement will be deemed part of the agreed results of the negotiations provided that no participant objects to such modifications. To enable all participants to examine any such modifications in advance of the date of signature, modifications should be notified to other participants through the Secretariat by 31 March 1994.

C. *Korea's Accession to the Agreement on Government Procurement*

1. *Korea's Application for Accession*

2.10 Korea was not a Party to the Tokyo Round Agreement. However, in a communication dated 25 June 1990, the Government of the Republic of Korea indicated its interest in exploring the possibility of acceding to the GPA. Attached to this communication was a note containing a list of purchasing entities and products for which coverage was proposed together with explanatory notes.[7]

2.11 Further, in a communication dated 20 September 1991[8], the Government of the Republic of Korea indicated that following submission of its initial offer to the Committee on Government Procurement on 25 June 1990, it had held bilateral consultations with the Parties in relation to its offer list. The communication also requested permission to participate in the Uruguay Round negotiations. This request was acceded to.[9]

2.12 Leading up to its accession to the GPA on 15 April 1994, Korea submitted to the Committee on Government Procurement, a series of offers concerning its commitments under the GPA upon accession.[10]

2. *Korea's Accession Offers*

(a) Offer of 25 June 1990

2.13 In its initial offer[11], Korea listed the purchasing entities for which GPA coverage would be provided without categorizing those entities. The offer did not contain thresholds above which the GPA would apply.

(i) Coverage of Entities

2.14 Korea's initial offer included primarily government ministries.[12] However, the offer also proposed coverage of a number of boards[13], agencies[14], offices[15] and administration bodies.[16] It also proposed coverage of one corporation (the Korea Na-

---

7 Letter from the Permanent Mission of the Republic of Korea to the Director-General, GATT, dated 25 June 1990.

8 Communication from the Delegation of the Republic of Korea, Document GPR/W/109, dated 20 September 1991.

9 GPR/M/50 indicates that the Republic of Korea was a full participant in the Uruguay Round negotiations.

10 The original offer was attached to a communication to the Director-General, dated 25 June 1990. Subsequent offers were submitted on 14 August 1992 in document GPR/Spec/73 and on 14 December 1993.

11 Document accompanying Korea's letter to the GATT, dated 25 June 1990.

12 Specifically, of the 37 entities that were proposed to be covered by Korea in its initial offer, 19 were ministries. Ibid. pp. 2-3.

13 The Board of Audit and Inspection, the Economic Planning Board and the National Unification Board.

14 The Government Legislation Agency and the Patriots and Veterans Affairs Agency.

15 The Office of Supply, the Supreme Public Prosecutors Office and the Korea Industrial Property Office.

16 The National Tax Administration, the Customs Administration, the Military Manpower Administration, the Rural Development Administration, the Forestry Administration, the Fisheries Admini-

tional Housing Corporation) and one authority (the Korea Telecommunication Authority).

2.15 Relevantly, Korea's offer proposed coverage of the Ministry of Construction, the Ministry of Transportation and the Office of Supply. The offer specified that the Office of Supply was only covered in relation to purchases made by the Office of Supply in its capacity as a central purchasing entity on behalf of entities referred to elsewhere on Korea's proposed list of covered entities.[17]

(ii) Coverage of Products and Services

2.16 By implication, the initial offer applied to all products. However, a limited list of products specified in Annex A applied to the Korea Telecommunication Authority.[18]

(iii) Explanations and Qualifications

2.17 Notes appeared at the end of the list of covered entities. Note 1 to the offer stated that:

> "Purchasing entities include all their subordinate linear organizations, special local administrative organs and attached organs as prescribed in the Government Organization Act of the Republic of Korea."

2.18 Note 2 stated that:

> "This Agreement shall not apply to the procurements with regard to which special procurement procedures are required and/or permitted in accordance with the laws and regulations of the Republic of Korea which are effective at the time of entry into force of this Agreement for the Republic of Korea."

2.19 The initial offer also contained four footnotes that qualified the scope of coverage in respect of some of the listed entities. Footnote 1 excluded coverage of procurement by the Ministry of Home Affairs for the purpose of maintaining public order. Footnote 2 excluded coverage of procurement by the Ministry of Agriculture, Forestry and Fisheries for the purposes of stabilizing the demand and supply situation of agricultural products and ensuring provision of basic national foodstuffs. Footnote 3 stated that procurement by the Office of Supply was only covered when the Office of Supply was acting for a listed centralized purchasing entity. Footnote 4 noted that the Korea Telecommunication Authority was covered only in relation to the goods listed in Annex A except for goods procured by the local branch offices of that Authority.

---

stration, the Industrial Advancement Administration and the Korea Maritime and Port Administration.

[17] Footnote 3 of document accompanying Korea's letter to the GATT, dated 25 June 1990.

[18] The listed products were vehicles, clothing, paper and stationery, tools, poles, conduits, cable splicing materials, line distributing materials, wire (except cables), power supplies and accessories, air conditioning and control equipment, circuit protective devices, test and measuring instruments, telegraph or telephone-type terminals (except for public terminals), other miscellaneous machinery, appliances and materials, computers (off-line or stand-alone use) and peripherals for off-line computer systems, data terminal equipment and modems, word processors and keyboard printers.

(b) *Supplementary Explanation* of Offer of 25 June 1990

2.20 By a communication, dated 28 February 1991, which was circulated at least to the United States[19] and the European Communities[20], Korea provided a *Supplementary Explanation* of its initial offer of 25 June 1990.[21]

(i) Entities

2.21 This *Supplementary Explanation* identified entities that had not been specifically listed in the initial offer but were proposed to be covered under the entities that had been listed in that offer. The *Supplementary Explanation* listed the following entities for which coverage was proposed under the Ministry of Transportation[22]: Regional Aviation Bureaus (2); CHEJU Regional Aviation Office; Flight Inspection Office; VOR-TAC Stations (5); and Marine Accident Inquiry Office (5).

2.22 The following entities were proposed to be covered under the Ministry of Construction[23]: National Construction Research Institute; Central Equipment Management Office; Regional Construction and Management Institutes; District Construction Offices; Cheju-do Development Construction Office; Flood Control Offices; Construction Officials Training Institute; and the National Geography Institute.

2.23 The following entities were proposed to be covered under the Ministry of Communications[24]: Regional Communications Offices; Post Offices; Communications Officials Training Institute; Postal Service Research Institute; Radio Research Laboratory; Postal Money Order and Giro Center; Central Radio Monitoring Office; and the Supply and Construction Office.

2.24 The following entities were proposed to be covered under the Office Supply[25]: Central Supply Office; and Regional Supply Offices (10).

(ii) Notes

2.25 The *Supplementary Explanation* also elaborated on the notes to Korea's initial offer.[26] Specifically, the explanation stated the following in relation to Note 1:

> "Note 1 is established to clarify the coverage of central government organs, which come under 35 of 37 purchasing entities.
>
> The meaning and categories of subordinate linear organizations, special local administrative organs and attached organs are prescribed in the Government Organization Act of Korea as follows:

---

[19] Questions 9, 10 and 14 of the United States' questions, entitled "Questions Relating to Korea's Request to Accede to the Agreement on Government Procurement," sent to Korea on 1 May 1991 indicate that the United States received a copy of this communication. (US Exhibit 4)

[20] Annex II to the European Communities' Answers to the Panel's Questions, dated 3 November 1999.

[21] Supplementary Explanation of the Note by the Republic of Korea, dated 29 June 1990, relating to the Agreement on Government Procurement, dated February 1991. (Exhibit Kor-117)

[22] Ibid. p. 11.

[23] Ibid. p. 10.

[24] Ibid. p. 11.

[25] Ibid.

[26] Ibid. pp. 26 -28.

- Subordinate linear organizations: office of the minister, vice-minister, assistant minister, director general, director etc.
- Special local administrative organs: the organs established in local regions by central government organs when necessary, for example, local tax offices by the National Tax Administration and local post offices by the Ministry of Communication.
- Attached organs: the organs established by central government organs for the purpose of R&D, training and education, culture, medical care, and consulting. These include the Central Officials Training Institute by the Ministry of Government Administration and the National Film Production Center by the Ministry of Information."

(c) Offer of 14 August 1992

2.26 The second offer made by Korea was first circulated informally to members of the Informal Working Group on 12 May 1992 and then formally to the Committee on Government Procurement on 14 August 1992 in document GPR/Spec/73. The offer was stated to be made in substitution for the initial offer made on 25 June 1990.[27] Korea further stated that it reserved the right to withdraw, amend or supplement its offer in the future taking into account the offers made by other Parties and the progress made during negotiations on the expansion of the Agreement.[28]

2.27 The offer listed the purchasing entities for which GPA coverage would be provided and specified the GPA Annexes under which coverage would be provided for those entities. The offer did not specify the products that would be covered by Korea's offer but, by implication, the offer applied to all products. The offer specified the services that would be covered in Annex 4 and construction services that would be covered in Annex 5. The offer also contained thresholds in Annexes 1, 2 and 3 above which the GPA would apply for all products and for the services and construction services referred to in Annexes 4 and 5.

(i) Coverage of Entities

2.28 The entities that were proposed to be covered under Annex 1 in Korea's offer of 14 August 1992 were substantially the same as the entities for which Korea proposed coverage in its initial offer. As in the case of the initial offer, Korea proposed coverage under Annex 1 of the Ministry of Construction, Ministry of Communication and the Ministry of Transportation. It also continued to propose coverage of the Office of Supply subject to the same limitation that was expressed in Korea's initial offer, namely that procurement by the Office of Supply was only covered in relation to purchasing undertaken on behalf of entities listed in Annex 1.

2.29 Korea also proposed coverage of entities at the sub-central level that had not been included in its initial offer. Specifically, Korea proposed coverage under Annex 2 of the Seoul Metropolitan Government, City of Pusan, City of Taegu, City of In-

27 Document GPR/Spec/73, p. 2.

28 Ibid.

chon, City of Kwangju and City of Taejon.[29] The offer indicated that the Offices of Subway Construction were not covered under Annex 2.

2.30 Finally, Korea proposed coverage under Annex 3 of the Office of Waterworks, Seoul Metropolitan Government; Office of Waterworks, City of Pusan; Office of Waterworks, City of Taegu; Office of Waterworks, City of Inchon; Office of Waterworks, City of Kwangju; Office of Waterworks, City of Taejon. It also proposed coverage of Korea Telecom, Korea National Railroad, Korea Container Terminal Authority, Korea Development Bank, Korea National Housing Corporation and Agricultural and Fishery Marketing Corporation under Annex 3.[30]

(ii) Coverage of Products and Services

2.31 Korea's offer of 14 August 1992 applied to all products except for goods referred to in parentheses next to the names of some of the listed entities. Further, unlike the initial offer, the offer of 14 August 1992 did propose coverage of services. It proposed coverage of a list of services specified in Annex 4. The offer also proposed coverage of construction services listed in Annex 5.

(iii) Explanations and Qualifications

2.32 Note 1, which appeared at the end of Korea's initial offer and stated that listed purchasing entities include "subordinate linear organizations, special local administrative organs and attached organs as prescribed in the *Government Organization Act,*" was repeated in identical terms in Korea's offer of 14 August 1992. However, in the case of the later offer, the qualification appeared as a preface to the list of entities contained in Annex 1 and purported to relate exclusively to "central government entities."[31] Note 2, which concerned procurements that were subject to special procurement procedures and qualified Korea's initial offer, appeared in similar terms in the offer of 14 August 1992 but only applied to Annex 5.[32]

2.33 In the offer of 14 August 1992, Annexes 4 and 5 were made subject to a new qualification which provided that the exceptions and restrictions contained in the Revised Conditional Offer of the Republic of Korea Concerning Initial Commitments on Trade in Services[33] would apply to services listed in those Annexes and that the Korean Government may impose restrictions on qualification, registration, licensing and/or other authorization requirements on service providers according to domestics laws and regulations.[34]

2.34 The qualifications that had appeared in footnotes 1 and 2 in the initial offer did not appear in the offer of 14 August 1992. However, other qualifications appeared in the later offer in parentheses next to the names of some listed entities.

---

[29] Ibid. p. 5.
[30] Ibid. p. 6.
[31] Ibid. p. 3.
[32] Ibid. p. 8.
[33] MTN.TNC/W/61/Rev.1, dated 19 February 1992.
[34] Document GPR/Spec/73, pp. 7-8.

(d) Offer of 14 December 1993

2.35 Korea made its final formal offer prior to accession on 14 December 1993.[35] The offer again stated that Korea reserved the right to make technical changes to the offer and to correct any errors, omissions or inaccuracies prior to 15 April 1994[36], being the date by which the Agreement on Government Procurement (1994) and the Final Act Embodying the Results of the Uruguay Round of Multilateral Trade Negotiations were scheduled to be signed.

2.36 The structure of Korea's final offer was largely the same as for Korea's offer dated 14 August 1992. Specifically, the offer again listed the purchasing entities for which GPA coverage would be provided and specified the GPA Annexes under which coverage would be provided for those entities. The offer purported to apply to all products. Further, it specified the services that would be covered in Annex 4 and construction services in Annex 5. The offer again contained thresholds in Annexes 1, 2, 3 and 4 and specified in Annex 5, a threshold for construction services of 5,000,000 SDR for Annex 1 entities, 15,000,000 SDR for Annex 2 entities and 15,000,000 SDR for Annex 3 entities.

(i) Coverage of Entities

2.37 Korea's final offer and its previous offer of 14 August 1992 were the same in all relevant respects in respect of coverage under Annex 1. However, the lists of entities covered under Annexes 2 and 3 were expanded in the final offer.

2.38 Specifically, in addition to the entities for which coverage was proposed under Annex 2 in its offer of 14 August 1992, Korea also proposed coverage of the following entities in its final offer: Kyonggi-do, Kang-won-do, Chungchongbuk-do, Chungchongnam-do, Kyongsangbuk-do, Kyongsangnam-do, Chollabuk-do, Chollanam-do and Cheju-do. Unlike the offer of 14 August 1992, the final offer did not state that the Offices of Subway Construction were not covered under Annex 2.

2.39 In relation to Annex 3, the final offer did not include the various Office of Waterworks that had been specified in the offer of 14 August 1992. However, the final proposal for Annex 3[37] included four banks (Korea Development Bank, Small and Medium Industry Bank, Citizens National Bank and Korea Housing Bank) and 17 corporations (Korea Tobacco & Ginseng Corporation, Korea Security Printing and Minting Corporation, Korea Electric Power Corporation, Dai Han Coal Corporation, Korea Mining Promotion Corporation, Korea Petroleum Development Corporation, Korea General Chemical Corporation, Korea Trade Promotion Corporation, Korea Highway Corporation, Korea National Housing Corporation, Korea Water Resources Corporation, Korea Land Development Corporation, Rural Development Corporation, Agricultural and Fishery Marketing Corporation, Korea National Tourism Corporation, Korea Labor Welfare Corporation, Korea Gas Corporation). It also included Korea Telecom and National Textbook Ltd.

---

35 "Korea's Offer in the Agreement on Government Procurement", dated 14 December 1993.

36 Ibid. p. 1.

37 Ibid. p. 9.

(ii) Coverage of Products and Services

2.40 As in the case of Korea's offer of 14 August 1992, the final offer applied to all products except for goods referred to in parentheses next to the names of some of the listed entities. It also applied to a list of services specified in Annex 4 which was broader than the list of services that were included in the offer of 14 August 1992.[38] Korea's final offer also included a range of construction services to be covered under Annex 5.[39]

(iii) Explanations and Qualifications

2.41 The note concerning the application of Annex 1 to "subordinate linear organizations, special local administrative organs, and attached organs as prescribed in the *Government Organization Act*" that appeared in Korea's initial offer and its offer of 14 August 1992 also appeared in its final offer as Note 1 to Annex 1.

2.42 The Note that appeared in Annex 5 of Korea's offer of 14 August 1992 concerning special procurement procedures was deleted from the final offer. The qualifications to Annexes 4 and 5 in the offer of 14 August 1992 regarding "the Revised Conditional Offer of the Republic of Korea Concerning Initial Commitments on Trade in Services" were also deleted from the final offer.

2.43 The final offer additionally contained the following note (Note 1) which applied to Annex 2:

> "The above sub-central administrative government entities include their subordinate organizations under direct control and offices as prescribed in the Local Autonomy Law of the Republic of Korea."

2.44 The final offer also introduced general notes that applied to all the Annexes.[40] General Note 1 provided:

> "Korea will not extend the benefit of this Agreement
>
> (a) as regards the award of contracts by National Railroad Administration,
>
> (b) as regards procurement for airports by the entities listed in Annex 1,
>
> (c) as regards procurement for urban transportation (including subways) by the entities listed in Annexes 1 and 2
>
> to the suppliers and service providers of member states of the European Community, Austria, Norway, Sweden, Finland and Switzerland, until such time as Korea has accepted that those countries give comparable and effective access for Korean undertakings to their relevant markets."

2.45 In the final offer, qualifications again appeared in parentheses next to the names of some listed entities.

---

[38] Ibid. p. 13.
[39] Ibid. p. 17.
[40] Ibid. p. 18.

(e) The Government Organization Act

2.46 As noted above at paragraph 2.41, Korea's final offer provided in Note 1 to Annex 1 that all central government entities listed in Annex 1 included their "subordinate linear organizations, special local administrative organs and attached organs as prescribed in the *Government Organization Act* of the Republic of Korea". This qualification also appeared in Korea's previous accession offers.[41]

2.47 As at 30 December 1989, Article 2 of the *Government Organization Act* entitled "Establishment and Organization of Central Administrative Organs" provided in sub-article (3) that:

> "The subordinate linear organizations of the central administrative organs shall be Cha-Gwan (Vice-Minister), Cha-Jang (Deputy Administrator), Sil-Jang (Office Director), Guk-Jang (Bureau Director) or Bu-Jang (Department Director) and Gwa-Jang (Division Director), under Vice-Minister or Deputy Administrator, as division not belonging to Office, Bureau or Department may be set up except those otherwise prescribed by special provisions in this Act or any other laws. The subordinate linear organizations undertaking national police affairs under the Ministry of Home Affairs, however shall be Bon-Bu-Jang (Chief Commissioner of Policy), Bu-Jang (Department Director) and Gwa-Jang (Division Director); and for those undertaking civil defense affairs, Bon-Bu-Jang (Chief of Civil Defense Headquarters), Guk-Jang (Bureau Director) and Gwa-Jang (Division Director)."

2.48 Article 3 of the 1989 *Government Organization Act* entitled "Establishment of Special Local Administrative Organs" provided in sub-article (1) that:

> "Each central administrative organ may have local administrative organs as prescribed by Presidential Decree except those especially prescribed by laws, in case they are necessary for the implementation of the duties under its jurisdiction."

2.49 Article 4 of the 1989 *Government Organization Act* entitled "Establishment of Attached Organizations" provided that:

> "In an administrative organ, there may be established by the Presidential Decree organizations for experiment and research, education and training, culture, medicine, manufacturing or advice, respectively, if necessary for the fulfilment duties under its jurisdiction."

2.50 The above provisions remained largely the same in all relevant respects despite various changes that were made to the *Government Organization Act* from 30 December 1989 until Korea's GPA obligations came into effect. However, the English translation of the title of Article 2(3) was amended to prescribe "subsidiary organs of central administrative agencies" rather than "subordinate linear organizations of the central administrative organs", the latter phrase being used in the 1989 version of the Act.

---

[41] See paras. 2.17 and 2.32.

3. Communication between the Parties During Korea's Accession

2.51 The United States began bilateral negotiations with Korea regarding its accession bid on 22 April 1991. During the course of these negotiations, the United States put a series of questions to Korea regarding its offer.[42] Question 6 asked:

> "How does the Airport Development Group relate to the Ministry of Communications? Does Korea's offer of coverage of the Ministry of Communications include purchases for the Airport Development Group? Please identify all Ministries that will be responsible for the procurement of goods and services related to new airport construction."

2.52 In response, Korea answered[43]:

> "The new airport construction is being conducted by the New Airport Development Group under the Ministry of Transportation. The new airport construction project is scheduled to be completed by 1997 after the completion of the basic plan by 1992 and the working plan by 1993. The US company, Bechtel, is taking part in the basic plan projects.
>
> The responsible organization for procurement of goods and services relating to the new airport construction is the Office of Supply. But at present, the concrete procurement plan has not been fixed because now the whole airport construction project is only in a basic planning stage."

4. Korea's Accession

2.53 Korea became a signatory to the Agreement on Government Procurement signed at Marrakesh on 15 April 1994. There were no further changes made to Korea's accession offer between the date of Korea's final offer, namely, 14 December 1993, and the signing of the new GPA at the Marrakesh Ministerial Conference in April 1994.

2.54 While the GPA entered into force for existing Parties on 1 January 1996, it entered into force for Korea on 1 January 1997.[44]

2.55 In its final form at accession, Korea's Appendix I to the GPA was identical in all relevant respects to Korea's final offer of 14 December 1993.

D. Korea's Implementation of the GPA

1. Modification of Korea's Appendix I

2.56 On 24 October 1997, Korea notified the Committee on Government Procurement of a proposed modification to Appendix I pursuant to Article XXIV:6(a) of the GPA.[45] Paragraph 3 of the relevant communication stated:

---

42 Letter from the US Trade Mission to the Mission of the Republic of Korea, dated 1 May 1991.

43 Korea's Answers to Questions from the USTR delivered on 1 May 1991, dated July 1991.

44 Article XXIV:3(a) of the GPA.

"Delete "Ministry of Construction" and "Ministry of Transportation." Add "Ministry of Construction and Transportation" instead. This rectification is based on the fact that the "Ministry of Construction" and the "Ministry of Transportation" have been merged to form the "Ministry of Construction and Transportation"."

2.57 In accordance with procedures of Article XXIV:6, the changes proposed by Korea entered into force on 23 November 1997.[46]

2. *Notification of National Implementing Legislation*

2.58 Korea notified its national implementing legislation to the Committee on Government Procurement in accordance with the Committee's Decision of 4 June 1996.[47]

E. *The Inchon International Airport Project*

1. *General Description of the Project*

2.59 The project in question concerns the construction of Inchon International Airport. The airport is being built on reclaimed land between two islands, Yongjong and Yongyu[48], and is 52 kilometres west of the centre of the Republic of Korea's capital, Seoul. More specifically, it is located in the official district of Unsee-Dong, Chung-Ku, Inchon City.

2.60 The project commenced in 1990. The first phase of construction (which includes airport start-up and commissioning) is scheduled to be completed by the end of 2000. Later phases of airport construction will continue until 2020 and will be based on future traffic demand.[49]

2.61 It is estimated that the first phase of construction will cost W 300.9 billion. This includes the cost of land acquisition, compensation for fishing rights, the actual cost of construction and support expenses including design and supervision. The total cost of the project is estimated to be in the vicinity of W 2,964 billion. According to a publication regarding the IIA project, the government contribution to the cost of the project is projected to be 40 per cent of the total cost and the remainder will come from other sources including domestic and overseas capital markets.[50]

---

45 Document GPA/W/59, dated 24 October 1997.

46 WT/Let/207.

47 GPA/1/Add.1 and GPA/12/Rev.1, dated 9 June 1997.

48 "Inchon International Airport: A Future-Oriented Airport, Increasing the Value of Time," p. 3.

49 Ibid. p. 14.

50 Ibid. p. 41.

2. *Chronology*

(a) Project Stages

2.62 On 14 June 1990 the site for the IIA project was selected.[51] In November 1990, the preparation of the Master Plan commenced.[52] On 24 December 1991, the Master Plan was completed[53] and was announced on 16 June 1992.[54] On 12 November 1992, the ground-breaking ceremony occurred at the IIA site and site preparation commenced.[55] As at February 1999, the first phase of construction (airport start-up and commissioning) was 62.7 per cent complete.[56]

(b) Entities

(i) Introduction

2.63 An act regarding the IIA project, entitled the *Act on the Promotion of a New Airport for Seoul Metropolitan Area Construction* ("*Seoul Airport Act*"), was enacted on 31 May 1991. Article 1 of the *Seoul Airport Act* provides that:

> "The purpose of this Act is, by specifying the matters necessary for the speedy construction of a new airport in the Seoul Metropolitan area, to push ahead efficiently with the new airport construction project to meet the rapidly growing demands for air transport service in the Seoul Metropolitan area and to contribute to the development of national economy."

2.64 While the Ministry of Transportation and, more specifically, the New Airport Development Group under that Ministry, was originally responsible for the IIA project[57], the *Seoul Airport Act* contemplated the appointment of an operator for the IIA project. However, the Act did not specify the identity of the operator. Rather, it left this issue open. Specifically, it provided in Article 6(1) that:

> "The new airport construction project shall be implemented by the state, local governments, or a government-invested institution as determined by the Presidential Decree."

2.65 Further, Article 6(2) provided that:

> "The Minister of Construction and Transportation may, where he deems it necessary for efficient execution of the new airport construction project, arrange for a person other than those referred to in paragraph (1) to implement part of the project."

---

51 History of KOACA (Document from KOACA website) and "Inchon International Airport: A Future-Oriented Airport, Increasing the Value of Time," p. 42.

52 Timeline of events relating to Inchon International Airport construction prepared by the US.

53 History of KOACA and "Inchon International Airport: A Future-Oriented Airport, Increasing the Value of Time," p. 42.

54 History of KOACA.

55 History of KOACA and "Inchon International Airport: A Future-Oriented Airport, Increasing the Value of Time," p. 42.

56 "Inchon International Airport: A Future-Oriented Airport, Increasing the Value of Time," p. 42.

57 Korea's Answers to Questions from the USTR delivered on 1 May 1991, dated July 1991.

2.66 Since the inception of the project, authority for the IIA project has been assigned to various authorities or "operators" by the Korean National Assembly. On 14 December 1991, authority was assigned to Korea Airports Authority (KAA). On 1 September 1994, authority was transferred to Korea Airport Construction Authority (KOACA). Finally, authority was transferred to the Inchon International Airport Corporation (IIAC) on 1 February 1999.

(ii) MOCT

2.67 The Ministry of Transportation originally had jurisdiction over the IIA project. Pursuant to Article 40 of the *Government Organization Act* as it existed in June 1993, it derived its authority from Article 40 of the *Government Organization Act*. Article 40(1) provided that:

> "The Minister of Transportation shall have jurisdiction over the affairs relating to land, air and marine transportation and tourism."

2.68 The current version of the *Government Organization Act* contains a similar provision in Article 42.

2.69 Of relevance is the *Aviation Act*, which was wholly amended on 14 December 1991. Article 1 of the Act as it then existed provided that:

> "The purpose of this Act is to contribute to the development of aviation and the promotion of public welfare by determining methods to assure the safety in air navigation, increasing the efficiency of installation and management of air navigation facilities, and establishing the order in the air transportation services, pursuant to the provisions of the International Civil Aviation Treaty and in conformity with standards and ways as adopted by the Annex to the said Treaty."

2.70 Article 1 of the current version of the *Aviation Act* contains a similar provision.

2.71 Additionally, Article 94(1) of the 14 December 1991 version of the *Aviation Act* provided that:

> "Except as provided otherwise by this Act or other laws and regulations, the airport development projects shall be carried out by the Minister of Transportation."

2.72 Article 94(1) of the current version of the *Aviation Act* which incorporates amendments up to and including 13 December 1997 contains a similar provision.

2.73 "Airport development projects" to which Article 94(1) of the December 1991 version of the *Aviation Act* referred was defined in Article 2(14) of the *Aviation Act* as "projects related to new construction, enlargement or improvement of airport facilities, executed under this Act". The current *Aviation Act* defines "airport development projects" in identical terms.

2.74 Article 94(2) of the December 1991 version of the *Aviation Act* provided that:

> "Any person other than the Minister of Transportation who desires to operate the airport development projects, shall obtain the permission of the Minister of Transportation under the conditions as prescribed by the Presidential Decree."

2.75 Article 94(2) of the current *Aviation Act* contains a similar provision but requires the operator to obtain permission from the Minister of Construction and Transportation rather than the Minister of Transportation.

2.76 The Ministry of Transportation and the Ministry of Construction merged on 23 December 1994[58] to create the Ministry of Construction and Transportation (MOCT). Accordingly, references to the Ministry of Transportation in Korean legislation including the *Government Organization Act* and the *Aviation Act* were replaced by references to MOCT.

2.77 The *Seoul Airport Act* also refers to the MOCT's role in relation to the IIA project. Article 3(1) of the Act provides:

> "The Minister of Construction and Transportation is empowered to designate an area necessary for the execution of the new airport construction project as the projected area for the construction of the new airport for the Seoul Metropolitan area ... or to effect a change in the already designated projected area."

2.78 Article 4(1) of the *Seoul Airport Act* vests MOCT with the responsibility for drawing up the Master Plan for the IIA project. It provides that:

> "Where the Minister of Construction and Transportation has designated and announced publicly the projected area pursuant to Article 3, he shall draw up a master plan relating to the new airport construction ... ."

2.79 Article 4-2 also empowers MOCT to make alterations to the master plan and Article 4-3 obliges MOCT to publicly notify the master plan upon its completion.

2.80 MOCT is required to approve execution plans prepared by the operator.[59] MOCT is also required to certify completion of the work undertaken by the project operator.[60] MOCT has the power to grant a subsidy or loan to the operator to help finance expenses associated with the project.[61] Further, MOCT may cancel or suspend permission of approval granted under the Act in certain circumstances.[62] Finally, Article 12-3(1) of the Act provides that:

> "The title to the land and facilities created or built as a consequence of the new airport construction project shall vest in the State upon completion ... ."

(iii) New Airport Development Group (NADG)

2.81 In June 1990, MOCT created an internal organization, which is generally referred to as the New Airport Development Group (NADG), to assume responsibility for the IIA project. NADG was created pursuant to the *Regulation on Establishment of the New International Airport Construction Working Group*, which was enacted by Ministerial Order of the Minister of Transportation on 1 June 1990. NADG has been referred to by a variety of names including the "New International Airport Construction Working Group," "Corps of the New International Airport Construction Project," the "New Airport Construction Planning Team" and the "IIA Construction Corps."

---

58 Excerpt from MOCT website, p. 2.
59 Ibid. Article 7(1).
60 Ibid. Article 12-2.
61 Ibid. Article 15.
62 Ibid. Article 13(1).

2.82 At present, 30 government employees are assigned to NADG.[63] Specifically, 1 director general, 3 directors, 10 deputy directors, 14 assistant directors and 2 secretaries have been assigned from the current operator to NADG.

2.83 NADG is divided into two divisions - a planning division and a technology division. Pursuant to Article 6(1) of NADG's Regulations, the planning division is responsible for a number of matters including those concerning the establishment, inspection, and analysis of the basic operation plan for the IIA project; the coordination and control of matters related to the project; the funding for construction of the project; and the development of laws and systems for the airport's construction.

2.84 Further elaboration of the role of the NADG in relation to the IIA project is found in the *Rules of the Corps of New International Airport Construction Project and Rapid Railway Construction Project Foundation*, which were created by a directive of MOCT on 3 November 1996. Among other matters, the Rules prescribe the structure of NADG. Specifically, Article 3 of the Rules provides that the Corps is to be comprised of a planning department, a facility department and an operation support team. Article 3 of the Rules also makes it clear that members of the Corps are MOCT public officials.

2.85 Article 6 of the Rules defines the responsibilities of the three departments of the Corps. Article 6(1) provides that the planning division has responsibility for various types of "work" related to a range of topics including the establishment and modification of the master planning for the IIA project; budgeting; IIA project funding; and IIA project control and analysis.

(iv) The Korean Airports Authority (KAA)

Origins

2.86 The predecessor to the KAA was the Korea International Airports Authority.[64] The Korea International Airports Authority was renamed as the Korea Airports Authority on 7 April 1990[65] but is referred to in all the relevant legislation as the Korea Airport Corporation.

2.87 The *Korea Airport Corporation Act,* which was originally enacted on 28 December 1979, constitutes and regulates the KAA. Article 1 of the 3 August 1994 version of the *Korea Airport Corporation Act* provides:

> "The purpose of this Act is to ensure smooth air transportation and to contribute to the totally integrated development of aviation by establishing the Korea Airport Corporation ... [which will be responsible for] constructing airport facilities, and managing and operating them efficiently."

Scope of Responsibility

2.88 The *Korea Airport Corporation Act* defines the rights and responsibilities of the KAA. Specifically, Article 7 provides that the Corporation shall carry out a range

---

63 Korea's Answer to Question 14 from the Panel, dated 29 November 1999.

64 KAA History from KAA website.

65 Ibid.

of projects including the management, operation, repair and maintenance of passenger and freight terminals, and their ancillary and supporting facilities; the management, operation, repair and maintenance of runways and moorings; the repair and maintenance of aeronautical communication facilities and aviation security facilities; landscaping and beautification of airports and installations; incidental projects; and other projects entrusted to KAA by the Minister of Construction and Transportation for management, operation and improvement of airport facilities.

2.89 The provisions in the Act are supplemented by the *By-Laws of Korea Airport Corporation*, the most recent amendment to which was made on 30 December 1991. Article 2 of the 30 December 1991 version of the *By-Laws* states that the objectives of KAA "shall be to build airport facilities and manage the airport, promoting smooth operation of air transportation, developing comprehensive air transportation businesses." Article 4 further elaborates on the projects that KAA is required to undertake.

Relationship with MOCT

2.90 Article 28 of the *Korea Airport Corporation Act*, entitled "Direction and Supervision," prescribes the relationship between KAA and MOCT. Specifically, it provides that:

> (1) The Minister of Construction and Transportation shall direct and control the Corporation, and if it is deemed necessary to do so, he may have the Corporation report matters concerning its affairs, accounting and property, or have a public official under his control inspect books, documents, facilities and other things of the Corporation.
>
> (2) If it is found that any unlawful or unreasonable acts are committed as a result of the inspection under the provisions of paragraph (1), the Minister of Construction and Transportation may order the Corporation to take corrective measures.
>
> (3) Any public official who conducts the inspection under the provisions of paragraph (1), shall produce a certificate indicating his competence to the persons concerned.

2.91 Among other things, MOCT is empowered to permit use of, lend or concede gratuitously any state property to KAA.[66] In addition, KAA is required to annually prepare business plans[67] and statements of account[68] for approval by the Minister of Construction and Transportation. Funds can be borrowed by KAA from various bodies with the approval of MOCT.[69]

66 *Korea Airport Corporation Act*, Article 16.
67 Ibid. Article 19.
68 Ibid. Article 20.
69 Ibid. Article 23.

Legal Status

2.92 Article 3 of the *Korea Airport Corporation Act* states that the Korea Airport Corporation (that is, KAA) is a juristic person. Article 4(1) further states that the "Corporation shall come into existence by making a registration of incorporation at the location of its principal office."

Composition

2.93 Article 8 of the *Korea Airport Corporation Act* prescribes the composition of the Corporation. Specifically, it provides that:

> (1) The Corporation shall be composed of officers falling under each of the following subparagraphs:
>
> 1. A president of the board of directors;
> 2. A vice-president;
> 3. Not more than five directors; and
> 4. An auditor.
>
> (2) The president, vice-president and auditor shall be appointed and dismissed by the Minister of Construction and Transportation.

2.94 KAA's board of directors[70] is required to decide on "important matters."[71] The Act provides that "the board of directors shall be composed of the president, vice-president and directors".[72] Article 8(3) of the Act provides that:

> "The directors shall be appointed and dismissed by the president with the approval of the Minister of Construction and Transportation."

2.95 The members of KAA's board of directors are not government employees.[73] Further, KAA employees are not government employees. However, Article 30 of the *Korea Airport Corporation Act* provides that officers and employees of KAA are to be considered public officials in the application of certain provision of Korea's *Criminal Act*. Further, Article 13 of the *Korea Airport Corporation Act* provides that the employees are employed and dismissed as prescribed by KAA's articles of incorporation.

Role in Relation to Inchon International Airport Project

2.96 On 14 December 1991, the Korea Airports Corporation or KAA was listed as a potential operator for the IIA project. This was achieved through an amendment to Article 6(1) of the *Seoul Airport Act*. Article 6(1) as amended provided:

> "The new airport construction project shall be implemented by the state, local governments, the Korea Airport Corporation established pursuant to the Korea Airport Corporation Act, or a government-invested institution as determined by the Presidential Decree."

---

[70] Exhibit Kor-110 lists KAA directors.

[71] *Korea Airport Corporation Act*, Article 12(1).

[72] Ibid. Article 12(2).

[73] Korea's Answer to Question 10 from the Panel, dated 3 November 1999.

2.97 Simultaneously, the *Korea Airport Corporation Act* was amended. As amended, Article 7, which defined the projects for which KAA is responsible, provided in sub-article 5-2 that KAA was responsible for:

> "New airport construction project pursuant to paragraph 2 of Article 2 of Act on the Promotion of a New Airport for Seoul Metropolitan Area Construction."

2.98 Article 2 of the *Seoul Airport Act* was also amended on 14 December 1991 to provide that:

> "2. The term "new airport construction project" means any of the following activities:
>
> (a) Construction of such airport facilities as stipulated in subparagraph 6 of Article 2 of the Aviation Act ...
>
> (c) Construction of urban railways, roads and port facilities etc. which are necessary to transport passengers and cargo using the Seoul Metropolitan area new airport
>
> (d) Creation of the infrastructure connected with airport services such as convenience facilities for airport users and persons etc. engaged in air transport service and such other aviation-related services as determined by the Presidential Decree ... air cargo distribution facilities and information communication facilities etc.
>
> (e) Creation of infrastructure for facilities beneficial to the living such as accommodation facilities, etc., in favor of persons engaged in aviation-related services and persons who will be deprived of their residence because of the new airport construction project; and
>
> (f) Reclamation of public water surface to create the projected area for the construction of the new airport."

2.99 Further, Article 4(6) of the *By-Laws of Korea Airport Corporation*[74] was amended with the approval of the Minister of Transportation on 30 December 1991 to provide that KAA was required to, among other things, "build the new capital area airport."

2.100 On 31 January 1992, KAA established the New Airport Construction Office to implement the IIA project.

Funding

2.101 During KAA's term as operator of the IIA project (that is, from 14 December 1991 until 14 August 1994), it exclusively relied upon government funds for the IIA project in 1992; 78 per cent government funds, 3.5 per cent debts and bonds and 18 per cent other means in 1993; 77 per cent government funding, 21 per cent debts and bonds and 1 per cent other means in 1994.[75]

---

[74] Exhibit Kor-15.

[75] Sources of Fund for KAA (Exhibit Kor-109).

Procurement

2.102 The rules according to which the Korea Airport Corporation procures are set out in the *Contract Procedure Rules of Korea Airport Authority.*[76] In addition, Article 90 of these rules provide that:

> "With respect to the provisions not stipulated herein, the government contract related laws, regulations and so on shall be applied."

2.103 Teams of approximately 23 KAA employees are used for the opening and evaluation of bids for contracts tendered by KAA.[77]

(v) The Korea Airport Construction Authority (KOACA)

Origins

2.104 The Korea Airport Construction Authority (KOACA) was created pursuant to the *Korea Airport Construction Authority Act,* which was enacted on 3 August 1994 and entered into force on 1 September 1994.[78] That Act purported to transfer KAA's rights and responsibilities in relation to the IIA project to KOACA. Specifically, Article 5 of the Addenda to the Act provided that:

> "(1) Property and rights/obligations of Korea Airport Corporation related to the New Airport Construction Project before the enforcement of this Act, shall be entirely assigned to KOACA...
>
> (4) Any acts conducted by Korea Airport Corporation or taken upon Korea Airport Corporation in relation to New Airport Construction Project before [KOACA's] foundation, shall be considered as those conducted by or taken upon Korea Airport Corporation."

Scope of Responsibility

2.105 Article 1 of the *Korea Airport Construction Authority Act* provided that KOACA:

> "... will carry out the New International Airport Construction Project ... around the Seoul metropolitan area for ensuring smooth air transportation and contributing to the national economic development."

2.106 Article 7 of the Act defines the projects for which KOACA is responsible. That Article specifically referred to the IIA project but also listed "other airport construction related projects entrusted by the government."[79]

2.107 Article 1 of the *By-Laws (Articles of Authority) of Korea Airport Construction Authority*[80] further provides that:

---

76 Exhibit Kor-18.

77 Korea's Answer to Question 15 from the Panel, dated 29 November 1999.

78 *Korea Airport Construction Authority Act*, Article 1 of Addenda.

79 Sub-articles 2 and 3 are blank.

80 Exhibit Kor-45.

> "The object of this Authority is to facilitate the air transportation and further to contribute to the development of national economy by efficiently propelling the New Capital Airport Construction Project … ."

2.108 The By-laws further elaborate on KOACA's responsibilities.

Relationship with MOCT

2.109 Article 31 of the *Korea Airport Construction Authority Act*, entitled "Direction and Supervision" is identical in all relevant respects to Article 28 of the *Korea Airport Corporation Act* which prescribes the relationship between MOCT and KAA and which is referred to above in paragraph 2.90.

2.110 MOCT's power and KOACA's responsibilities *vis-à-vis* MOCT are essentially the same as for KAA.[81] In addition, the *Korea Airport Construction Authority Act* provides that "the title the land and facilities of new airport created or built as the consequence of the new airport construction project by KOACA … shall be vested to the State upon completion."[82]

Legal Status

2.111 As in the case of KAA, KOACA is a juristic person and has corporate status.[83]

Composition

2.112 The composition of KOACA's board of directors is identical in all relevant respects to KAA.[84] As with KAA, KOACA's board of directors (which, according to the *Korea Airport Construction Authority Act*, shall be composed of the president, vice-president and directors)[85] is required to decide on "important matters."[86]

2.113 As in the case of KAA, KOACA's board of directors are not government employees[87] and neither are its employees. Again, similarly with KAA's empowering legislation, Article 35 of the *Korea Airport Construction Authority Act* provides that officers and employees of KOACA are to be considered public officials in the appli-

---

81 See para. 2.91.

82 *Korea Airport Construction Authority Act*, Article 19(1).

83 Article 3 of the *Korea Airport Construction Authority Act* states that the KOACA is a juristic person. Article 4(1) states that "KOACA shall come into existence by making a registration of incorporation at the location of its principal office".

84 Article 8 of the *Korea Airport Construction Authority Act* prescribes the composition of the KOACA. Specifically, it provides that:

> (1) Officers of KOACA shall be composed of five directors including a president of the board of directors and a vice president and an auditor.
>
> (2) The president and auditor shall be appointed and dismissed by the Minister of Construction and Transportation.
>
> (3) The vice president and auditor shall be appointed and dismissed by the president of KOACA with the approval of the Minister of Construction and Transportation.

85 *Korea Airport Construction Authority Act*, Article 14(2). Exhibit Kor-110 lists KOACA directors.

86 *Korea Airport Construction Authority Act*, Article 14(1).

87 Korea's Answer to Question 10 from the Panel, dated 3 November 1999.

cation of certain provision of Korea's *Criminal Act* and Article 15 provides that the employees are employed and dismissed as prescribed by KOACA's articles of incorporation.

Role in Relation to Inchon International Airport Project

2.114 KOACA's role in relation to the IIA project was defined by the *Korea Airport Construction Authority Act* and the *By-Laws (Articles of Authority) of Korea Airport Construction Authority*. Further, at the time that KOACA was created, the *Korea Airport Corporation Act* was also amended. Specifically, Article 7(5-2) which vested KAA with jurisdiction in respect of "the new airport construction project" was deleted.

Funding

2.115 During KOACA's term as operator of the IIA project (that is, from September 1994 until 1 February 1999), it relied upon 78 per cent government funding, 14 per cent domestic and foreign debt, 7 per cent bonds and 1 per cent other means for the IIA project in 1994; 80 per cent government funding, 19 per cent domestic and foreign debt, 2 per cent bonds in 1995; 69 per cent government funding, 28 per cent domestic and foreign debt, 4 per cent bonds in 1996; 38 per cent government funding, 58 per cent domestic and foreign debt, 2 per cent bonds in 1997; 41 per cent government funding, 46 per cent domestic and foreign debt, 14 per cent bonds in 1998.[88]

Procurement

2.116 The rules according to which the KOACA procures are set out in the *Contract Administration Regulations of Korea Airport Construction Authority*.[89] In addition, Article 3 of these regulations provide that:

> "With respect to all contract administration matters of the KOACA, it shall be governed by the provisions of this contract administration regulations. Matters not stipulated in this contract administrations regulations shall be governed by Contracts to which the State is a Party...such as government procurement contracts."

2.117 As in the case of KAA, teams of approximately 23 KOACA employees are used for the opening and evaluation of bids for contracts tendered by KOACA.[90]

(vi) The Inchon International Airport Corporation (IIAC)

Origins

2.118 The Inchon International Airport Corporation (IIAC) was created on 1 February 1999 pursuant to the *Law on Inchon International Airport Corporation*. That law

---

88 Sources of Fund for New Airport Construction (KOACA and IIAC) (Exhibit Kor-109).
89 Exhibit Kor-47.
90 Korea's Answer to Question 15 from the Panel, dated 29 November 1999.

also purported to amend the *Korea Airport Corporation Act* and the *Seoul Airport Act*.[91] It was enacted on 26 January 1999 and came into effect on 1 February 1999.[92] The effect of those amendments was that KOACA was reconstituted as IIAC. This is evident from Article 5 of the Additional Rule contained in the *Law on Inchon International Airport Corporation*, which provides that:

> "(1) The IIAC inherits the assets, right and responsibilities of the Metropolitan New Airport Public Corporation (KOACA) when this law is enforced the moment the IIAC is established...
>
> (4) All the activities related with the Metropolitan New Airport Public Corporation (KOACA) and activities performed toward this IIAC are regarded as the ones that the IIAC conducted or are conducted toward the IIAC."

Scope of Responsibility

2.119 Article 1 of the *Law on Inchon International Airport Corporation* provides that:

> "This law is focused on effective operation of air freight delivery and improvement of national economy by managing efficiently Inchon International Airport ... with [the] establishment of Inchon International Airport Corporation."

2.120 Article 10(1) of the Law defines the projects for which IIAC is responsible. Specifically it states that the IIAC is responsible for, among other things, "construction business" associated with the IIA project; management, operation and maintenance of IIA; the development of businesses in areas adjacent to the airport to ensure the efficient management and operation of the IIA; and "other business" related to construction, management and operation, for which it has a licence from the Korean Government or other autonomous entities.

2.121 Article 2(1) of the *By-Laws (Articles of Incorporation) of Inchon International Airport Corporation*[93] further provides that the IIAC has authority, among other things, to construct the IIA in accordance with Article 2 of the *Seoul Airport Act*; to maintain, operate and repair the IIA; to develop neighbouring areas which are necessary for the effective operation and maintenance of the IIA; and "other businesses" related to construction and operation of the IIA which are delegated to IIAC by national local governments.

Relationship with MOCT

2.122 Article 16 of the *Law on Inchon International Airport Corporation*, entitled "Direction and Supervision," prescribes the relationship between IIAC and MOCT

---

91 *Law on Inchon International Airport Corporation*, Article 10 of the Additional Rule.

92 Ibid. Article 1 of the Additional Rule.

93 Exhibit Kor-54.

but in somewhat different terms to that prescribed as between MOCT and KAA[94] and also as between MOCT and KOACA.[95] Specifically, Article 16 provides that:

> "The Minister of Construction and Transportation can direct and supervise the IIAC about the matters that are necessary for increase of public goods which are designated by the Presidential Decree in managing the Airport. However, this isn't applied to the jobs related with the managing object promised by the law of the paragraph 1 of Article 13 which is about the improvement of the corporation's managing environment and about privatization."

2.123 Moreover, MOCT is empowered to permit the use of, lend or concede gratuitously national assets to IIAC.[96]

Legal Status

2.124 Article 2 of the *Law on Inchon International Airport Corporation* provides that "IIAC is supposed to be incorporated body." IIAC's corporate status is confirmed in Article 1 of *By-Laws (Articles of Incorporation) of Inchon International Airport Corporation* which provides that:

> "This Corporation is established by Inchon International Airport Corporation Law and shall be called ... Inchon International Airport Corporation ... ."

Composition

2.125 According to Article 6(1) of the Additional Rule of the *Law on Inchon International Airport Corporation*, the composition of the IIAC, at least at the time of it creation, was identical to the composition of KOACA. Article 6(1), entitled "Interim measures for staffs and workers of the KOACA" provides that:

> "(1) The president, chief director and the auditor of the Metropolitan New Airport Public Corporation (KOACA) shall be regarded as the president, chief director and auditor according to this law, however the term of office shall be till new president, chief director and auditor are newly appointed.
>
> (2) The workers of the Metropolitan New Airport Public Corporation (KOACA) shall be employed as the workers of the IIAC."

2.126 The Law additionally provides that the board of directors is "implemented to process the works related with establishing the corporation"[97] and that "the board [of directors] for establishment consists of less than seven members appointed by the Minister of Construction and Transportation, and he becomes the chairman of the board."[98]

---

94 See para. 2.90.

95 See para. 2.109.

96 *Law on Inchon International Airport Corporation*, Article 11.

97 *Law on Inchon International Airport Corporation*, Article 3(1) of the Additional Rule.

98 Ibid. Article 3(2).

2.127 Under IIAC's articles of incorporation, the Corporation is governed by twelve directors, six of whom, as non-standing directors, are elected by the Corporation's stockholders and constitute the board of directors. IIAC's president, as one of the six standing directors, is nominated by a nominating committee and elected by the stockholders, while the remaining five standing directors are simply elected by stockholders.[99]

2.128 Again, as in the case of KAA and KOACA, neither IIAC's members of its board of directors are government employees[100] nor are its staff. IIAC currently employs 557 persons.

Role in Relation to Inchon International Airport Project

2.129 On 26 January 1999, IIAC was listed as a potential operator for the Inchon International Airport through an amendment to Article 6(1) of the *Seoul Airport Act.* Article 6(1) as amended provides:

> "The new airport construction project shall be implemented by the state, local governments, the Inchon International Airport Corporation established pursuant to the Inchon International Airport Corporation Act, or a government-invested institution as determined by the Presidential Decree."

Funding

2.130 During IIAC's term as operator of the IIA project (that is, from 2 February 1999 onwards), it relied upon 25 per cent government funding, 24 per cent domestic and foreign debt, 41 per cent bonds and 10 per cent other means in 1999.[101]

Procurement

2.131 The rules according to which the IIAC procures are set out in the *Contract Administration Regulations of Inchon International Airport Corporation.*[102] In addition, Article 3 of these regulations provides that:

> "With respect to all contract administration matters of the IIAC, it shall be governed by the provisions of this contract administration regulations. Matters not stipulated in this contract administrations regulations shall be governed by Contracts to which the State is a Party ... such as government procurement contracts."

2.132 Again, as in the cases of KAA and KOACA, a "Property Management & Contract" team of approximately 23 IIAC employees is used for the opening and evaluation of bids for contracts tendered by the IIAC.[103]

---

[99] IIAC Articles of Incorporation, Articles 26, 27, 35.

[100] Exhibit Kor-110 lists IIAC directors. In Korea's Answers to Question 10 from the Panel, dated 3 November 1999, Korea notes that none of these directors are government employees.

[101] Sources of Fund for New Airport Construction (KOACA and IIAC).

[102] Exhibit Kor-55.

[103] Korea's Answer to Question 15 from the Panel, dated 29 November 1999.

(vii) Office of Supply

2.133 The *Procurement Fund Act* provides that the Office of Supply is primarily responsible for procurement using government procurement funds ("the Fund").[104] The projects for which the Fund may be used are set out in Article 6 of the Act:

> "The Fund shall be used for the following projects:
>
> 1. Purchasing, transport, manufacturing, storing, supplying and their accompanying projects
> 2. Management and operation of facilities and their accompanying projects
> 3. Other projects necessary in operation of the Fund."

2.134 The procurement procedures, which the Office of Supply is obliged to follow are referred to in Article 13 of the *Procurement Fund Act*. Specifically, Article 13 provides:

> "Matters necessary for the procurement procedures and ranges, such as purchasing, saving for emergency, manufacturing, and supplying of procurement goods and contracts for construction of facilities shall be provided for by the Presidential Decree."

2.135 The bodies for which the Office of Supply is required to procure are defined pursuant to a series of provisions in the *Procurement Fund Act*. First, the goods procured are defined in Article 2(2) and 2(3) of the Act:

> "(2) Procurement goods refers to goods demanded...
>
> (3) Goods demanded refers to goods required by a demanding agency pursuant to paragraph 5 and designated by Presidential Decree."

2.136 Secondly, Article 2(5) defines a "demanding agency" as a national agency, a local government organization or other agencies designated by Presidential Decree.

III. FINDINGS AND RECOMMENDATIONS REQUESTED BY THE PARTIES

A. United States

3.1 The United States requested the Panel to make the following findings:

"That MOCT (including the New Airport Development Group under MOCT), KAA, KOACA, and IIAC, all of which are or have been in the past Korean Government entities involved in procurement for the Inchon International Airport project, are covered under Korea's Appendix I of the GPA and:

(a) That by imposing bid deadlines for the receipt of tenders that are shorter than the GPA-required 40 days, Korea is in violation of Article XI:1(a) and XI:2(a) of the GPA.

(b) That by imposing qualification requirements specifying that an interested foreign supplier must have a licence that in turn re-

---

104 *Procurement Fund Act*, Article 4(1).

quires that supplier to build or purchase manufacturing facilities in Korea, just so the supplier may be eligible to bid as a prime contractor, Korea is in violation of Articles III:1(a), VIII first sentence, and VIII(b) of the GPA.

(c) That by imposing domestic partnering requirements that force foreign firms to partner with, or act as subcontractors to, local Korean firms, just so the foreign firms may participate in tendering procedures, Korea is in violation of Articles III:1(a), VIII first sentence, and VIII(b) of the GPA.

(d) That by not establishing effective domestic procedures enabling foreign suppliers to challenge alleged breaches of the GPA for procurements related to the Inchon International Airport project, Korea is in violation of Article XX of the GPA."

3.2 The United States also requested the Panel to make the following finding:

"That should the Panel determine that the above measures do not violate the GPA, the measures nevertheless nullify or impair benefits accruing to the United States under the GPA, pursuant to Article XXII:2 of the GPA."

B. Korea

3.3 Korea requested the Panel to reject the complaints to the United States on the basis of the following finding:

"That the entities conducting procurement for the Inchon International Airport are not covered entities under Korea's Appendix I of the GPA."

IV. ARGUMENTS OF THE PARTIES

A. Entities covered under Korea's Appendix I of the GPA

1. Interpretation of Appendix I and Notes

4.1 **Both parties argue** that regard should be had to the *Vienna Convention on the Law of Treaties* in interpreting Korea's Appendix I to the GPA.

4.2 In support of its argument that regard should be had to Articles 31 and 32 of the *Vienna Convention on the Law of Treaties* in interpreting Korea's Appendix I to the GPA, the **United States notes** that the Appellate Body and previous panels have consistently looked to Articles 31 and 32 of the *Vienna Convention on the Law of Treaties* for guidance in interpreting the provisions of the WTO agreements and that these articles have "attained the status of a rule of customary or general international law."[105]

[105] The United States refers to Appellate Body Report on *Japan - Taxes on Alcoholic Beverages* ("*Japan - Alcoholic Beverages II*"), WT/DS8/AB/R, WT/DS10/AB/R, WT/DS11/AB/R, adopted 1 November 1996, DSR 1996:I, 97, at 104, and to Appellate Body Report, *United States - Standards for Reformulated and Conventional Gasoline* ("*US - Gasoline*"), WT/DS2/AB/R, adopted 20 May

4.3 **Korea agrees** that the *Vienna Convention on the Law of Treaties* contains customary rules of interpretation that should be used in interpreting Korea's Note 1 to Annex 1.[106]

2. *Appendix I, Annex 1: Branch Offices and Subsidiary Organizations*

(a) Status of Notes, Annexes and Appendices to the GPA

4.4 **Both parties argue** that, according to Article XXIV:12 of the GPA, which states that the "Notes, Appendices and Annexes to this Agreement constitute an integral part thereof," Annex 1 and, specifically, the term "central government entity," must be interpreted "in accordance with customary rules of interpretation of public international law," pursuant to Article 3:2 of the DSU.[107]

(b) Interpretation of "Central Government Entity" according to the Ordinary Meaning

4.5 **The United States argues** that when interpreted according to its ordinary meaning, in its context and in light of the object and purpose of the GPA, the scope of "central government entity" in Annex 1 of the GPA includes coverage of its branch offices and subsidiary organizations unless otherwise provided for in the GPA. The United States asserts that its argument is based on a textual interpretation of the GPA, pursuant to Article 31 of the *Vienna Convention on the Law of Treaties*.

4.6 To further explain its argument, the United States contends that since all "central government entities" are composed of branch offices and subsidiary organizations, *a fortiori*, the scope of coverage of a "central government entity" must include these subordinate units, unless otherwise specified. The United States further argues that coverage of an entity that excludes its subordinate units actually amounts to no coverage at all. In support, the United States refers to its arguments in paragraphs 4.323 and 4.324.

4.7 **In response, Korea argues** that the claim that, "the coverage of a 'central government entity' under Annex 1 of the GPA includes coverage of its subordinate units, i.e. its branch offices and subsidiary organizations" is unsupported by any text of the GPA. Korea notes in this respect that the words "branch office" or "subsidiary

---

1996, DSR 1996:I, 3, at 16, and Panel Report, *United States - Standards for Reformulated and Conventional Gasoline* ("*US - Gasoline*"), WT/DS2/R, adopted 20 May, 1996, DSR 1996:I, 29, para 6.7.

[106] Korea further notes that the Appellate Body has stated that tariff concessions in a Member's Schedule - much like commitments in a GPA signatory's Appendix I - are "part of the terms of the treaty," to be interpreted by resort to the rules of interpretation included in the Vienna Convention. Appellate Body Report, *European Communities - Customs Classification of Certain Computer Equipment* ("*EC - LAN*"), WT/DS62/AB/R, WT/DS67/AB/R, WT/DS68/AB/R, adopted 22 June 1998, DSR 1998:V, 1851, para. 84. Korea also refers to Apellate Body Report, *United States - Import Prohibition of Certain Shrimp and Shrimp Products* ("*US – Shrimp*"), WT/DS58/AB/R, adopted 6 November 1998, DSR 1998:VII, 2755, para. 114 ("A treaty interpreter must begin with, and focus upon, the text of the particular provision to be interpreted").

[107] Appellate Body Report, *EC - Lan, supra*, footnote 106, para. 84.

organization" do not appear anywhere in the text of the GPA or in Korea's Appendix I.

4.8 Korea states that the United States is using the rules of the *Vienna Convention on the Law of Treaties* to interpret the "ordinary meaning" of treaty language that does not appear in the treaty. According to Korea, the terms "branch office" and "subsidiary organization," are terms that do not appear in the GPA and are, instead, merely labels with no significance in and of themselves.

4.9 **The United States argues in response** that the terms "branch offices" and "subsidiary organizations" are merely used as generic terms to depict the different types of subdivisions within a given entity. In support of this assertion, the United States notes that, as quoted often by Korea from a United States International Trade Commission Report, the GPA "is aimed at government ministries [sic] and their subdivisions,"[108] and these subdivisions necessarily include branch offices and subsidiary organizations.

4.10 In support of its argument that branch offices and subsidiary organisations are not covered under the GPA, **Korea uses** an analogy to corporate law. Korea states that, in that field, a "branch" is defined as a "division, office, or other unit of business located at a different location from main office or headquarters."[109] Korea states that a subsidiary corporation, on the other hand, is "one in which another corporation (i.e. parent corporation) owns at least a majority of the shares and thus has control."[110] Korea argues that what is significant about these definitions, for the purposes of this case, is that a "branch" normally is not an independent entity, but is simply a division, office or other unit located somewhere else. Korea states that special local administrative organs could be considered branches, because they generally are located at some place other than the main office or headquarters.

4.11 Korea further argues that a branch has the same GPA obligations as the parent entity. On the other hand, it is Korea's view that a subsidiary is a separate legal entity. According to Korea, a subsidiary does not necessarily acquire the GPA obligations of another entity, even another entity that controls it to some extent.

(c) Application of the Ordinary Meaning of "Central Government Entity" to the Present Case

4.12 **The United States argues** that MOCT, like all other Korean "central government entities," is composed of branch offices and subsidiary organizations. In support, the United States refers to its arguments in paragraphs 4.435 and 4.436. The United States further argues that since the NADG, KAA, KOACA, and IIAC are either branch offices or subsidiary organizations of a covered "central government entity," namely, MOCT, coverage of MOCT under the GPA includes coverage of NADG, KAA, KOACA, and IIAC.

---

108 *Agreements Being Negotiated at the Multilateral Trade Negotiations in Geneva*, US International Trade Commission Investigation No. 332-101 (MTN Studies, August 1979).

109 Black's Law Dictionary (1990).

110 Ibid.

(i) NADG

4.13 **The United States notes** that the ordinary meaning of "entity" is an organization, a "being...the existence of a thing...all that exists...a thing that has a real existence."[111] The United States further notes that "central government" describes the level within a government structure at which the entity exists, i.e., at the national level as opposed to the state or local level. The United States argues that MOCT is, therefore, a GPA-covered entity at the national level of the Korean government structure. The United States argues that as with most, if not all, national-level entities in Korea, MOCT is organized into many branch offices and that the NADG is such an office. The United States asserts that it is undisputed that a listing of a "central government entity" under Annex 1 encompasses its branch offices, unless otherwise specified because, according to the United States, the two cannot be naturally separated for the purposes of GPA coverage. The United States refers to its arguments in 4.344.

4.14 **In response, Korea argues** that NADG is a not a "branch office" of MOCT and that the term "branch office" is not used by Korea for NADG. Korea states that NADG is, in fact, specially organized, ad hoc MOCT task force, and is not itself a legal person under Korean law.[112] Korea states that, as a result, NADG has no authority to undertake binding legal actions, such as contracting, on its own behalf. Korea further notes that NADG's regulations do not provide authority for procurement by NADG for IIA. Korea states that, therefore, both as to procurement and all other activities, NADG is MOCT itself - the entity listed on Annex 1. In support of this argument, Korea notes that Article 3 of NADG's regulations names MOCT's Assistant Minister of Planning and Management as the head of the task force, and MOCT's Director General of MOCT's Civil Aviation Bureau as the second in charge.

4.15 **In response to Korea's argument that NADG is MOCT itself, the United States questions** why the New Airport Development Group has a different name than MOCT, why did Korea in 1991 refer to the New Airport Development Group as "the New Airport Development Group under" MOCT, and not just as MOCT and how can the New Airport Development Group be "established within" MOCT in one instance yet be MOCT in another?

(ii) KAA, KOACA and IIAC

4.16 **Korea argues** that KAA, KOACA and IIAC are not subsidiary organizations of MOCT. In support of this argument, Korea notes that KAA, KOACA and IIAC are independent legal persons under Korean law. Korea further states that KAA, KOACA and IIAC, like the entities included on Korea's Annex 3, were established individually by special law. Korea states that each is identified as a legal or "juristic" person, rather than as an agency or instrumentality of MOCT or any other ministry. Korea further states that, as a separate legal person, each entity contracts on its own behalf, pursuant to its own bid announcements and its own procurement regulations.

---

[111] The New Shorter Oxford English Dictionary (1993 ed.), p. 830.

[112] *Regulation on Establishment of the New International Airport Construction Working Group*, MOT Order No. 902, 1 June 1990, Article 2 ("The Working Group is to be established under the authority of the Minister of Transportation.").

Each has its own officers and directors, and its employees are not government civil servants or employees.

4.17 **In response, the United States refers** to its arguments in paragraph 4.587. The United States also notes that, in fact, the affairs of KAA have always been the responsibility of the Civil Aviation Bureau, a branch office of MOCT.[113]

4.18 **In response to a question from the United States, Korea asserts** that all non-listed entities that are "independent legal persons" under domestic law are not covered under Annex 1 of the GPA. Korea states in this respect that Article I of the GPA and Annex 1 speak of "entities." Korea notes that the New Shorter Oxford English Dictionary defines "entity" as a "thing that has a real existence." In the context of the GPA, in Korea's view, an "entity" has real existence when it is a juristic or legal person in its own right, with its own officers, its own directors, its own rules and regulations. Korea argues that KAA, KOACA, IIAC are such entities.

4.19 **In response, the United States argues** that, merely because an entity is a separate legal person does not automatically mean it cannot be a subsidiary organization of another entity. The United States refers to its arguments in paragraph 4.435 for support. In support of its argument, the United States notes that "subsidiary" is defined as "serving to help, assist, or supplement, auxiliary, supplementary ... subordinate, secondary." Thus, according to the United States, if one entity is supplementary or subordinate to another entity, it is a subsidiary organization of that other entity, regardless of its domestic legal status. The United States also refers to its arguments in paragraph 4.252.

(d) Significance of Note 1 to Annex 1

4.20 **Korea argues** that even if the ordinary meaning of "central government entity" includes "branch offices" and "subsidiary organizations," the United States' argument must be rejected because it ignores the ordinary meaning of Note 1 to Korea's Annex 1, which identifies the universe of bodies included within an entity listed on Annex 1, and which renders the ordinary meaning of the term "central government entity" irrelevant. Korea further argues that its commitments in Note 1 do not permit expansion of GPA coverage beyond those entities identified as "subordinate linear organizations, special local administrative organs, and attached organs as prescribed in the *Government Organization Act* of the Republic of Korea." In support of this argument, Korea states that Note 1 provides specific, textual evidence of the intent and the agreement of the parties to the GPA, and as an "integral part"[114] of the GPA, it must be accorded both its ordinary meaning, and the "special meaning" it imposes upon the term "central government entity" for the purposes of Korea's Annex 1. Korea further states that Note 1 evidences and itself provides a "special meaning," under Article 31(4) of the *Vienna Convention on the Law of Treaties*, for the term "central government entity."[115]

---

[113] The Presidential Order on the Organization of the Ministry of Construction and Transportation, Article 16 (US Exhibit 71).

[114] GPA Article XXIV:12.

[115] *Vienna Convention*, Article 31(4) ("A special meaning shall be given to a term if it is established that the parties so intended.").

4.21 **The United States responds** that, in its view, the text of Korea's Annex 1 fully supports the interpretation put forward by the United States. The United States asserts that it is wrong to argue that Note 1 exclusively governs the means of identifying the universe of entities internal to an Annex 1 entity that, while not themselves listed in Annex 1, are nevertheless covered under Annex 1 by virtue of their relationship to listed "central government entities." In support of its argument, the United States refers to the fact that Korea has admitted coverage of branch offices, such as the New Airport Development Group, which are neither "subordinate linear organizations," "special local administrative organs," nor "attached organs." Thus, according to the United States, these three terms cannot be exhaustive with regard to the "universe" of subordinate units within Korean "central government entities."

4.22 Further, the United States argues that Note 1 does not define the scope of "central government entity." Rather, according to the United States, Note 1 expands it. The United States contends that such an interpretation is consistent with the principle of effectiveness. The United States further asserts that such an interpretation is also consistent with the reasoning that Note 1 cannot both define and expand the scope of "central government entity." The United States refers to its arguments in paragraphs 4.159 and 4.161 and 4.163.

(e) Relevance of the Annex 1 List

(i) Explicit Listing

4.23 **The United States notes** that it is undisputed that the New Airport Development Group, a branch office of MOCT, is covered by virtue of the listing of MOCT in Annex 1, and not by its own listing. The United States argues that, therefore, the mere fact that the name of a branch office or a subsidiary organization is not explicitly listed in Annex 1 does not automatically mean that the branch office or subsidiary organization is outside the purview of the GPA.

4.24 The United States further argues that if all unlisted branch offices of enumerated "central government entities" were deemed excluded from Annex 1 coverage, then most Korean "central government entities" would not be effectively covered, since most of these entities are made up of branch offices, of which none are listed by name in Korea's Annex 1. The United States contends that, moreover, if the GPA only applied to enumerated subsidiary organizations, a Party, after agreeing to cover a "central government entity," could then unilaterally and without compensatory adjustments transfer procurement authority from the "central government entity" to its unlisted subsidiary organization, all the while retaining control of the procurements by this subsidiary organization within the "central government entity." According to the United States, the result would be a GPA emptied of its substance.

4.25 **In response, Korea refers** to its arguments in paragraphs 4.160, 4.31, and 4.290.

(ii) Transfer of Procurement Authority

4.26 **Korea notes** that since the United States considers KAA, KOACA and IIAC to be the same and interchangeable, "transfers" between them could have no cognizable effect under the terms of the GPA at issue in this case. Korea asserts that the only remaining "transfer" about which the United States apparently complains, must be the Korean National Assembly's decision to assign responsibility for the IIA project to KAA. Korea states that it was fully within its right to undertake this so-called "transfer unilaterally and without compensatory adjustments" because it occurred in December 1991, two years before Korea submitted its final offer for accession to the GPA, and five years before the effective date of the GPA for Korea. Korea notes that if a similar "transfer" occurred today, a GPA signatory would not be able to accomplish it "unilaterally and without compensatory adjustments." It would be required, under Article XXIV:6(a), to address claims for compensatory adjustments. Korea further asserts that it is one thing to transfer procurement authority from a not yet covered entity (MOCT in 1991) to a non-covered entity (KAA), and something else to transfer it from a covered entity to a non-covered entity. Korea states that the United States submissions do not appear to make this distinction, or to allow for the application of Article XXIV:6.

4.27 **In response, the United States argues** that it is irrelevant that Korea did not make its final offer until three years after the shift of procurement authority to KAA. As a subsidiary organization of MOCT, KAA remains covered under Annex 1 of the GPA because (1) all branch offices and subsidiary organizations of "central government entities" are automatically covered under Annex 1, unless otherwise specified, and (2) procurements by a subsidiary organizations are in fact procurements by a listed "central government entity" - pursuant to Article I of the GPA. Furthermore, the United States argues that pursuant to Article I, KAA remains covered regardless of whether or not it is a subsidiary organization of MOCT because KAA was merely the operator of the IIA construction project, and MOCT remained the entity responsible for IIA construction.

4.28 **Korea also states** that it has demonstrated that the Korean National Assembly made the various transfers of responsibility for the IIA project for entirely legitimate reasons. To illustrate that governments transfer authority over projects or portfolios for many legitimate reasons, Korea states that prior to passage of the *Energy Policy Act of 1992*[116], the United States Department of Energy was responsible for the production and sale of uranium fuel enrichment services for commercial nuclear power plants.[117] Korea states that this responsibility involved procurement authority for the various facilities associated with uranium enrichment, including the Department of Energy's gaseous diffusion enrichment plants.[118] Korea notes that the *Energy Policy Act of 1992* created the United States Enrichment Corporation, and transferred the Energy Department's responsibility for the sale and production of uranium enrichment services to the Corporation. Korea further notes that the transfer took effect when the Corporation commenced operations on 1 July 1993.[119] Korea states that the

[116] Public Law No. 102-486, Title IX.

[117] The testimony of William H. Timbers, Jr., President and Chief Executive Officer, United States Enrichment Corporation, before the Subcommittee on Energy and Power of the House Committee on Commerce, 21 February 1995, pp. 3, 4 (Testimony of USEC President and CEO); Uranium Enrichment Activities Leading to Establishment of the US Enrichment Corporation, GAO Report GAO/RCED-94-227FS, 27 July 1994, p. 4 (1994 GAO Report); United States General Accounting Office, *Status of Open Recommendations FY97*,
at http://www.gao.gov/openrecs97/abstracts/rc95245.htm.

[118] Uranium Enrichment: Process to Privatize the US Enrichment Corporation Needs to be Strengthened, GAO Report GAO/RCED-95-245, 14 September 1995, p. 5 (1995 GAO Report).

[119] 1994 GAO Report, p. 4.

transfer from the Energy Department extended the procurement authority associated with the project to the Corporation, although the Act exempted the Corporation from many of the federal procurement requirements included in the *Federal Property and Administrative Services Act* of 1949, as amended, and the *Competition in Contracting Act* of 1984, as amended.[120] The Corporation issued its own procurement policies and procedures, which it contends, adhere to the United States' Federal Acquisition Regulations.[121]

4.29 Korea further states that subsequent to this transfer, and pursuant to the *United States Enrichment Corporation Privatization Act* of 1996 (passed on 26 April 1996, months after the effective date of the GPA), the United States privatized the Corporation, ultimately selling its shares in the Corporation on the New York Stock Exchange on 23 July 1998.[122]

4.30 Korea notes that this involved, effectively, two transfers and three entities for the same activity in a period of five years. Korea further notes that there is nothing unusual or dubious about these transfers and nor is there anything unusual or dubious about the transfer of responsibility for the IIA project between the various Korean entities.

(f) Article I:3 of the GPA

4.31 **Korea argues** that the GPA does, in fact, provide a means of attaining coverage for procurements by non-listed entities. More specifically, Korea refers to Article I:3 which provides as follows:

> "Where entities, in the context of procurement covered under this Agreement, require enterprises not included in Appendix I to award contracts in accordance with particular requirements, Article III shall apply *mutatis mutandis* to such requirements."

4.32 Korea interprets this Article as meaning that where covered entities ("entities, in the context of a procurement covered by this Agreement")[123] require non-covered entities ("enterprises not included in Appendix I")[124] to adhere to particular requirements in awarding contracts pursuant to the latter's procurement responsibilities, the substantive national treatment and non-discrimination obligations included in Article

[120] *Energy Policy Act*, Section 1312(f) and 1994 GAO Report, p. 7 and Testimony of USEC President and CEO, p. 6.

[121] 1994 GAO Report, p. 7.

[122] United States Enrichment Corporation website, http://www.usec.com/Content/ThirdTier/whoweare/cnt_about_privatization.html.

[123] Korea argues that the GPA does not use the terms "covered" versus "non-covered" entities. The terms "covered" and "non-covered" are shorthand terms adopted by the parties to this dispute. In the GPA, the use of the term "entity" automatically signifies coverage. See, e.g., the reference to simply "entities" in GPA Articles III:2(a), III:2(b), VI:1, VI:2, VI:4. The phrase "in the context of a procurement covered by this Agreement," therefore, clarifies that the procurement at issue, besides being conducted by a covered entity, must also be for a good or service for which the signatory has committed.

[124] Korea argues that the use of the term "entity" in the GPA automatically signifies coverage. Therefore, the term "enterprises" was most likely adopted in Article I:3 to distinguish such bodies from "entities," and to convey the intent to address in that Article the relevance of requirements imposed by covered entities upon bodies that are not covered.

III of the GPA must be observed. In Korea's view, Article I:3 effectively provides a standard to convert non-covered entities into de facto covered entities.

4.33 Further, in response to a question from the Panel, Korea argues that Article I:3 provides, "a formulation which offers a way of distinguishing between those [non-listed] 'organs' or 'organisations' which are 'attached/connected/affiliated' etc. to MOCT and are, therefore, covered entities for the purposes of the GPA and those which are not."[125]

4.34 Korea notes that if MOCT required KAA to award contracts with particular requirements, then, by operation of Article I:3, KAA would be covered by the national treatment and non-discrimination requirements of Article III of the GPA. However, Korea argues that there is no evidence suggesting that MOCT requires KAA, KOACA or IIAC to award IIA procurement contracts in accordance with Article I:3.

4.35 **In response, the United States argues** that Article I:3 cannot be used in this dispute because KAA, KOACA, and IIAC are not entities "not included in Appendix I." The United States further argues that a plain reading of Article I:3 makes it clear that it addresses the issue of subcontracts, not primary contracts. The United States questions how else can a non-covered entity be conducting a "procurement covered under this Agreement"? Further, the United States argues that adopting the approach proposed by Korea in relation to Article I:3 would mean that rectifications and modifications could be effected without the use of Article XXIV:6. The United States contends that this would render Article XXIV:6 an inutility. The United States emphasizes that Article I:3 cannot be interpreted as a means of expanding GPA coverage "beyond the list of entities included in a signatory's Appendix I."

4.36 The United States also contends that Korea's arguments contained in paragraphs 4.20, 4.31 and 4.296 regarding Article I:3 would lead to the result that, with the exception of Korea, every GPA Party's non-listed subdivisions of its "central government entities" would not be covered, because "only named entities, not other entities over which they may exert some control, are covered." The United States further contends that because these "non-covered" subdivisions are required by their covered "central government entities" "to award contracts in accordance with particular requirements," these subdivisions would then be subject to Article III of the GPA (non-discrimination), but not to the rest of the GPA disciplines. In contrast, Korea's non-listed subdivisions (*i.e.,* the "subordinate linear organizations," "special local administrative organs," and "attached organs" of listed entities) would be subject to all GPA disciplines, because "central government entity" for Korea - according to its Note 1 to Annex 1 - encompasses the entities' subdivisions. The United States concludes that, in short, Korea's arguments would result in major reductions of concessions for all GPA Parties, while singling out Korea as the sole Party providing full coverage of its non-listed entities. The United States argues that the text of the GPA does not support such a conclusion.[126]

[125] Korea's Answer to Question 11 from the Panel, dated 29 November 1999.

[126] US Response to Korea's Answer to Question 5 from the Panel, dated 29 November 1999.

3. *Appendix I, Annex 1: The Scope of "Central Government Entities"*

(a) The "Control" Test

4.37 Article I:1 of the GPA provides as follows:

> "This Agreement applies to any law, regulation or practice regarding any procurement by entities covered by this Agreement as specified in Appendix I."

4.38 **The United States argues** that Article I:1 should be considered to determine whether procurements by KAA, KOACA, and IIAC are in fact procurements by MOCT.

4.39 The United States contends that a textual interpretation of Article I:1, and specifically of the word, "by," suggests an analysis of the relationship between MOCT and these three entities *vis-à-vis* the procurement of IIA construction. According to the United States, in making this analysis, factors such as control, funding, ownership, and benefit may be considered. The United States argues that in the present dispute, MOCT controls, finances, benefits from, and owns the procurements of KAA, KOACA, and IIAC. The United States refers in this respect to a list of provisions from Korean law that, according to the United States, evidences MOCT's ultimate control and responsibility over the IIA project, the entities related to this project, and the procurements of these entities.[127]

4.40 The United States concludes that procurements by KAA, KOACA, and IIAC are procurements by MOCT and that, therefore, they are covered under Annex 1 of the GPA pursuant to Article I:1 of the Agreement.

(b) Factors Illustrating Control

(i) Status of Project Operators

4.41 **The United States notes** that the term "project operators" is defined in Article 95(1) of Korea's *Aviation Act*, which states:

> "Any operator of the airport development projects as prescribed in Article 94(2) [is] (hereinafter referred to as "project operator")... ."[128]

4.42 The United States also notes that Article 94(2) of that Act, in turn, describes a "project operator" as "any person other than the Minister of Construction and Transportation" who has obtained "the permission of the Minister of Construction and Transportation" "to operate the airport development projects."[129]

4.43 The United States contends that in further defining "project operator," the *Aviation Act* goes into explicit detail regarding the role and duties of project operators and the authority of MOCT over project operators carrying out airport development projects. The United States notes that, for example, project operators can only carry out airport development projects with the approval, permission, and consent of

---

127 US Exhibit 77.

128 US Answer to Question 19 from the Panel, dated 29 November 1999.

129 Ibid. The United States also notes that "airport development projects" are defined in Article 2(8) of the *Aviation Act* as "projects related to new construction, enlargement or improvement of airport facilities... ."

MOCT.[130] The United States further notes that the *Aviation Act* requires potential project operators to obtain approval from MOCT of their proposed operational plan, which must "specify or be accompanied by design drawings necessary for operating the projects, financing scheme, period of operation, and other matters prescribed by the Ordinance of the Ministry of Construction and Transportation."[131] The United States notes that, moreover, project operators must obtain approval from MOCT that the work performed conforms to project requirements.[132]

4.44 The United States further notes that the *Enforcement Decree of the Aviation Act* supplements the *Aviation Act* as follows:

> "Any person who desires to execute the airport development projects under Article 94(2) of the [Aviation] Act, shall submit to the Minister of Construction and Transportation an application for permission specifying the following matters ... [o]bject and details of projects, [p]eriod and method of execution of projects; and [o]ther matters necessary for executing projects .... ."[133]

4.45 Furthermore, according to the United States, the *Act on the Promotion of a New Airport for the Seoul Metropolitan Area Construction* notes that MOCT may designate a "project operator" to implement the Inchon International Airport construction project.[134] However, "the operator of the new airport construction project as provided for in Article 6 (hereinafter referred to as the "project operator") shall draw up the execution plan for the new airport construction project (hereinafter referred to as the "execution plan") containing the scale and contents of the project, the execution period, a financing scheme and such other matters as determined by the Presidential Decree, and obtain approval from the Minister of Construction and Transportation. The same shall apply where he intends to modify the matters already approved ... ."[135]

4.46 The United States argues that aside from the *Aviation Act*, no other law submitted in this case defines the term "project operators." Instead, argues the United States, they merely confirm the designation of KAA, KOACA, and IIAC as IIA project operators. Specifically, the United States notes that the *Seoul Airport Act*, lists the "Operator[s] of New Airport Construction Project."[136] The United States notes that the relevant article of the *Seoul Airport Act* was revised on a number of occasions since its passage in 1991 to include KAA and KOACA in the list of potential IIA project operators.[137] The United States notes that Korea confirms KAA, KOACA and

---

[130] *Aviation Act*, Article 96 (describing MOCT approval of a project operator's "operational plan." Article 95(1) indicates that the purpose of an operational plan is to obtain the permission of the Minister of Construction and Transportation with regard to an airport development project).

[131] Ibid. Article 95.

[132] US Answer to Question 19 from the Panel, dated 29 November 1999, citing Article 104 of the *Aviation Act*.

[133] US Answer to Question 19 from the Panel, dated 29 November 1999, citing Article 27 of the *Enforcement Decree of the Aviation Act*.

[134] *Act on the Promotion of a New Airport for the Seoul Metropolitan Area Construction, US Exhibit 11, Article 6.*

[135] Ibid. at Article 7(1).

[136] *Seoul Airport Act*, Article 6.

[137] US Answer to Question 19 from the Panel, dated 29 November 1999.

IIAC as IIA project operators by specifically referring to them as "project operators" throughout Korea's submissions.

4.47 Finally, the United States argues that consistent with Article 94 of the *Aviation Act*, the *Seoul Airport Act* gives MOCT authority to choose a different procurement operator at any time, stating that, "[t]he Minister of Construction and Transportation may, where he deems it necessary for the efficient execution of the new airport construction project, arrange for a person other than those referred to in paragraph (1) to implement part of the project."[138] The United States argues that MOCT did just that when it made KAA the IIA project operator in December 1991, KOACA the project operator in August of 1994, and IIAC the project operator in 1999. However, the United States asserts that it is clear that throughout this eight-year period of switching project operators, MOCT retained statutory authority and ultimate control over the entire IIA airport development project.[139]

4.48 **Korea notes** that according to Article 6(1) of the *Seoul Airport Act*, "[t]he new airport construction project shall be implemented by" the operator identified therein. Korea states that although the term "operator" is not defined beyond the entity identified in Article 6(1), the term "new airport construction project" is defined, in Article 2(2) of the *Seoul Airport Act* to include various types of construction. In their respective authorizing statutes, KAA, KOACA and IIAC are charged with undertaking these types of construction projects.[140]

4.49 Korea further notes that the title of Article 6 of the 1991 *Seoul Airport Act* - which gave KAA responsibility for the IIA project - is "Operator of New Airport Construction Project."[141] Korea asserts that the wording of this title, and not anything from the *Aviation Act*, is precisely why Korea and the United States used the shorthand term "project operator" when referring to KAA's role.[142] Korea asserts that the United States has specifically stated that a "project operator" may be designated for IIA construction under Article 6 of the *Seoul Airport Act*. Korea further asserts that the United States did not rely on the *Aviation Act* as its source for the term "project operator."[143]

---

138 *Seoul Airport Act*, Article 6(2).

139 US Answer to Question 19 from the Panel, dated 29 November 1999.

140 Korea's Answer to Question 10 from the Panel, dated 29 November 1999, citing *Korea Airport Corporation Act*, Article 7(5-2) (assigning KAA responsibility for "New airport construction projects as referred to subparagraph 2 of Article 2 of the Act on the promotion of New Airport Construction in Seoul Metropolitan Area."); *Korea Airport Construction Authority Act*, Article 2 (defining "project" for which KOACA is responsible as "any of the activities stipulated in the subparagraph 2, Article 2, '*Seoul Airport Act*.'"); *Law on Inchon International Airport Corporation*, Article 10(1)(1) (assigning IIAC responsibility for "Construction business of the Metropolitan New Airport (hereinafter referred to as Inchon International Airport) in accordance with the Article 2 of the promotional law on Metropolitan New Airport Construction.").

141 1991 *Seoul Airport Act*, Article 6.

142 Korea's Response to the US Answer to Question 19 from the Panel, dated 29 November 1999.

143 Korea's Response to the US Answer to Question 19 from the Panel, dated 29 November 1999, *quoting* US First Written Submission, para. 20.

(ii) Independent Legal Persons

4.50 **Korea argues** that MOCT does not control procurements by KAA, KOACA and IIAC. In support of this argument, Korea states that, as specified in their authorizing statutes, KAA, KOACA and IIAC were established by an act of the National Assembly as separate legal persons[144] and are, therefore, independent legal persons under Korean law. Korea further states that these entities authored and adopted their own by-laws, they authored and adopted their own Contract Administration Regulations governing all procurement matters[145], they issue their own requests for proposals and bid announcements, they publish bid announcements and requests for proposals of their own accord, and they conclude contracts with successful bidders on their own behalf. Korea argues that MOCT does not ask these entities, much less require them, to award contracts in accordance with particular requirements.

4.51 **The United States argues**, on the other hand, that a separate legal person may still be an agent or instrumentality of another entity. The United States refers to Black's Law Dictionary, which notes that an "agent" can be an "independent contractor," - that is, a separate legal entity. Further, in the view of the United States, merely having the status of a separate legal person does not in and of itself guarantee independence. The United States refers to its arguments in paragraph 4.424.

4.52 The United States continues by stating that "control" has nothing to do with an entity's legal status. According to the United States, a separate legal entity can be controlled. The United States refers in this respect to the concept of "subsidiary corporation" in corporate law, in which a separate legal entity is a subsidiary by means of control. The United States argues that this does not mean that the subsidiary corporation ceases to be a separate legal entity. The United States contends that while it agrees with Korea that MOCT's control would not lead to the surrender of KAA, KOACA, and IIAC's status as separate legal entities, this fact does not mean that the existence of separate legal entities make them *per se* incapable of being controlled. The United States further argues that laws creating KAA, KOACA and IIAC demonstrate that MOCT "guides", "supervises", "inspects" and "directs" the New Airport Development Group, KAA, KOACA and IIAC.[146]

4.53 The United States also states that if Korea's argument were to be accepted, then any Party to the GPA could unilaterally transform one of its covered entity's subdivisions into a "separate 'juristic' person" and then claim successfully that this "separate juristic" subdivision is no longer covered under the GPA. The United States further states that if other Parties were to object to this unilateral erosion of bargained-for coverage, the Party making this transformation could - according to Korea - simply claim that the objecting Parties have no rights in the matter because "separate 'juristic' persons" cannot possibly be subdivisions of "central government entities." The United States argues that this would reduce Article XXIV:6 - and the

---

[144] *Korean Airport Corporation Act*, Article 3; *Korea Airport Construction Authority Act*, Article 3; *Law on Inchon International Airport Corporation*, Article 2.

[145] *KAA Contract Administration Regulations*, Article 90; *KOACA Contract Administration Regulations*, Article 3; *IIAC Contract Administration Regulations*, Article 3.

[146] In support of this argument, the United States refers to Article 28 of the *Korea Airport Corporation Act*, Article 31 of the *Korea Airport Construction Authority Act* and Article 16 of the *Law on Inchon International Airport Corporation*.

schedules - to inutility, contrary to the customary rules of interpretation of public international law.[147]

(iii) Oversight for Public Safety and Fiscal Propriety

4.54 **Korea also argues** that "control" exercised by a central government entity does not undermine the independence of separate legal persons such as KAA, KOACA and IIAC and, rather, is the minimum degree of oversight required to fulfill a government's fiduciary duty. Korea notes that constructing an airport, like any other public purpose project, is intimately linked to public welfare, safety and finance. In Korea's view, any responsible government will maintain oversight over the entities responsible for the project in order to guarantee to the public that the highest standards of safety and fiscal propriety are observed. Korea argues that this type of oversight does not surrender an entity's status as a separate legal person.

4.55 Korea argues that the MOCT's authority to appoint board members, the reporting requirements incumbent upon KAA, KOACA and IIAC, MOCT's oversight of fiscal decision-making, and its maintenance of blue-ribbon consultative commissions regarding the IIA project is consistent with the nature of the task with which KAA, KOACA and IIAC have been charged. Korea further argues that, apart from the obvious public safety issues associated with the construction of an airport, a certain amount of government oversight is justified to ensure that appropriate standards of fiscal propriety are observed. Korea notes that the budget for the IIA project stands at approximately $6 billion, with 40 per cent derived from public funds. According to Korea, accountability is needed to guarantee the observation of the highest standards of fiscal responsibility.

4.56 Additionally, Korea argues that the type of oversight referred to by the United States - the requirement that KAA, KOACA or IIAC seek approval for and report on certain of its actions - also ensures accountability. Korea argues that the approval and reporting requirements to which KAA, KOACA and IIAC are subject ensures that there is a public record evidencing their accountability for what they do. Korea states that they do not surrender their status as separate legal persons merely because they are called to account for their actions.

4.57 Finally, Korea argues that, even assuming for the sake of argument that the United States' control test applies, KAA, KOACA and IIAC cannot be considered to be controlled by MOCT under this test. Korea argues that this follows from the fact that the degree of control is not extreme but, rather, is only the degree of control necessary to ensure that the interests of the public are reflected in the operations of each corporation. Korea asserts that the United States itself, in discussing the control exercised over its own Amtrak and Comsat by central government entities, reasoned that "the retained links with the government may be seen as only those necessary to ensure that the interests of the public are reflected in the operations of [Amtrak and Comsat]," and that these links do not support the extension of GPA coverage to Amtrak and Comsat since "the code is aimed at government ministeries [sic] and their

[147] US Response to Korea's Answer to Question 2 from the Panel, dated 29 November 1999.

subdivisions - not the myriad organizations tangential to the essential function of government."[148]

4.58 **In response, the United States argues** that there is no support for the argument that MOCT's direction and supervision of KAA and KOACA are merely aimed at public policy matters in the texts of the *Korea Airport Corporation Act*, the *Korea Airport Construction Authority Act*, and the *Inchon International Airport Corporation Act.*

(iv) Master Plan for IIA Project

4.59 **In support of its argument** that MOCT remains in ultimate control of the IIA project, **the United States refers** to Article 4(1) of the *Seoul Airport Act*, which requires the MOCT to establish the "master plan" for the IIA project. The United States notes that Article 4(2) stipulates that the master plan includes: 1. General direction of construction; 2. Outline of the construction plan; 3. Construction period; 4. Financing plan; and 5. Such other matters as the Minister of Construction and Transportation deems necessary.

4.60 **Korea argues in response** that Article 4 of the *Seoul Airport Act* does not authorize MOCT to undertake procurement for IIA or to require the project operator to award contracts for IIA procurements in accordance with any particular requirements.

4.61 **The United States also notes** that as project operators, NADG, KAA, KOACA and IIAC were and are required to follow the "master plan." The United States further notes that the NADG, KAA, KOACA, and IIAC are required to obtain MOCT approval for their project execution plans.

(v) Reporting Obligations

4.62 In further support of its argument that MOCT controls the IIA project operators, the **United States notes** that MOCT may:

> "where necessary for the implementation of the Act, order the project operator to make necessary reports on the new airport construction project or to submit necessary data, and may have public officials serving at his Ministry enter the project operator's office, the workplace or other relevant places to inspect the business of the new airport construction project"[149]

4.63 The United States also notes that if and when the project operator:

> "has completed the work on the new airport construction project, [he shall] submit a work completion report to the Minister of Construction and Transportation and obtain confirmation of the completion of work"[150]

---

[148] *Agreements Being Negotiated at the Multilateral Trade Negotiations in Geneva*, US International Trade Commission Investigation No. 332-101 (MTN Studies, August 1979), p. 44.

[149] US Answer to Question 19 from the Panel, dated 29 November 1999, citing Article 14(1) of the *Seoul Airport Act.*

[150] Ibid. citing Article 12-2(1) of the *Seoul Airport Act.*

(vi) Appointment and Dismissal

4.64 Also, in further support of its argument that MOCT controls each of the IIA "project operators," the **United States contends** that directors of NADG are accountable to the MOCT. Further, the presidents, vice-presidents, and auditors of KAA, KOACA, and IIAC are appointed and dismissed by MOCT while the rest of their boards are appointed and dismissed by the president "with the approval of" MOCT.

4.65 **In response, Korea argues that** KAA, KOACA and IIAC are governed by their own boards of directors that control all matters related to major corporate investments and all other major corporate issues of any significance.[151] Further, Korea states that KAA, KOACA and IIAC hire and fire a workforce that is not in the government's employ.[152]

(vii) Power to Cancel Permission or Approval

4.66 **In further support** of its control argument, **the United States notes** that Article 13(1) of the *Seoul Airport Act* provides that the MOCT retains final authority to:

> "cancel the permission or approval granted pursuant to this Act or order the suspension of or alteration in the work, or the reconstruction, modification or relocation of facilities:
>
> 1. Where the operator has obtained permission or approval under this Act by deceit or other wrongful means;
> 2. Where the operator has breached an order or disposition issued under this Act; and
> 3. Where continued execution of the new airport construction project has been made impossible owing to change of circumstances"[153]

4.67 **Korea argues in response** that MOCT's oversight authority is related to MOCT's mandate to police any potential criminal conduct by KAA, KOACA and IIAC. More specifically, Korea argues that MOCT is able to cancel, suspend or alter any action undertaken by KAA, KOACA or IIAC only where conduct by those entities is illegal or otherwise wrongful. Korea notes in this respect that it is only in exceptional situations, where KAA employees have committed certain criminal violations, that they will be treated as public officials. Korea further notes that under Article 30 of the *Korea Airport Corporation Act*, this "legal fiction" will result in the application of Chapter VII of the *Korean Criminal Act* to KAA employees.[154] Korea argues that MOCT oversight of the type described in Article 8(2) of the *Korea Airport Corporation Act* is aimed at policing such conduct. Korea states that it is "good

[151] Korea refers to, for example, *KAA By-laws*, Articles 4(3), 4(1)(6), 14, 25; *KOACA By-laws*, Articles 7(1), 30; *IIAC Articles of Incorporation*, Articles 17, 47.

[152] *Korea Airport Corporation Act*, Article 13; *Korea Airport Construction Authority Act*, Article 15; *Law on Inchon International Airport Corporation*, Additional Rule Article 6(2) (KOACA employees, who were by virtue of Article 15 of the *Korea Airport Construction Authority Act* not government employees, became employees of IIAC).

[153] US Answer to Question 19 from the Panel, dated 29 November 1999.

[154] *Criminal Act*, Act No. 293, 14 September 1953 (as amended by Act No. 2745, 25 March 1975).

government" to police the conduct of KAA, KOACA or IIAC officials, routing out any potential criminal conduct, or cancelling or suspending any "wrongful" or "deceitful" actions that might be undertaken by those officials.

(viii) Power to Dictate Technical and Non-Technical Requirements

4.68 In further support of its argument that MOCT controls the IIA procuring entities, the **United States argues** that MOCT dictates what technical or non-technical requirements are necessary for each procurement, the decision of which determines the final selection of the products or services. The United States notes that through its New Airport Development Group and its "New Airport Construction Deliberation Commission", MOCT *inter alia* deliberates on "important issues relating to building techniques, construction technology and traffic impact, etc. of the new airport construction project"; researches and develops "systems and regulations" concerning the airport; and plans, designs and oversees "actual works of [the airport's] civil engineering facilities, site preparation, supporting complex construction supporting facilities and accessible transport facilities."

4.69 **In response, Korea notes** that there is no evidence to demonstrate that MOCT dictates technical or non-technical requirements for procurements by KAA, KOACA or IIAC. Korea argues that the United States has not established that KAA, KOACA or IIAC are "required" by MOCT or any other covered entity "to award contracts in accordance with particular requirements," which is the standard provided in Article I:3 of the GPA to extend coverage to unlisted entities. According to Korea, neither the statutory provisions regarding MOCT's responsibility for the Inchon airport's basic plan, nor the statutory provisions requiring KAA, KOACA and IIAC to request approval for and report on certain of their actions, instruct MOCT to require KAA, KOACA or IIAC to award Inchon airport contracts in accordance with any particular requirements. Korea argues that it has in fact demonstrated that no such requirements exist, given its demonstration that KAA, KOACA and IIAC: are separate legal persons; have adopted their own procurement regulations; are empowered to and have in fact conducted procurements on their own behalf; and, have signed contracts on their own behalf.

(ix) Financing of IIA Project

4.70 **The United States also argues** that MOCT is responsible for all budget and funding matters related to the airport and, more particularly, that MOCT finances all IIA procurements. In support of this argument, the United States refers to Article 15 of the *Seoul Airport Act,* which, it argues, permits the Government of Korea - that is, MOCT - to grant a subsidy or a fiscal loan to the project operator to help him finance all or part of the expenses needed for the new airport construction project. The United States further argues that MOCT provides free loans of national assets, it concedes gratuitously any state property to KAA, KOACA and IIAC, it guarantees the bonds issued by these entities, and establishes the financial plans for the repayment of debt incurred by these entities from the construction of the airport. The United States also states that if these entities attempt to collect rents or charges for the use of airport facilities, borrow funds, or sell airport property, they must obtain MOCT's approval. Finally, the United States argues that MOCT funds the NADG.

4.71 **Korea argues in response** that there is no evidence indicating that MOCT finances all IIA procurements. Further, Korea argues that KAA, KOACA and IIAC fund portions of IIA procurement with their own funds.

4.72 In support of its argument regarding finance of the IIA project, **the United States refers** to a document entitled, "Inchon International Airport: A Future-Oriented Airport, Increasing the Value of Time." The United States contends that this document shows that 40 per cent of the funding for the IIA construction project will come from government grant. The United States further states that the remaining IIA funding will come from borrowing guaranteed by the government, government land sales, and KAA. The United States notes that Korea is anticipating at this time that only 11.7 per cent of the IIA funding will come from private investment and that IIAC may not be privatized.

(x) Property in IIA Project

4.73 **The United States also argues** that MOCT retains possession of all products or services procured for the IIA project. The United States argues that the *Seoul Airport Act* confirms that the title to the land and facilities created or built as a consequence of the new airport construction project shall vest in the State upon completion. The United States also notes that the *Korea Airport Construction Authority Act* states that the ownership of new airport facilities constructed through the new airport construction project belongs to MOCT as soon as the construction is finished.

4.74 The United States also notes that the *Seoul Airport Act* provides that if the project operator chooses to "set up or expand in or relocate to the projected area or its adjoining area such facilities for the production of various construction materials as are required for the new airport construction project,"[155] "receive advance money for all or part of the land price from the persons who will be provided with a portion of the land to be created by the implementation of the new airport construction project,"[156] or "issue bonds convertible to land (hereinafter referred to as the "land redemption bonds")[157] the project operator must obtain the approval of MOCT."[158]

(c) Is Control Related to Procurement?

4.75 **Korea asserts** that the "control" factors identified by the United States are essentially two-fold: "control" stemming from MOCT's responsibility for formulating and amending the basic plan; and, "control" stemming from the statutory requirement that KAA, KOACA and IIAC request approval for and report on certain of their actions.

4.76 Korea argues that these factors are not related to procurement. Further, Korea argues that these factors do not demonstrate that MOCT requires KAA, KOACA and IIAC to award contracts in accordance with particular requirements.

4.77 Regarding the first category of control referred to in paragraph 4.75, Korea notes that Article 4(2) of the *Seoul Airport Act* describes what should be included in

155 *Seoul Airport Act*, Article 8-2(3).
156 Ibid. Article 11.
157 *Ibid.*
158 US Answer to Question 19 from the Panel, dated 29 November 1999.

the basic or master plan. Korea argues that the Act does not direct or authorize MOCT to undertake procurement for IIA nor does it instruct MOCT to require KAA, KOACA or IIAC to award IIA contracts in accordance with any particular requirements.

4.78 Regarding the second category of MOCT control referred to in paragraph 4.75, Korea states that the United States only provides one example where MOCT oversight was connected to procurement by KAA, KOACA and IIAC. Korea makes specific reference to the assertion by the United States that MOCT's authority to cancel, suspend or alter actions undertaken by KAA, KOACA or IIAC, under Article 13(1) of the *Seoul Airport Act*, includes the right to cancel, suspend, or change any procurement decision. Korea argues that MOCT is authorized to exercise this discretionary authority only in instances where conduct by KAA, KOACA or IIAC is illegal, otherwise wrongful or unenforceable.[159] Korea reiterates that this power is related simply to MOCT's task to police any potentially criminal conduct by KAA, KOACA or IIAC.

4.79 **The United States argues** that MOCT is responsible for all "affairs relating to air transportation" and it oversees the "construction and administration of...airports and all other matters concerning construction and transport safety affairs." The United States asserts that although the New Airport Development Group, KAA, KOACA or IIAC may purport to have the procuring authority for the IIA project, they are merely procurement agencies acting on behalf of MOCT. The United States maintains that such procurements are, in fact, conducted by MOCT and, therefore, are within the scope and meaning of Korea's Annex 1 of the GPA.

(d) Relevance of the Aviation Act to the IIA Project

(i) MOCT and the Aviation Act

4.80 **The United States argues** that Article 94(1) of the *Aviation Act* confers on MOCT authority over airport development projects. The United States also argues that the *Aviation Act* confirms MOCT's control. The United States refers to the following provisions of that Act in support of its argument:[160]

> "The airport development projects shall be carried out by the Minister of Construction and Transportation ... Any person other than the Minister of Construction and Transportation, who desires to operate the airport development projects, shall obtain the permission of the Minister of Construction and Transportation ....[161]

[159] *Seoul Airport Act*, Article 13(1). Article 13(1)(3) lists impossibility owing to changed circumstances as a reason justifying MOCT cancellation, suspension or alteration of action by KAA, KOACA or IIAC. "Impossibility" is a general term of contract law dictating that in exceptional circumstances, changed circumstances can excuse a party from performance of a contract. See generally E. Allan Farnsworth, CONTRACTS, § 9.5 (2nd Ed., 1990) (Little, Brown, Boston). Thus, "impossibility" owing to changed circumstances leads to the same result as illegality or other wrong - the action by KAA, KOACA or IIAC is *unenforceable* as a matter of law.

[160] US Answer to Question 18 from the Panel, dated 29 November 1999.

[161] *Aviation Act*, Article 94.

Any operator of the airport development projects ... shall make an operational plan before he undertakes the work under the conditions as prescribed by the Presidential Decree. In this case, the project operator as prescribed in Article 94(2) shall produce an operational plan to obtain the permission of the Minister of Construction and Transportation ... The operational plan ... shall specify or be accompanied by design drawings necessary for operating the projects, financing scheme, period of operation and matters as prescribed by the Ordinance of the Ministry of Construction and Transportation ..."[162]

4.81 The United States notes that the *Aviation Act* defines "airport development projects" as "projects related to new construction, enlargement or improvement of airport facilities."[163]

4.82 Further, the United States relies upon the *Enforcement Decree of the Aviation Act* which, it says, supplements the *Aviation Act*:

"Any person who desires to execute the airport development projects under Article 94(2) of the Act, shall submit to the Minister of Construction and Transportation an application for permission specifying the following matters ... [o]bject and details of projects, [p]eriod and method of execution of projects; and [o]ther matters necessary for executing projects ... ."[164]

4.83 The United States argues that, according to the *Aviation Act*, MOCT not only carried out past "projects related to new construction, enlargement or improvement of airport facilities," but is also presently carrying out the IIA construction project.[165] The United States notes that MOCT has the authority to choose and transfer the project operators of the construction project at will: it was MOCT that transferred IIA procurement responsibility from KAA to KOACA and from KOACA to IIAC. As project operators, according to the United States, KAA, KOACA amd IIAC are mere tools used by MOCT to construct the IIA.

4.84 Finally, the United States argues that various provisions in the *Aviation Act* confirm the subordinate nature of project operators.[166]

4.85 **In response, Korea argues** that although some Articles of the *Aviation Act* were incorporated by reference into the *Seoul Airport Act*, the Articles mentioned by the United States - Articles 2(8), 94(1), 94(2), 103, 103(1), 104(2), 107 and 108 of the *Aviation Act* - were not so incorporated. Korea concludes that the United States' arguments must, therefore, be rejected.[167]

162 Ibid. Article 95.

163 US Answer to Question 18 from the Panel, dated 29 November 1999, citing Article 2(8) of the *Aviation Act*.

164 *Enforcement Decree of the Aviation Act*, Article 27.

165 *Aviation Act*, Articles 94 and 2(8).

166 Articles 95, 96, 103, and 104 of the *Aviation Act*.

167 Korea's Response to the US Answer to Question 18 from the Panel, dated 29 November 1999.

(ii) Applicability of the Aviation Act

Later Act Supersedes the Former

4.86 **Korea argues** that the *Aviation Act* is not applicable to the IIA project because, in May 1991, the National Assembly enacted the *Seoul Airport Act.* Korea argues that this Act governs the IIA project.

4.87 In support of its argument, Korea notes that Article 1 of the *Seoul Airport Act* provides that:

> "The purpose of this Act is, by specifying the matters necessary for the speedy construction of a new airport in the Seoul Metropolitan area, to push ahead efficiently with the new airport construction project to meet the rapidly growing demands for air transport service in the Seoul Metropolitan area and to contribute to the development of national economy."[168]

4.88 Korea notes that one reason to consider the *Seoul Airport Act*, rather than the *Aviation Act*, as determinative for questions regarding the construction of IIA, is that the *Seoul Airport Act* was enacted subsequent to the *Aviation Act.*[169]

4.89 Korea notes as a matter of clarification that the *Aviation Act* was superseded by the *Seoul Airport Act* for the purposes of IIA construction only. Korea notes that the *Aviation Act* still exists and is operative for other purposes.[170] Specifically, Korea states that apart from Section 2 of its Chapter V, titled "Airport," the *Aviation Act* regulates a variety of areas irrelevant to an airport like IIA that is not yet completed or operating: Chapter II, regarding "Aircraft"; Chapter III, "Airman"; Chapter IV, "Operation of Aircraft"; Chapter VI, "Air Transportation Business, Etc."; Chapter VII, "Aircraft Handling Business, Etc."; Chapter VIII, "Foreign Aircraft"; Chapter VIII-2, "Investigation of Aviation Accident"; Chapter IX, "Supplementary Provisions"; and, Chapter X, "Penal Provisions". Korea states that, furthermore, the provisions of Section 2 of Chapter V of the *Aviation Act* continue to apply to other airport construction projects in Korea, in the absence of "other Acts" or "other laws" providing otherwise.[171]

4.90 **In response, the United States argues** that Korea cites no provision in the *Seoul Airport Act* that would support a conclusion that the *Seoul Airport Act* supersedes the *Aviation Act.*[172]

4.91 The United States notes specifically that nowhere in Article 8 of the *Seoul Airport Act* entitled "Relations with Other Acts" does it say that the *Seoul Airport Act* supersedes the *Aviation Act.* On the contrary, the United States argues that Article 8 of the *Seoul Airport Act* specifically cross-references the *Aviation Act* and states that

168 1997 *Seoul Airport Act*, Article 1.

169 Korea's Answer to Question 9 from the Panel, dated 29 November 1999.

170 Korea's Answer to Question 1 from the Panel, dated 29 November 1999.

171 Korea's Answer to Question 9 from the Panel, dated 29 November 1999.

172 US Response to Korea's Answer to Question 1 from the Panel, dated 29 November 1999.

the approval of the "execution plans" under the *Seoul Airport Act* shall constitute approval under the *Aviation Act*.[173]

4.92 The United States argues that if the *Seoul Airport Act* were intended to supersede provisions of the *Aviation Act* relating to airport development projects, as Korea argues, there would be no need for the *Seoul Airport Act* to indicate that approval of the execution plan would also constitute approval under Article 95(1) of the *Aviation Act*, i.e., Article 95(1) of the *Aviation Act* would simply not apply to the IIA project. Thus, according to the United States, Article 8 of the *Seoul Airport Act* clearly demonstrates first, that the *Aviation Act* is not superseded by the *Seoul Airport Act*, and secondly, that the IIA project is included in the airport development projects to which the *Aviation Act* applies.[174]

4.93 The United States notes that other Korean statutes illustrate that when one law "replaces" or "supersedes" another, this change is clearly and unambiguously stated in law as a matter of statutory drafting. The United States notes that, for example, when Korea enacted the law creating the IIAC, which superseded the KOACA law and transferred the duties of IIA project operator from KOACA to IIAC, the new IIAC law made it clear that the IIAC law displaced the KOACA law. The United States refers for support of its argument to Article 2 (Additional Rule) of the *Law on Inchon International Airport Corporation* which states:

> "Article 2. (Abolition of other law) The law on Metropolitan New Airport Public Corporation shall be abolished."[175]

4.94 The United States concludes that there is no indication in the *Seoul Airport Act*, the laws establishing KAA, KOACA, or IIAC (or any of the by-laws for those entities), or in any other law or regulation that the *Seoul Airport Act* supersedes the *Aviation Act* in any way.[176]

Specific Act Takes Precedence over General

4.95 **Korea argues** that the material articles of the *Seoul Airport Act* replace often in virtually verbatim form parallel Articles in the *Aviation Act* dealing with the construction of an airport. Korea argues that it is axiomatic that a more specific rule, i.e.,

---

173 US Response to Korea's Answer to Question 1 from the Panel, dated 29 November 1999, citing Article 8 of the *Seoul Airport Act* which states, in relevant part:

Article 8 (Relations with Other Acts)

(1) Where the project operator obtains approval for the execution plan pursuant to Article 7, it shall be presumed that the following approval, permission, authorization, decision, designation, licensing, consultation, consent...have been granted or made...and where the Minister of Construction and Transportation brings to public notice of the approval of the execution plan, it shall be presumed that a public notification or announcement of authorization and permission, etc. has been made or granted pursuant to on the of following Acts:

...

16. Approval of an execution plan as stipulated in Article 95(1) of the Aviation Act...

174 US Response to Korea's Answer to Question 1 from the Panel, dated 29 November 1999.

175 Ibid.

176 Ibid.

one narrowly targeted at a particular project like the IIA, replaces a more general, albeit co-existing rule, i.e., one broadly addressed to any airport project.[177]

4.96 Korea also submits that as to construction of the IIA, where the *Seoul Airport Act* contains Articles corresponding directly with identical or similar Articles contained in the *Aviation Act* - the purpose of which is, considerably more general, "to contribute to the development of aviation and the promotion of public welfare" - the provisions of the *Seoul Airport Act* apply.[178]

4.97 Korea notes that, for example, Article 94 of the 1997 *Aviation Act*, entitled "Operator of Airport Development," states at subparagraph (1) that MOCT shall carry out airport development projects.[179] Korea notes that Article 6 of the 1997 *Seoul Airport Act*, not coincidentally entitled "Operator of New Airport Construction Project," states at subparagraph (1) that KOACA (by its alias, the Seoul Metropolitan Area New Airport Construction Corporation) shall implement the IIA project.[180]

4.98 Korea notes that, similarly, the 1991 *Aviation Act*, at Article 94(1), under the title "Operator of Airport Development Projects," states that MOCT shall carry out airport development projects[181] while the 1991 *Seoul Airport Act*, at Article 6(1), under the title "Operator of New Airport Construction Project," states that KAA shall implement the IIA project.[182]

4.99 Korea argues that, therefore, with regard to the IIA project, the more specific provision of *Seoul Airport Act* take precedence over the more general provision of the *Aviation Act*, with the result being that KAA, KOACA or IIAC, rather than MOCT, carry responsibility for the IIA project.[183]

4.100 Korea notes that examples of the National Assembly's substitution of Articles in the *Aviation Act* with Articles from the *Seoul Airport Act* are plentiful. Korea refers to the charts below, which compare the two Acts in 1997 and 1991. Korea notes that the Korean National Assembly elected, for the purposes of IIA construction, to replicate and replace the terms of Section 2 of Chapter V of the *Aviation Act* with the terms of the *Seoul Airport Act*. Korea notes that the titles of the corresponding articles are often virtually identical, which, according to Korea, establishes the clear intent of the National Assembly to replace the regulatory framework of the *Aviation Act*, for purposes of construction of the IIA, with the new framework of the *Seoul Airport Act*.[184]

---

177 Korea's Answer to Question 9 from the Panel, dated 29 November 1999.

178 Ibid.

179 Ibid. citing 1997 *Aviation Act*, Article 94(1).

180 Ibid. citing Article 6(1) of the 1997 *Seoul Airport Act*.

181 1991 *Aviation Act*, Article 94(1).

182 Korea's Answer to Question 9 from the Panel, dated 29 November 1999, citing Article 6(1) of the 1991 *Seoul Airport Act*.

183 Ibid.

184 Korea's Answer to Question 9 from the Panel, dated 29 November 1999.

1997 Aviation Act	*1997 Seoul Airport Act*
Article 89 (Establishment of Basic Airport Development Plan)	Article 4 (Drawing-up of Master Plan for New Airport Construction)
Article 90 (Modification, etc. of Basic Plan)	Article 4-2 (Alterations, etc. to Master Plan)
Article 91 (Public Announcement on Basic Plan)	Article 4-3 (Public Notice of Master Plan)
Article 92 (Contents of Basic Plan)	Article 4 (Drawing-up of Master Plan for New Airport Construction)
Article 93 (Restriction on Act, etc.)	Article 5 (Restriction on Acts, etc.)
Article 94 (Operator of Airport Development Projects)	Article 6 (Operator of New Airport Construction Project)
Article 95 (Establishment, Approval, etc. of Operational Plan)	Article 7 (Approval of Execution Plan)
Article 96 (Relations With Other Acts)	Article 8 (Relations With Other Acts)
Article 97 (Access to and Use of Land)	Article 9 (Entry Into and Use of Land)
Article 98 (Expropriation of Land, etc.)	Article 10 (Expropriation of Lands, etc.)
Article 99 (Restriction, etc. on Disposal of State-owned Land)	Article 12 (Restriction, etc. on Disposal of State and Public Lands)
Article 100 (Entrustment With Affairs Concerning Land Purchase, etc.)	Article 16 (Entrustment of Land Purchase Business, etc.)
Article 101 (Execution of Appurtenant Work)	Article 7-2 (Execution of Appurtenant Work)
Article 104 (Inspection of Completion)	Article 12-2 (Confirmation of Completion of Work)
Article 104 (Inspection of Completion)	Article 14 (Report and Inspection, etc.)
Article 105 (Reversion of Airport Facilities and Exemption From Rent)	Article 12-3 (Title, etc., to Facilities)
Article 110 (Supervision)	Article 13 (Supervision)

1991 Aviation Act	*1991 Seoul Airport Act*
Article 89 (Establishment of Basic Airport Development Plan)	Article 4 (Drawing-up of Master Plan for New Airport Construction)
Article 93 (Restriction on Act, etc.)	Article 5 (Restriction on Acts, etc.)
Article 94 (Operator of Airport Development Projects)	Article 6 (Operator of New Airport Construction Project)
Article 95 (Establishment, Approval, etc. of Operational Plan)	Article 7 (Approval of Project Plan)
Article 96 (Relations With Other Laws)	Article 8 (Relations With Other Acts)
Article 97 (Access to and Use of Land)	Article 9 (Entry Into and Use of Land)
Article 98 (Expropriation of Land, etc.)	Article 10 (Expropriation of Lands, etc.)
Article 99 (Restriction, etc. on Disposal of State-owned Land)	Article 12 (Restriction, etc. on Disposal of State and Public Lands)
Article 100 (Entrustment with Affairs Concerning Land Purchase, etc.)	Article 16 (Entrustment of Land Purchase Business, etc.)

4.101 **In response, the United States argues** that, first, there is an inherent contradiction in Korea's argument that the articles of the *Seoul Airport Act* " replace" certain articles in the *Aviation Act*, when these very articles in the *Aviation Act* are still in force today.[185] The United States contends that Korea cites no provision in any act that suggests this to be true, nor can Korea provide evidence that the provisions of the *Aviation Act* apply to all airport development projects except the IIA project.[186]

4.102 Second, the United States refers to the above charts in which Korea points to 17 articles in the 1997 *Aviation Act* that have "similar" titles to Articles in the 1997 *Seoul Airport Act*. The United States argues that, however, given that the 1997 *Aviation Act* contains 184 Articles (not including six addenda articles), the mere fact that 17 of these 184 articles (less than 10 per cent) have "similar" titles to another act is not persuasive. According to the United States, if a Korean statute could "take precedence over," "supersede," or "replace" another statute, simply by showing that its article titles are "similar" to 10 per cent of the titles in the second statute, then a large number of Korea laws would no longer be in existence. In addition, contends the United States, many of the "similar" titles in Korea's chart can be found in acts other than the *Aviation Act*. The United States notes, for example, such article titles as "Relations With Other Acts," "Restriction, etc. on Disposal of States and Public Lands," "Entrustment of Land Purchase Business, etc.," and "Supervision" can be found in the KAA law, the law establishing KOACA, and the IIAC law. Moreover, the United States submits that many of the titles of Korea's 17 articles are neither similar, nor virtually identical. For example, "Reversion of Airport Facilities and Exemption From Rent" is not identical to "Title, etc., to Facilities." Likewise, "Contents of Basic Plan" is not identical to "Drawing up Master Plan for New Airport Construction."[187]

4.103 The United States notes, third, that the substance of the articles that Korea maintains as "similar" or "identical" are not always so. The United States notes that, for example, while the titles of Article 104 of the *Aviation Act* (Inspection of Completion) and Article 14 of the *Seoul Airport Act* (Report and Inspection, etc.) appear similar, their texts are quite different. The United States refers to the following side-by-side chart of the two articles[188]:

1997 Aviation Act	*1997 Seoul Airport Act*
Article 104 (Inspection of Completion) (1) When a project operator, as described in Article 94(2) has completed the work, he shall submit without delay a report on work completion to the Minister of Construction and Transportation to undergo the inspection of completion.	**Article 14 (Report of Inspection, etc.)** (1) The Minister of Construction and Transportation may, where necessary for the implementation of the Act, order the project operator to make necessary reports on the new airport construction project or to submit necessary data, and may have public officials serving at his Ministry enter the project operator's office, the workplace or other relevant places to inspect the business of the new airport construction project.

[185] The US notes that in its Response to Question 9 from the Panel, dated 29 November 1999, Korea states that, "The *Aviation Act* is, of course, still in effect."

[186] US Response to Korea's Answer to Question 9 from the Panel, dated 29 November 1999.

[187] Ibid.

[188] Ibid.

1997 Aviation Act	*1997 Seoul Airport Act*
(2) The Minister of Construction and Transportation shall, upon receiving an application for inspection and completion under paragraph (1), conduct the inspection of completion, and in a case where he deems that the work has been executed in conformity with the permission on the work, he shall deliver a certificate of completion to the applicant.	(2) The public officials conducting an inspection of the affairs pertaining to the new airport construction project under paragraph (1) shall carry a certificate indicating his mandated powers and produce it to relevant personnel.
(3) When the certificate of completion inspection is delivered under paragraph (2), the inspection, authorization, etc. of completion on the work according to approval, permission, license, etc. under the subparagraphs of Article 96(1) shall be considered to be obtained.	(3) Matters necessary for the certificate as provided for in paragraph (2) shall be determined by the Ordinance of the Ministry of Construction and Transportation.
(4) The land and airport facilities which are created or installed by the airport development projects, shall not be used before a certificate or completion inspection as referred to in paragraph (2) is delivered: Provided, That this shall not apply in a case where a permission on use prior to completion is granted by the Minister of Construction and Transportation.	

4.104 The United States asserts that each of the examples above shows the weaknesses in Korea's argument, and reinforces the US position that the *Seoul Airport Act* does not replace the *Aviation Act.* The United States reiterates that the acts are entirely consistent with one another. The United States concludes that, indeed, to the extent that certain articles are similar, it is because the *Aviation Act* is the foundation upon which supplementary laws like the *Seoul Airport Act* are based.[189]

Incorporation by Reference

4.105 **Korea acknowledges** that the National Assembly chose to incorporate certain provisions of the *Aviation Act* into the *Seoul Airport Act*, placing occasional specific references to the former in the latter. Korea notes that the 1997 *Seoul Airport Act* does, for example, at Article 2(2)(a), list Article 2(6) of the *Aviation Act* as the source for the definition of the term "airport facilities." Korea notes that, similarly, Article 2(1) of the 1997 *Seoul Airport Act* incorporates Article 111 of the *Aviation Act*; Article 111 in turn refers to certain of the Articles in Section 1 of Chapter V of the Aviation Act, concerning "Aerodrome and Navigation Aids" (navaids). Korea states that pursuant to Article 111, Article 75 of the *Aviation Act*, regarding the installation of navaids by MOCT or another entity granted permission to so install, does not apply. Korea states that Articles 77(1), 81 or 87, each of which address subsequent acts regarding entities granted permission to install navaids, also do not apply. However,

[189] Ibid.

Korea notes that Article 111 of the *Aviation Act* refers to and thus incorporates into the *Seoul Airport Act*, Article 76 of the *Aviation Act*, regarding public notice of navaid installation; Article 77(2), regarding inspection and further public announcement of installed navaids; Article 79, regarding delayed or discontinued use of navaids; Article 80, regarding management of navaids; Article 82, regarding the restriction of various "obstacles"; Article 83, regarding the requirement of aviation obstacle lights and beacons; Article 85, regarding forbidden or illegal acts; and, Article 86, regarding rent due to parties using navaids once they are installed. Finally, Korea notes that Articles 105(3) and 105(4) of the 1997 *Aviation Act*, by virtue of Article 12-3(2) of the 1997 *Seoul Airport Act*, permit investors or project operators to operate and derive revenue from airport facilities.[190]

4.106 Korea notes that the 1991 *Seoul Airport Act* similarly incorporates by reference several provisions of the 1991 *Aviation Act*. Article 2(2)(b) of the 1991 *Seoul Airport Act* turns to the 1991 *Aviation Act* for a definition of the term "aircraft handling business."[191] Korea states that, moreover, the reference in Article 2(1) of the 1991 *Seoul Airport Act* to Article 111 of the 1991 *Aviation Act* is identical to the parallel reference in the 1997 Acts, incorporating by reference Articles 76, 77(2), 79, 80, 82, 83, 85 and 86 of the 1991 *Aviation Act*. Korea states that, finally, by virtue of Article 8(1) of the 1991 *Seoul Airport Act*, subparagraph 16, KAA's "operational plan" is to be approved by the Minister of Transportation under Article 95(1) of the 1991 *Aviation Act*. Korea notes that such approval was already required under Article 7 of the 1991 *Seoul Airport Act*.[192]

4.107 Korea argues that these specific Articles of the *Aviation Act*, while incorporated by reference into the *Seoul Airport Act*, do not demonstrate that MOCT, rather than KAA, KOACA or IIAC, is the entity responsible for procurement for the IIA construction project. Korea argues that even if the United States' "control" test was determinative of GPA coverage, these specific Articles do not demonstrate "control" by MOCT over KAA, KOACA or IIAC. Further, Korea argues that they do not demonstrate, under the test included in Article I:3 of the GPA, that MOCT "requires" KAA, KOACA or IIAC "to award contracts in accordance with particular requirements." In support of its argument, Korea refers to evidence showing that KAA, KOACA and IIAC conduct their own procurements and conclude their own contracts, pursuant to their own *Contract Administration Regulations*.[193]

4.108 Korea concludes that it has demonstrated that the National Assembly enacted amendments to the *Seoul Airport Act* and the *Korea Airport Corporation Act*, rather than the *Aviation Act*, in order to appoint KAA as the entity responsible for IIA construction in December 1991. Korea further states that along with Article 6(1) of the *Seoul Airport Act*, which was amended in December 1991 to appoint KAA to the IIA project, amendments to KAA's authorizing statute, the *Korea Airport Corporation*

---

190 Korea's Answer to Question 9 from the Panel, dated 29 November 1999.

191 Korea notes that there appears to be a typographical error in Article 2(2)(b). Rather than Article 2(26) of the 1991 *Aviation Act*, the definition of the term "aircraft handling business" is found at Article 2(30) of the 1991 *Aviation Act*.

192 Korea's Answer to Question 9 from the Panel, dated 29 November 1999.

193 Ibid.

Act, assigned to KAA the IIA project "as referred to [in] subparagraph 2 of Article 2 of the *Seoul Airport Act*."[194]

4.109 **In response, the United States argues** that the *Seoul Airport Act* does not appoint the entity responsible for the IIA project — it merely lists a range of entities that could be IIA project operators. It then grants MOCT ultimate authority to select any entity to be the project operator for the IIA project.

4.110 The United States further argues that the *Aviation Act* is the primary Korean law relating to aviation matters, and it addresses a range of aviation-related issues, including aircraft registration, aviation safety, air transportation businesses, and airport development projects. According to the United States, this *Act* is then supplemented by a host of additional Korean laws and measures in these areas.[195] The United States argues that the *Seoul Airport Act* is just one such law, that it provides ancillary rules for the IIA project.[196]

4.111 As such, the United States argues that the *Seoul Airport Act* is entirely consistent with the *Aviation Act*. The United States notes that, for instance, Article 2(2) of the *Seoul Airport Act* cross-references the *Aviation Act* by defining the term "new airport construction project" as "[c]onstruction of such airport facilities as stipulated in subparagraph 6 of Article 2 of the *Aviation Act*. In fact, the United States notes that there is no provision in either act (or in any other Korean law) that expressly or implicitly suggests that the *Seoul Airport Act* "replaces" or "supersedes" the *Aviation Act*.[197]

(iii) Proviso in Article 94(1) of the Aviation Act

4.112 **Korea notes** that Article 94(1) of the 1997 *Aviation Act* states that MOCT shall carry out airport development projects, "provided that this shall not apply in case (of) provided otherwise by this Act or other Acts and subordinate statutes." Korea notes that, similarly, Article 94(1) of the 1991 *Aviation Act* states that "[e]xcept as provided otherwise by this Act or other laws and regulations," MOT shall carry out airport development projects.[198]

4.113 Korea states that the "other Acts" and "other laws" providing that an entity other than MOCT is to implement IIA construction are the *Seoul Airport Act*, the *Korea Airport Corporation Act*, the *Korea Airport Construction Authority Act*, and the *Law on Inchon International Airport Corporation*. Korea also notes that December 1991 amendments to the *Seoul Airport Act* and the *Korea Airport Corporation Act* appointed KAA as the entity responsible for the IIA project, August 1994 amendments to the *Seoul Airport Act* and the September 1994 enactment of the *Korea Airport Construction Authority Act* appointed KOACA to that role and February 1999 amendments to the *Seoul Airport Act*, together with passage of the *Law on Inchon International Airport Corporation*, similarly appointed IIAC to perform this

194 Korea's Response to the US Answer to Question 18 from the Panel, dated 29 November 1999, citing *Korea Airport Corporation Act*, Article 7(5-2). Korea also notes that Footnotes 46 and 47 to Korea's response to Question 9 make the same point with regard to KOACA and IIAC.

195 Articles 15, 24, 39, 74, 108, and 112 of the *Aviation Act*.

196 US Response to Korea's Answer to Question 9 from the Panel, dated 29 November 1999.

197 Ibid.

198 Korea's Answer to Question 9 from the Panel, dated 29 November 1999.

task. Korea argues that in each case, the *proviso* in Article 94(1) of the *Aviation Act* was triggered.[199]

4.114 **In response, the United States argues** that this argument is inconsistent with Korea's argument that the *Aviation Act* was "replaced" and "superseded by the *Seoul Airport Act*." The United States asserts that Korea now argues that the *Aviation Act* in fact does apply to the Inchon International Airport project, and that the *Seoul Airport Act* and other laws "trigger" the *proviso* in Article 94(1). The United States argues that neither the *Aviation Act* was replaced and superseded by the *Seoul Airport Act*, nor was the *proviso* in Article 94(1) triggered by the *Seoul Airport Act*. The United States notes in this respect that Korea concedes that KAA, KOACA, and IIAC are "project operators," as designated by the *Seoul Airport Act*. The United States argues that if the *Seoul Airport Act* designates these entities as "project operators," then this Act cannot trigger the *proviso* in Article 94(1) of the *Aviation Act* as Korea suggests, because the *proviso* relates to MOCT's authority over airport development projects and not to the designation of project operators. The United States asserts that the designation of project operators is addressed in Article 94(2).[200]

4.115 The United States acknowledges that the proviso contained in Article 94(1) of the *Aviation Act* appears to indicate that the statutory authority of MOCT over airport development projects can be modified when specifically provided for in the *Aviation Act* or other statutes. However, the United States argues that there is nothing in the *Aviation Act* or any other Korean law that indicates that MOCT no longer has statutory authority over the IIA project or that this authority has been granted to any entity other than MOCT. Instead, the United States argues that the Korean laws that relate to the IIA project merely confirm the designation of entities such as KAA, KOACA, and IIAC as "project operators" of the IIA project pursuant to Article 94(2) of the *Aviation Act*. The United States further argues that Article 94(2) is separate and distinct from Article 94(1), and does not affect MOCT's statutory authority over the airport construction project.[201]

4.116 The United States argues that the *Aviation Act* provides support that MOCT retains authority over airport development projects following the selection of a project operator. The United States notes that Article 103(1) of the *Aviation Act* states, for example, that: "[i]f there is a person who performs a work or an act to damage or destroy the airport facilities under control of the Minister of Construction and Transportation, the Minister may have the operator of such work or the person doing such act bear the whole or part of the expenses..." According to the United States, this provision recognizes that even when there is a project operator on an airport development project, MOCT maintains its statutory authority over the project. The United States contends that, moreover, after the designation of a project operator, MOCT continues to have authority to direct the project operator[202] and ultimately is respon-

199 Ibid.

200 US Response to Korea's Answer to Question 9 from the Panel, dated 29 November 1999.

201 US Answer to Question 18 from the Panel, dated 29 November 1999.

202 *Aviation Act*, Articles 103, 107, 108.

sible for making the determination as to whether the project operator's work "has been executed in conformity with the permission on the work."[203]

(e) Is the Control Test Justified Under the GPA?

(i) Does a Control Test Exist in the GPA?

4.117 **Korea argues** that the United States' test does not exist in the GPA. More specifically, Korea argues that the test itself, the categories of "control" identified by the United States as relevant and the degree of control identified by the United States as sufficient to deem an entity "controlled" are not referred to anywhere in the GPA. Korea further argues that the non-textually-based test proposed by the United States would have the effect of overriding the basis upon which signatories negotiated their GPA commitments - that is, the specific enumeration of lists of entities to which the substantive obligations of the Agreement were to apply. Korea refers to its arguments in paragraphs 4.291 - 4.312.

4.118 **In response, the United States acknowledges** that the *Vienna Convention* requires first and foremost a textual interpretation of a treaty, which would ensure that an explicit enumeration of lists of entities would override everything else. However, the United States argues that the relationship between a listed entity and a non-listed entity is a legitimate factor to consider in determining whether certain procurements are covered under the GPA.

4.119 The United States further argues that the notion of "control" does exist in the current GPA. In addition, although it is not applicable to this dispute, the United States notes that Article XXIV:6(b) also relies on the concept of "control":

> Where a Party wishes, in exercise of its rights, to withdraw an entity from Appendix I on the grounds that government control or influence over it has been effectively eliminated, that Party shall notify the Committee ... In considering the proposed modification to Appendix I and any consequential compensatory adjustment, allowance shall be made for the market-opening effects of the removal of government control or influence.

4.120 The United States contends that, indeed, if "control" did not exist in the Agreement, then the coverage of non-listed entities that are "'attached/connected/affiliated' etc." to a listed entity (*e.g.*, branch offices, subsidiary organizations, and other subdivisions) would not be achieved.[204]

4.121 The United States further argues that if the notion of control did not exist in the GPA, the GPA would be rendered a nullity, in contravention of numerous Appellate Body decisions. According to the United States, the implication of Korea's "no control" interpretation would be to allow GPA Members to transfer procurement authority from a listed entity to a non-listed entity that is controlled by the listed entity, thus effectively avoiding being subject to GPA disciplines. The United States argues that, in the context of this dispute, Korea's argument would allow a covered entity such as MOCT to simply designate a new project manager to avoid subjecting

[203] US Answer to Question 18 from the Panel, dated 29 November 1999, citing Article 104(2) of the *Aviation Act*.

[204] US Response to Korea's Answer to Question 5 from the Panel, dated 29 November 1999.

the IIA project to the GPA. According to the United States, such a result would be contrary to the object and purpose of the GPA as reflected in its text and context, and cannot be what the drafters of the GPA intended. The United States argues that such an interpretation would have significant negative ramifications on the future applications and interpretations of the Agreement.[205]

4.122 **Korea argues in response** that the United States is wrong when it argues that without a "control" test, GPA signatories would be able to transfer procurement authority from a listed entity to a non-listed entity that is controlled by the listed entity, thus effectively avoiding being subject to GPA disciplines. Korea reiterates that Article I:3 of the GPA in fact provides for the extension of coverage to non-listed bodies where those non-listed bodies are required by covered entities to award contracts in accordance with particular requirements.[206]

4.123 Korea notes that, moreover, the United States contended previously that the concept of "compensatory adjustments" under Article XXIV:6 of the GPA would provide a remedy in these circumstances.[207] Korea refers to its arguments contained in paragraphs 4.26 and 4.560.

(ii) Relevant Appellate Body Decisions

4.124 **The United States emphasizes** that the absence of the word "control" in the GPA text does not mean that such a test cannot and should not be applied. To support this argument, the United States refers to *Canada - Measures Affecting the Importation of Milk and the Exportation of Dairy Products* (*Canada - Dairy*).[208] The United States contends that in the *Canada - Dairy* decision, the Appellate Body applied a control test to determine whether a provincial board made up of milk producers was actually a "government" for the purposes of Article 9.1(a) of the *Agreement on Agriculture*. The United States argues that there is no reference to "control" in Article 9.1(a), yet the Appellate Body applied such a test to pierce through the fiction created by the provincial board to find that the board was actually a "government." In the view of the United States, the instant case is closely analogous.

4.125 The United States also asserts that the Appellate Body decision provides guidance on the determination of "control" in its report. The United States makes reference to the following excerpts from that decision:

> "A "government agency" is, in our view, an entity which exercises powers vested in it by a "government" for the purpose of performing functions of a "governmental" character, that is, to "regulate," "restrain," "supervise" or "control" the conduct of private citizens. As with any agency relationship, a "government agency" may enjoy a degree of discretion in the exercise of its functions ...

---

205 US Answer to Question 20 from the Panel, dated 29 November 1999.

206 Korea's Response to the US Answer to Question 20 from the Panel, dated 29 November 1999.

207 Ibid.

208 Appellate Body Report, *Canada - Measures Affecting the Importation of Milk and the Exportation of Dairy Products* ("*Canada - Dairy*"), WT/DS103/AB/R, WT/DS113/AB/R, adopted 27 October 1999, DSR 1999:V, 2057.

The "governmental" character of the boards' functions, as well as the extent of their regulatory control is underlined by the fact that their orders and regulations are enforceable in courts of law. Thus, the powers of the provincial boards are augmented by the machinery of the State itself, and the boards have at their disposal the public force to ensure that their regulatory functions and decisions are carried out. Although the provincial boards enjoy a high degree of discretion in the exercise of their powers, governments retain "ultimate control" over them. The Panel was, therefore, correct to conclude that the provincial milk marketing boards are "government agencies.""[209]

4.126 The United States argues that the Appellate Body in the *Canada - Dairy* case agreed with the panel's analysis that the Government of Canada had "ultimate control" over Canada's provincial milk marketing boards based on two factors: delegation of power (that is, whether the marketing boards acted under explicit authority granted to them by the government), and function (that is, whether the marketing boards acted in the manner in which the government would have acted otherwise).

4.127 The United States asserts that the Appellate Body decision supports the United States' interpretation of Article I:1. Further, the United States argues that it uses the same analysis in this dispute as the Appellate Body in the *Canada - Dairy* case to determine whether KAA, KOACA and IIAC are subdivisions of MOCT. The United States argues that it verified, through the use of Korea's laws, that KAA's, KOACA's and IIAC's powers derive from authority explicitly delegated to them as project operators by MOCT and that they cannot act outside the purview of their delegated powers. The United States also argues that its "control" analysis confirms that KAA, KOACA and IIAC are only performing functions that, had the authority not been delegated to them, MOCT would itself be performing.

4.128 **In response, Korea notes** that there is no evidence to indicate that the authority of KAA (and KOACA and IIAC) has been delegated from MOCT. Korea argues that, rather, the authority of KAA and its successors was derived from legislation, passed by the National Assembly.

4.129 Korea also notes that in *Canada - Dairy*, the issue was whether provincial milk marketing boards, composed in part of private citizens, that exercised government power, were "government" for purposes of the *Agreement on Agriculture*. Korea argues that this issue is very different from the issue presented by MOCT and KAA. According to Korea, the question is not whether KAA (and KOACA and IIAC) are government entities. Rather, the question is whether they are covered government entities.

4.130 Korea further notes that the United States cites the opinion of the Appellate Body in the *Canada - Dairy* case for the proposition that the degree of control allegedly exercised by MOCT over KAA, KOACA and IIAC requires a determination that those independent entities are MOCT. In Korea's view, in fact, *Canada - Dairy* establishes the opposite.

---

[209] Appellate Body Report, *Canada - Dairy*, *supra*, footnote 208, paras. 97 and 100.

(f) The Implications of a Control Test for Parties' Annex 1

(i) Amtrak

4.131 **Korea argues** that if the United States' "control test" were to prevail, a signatory's express decision to leave entities off its lists of commitments would have no effect. To illustrate its point, Korea considers the case of Amtrak, an entity created by the US Congress in 1970 for the purpose of operating the nation's intercity passenger rail service. Amtrak is not included in the United States' commitments. Korea argues that Amtrak is, nonetheless, subject to the control of the Executive Office of the President, which is itself an Annex 1 covered entity. Korea makes the following comments in support of its argument.

4.132 First, Korea notes that Amtrak's board, consists of seven voting members, all of whom are appointed by the Executive Office of the President. Korea states that the Secretary of Transportation, head of another Annex 1 covered entity, the US Department of Transportation, is a voting member of the Amtrak board.

4.133 Secondly, Korea notes that Amtrak is required to submit an annual report to the Executive Office of the President detailing its operations, activities, revenues, expenditures and accomplishments for the previous fiscal year. Korea states that the Secretary of Transportation is also required to prepare an annual report on Amtrak's effectiveness in helping to meet the requirements for a balanced US transportation system. Korea further states that this report is to include recommendations for further legislation regulating Amtrak's activities.

4.134 Thirdly, Korea notes that the Executive Office of the President submits a proposed budget to the US Congress on Amtrak's behalf, and any congressional appropriation is made to the Secretary of Transportation, rather than to Amtrak itself. Korea states in this respect that federal subsidies for Amtrak's operation are massive. Korea specifically states that since 1971, the United States Government has provided a total of $21 billion in federal subsidies to Amtrak. Most recently, the *Amtrak Reform and Accountability Act* of 1997 authorized appropriations to Amtrak of over $5 billion in capital and operating funds for the period 1998-2002 alone.

4.135 Korea further states that despite the fact that KAA, KOACA and IIAC are independent legal persons under Korean law, each of the factors discussed above in relation to Amtrak - authority to appoint board members, composition of the board, reporting requirements, oversight of fiscal decision-making and source of funding - was used by the United States to argue that KAA, KOACA and IIAC are subject to control by MOCT, and by virtue of that control should be considered covered entities. Korea concludes that, similarly, under the United States' test, Amtrak would, by virtue of the control exercised by the Executive Office of the President and the Department of Transportation, be considered a covered entity.

4.136 Korea argues that this outcome would, presumably, prove problematic for the United States since Amtrak's procurement authority includes an explicit requirement that it exclusively buy "unmanufactured articles, material, and supplies mined or produced in the United States," and "manufactured articles, material, and supplies manufactured in the United States substantially from articles, material, and supplies mined, produced, or manufactured in the United States." Korea also argues that the United States' proposed "control" test would have a broad effect on GPA signatories' commitments generally.

(ii) Comsat

4.137 **To further illustrate its argument, Korea notes** the impact of the United States' "control" test on Comsat, another entity not included in the United States' GPA commitments. Korea states that pursuant to the *Communication Satellite Act* of 1962, the US Congress authorized the creation of Comsat, for the purpose of facilitating the establishment of a commercial communications satellite system. Korea asserts that like Amtrak's authorizing statute, the *Communication Satellite Act* of 1962 states that Comsat "will not be an agency or establishment of the United States Government."[210]

4.138 Korea states that along with the appointment of members to Comsat's board, the Executive Office of the President, an Annex 1 covered entity, undertakes considerable oversight of Comsat's activities. Korea specifically, notes that the President shall "provide for continuous review of all phases of the development and operation of [a communications satellite] system, including the activities of [Comsat]."[211] Korea further notes that Comsat is also required to provide to the Executive Office of the President "annually and at such other times as it deems desirable, a comprehensive and detailed report of its operations, activities, and accomplishments."[212]

4.139 Korea states that, additionally, the US Federal Communications Commission ("FCC"), another Annex 1 covered entity, is directed to perform a number of oversight functions regarding Comsat. Korea notes that, for example, the FCC is empowered "to authorize [Comsat] to issue any shares of capital stock ... or to borrow any moneys, or to assume any obligation in respect of the securities of any other person, upon a finding that such issuance, borrowing, or assumption is compatible with the public interest, convenience, and necessity."[213]

4.140 Korea further notes that the FCC's control extends to Comsat's procurement. Korea states, more specifically, that the FCC shall "insure effective competition, including the use of competitive bidding where appropriate, in the procurement by [Comsat] ... of apparatus, equipment, and services required for ... the communications satellite system."[214] The FCC shall also "approve technical characteristics of the operational communications satellite system to be employed by [Comsat]."[215]

4.141 Korea argues that under the United States' "control" test, the control exercised by the Executive Office of the President and the FCC would make Comsat a covered entity. Korea states that as with Amtrak, the factors mentioned with regard to Comsat - authority to appoint board members, reporting requirements, oversight and virtual direction of fiscal decision-making and oversight of the technical and procedural aspects of procurement - were specifically used by the United States to argue that KAA, KOACA and IIAC are subject to control by MOCT, and by virtue of that control should be considered covered entities. Korea argues that, in contrast to the FCC's control over Comsat, MOCT does not require KAA, KOACA or IIAC to award contracts in accordance with particular requirements.

---

210 47 U.S.C. § 731.
211 47 U.S.C. § 721(a)(2).
212 47 U.S.C. § 744.
213 47 U.S.C. § 721(c)(8).
214 47 U.S.C. § 721(c)(1).
215 47 U.S.C. § 721(c)(6).

(iii) Conclusions from Amtrak and Comsat Examples

4.142 **Korea argues** that it is clear from the Amtrak and Comsat examples that, were the United States' "control" test to be accepted, it would have broad, unintended and unpredictable effects upon signatories' express decisions to leave entities off their Appendix I lists of commitments.

4.143 Korea refers to the fact that in discussing the control exercised by central government entities over Amtrak and Comsat, the United States has noted that "the retained links with the Government may be seen as only those necessary to ensure that the interests of the public are reflected in the operations of each corporation."[216] Korea further notes that the United States has observed that a strong and logical argument against coverage of Amtrak and Comsat is that "the code is aimed at government ministries [sic] and their subdivisions - not the myriad organizations tangential to the essential function of government."[217] Korea states that it agrees with this observation and on the basis of these comments made by the United States, argues that the broad expansion of GPA signatories' commitments that would result from the imposition of the United States' "control" test should be rejected.

(g) Implications of a Control Test for Annex 3

4.144 **Korea notes** that every entity on Korea's Annex 3 is controlled by an Annex 1 entity in the same sense that KAA is "controlled" by MOCT. Korea refers to several examples discussed in paragraphs 4.262 - 4.269. Korea states that it believes that most, if not all, Annex 3 entities of other parties are also controlled by their Annex 1 entities. In support of this belief, Korea refers to the control exercised by Japan's Ministry of Transport, an Annex 1 entity, over the New Tokyo International Airport Authority, an Annex 3 entity. Korea refers to paragraph 4.250 where this example is further discussed.

4.145 Korea argues that, if control converts an entity not on Annex 1 into an Annex 1 entity, then Annex 3 would be greatly diminished, if not reduced to a nullity. First, Korea argues that under the US "control" test, entities listed on a Member's Annex 3 will be considered covered under Annex 1 by virtue of the "control" over them by Annex 1 entities. Korea cites Japan's New Tokyo International Airport Authority as an example. Second, Korea argues that separate and distinct entities, like the United States' Amtrak and Comsat, will be nonetheless subject to the same degree of control by Annex 1 entities as that allegedly exercised by MOCT over KAA despite their intentional exclusion from Annex 3.[218] Korea further argues that given the differences in thresholds between Annex 1 and Annex 3, this would have the effect of greatly changing the commitments of the parties to the GPA and this is a result to be avoided. Korea notes that all GPA signatories except Japan committed to substantially lower thresholds for goods and services procurements by Annex 1 entities than for such procurements by Annex 3 entities.

---

[216] *Agreements Being Negotiated at the Multilateral Trade Negotiations in Geneva*, US International Trade Commission Investigation No. 332-101 (MTN Studies, August 1979), p. 44.
[217] *Ibid.*
[218] Korea's Answer to Question 11 from the Panel, dated 29 November 1999.

4.146 **In response, the United States argues** that a control analysis will not reduce Annex 3 to a nullity because, pursuant to Articles 31 and 32 of the *Vienna Convention*, an interpretation of the GPA will be first and foremost based on its text. The United States contends that, therefore, the text of Annex 3 will always take precedence over any control analysis. The United States reiterates that "control" is useful in determining whether non-listed entities should be covered under the GPA because they are "'attached/connected/affiliated' etc." to a listed entity. The United States argues that this in no way expands any GPA Party's obligations beyond what was agreed to at the close of negotiations on 15 April 1994. The United States asserts that, in fact, it ensures that the balance of rights and obligations and the comparable level of mutually agreed coverage among the Parties, as provided in the GPA, are preserved.[219]

(h) Article I:3

4.147 **Korea argues** that the "control" test proposed by the United States does not comport to the standard included in Article I:3. More specifically, Korea argues that none of the factors submitted by the United States as illustrative of the "control" exercised by MOCT over KAA, KOACA and IIAC suggests that MOCT requires those three entities to adhere to any particular requirements in awarding contracts for the IIA project.

4.148 Korea further argues that it has demonstrated that KAA, KOACA and IIAC are separate legal persons under Korean law, that each entity has adopted its own procurement regulations, and that each entity is, as a result of its status as a legal person, empowered to and has in fact conducted procurements and signed contracts on its own behalf.

4.149 Korea also reiterates that the United States has offered no evidence supporting a conclusion that MOCT or any other covered entity has ever "required" KAA (or KOACA or IIAC) "to award contracts in accordance with particular requirements." Korea states that it has, in fact, affirmatively demonstrated that no such requirements exist.[220]

(i) Relevance of Lists in Annexes

4.150 **Korea argues** that the control test cannot be sustained because, according to that test, entities need not be listed in Annex 1 or included via any notes thereto, for their procurements to be subject to the GPA. Rather, under the United States' test, if a central government entity listed on a signatory's Annex 1 "retain[s] control of the procurements by" another entity, or "remains in ultimate control" of "procurement authority," procurements are de facto made by that central government entity. In Korea's view, "de facto" coverage of unlisted entities would undermine the entire basis upon which signatories negotiated their GPA commitments - the specific enumeration of lists of entities to which the substantive obligations of the Agreement were to apply. It would, according to Korea, have broad, unintended effects upon signatories'

219 US Response to Korea's Answer to Question 22 from the Panel, dated 29 November 1999.
220 Korea's Response to the US Answer to Question 20 from the Panel, dated 29 November 1999.

express decisions to leave entities off their Appendix I lists of commitments. Korea also refers to its arguments in paragraphs 4.31, 4.117 and 4.142.

(j) Relevance of Note 1 to Annex 1

4.151 **Korea argues** that the US "control" test does not exist in the language of the GPA and that, instead, Note 1 to Korea's Annex 1 specifically, and exclusively, governs the means of identifying "covered entities," which, while not themselves listed on Annex 1, are nonetheless considered covered. Note 1 states that "subordinate linear organizations, special local administrative organs, and attached organs as prescribed in the *Government Organization Act*" are such entities.

(k) Relevance of Domestic Practices and Laws

4.152 **Korea also argues** that the "control" test proposed by the United States in these proceedings is inconsistent with the test that would apply under US procurement law to determine whether a private entity undertaking procurement for a central government entity is effectively under the control of that central government entity, as an "agent" or "conduit."

4.153 Korea argues that even where a central government entity: (i) approved the private entity's decision to conduct the procurement; (ii) was the final selection authority for the procurement; (iii) would take title to the material procured; and (iv) would pay for the system procured with government funds, US courts have held that the private procurement entity was not sufficiently controlled by the central government entity to confer jurisdiction over challenges to allegedly unlawful procurement practices undertaken by the private procurement entity.[221] Korea further argues that for jurisdiction to attach, the private procurement entity would have to have been identified contractually as an "agent" for the central government entity.

4.154 Korea argues that under this standard, KAA, KOACA and IIAC could not be considered "stand-ins" for MOCT, and considered covered entities by virtue of their relationship thereto. Korea contends that IIA procurements by KAA, KOACA and IIAC are not nearly as closely tied to MOCT as are procurements by the US private procurement entities to US central government entities in the cases described above, under factors (i) - (iv).

4.155 In support of its argument, Korea notes that it has demonstrated that KAA, KOACA and IIAC are the "final selection authorities" for IIA procurements rather than MOCT. Moreover, MOCT does not finance all of the procurements related to the Inchon project. Korea states that, moreover, and most importantly, the authorizing statutes for KAA, KOACA and IIAC - like a contract governing the relationship between a private US procurement entity and a US central government entity - expressly state that those three entities are legal persons under Korean law.[222] For all of these reasons, Korea asserts that they are not agents for MOCT or any other Korean

---

[221] *US West Communications Services, Inc. v. United States*, 940 F.2d 622, 629-630 (Fed. Cir. 1991). See also *Phoenix Engineering, Inc. v. M-K Ferguson of Oak Ridge Co.*, 966 F.2d 1513, 1526 (6th Cir. 1992), *cert. denied*, 507 US 984 (1993).

[222] *Korean Airport Corporation Act*, Article 3; *Korea Airport Construction Authority Act*, Article 3; *Law on Inchon International Airport Corporation*, Article 2.

central government entity. Korea concludes that under the test imposed under US law, KAA, KOACA and IIAC could not be considered covered entities *via* MOCT.

4.156 **In response to Korea's argument** that US courts have held that one cannot challenge a "central government entity" over "unlawful procurement practices undertaken by a private entity" under its control, the **United States notes** that Korea's argument merely confirms that control is unrelated to an entity's legal status. According to the United States, no matter how much the control, an entity's separate legal status cannot be pierced, unless for non-control reasons. Thus, the United States argues that not only is US case law irrelevant to the interpretation of the GPA, this particular case does not even support Korea's position in this dispute. The United States also responds by noting that the relationship between a listed and non-listed entity is a legitimate factor to consider in determining whether certain procurements are covered under the GPA. According to the United States, Korea itself uses this factor when, in discussing its position regarding Note 1, it mentions Note 1 to Korea's Annex 1 provides the exclusive means by which to identify as Annex 1 covered entities those entities that, while not literally listed on Annex 1, are nonetheless considered Annex 1 covered entities by virtue of their relationship with entities listed on Annex 1.

4. *Appendix I, Annex 1: Note 1*

(a) Interpretation of Note 1

4.157 **Korea argues** that the *Vienna Convention on the Law of Treaties* contains customary rules of interpretation that should be used in interpreting Korea's Note 1 to Annex 1. Korea further argues that pursuant to Article 31 of the *Vienna Convention on the Law of Treaties*, the first step is to consult the ordinary meaning of Note 1.[223]

4.158 **The United States argues** that the fundamental principle of *effet utile* ("principle of effectiveness") applies to the interpretation of Note 1. The United States claims that, according to this principle, "a treaty interpreter is not free to adopt a meaning that would reduce parts of a treaty to redundancy or inutility."[224] The United States further argues that this principle must apply to any interpretation of Note 1.

(b) Expansive or Restrictive Interpretation of Note 1 to Annex 1?

4.159 **The United States further states** that it is arguable that Note 1 serves both to clarify that Annex 1 covers all possible categories of subordinate units of "central government entities," particularly given Korea's exclusive terminology of certain subordinate units and also to expand Korea's Annex 1 coverage to include those entities that may not be subordinate units, but may nevertheless be considered "subor-

---

223 *US - Shrimps, supra,* footnote 106, para. 114 ("A treaty interpreter must begin with, and focus upon, the text of the particular provision to be interpreted").

224 Appellate Body Report, *Canada - Dairy, supra,* footnote 208, para. 133; Appellate Body Report, *US - Gasoline, supra,* footnote 105, at 21; and Appellate Body Report, *Japan - Alcoholic Beverages II, supra,* footnote 105, at 106.

dinate linear organizations," "special local administrative organs," or "attached organs."

4.160 **On the other hand, Korea argues** that Note 1 to Korea's Annex 1 specifically, and exclusively, governs the means of identifying "covered entities," which while not themselves listed on Annex 1, are nonetheless considered covered. Korea notes in this respect that Note 1 states that "subordinate linear organizations, special local administrative organs, and attached organs as prescribed in the *Government Organization Act*" are such entities.

4.161 **The United States notes in response** that Annex 1 cannot contain the universe of bodies internal to central government entities under Korean law because it does not contain the New Airport Development Group. The United States argues that this is obvious since Korea acknowledges that the New Airport Development Group is internal to MOCT. However, the New Airport Development Group is not included within Annex 1. The United States argues that, similarly, the entirety of the Korean central government structure cannot be embodied in the *Government Organization Act* because Korea further admits that the New Airport Development Group is neither a "subordinate linear organization," a "special local administrative organ," or an "attached organ" of MOCT. The United States asserts that these statements are inconsistent with each other.

4.162 The United States further argues that Note 1 cannot define "central government entity" by giving the term a special meaning, unique only to Korea thus displacing the ordinary meaning of "central government entity." In support of its argument, the United States notes that nowhere in this provision is there any indication, explicit or implicit, that Note 1 is meant to define "central government entity."

4.163 The United States additionally argues that the verb "includes" in Note 1 makes clear that Korea's Annex 1 entities cover more than just the three categories of sub-entities referred to in the Note. The United States argues that Korea's interpretation, therefore, suggests that every single party to the GPA has agreed to provide Korea with its own unique definition of "central government entity", different from the common definition of "central government entity" they use. The United States questions whether the European Communities, Hong Kong, Japan, Liechtenstein, Norway and Switzerland agreed to this and notes that the United States did not. The United States argues that Korea offered no supplementary means of interpretation to back this claim up. Further, the United States argues that Note 1 does not define the scope of "central government entity."

(c) Ordinary Meaning of "Prescribed in the Government Organization Act"

(i) Status of Government Organization Act in the context of Note 1 to Annex 1

4.164 **The United States argues** that KAA, KOACA and IIAC are covered under Annex 1 on the ground that they are "subordinate linear organizations" within the meaning of Korea's Note 1 to Annex 1 of the GPA.

4.165 In support of its argument, the United States contends that Note 1 explains that the term, "subordinate linear organization," is "prescribed in the *Government Organization Act* of the Republic of Korea." According to the United States, the ordinary meaning of "prescribe" is conveyed by the definition of "prescriptive," which means "giving definite precise directions or instructions ... laying down rules of usage ..."[225] The United States argues that, therefore, the *Government Organization Act* in Note 1 merely lays down the rules of usage for "subordinate linear organization."

4.166 The United States argues that Article 1 of the *Government Organization Act* confirms the interpretation that the *Government Organization Act* merely lays down the rules of usage for "subordinate linear organizations" by stating that its aim is to provide "guidelines for the establishment, organization and the scope of function of national administrative organs for the systematic and efficient execution of national administrative affairs."[226] The United States contends that, further, Article 2 of the *Government Organization Act* does not define "subordinate linear organization," but instead offers a list of what "subordinate linear organizations" "shall be" for all "central government entities." According to the United States, Korea itself admits that the Act does not provide a definition for "subordinate linear organizations" but instead offers a list that "identifies not entities but officials within a ministry's hierarchy". Article 2 of the Act states that the subordinate linear organizations of the central administrative organs shall be Cha-Gwan (Vice-Minister), Cha-Jang (Deputy Administrator), Sil-Jang (Office Director), Guk-Jang (Bureau Director) or Bu-Jang (Department Director) and Gwa-Jang (Division Director), under Vice-Minister or Deputy Administrator, as division not belonging to Office, Bureau or Department may be set up except those otherwise prescribed by special provisions in this Act or any other laws. The subordinate linear organizations undertaking national police affairs under the Ministry of Home Affairs, however, shall be Bon-Bu-Jang (Chief Commissioner of Policy), Bu-Jang (Department Director) and Gwa-Jang (Division Director); and for those undertaking civil defense affairs, Bon-Bu-Jang (Chief of Civil Defense Headquarters), Guk-Jang (Bureau Director) and Gwa-Jang (Division Director).[227]

4.167 The United States argues that Note 1 of Korea's Annex 1 of the GPA expands Korea's Annex 1 coverage by including "subordinate linear organizations," a category of subdivisions in Korea. The United States argues that according to the *Vienna Convention* rules of interpretation, "subordinate linear organization" is virtually synonymous with subsidiary organization. Therefore, as subsidiary organizations of MOCT, KAA, KOACA and IIAC are also "subordinate linear organizations" of MOCT.

4.168 **In response, Korea argues** that the ordinary meaning of Note 1 is such that the *Government Organization Act* "limits," "restricts," "imposes authoritatively," "appoints," "dictates" and "directs" the identification of those entities that constitute subordinate linear organizations, special local administrative organs and attached organs. Korea further argues that the *Government Organization Act* does not have mere suggestive force. Korea states that, rather, it carries "imperative force," and offers "definite precise directions or instructions" regarding the identification of subordinate linear organizations, special local administrative organs and attached organs. The ordinary meaning of "subordinate linear organizations, special local administrative organs and attached organs" is irrelevant; the only relevant meaning is that prescribed by the *Government Organization Act*.

---

225 The New Shorter Oxford English Dictionary (1993 ed.), p. 2339.

226 *Government Organization Act*, Article 1.

227 Article 2(3) of the *Government Organization Act* of the Republic of Korea (version submitted by Korea in 1991, official English translation).

4.169 In support of its argument, Korea notes that the verb "prescribe" means to "[l]imit, restrict; confine within bounds," or to "[w]rite or lay down as a rule or direction; impose authoritatively; appoint, dictate, direct."[228] Korea argues that, similarly, something that is "prescriptive" is something that "giv[es] definite precise directions or instructions," or "ha[s] or impl[ies] an imperative force."[229]

(ii) "Prescribe" versus "Define"

4.170 **The United States argues** that Korea is essentially arguing that the term "subordinate linear organizations" is defined by the *Government Organization Act.* However, according to the United States "prescribe" and "define" are not synonyms. In support of this argument, the United States refers to The New Shorter Oxford English Dictionary for the ordinary meanings of "prescribe" and "prescriptive" none of which, according to the United States, define "prescribe" as "define." According to the United States, the ordinary meaning of "prescribe" means "giving definite precise directions or instructions" and "laying down rules of usage."

4.171 The United States argues that it is clear from considering the text of the *Government Organization Act* itself that the Act does not provide a definition for "subordinate linear organization." The United States notes that all the Act does is, in Korea's words, to identify "officials within a ministry's hierarchy."

4.172 The United States further argues that the textual interpretation that "prescribed in" is not the same as "defined by" is further supported by Note 1 of Korea's Annex 2, which states, "The above sub-central administrative government entities include their subordinate organizations under direct control and offices as prescribed in the Local Autonomy Law of the Republic of Korea." The United States argues that, analogous to Note 1 of Korea's Annex 1, the two terms used in Korea's Note 1 of Annex 2 are "subordinate organizations under direct control" and "offices." The United States notes that these terms are found in Articles 104 and 105 of the *Local Autonomy Law*, respectively.[230] The United States further notes that, like the *Government Organization Act*, the *Local Autonomy Law* does not define the two terms. In the view of the United States, these terms are not terms of art and should, therefore, be interpreted according to their ordinary meanings.

4.173 **In response, Korea states** that the United States makes too much of the minor difference between the verbs "prescribe" and "define." Korea notes that, in fact, the definition of the verbs "prescribe" and "define" employ many of the same terms, challenging the argument that they are not synonymous. Korea further notes that both definitions refer to the drawing of "bounds" or "boundaries," both make ample use of the term "precise" or "precisely," and both contain the term "restrict."[231] Korea finally notes that the definition of "define" includes the verb "prescribe," and the definition of "prescriptive" includes the term "definitive."[232]

4.174 Second, Korea asserts that the fact that Article 2(3) of the *Government Organization Act* lists officials within a ministry's hierarchy, does not mean that Article

[228] The New Shorter Oxford English Dictionary (1993 ed.), p. 2339.

[229] Ibid.

[230] *Local Autonomy Law* Act. No. 4004.

[231] The New Shorter Oxford English Dictionary (1993 ed.), pp. 618 and 2339.

[232] *Ibid.*

2(3) fails to provide a definition for the term "subordinate linear organizations." Korea argues that the Act does provide a definition of the term "subordinate linear organization" and that Article 2(3) of the Act is that definition.

4.175 Korea further argues that it had every right to define a term in its GPA commitments by reference to domestic law. Korea notes in this respect that it has been joined in so doing by the European Communities, Hong Kong, Japan, Liechtenstein, Norway, Switzerland and the United States, which, according to Korea, confirms the legitimacy of this practice. More specifically, Korea notes that within the context of the GPA, Annex 1 to the United States' GPA Appendix I defines certain excepted Department of Energy procurements with reference to the *Atomic Energy Act*. Korea further notes that, similarly, US Annex 2 commitments regarding the state of Oklahoma likewise identify covered entities as those "state agencies and departments subject of the *Oklahoma Central Purchasing Act*."[233]

[233] See also European Communities' GPA Appendix I, General Note 11 (refers to the Public Procurement Act for the meaning and identification of entities which are themselves contracting authorities); Hong Kong, China's GPA Appendix I, General Note 2 ("Hong Kong's commitments on telecommunications services are subject to the terms of the licence held by Hong Kong Telecommunications International Ltd. ... ."); Japan's GPA Appendix I, Annex 1, Note 1 ("Entities covered by the Accounts Law include all their internal sub-divisions, independent organs, attached organizations and other organizations and local branch offices provided for in the National Government Organization Law."); Japan's GPA Appendix I, Annex 2, Note 1 ("'To', 'Do', 'Fu', 'Ken' and 'Shitei-toshi' covered by the Local Autonomy Law include all internal sub-divisions, attached organizations and branch offices of all their governors or mayors, committees and other organizations provided for in the Local Autonomy Law."); Liechtenstein's GPA Appendix I, Annex 3, Title II (Defines Annex 3 covered entities associated with the provision of electricity as those "[p]ublic authorities and public undertakings ... operating on the basis of authorizations for expropriation pursuant to the Gesetz vom 16.Juni 1947 betreffend die 'Liechtensteinischen Kraftwerke' (LKWG)."); Liechtenstein's GPA Appendix I, Annex 3, Title III (Defines certain Annex 3 covered entities in the field of transport services with reference to "Vertrag vom 9.Januar 1978 zwischen dem Fürstentum Liechtenstein und der Schweizerischen Eidgenossenschaft über die Besorgung der Post- und Fernmeldedienste im Fürstentum Liechtenstein durch die Schweizerischen Post-, Telefon- und Telegrafenbetriebe (PTT)."); Norway's GPA Appendix I, Annex 3, Number 1 (Defines Annex 3 covered entities in the electricity sector as those "[p]ublic entities producing, transporting or distributing electricity pursuant to Lov om Bygging og drift av elektriske anlegg (LOV 1969-06-19), Lov om erverv av vannfall, bergverk og annen fast wiendom m.v., Kap. I, jf. Kap. V (LOV 19-17-24 16, kap. I), or Vassdragsreguleringsloven (LOV 1917-12-14 17) or Energiloven (LOV 1990-06-29 50)."); Norway's GPA Appendix I, Annex 3, Number 2 (Defines Annex 3 covered entities in the urban transport sector as those public entities "providing a service to the public in the field of transport ... according to Lov om anlegg og drift av jernbane, herunder sporvei, tunellbane og forstadsbane m.m. (LOV 1993-06-11 100), or Lov om samferdsel (LOV 1976-06-04 63) or Lov om anlegg av taugbaner og løipestrenger (LOV 1912-06-14 1)."); Norway's GPA Appendix I, Annex 3, Number 3 (Defines Annex 3 covered entities as those "[p]ublic entities providing airport facilities pursuant to Lov om luftfart (LOV 1960-12-16 1)."); Norway's GPA Appendix I, Annex 3, Number 4 (Defines Annex 3 covered entities providing port services as those "[p]ublic entities operating pursuant to Havneloven (LOV 1984-06-08 51)."); Norway's GPA Appendix I, Annex 3, Number 5 (Defines Annex 3 covered entities as those "[p]ublic entities producing or distributing water pursuant to Forskrift om Drikkevann og Vannforsyning (FOR 1951-09-28)."); Norway's GPA Appendix I, General Note 6 (States that with regard to Annex 4, the GPA is not applicable to "contracts awarded to an entity which is itself a contracting authority within the meaning of the Public Procurement Act: 'Lov om offentlige anskaffelser m.v.' (LOV 1992-11-27 116) on the basis of an exclusive right which it enjoys pursuant to a published law, regulation or administrative provision."); Switzerland's GPA Appendix I, Annex 3, Title II (Defines Annex 3

4.176 Korea states that in proposing and accepting the incorporation by reference of provisions of domestic law in each of these instances, GPA signatories agreed to the meaning ascribed to a particular term in domestic law. Korea states that this was also the case with the signatories' acceptance of the meaning accorded by Korea's circumscription of the term "central government entity" to include listed entities and their subordinate linear organizations, special local administrative organs and attached organs, "as prescribed in the Government Organization Act of the Republic of Korea."

4.177 Korea finally argues that it has the right to define "subordinate linear organization" in the way that it has in Article 2(3) of the *Government Organization Act.* Nothing in the GPA requires that Korea define the term "subordinate linear organization" in its domestic law in any particular way.

(d) Ordinary Meaning of "Subsidiary Linear Organizations"

4.178 **The United States argues** that the interpretation of Note 1 to Korea's Annex 1, based on Articles 31 and 32 of the *Vienna Convention*, confirms that in "prescribing" the terms "subordinate linear organization," "special local administrative organ," and "attached organ," the *Government Organization Act* does not define these terms. Hence, according to the United States, a textual interpretation is to be applied. The United States argues that in doing so, "subordinate linear organization" is found to be synonymous with subsidiary organization.

4.179 The United States argues that the ordinary meaning of "subordinate," according to The New Shorter Oxford English Dictionary, is "of inferior rank; dependent upon the authority or power of another ... dependent on or subservient to a chief or principle thing of the same kind ... submissive ... of inferior importance; secondary, minor ... ."[234] The United States further argues that the ordinary meaning of "linear" is, *inter alia*, "progressing in a single direction by regular steps or stages, sequential."[235] Finally, the United States argues that the ordinary meaning of "organization" is "an organized structure, body, or being."[236] The United States asserts

covered entities in the electricity sector as those "[p]ouvoirs publics ou entreprises publiques" operating "conformément à la 'loi fédérale du 24 juin 1902 concernant les installations électriques à faible et à fort courant'" or "conformément à la 'loi fédérale du 22 décembre 1916 sur l'utilisation des forces hydrauliques' et á la 'loi fédérale du 23 décembre 1959 sur l'utilisation pacifique de l'énergie atomique et la protection contre les radiations'."); Switzerland's GPA Appendix I, Annex 3, Title III (Defines Annex 3 covered entities in the transport as those entities operating "au sens de l'article 2, 1er alinéa, de la 'loi fédérale du 20 décembre 1957 sur les chemins de fer,'" "au sens de l'article 4, 1er alinéa, de la 'loi fédérale du 29 mars 1950 sur les entreprises de trolleybus,'" "au sens de l'article 2 de la 'loi fédérale du 18 juin 1993 sur le transport de voyageurs et les entreprises de transport par route,'" and "au sens de l'article 4 de la 'loi fédérale du 18 juin 1993 sur le transport de voyageurs et les entreprises de transport par route.'"); Switzerland's GPA Appendix I, Annex 3, Title IV (Defines Annex 3 covered entities providing airport services as those "[p]ouvoirs publics ou entreprises publiques exploitant des aéroports en vertu d'une concession au sens de l'article 37 de la 'loi fédérale du 21 décembre 1948 sur la navigation aérienne.'").

[234] The New Shorter Oxford English Dictionary (1993 ed.), p. 3121.

[235] Ibid. p. 1596.

[236] Ibid. p. 2020.

that, taken together, the term "subordinate linear organization" suggests an organization that is directly controlled by, dependent upon, and secondary to another organization - that is, it is a subsidiary organization.

4.180 **In response, Korea argues** that to suggest that the term "subordinate linear organization" is synonymous with the terms "subsidiary organizations" or "subsidiary or subordinate body" is not possible given the ordinary meaning of Note 1 which states that the term "subordinate linear organization" is "prescribed in the Government Organization Act of the Republic of Korea." Korea also questions the United States' use of the principles of interpretation of the *Vienna Convention of the Law of Treaties* to determine the ordinary meaning of a term such as "subsidiary organization," which is not in fact found in the GPA.

4.181 In support of its argument that the term, "subordinate linear organization," is synonymous with "subsidiary organization," **the United States refers** to the fact that Korea re-translated "subordinate linear organization" as "subsidiary organs." The United States quotes Korea: "The re-translation did not, however, alter the substantive effect of Note 1 to Annex 1." The United States argues that by amending its English translation, Korea determined that the English phrase, "subsidiary organs," is not only synonymous with "subordinate linear organizations," but is probably a better representation of what "subordinate linear organizations" was originally intended to mean. The United States also refers to its arguments in paragraph 4.435.

4.182 The United States concludes that given that KAA, KOACA and IIAC are subsidiary organizations of MOCT then they are also "subordinate linear organizations" of MOCT and are, therefore, covered under Annex 1 of the GPA.

4.183 **In response, Korea argues** that KAA, KOACA and IIAC were not converted to GPA covered entities when the term "subordinate linear organizations" was re-translated in English to "subsidiary organs" in Article 2(3) of the *Government Organization Act*. Korea notes in this respect that the term "subordinate linear organization" was re-translated by the Korean Legislation Institute as "subsidiary organs" by an amendment to the *Government Organization Act* that was enacted on 28 February 1998. Korea notes that the Korean version of the term remained the same, as did, the Korean and English versions of the enumerated list of "subordinate linear organizations" included in Article 2(3) of the Act.

(e) Subordinate Linear Organizations: Officials or Entities?

4.184 **In response to a question from the Panel, Korea notes** that it is Korean practice to refer to an organization through its head. For example, rather than say that a particular "Ministry" has authority to take certain action, Korea notes that it would say that a particular "Minister" has the authority.[237] Korea further notes that, in Korean law as embodied in the *Government Organization Act*, authority is delegated from the chief of a government agency to individual officials in the vertical chain of command, who are in some instances, in turn, authorized to delegate to other individual officials further down the chain of command. Korea notes that, in addition to the Minister and Vice-Minister, all divisions, offices and bureaus are led by "Divi-

[237] Korea's Answer to Question 11(b) from the Panel, dated 3 November 1999.

sion Directors," "Office Directors" or "Bureau Directors" listed in Article 2(3) of the *Government Organization Act* as "subordinate linear organizations."[238] Korea further notes that all legislation envisions government activity in terms of the people undertaking that activity and the chain of command under which decisions regarding that activity is made. Korea finally notes that this system may be divergent from western legal systems, but nothing in the WTO Agreements, including the GPA, prohibits it. Korea also refers to its arguments in paragraphs 4.175, 4.177 and 4.376.

4.185 **In response to Korea's argument, the United States asserts** that Korea's description of the relationship between the chief of a government agency and subsidiary linear organizations is precisely what "control" is all about. The United States argues that control exists when one entity's power to act is delegated to it by another entity, and when these acts are done on behalf of this other entity. The United States notes that this analysis was affirmed by the Appellate Body in the recent *Canada - Dairy* dispute.[239] The United States contends that KAA, KOACA and IIAC are mere project operators of the IIA project whose authorities are delegated from MOCT, and whose acts are only done on behalf of MOCT, for the benefit of MOCT. The United States further states that if "subordinate linear organizations" also act in this manner, then KAA, KOACA and IIAC must be "subordinate linear organizations" of MOCT.

4.186 **In response to a question from the Panel regarding MOCT's organization chart, Korea notes** that all of the "organs" or "organizations" included on the chart are in fact prescribed in the *Government Organization Act.* The listed "divisions, offices and bureaus" are according to Korea covered under the GPA because they are led by "Division Directors," "Office Directors" or "Bureau Directors," which are listed in Article 2(3) of the *Government Organization Act* as "subordinate linear organizations" and therefore covered by virtue of Note 1 to Korea's Annex 1. The other organizations listed on page 2 of the chart are MOCT's "special local administrative organs" and "attached organs" under the *Government Organization Act.*[240]

4.187 **The United States argues** that Korea's argument that the divisions, offices, and bureaus of MOCT are covered under Annex 1 of the GPA because they are "subordinate linear organizations" of MOCT is flawed. The United States notes that MOCT's divisions, offices, and bureaus are already covered under Annex 1 of the GPA because they are "'attached/connected/affiliated' etc. to MOCT." According to the United States, for Korea to now interpret the term, "subordinate linear organizations," as encompassing these entities would make this term redundant, because "subordinate linear organization" would merely provide for the coverage of entities that are already covered. According to the United States, such an interpretation is contrary to the "principle of effectiveness."[241]

---

238 Korea's Answer to Question 11 from the Panel, dated 29 November 1999, citing the *Government Organization Act.*

239 Appellate Body Report, *Canada - Dairy, supra,* footnote 208, paras. 96-102. Also see Panel Report, *Canada - Measures Affecting the Importation of Milk and the Exportation of Dairy Products* ("*Canada – Dairy*"), WT/DS103/R, WT/DS113/R, adopted 27 October 1999, DSR 1999:VI, 2097, para. 7.78.

240 Korea's Answer to Question 11 from the Panel, dated 29 November 1999.

241 US Response to Korea's Answer to Question 11 from the Panel, dated 29 November 1999, citing Appellate Body Report, *Canada - Dairy, supra,* footnote 208, para. 133; Appellate Body Report, *US*

4.188 **In response to a question from the Panel, Korea also notes** that the reference to individuals in Article 2(3) of the *Government Organization Act* is not a reference to these people as natural persons, but as titles of officials who head an office or bureau in the line of command within a government agency.[242] Further, in response to a question from the United States, Korea states that in Korea's terminology, reference to an "official" within the hierarchy is a reference to the position and the office itself.[243] Korea notes that the officials listed as "subordinate linear organizations" in Article 2(3) of the *Government Organization Act* are those authorized to act on behalf of the chief of the government agency concerned. Korea further states that the "subordinate linear organizations" are not the "organizations" that report to a listed individual but, rather, they are the titles of officers who report on behalf of the division or bureau. Thus, in interpreting the term "subordinate linear organization" Korea suggests that the organizational unit (ministry, bureau, division, etc.) represented by the title should be considered.[244] Korea also argues that the structure of Article 2(3) does not mean that only procurements undertaken personally by an official in Article 2(3) are covered under Annex 1. Korea argues that, rather, the entirety of that official's office is considered covered. Finally, Korea notes that all central government entities may not necessarily have each of the listed subordinate linear organizations provided for in Article 2(3) of the *Government Organization Act*.[245]

4.189 **In response, the United States argues** that the organizational units that represent the titles referred to in Article 2(3) of the *Government Organization Act* are merely branch offices of "central government entities," and are already covered pursuant to the ordinary meaning of "central government entity."

(f) Are KAA, KOACA and IIAC "Subordinate Linear Organizations"?

4.190 **In response to the argument by the United States** that KAA, KOACA and IIAC are "subordinate linear organizations" of MOCT under Note 1 to Korea's Annex 1 in paragraph 4.164, **Korea notes** that KAA, KOACA and IIAC are not identified as "subordinate linear organizations" (or the re-translated term, "subsidiary organs") in Article 2(3) of the *Government Organization Act*. Note 1 to Korea's Annex 1 states that Korea's Annex 1 includes those "subordinate linear organizations ... prescribed in the Government Organization Act of the Republic of Korea." Korea further notes that both in its current form and as it existed during the negotiations leading up to the submission by Korea of its final offer list for accession to the GPA, Article 2(3) identifies not entities, but officials within a ministry's hierarchy.

4.191 **In response, the United States argues** that it is illogical for Korea to make the claim that KAA, KOACA and IIAC are not identified as "subordinate linear organizations," given the structure of and information in the *Government Organization Act*. Specifically, the United States refers to the fact that that the *Government Or-*

- *Gasoline*, *supra*, footnote 105, at 21; and Appellate Body Report, *Japan - Alcoholic Beverages II*, *supra*, footnote 105, at 106.

242 Korea's Answer to Question 11(b) from the Panel, dated 3 November 1999.

243 Korea's Answer to Question 3 from the US, dated 3 November 1999.

244 Korea's Answer to Question 11(b) from the Panel, dated 3 November 1999.

245 Korea's Answer to Question 6 from the US, dated 3 November 1999.

ganization Act does not identify entities as "subordinate linear organizations," but only as "officials within a ministry's hierarchy." The United States additionally notes that the *Government Organization Act* does not specifically name any entities as "special local administrative organs" or "attached organs."

(g) Is NADG a "**Subordinate** Linear Organization"?

4.192 **In response to a question from the United States, Korea states** that the New Airport Development Group was established within the Ministry of Transportation. Korea further states that it drew personnel from several subordinate linear organizations, as defined in the *Government Organization Act*, within the Ministry. Korea notes that NADG is not a separate legal person but, rather, it is an ad hoc group within the Ministry. Korea concludes that NADG is not a subordinate linear organization as defined in Article 2(3) of the Act.[246]

(h) Ordinary Meaning of "Special Local Administrative Organs"

4.193 **Korea discusses** those entities identified as MOCT's "special local administrative organs," which are by virtue of Note 1 to Korea's Annex 1 considered covered entities. Korea states that among MOCT's special local administrative organs are its two Regional Aviation Offices - the Seoul Regional Aviation Office and the Pusan Regional Aviation Office.[247] Korea notes that these regional aviation offices conduct procurement for existing airports in their regions. Korea further notes that where not otherwise provided by special law, as in the case of the legal authority for the construction of IIA[248], these Offices are responsible for construction and maintenance of Korean airports, including Yangyang, Yeosoo, Muan, Daegu, Pohang, Yecheoon and Uljin Airports.

4.194 **The United States argues** that Korea, by implication, uses the ordinary meaning to interpret "special local administrative organ," and that, therefore, it is not a term of art. The United States points out that in defining "special local administrative organs", Korea chooses to use the ordinary meaning by stating, "As the term suggests, special local administrative organs carry regional portfolios". By doing so, according to the United States, Korea essentially confirms that Note 1 does not require "subordinate linear organizations", "special local administrative organs" or "affiliate organs" to be defined by the *Government Organization Act*. The United States further asserts that, indeed, "subordinate linear organization," "special local administrative organs," and "attached organs" are used uniquely by Korea to categorize the subordinate units of its "central government entities." However, according to the United States, since they are not unique terms of art and they are not defined by

246 Korea's Answer to Question 7 from the US, dated 3 November 1999.

247 Korea states that, as the term suggests, special local administrative organs carry regional portfolios. MOCT maintains other special local administrative organs, including five National Territory Management Offices (Seoul, Wonju, Taejon, Iksan and Pusan) and five River Flood Control Offices (Han River, Nakdong River, Keum River, Sumjin River and Yeongsan River).

248 See, e.g., the *Seoul Airport Act*, Article 7(5-2) of the *Korea Airport Corporation Act*, Article 7 of the *Korea Airport Construction Authority Act*, or Article 10 of the *Law on Inchon International Airport Corporation.*

the *Government Organization Act*, their ordinary meaning should apply. Further, the United States notes that the *Government Organization Act* does not identify the Seoul Regional Aviation Office and the Pusan Regional Aviation Office as "special local administrative organs."

4.195 **Korea argues** that the terms "subordinate linear organization," "special local administrative organ" and "attached organ" are in fact "unique terms of art" found in the *Government Organization Act*.

4.196 In response to a question from the United States requesting Korea to reconcile its statement that the Seoul Regional Aviation Office and the Pusan Regional Aviation office are special local administrative organs although they are not identified in the *Government Organization Act* and its statement that Note 1 to Korea's Annex 1 provides the exclusive means by which to identify as Annex 1 covered entities those entities, Korea makes the following argument. First, Korea argues that Article I:1 of the GPA limits coverage to "entities." Korea states that one of the "entities" covered by Korea's commitment is MOCT, which is a central government entity within the meaning of Annex 1 to Appendix I of Korea's GPA Schedule. Korea further states that the Seoul Regional Aviation Office and the Pusan Regional Aviation Office, which conduct the implementation of the affairs of MOCT in their respective regions, are special local administrative organs of MOCT. Korea asserts that, unlike, for example, KAA, KOACA and IIAC, they are not separate legal entities in their own right. According to Korea, MOCT has determined that its aviation responsibilities in those regions will be most efficiently administered by the use of these regional offices, as provided for in Article 3(2) of the *Government Organization Act*. Korea concludes that any body identified as a special local administrative organ pursuant to Article 3(2) of the *Government Organization Act* is an Annex 1 covered entity by virtue of Note 1.[249]

5. *Responses to Panel Question Regarding KAA*

(a) Arguments by the United States

4.197 The Panel asked both Parties to explain why KAA should or should not be considered as "'attached/connected/affiliated' etc." to MOCT and, therefore, a covered entity for the purposes of the GPA.[250]

4.198 **In response to the Panel's question, the United States argues** that KAA should be considered "'attached/connected/affiliated' etc." to MOCT because of MOCT's pervasive links to, authority over, and control of KAA.[251]

4.199 In support of its argument, the United States notes that KAA, formerly known as the "International Airport Management Committee," was created in 1979 "under the Construction and Transportation Ministry ... to bring about efficiency of International Airport management ... ."[252]

[249] Korea's Answer to Question 1 from the US, dated 3 November 1999.

[250] Question 20 from the Panel, dated 15 November 1999.

[251] US Answer to Question 22 from the Panel, dated 29 November 1999.

[252] US Answer to Question 22 from the Panel, dated 29 November 1999, citing Article 1 of the *International Airport Management Act*, Presidential Decree 9549.

4.200 The United States refers to the composition of the KAA and the projects for which KAA is responsible.[253] The United States notes that KAA may "establish a branch office,"[254] "lend or sublease any property contributed or leased,"[255] "collect rents or charges for use from those who use or utilize airport facilities managed and operated by it,"[256] "borrow funds[257], "have beneficiaries of its projects bear expenses required for the projects,"[258] and "dispose of important property,"[259] but only with the approval of MOCT.[260]

4.201 The United States also notes that KAA must: [261]

> prepare a business plan and budget bill for each business year ... and submit them to the Minister of Construction and Transportation to obtain his approval. The same shall also apply, if it wishes to modify them ...[262]
>
> [and] prepare a settlement of accounts on revenues and expenditures for each business year ... and submit it to the Minister of Construction and Transportation after undergoing an audit by a certified public accountant designated by the Minister of Construction and Transportation ...[263]
>
> [and] make rules relating to organization, accounting, personnel affairs, remuneration, etc. and obtain the approval of the Minister of Construction and Transportation. The same shall also apply, if [KAA] wishes to modify such rules.[264]

4.202 The United States refers to Article 28 of the *Korea Airport Corporation Act* which states:

> "The Minister of Construction and Transportation shall direct and control [KAA], and if it is deemed necessary to do so, he may have [KAA] report matters concerning its affairs, accounting and property, or have a public official under his control inspect books, documents, facilities and other things of [KAA]."[265]

4.203 The United States notes that the Civil Aviation Bureau within MOCT provides "guidance and supervision" for KAA[266], that KAA is listed on MOCT's Internet

[253] US Answer to Question 22 from the Panel, dated 29 November 1999.
[254] *International Airport Management Act* Article 5.
[255] Ibid. Article 17.
[256] Ibid. Article 18.
[257] Ibid. Article 23.
[258] Ibid. Article 24.
[259] Ibid. Article 26.
[260] US Answer to Question 22 from the Panel, dated 29 November 1999.
[261] US Answer to Question 22 from the Panel, dated 29 November 1999.
[262] *International Airport Management Act,* Article 20.
[263] Ibid. Article 20.
[264] Ibid. Article 22.
[265] US Answer to Question 22 from the Panel, dated 29 November 1999.
[266] See Duties of Civil Aviation Bureau, *in* MOCT Internet website document, *http://www.moct.go.kr/mcte/ mct_about/aboutml/mcthpg_air.htm.*

website as a "subsidiary organization" of MOCT[267] and that during the time-period KAA supposedly had procurement authority for the IIA project, procurements related to the project were announced as MOCT procurements.[268] The United States contends that, moreover, during the period KAA was involved in the IIA project, MOCT retained ultimate authority and control over the project. According to the United States, this further confirms that KAA is "'attached/connected/affiliated' etc." to MOCT. The United States notes that during the period KAA was involved in the IIA project the United States argues that MOCT retained jurisdiction "over the affairs relating to land, air and marine transportation, and tourism,"[269] pursuant to the *Government Organization Act of the Republic of Korea* and that it was the responsibility of MOCT to *inter alia* "designate" and "publicly announce" the Inchon Airport construction project[270] to "designate an area necessary for the execution of the new airport construction project as the project area for the construction of the new airport"[271] and to "draw up a master plan relating to the new airport construction."[272] The United States notes that the "master plan" shall include the following matters: General direction of construction; outline of the construction plan; construction period; financing plan; and such other matters as the Minister of Construction and Transportation deems necessary.[273] The United States also notes that MOCT could "change the master plan formulated pursuant to the provisions [of the *Act on the Promotion of a New Airport for the Seoul Metropolitan Area Construction*, and] make alterations therein."[274]

4.204 The United States contends that Korea's *Aviation Act* confirmed that:

> "The airport development projects shall be carried out by the Minister of Construction and Transportation ... Any person other than the Minister of Construction and Transportation, who desires to operate the airport development projects, shall obtain the permission of the Minister of Construction and Transportation ..."[275]

---

267 See MOCT List of Subsidiary Organizations, from the MOCT Internet website, *http://www.moct.go.kr/ ours/e-o023.html.* MOCT's website is also discussed at para. 4.432 *et seq.*

268 See, e.g., *Transportation Department Announcement 1993-33*, from MOCT for a procurement relating to railway connection from the Inchon Airport.

269 *Government Organization Act*, Article 40. The most recent version of the *Government Organization Act* states in its Article 42:

> "The Minister of Construction and Transportation shall take charge of the affairs relating to the establishment and adjustment of comprehensive plans for construction in national territory, the conservation, utilization, and development of national territory and water resources, the construction of cities, roads, and housing, coasts, rivers, and reclamation, land transportation, and air services."

270 *Seoul Airport Act*, Article 2(1).

271 Ibid. Article 3(1).

272 Ibid. Article 4(1).

273 Ibid. Article 4(2).

274 US Answer to Question 22 from the Panel, dated 29 November 1999, citing *Seoul Airport Act* Article 4-2(1).

275 US Answer to Question 22 from the Panel, dated 29 November 1999, citing *Aviation Act* Article 94.

4.205 The United States argues that MOCT has ultimate authority to carry out the IIA project.[276] KAA was merely a project operator, designated and used by MOCT to construct the Inchon International Airport.[277]

4.206 The United States also notes that the New Airport Construction Deliberation Commission under MOCT was established:

> "to deliberate on important issues relating to building techniques, construction technology and traffic impact, etc. of the new airport construction project ...[278]
>
> [The Commission] comprised of members, including Chairman, not exceeding one hundred persons who shall be appointed or commissioned by the Minister of Construction and Transportation from among persons coming under one of the following subparagraphs:
>
> 1. Public officials in the fourth grade or above serving at a central or local administrative organ or a local government concerned with the affairs of the new airport construction project;
> 2. Members on the board of directors of public entities or research institutions; and
> 3. Persons of such professional learning and experience in airport, building, civil engineering, fire fighting and the environment, etc. as determined by the Minister of Construction and Transportation."[279]

4.207 According to the United States, many of the exhibits provided by Korea corroborate the United States argument that regardless of KAA, KOACA and IIAC's status as subsidiary organizations of MOCT, they nevertheless remain covered under the GPA because procurements by KAA, KOACA and IIAC are, in fact, procurements by MOCT. The United States notes that MOCT not only controls procurements by KAA, KOACA and IIAC, but it also funds, owns and benefits from these procurements.

4.208 The United States refers also to the *Rules of the New Airport Development Group* which state in Article 5 that the "head of the Aviation Office shall assume the overall authority to supervise and control the construction and operation of the New International Airport."[280] The United States notes that the New Airport Development Group under MOCT retained the following responsibilities: establishing and coordinating basic plans for the airport; budget and funding matters related to the airport; researching and developing "systems and regulations" concerning the airport; planning, designing and overseeing "actual works of [the airport's] civil engineering facilities, site preparation, supporting complex construction supporting facilities and

---

276 See Articles 94 and 2(8) of the *Aviation Act*.

277 US Answer to Question 22 from the Panel, dated 29 November 1999, referring to, e.g., Articles 95, 96, 103, and 104 of the *Aviation Act*. The United States contends that these and other provisions confirm the subordinate nature of project operators.

278 *Seoul Airport Act*, Article 7-3(1).

279 US Answer to Question 22 from the Panel, dated 29 November 1999, citing the *Seoul Airport Act*, Article 7-3(3).

280 US Answer to Question 22 from the Panel, dated 29 November 1999.

accessible transport facilities"; analysing and controlling "all [airport] work processes;" planning, designing and overseeing "actual works of the [airport's] structural, mechanical, communication electronics and power facilities; supervising the operation of the "[t]he New Airport Construction Deliberation Commission;" and establishing "financial plans for repayment of debt incurred from the construction [of the airport] and securing ... funds for operation" of the airport.

4.209 The United States notes that a Korean business guide touted MOCT as the entity controlling the IIA project[281], that KAA utilized the Office of Supply and its regulations for procurement purposes, just as MOCT would and that employees of KAA in certain circumstances were "treated as public officials."[282]

4.210 **In response to this argument, Korea states** that there is no evidence that even remotely suggests that KAA has, as the United States argues, "utilised the Office of Supply and its regulations for procurement purposes, just as MOCT would."[283] Korea states that the procurements referred to by the United States for which KAA requested Office of Supply assistance, were not for the IIA - which is, exclusively, the subject of the Panel's terms of reference in this case. In any event, Korea notes that Korea's Annex 1 specifically states that Office of Supply coverage is "limited to purchases for entities in this [Annex 1] list only." Korea further notes that KAA is not listed on Annex 1.[284]

4.211 Korea argues that a publication by the US Foreign Commercial Service of the American Embassy, Seoul, produced in conjunction with a Korean trade association (the Association of Foreign Trading Agents) can scarcely be considered to bind the Korean Government to GPA obligations, including the proposition offered by the United States that this joint US-private sector publication proves MOCT's role "as the entity controlling the IIA project."[285]

4.212 **The United States concludes** that, therefore, due to the fact that KAA is "'attached/connected/affiliated' etc." to MOCT, KAA should be considered a covered entity for the purposes of the GPA because:

(1) Annex 1 of the GPA, which covers MOCT as a "central government entity," also covers the subdivisions of MOCT. KAA is a subdivision of MOCT because it is "'attached/connected/affiliated' etc." to MOCT.

(2) Article I:1 of the GPA, which states that the GPA "applies to any law, regulation, procedure or practice regarding any procurement by entities covered by this Agreement," applies to

---

281 American Business in Korea: Guide & Directory 1992-93, p. 126. This guide was published by the Association of Foreign Trading Agents of Korea, a Korean business association, in conjunction with the Foreign Commercial Service of the American Embassy, Seoul. The United States notes that the Inchon International Airport is also known as the "Youngjong-do" project, as it is being constructed on Youngjong Island near Inchon.

282 US Answer to Question 22 from the Panel, dated 29 November 1999. Further arguments regarding publications that the US argues evidence MOCT's control over the IIA project are contained in para. 4.420.

283 Korea's Response to the US Answer to Question 22 from the Panel, dated 29 November 1999, quoting US Answer to Question 22.

284 Korea's Response to the US Answer to Question 20 from the Panel, dated 29 November 1999.

285 Ibid.

KAA because, as an entity "'attached/connected/affiliated' etc." to MOCT, any procurement by KAA is in fact a procurement by MOCT.

(3) Note 1 of Korea's Annex 1 of the GPA, which states that coverage of the listed "central government entities" "include[s] their subordinate linear organizations, special local administrative organs, and attached organs as prescribed in the Government Organization Act of the Republic of Korea," also covers KAA because - as an entity "'attached/connected/affiliated' etc." to MOCT - KAA is a "subordinate linear organization" of MOCT.[286]

4.213 The United States argues that KAA is covered pursuant to: Korea's Annex 1 of the GPA, which lists MOCT as a covered "central government entity;" Note 1 to Korea's Annex 1 of the GPA, which states that "subordinate linear organizations" of MOCT are also covered; and Article I:1 of the GPA. The United States further argues that given that KAA is a covered entity, as a factual matter, any procurement conducted by KAA that is within the scope of the GPA (*i.e.*, above the Agreement's thresholds and not subject to any of the exceptions enumerated in the Agreement's text) is covered. This includes procurements related to the other regional airports for which KAA is responsible.[287]

4.214 The United States notes that KAA was involved in the IIA airport development project from 1992 until KOACA's creation in 1994. The United States contends that, apparently, this was the only "new airport construction" which KAA participated in. With regard to the procurement for this "new airport construction," the United States contends that it expected KAA to be covered, given its May 1991 question[288] to Korea. The United States also notes that as for the rest of KAA's work, which according to Korea, "has traditionally been limited to the management and maintenance of [existing] Korean airports," the US May 1991 question did not focus on these procurements. However, the United States argues that they are nevertheless covered by the GPA because of the coverage of KAA as a subdivision of MOCT.

4.215 **In response, Korea argues** that the US May 1991 question was not about just any generic airport procurement. Korea notes that the actual text of the United States' question was:

> "How does the Airport Development Group relate to the Ministry of Communication? Does Korea's offer of coverage of the Ministry of Communications include purchases for the Airport Development Group? Please identify all Ministries that will be responsible for the procurement of goods and services related to new airport construction."

---

[286] US Answer to Question 22 from the Panel, dated 29 November 1999.

[287] US Answer to Question 16 from the Panel, dated 29 November 1999.

[288] The US May 1991 question is discussed further below at para. 4.328 *et seq*.

4.216 Korea states that its reasonable interpretation of this question was that the United States was interested in the NADG - the New Airport Development Group.[289] Korea states that, therefore, its response dealt with NADG and its relationship with MOCT, and the Office of Supply, as the entity that would in principle be responsible for procurement for the IIA under the terms of the *Government Procurement Fund Act*, had there even been any procurements for IIA construction at the time. Korea states that it reasonably considered that the United States was not asking a question about airport procurement in general.

4.217 **The United States further argues** that the coverage of procurement resulting from KAA's management and maintenance of Korea's regional airports is similar to the coverage of procurement by the Seoul and Pusan Regional Aviation offices which are covered under Korea's GPA obligations. The United States contends that these regional offices conduct procurement for new airport construction of certain airports other than the IIA. In addition, they also conduct procurement for the maintenance of these airports. The United States argues that regardless of whether the Seoul and Pusan Regional Aviation offices are procuring for the construction or the maintenance of these airports, their procurements are covered under the GPA because they, as subdivisions of MOCT, are covered under the GPA.[290]

4.218 The United States notes that it has not uncovered any additional documentation not already provided that demonstrates the contemplation of the coverage of KAA over the "management and maintenance" of these other regional airports. However, it notes that it is not unheard of for a country to find that it has "GPA benefits" that "it had not anticipated," due to the coverage of an entity that, although originally covered for a particular purpose, engages in the procurement of other projects or sectors that were not explicitly excluded from GPA coverage.[291]

4.219 In response to a question from the Panel regarding evaluation of the Korean accession offer by the United States, the United States notes that throughout the GPA accession process, it has analysed the offers of countries acceding to the GPA on an ongoing basis but does not routinely prepare formal "studies". With regard to assessment of the value of Korea's accession offer, the United States notes that the potential monetary value of a country's GPA accession offer is often not as important to the United States as the quality of the overall package (including coverage of key entities and projects/sectors of interest). The United States recognizes that the US procurement market is substantially larger than that of most of its trading partners and that the monetary value of the opportunities offered by an acceding country is unlikely to be equivalent to the monetary value of opportunities offered by the United States. Therefore, the United States notes that its acceptance of another country's accession package is often based on the extent to which the offer includes coverage of areas of key interest to US suppliers and services providers, i.e., the coverage of key entities, projects and sectors of interest to the United States. The United States argues that airport was such a priority.[292]

---

[289] Further discussion of Korea's interpretation of the US May 1991 question is contained below at para. 4.343.

[290] US Answer to Question 16 from the Panel, dated 29 November 1999.

[291] Ibid.

[292] US Answer to Question 24 from the Panel, dated 29 November 1999.

(b) Arguments by Korea

4.220 In response to the Panel's question referred to above in paragraph 4.197 Korea, on the other hand, argues that KAA should not be considered as "'attached/connected/affiliated' etc. to MOCT" for the purposes of determining GPA coverage, for the following reasons.[293]

4.221 First, Korea states that Note 1 to its Annex 1 governs the determination of which non-listed entities are covered by virtue of their relationship with entities listed on Annex 1. Korea states that, specifically, Note 1 refers to the *Government Organization Act of the Republic of Korea*, which "prescribes" those entities that, as "subordinate linear organizations," "special local administrative organs" or "attached organs," are considered covered despite their absence from Annex 1.[294]

4.222 Korea notes that Note 1, with its incorporation by reference of the *Government Organization Act*, evidences and itself provides a "special meaning," under Article 31(4) of the *Vienna Convention on the Law of Treaties*. According to Korea, Note 1 provides specific, textual evidence of the intent and the agreement of the parties to the GPA, and as an "integral part" of the GPA, under Article XXIV:12 thereto, must be accorded both its ordinary meaning, and the "special meaning" it imposes upon the term "central government entity" for the purposes of Korea's Annex 1.[295]

4.223 Korea argues that KAA is not considered a covered entity by virtue of Note 1. Specifically, Korea argues that KAA is not a "subordinate linear organization," "special local administrative organ" or "attached organ," within the meaning of the *Government Organization Act*, and its status as a separate legal person with the authority to conduct its own procurements distinguishes it from a body such as NADG, which is effectively MOCT itself.[296]

4.224 Korea also notes that unlike the entities prescribed by the *Government Organization Act*, KAA has the following characteristics[297]: KAA was established by an act of the National Assembly as a separate legal person[298]; KAA authored and adopted its own by-laws[299]; KAA is governed by its own board of directors that controls all matters related to major corporate investments and all other major corporate issues of any significance[300]; KAA hires and fires its own workforce that is not in the government's employ[301]; KAA authored and adopted its own Contract Administration Regulations[302] distinct from the government procurement rules included in the *Korean Budget and Accounting Act* and used those Regulations for IIA procurements;

[293] Korea's Answer to Question 22 from the Panel, dated 29 November 1999.
[294] Ibid.
[295] Ibid.
[296] Korea's Answer to Question 22 from the Panel, dated 29 November 1999.
[297] Korea's Answer to Question 11 from the Panel, dated 29 November 1999.
[298] *Korea Airport Corporation Act*, Article 3. See also Notification of Act No. 3219, *Official Gazette*, 28 December 1979, p. 5892.
[299] KAA By-laws.
[300] *Ibid.* Articles 4(3), 4(1)(6), 14, 25.
[301] *Korea Airport Corporation Act*, Article 13.
[302] KAA Contract Administration Regulations, Article 90.

KAA published bid announcements and requests for proposals of its own accord[303]; and, KAA concluded contracts with successful bidders on its own behalf.[304]

4.225 Korea argues that each of these factors demonstrates that KAA is an entity in its own right, separate and distinct from MOCT. Korea also argues, in response to a question from the Panel, that all of the "organs" or "organizations" included on the MOCT organization chart are in fact prescribed by the *Government Organization Act*, and covered under the GPA, as subordinate linear organizations, special local administrative organs or attached organs.[305]

4.226 Second, Korea argues that even if Note 1 is not controlling, the "control" test proposed by the United States enjoys no support in the GPA. Although Article I:1(c) of the Tokyo Round GPA[306] included what the United States has styled a "normative" control test[307] this test was not included in the Uruguay Round GPA[308], in either a normative or a binding form. Korea argues that according to the Appellate Body, the disappearance of a provision during negotiations "strongly reinforces the presumption" that prior practice has changed.[309] Quoting the Appellate Body, Korea states that rejecting prior practice in these circumstances "is the commonplace inference that is properly drawn from such disappearance," and an interpreter is "not entitled to assume that that disappearance was merely accidental or an inadvertent oversight on the part of either harassed negotiators or inattentive draftsmen."[310]

4.227 Korea states that the United States itself agrees that the "control" test included in Article I:1(3) of the Tokyo Round GPA was "excluded" from the Uruguay Round GPA, but argues that rather than rejecting the "'control' concept, ... Annex 3 made it unnecessary." Korea states that this argument does not explain why the United States argues in these proceedings for importation of the "control" test into *Annex 1*, which is the locus of its claim for KAA coverage. Korea states that, more importantly, if Annex 3 made the Tokyo Round "control" test unnecessary, then reference to Annex 3 for evidence of KAA coverage is appropriate. Korea notes that KAA is not included on Korea's Annex 3.[311]

4.228 Korea argues that in either case, whether the Tokyo Round "control" test was rejected altogether by the Uruguay Round GPA negotiators, or whether the negotiators intended Annex 3 to encompass the concept of "control," the importation by the

---

303 Exhibits Kor-19A through Kor-19D.

304 *Ibid.*

305 Korea Answer to Question 11 from the Panel, dated 29 November 1999.

306 The Tokyo Round GPA and, more particularly, Article I:1(c) is discussed below at para. 4.291 *et seq.*

307 *Agreements Being Negotiated at the Multilateral Trade Negotiations in Geneva*, US International Trade Commission Investigation No. 332-101 (MTN Studies, August 1979), pp. 26, 27-28, 38, 44.

308 The removal of the control test from the Uruguay Round GPA is discussed below at para. 4.296 *et seq.*

309 See para. 4.300 *et seq.*

310 Korea's Answer to Question 22 from the Panel, dated 29 November 1999, quoting Appellate Body Report, *United States - Restrictions on Imports of Cotton and Man-made Fibre Underwear*, WT/DS24/AB/R, adopted 25 February 1997, DSR 1997:I, 11, at 25.

311 Korea's Answer to Question 22 from the Panel, dated 29 November 1999. The Annex 3 issue is discussed further at para. 4.307 *et seq.*

United States of a "control" test into Annex 1, and its claim that KAA is an Annex 1 covered entity by virtue of the control allegedly exercised over it by MOCT, must be rejected.[312]

4.229 Third, Korea argues that the test included in the Uruguay Round GPA to extend coverage beyond the list of entities included in a signatory's Appendix I - Article I:3 - is not met in the circumstances of this case. Korea argues that the United States' "control" test, either as drafted or as applied by the United States, does not comport to the requirements of Article I:3, and that there is no evidence that suggests that KAA was even asked by MOCT or any other covered entity, let alone required, to award contracts for IIA procurements in accordance with particular requirements. Korea states that the United States' list of "control" factors speaks largely to the statutory requirement that KAA request approval for and report on certain of its actions. Korea argues that neither of these factors, nor any other evidence offered by the United States, demonstrate that KAA is required to apply particular requirements in awarding IIA procurements.[313]

4.230 Fourth, Korea argues that considering KAA to be a covered entity by virtue of a "control" test that (i) utilizes categories of "control" without textual basis in the GPA, and (ii) adopts an arbitrary degree of "control," also without any textual base, sufficient to deem an entity controlled and, therefore, covered, will seriously disrupt the delicate balance of rights and obligations agreed to by signatories to the GPA. Korea states that a decision that this non-textually-based test should trump the entire basis upon which signatories negotiated their GPA commitments - the positive enumeration of entities subject to the terms of the GPA - will have effects well beyond KAA.[314]

4.231 Korea states that each entity included on Korea's Annex 3 is controlled by an Annex 1 entity in the same sense that KAA is "controlled" by MOCT.[315] Korea states that whether discussing entities included on Annex 3, or entities excluded from but susceptible to inclusion on Annex 3 such as Amtrak, Comsat and KAA, the result of the United States' "control" test would be to subject those entities to coverage under Annex 1. Given the lower thresholds applicable to procurements by Annex 1 entities, the result of the United States' test would be not only to reduce Annex 3 to a nullity, but also to expand greatly signatories' GPA obligations.[316]

4.232 Korea argues that for the four reasons mentioned above, KAA should not be considered covered by virtue of its "attachment," "connection" or "affiliation" to MOCT. Korea states that there is no textual basis in the GPA to expand Korea's GPA commitments to KAA in the manner proposed by the United States, and the test provided by the GPA to secure coverage of non-listed entities - Article I:3 - is not satisfied under the factual circumstances of this case.[317]

4.233 **In response, the United States refers** to its arguments in paragraphs 4.118 and 4.146.

---

[312] Ibid.
[313] Ibid.
[314] Ibid.
[315] Ibid.
[316] Ibid.
[317] Ibid.

4.234 **Further, Korea argues** that it did not commit, or intend to commit, to GPA coverage for KAA, whether procurements were for the IIA or "other regional airports for which KAA is responsible." Korea reiterates that KAA is responsible for the management of existing regional airport operations, a task that may involve incidental repair and maintenance, and procurements therefor. Korea states that the only significant construction authority possessed by KAA was its responsibility for procurement for the IIA project, during the period December 1991 - August 1994. Korea argues that there is no evidence suggesting that Korea committed to coverage for KAA's procurements. Korea also argues that it did not commit to coverage for procurements undertaken on KAA's behalf by the Office of Supply since Korea's commitment to Annex 1 coverage for the Office of Supply is limited to purchases for entities on Annex 1 only and KAA is not on Annex 1.[318]

6. *Appendix I: General Note 1(b)*

(a) Ordinary Meaning of Note 1(b)

4.235 **The United States argues** that General Note 1(b) confirms that there are in fact "entities listed in Annex 1" responsible for "procurement of airports." The United States asserts that the reference to airport procurement entities can only be a reference to MOCT given that it is the only enumerated entity under Korea's Annex 1 with a mandate to oversee "all matters concerning public roads, railways, air and maritime transport ... [such as the] construction and administration of roads and airports and all other matters concerning construction and transport safety affairs ... [including] the construction of the ... Inchon International Airport"[319] and MOCT, the NADG, KAA, KOACA, and IIAC are the only entities Korea has held out as being "responsible" for procurements of airports.

4.236 **In response, Korea argues** that General Note 1(b) to Korea's GPA Appendix I does not convert KAA, KOACA or IIAC into covered entities. Korea notes in this respect that since December 1991, KAA, KOACA and IIAC have been the entities responsible for IIA procurement, and that KAA, KOACA and IIAC are not covered entities by virtue of Korea's Annex 1 or the Notes thereto. Korea argues that even an *a contrario* reading of General Note 1(b) does not imply that IIA procurement is extended to US suppliers and service providers under the terms of the GPA since the Korean entities conducting such procurements are not "entities listed in Annex 1."

4.237 Korea further notes that as a matter of reciprocity, General Note 1(b) withholds GPA benefits for "procurement for airports by the entities listed in Annex 1" from suppliers and service providers of the member States of the European Communities, Norway and Switzerland.

---

318 Korea's Answer to Question 21 from the Panel, dated 29 November 1999.

319 "History of the Ministry of Construction and Transportation," found on MOCT's Internet website at http://www.moct.go.kr/mcte/mct_about/mctha2.htm.

(b) Entities to Which General Note 1(b) Refers

(i) Seoul and Pusan Regional Aviation Offices

4.238 **Korea states** that the reference to airport procuring authorities in General Note 1(b) is a reference to the Seoul and Pusan Regional Aviation Offices. Korea notes that these are MOCT's "special local administrative organs," and, therefore, as covered entities pursuant to Note 1 to Korea's Annex 1, are charged with procurement responsibility associated with construction and maintenance of Yangyang, Yeosoo, Muan, Daegu, Pohang, Yecheoon and Uljin Airports. Korea further notes that the Regional Aviation Offices may conduct such procurement or request that Office of Supply procure on their behalf. Korea asserts that, in either case, procurement for these airports is subject to the GPA.

4.239 In response to a question from the Panel, Korea provides details of the construction projects (including value) that have been undertaken by the Seoul and Pusan Regional Aviation Offices since 1990.[320] Further, Korea refers to examples of contracts awarded by the Office of Supply, in conjunction with MOCT's Seoul and Pusan Regional Aviation Offices.[321]

4.240 **In response, the United States refers** to its arguments in paragraphs 4.340, 4.402 and 4.403.

(ii) Covered and Uncovered Entities

4.241 **Korea explains** its rationale for dividing airport procurement between various entities and, for submitting some, rather than all, of those procurement entities to coverage under Annex 1 of the GPA. Korea states that there are differences between construction of and attendant procurement for a $6 billion off-shore airport on reclaimed land, and procurement for the considerably smaller projects.

4.242 Korea also states that it had a right to commit to coverage for certain entities, and to exclude others. Korea asserts that every single GPA signatory did likewise. Korea notes that the United States, for example, excluded the Federal Aviation Administration ("FAA") and its Office of Airports from coverage under Annex 1, but included other airport procurement authorities such as the Port Authority of New York and New Jersey under Annex 3. Korea further notes that although both the FAA's Office of Airports and entities like the Port Authority of New York and New Jersey each have airport procurement responsibilities, the United States considered it legitimate to exclude the FAA from coverage while including the Port Authority.

4.243 In response to a question from the Panel concerning the difference in categorization of the IIA authorities on the one hand and Seoul and Pusan Regional Airport Authorities on the other, Korea also states that the procurement responsibility associated with construction and maintenance of existing airports conducted by the Regional Aviation Offices is in the nature of routine maintenance and relatively minor construction, which is not on the scale of the construction of a new airport of the magnitude of IIA. Korea further states that since this construction and maintenance is well within the capabilities of the Regional Aviation Offices, Korea has lodged it

---

[320] Korea's Answer to Question 17 from the Panel, dated 3 November 1999.

[321] Exhibits Kor-61A - Kor-61B.

there, along with the authority for any necessary procurement. Korea finally states that, because of the magnitude of the IIA project, Korea found that an entirely separate entity, devoted only to that task, was needed. Korea also refers to its arguments in paragraphs 4.443 - 4.445.

(c) Coverage of "New Airport Construction" under Korea's Annex 1

4.244 **In response to a question from the Panel, the United States says** that it interpreted the reciprocal derogations between the EC and Korea regarding airports as an indication that Korea and the EC could not agree that each was offering "comparable and effective access [to their] relevant markets."[322] The United States further states that, moreover, the United States interpreted these derogations as a confirmation that Korea's GPA offer indeed included coverage of "new airport construction" under its Annex 1, consistent with Korea's July 1991 statement regarding the coverage of MOCT and the Office of Supply - as entities responsible for the IIA project - under Annex 1. The United States contends that it was able to draw this conclusion because Korea's country-specific derogation, which listed the EC and others, did not include the United States when carving out "procurement for airports by the entities listed in Annex 1."[323]

4.245 **Korea argues that** it is not at all apparent why Korea's General Note 1(b) is confirmation that Korea's GPA offer indeed included coverage of "new airport construction" under its Annex 1 as postulated by the United States. Korea argues that if an *a contrario* interpretation of General Note 1(b) is adopted, one could presume that "procurement for airports by the entities listed in Annex 1" - the actual language of General Note 1(b) - would be subject to GPA-consistent terms for US suppliers and service providers. However, Korea states that there is no specification of "new airport construction," as asserted by the United States; rather, any "procurement for airports" by any Annex 1 entity is covered.[324]

7. *Appendix I: Annex 3*

(a) Procuring Entities under Annex 3

4.246 **Korea argues** that if, in fact, it had intended to cover KAA, KOACA and the IIAC under the GPA, it would have listed those entities under Annex 3 rather than Annex 1 of Appendix I to the GPA given their independent legal existence and their association with a public-purpose project.

(i) Independent Legal Persons

4.247 **Korea argues** that like KAA, KOACA and IIAC, each of the entities listed on Annex 3 of Korea's Appendix I were established by a special legislative act, rather than by an order or directive issued by an entity included on Annex 1 and were created to engage in particular public-purpose commercial or non-commercial tasks.

322 See EC General Note 1 and Korea General Note 1 to Appendix I of the GPA.

323 US Answer to Question 17 from the Panel, dated 29 November 1999.

324 Korea's Response to the US Answer to Question 17 from the Panel, dated 29 November 1999.

4.248 Korea also argues that the entities listed on Annex 3 are, like KAA, KOACA and IIAC, independent legal or "juristic" persons under Korean law, as stated in their authorizing statutes. Korea states that this is not the case with an entity, such as NADG, established by an Annex 1 entity on its own authority.

4.249 Korea argues that as legal persons under Korean law, Annex 3 entities, like KAA, KOACA and IIAC, are able to enter into binding legal commitments on their own behalf. Each has its own officers and directors, and its employees are not government civil servants or employees.

4.250 In support of its argument, Korea notes that Japan's New Tokyo International Airport Authority ("NTIAA"), like KAA, KOACA and IIAC, is a "juridical person."[325] Korea notes that NTIAA is led by officers who are appointed and dismissed by, or subject to the approval of, the Japanese Minister of Transport.[326] Korea further notes that NTIAA employees are not government civil servants but, rather, are hired and fired by the president of NTIAA itself. Finally, Korea notes that despite their private sector status, NTIAA officers and employees are considered "employees engaged in public duties" for the purposes of the Japanese *Criminal Act*.[327]

4.251 **In response, the United States argues** that whether an entity is a separate legal entity or not is irrelevant. In support of its argument, the United States asserts that a GPA member can choose to put any of its entities in Annex 1 or Annex 3, provided that the other GPA members agree to this. Therefore, whether an entity is a separate legal entity or not is irrelevant.

4.252 Further, the United States argues that a separate legal entity is normally created for the purposes of limiting liability and providing continuity. The United States also argues that an organization need not possess this legal fiction to be considered an "entity." The United States refers to Black's Law Dictionary which defines a separate legal entity of a corporation as follows:

> "An artificial person or legal entity created by or under the authority of the laws of a state. An association of persons created by statute as a legal entity. The law treats the corporation itself as a person, which can sue and be sued. The corporation is distinct from the individuals who comprise it ... [and it] survives the death of its investors, as the shares can usually be transferred."[328]

4.253 Accordingly, the United States argues that applying these notions to the facts of this case, subdivisions such as the New Airport Development Group are "entities," even though they are not separately legal. The United States additionally argues that, in fact, the New Airport Development Group has its own director and its own regulations. The United States asserts that an Annex 1 entity does not automatically become an Annex 3 entity because it becomes a separate legal entity. The United States asserts that Korea's own National Railway Administration confirms this principle. The United States concludes that, thus, the status of an entity is irrelevant to the determination of this dispute.

---

325 *New Tokyo International Airport Authority Act*, Article 3.

326 *Ibid.* Articles 11, 14.

327 *Ibid.* Article 19.

328 Black's Law Dictionary (6th ed., 1990), p. 340.

(ii) Specific Task or Purpose

4.254 **Korea argues** that like KAA, KOACA and IIAC, the entities included on Korea's Annex 3 list were established to engage in tasks that, while closely linked to the public interest, are for self-evident reasons generally considered better or more efficiently performed by an entity outside the traditional central government apparatus. Korea states that constructing or maintaining major utility or transportation projects is just such a task. Korea notes that Korea's Annex 3 list includes the Korea Highway Corporation and the Korea Gas Corporation. Korea also notes that, similarly, the United States' Annex 3 list includes the Port Authority of New York and New Jersey, which, among other things, oversees metropolitan New York's three major airports - JFK International, Newark International and LaGuardia. Korea asserts that building or maintaining an airport fits in this category.

4.255 To elaborate on this point, Korea also notes that each Annex 3 entity, as with KAA, KOACA and IIAC, is associated with a relatively narrow task or large-scale public project, rather than with the broad portfolio typically associated with a government ministry. Korea further notes that, like the IIA project, the tasks or projects with which Annex 3 entities are charged, while closely linked to the public interest, are still rather "tangential to the essential function of government," in the words of the United States itself.[329] Korea states that placing those tasks in the hands of entities isolated from the constraints of large government bureaucracy and structured to more readily attract private capital facilitates prompt completion of the project.

(iii) Subject to Central Government Oversight

4.256 **Korea argues** that its Annex 3 entities are, like KAA, KOACA and IIAC, subject to certain oversight by central government entities, despite their status as independent legal persons under Korean law. Korea further argues that given their key roles in major public purpose projects, and the implications of their actions on public safety and welfare, this oversight is necessary and justifiable to ensure that the public interests inextricably linked to the performance of their tasks are adequately protected and observed. Korea asserts that there is nothing inconsistent with government oversight of Annex 3 entities. Korea further asserts that MOCT oversight to which KAA, KOACA and IIAC are subject would not prevent Korea from placing those entities on its Annex 3 list, had it decided to do so or had its negotiating partners demanded that it do so. Korea notes that the IIA project and the projects with which Korea's Annex 3 entities are charged are linked closely enough to the public interest to require, as the United States itself has stated, "retained links with the Government" sufficient "to ensure that the interests of the public are reflected ... ."

4.257 In support of this argument, Korea notes that Japan's New Tokyo International Airport Authority (NTIAA), is included on Japan's Annex 3 despite the significant oversight by Japan's Ministry of Transport to which the Authority is subject.

---

[329] *Agreements Being Negotiated at the Multilateral Trade Negotiations in Geneva*, US International Trade Commission Investigation No. 332-101 (MTN Studies, August 1979), p. 44 (describing the activities of Amtrak, which is charged with development and maintenance of a national railway system, and Comsat, which is charged with the establishment of a commercial communications satellite system).

Korea states that reference to the *New Tokyo International Airport Authority Act*, which bears remarkable resemblance to the *Seoul Airport Act*, the *Korea Airport Corporation Act* and the *Korea Airport Construction Authority Act*, demonstrates this fact.

4.258 **In response, the United States argues** that, as a factual matter, KAA and KOACA are different in nature from the entities found in Korea's Annex 3. The United States notes that as the Panel itself noted in a question to the Parties, "[t]he entities listed in Annex 3 are all referred to as 'Corporations' while the KAA and [KOACA] is an 'Authority'." The United States refers to its arguments in paragraph 4.442.

4.259 **Korea further states** that while the Japanese Minister of Transportation is responsible for drawing up a "master plan" for the airport[330], NTIAA is charged with executing the plan[331], pursuant to a "Program of Duty" authored by NTIAA and subject to approval by the Minister.[332] Further, Korea notes that similar to the entities responsible for IIA procurement, NTIAA is subject to the "supervision and inspection" of the Japanese Minister of Transportation.[333] Korea states that like KAA, KOACA and IIAC, NTIAA is required to observe significant reporting requirements, submitting for the Minister of Transportation's approval, prospectively, an annual business plan, budget plan and funding plan[334], and retrospectively, detailed financial statements and statements of accounts.[335] NTIAA may also be instructed by the Minister to submit reports on various financial matters, and must open its books for inspection by individuals sent by the Minister.[336] Finally, Korea states that, like the entities responsible for IIA procurement[337], NTIAA may obtain loans or issue airport bonds[338], after receiving approval from the appropriate Minister.

4.260 Korea argues that this example demonstrates that GPA signatories have included airport authorities on Annex 3 despite the subjection of those authorities to at least the degree of oversight by an Annex 1 entity as is maintained in the case of the Korean entities responsible for IIA procurement.

4.261 **In response, the United States argues** that Korea is one GPA signatory that included airport authorities in Annex 1 since it has repeatedly maintained that the Seoul and Pusan regional airport authorities are covered under Korea's Annex 1.[339]

4.262 **In further support of its argument, Korea refers** to the Act authorizing the activities of the Small and Medium Industry Bank, an entity listed on Korea's Annex 3.[340] Korea notes that despite the Bank's status as an independent legal person[341],

---

330 *New Tokyo International Airport Authority Act*, Article 21.

331 *Ibid*. Article 22.

332 *Ibid*. Article 24.

333 *Ibid*. Articles 36-37.

334 *Ibid*. Article 26.

335 *Ibid*. Article 27.

336 *Ibid*. Article 37.

337 *KAA By-laws*, Article 7(3); *Korea Airport Construction Authority Act*, Articles 16, 28, 25.

338 *New Tokyo International Airport Authority Act*, Article 29.

339 US Response to Korea's Answer to Question 11 from the Panel, dated 29 November 1999.

340 *Industrial Bank of Korea Act* Act No. 641, 1 July 1961 (as amended by Act No. 5529, 28 February 1998).

341 *Ibid*. Article 3(1).

oversight by the Minister of Finance and Economy, an Annex 1 entity, is noted in this Act in a number of provisions.[342]

4.263 Korea notes that, in a similar fashion to KAA and KOACA, officers and directors of the Small and Medium Industry Bank are appointed and dismissed by either the President of Korea or the Minister of Finance and Economy.[343] Like KAA, KOACA and IIAC, Bank employees are not government civil service employees, but are appointed and dismissed by the Bank itself.[344] Although not public officials, officers of the Bank, as in the case of the entities responsible for IIA procurement, are in the case of criminal acts treated as such and subject to the terms of the *Korean Criminal Act*.[345]

4.264 Korea notes that to engage in activities beyond those specifically enumerated by the *Industrial Bank of Korea Act*, the Small and Medium Industry Bank must obtain the approval of the Minister of Finance and Economy[346]; KAA, KOACA and IIAC must similarly receive MOCT approval to go beyond the scope of their specifically-enumerated portfolios.[347]

4.265 Korea further notes that the Bank, KAA, KOACA and IIAC all have provisions in their respective statutes subjecting them to the "supervision and management" or the "direction and supervision" of the relevant ministry.[348] Korea states that the Bank is also required to prepare for the Minister's review, and to obtain approval from the Minister for, its business plans, its operations manual and its annual budgets and reports.[349] Korea also states that the Bank may, moreover, be instructed by the Minister to submit reports on any matters "as may be deemed necessary," and must open its books to designated officials upon request by the Minister.[350] Korea asserts that the entities responsible for IIA procurement are subject to nearly identical reporting requirements.[351]

4.266 As yet another example, Korea refers to the Act authorizing the activities of the Korea Development Bank, another Annex 3 entity.[352] Korea states that despite the

---

342 Ibid. Article 6(2), Article 26(1), Article 26(2), Article 26(3), Article 28, Article 33-2(1), Article 33(2-2), Article 33(9), Article 35(1), Article 35-2, Article 37(2), Article 37(3), Article 44(1), Article 44(2), Article 46(1), Article 46(2), Article 48(1) Article 48(3) Article 48(4) Article 49.

343 *Industrial Bank of Korea Act*, Article 26.

344 *Ibid*. Article 31.

345 *Ibid*. Article 32.

346 *Industrial Bank of Korea Act*, Article 33(9).

347 *Korea Airport Corporation Act*, Article 7(7); *Korea Airport Construction Authority Act*, Article 7(4); *Law on Inchon International Airport Corporation*, Article 10(1)(6).

348 *Industrial Bank of Korea Act*, Article 46; *Korea Airport Corporation Act*, Article 28; *Korea Airport Construction Authority Act*, Article 31; *Law on Inchon International Airport Corporation*, Article 16.

349 *Industrial Bank of Korea Act*, Articles 35, 35-2, 37, 49.

350 *Ibid*. Article 48.

351 *Korea Airport Corporation Act*, Articles 19, 20; *Korea Airport Construction Authority Act*, Articles 21, 22; *Law on Inchon International Airport Corporation*, Article 17.

352 *Korea Development Bank Act*, Act No. 302, 30 December 1953 (as amended by Act No. 5505, 13 January 1998).

Bank's status as an independent legal person[353], oversight by the Minister of Finance and Economy, an Annex 1 entity, is noted in this Act in a number of provisions.[354]
4.267 Korea states that, like KAA and KOACA, officers and directors of the Korea Development Bank are appointed by either the President of Korea or the Minister of Finance and Economy.[355] Korea further states that like KAA, KOACA and IIAC, Bank employees are appointed and dismissed by the Bank itself, and therefore are not government employees.[356] Korea notes that Bank officers, while not public officials, are, like officers of the IIA procurement entities, treated as public officials and subjected to the terms of the *Korean Criminal Act* if criminal acts are committed.[357]
4.268 Further, Korea notes that if the Bank wishes to engage in activities beyond those specifically enumerated by the *Korea Development Bank Act,* it must obtain the approval of the Minister of Finance and Economy.[358] The entities responsible for IIA procurement would in this situation also need MOCT approval.
4.269 Korea states that the Bank is subject to overall supervision by the Minister of Finance and Economy.[359] Korea further states that the Bank must also prepare for the Minister's review, and obtain approval from the Minister for, its operational programme, its service manual and its annual budgets and reports.[360] Korea notes that the Minister may also instruct the Bank to submit reports on any matters "as he deems it necessary," and must open its books to designated officials upon request by the Minister.[361] Korea argues that the entities responsible for IIA procurement are subject to nearly identical reporting requirements.[362]

(iv) Choice between Annex 1 and Annex 3

4.270 **In response to a question from the United States** as to whether members of the GPA could choose to place any entity within Annex 1 or Annex 3, regardless of the project or sector that entity is procuring for, **Korea** confirms that this was its understanding.
4.271 Korea states that it is aware of nothing in the GPA that, in principle, would control the Annex in which a covered entity is placed. However, Korea notes that Annex 1 covers "central government entities" while Annex 3 covers "other entities." Korea notes further that Korea and other parties to the GPA have tended to put ministries and the like in Annex 1 and "other entities," such as Airport Authorities and

---

[353] *Ibid.* Article 2(1).
[354] Article 5(2), Article 12(1), Article 12(2), Article 12(3), Article 14, Article 17, Article 18(8), Article 20(1), Article 21, Article 24, Article 37(2), Article 37(3), Article 37(6), Article 47(1), Article 47(2), Article 48(1), Article 48(2), Article 48(3), Article 49(1), Article 49(2), Article 54-3(2), Article 54-3(3), Article 54-3(4), Article 55(1), Article 55(2), Article 55(3), Article 57.
[355] *Ibid.* Article 12.
[356] *Ibid.* Article 16.
[357] *Ibid.* Article 17.
[358] *Ibid.* Article 18(8).
[359] *Ibid.* Article 47.
[360] *Ibid.* Articles 20, 21, 24, 37.
[361] *Ibid.* Article 49.
[362] *Korea Airport Corporation Act*, Articles 19, 20; *Korea Airport Construction Authority Act*, Articles 21, 22; *Law on Inchon International Airport Corporation*, Article 17.

government-invested corporations, in Annex 3.[363] Korea further notes that Annex 2, is reserved for specific kinds of entities, while Annexes 4 and 5 are reserved for specific kinds of procurements.

4.272 Korea argues that it would not have been alone in listing KAA, KOACA and the IIAC under Annex 3 rather than Annex 1 of Appendix I to the GPA. In support of this argument, Korea notes that on their respective Annex 3 lists, the United States has included the Port Authority of New York and New Jersey, which has jurisdiction over metropolitan New York's three major airports; Hong Kong has included its Airport Authority; and Japan has included the New Tokyo International Airport Authority. Similarly, on their Annex 3 lists, Israel has included its Airport Authority; Norway has included its National Civil Aviation Administration; Switzerland has included its various airport authorities; and Belgium, Denmark, Germany, Greece, Spain, France, Ireland, Italy, Luxembourg, the Netherlands, Portugal and the United Kingdom, as member States of the European Communities, have listed their airport authorities.

4.273 **In response, the United States argues** Korea's assertion that it and other parties to the GPA have tended to put ministries and the like in Annex 1 and "other entities," such as Airport Authorities and government-invested corporations, in Annex 3 is contradicted by the fact that Korea's Regional Aviation Authorities are placed in Annex 1. Further, the United States notes that Korea's attempt to define Annex 3's "other entity" is without textual support. The United States argues that it is clear that the text of the GPA does not define this term, and there is no basis to interpret the term by way of "trends" that Korea itself does not follow.

4.274 **In response to a question from the United States** as to why the Seoul and Pusan Regional Aviation Offices are covered under Annex 1 rather than Annex 3, **Korea states** that the procurement responsibility associated with construction and maintenance of airports conducted by the Regional Aviation Offices is in the nature of routine maintenance and relatively minor construction and not on the scale of the construction of a new airport of the magnitude of IIA. Korea states that since the task is well within the capabilities of those Offices, Korea chooses to assign it to them. Korea notes that because they are internal to MOCT, and not separate legal entities, they are covered by the GPA.[364]

4.275 **In response, the United States notes** that, on the one hand, Korea claims that the activities of building and maintaining an airport must be conducted by Annex 3-type entities and, on the other hand it represents that the Seoul and Pusan Regional Airport Offices, which are responsible for the construction and maintenance of airports, are covered under Annex 1. The United States contends that a GPA Party can choose to place an entity under either Annex 1 or Annex 3, subject to agreement with other Parties, regardless of the procurement subject-matter or the type of entity. The United States notes that Korea has acknowledged this fact.

4.276 The United States argues that, moreover, as a factual matter, KAA and KOACA are different in nature from the entities found in Korea's Annex 3. Specifi-

---

[363] Korea's Answer to Question 12 from the US, dated 3 November 1999.

[364] Korea's Answer to Question 11 from the US, dated 3 November 1999.

cally, the entities listed in Annex 3 are all referred to as "Corporations" while the KAA (and KOACA) is an "Authority".

4.277 **In response to a question from the Panel, Korea notes** that there is no significance in the use of the term "authority" or "corporation" in the context of Korean Government entities. Korea states that the terms are used interchangeably. For example, the English translation of the *Korea Airport Corporation Act* of 14 December 1991 refers to the "Korea Airport Corporation" which in fact is KAA. Korea notes that KAA (or "KAC") is a separate juridical person, as are the other entities in its Annex 3. Under Korean law, both authorities and corporations must have by-laws and be registered.[365]

(b) Shifting of an Entity from Annex 1 to Annex 3

4.278 The Panel pointed out to the Parties that the Korean National Railway Administration is listed as an Annex 1 entity but with a note that it may be made into a public corporation and shifted to Annex 3 without further compensation. The Parties were asked to discuss the relevance of this, if any, to the interpretation of the Korean Schedule.[366] **In response, Korea notes** that the Korean National Railway Administration was placed in Annex 1 because it is a central government entity. With privatization (which has not yet occurred) it would become a separate legal person, and therefore, would be more appropriate for Korea's Annex 3, which consists of separate legal persons. Korea states that it is because KAA is a separate legal person that Korea would have placed it on its Annex 3 offer had Korea intended KAA to be a covered entity.[367]

4.279 **In response to Korea's answer, the United States notes** that the "privatization" of an entity has nothing to do with its becoming a "separate legal entity." In the view of the United States, these are two completely different concepts that have no relevance to each other.

4.280 In response to the Panel's question, the United States notes that Korea's explanatory note concerning the Korean National Railway Administration implicitly recognizes two legal points. First, shifting an entity from one Annex to another is a substantive alteration in a mutually agreed balance of concessions between Members. Second, if a GPA concession is unqualified, and does not provide explicitly for the possibility that an entity will be shifted to another Annex, then any such shift in coverage is inconsistent with the concession.[368]

4.281 The United States argues that this legal point can be understood all the more clearly by drawing an analogy to the law of tariff concessions. According to the United States, it is possible to make a tariff concession subject to a qualification regarding future changes in treatment. To illustrate, the United States considers the example of a US concession on Vitamin B12, which was made subject to a general note reserving the ability of the importing country to adjust the duty rate in the event that a particular customs valuation method was eliminated; because of this general

365 Korea's Answer to Question 8 from the Panel, dated 3 November 1999.

366 Panel's Question 30 to the Parties, dated 20 October 1999.

367 Korea's Answer to Question 30 from the Panel, dated 3 November 1999.

368 US Answer to Question 30 from the Panel, dated 3 November 1999.

note (and the factual circumstances of its application).[369] The United States notes that a panel found that conversion of the duty rate in question was not inconsistent with US obligations. The United States further states that where a tariff concession is unqualified, any excess of the duty rate over the bound rate or a switch in the basis for levying duties (*e.g.*, from specific to *ad valorem* or vice versa) is inconsistent with the legal obligations of that Member under Article II.[370]

8. Coverage of Entities versus Coverage of Projects

4.282 **The United States argues** that all airport construction in Korea should be covered by Korea's GPA commitments. The United States further argues that the GPA covers projects and sectors by way of entities and that all airport construction in Korea should be covered by Korea's GPA commitments. The United States asserts that this is apparent throughout the text of the GPA, where Members often refer to sectors rather than entities. The United States notes that, for instance, Korea's General Note 1(b) refers to "procurement for airports by the entities listed in Annex 1," Korea's General Note 1(c) refers to "procurement for urban transportation," and Korea's Annex 3 refers to "purchases of common telecommunication commodity products." The United States notes that in all three cases, entities are identified by what they procure, that is, their projects or sectors, and not by their names. The United States notes that, likewise, exceptions to coverage under the GPA are often expressed in terms of projects or sectors, rather than entity names. Finally, Annex 4 of the GPA does not even refer to entities, but solely to sectors.

4.283 **Korea argues** that the United States' claim that "all airport construction in Korea" should be covered by Korea's GPA commitments, regardless of which entity conducts procurement for such construction, must be rejected as anathematic to the underlying premises of the GPA. In Korea's view, the United States argues that it bargained for coverage of IIA procurement under Korea's Annex 1. However, Korea asserts that Korea's Annex 1 does not identify projects subject to the GPA. Korea further argues that the GPA does not identify "covered projects." Rather, according to Korea, Korea's Annex 1 and the Notes thereto identify "covered entities."

4.284 **The United States argues in response** that if the GPA merely covers particular entities and not particular projects, Members could then transfer procurement authority out of a covered entity without notification or compensation, and still claim to be acting consistently with the Agreement. According to the United States, this would render the GPA a nullity, because the GPA would only end up covering entities that lack procurement authority.

4.285 **In response, Korea refers** to its arguments in paragraph 4.26.

9. Amendments to Appendix under Article XXIV:6

4.286 **The United States argues** that Article XXIV:6 provides the only procedure within the GPA according to which a Party may alter its annexes. The United States contends that any changes to a Party's schedule of concessions, no matter how minor,

[369] Analytical Index notes at p. 71.

[370] US Answer to Question 30 from the Panel, dated 3 November 1999.

must be notified to the WTO Committee on Government Procurement. This includes transfers of procurement authority from a covered entity to a non-covered entity, since such transfers will disrupt the balance of rights and obligations between the Parties to the GPA. The United States argues that Korea has never used Article XXIV:6 to notify the Committee of any of its transfers of procurement authority for the IIA construction project. The United States argues that, by not notifying the Committee (assuming Korea did not violate Article XXIV:6), Korea is in essence confirming that these transfers took place within one "central government entity" - namely, MOCT.

4.287 The United States further argues that any transfer of procurement authority from a branch office of a covered entity to a subsidiary organization of the same entity or from a subsidiary organization of a covered entity to another subsidiary organization of the same entity, need not be notified to the Committee, for the procurement authority remains within that covered entity. The schedule of concessions do not change and the "balance of rights and obligations" is not disrupted. The United States concludes that Korea need not utilize the procedures of Article XXIV:6 for no changes were made to its schedule of concessions with regard to airport procurement for the IIA project.

4.288 **Korea argues** in response that Article XXIV:6 of the GPA does not apply given that authority had been transferred from a non-covered entity to other non-covered entities. It argues that Korea has not shifted procurement responsibilities from covered to non-covered entities in order to circumvent its obligations under the GPA. Rather, Korea asserts that those procurement responsibilities have, since December 1991, always rested with non-covered entities.[371]

4.289 Korea argues that neither the United States nor the European Communities claim that the transfer of responsibility for IIA procurement from KAA to KOACA, or from KOACA to IIAC, effected any change cognizable under the provisions of the GPA since, for the purposes of the United States' and the European Communities' claims, KAA, KOACA and IIAC are essentially the same. Korea states that it agrees with this position. Korea argues that, accordingly, the only remaining transfer of responsibilities about which the United States and the European Communities apparently complain is the "transfer" of responsibility for IIA procurement from MOCT to KAA. Korea reiterates that that event occurred in December 1991, five years before the effective date of the GPA for Korea, and two years before Korea submitted its final offer for accession to the GPA on 15 December 1993. Korea states that no GPA commitments were incumbent upon Korea at that time.

4.290 Finally, Korea notes that any alleged violation of Article XXIV:6 is not within the Panel's terms of reference.

[371] Korea notes that since obligations under the GPA were not effective until 1 January 1997, it is more accurate to state that IIA procurement has since December 1991 rested with entities that would not have been covered entities, had the GPA been effective at the time.

B. Preparatory Work and Other Evidence

1. Negotiation of the GPA

(a) Article I:1(c) of the Tokyo Round GPA and Annex 3 of the Uruguay Round GPA

4.291 **Korea notes** that like the Uruguay Round GPA, the Tokyo Round GPA applied only to procurements "by the entities subject to this Agreement."[372] Article I:1(c) of the Tokyo Round GPA, however, spoke directly to the issue of "control" raised by the United States' proposed "control" test:

> "1. This Agreement applies to:
>
> ...
>
> (c) procurement by the entities under the direct or substantial control of Parties and other designated entities, with respect to their procurement procedures and practices. Until the review and further negotiations referred to in the Final Provisions, the coverage of this Agreement is specified by the list of entities, and to the extent that rectifications, modifications or amendments may have been made, their successor entities, in Annex I."[373]

4.292 Korea states that the United States discussed the implications of Article I:1(c) extensively in a report issued by its International Trade Commission regarding the Tokyo Round GPA.[374] According to Korea, in that report, the United States concludes that the "direct or substantial control" test included in Article I:1(c) was merely a "normative rule" and that "Annex I is clearly the sole determinant of entities covered."[375]

4.293 Korea states that, according to the United States, however, the "normative" control test in Article I:1(c) was important, as it was to be "the guide for future negotiations on expanded coverage."[376] Korea further quotes: "the code is aimed at government ministries [sic] and their subdivisions - not the myriad organizations tangential to the essential function of government."[377] Korea states that the United States cited in the USITC report examples including the United States' National Rail Passenger Corporation, known as "Amtrak," and the Communications Satellite Corporation, known as "Comsat."[378] Determining whether coverage should be extended to these types of "myriad organizations tangential to the essential function of gov-

---

372 Tokyo Round GPA, Article I:1(a).

373 Ibid. Article I:1(c).

374 *Agreements Being Negotiated at the Multilateral Trade Negotiations in Geneva*, US International Trade Commission Investigation No. 332-101 (MTN Studies, August 1979), pp. 26-28, 38-46.

375 *Ibid.* p. 26. See also *Ibid.* pp. 27-28 ("The Annex is in fact the exclusive rule for code application."); p. 28 ("The control test thus appears to impose no real obligation in implementation of the code ..."); p. 38 (Covered entities "are only those found in Annex I."); p. 44 ("[T]he operations of entities not on Annex I will continue unaffected by the agreement.").

376 *Ibid.* p. 26.

377 *Ibid.* p. 44.

378 *Ibid.*

ernment," the United States concluded, was to be left to future negotiations; "negotiations rather than normative rules will always be determinative."[379]

4.294 Korea states that, thus, while the control test included in Article I:1(c) of the Tokyo Round GPA was, according to the United States, not binding, the United States characterized it as "the guide for future negotiations" and "perhaps ... the objective to which parties will refer when establishing the initial list and later in review and negotiation."[380]

4.295 **The United States notes** that Article I:1(c) did "serve as the starting point for future negotiations," for it was during the Uruguay Round that a new category of covered entities, Annex 3, was conceived. Article I:1(c) was excluded from the new GPA, not because the negotiators rejected the "control" concept, but because Annex 3 made it unnecessary.

(i) Deletion of Article I:1(c)

4.296 **Korea agrees that** while there was a control test in Article I:1(c) of the Tokyo Round GPA and despite the fact that the "control" concept was to serve as the starting point for future negotiations, the negotiators excluded such a test for the Uruguay Round GPA. Korea notes that, in other words, the Uruguay Round negotiators rejected the notion of covering unnamed entities based on their control by named entities.

4.297 Korea also argues that not even the "normative" version of the "control" test included in Article I:1(c) of the Tokyo Round GPA was retained in the Uruguay Round GPA and that no remnant of the "control" test remains. In Korea's view, if the negotiators of the Uruguay Round GPA had intended to take up the invitation from the Tokyo Round negotiators to change the merely "normative" version of the control test included in Article I:1(c) of the Tokyo Round GPA into a binding, determinative test in the Uruguay Round GPA, they would have made some indication that they so intended in the text of the Agreement. Instead, states Korea, they rejected even the Tokyo Round's "normative" control test.

4.298 Korea states that it is implausible to accept that the GPA negotiators, who thought the "control" test important enough even in its strictly "normative" form to include it in the text of the Tokyo Round GPA, would have eliminated any mention of such a test from the text of the Uruguay Round GPA while still intending to impose it as binding upon signatories to that Agreement. Korea states that in these circumstances, the United States' assertion that KAA, KOACA and IIAC should be subject to the GPA by virtue of a "control" test must be rejected.

4.299 **In response, the United States argues** that the language in Article I:1(c) of the Code is not found in the new GPA because it is no longer needed in the new Agreement. The United States reiterates that Article I:1(c) is merely a "guide for future negotiations on expanded coverage."[381] The United States contends that these "future negotiations" had already taken place in the Uruguay Round, during which time the goals that Article I:1(c) set forth were fulfilled when additional annexes to

[379] *Ibid.*
[380] *Ibid.* pp. 26, 28.
[381] USITC Report, p. 26.

the GPA were agreed upon to cover "quasi-governmental purchasing agents" and other entities such as "political subdivisions" and "provincial governments." According to the United States, in other words, Article I:1(c) no longer exists in the new GPA, not because the Uruguay Round negotiators rejected the "control" concept, but because the additional annexes of the GPA made the provision redundant and unnecessary.[382]

4.300 **In response, Korea** refers to its arguments in paragraphs 4.310 and 4.311. Further, in support of its argument regarding the deletion of Article I:1(c) of the Tokyo round GPA, Korea notes that a similar situation was presented in *United States - Restrictions on Imports of Cotton and Man-made Fibre Underwear.* Korea, noting that a provision of the prior *MFA* was not carried over into the *Agreement on Textiles and Clothing*, states that the Appellate Body said that the disappearance of the provision "strongly reinforces the presumption" that a prior practice no longer was permissible. "This is the commonplace inference that is properly drawn from such disappearance," the Appellate Body observed. "We are not entitled to assume that that disappearance was merely accidental or an inadvertent oversight on the part of either harassed negotiators or inattentive draftsmen."[383]

4.301 Korea argues that the disappearance of the control test was not accidental or inadvertent oversight either. Korea argues that it was tried and found wanting, and was not continued. In Korea's view, the message from its disappearance is that only named entities, not other entities over which they may exert some control, are covered.

4.302 **In response, the United States argues** that Korea wrongly suggests that, on the basis of the *United States - Underwear* Appellate Body decision, a "presumption" exists in this case that a control test is not included in the GPA. First, the United States argues that such presumptions cannot be independently derived from the disappearance of language but must, instead, come from a *Vienna Convention* interpretation of the GPA. With the disappearance of the language acting as mere "reinforcement" of the presumption[384] the above explanation regarding the fulfilment of the goals of Article I:1(c) in the new GPA can easily distinguish the present dispute from that of *United States - Underwear.*[385]

4.303 Secondly, the United States argues that the "presumption" identified by the Appellate Body in *United States - Underwear* resulted from the Appellate Body's interpretation of Article 6.10 of the ATC[386] and not from the absence of language on retroactive application that had been in the Multifiber Arrangement.[387] Thus, according to the United States, the issue is whether the absence of a provision in a new text is evidence (not a presumption) that the new text does not include the meaning or concepts in the old text.

4.304 The United States notes that it believes that the instant case is distinguishable from the *United States - Underwear* case for the reasons set forth in the 1979 USITC

---

[382] US Answer to Question 20 from the Panel, dated 29 November 1999.
[383] Appellate Body Report, *United States - Underwear, supra*, footnote 310, at 25.
[384] Ibid.
[385] US Answer to Question 20 from the Panel, dated 29 November 1999.
[386] Appellate Body Report, *United States - Underwear, supra*, footnote 310, at 22-23.
[387] Ibid. pp. 16-17.

report and, more specifically, the explanation regarding the fulfilment of the goals of Article I:1(c) in the new GPA. The United States notes that in *United States - Underwear*, the Appellate Body stated that when:

> "The above underscored clause of Article 3(5)(i), MFA, ... disappeared with the supersession of the MFA by the new ATC; no comparable clause was carried over into Article 6.10 of the ATC. [Also, t]he Panel did not draw any operable inference from the disappearance of the MFA clause."[388]

4.305 However, according to the United States, unlike *United States - Underwear*, Article I:1(c) of the Code was in fact replaced by the additional annexes in the new GPA. The United States asserts that these annexes are "comparable clauses" that allow for the coverage of "quasi-governmental purchasing agents" and "political subdivisions." The United States further states that, unlike *United States - Underwear*, an "operable inference" may be drawn from the disappearance of Article I:1(c) of the Code, for with the creation of the additional annexes in the new GPA, Article I:1(c) - if maintained - would be redundant.[389]

4.306 The United States contends that, in addition, in this case, the absence of direct references to control in the GPA that had existed in the Tokyo Round GPA does not mean that the notion of control cannot exist in determining the coverage of entities under the GPA. The United States further states that, indeed, if the notion of control did not exist in the GPA, such an interpretation would render the interpretation of the GPA a nullity in contravention of numerous Appellate Body decisions. The United States argues that the implication of Korea's "no control" interpretation would be to allow GPA members to create new entities with exactly the same functions, personnel, and operation as listed entities. The United States contends that by eliminating the old listed entities, and preventing the piercing of the legal fiction of the new entity, Members could effectively avoid GPA disciplines. According to the United States, such a result would be contrary to the object and purpose of the GPA as reflected in its text and context.

(ii) Annex 3

4.307 **Korea notes** that, in relation to the comment by the United States referred to above at paragraph 4.295, the reason the Uruguay Round negotiators rejected the control test is "because Annex 3 made it unnecessary," Korea submits that this can only mean that entities controlled by Annex 1 entities are not subject to GPA coverage by virtue of that control, but by virtue of their inclusion in Annex 3.

4.308 Korea states, in agreeing with this conclusion, that at least four entities, legal persons in their own right but subject to the same supervisory control by MOCT that KAA, KOACA and IIAC are subject, are on Korea's Annex 3. Korea notes that they are the National Housing Corporation, the Water Resources Corporation, the Land Corporation and the Highway Corporation. Korea further notes, however, that KAA, KOACA and IIAC are not on Annex 3 and never have been. Korea argues that, by

---

388 US Answer to Question 20 from the Panel, dated 29 November 1999 citing Appellate Body Report, *United States - Underwear*, *supra*, footnote 310, at 24-25.

389 US Answer to Question 20 from the Panel, dated 29 November 1999.

the analysis proposed by the United States and agreed to by Korea, the only place they could be listed is Annex 3, and because they are not there, they are not and never have been covered entities.

4.309 **The United States argues** that a GPA Party can choose to place an entity under either Annex 1 or Annex 3, subject to agreement with other Parties, regardless of the procurement subject matter or the type of entity. According to the United States, the negotiating history of Annex 3 confirms this:

> "The definition of Group C entities is of interest. The heading of Group C (or Annex 3) entities in the new Agreement, reads: "Other entities which procure in accordance with the provisions of this Agreement." The title suggests problems in defining what Annex 3 (Group C) would eventually cover. In the end, this heading was chosen as a compromise to refrain from defining Group C (Annex 3) entities and to leave it up to each delegation to list in Annex 3 what is wished to list, subject of course, to acceptance by its negotiating parties."[390]

4.310 **Korea states** that the United States' assertion that the additional annexes of the Uruguay Round GPA made Article I:1(c) of the Tokyo Round GPA redundant and unnecessary are unsupported by any evidence. Korea states that the United States proposes to overturn the principles of treaty interpretation included in the *Vienna Convention*, and the Appellate Body's reasoning regarding "the commonplace inference that is properly drawn from [the] disappearance" of the "direct or substantial control" test from the GPA, on the basis of nothing more than its own unsupported assertion that the drafters of the Uruguay Round GPA theoretically could have meant for Annexes 2 or 3 to replace or encompass the "control" concept.[391]

4.311 Korea states that, assuming, however, that the United States is correct, it has not explained why the result of its analysis is not merely to refer the Panel to the lists of Korean entities included in Annexes 2 or 3 of the Uruguay Round GPA. Korea notes that KAA does not appear on either of these lists. Korea asks why the United States insists that KAA is included on Annex 1 by virtue of the "control" allegedly exercised over it by MOCT, an Annex 1 entity, if the negotiators of the Uruguay Round GPA intended, when they "excluded" the control test included in Article I:1(c) of the Tokyo Round GPA to incorporate the concept of "control" in Annexes 2 or 3. Korea asserts that the result of the United States' theory should rather be to direct an interpreter of the GPA, and Korea's Appendix I, to Korea's Annexes 2 and 3.[392]

4.312 **In response, the United States argues** that Korea's argument takes the United States' comments out of context, and attributes an incorrect conclusion to its analysis of Article I:1(c) of the Code.[393]

---

390 Blank and Marceau, "The History of the Government Procurement Negotiations Since 1945," p. 113.

391 Korea's Response to the US Answer to Question 20 from the Panel, dated 29 November 1999.

392 Ibid.

393 US Response to Korea's Answer to Question 5 from the Panel, dated 29 November 1999. The United States refers to the US Answer to Question 20 from the Panel, dated 29 November 1999, for

(b) Relevance of Control to 1991 Amendments to IIA Legislation

4.313 **In response to a question from the Panel, Korea argues** that the reference to control in the Tokyo Round GPA, and its absence from the Uruguay Round GPA, is fatal to the US claim that KAA, KOACA and IIAC are covered under the GPA by virtue of the "control" allegedly exercised over them by MOCT. In Korea's view, even if, when responsibility for the Inchon airport project was assigned to KAA in December 1991, the United States relied on the Tokyo Round "control" test to assume that MOCT "control" over KAA would subject KAA to GPA coverage, everything changed when the Uruguay Round negotiators subsequently dropped the "control" test from the GPA. From that point on, the United States could no longer have reasonably expected that unlisted entities, not themselves listed on an Annex, would be covered by virtue of the control exercised over them by listed entities. As a matter of law, according to Korea, entities controlled by named entities, but not themselves named, no longer would be covered. Korea argues that to the extent the United States relied on the Tokyo Round GPA's "control" test, it did so at its peril once that test was eliminated by the Uruguay Round GPA negotiators.[394]

4.314 **In response to the same question from the Panel, the United States argues** that the reference to control in the Tokyo Round Procurement Code is irrelevant to any analysis about the US response (or lack thereof) to the 1991 amendments made to the *Act on Promotion of a New Airport for Seoul Metropolitan Area Construction*, the *Korea Airport Corporation Act* and the *By-Laws of Korea Airport Corporation* since the reference to control, found in Article I:1(c) of the Tokyo Round Procurement Code ("Code"), is actually unrelated to "central government entities."[395]

4.315 The United States argues that according to the 1979 USITC report, Article I:1(c) is essentially a "guide for future negotiations" to expand the Code coverage in two directions.[396] First, it suggests expanding the Code to apply to procurement by the "entities under the direct or substantial control of Parties." Secondly, it also suggests expanding the Code to apply to procurement by "other designated entities."

4.316 The United States argues that with regard to the expansion of coverage to procurements by "entities under the direct or substantial control of Parties," the 1979 USITC report states that "[t]he broader language 'direct or substantial control' apparently is intended to encompass not only governmental units but quasi-governmental purchasing agents as well." In other words, this control reference is not related to the control of "central government entities" over their subdivisions. Instead, it is referring to the control of Code parties (*i.e.*, the governments themselves) over their "quasi-governmental purchasing agents."[397]

4.317 As for the expansion of coverage to procurements by "other designated entities," the United States argues that the USITC report makes clear that this reference is not related to the concept of control and in addition, this reference is unrelated to

---

what it says is an accurate presentation of its views regarding the normative "control" test of Article I:1(c) of the Code.

[394] Korea's Answer to Question 20 from the Panel, dated 29 November 1999.

[395] US Answer to Question 20 from the Panel, dated 29 November 1999.

[396] USITC report, p. 26.

[397] US Answer to Question 20 from the Panel, dated 29 November 1999.

"central government entities." According to the United States, instead, it is referring to procurement by those entities that are not "specified by the lists" in the Code[398] and are not "under the direct or substantial control of Parties" to the Code[399] but would nevertheless fall under the rubric of "government" procurement. The United States further argues that, according to the USITC report, this reference encompasses such entities as "political subdivisions" and "provincial governments."[400]

4.318 The United States concludes that it did not respond to the 1991 amendments made to the *Act on Promotion of a New Airport for Seoul Metropolitan Area Construction*, the *Korea Airport Corporation Act* and the *By-Laws of Korea Airport Corporation* because these amendments came about merely as a result of MOCT's decision to designate KAA as a project operator of the IIA project, with MOCT itself retaining ultimate authority and control over the project and over KAA. The United States argues that this is an example of an entity being controlled by another entity, and is irrelevant to the control reference in the Code because Article I:1(c) of the Code has nothing to do with the control of entities by "other entities." Instead, according to the United States, Article I:1(c) is referring to the control of entities by "Parties" to the Agreement.[401] The United States further argues that it is alluding to the coverage under the GPA of what the USITC calls "quasi-governmental purchasing agents," i.e., entities that are controlled by the governments themselves, and not by other entities.[402]

4.319 **In response, Korea argues that**, the United States' assertion that the "control" test in Article I:1(c) of the Tokyo Round GPA "is not related to the control of 'central government entities' over their subdivisions," and instead refers to "the control of Code parties (*i.e.*, the governments themselves) over their 'quasi-governmental purchasing agents'" is not supported by the 1979 US International Trade Commission Report, as the United States claims.[403]

4.320 Korea states that the quote extracted by the United States from the Report confirms, first of all, that Article I:1(c) refers to "governmental units" as well as "quasi-governmental purchasing agents."[404] Korea states that, moreover, in discussing the impact of the "control" test in Article I:1(c), the Report specifically considers whether Amtrak and Comsat would be covered under "the normative 'direct substantial control' rule," and goes on to catalogue the control exercised over those entities by central government entities listed on the United States' Annex I.[405] Korea states that whether characterized as "governmental units" or "quasi-governmental purchasing agents," Korea had demonstrated that the MOCT "control" to which the United States alleges KAA is subject is remarkably similar to the control to which Amtrak and Comsat are subject by US Annex 1 entities. Korea states that if KAA is subject

---

398 Article I:1(c) of the Code, second sentence.

399 Ibid. first sentence.

400 US Answer to Question 20 from the Panel, dated 29 November 1999, citing USITC report, pp. 25-26.

401 Article I:1(c) of the Code.

402 US Answer to Question 20 from the Panel, dated 29 November 1999.

403 Korea's Response to the US Answer to Question 20 from the Panel, dated 29 November 1999.

404 USITC Report, p. 25.

405 *Ibid.* pp. 41-44.

to GPA coverage by virtue of this "control" test, so are Amtrak, Comsat, and many other non-listed "myriad organizations tangential to the essential function of government."[406]

(c) Coverage of Entities or Sectors

4.321 **The United States asserts** that the GPA's negotiating history confirms the interpretation that the GPA provides for the coverage of sectors by way of entities. Specifically, the United States notes that in the 1979 independent USITC report, the Commission made clear that, with regard to coverage, "The code approach is to define coverage in terms of procuring entities ... and value of contracts, together with numerous exceptions." However, the goal of "maximum coverage of procuring entities must be attained while achieving an agreeable balance of coverage in terms of quality (type) and quantity (value) of goods procured," which meant that coverage is actually:

> "a function of four factors: (1) types of procurement actions; (2) value of the procured product; (3) identity of procuring entity; and (4) specific exclusions from coverage. Each of these factors must be taken into account when determining the applicability of the code to any government contract action."

4.322 The United States argues that it is apparent from this excerpt that entities were covered based on the sectors and projects that they procure for, and not on the identities of the entities themselves. In other words, the sectors and projects that an entity was responsible for were the major factors for countries in considering which entities they would seek to be covered under the GPA. The United States contends that when a balance of rights and obligations was established between two of these negotiating countries, the balance was often considered not in terms of the number or the names of the entities, but in terms of total procurement value and/or the quality (for example, future procurement opportunities for domestic industry) of the concession packages. The United States asserts that, in short, GPA negotiators bargained for what the entities bought, not for who the entities were.

(d) "The History of the Government Procurement Negotiations Since 1945"

4.323 **The United States argues** that when interpreted according to its ordinary meaning, in its context and in light of the object and purpose of the GPA, the scope of "central government entity" in Annex 1 of the GPA includes coverage of its branch offices and subsidiary organizations unless otherwise provided for in the GPA.

4.324 The United States contends that the negotiating history of the GPA confirms this interpretation. Specifically, the United States refers to an article entitled, "The History of the Government Procurement Negotiations Since 1945" which notes that "[i]t was necessary for the Agreement to have the widest possible coverage. This

---

406 Korea's Response to the US Answer to Question 20 from the Panel, dated 29 November 1999, citing USITC Report at p. 44.

principle was agreed in the OECD."[407] The United States contends that, to now exclude coverage of a listed entity's subordinate units would not only be contrary to the above, but would also rid the GPA of most of its substantive coverage, for coverage of an entity that excludes its subordinate units actually amounts to no coverage at all.

2. *History of Korea's Accession*

(a) Bilateral Negotiations Prior to Korea's Accession

4.325 In order to confirm its interpretation of "central government entity" in Korea's Annex 1, **the United States** looks to the preparatory work of the GPA and the circumstances of its conclusion pursuant to Article 32 of the *Vienna Convention*. According to the United States, during Korea's accession negotiations, the United States explicitly bargained for and received coverage of all Korean Government entities responsible for the procurement of products and services related to new airport construction projects under Annex 1.

4.326 The United States submits that, from the outset of negotiations with Korea, it was made clear that the United States would only accept from the Government of Korea, a "credible offer with respect to ongoing negotiations to expand [the Procurement Code's] coverage,"[408] which included coverage of "all entities in the telecommunications, energy, transportation, and water sectors;" as well as "services and construction contracts."[409]

4.327 **Korea responds** that despite the United States' claim that it would have accepted nothing less, in negotiations with Korea, than coverage of "all entities in the ... transportation ... sector[]," it has acknowledged that it failed to achieve this goal.[410]

(i) The July 1991 Communication from Korea

Contents of the Communication

4.328 **The United States notes** that on 1 May 1991, pursuant to issues raised during the 22 April bilateral negotiations, the United States sent a list of follow-up questions to Korea regarding its accession package.[411] In it, the United States notes that it explicitly asked:

---

[407] Annet Blank and Gabrielle Marceau, "The History of the Government Procurement Negotiations Since 1945," 5 *Public Procurement Law Review* 77, p. 99 (1996). The reference to the OECD alludes to "the research and negotiating work undertaken by the OECD from 1963 onwards" that attempted "to re-introduce government procurement into the general multilateral trade rules." Ibid. p. 77.

[408] US Department of Commerce Reporting Cable (Geneva 05022, May 91), para. 1. The "ongoing negotiations" is in reference to the Uruguay Round negotiations to expand coverage of the Procurement Code.

[409] Ibid. para. 5.

[410] Korea refers here to the US Department of Commerce Memorandum, referred to below in para. 4.388 *et seq.*

[411] US Questions Relating to Korea's Request to Accede to the Agreement on Government Procurement, May 1991.

> "How does the Airport Development Group relate to the Ministry of Communications? Does Korea's offer of coverage of the Ministry of Communications include purchases for the Airport Development Group? Please identify all Ministries that will be responsible for the procurement of goods and services related to new airport construction."

4.329 In response to a question from the Panel as to what prompted these questions, the United States notes as follows. To assist US officials negotiating Korea's accession to the GPA following Korea's initial accession offer of 25 June 1990, the American Embassy in Seoul conducted a survey of US companies regarding areas of interest in the Korean procurement market. Specifically mentioned by American companies as priority areas of interest were coverage of the "Airport Development Group" with its responsibility over procurement for the new airport construction, as well as procurement of specific sectors including "airport systems," and "air and maritime communication and navigation equipment."[412]

4.330 The United States refers to Korea's response to the follow-up questions which was received in July 1991:

> "The new airport construction is being conducted by the New Airport Development Group under the Ministry of Transportation. The new airport construction project is scheduled to be completed by 1997 after the completion of the basic plan by 1992 and the working plan by 1993. The US company, Bechtel, is taking part in the basic plan projects.
>
> The responsible organization for procurement of goods and services relating to the new airport construction is the Office of Supply. But at present, the concrete procurement plan has not been fixed because now the whole airport construction project is only in a basic planning stage."[413]

Procuring Entities Referred to in Communication

4.331 **The United States notes** that at the time the July 1991 response was received from Korea, the two entities Korea represented as being responsible for new airport construction projects in the response - the Ministry of Transportation and the Office of Supply - had already been listed in Korea's initial GPA offer. The United States further notes that coverage under Annex 1 of the same two entities was finalized on 15 April 1994 when Korea became a Party to the GPA.

4.332 The United States argues that following July 1991 when Korea represented that the Ministry of Transportation and the Office of Supply would be responsible for airport procurement, Korea did not broach the subject of airport procurement again. Further, the United States asserts that Korea did not attempt to amend the statements made in July 1991. According to the United States, given this series of communica-

[412] US Answer to Question 21 from the Panel, dated 3 November 1999.

[413] Korea's Answers to the Questions from USTR Relating to Korea's Request to Accede to the GPA, 1 July 1991, p. 6.

tions and subsequent silence by Korean officials, it is reasonable for the United States to conclude that MOCT and the Office of Supply were indeed the only entities engaging in procurements for new airport construction projects. **Korea acknowledges** that its July 1991 response identified the Office of Supply as the "responsible organization" for IIA procurement. Korea states that pursuant to Article 2(5) of the *Government Procurement Fund Act*[414], the Korean Office of Supply would in principle have assumed procurement responsibility in respect of the IIA project. However, Korea argues that since the plan for the IIA project had not been completed and that site preparation for the project was not to commence for at least 16 months from the time Korea provided its response to the United States, Korea emphasized in its response that "the concrete procurement plan has not been fixed because now the whole airport construction project is only in a basic planning stage."[415] In response to a question from the United States, Korea states that these words should have served to alert any reasonable person that, at that point, nothing with regard to procurement was fixed. According to Korea, that would include the entity ultimately responsible for procurement.[416]

4.333 **In response, the United States notes** that with regard to the specifics of the 1991 Korean response, the United States does not consider the Korean statement "[b]ut at present, the concrete procurement plan has not been fixed..." as indicating a possible change in the entities responsible for procurement for the IIA project. According to the United States, Korea's response merely notes that the specifics of the procurement plan (i.e. the tendering schedule, estimated value of tenders etc.) have not yet been determined. The logical reading of Korea's statement is that the entities responsible for the procurement of the new airport construction are the New Airport Development Group under MOCT and the Office of Supply. However, exactly how these entities will construct the airport and what value of the associated procurements will be, has not yet been determined. The United States argues that had Korea intended to focus on which entities are responsible for airport procurement, it would have stated that the "procuring entities have not been fixed..." rather than the "procurement plan has not been fixed."

4.334 Moreover, the United States argues that Korea was clear and unequivocal regarding which entities were responsible for IIA procurement. The United States notes that in response to the United States question, the statement that the construction "is being conducted by the New Airport Development Group under the Ministry of Transportation," appears in an earlier paragraph before Korea's "qualification," and precedes a discussion of the possible timetable for the new project. Finally, the United States argues that by noting in its response that Bechtel was taking part in the basic plan project, Korea acknowledges that procurement had already begun for the airport project, with the assumption that the entities named were responsible for conducting this procurement.

4.335 **Further, in response to a question from the Panel, Korea notes** that the July 1991 communication should be put in context. Korea states that the inquiry from

---

414 Act No. 3580, 27 December 1982.

415 Korea's Answers to Questions 15 & 16 from the US, dated 3 November 1999.

416 Korea's Answer to Question 15 from the US, dated 3 November 1999.

the United States was to Korea, largely academic when it was received. Korea states that its response was an accurate, good faith, honest response to an inquiry in another language. Korea further states that it was drafted - probably dictated to a stenographer in the drafter's second language - without reference to the New Shorter Oxford English Dictionary. Korea states that it believed it honestly and reasonably informed the United States that as of July 1991 the relevant entities were the Ministry of Transportation and the Office of Supply, but that nothing, as of that date, was fixed, and that a reasonable reader of that communication would have concluded that the existing situation was temporary.[417] Korea argues that this interpretation is warranted by the structure of the second paragraph of Korea's July 1991 response. Korea notes that immediately after the reference to the Office of Supply, Korea wrote, "But at present the concrete procurement plan ... ." Korea argues that the reference to the entity in principle responsible for IIA procurement at that time, followed immediately by the statement that the "concrete procurement plan has not been fixed," coupled with the qualifier, "But at present," would lead any reasonable reader to conclude that the entire IIA project was in its infancy and undecided.[418]

4.336 **The United States responds by arguing** that Korea appears to suggest that it is exempt from the normal rules of treaty interpretation and of state responsibility with respect to its GPA schedules and other official documents merely because those documents were translated from Korean to English. The United States notes that Korea has already agreed that its schedule to the GPA be "[a]uthentic in the English language only." Indeed, the United States notes that all negotiating documents provided by Korea including the *Government Organization Act* were provided in English. Moreover, according to the United States, Korea has in many other instances argued for precise textual interpretations of translated Korean documents.

4.337 **In further support of its argument that it had not made any commitments regarding entities responsible for airport procurement, Korea refers** to a European Communities report regarding the progress of the Uruguay Round negotiations dated March 1993. Korea notes that the European Communities explicitly stated in the report that Korea had given "no offer regarding airports."

4.338 **In response, the United States notes** that Korea has not reconciled the statement in the EC report with its earlier statement that the Seoul and Pusan Regional Aviation Offices, responsible for airport projects "during the period 1992-1998," are covered under Annex 1 of the GPA. The United States argues that as "special local administrative organs" of MOCT, these Regional Aviation Offices should have been covered from the time MOCT was first placed on Korea's GPA accession offer in June of 1990.

4.339 The United States further notes that given the fact that Korea previously represented to the United States that IIA construction is the only airport project currently underway and that GPA Parties can choose to cover any entity under Annexes 1 or 3 regardless of the entity's procurement subject-matter or domestic legal status, Korea's position regarding the Regional Aviation Offices *vis-à-vis* General Note 1 remains

417 Korea's Answer to Question 16 from the Panel, dated 3 November 1999.

418 Ibid.

highly problematic with respect to Korea's overall defense that KAA, KOACA and IIAC are not covered under Korea's GPA obligations.

Seoul and Pusan Regional Aviation Offices

4.340 **The United States argues** that in 1991, when the United States asked Korea for a list of entities responsible for new airport construction procurements, Korea made no mention of the Seoul and Pusan Regional Aviation Offices. The United States contends that this answer appears to contradict Korea's present argument that the Regional Aviation Offices have been awarding airport procurement contracts "during the period 1992-1998."

4.341 **Korea argues** that if the United States was intent on achieving GPA coverage for IIA procurement, it surely would have consulted industry regarding airport procurement. Korea asserts that, in that case, the United States would have been aware of the numerous examples of contracts awarded by the Regional Aviation Offices or the Office of Supply, during the period while the GPA negotiations were pending, for projects associated with the relevant airports. Korea refers to the evidence referred to in paragraph 4.239.

4.342 Korea further notes that in describing Korea's alleged failure in July 1991 to mention the Regional Aviation Offices in response to a question regarding the IIA project, the United States contends that its question "asked Korea for a list of entities responsible for new airport construction procurements." Korea states that this assertion is in error. Korea notes that the actual text of the United States' question was:

> "How does the *Airport Development Group* relate to the Ministry of Communication? Does Korea's offer of coverage of the Ministry of Communications include purchases for the *Airport Development Group*? Please identify all Ministries that will be responsible for the procurement of goods and services related to new airport construction."

4.343 Korea argues that its impression was that the United States was not asking about just any generic airport procurement. Given the United States' obvious emphasis on the Airport Development Group, NADG, Korea states that its response was entirely focused upon the airport with which NADG was associated - IIA. Korea states that its entirely reasonable assumption was that the United States' question was about the IIA project and that its response was to give as much information as was available about what was, at the time, a fledgling project.

Coverage of Entities or Projects

4.344 **The United States argues** that, in response to a direct question regarding the coverage of new airport construction from the United States, Korea explicitly represented that the New Airport Development Group of MOCT and the Office of Supply would be responsible for procurement of new airport construction. The United States asserts that by phrasing the question in sectoral terms, it is clear that the United States was interested in projects related to airport procurements. The United States further argues that Korea's response, in entity terms, created an expectation that airport procurements would be covered through the listing of MOCT and the Office of Supply. The United States concludes that it could reasonably expect airport procurement to be subject to the disciplines of the GPA through coverage of MOCT and the Office of Supply.

4.345 The United States further argues that the sectors and projects that an entity was responsible for were the major factors for countries in considering which entities they would seek coverage for under the GPA. In relation to this case, the United States contends that it sought to cover "new airport construction." The United States notes that Korea responded in July of 1991 that MOCT and the Office of Supply were responsible for "new airport construction."[419] The United States argues that, therefore, MOCT and the Office of Supply became covered, not just for procurements related to "new airport construction," but, pursuant to Article I:1 of the GPA for "any procurement by [these] entities," subject to explicit exceptions.[420]

4.346 **In response to a question from the Panel, Korea states** that its Annex 1 commitments were negotiated on the basis of entities, rather than projects. Korea notes that Annex 1 does list entities rather than projects. Korea states that it fails to see how this fact can be disputed. Korea further notes that neither Korea's initial offer nor its second offer nor its third and final offer, submitted in December 1993, include a list of projects for Annex 1.[421] In any event, Korea argues that since KAA was the entity responsible for IIA procurement from December 1991 through August 1994, if it was not covered, then the IIA was not covered.[422]

4.347 **The United States argues in response** that to accept Korea's position that the GPA provides pure entity coverage is to make the GPA a nullity. According to the United States, a Party could transfer procurement authority from listed entities to non-listed entities and not have to notify or compensate other Parties for such transfers because, as an agreement covering purely on the basis of entities, the listed entities are technically still "covered." The United States argues that, needless to say, the GPA would quickly be emptied of substance.

4.348 **Further, in response to the United States' argument, Korea reiterates** that procurements by MOCT and NADG (were any to exist) are indeed subject to the GPA, as are procurements by the Office of Supply for Annex 1 entities. However, according to Korea, this result does not flow from Korea's July 1991 response. Korea states that its July 1991 response was a reply to a factual question from the United States about NADG, and did not speak in any way whatsoever to the question of GPA coverage.[423]

4.349 Korea states that, moreover, its July 1991 response did not speak to "new airport construction." Korea stresses that neither the question nor the answer spoke to a commitment to GPA coverage for anything at all - neither an entity, nor a sector called "new airport construction." Korea asserts that both the May 1991 question and the July 1991 answer were factual, and spoke to NADG and the IIA. Korea further states that the July 1991 response spoke to an entity that would in principle have

---

[419] The United States notes that both these entities were already in Korea's GPA accession offer, and in fact MOCT was already responsible for awarding the first IIA procurement contracts for the basic plans.

[420] US Answer to Question 16 from the Panel, dated 29 November 1999.

[421] Korea's Answer to Question 4 from the Panel, dated 29 November 1999.

[422] Korea's Answer to Question 5 from the Panel, dated 29 November 1999.

[423] Korea's Response to US Answer to Question 17 from the Panel, dated 29 November 1999.

been responsible for procurements for a particular airport, had there even been any at the time. Korea states that it is inaccurate to say that, in its July 1991 response, made two and one-half years before it signed the GPA, Korea committed to GPA coverage at all, much less GPA coverage for a sector called "new airport construction." Korea argues that the United States is using its own question, and not Korea's response, as evidence of Korea's commitments. This, states Korea, is no evidence at all.[424]

The February 1991 Supplementary Explanation *of Korea's GPA Offer*

4.350 Korea argues that during negotiations regarding Korea's accession to the GPA, the United States was aware of the existence and activities of Annex 1 entities undertaking "procurement for airports," whether related to new airport construction or work on existing airports. Korea further argues that the United States was aware that entities other than KAA - namely, the Regional Aviation Offices - existed, procured for Korean airports other than IIA and were included in Korea's offer.[425]

4.351 Korea notes that the Korean cable report[426], the questions put to Korea by the United States in May 1991[427] and a May 1991 US Department of Commerce cable report[428] all note the United States' receipt of a February 1991 document entitled "*Supplementary Explanation of the Note by the Republic of Korea, dated 29 June 1990, relating to the Agreement on Government Procurement.*"[429] Korea further notes that page 11 of this *Supplementary Explanation*, explaining Korea's initial offer, lists the Regional Aviation Offices or Bureaus as included within Korea's commitment of the Ministry of Transportation. Korea notes that it does not list KAA.

The Act on the Promotion of a New Airport for Seoul Metropolitan Area Construction

Reference to Act in 1991

4.352 **In response to a question from the Panel** requesting an explanation why Korea did not mention the 1991 *Seoul Airport Act* in its July 1991 response, **Korea notes** that the United States posed 17 questions, which deal with a wide variety of issues. Korea notes that only one question deals with the IIA. Korea asserts that an employee of the Ministry of Commerce provided good faith answers to all of these questions on 1 July 1991. Korea further states that the answers provided were, moreover, in depth and thorough.[430]

4.353 Korea argues that as is evident from Korea's July 1991 responses, it went to considerable lengths to answer the United States' questions, providing a 29-page response to two pages of questions from the United States. Korea states that it took the inquiries seriously, and provided thorough, detailed responses to anything that

---

424 Korea's Response to US Answer to Question 16 from the Panel, dated 29 November 1999.

425 Korea's Response to US Answer to Question 17 from the Panel, dated 29 November 1999.

426 Exhibit Kor-118.

427 US Exhibit 4, Questions 9, 10, 11, 14, 15.

428 US Exhibit 2, p. 2.

429 Exhibit Kor-117.

430 Korea's Answer to Question 1 from the Panel, dated 29 November 1999.

was asked of it. Korea states that it did not read into the United States' inquiry, questions that were not posed, including questions about the *Seoul Airport Act* or any other legislation related to the IIA, such as the *Korea Airport Corporation Act.*[431]

4.354 Korea argues that given the diversity of topics raised by the United States, and the breadth of the answers given, it is not reasonable to expect Korea, or any Member, to go well beyond what was asked, and to provide information in each case about whatever it may have considered that the United States might possibly have considered interesting. Korea states that were it or any other Member to accept such a burden, the virtual impossibility of successfully addressing every possible issue would virtually guarantee failure, and subject it to certain liability in later disputes.[432]

4.355 In support of its position, Korea states that this undoubtedly is one reason why the Appellate Body, in the *Computer Equipment* case, rejected the notion that the "importing party" (here, Korea) bore the responsibility for the clarity of its tariff schedule. Korea states that according to the Appellate Body, "exporting Members" (here, the United States) have to ensure that their corresponding rights are described in such a manner in the Schedules of importing Members that their export interests, as agreed in the negotiations, are guaranteed.[433] Korea notes that in July 1991, Korea offered 29 pages of good faith responses to 17 questions posed by the United States. Korea asserts that under the principles enunciated by the Appellate Body in the *Computer Equipment* case, it can be charged with nothing more, without forcing upon it a burden properly put upon the United States.[434]

Status of Act at Time of July 1991 Response

4.356 **In response to a question from the Panel** that requested details regarding the progress of the *Seoul Airport Act* from the policy phase to the legislation phase, **Korea argues** that, in the abstract, it is impossible to say with any precision how long it takes for legislation to run its course. Korea argues that as with most other Members with legislatures independent of the executive, the time required to pass legislation depends on many factors, including the degree and intensity of opposition.[435]

4.357 Korea states that the following timeline, applied to the December 1991 amendments to the *Seoul Airport Act*, by which KAA was nominated as the entity responsible for the IIA project:[436]

431 Ibid.

432 Ibid.

433 Appellate Body Report, *EC – Computer Equipment*, *supra*, footnote 106, para. 109.

434 Korea's Answer to Question 1 from the Panel, dated 29 November 1999.

435 Korea's Answer to Question 3 from the Panel, dated 29 November 1999.

436 Ibid.

26 June 1991:	MOT makes an internal decision to recommend that KAA be assigned by the National Assembly as the entity responsible for the IIA project, in draft legislation proposed to amend the *Seoul Airport Act*
10 July 1991:	MOT publishes a public notice of draft legislation containing proposed amendments to the *Seoul Airport Act*
29 July 1991:	Vice-Ministers of concerned Ministries meet to discuss the draft legislation
6 August 1991:	Directors General of these same concerned ministries meet to discuss the draft legislation
14 August 1991:	The draft legislation is approved at a meeting of the Vice-Ministers of the Economic Ministries
8 October 1991:	The draft legislation is approved at a meeting of all Vice-Ministers
9 October 1991:	The draft legislation is approved at a Cabinet meeting of the all Ministers
16 October 1991:	The draft legislation is approved by the President of Korea
21 October 1991:	The draft legislation is transferred to the National Assembly
12 November 1991:	The draft legislation is tabled with the National Assembly's Committee on Transport and Communication
19 November 1991:	The draft legislation is approved by the National Assembly's Committee on Transport and Communication
20 November 1991:	The legislation is adopted at a plenary session of the National Assembly
29 November 1991:	The legislation is transferred to the President of Korea
14 December 1991:	The legislation is signed by the President, promulgated as Law No. 4436 and published in the *Official Gazette*

4.358 Korea notes that the legislation in question was not particularly controversial, and, thus, was enacted in a comparatively short time. Korea states that, as is evident from this timeline, the Ministry of Transportation made an internal decision to recommend that the National Assembly appoint KAA as the entity responsible for the IIA project on 26 June 1991. Korea notes that a public notice was not issued by the Ministry of Transportation until 10 July, 10 days after the 1 July response from the Ministry of Commerce, an entirely different agency. The Ministry of Transportation's decision to recommend KAA was not discussed with other ministries until the 29 July and 6 August meetings of interested vice-ministers and directors general.[437]

4.359 Korea states that the Ministry of Commerce, which prepared Korea's responses to the United States' questions, was simply not aware of the Ministry of Transportation's internal decision when it provided those responses to the United States on 1 July 1991. Korea further states that, moreover, the employee of the Ministry of Commerce who drafted responses to the United States' questions would have completed a draft before 26 June 1991, to allow for review by his superiors in advance of the 1 July 1991 submission. Korea argues that for either or both of these reasons, the decision to recommend KAA's involvement in the IIA project would not have been known to the Ministry and individual preparing Korea's 1 July 1991 response.[438]

[437] Ibid.
[438] Ibid.

4.360 Korea argues that even if the individual preparing Korea's 1 July 1991 response had been aware of the Ministry of Transport's 26 June decision, it would have been highly presumptuous for an employee of the Ministry of Commerce to communicate to the United States the inclusion of KAA in draft legislation yet to be discussed, let alone approved, by the relevant directors general, vice-ministers and ministers, along with the President of Korea and the National Assembly. Korea states that on 1 July 1991, when Korea provided its response to the United States, the draft legislation with proposed amendments to the *Seoul Airport Act* was little more than a proposal.[439]

4.361 Korea offers a parallel example to illustrate its point. In Korea's view, it would be politically impossible for an employee of the Office of the United States Trade Representative to offer preliminary information or assurances to a foreign negotiating partner regarding specific terms of not-yet-introduced legislation before domestic approval of the legislation was secured from the Cabinet and the President, if not of the Congress. According to Korea, conduct by the USTR suggesting that any of these approvals was merely a technical formality would engender serious political ramifications, and would counsel against providing the information to the foreign negotiating partner in the first place. Korea states that it should not be held to a different standard.[440]

4.362 **In response, the United States notes** that Korea's responses themselves do not indicate on which day in July they were provided. The United States notes that these responses merely read, "July 1991." The United States asserts that Korea offers no basis for its arbitrarily determined date of 1 July.[441]

4.363 The United States further notes that, in any case, it remains uncontested that the Ministry of Transportation's internal decision to recommend that KAA be assigned as the IIA project operator was made prior to the date on which Korea provided its responses to the United States, and that Korea did not inform the United States of MOT's internal decision in its July 1991 responses. The United States argues that because it remains unclear on what day in July 1991 Korea provided its responses, it is quite possible that MOT had already published the public notice of draft legislation containing proposed amendments to the *Seoul Airport Act*[442] and that the Vice-Ministers had already met to discuss this draft legislation[443] before Korea provided the United States with its July 1991 responses.[444]

4.364 The United States argues that, finally, it is important to keep the above discussion in perspective, and remember that the December 1991 amendment to the *Seoul Airport Act* did not alter MOCT's ultimate authority over the IIA project, and merely added KAA to the list of potential project operators.[445]

---

439 Ibid.

440 *Ibid.*

441 US Response to Korea's Answer to Question 3 from the Panel, dated 29 November 1999.

442 Korea indicates that this took place on 10 July 1999.

443 Korea indicates that this took place on 29 July 1991.

444 US Response to Korea's Answer to Question 3 from the Panel, dated 29 November 1999.

445 Ibid.

Completion Date of the Project

4.365 **In response to a question from the Panel, Korea notes** that its July 1991 response which states that the project would be completed by 1997, was provided six months before the basic plan was completed by a US company, Bechtel, in December 1991.[446] Korea notes that even though the statement in July 1991 regarding the 1997 completion date was apparently for the entire project, it was obviously based on very preliminary estimates by the Korean Government. Korea asserts that 1997 was simply a target time. Korea argues that while the schedule for the IIA project has, as with most large construction projects, been subject to considerable change over the years, the airport is currently scheduled to open in January 2001.[447]

4.366 The United States argues in response that although the airport is currently scheduled to open in January 2001, according to a 1998 revision to the airport plan, the Inchon airport development project will not be fully completed until 2020.[448] The United States asserts that, thus, Korea's discriminatory procurement practices have the potential of adversely affecting US companies for the next two decades.[449]

(ii) The May 1991 US Cable Report

Contents of the Cable Report

4.367 **The United States argues** that the arguments advanced by Korea would merely diminish Korea's obligations under Annex 1, which would then be in conflict with Korea's previous representations. Specifically, the United States refers to a May 1991 US Department of Commerce reporting cable, which, according to the United States, provides a factual account of the first round of GPA bilateral negotiations between the United States and Korea, held on 22 April 1991:

> "The Korean Del was asked to clarify Note 1 [of Korea's Annex 1]. The Korean Rep said that this Note was meant to "explain, not to derogate." The US Del noted that it seemed to be obvious that if an entity were covered, then all its subsidiary bodies would also be covered unless an explicit exception were stated [sic] in the offer. Therefore, it was unclear what the note was meant to add. The Korean Rep reiterated that the Note was not intended to limit their offer in any way and suggested that if it was causing concern they could consider dropping it."[450]

Meaning of the Cable Report

4.368 **According to the United States**, the May 1991 US Department of Commerce reporting cable summarizes the discussion between Korea and the United States as

446 Inchon International Airport: A Future-Oriented Airport, Increasing the Value of Time, p. 42. See also Exhibit Kor-11 (Contract for the basic plan).
447 Korea's Answer to Question 13 from the Panel, dated 29 November 1999.
448 US Exhibit 18.
449 US Response to Korea's Answer to Question 13 from the Panel, dated 29 November 1999.
450 Department of Commerce Reporting Cable (Geneva 05022, May 1991), para. 14.

they tried to reach a mutual understanding regarding the meaning of Note 1.[451] The United States contends that the cable records the parties' agreement regarding Note 1's intent to cover all "subsidiary bodies" of "central government entities" under Korea's Annex 1, unless "an explicit exception were stated in the offer." The United States asserts that, as Korea represented, Note 1 was not meant to "derogate," nor to "limit [Korea's] offer in any way;" Note 1 was never intended to exclude subsidiary organs from Annex 1 coverage. The United States concludes that, therefore, as subsidiary organizations of MOCT, KAA, KOACA and IIAC are also covered under Korea's Annex 1 pursuant to Note 1.

4.369 The United States further argues that Note 1 does not embody the "universe of bodies internal to central government entities under Korean law" and the *Government Organization Act* does not encompass the "entirety of the Korean central government structure". The United States argues that Note 1 does not define the scope of "central government entity" but, rather, expands it. The United States asserts that this interpretation has been confirmed by Korea when it states that, "Note 1 was not meant to 'limit' its Annex 1 offer." The United States argues that such an interpretation is consistent with the principle of effectiveness. The United States further argues that it is also consistent with the reasoning that Note 1 cannot both define and expand the scope of "central government entity."

4.370 The United States notes that the negotiating history may be used as a supplementary means of interpretation pursuant to Article 32 of the *Vienna Convention* should there remain any uncertainty or ambiguity about the meaning of Note 1. For example, in its recent report on *Canada - Measures Affecting the Importation of Milk and the Exportation of Dairy Products*, the Appellate Body, after determining that "the language in the notation in Canada's Schedule is not clear on its face...the language is general and ambiguous and, therefore, requires special care on the part of the treaty interpreter," found it "necessary, in this case, to turn to 'supplementary means of interpretation' pursuant to Article 32 of the *Vienna Convention*."

4.371 According to the United States, in the May 1991 US Department of Commerce reporting cable, Korea agreed with the United States that, "if an entity were covered, then all its subsidiary bodies would also be covered unless an explicit exception" were stated otherwise, and then conceded that Note 1 "is not intended to limit their offer in any way." Thus, the United States maintains that it is clear that Note 1 does not diminish the scope of coverage of Korea's Annex 1, i.e., branch offices and subsidiary organizations are still covered. The United States argues that in order to avoid interpreting Note 1 as being redundant or useless then one must interpret it as expanding Korea's Annex 1 coverage to include entities that might not be branch offices or subsidiary organizations of listed "central government entities" but are still a "subordinate linear organization," "special local administrative organ" or "attached organ" pursuant to Note 1.

---

[451] The United States notes that it is the common practice of US government officials to provide just such a factual report after each negotiating round. Although it might be argued that such a description is one-sided or capable of being inaccurate, the United States contends that it must be kept in mind that the US negotiator is under a duty to observe, report, and record these negotiations properly and factually, without any attempt at analysis. These reports are made in the "ordinary course" of a negotiator's business, and therefore should be considered reliable.

4.372 **In response, Korea notes** that despite the fact that Note 1 to Korea's Annex 1 specifically and unambiguously defines the terms "subordinate linear organization," "special local administrative organ" and "attached organ" by reference to the *Government Organization Act*, and despite the fact that the *Government Organization Act* does not include KAA, KOACA or IIAC within the definition of "subordinate linear organization," "special local administrative organ" or "attached organ," the United States argues that this cable, alone, subjects procurement by KAA, KOACA and IIAC to the terms of the GPA. Korea states that this position cannot be accepted.

4.373 Korea argues that the cable does not state, and Korea did not agree, as the United States alleges, "to cover all 'subsidiary bodies' of 'central government entities' ... unless 'an explicit exception were stated in the offer'." Korea states that Note 1 clarifies and defines the scope of those bodies internal to ministries listed on Annex 1. Korea further argues that Note 1 "excludes" or "excepts" nothing that would otherwise be included in these ministries under Korean law. Rather, in listing "subordinate linear organizations, special local administrative organs, and attached organs as prescribed by the *Government Organization Act* of the Republic of Korea," Korea argues that Note 1 includes the universe of bodies that are internal to an Annex 1 entity, and are, therefore, logically covered.

Status of the Cable Report

4.374 With respect to the status of the cable, **Korea argues** that this document cannot be considered "preparatory work," for two reasons. Korea argues that, first, it was not available to Korea before its accession to the GPA, and as a result cannot possibly be part of the commitments Korea accepted upon accession.[452] Korea states that had it seen the cable report prior to accession and therefore known the United States' view, it would have objected to or at least clarified the United States' interpretation of statements made by Korea at the 22 April 1991 meeting that the US cable purports to record. Korea states that, secondly, the cable report speaks only to the United States' expectations of what it had secured. Korea notes that the United States' expectations are relevant only in the context of its non-violation claim.[453]

4.375 Korea states that even if the cable report is considered "preparatory work," Article 32 of the *Vienna Convention* provides that "preparatory work" is relevant only where the ordinary meaning of an agreement is ambiguous, obscure, or leads to an absurd result. Alternatively, it may be used to "confirm" an interpretation derived through the application of Article 31.

4.376 Korea states that the circumstances surrounding the United States' reliance on the May 1991 cable do not satisfy the requirements of Article 32. According to Ko-

---

[452] Sir Ian Sinclair, The Vienna Convention on the Law of Treaties (2nd Ed., 1984), p. 144. Korea notes that Professor Sinclair reasons that preparatory works must be "in the public domain" so that subsequently acceding States can know to what they are being bound. There is no logical reason why original signatory States should not also have the benefit of knowing about any documents that purport to bind them to something of which they were not aware.

[453] Appellate Body Report, *EC - LAN*, *supra*, footnote 106, para. 80 (Reference to a complainant's reasonable expectations "in the context of a violation complaint 'melds the legally-distinct bases for violation and non-violation complaints ... into one uniform cause of action,' and is not in accordance with established GATT practice.").

rea, the reference in Note 1 to the *Government Organization Act* as the source of the definition for the term "subordinate linear organizations" is anything but ambiguous. Further, Korea states that Article 2(3) of the Act is clear, even if it does not correspond to a list the United States might adopt in its own domestic law. Korea argues that, furthermore, the fact that the United States, the European Communities, Hong Kong, Japan, Liechtenstein, Norway and Switzerland all define terms in their respective GPA Appendix I by reference to provisions of their domestic law indicates that to do so is far from an obscure or an absurd practice. Korea also states that the fact that the United States had the *Government Organization Act* at its disposal during negotiations with Korea regarding its GPA commitments demonstrates that giving the reference in Note 1 to the *Government Organization Act* effect is far from absurd. Finally, Korea asserts that the United States is not relying on this so-called preparatory work to "confirm" an interpretation derived through the application of Article 31. According to Korea, it is, rather, using the cable in an attempt to overturn the ordinary meaning of Korea's Note 1.

4.377 Korea states that, at most, the cable constitutes one party's record of discussions regarding the GPA. Korea argues that this type of evidence is self-serving. Korea states that it does not accept the unilateral characterization of the April 1991 meeting made by the United States. Korea further argues that Article 32 of the *Vienna Convention* does not, for good reason, permit the notes of a party with a vested interest in a particular interpretation to trump the unambiguous ordinary meaning of the terms included in an agreement, particularly where both the accuracy and the interpretation of those notes is disputed, as it is in this case.

4.378 **In response, the United States argues** that the cable report should be taken into account because Article 32 of the *Vienna Convention* explicitly permits the use of "circumstances of [the GPA's] conclusion" as a supplementary means of interpretation.

4.379 The United States further argues that the *Vienna Convention* rightly accords only a subordinate role to "supplementary means of interpretation" precisely because the documentary record of preparatory work or the circumstances of a treaty's conclusion may be incomplete, one-sided, or inconclusive. The United States argues that the Panel can and should determine through an interpretation under Article 31 that airport procurement is covered within the scope of Korea's GPA commitments. According to the United States, this interpretation is neither ambiguous nor obscure and does not lead to an absurd or unreasonable result. The United States asserts that, to the contrary, an interpretation that this procurement is not covered would be absurd and unreasonable. The United States argues that it is not necessary for the Panel to have recourse to any supplementary means to confirm the reading that the United States has given to Korea's Schedule under Article 31.

Accuracy of the Cable Report

4.380 Regarding the accuracy of the US cable, **Korea notes** that the document discussed at the meeting to which the cable relates was Korea's 25 June 1990 offer, which contained both notes and footnotes. Korea states that its notes of the April 1991 meeting, which are included in a Korean reporting memorandum written the day after the meeting, confirm that the United States indeed asked a question regarding whether attached organs, supporting organs and offices were included in

Korea's offer.[454] Korea states that the notes also confirm that the United States asked a question about "the reason for setting up 'Footnote 1', 'Footnote 3', and 'Note 1', 'Note 2', 'Note 3', 'Note 4' and 'Note 5'; and the possibility of removing these 'Footnotes' and 'Notes'." The specific offer under consideration was Korea's first offer, dated 25 June 1990. Korea notes that that offer included a list of "Purchasing Entities," along with four footnotes and five notes thereto.

4.381 Korea states that the accuracy of the United States' May 1991 cable, however, ends there. Korea states that it offered to drop footnote 1 and not Note 1. Korea states that, indeed, footnote 1 was dropped and Note 1 was not dropped. Korea states that the memorandum containing Korea's report of the meeting records no discussion about Note 1, and instead includes a conditional offer to delete Footnote 1, which exempted "purchases for the purpose of maintaining public order" from Korea's offer to include procurements by the Ministry of Home Affairs. Specifically, the Korean memorandum states:

> "Regarding 'Footnote 1' and 'Note 2' and 'Note 3,' Korea stated that if Korea and US had a clear mutual understanding of the GPA and GATT agreements, it may be possible to delete these points."

4.382 Korea states that it did not, therefore, offer to delete Note 1 from its offer, that any discussion about the "explanatory" as opposed to the "limiting" effect of its offer was, like its conditional offer regarding deletion, relevant to Footnote 1, Note 2 and Note 3. Korea notes that while a slightly amended version of what was Note 3 to Korea's initial offer appears in Korea's Annex 1 as Note 2, Footnote 1 and Note 2 to Korea's initial offer were deleted, and do not appear in its Annex 1.

4.383 Korea states that, moreover, and assuming, *arguendo*, that Korea's offer was to delete Note 1 rather than Footnote 1, the Korean memorandum reporting on this same meeting stated that the offer to do so was conditional on reaching a "clear mutual understanding" with the United States regarding the GPA. Korea states that such an understanding would have to include an agreement of the whole point to Note 1 in the context of the Korean Government system.

4.384 Korea notes that it is true that Note 1 was not meant to "limit" its Annex 1 offer. Korea notes that when it committed to coverage for the entities listed on Annex 1, along with their "subordinate linear organizations, special local administrative organs, and attached organs as prescribed by the *Government Organization Act*," Korea committed the universe of bodies internal to central government entities under Korean law.

4.385 Korea notes that if, indeed, it stated that Note 1 was "meant to 'explain, not to derogate'" or "to limit," it said so with the knowledge that it was committing everything that belongs to any of the central government entities listed on Annex 1, under the Korea system of government represented in the *Government Organization Act*. The entirety of the Korean central government structure is embodied in the *Government Organization Act*, and all of it, with regard to the entities listed on Annex 1, is included in Korea's Annex 1 commitment.

---

[454] Memorandum from the Permanent Mission of the Republic of Korea, 23 April 1991, p. 2. Korea states that the notes contained in this memorandum report on 22 April 1991 bilateral GPA negotiations with both the European Communities and the United States.

4.386 Korea notes that according to the United States, the May 1991 US cable report indicates an "agreement" between the parties. Korea states that the cable report makes clear that Korea made no such commitment. Further, Korea states that it does not accept the unilateral characterization of the April 1991 meeting by the United States.

Timing of Cable Report

4.387 **Korea states** that even if it were assumed for the sake of analysis that the May 1991 US cable report is correct in its description of events, Korea submits that it establishes nothing in relation to Korea's GPA obligations. Korea notes in this respect that April 1991 was a full three years before the GPA was signed and July of 1991 was more than two and one-half years before the GPA was signed. Korea further notes that these events were some two years and two and one-half years, respectively, before Korea's final offer. Korea notes that it didn't have any GPA obligations at that time.

(iii) US Department of Commerce Memorandum

4.388 **Korea also states** that despite the United States' claim that it would have accepted nothing less, in negotiations with Korea, than coverage of "all entities in the telecommunications, energy, transportation, and water sectors," it has acknowledged that it did not achieve this goal. In a Department of Commerce memorandum regarding the GPA, the United States explains that "major purchasers of transportation and telecommunications equipment" are absent from its own GPA commitments "because other GPA signatory countries were unwilling to offer these entities for coverage ... ."[455]

4.389 Korea notes that in similar circumstances, the International Court of Justice has attached particular significance to "statements against interest," such as these, placing them on equal footing with evidence offered by disinterested witnesses, and deeming them to be "of superior credibility."[456] Korea notes that, for example, in the Nicaragua case, the Court considered such statements tantamount to admissions:

> "The material before the Court ... includes statements by representatives of States, sometimes at the highest political level. Some of these statements were made before official organs of the State or of an international or regional organization, and appear in the official records of those bodies. Others, made during press conferences or interviews, were reported by the local or international press. The Court takes the view that statements of this kind, emanating from high-ranking official political figures, sometimes indeed of the highest rank, are of particular probative value when they acknowledge facts or conduct unfa-

---

[455] US Department of Commerce, International Trade Administration, Government Procurement Agreement, Publication No. 4019, undated, pp. 6 -7.

[456] *Case Concerning Military and Paramilitary Activities in and against Nicaragua*, 1986 I.C.J. 14, 42-43 (para. 69).

vourable to the State represented by the person who made them. They may then be construed as a form of admission."[457]

4.390 Korea submits that the statements by the United States and the European Communities (in the EC Commission report of March 1993), as "statements against interest," should be considered as admissions of the fact that the entities responsible for IIA procurement are not covered entities under the terms of the GPA.

4.391 **In response, the United States argues** that one glance at the Department of Commerce memorandum will tell the reader that the memorandum is not about what Korea excluded from its coverage. The United States asserts that, instead, it is about broader issues, such as the European Community's General Note 6, which explicitly states that "contracts awarded by entities in Annexes 1 and 2 in connection with activities in the fields of drinking water, energy, transport or telecommunications, are not included." In contrast, argues the United States, Korea's argument enjoys no such textual support.

(b) Communications Following Korea's Accession

(i) July 1998 Communication from the United States

Interpretation of Contents of Letter

4.392 **Korea refers** to a letter from the United States Embassy in Seoul to the Korean Ministry of Foreign Affairs and Trade, dated July 1998, in which the United States proposed that:

> "During the period before KOACA formally is brought under the GPA, ... [KOACA] agree to measures that would bring its procurement policies and practices de facto into conformity with the internationally-acceptable provisions of the GPA ... ."

4.393 Korea argues that if the time at which the above letter was written, namely, July 1998, was "before" the entities responsible for IIA procurement were "formally" covered, then those entities were not covered at all at that time. Korea further argues that there is no such thing as informal coverage and that if the entities referred to in the United States were "formally" covered in July 1998, the United States would not have requested de facto compliance with the GPA. Rather, it would have demanded *de jure* compliance.

4.394 In response to a question from the Panel requesting clarification of the July 1998 letter, the **United States notes** that at all times, including in the July 1998 letter from the US Commercial Officer, the United States has maintained that procurement by entities responsible for the construction of the Inchon International Airport were covered under Korea's obligations under the WTO GPA. The United States asserts that its position that KOACA was a covered entity has never changed.[458]

4.395 Further, the United States argues that Korea's argument was based on a single sentence taken out of context. The United States notes that had Korea quoted the entire relevant paragraph, it would have included the sentence indicating that the

---

[457] *Ibid.* para. 64, p. 41.

[458] US Answer to Question 27 from the Panel, dated 3 November 1999.

United States, "hold[s] firm to our position that KOACA should be covered by GPA disciplines."[459]

4.396 The United States also notes that following this statement of the US position, the letter goes on to urge the Korean Government to ensure that KOACA bring its procurement policies and practices de facto into conformity with the GPA. The United States contends that this is entirely consistent with the US position that KOACA and other entities procuring for the Inchon International Airport, were, and, as far as is known, continue to be as a matter of fact, acting in violation of the GPA. The United States notes that in the letter, the United States urges Korea, as a factual matter, to discontinue these discriminatory practices.[460]

Interpretation in light of the Vienna Convention on the Law of Treaties

4.397 **In response to a question from the Panel, Korea argues** that while the July 1998 letter is not itself treaty language, Korea believes it has great relevance to the interpretation of Korea's obligations under the GPA in light of Articles 31 and 32 of the *Vienna Convention on the Law of Treaties*. Korea argues that, first, with regard to the good faith requirement of Article 31.1, the United States cannot now claim that KOACA is a covered entity when only last year the United States explicitly took the position that KOACA was not covered. Second, Korea argues that with regard to Article 31.2(a), the letter is evidence of an agreement (in the sense of a common understanding) between the parties that KOACA was not covered. In Korea's view, this letter, four years subsequent to the treaty, clearly shows that both parties agreed on an interpretation of the provisions of the GPA that do not cover KOACA. Third, Korea states that with regard to Article 31.3(a), the letter is evidence of subsequent agreement between the parties regarding the interpretation of the GPA or the application of Article I and Appendix I. Fourth, Korea states that with regard to Article 31.3(b), the letter is practice that establishes the agreement of the parties regarding the GPA's interpretation. Fifth, Korea states that with regard to Article 31.3(c), the principle of equitable estoppel is a rule of international law[461]; Korea states that it reasonably relied on the United States' letter as evidence of its position and argues that the United States should not now be permitted to change its position to the detriment of Korea. Sixth, Korea states that it does not believe resort to Article 32 is necessary, but if it were, the letter clearly is a "supplementary means of interpretation" that confirms Korea's reading of its GPA obligations. Finally, Korea states that while not directly relevant to Articles 31 and 32, the July 1998 letter, in the context of this dispute, constitutes a statement against interest, which, as the International Court of Justice has noted, may be construed as a form of admission, as discussed in paragraph 4.389.[462]

---

[459] Ibid.

[460] Ibid.

[461] J.L. Brierly, The Law of Nations 63 (Oxford 1963); Ian Brownlie, Principles of Public International Law 18 (Oxford 1990).

[462] *Case Concerning Military and Paramilitary Activities in and against Nicaragua*, 1986 I.C.J. 14, 42-43 (para. 69).

4.398 **In response to the same question from the Panel, the United States argues** that in its view, its July 1998 letter does not fit within the customary rules of treaty interpretation, as set forth in Articles 31 and 32 of the *Vienna Convention on the Law of Treaties*. Article 31 states that a "treaty shall be interpreted in good faith in accordance with the ordinary meaning to be given to the terms of the treaty in their context and in the light of its object and purpose." The United States contends that as the letter in question post-dates the concession, it cannot be used to determine the object or purpose of Korea's concessions. In addition, the United States contends that this letter does not provide evidence of "any subsequent practice in the application of a treaty which establishes the agreement of the parties regarding its interpretation" under Article 31.3(b). The United States contends that, indeed, the letter was drafted at a time when Korea and the United States were on a pre-litigation footing. The United States contends that, thus, it cannot be construed as evidencing any type of either agreement or practice between the United States and Korea. The United States further states that it does not suggest that there is any "subsequent agreement between the parties regarding the interpretation of the treaty or the application of its provisions" as provided for in Article 31.3(a) of the *Vienna Convention*, particularly given the clear disagreement between the United States and Korea regarding what the letter says. The United States argues that, moreover, the meaning of Korea's concession in this case is not ambiguous or obscure, so an interpretation under Article 32 is inappropriate.[463]

Impact of Interpretation of Letter on other Arguments

4.399 In response to a question requesting clarification of how the fact that KOACA was not a covered entity would impact on the argument that KAA and IIAC are covered, **the United States argues** as follows. The United States asserts that if it is determined that KOACA was not a covered entity, there would be no impact on the US argument that KAA is covered because (1) KAA is still a subsidiary organization of MOCT, and all subsidiary organizations of "central government entities" are automatically covered under Annex 1 unless otherwise specified, and (2) KAA's procurements are in fact procurements by MOCT, pursuant to Article I of the GPA. The United States argues that as to the question of whether IIAC would be covered, that would depend on the reason why KOACA is not covered. In any case, if KOACA was determined not to be covered, the United States asserts that the result would be a shift in the mutually agreed balance of concession — MOCT responsibility for IIA procurement was transferred out of a covered entity. The United States argues that, therefore, Korea is obliged to make compensatory adjustment for its unilateral exclusion of airport procurement in order to re-balance the rights and obligations between the two countries.[464]

---

[463] US Answer to Question 31 from the Panel, dated 3 November 1999.

[464] US Answer to Question 28 from the Panel, dated 3 November 1999.

(ii) Letters from US Government Officials to Korean Government Officials

4.400 **The United States contends** that it has made its position undeniably clear on many occasions that KOACA is covered under Korea's GPA obligations and that KOACA's discrimination against US bidders on IIA projects is inconsistent with Korea's GPA obligations. In this respect, the United States refers to the fact that senior United States officials sent at least six letters to Korean Government officials unequivocally asserting the US position that KOACA was covered under Korea's GPA obligations, and that KOACA's procurement practices were in violation of Korea's obligations under the GPA.[465] These letters include: a letter dated 3 June 1997 from Charge d'Affaires Richard Christenson of the American Embassy in Seoul to KOACA Chairman Kang, Dong-Suk; a letter sent 17 August 1998 from United States Under Secretary of Commerce David Aaron to Korean Minister of State for Trade Han, Duck-Soo; a letter sent 17 August 1998 from United States Under Secretary of Commerce David Aaron to KOACA Chairman Kang, Dong-Suk; a letter dated 11 September 1998 from US Ambassador to the WTO Rita Hayes to Korean Ambassador to the WTO Man-Soon Chang; a letter dated 15 September 1998 from United States Under Secretary of Commerce David Aaron to Minister of Construction and Transportation Lee Jung; a joint letter dated 14 January 1999 from Secretary of Commerce William Daley and US Trade Representative Charlene Barshefsky to Korean Minister of Foreign Affairs and Trade Hong Soon-Young.

(iii) Memorandum from Korea's Ministry of Foreign Affairs and Trade to KOACA

4.401 **The United States also refers** to a memorandum from Korea's Ministry of Foreign Affairs and Trade (MOFAT) to KOACA, which it says reveals that Korea never had any misunderstanding regarding the US position that KOACA and IIA procurement are covered under Korea's GPA obligations. The United States notes that the memorandum was sent shortly after the July 1998 letter from the US Commercial Officer, Karen Ware. The United States further notes that the subject of the memorandum is "GPA application to KOACA," and states, in relevant part, "Ms. Karen Ware, Commercial attaché of US Embassy pointed out as per the attached letter that GPA should be applied by KOACA tender... ."[466]

(iv) Representations made in September 1998

4.402 **The United States argues** that in September 1998, in response to a question from the United States regarding the scope of KOACA's responsibility and whether KOACA was "responsible for all airport construction projects currently being planned or implemented by government entities in Korea," Korea did not mention procurements for other airports by the Office of Supply or the Regional Aviation Offices, and instead replied:

---

465 US Answer to Question 27 from the Panel, dated 3 November 1999.

466 Ibid.

> "KOACA is responsible for the construction of the Inchon International Airport. At present, there are no other plans for airport construction."[467]

4.403 The United States argues that throughout Korea's GPA accession negotiation, and even after the GPA came into force for it, Korea never once referred to these Regional Aviation Offices in the context of Annex 1 coverage of airport procurement. Further, the United States contends that Korea's answer appears to contradict Korea's present argument that the Regional Aviation Offices have been awarding airport procurement contracts during the period 1992-1998.

4.404 The United States also notes that in the question immediately preceding the question posed by the United States mentioned above, the United States asked:

> "Please identify all government entities that were responsible for airport construction projects at [the time bilateral negotiations between the United States and Korea relating to Korea's participation in the GPA were concluded (1993)] and the relationship of those entities to KOACA, which was established subsequently."

4.405 The United States notes that Korea responded as follows:

> "No other institutions besides the New Airport Development Group was involved in the construction of the airport."[468]

4.406 The United States notes that, again, Korea neglected to mention the Seoul and Pusan Regional Aviation Offices. The United States state that, in fact, Korea even neglected to mention KAA, thus admitting that, as of 1993, the New Airport Development Group of MOCT was still responsible for IIA construction.

4.407 **Korea argues in response** that the United States neglects to mention that the entire backdrop to the series of 27 questions raised in the September 1998 questionnaire was a growing dispute with Korea regarding the applicability of the GPA to, specifically, KOACA, as an entity responsible, again specifically, for IIA procurement. Korea refers to the minutes of the 18 February 1998 and 25 June 1998 meetings of the Committee on Government Procurement, which record the disagreement and characterize it as one regarding the "*Korea Airport Construction Authority*" and the "*International Airport Construction Corporation.*"[469] Korea also refers to a letter from Ambassador David Aaron of the US Department of Commerce, dated 17 August 1998, specifically discussing *KOACA's* procurement procedures for the IIA project.[470] Korea notes that the questionnaire was sent to Korea by the United States shortly after this letter, on 11 September 1998.[471]

---

[467] Korean response to US Question 7(a), dated September 1998, (GPA/W/76).

[468] Questions 6(a) and 6(b) (GPA/W/76).

[469] GPA/M/8, 24 May 1998, *Minutes of the Meeting Held on 18 February 1998*, pp. 1, 5; GPA/M/9, 1 September 1998, *Minutes of the Meeting Held on 25 June 1998*, pp. 1, 6.

[470] Letter from Ambassador David L. Aaron, Under Secretary for International Trade, US Department of Commerce (with cover letter from Karen L. Ware, Acting Minister Counsellor for Commercial Affairs, US Embassy Seoul), to Mr. Kang, Dong-Suk, Chairman and President, KOACA, dated 17 August 1998.

[471] GPA/W/76, 18 September 1998, *Request for Information Pursuant to Paragraphs 1 and 2 of Article XIX of the Agreement on Government Procurement, Communication from the United States.*

4.408 Korea argues that the context and content of the questionnaire, therefore, was entirely focused on KOACA and its role in the IIA project. Korea states that it is understandable that Korea's response to the United States' questions would, therefore, focus on KOACA and the IIA project.

4.409 Korea argues that it is not incumbent upon Korea to mention something about which the United States did not ask, such as the Regional Aviation Offices. Korea states that for practical reasons alone, guessing what would have been important to the United States or any other negotiating partner would have been impossible. If any participant in a negotiation were to accept such a burden, the sheer impossibility of fulfilling it would subject it to almost certain liability. Korea questions whether any deleterious impact on the United States or any other signatory could be alleged with regard to the "failure" by Korea to raise the role of the Regional Airport Offices in procurement for airports have had on the United States or any other signatory, and what the effect it would it have on this dispute. In any event, Korea notes that if the United States consulted with US industry carefully and extensively with regard to airport procurement, it surely would have been aware of both the potential bidding opportunities available to and the contracts secured by US companies from the Office of Supply and the Regional Aviation Offices during the period while the GPA negotiations were pending.

4.410 Korea also notes that the United States was in fact aware of the Regional Aviation Offices during negotiations regarding Korea's accession to the GPA. Korea points to a February 1991 document, titled "*Supplementary Explanation of the Note by the Republic of Korea, dated 29 June 1990, relating to the Agreement on Government Procurement,*" that lists the Regional Aviation Offices as included within Korea's offer by virtue of its inclusion of MOCT. Korea provides evidence demonstrating that the United States received this document in February 1991.[472]

4.411 **In response, the United States** notes that Korea argues that when the United States asked Korea to "identify all Ministries that will be responsible for the procurement of goods and services related to new airport construction" in 1998, Korea neglected to mention the Regional Aviation Offices because the United States was focused only on the New Airport Development Group. However, the United States queries as to why it would ask about other entities if the United States was focused only on the New Airport Development Group. The United States also notes that Korea argues that when the United States asked about "all airport construction projects currently being planned or implemented by government entities in Korea," Korea neglected to mention the projects by the Regional Aviation Offices because the United States was focused only on the IIA project. The United States again queries as to why it would ask about other projects if the United States was focused only on the IIA project. The United States contends that if Korea's responses to these questions are to be taken seriously, then Korea should be estopped from arguing that General Note 1 is not referring to the New Airport Development Group or the IIA project.

[472] Korea's Answer to Question 21 from the Panel, dated 29 November 1999.

(c) Statements against Interest

4.412 **The United States notes** that Korea was the Party that initially raised the issue of "statements against interest". The United States then lists "statements against interest" made by Korea.[473] For example, the United States notes that when MOCT's website states that KAA, KOACA and IIAC are its "subsidiary linear organizations," this could be interpreted as a statement against interest and an admission that these entities are in fact MOCT's subsidiary organizations. The United States argues that, furthermore, Korea's 1991 statements that the New Airport Development Group under MOCT and the Office of Supply are responsible for IIA construction could also be interpreted as statements against interest and as government admissions of the coverage of airport construction under the GPA. According to the United States, throughout this dispute, Korea makes many statements against its interest.

4.413 **Korea refers** to the United States list of "statements against interest" and challenges the "inconsistencies" alleged by the United States. In each instance, Korea argues that "Korea" (not a monolith, but many individuals) was asked a question in a foreign language and answered, also in a foreign language. Korea states that, later the question was asked again, and a different set of words was used to convey the same meaning or two different statements were issued by different people at different times referring to the same subject, using different verbal formulas. Korea states that the list of statements against interest to which the US refers then takes these "different" responses and suggests that they constitute contradictions or statements against interest, and that the doctrine of estoppel is relevant. Korea states that, in any case, Korea made its best efforts to respond to questions that came from the United States. If the United States did not understand an answer, Korea tried a different verbal formula to convey the same meaning.

(d) Doctrine of Estoppel

4.414 **The United States refers** to the international law doctrine of estoppel and, more specifically, quotes from a decision of the International Court of Justice:

> "Estoppel may be inferred from the conduct, declarations and the like made by a State which not only clearly and convincingly evinced acceptance by that State of a particular regime, but also had caused another State, in reliance on such conduct, detrimentally to change position or suffer some prejudice."[474]

4.415 The United States argues that Korea made repeated declarations concerning whether airport procurement would be within the scope of its GPA offer. The United States contends that it relied upon these declarations in agreeing to Korea's terms of accession. The United States argues that, therefore, Korea is now estopped from changing its position on the very facts it held out to be true during negotiations.

---

[473] US Exhibit 79.

[474] Military and Paramilitary Activities in and against Nicaragua, Jurisdiction and Admissibility, Judgment, *ICJ Reports 1984*, p. 415, para. 51.

3. *Subsequent Practice*

(a) Coverage of Entities or Projects

4.416 **The United States argues** that subsequent practice in the application of the GPA confirms that the GPA does not contemplate pure entity coverage. The United States notes that, for instance, in considering "the greatest possible extension of [GPA] coverage," pursuant to Article XXIV:7(b) of the Agreement, the Parties at informal consultations suggested:

> "Identification of potential sectors for extended coverage. Reference was made to the inclusion of the telecommunications, transportation and steel *sectors*. In response to this suggestion, the appropriateness of focusing work on the expansion of coverage in the telecommunications and transportation sectors has been questioned since many countries had made significant progress towards privatization in these sectors. It has been suggested that the review relating to this element should focus on the elimination of the derogations from coverage in some other *sectors* existing in Appendix I of Parties."[475]

(b) Discussion in relation to GPA Requirements

4.417 **The United States argues** that it first became aware that Korea was not conducting procurement for the IIA project in a manner consistent with its GPA obligations approximately two years ago in 1997, when US companies began informing the United States Government that they were being treated unfairly and in a manner that was inconsistent with GPA requirements when bidding for contracts relating to the Inchon International Airport construction project. At that time, the United States began looking into these practices, and when the United States contacted Korea to discuss the situation, Korea informed the United States that it did not consider the IIA project to be covered by the GPA.[476]

4.418 The United States contends that it continued to discuss this issue with Korean Government officials in Seoul and on the margins of meetings of the WTO Committee on Government Procurement. The United States contends that when it became clear that this matter was not going to be quickly resolved by informing Korean trade officials of KOACA's discriminatory procurement practices and reminding Korea of its obligations under the GPA, the United States began raising this issue formally in the WTO Committee on Government Procurement, sending letters to the Korean Government, and raising this matter in bilateral negotiating fora.[477]

4.419 The United States notes that prior to initial complaints from US companies in mid-1997, the United States continued to believe that it was undisputed that IIA procurement was covered under the Ministry of Transportation, and was part of Korea's GPA commitments. The United States notes, for example, that a 1992-1993 publication jointly produced by Commercial Service Seoul and the Association of Foreign

---

[475] Committee on Government Procurement, "Checklist of Issues Raised in Informal Consultations Regarding Modalities for the Review of the Agreement on Government procurement," (7th revision) Job No. 369, 25 January 1999, p. 29.

[476] US Answer to Question 29 from the Panel, dated 3 November 1999.

[477] US Answers to Questions 27 and 29 from the Panel, dated 3 November 1999.

Trading Agents of Korea (AFTAK)[478], listing major projects in Korea, indicates that the new international airport project as being conducted by the Ministry of Transportation.[479] The United States notes that, in addition, a United States Government reporting cable describing Korea's new GPA obligations, sent on 1 May 1997, specifically notes that infrastructure projects such as the new Inchon Airport are subject to the new conditions of the GPA.[480]

4. *Press Releases and Other Publications*

(a) Procurements Announced as MOCT Procurements

4.420 **The United States argues** that MOCT's control is so prevalent that, at times, procurements for the IIA construction project are announced as "MOCT" procurements. The United States further argues that such thorough control of these entities has led the public to view MOCT as being responsible for making the award determinations for IIA procurements.

4.421 In support, the United States refers to a 1996 article in the Korea-Herald, which notes that "The tender contract for the project to build and operate refuelling facilities at the Inchon International Airport in South Korea, has been awarded to a consortium led by Hanjin Group. The decision by MOCT to select the Hanjin-led consortium ended the month-long squabble for the project between Hanjin and Kumho Group ... ."[481] The United States asserts that even awardees of Inchon International Airport contracts considered their awards to have been made by MOCT: A press release on the PR Newswire specifies that the "Korean Ministry of Construction and Transportation awarded a Samsung and Lockheed Martin team a contract for the Korean Area Control Center (KACC) system to be installed at the new airport and facility in Inchon, Korea."[482] The United States argues that there is no indication that Korean officials ever disputed or sought to change these characterizations of the role of MOCT.

4.422 **In response, Korea notes** that the selection of a consortium to build and operate the refuelling facility was not a "procurement." Korea states that, to the contrary, it was the award of a franchise or concession to build and operate the refuelling facility. Korea further states that such arrangements are common at airports. As to the KACC system, Korea notes that this was not a procurement for the IIA, but for a replacement for the nationwide air traffic control system presently located at Taegu.

---

478 The United States notes that AFTAK is a private trade association of over 10,000 Korean agents and distributors.

479 *American Business in Korea, Guide & Directory 1992-93*, the Association of Foreign Trading Agents of Korea in cooperation with the Foreign Commercial Service, American Embassy, Seoul. The United States notes that while many projects contained in the chart of "Major Projects Status as of October 1992" list the entity responsible for the project as a government invested corporation (*i.e.* Korea Gas Corp.), and not a central government entity, the Ministry of Transportation is listed with regard to the new international airport.

480 US Answer to Question 29 from the Panel, dated 3 November 1999, citing US Department of State Reporting Cable, (prepared 1 May 1997), para. 10.

481 "Hanjin-Led Consortium Wins Deal," *Korea-Herald*, 28 August 1996, p. 8.

482 "Korean Ministry of Construction and Transportation Awards Air Traffic Center Contract to Samsung/Lockheed Martin," *PR Newswire*, 26 May 1998.

Korea states that the new system will indeed be located at Inchon, rather than Taegu, but it will direct air traffic on a national basis, not for the airport. The air traffic control systems for the airport are being procured by KOACA and IIAC. Korea further notes that the award regarding refuelling predated the effective date of GPA obligations for Korea.[483]

4.423 The United States also notes that in an article that appeared in the February 1998 edition of the magazine, "Air Transport World" it was stated that:

> "Since the national government controls both the airport construction authority and the Korea Airports Authority - which operates South Korea's major airports and is expected to manage IIA - it will set the fees."[484]

4.424 **The United States also refers** to press clippings and publications in support of its assertion that MOCT maintains managerial responsibility (including the approval of budgets and implementation plans) over the IIA project as a whole. Specifically, the United States refers to publications, which it says, establish that: (a) primary facilities of the IIA, such as the passenger terminals, the concourses, and the runways, must by law be paid for by the government, controlled by the government, and owned by the government[485]; (b) although "[p]rivate investment for the construction of certain IIA facilities [called 'secondary facilities,' which include cargo terminals, refuelling facilities, and catering facilities] is also actively solicited by IIAC, and is authorized by the *Private Capital Inducement Act for the Expansion of Social Overhead Capital*," these facilities must nevertheless "be turned over to the government after a certain period of time"[486]; (c) during the period that KAA, KOACA and IIAC were responsible for IIA construction, MOCT was issuing its own bid announcements related to IIA construction, while other bid announcements noted MOCT's "control" over KOACA.[487]

4.425 With respect to the bid announcements to which the United States refers to illustrate MOCT's "control" over KOACA, **Korea states** that they both pre-date Korea's GPA obligations and they are not Korean documents. Korea states that, rather, they are reports from the US Embassy in Seoul.

4.426 Specifically, Korea notes that one of the examples referred to by the United States begins, in its substantive part, with the statement, "The Korea Airport Construction Authority (KOACA), under the control of the Ministry of Construction and Transportation … ." Korea states that it appears that this is a statement from KOACA or MOCT, but Korea states that this is not the case. Korea notes that the original bid

---

[483] Korea's Answer to Question 1 from the Panel, dated 3 November 1999.

[484] Adele C. Schwartz, "Return to Inchon," Air Transport World (February 1998), p. 89.

[485] "SOC Project in 1996," Business Korea, March 1996, Vol. 13, Issue 2, p. 3. Also see section 22 of the Private Capital Inducement Act for the Expansion of Social Overhead Capital.

[486] Inchon International Airport brochure, p. 41.

[487] "Korea: Invitation to Bids for New Seoul Int'l Airport Soil and Concrete Testing Equipment" (6 June 1995), para. 1. For more evidence of MOCT's control over KOACA, also see "Korea: Yongjongdo Airport Co-Gen Power Plant Proj: Opp'ties" (25 January 1996), which states in its para. 1 that "With the approval of the Ministry of Construction and Transportation (MOCT), the Korea Airport Construction Authority (KOACA) recently held an orientation and question/answer session regarding Request For Proposal (RFP) for the Yongjongdo co-generation project on 12 January 1996."

announcement states simply, "The Korea Airport Construction Authority (KOACA) invites bids for the procurement of the Soil and Concrete Testing Equipments on the following conditions." Korea further notes that there is no mention of MOCT or control in this bid announcement.

4.427 Korea further notes that another example to which the United States refers concerns a co-generation power plant. Korea states that this is not a procurement but the award of a franchise or concession to build and operate a power plant.

4.428 Korea provides press materials which it says challenges the United States' argument that press clippings and publications support the view that MOCT controls the IIA project. Korea provides press releases by US companies identifying KOACA as the contracting entity for IIA projects during its tenure in that role[488], and news articles identifying KAA as the entity in charge of IIA procurement while it held that responsibility.[489]

(b) MOCT Officials Take Credit

4.429 **The United States also states** that MOCT officials themselves have also taken credit for major decisions related to the construction of the Inchon International Airport. The United States refers, for instance, to a March 1996 article in the Korea-Economic Daily in which an MOCT spokesman announcing the decision by MOCT to formally name the Inchon International Airport the "Seoul-Inchon International Airport."[490] In addition, the United States notes that the Korea-Herald quotes an MOCT official declaring that MOCT had re-estimated the cost for the Inchon International Airport from W 5.7 trillion to W 7.48 trillion (US$5.8 billion), that MOCT did not see any problem in meeting the planned date for opening, and that MOCT would complete the first phase of the construction by mid-2000.[491] This official was identified as MOCT's "director general who is in charge of the new airport construction."[492]

(c) Publications Concerning Airport Projects

4.430 **The United States argues** that the airport procurements referred to in General Note 1(b) can only mean those of the IIA construction project. The United States contends that from the time Korea tabled its GPA commitment offer on 29 June 1990, to the present, the United States knows of no new major airport construction projects in Korea, other than the Inchon project. According to the United States, this is the understanding, not only of the United States, but also of other countries interested in the Korean procurement market.

4.431 In support of its argument, the United States notes that, for example, in a 1998 publication by the European Communities ("EC"), entitled "Business Opportunities and the Government Procurement Agreement: A Handbook for EU Compa-

488 Exhibits Kor-50 and Kor-51.

489 Exhibits Kor-102 and Kor-103.

490 "New Airport to be Called Seoul-Inchon International Airport," *Korea-Economic Daily*, 25 March 1996.

491 "Inchon Airport Cost Balloons 31 Percent to W 7.5 Trillion," *The Korea Herald*, 22 July 1998.

492 Ibid.

nies," a list of "major construction and transportation projects" in Korea is provided, in which the IIA is the only airport procurement project enumerated. Furthermore, the publication offers a list of "major purchasing entities in Korea." The United States contends that the publication also identifies "MOCT, Korea Airport Authority Corp." as the "competent ministry" for the IIA project.[493] The United States asserts that if, in fact, another entity was responsible for procurements for the Inchon project, or other airport procurements, surely it would have been included on this list. The United States contends that, moreover, if the "Korea Airport Authority Corp." is an entity independent of MOCT, it would have been listed separately. The United States notes that, however, MOCT is the only entity listed as being responsible for airport procurement, and "Korea Airport Authority Corp." is not listed separately.

5. *MOCT's Website and Other Entities' Websites*

4.432 **The United States argues** that in interpreting Annex 1 of the GPA reliance must be placed on the "ordinary meaning" of its text, in its context and in light of the object and purpose of the GPA, in accordance with Article 31 of the *Vienna Convention.*[494] The United States notes that it then looks to MOCT's website to confirm this interpretation. The United States asserts that this is a proper use of the information on MOCT's website and, therefore, should be fully considered in this dispute.

4.433 The United States argues that throughout the Inchon International Airport construction process, MOCT let it be known that it is the entity responsible for the construction of the new Inchon International Airport.

4.434 In support of this argument, the United States refers to the Internet website of MOCT, which proclaims, "In preparation for the 21st century, this ministry is ... dedicated to the construction of the Seoul-Pusan high-speed rail and the Inchon International Airport." The United States contends that the website also declares that "As of today, MOCT's organization consists of 3 offices, 5 bureaus and 47 divisions which overlook the affairs on national development planning, housing, city planning, land policy, water resources policy, construction and administration of roads and airports and all other matters concerning construction and transport safety affairs."[495]

4.435 The United States also asserts that national-level entities in Korea have subsidiary organizations, and unless otherwise specified, a listing of a "central government entity" under Annex 1 also embodies its subsidiary organizations. In support of this argument, the United States refers to the fact that Korea specifically uses the

---

493 The United States asserts that although it appears unclear as to whether "Korea Airport Authority Corp." is referring to KAA or KOACA, either way, it is evident that "Korea Airport Authority Corp." is considered by the European Communities to be a subordinate organization of MOCT.

494 Article 31 of the *Vienna Convention*. In addition, Article 32 permits the use of supplementary means to either confirm an Article 31 interpretation, or to interpret the treaty when an Article 31 interpretation "leaves the meaning ambiguous or obscure, or leads to a result which is manifestly absurd or unreasonable."

495 The United States contends that, in addition, Article 16(34) of the *Presidential Order on the Organization of the Ministry of Construction and Transportation* provides that the Civil Aviation Bureau within MOCT is responsible for "[a]ffairs relevant to construction, maintenance, improvement and operation of airport facilities."

term, "subsidiary organization," on MOCT's website to describe KAA, KOACA and IIAC.

4.436 The United States also argues that the New Airport Development Group which, Korea represented in July of 1991 as the entity responsible for IIA construction and which exists to this day as the "New Airport Construction Planning Team" is a branch office of MOCT. The United States notes that MOCT lists the New Airport Construction Planning Team on the organizational chart located on its webpage.

4.437 **In response, Korea argues** that it is irrelevant for the purposes of interpreting Korea's Annex 1 and Note 1 that MOCT's website (which has been prepared by MOCT's public affairs office) refers to KAA, IIAC and eight other entities as "subsidiary organizations." Korea notes in this respect that Note 1 to Annex 1 states that the term "subordinate linear organizations" is to be interpreted "as prescribed in the *Government Organization Act*," and not as referred to on MOCT's website.

4.438 Korea also notes that in other parts of the organizational chart included on the MOCT website, KAA is described, along with 47 other entities, as a "Related Organization" to MOCT, rather than a "subsidiary organization." Korea further states that the relevant excerpt of the MOCT website, while a useful informational guide, is, for purposes of interpreting legal terms of art, imprecise. Korea states that it is for this reason, undoubtedly, that Note 1 does not state that the central government entities listed on Annex 1 include their subordinate linear organizations "as prescribed by the website of the Ministry of Construction and Transportation of the Republic of Korea."

4.439 Further, in response to a question from the United States, Korea argues that the organizational chart included on the MOCT website is an unofficial "Organizations Chart" printed out from MOCT's website, which post-dates the 15 April 1994 signing of the GPA, which explicitly references the *Government Organization Act*. Korea notes that the website, which was first put online in 1997, could not have contributed to the United States' expectations concerning coverage of KAA at the time the GPA was signed.[496]

4.440 **In response, the United States contends** that the excerpt of the MOCT webpage to which Korea refers that categorizes KAA as a "related organization" instead of a "subsidiary organization" is simply a more recent version of the website that categorized KAA and KOACA as "subsidiary organizations." The United States asserts that it was only after the consultations with the United States in March of 1999 that Korea replaced the term, "subsidiary organization," with "related organization," on every page of MOCT's website. However, the United States asserts that there is still one page that labels KAA and IIAC as "subsidiary organizations."

4.441 **Korea states in response** that it does not see how a website put up in 1997 could have influenced a Member's attitude when it signed the GPA in 1994. Korea also has noted that KAA and KOACA are not the only entities that appear on that website as somehow related or subordinate to MOCT. At least four of Korea's Annex 3 entities also are listed: Korea National Housing Corporation; Korea Water Resources Corporation; Korea Land Corporation; and Korea Highway Corporation. Korea submits that if "control" by an Annex 1 entity subjects another entity, not on

[496] Korea's Answer to Question 10 from the US, dated 3 November 1999.

Annex 1, to GPA coverage under that Annex, then it does so to these four entities as well as to those responsible for Inchon Airport procurement. Korea asserts that the "control" is the same in all instances. Korea argues that, however, if "control" subjects these entities to Annex 1 coverage, it is unclear what the consequences are given their placement on Annex 3 and the higher thresholds that apply.

4.442 **The United States also states** that, in fact, on MOCT's webpage, subsidiary organizations are separated into three distinct and separate categories: "Government Investment Corporations," "Government Contribution Authorities," and "Government Contribution Research Institutes." The United States contends that the subsidiary organizations cited under "Government Investment Corporations" are all listed in Korea's Annex 3, while the "Government Contribution Authorities" (which include KAA and KOACA) and the "Government Contribution Research Institutes" are not. The United States argues that this is consistent with the textual interpretation that all subsidiary organizations are covered within the scope of "central government entity" under Annex 1, unless otherwise specified (as in the case of "Government Investment Corporations"). The United States argues that, moreover, only the "Government Investment Corporations" are subject to a special legislative act, the *Framework Act on the Management of Government-Invested Corporations*; there is no analogous legislation for "Government Contribution Authorities" or "Government Contribution Research Institutes."

4.443 **In support of its arguments made in paragraph 4.243** regarding the categorization of IIA entities on the one hand and the Seoul and Pusan Aviation Authorities on the other hand, **Korea refers** to a list of "Airport Profiles" from the Japanese Ministry of Transportation website.[497] Korea notes that while the "founder" and "administrator" for many Japanese airports is the Japanese Ministry of Transportation itself, the New Tokyo International Airport Authority is listed as the founder and administrator of the New Tokyo International (Narita) Airport.

4.444 Korea refers to another extract, from the New Tokyo International Airport's website, which it says explains that although "[i]n the past, the national government has directly administered the establishment and management of international airports in Japan ... it was decided that the New Tokyo International Airport Authority would perform the construction, management, and operation of [the New Tokyo International Airport] ... ."[498] Korea notes that Japan offers several reasons for this decision, including the need to attract "massive amounts" of private capital to fund such a large project[499], the need for greater flexibility than a traditional government bureaucracy could offer[500], and the need for greater efficiency, demanded by the complex operat-

[497] Japanese Ministry of Transportation website, *Airport Profiles*, http://www.motnet.go.jp/info/kuko03.htm.

[498] New Tokyo International (Narita) Airport website, *Adoption of Airport Authority Format and the First Step Toward Construction of New Airport*, http://www.narita-airport.or.jp/airporte/prpf_e/keii_e/koudan1_e.html.

[499] *Ibid.* ("[B]ecause the construction of a new airport requires massive amounts of capital, it would be necessary to obtain some project funds from the private sector.").

[500] *Ibid.* ("[F]lexibility would be needed in the areas of organization, personnel, and accounting.").

ing demands of the project, than could be generated through a traditional government bureaucracy.[501]

4.445 Korea's asserts that its decision to separate the implementation of the IIA project from other airport construction was motivated by similar reasons, and was entirely legitimate.

C. Practices in Violation of the GPA

1. Bid Deadlines

4.446 **The United States argues** that Korea routinely imposes inadequate bid deadlines that are shorter than the durations required by the GPA. The United States provides the following examples in support of its claim:

- Korea announced the procurement of a radar and communication system on 13 June 1998, then required tenders to be received less than 26 days later on 8 July 1998.[502]
- Korea announced the procurement of a contract for the ventilation systems on 9 November 1998, then required tenders to be received less than 23 days later on 1 December 1998.[503]
- Korea announced the procurement of a 22.9 KV electrical cable on 23 November 1998, then required tenders for Part I of the procurement to be received less than 17 days later on 9 December 1998, with tenders for Part II to be received less than 29 days later on 21 December 1998.[504]
- Korea announced the procurement of electrical wire facilities on 23 November 1998, then required tenders to be received less than 25 days later on 17 December 1998.[505]
- Korea announced the procurement of outdoor lighting equipment on 24 November 1998, then required tenders for Part I of the procurement to be received less than 15 days later on 11 December 1998, with tenders for Part II to be received less than 28 days later on 22 December 1998.[506]

4.447 The United States contends that the imposition by Korea of deadlines of less than 40 days for receiving tenders from the date of publication of the procurement announcements was inconsistent with the requirements of Article XI:1(a) and XI:2(a).

---

[501] *Ibid.* ("[T]he complexity of airport operation would require an efficient, self-supporting system.").

[502] Announcement of Bid for Radars and ATC Communication System for Inchon International Airport (IAA), KOACA Publication 98-39 (18 June 1998).

[503] Passenger Terminal and Attached Building Machine Installation and TAB Operation, New Airport Construction Corporation Announcement No. 98-69 (9 November 1998).

[504] 22.9 KV Electrical Cable Manufacture/Purchase Project (I) and (II), New Airport Construction Corporation Announcement No. 98-70 (23 November 1998).

[505] 22.9 KV Electrical Wire Facilities Construction, New Airport Construction Corporation Announcement No. 98-71 (23 November 1998).

[506] Inchon International Airport Outside Lighting Fixtures Manufacture Purchase Project (I) and (II), New Airport Construction Corporation Announcement No. 98-72 (24 November 1998).

2. *Qualification Requirements*

4.448 **The United States argues** that Korea imposes qualification requirements that require domestic investment while favouring domestic bidders. The United States contends that, for example, in the procurement of vertical transportation equipment - that is, elevators and escalators - Korea limited participation of parties as prime contractors to those that "completed the registration for manufacturing business of [elevators and escalators] under the laws of lift manufacturing and management and [to those that possess] both the licence of lift installation business under *Construction Industry Basic Act* and the licence of the first class electrical construction business under *Electricity Work Business Act*."[507] The United States argues that, in other words, this condition required firms bidding as prime contractor to have four Korean-issued licences: an elevator manufacturing licence, an escalator manufacturing licence, an elevator installation licence, and an electrical construction licence. The United States contends that two of these licences could only be obtained by firms that had committed substantial investment in Korea by either building or purchasing local manufacturing facilities. The United States argues that one can see the difficulties faced by foreign suppliers in becoming prime contractors as compared to domestic suppliers who no doubt already have manufacturing facilities in their home country. The United States argues that the discriminatory nature of this condition is further highlighted by the fact that the actual equipment used to satisfy the requirements of this specific contract need not be produced in the local manufacturing facilities in Korea.[508]

(a) Article III:1(a) of the GPA

4.449 **The United States argues** that Article III:1(a) requires non-discriminatory treatment between foreign and domestic products, services, and suppliers in government procurement. According to the United States, the standard of this non-discrimination obligation in the GPA is expressed in terms of "treatment no less favourable." The United States notes that similar, though not identical, language is found in Article III:4 of the General Agreement on Tariffs and Trade (GATT 1994).

> "The products of the territory of any contracting party imported into the territory of any other contracting party shall be accorded treatment no less favourable than that accorded to like products of national origin in respect of all laws, regulations, and requirements affecting their internal sale, offering for sale, purchase, transportation, distribution or use ... ."

4.450 The United States contends that there are strong similarities between Article III:4 of the GATT 1994 and Article III:1 of the GPA that should guide the interpretation of the GPA. The United States argues that, for example, both provisions prohibit discriminatory treatment based on product origin. Further, according to the United States, both utilize the "treatment no less favourable" standard. Under Article III:4 of

---

507 Announcement for the Procurement of the Manufacture and Installation of Vertical Transportation Equipment (15 May 1998), Item 2.1 of Information for Proposal.
508 Ibid.

the GATT 1994, this standard requires "equal treatment with respect to competitive opportunities."

4.451 The United States notes that, as first articulated by the panel in Section 337 of the *Tariff Act* of 1930:

> "These words ["treatment no less favourable,"] are to be found throughout the General Agreement and later agreements negotiated in the GATT framework as an expression of the underlying principle of equality of treatment of imported products as compared to the treatment given either to other foreign products, under the most favoured nation standard, or to domestic products, under the national treatment standard of Article III ... The Panel therefore considered that, in order to establish whether the "no less favourable" treatment standard of Article III:4 is met, it had to assess whether or not Section 337 in itself may lead to the application to imported products of treatment less favourable than that accorded to products of United States origin. It noted that this approach is in accordance with previous practice of the Contracting Parties in applying Article III, which has been to base their decisions on the distinctions made by the laws, regulations or requirements themselves and on their potential impact, rather than on the actual consequences for specific imported products."[509]

4.452 The United States contends that this interpretation of "no less favourable treatment" in Article III of GATT 1994 as requiring equality in terms of competitive opportunities has been followed consistently in subsequent panel and Appellate Body reports.[510]

4.453 The United States argues that Korea's qualification requirements are inconsistent with the GPA's national treatment requirements in Article III:1(a) because they unfairly discriminate against foreign suppliers in favour of domestic suppliers.

4.454 The United States further argues that by using "treatment no less favourable" in the GPA, the Parties to the GPA obviously intended to create a standard that also refers to less favourable competitive opportunities. The United States argues that, thus, if Korea's procurement practices have modified the competitive opportunities against foreign suppliers in favour of domestic suppliers, Korea should be deemed to have provided "less favourable treatment" to foreign suppliers, in violation of Article III:1(a) of the GPA.

4.455 The United States further argues that, in fact, the qualification requirements imposed by Korea in the vertical transportation equipment procurement accorded less

---

509 GATT Panel Report, *United States - Section 337*, paras. 5.11 and 5.13.

510 See, e.g. Panel Report, *Japan - Measures Affecting Consumer Photographic Film and Paper* ("*Japan - Film*"), WT/DS44/R, adopted 22 April 1998, DSR 1998:IV, 1179, para. 10.379; GATT Panel Report, *Canada - Import, Distribution and Sale of Certain Alcoholic Drinks by Provincial Marketing Agencies* (adopted on 18 February 1992), BISD 39S/27, paras. 5.12-5.14 and 5.30; *US - Malt Beverages*, BISD 39S/206, para. 5.30; Panel Report, *US - Gasoline, supra*, footnote 105, para. 6.10; Panel Report, *Canada - Certain Measures Concerning Periodicals* ("*Canada - Periodicals*"), WT/DS31/R, adopted 30 July 1997, DSR 1997:I, 481, para. 515; Panel Report, *European Communities - Regime for the Importation, Sale and Distribution of Bananas*, WT/DS27/R, adopted 25 September 1997, DSR 1997:II, 943, paras. 7.179-7.180.

favourable competitive opportunities for foreign firms than for domestic firms. According to the United States, in that procedure, a firm could not bid as a prime contractor unless it possessed by building or purchasing certain manufacturing facilities in Korea. The United States further states that foreign suppliers (who more often than not do not maintain manufacturing facilities in Korea) could, therefore, only bid as prime contractors if they invested considerable resources towards building or purchasing these local manufacturing facilities. The United States argues that this requirement provides less favourable conditions to foreign suppliers, since competing Korean suppliers need not expend the same amounts of additional resources in order to submit bids as prime contractors. The United States argues that, as such, this measure constitutes "less favourable treatment" within the meaning of GPA Article III:1(a).

(b) Article VIII first sentence of the GPA

4.456 **The United States contends** that qualification procedures set forth by Parties to the GPA must be consistent with the provisions of Article VIII. The United States further states that Korea's qualification requirements are all requirements within qualification procedures for procurements related to the IIA project. However, the United States argues that since it has already established that these requirements discriminate against foreign suppliers generally within the meaning of Article III:1(a) of the GPA, *a fortiori*, they also discriminate against foreign suppliers in violation of Article VIII, first sentence.

(c) Article VIII(b) of the GPA

4.457 **The United States argues** that Article VIII(b) establishes that any qualification requirements must be "essential" in order to ensure the "capability" of the firm to fulfill the contract. The United States argues that in applying Article 31 of the *Vienna Convention on the Law of Treaties*, one finds that the ordinary meaning of the term "essential," is "absolutely indispensable or necessary."[511] The United States argues that under Article VIII(b), such conditions for participation may include "financial guarantees, technical qualifications and information necessary for establishing the financial commercial and technical capacity of suppliers, as well as the verification of qualifications." Bearing in mind that, under the first sentence of Article VIII, the qualification process must not be discriminatory, the United States asserts that the question is whether a qualification requirement is really necessary to guarantee that a winning bidder will in fact be able to perform the very contract it has been awarded. The United States contends that it can thus be determined that Korea's qualification requirements are not "essential" in the sense of Article VIII(b).

4.458 The United States further argues that Korea's qualification requirements are inconsistent with Article VIII(b) of the GPA because, as conditions for participating in the tender procedures, they are not "essential" to a firm's "capability to fulfill the contract." Rather, it appears that these conditions were put in place to ensure that Korean suppliers would be able to benefit from and better participate in these valuable procurements.

---

[511] The New Shorter Oxford English Dictionary (1993 ed.), p. 852.

4.459 Additionally, the United States argues that Korea's requirement for a firm to maintain elevator or escalator manufacturing facilities in Korea, just so the firm can participate in a tender proceeding for vertical transportation equipment, is clearly not "essential to ensure the firm's capability to fulfill the contract." The United States contends that the elements that make it possible for a firm to supply and install an elevator or escalator - reliability, technical expertise, solvency - have no necessary relation to whether the firm owns a manufacturing facility located in Korea (as opposed to some other country), nor to whether the firm owns any factories at all. In fact, the factory requirement at best imposes a buy-national or local-content requirement. The United States asserts that if such a requirement is "essential to ensure the firm's capability to fulfill the contract," then any other GPA Party could exclude from its tender proceedings any bidder that does not have a factory in that country. In the view of the United States, this would eliminate any possibility that a bidder located wholly abroad could bid on a GPA-covered tender and supply the product from a foreign factory. The United States concludes that a key objective of the drafters of the GPA, to ensure that procurement rules and practices are not applied "so as to afford protection to domestic products or services or domestic suppliers,"[512] would be defeated.

3. Domestic Partnering Requirements

4.460 **The United States argues** that Korea has conducted procurements under bidding rules specifying that foreign suppliers can participate only if they partner with or act as a subcontractor to domestic suppliers. The United States notes that, for example, in a procurement for "site preparation and weak foundation enforcement," Korea established the requirement that any "company that has its base outside the Inchon Metropolitan Area must enter into a joint venture for at least 10 per cent of the contract with an Inchon-based company that possesses a Civil Engineering and Construction Licence (including Civil Engineering) issued in the Inchon Metropolitan Area."[513] The United States asserts that, in other words, foreign companies, since they are obviously based outside of the Inchon Metropolitan Area, must enter into joint ventures with local companies in order to even participate in the tendering process. The United States asserts that Korea used similar language to limit the participation of foreign firms in a procurement for electrical wire facilities.[514]

4.461 The United States further argues that in a procurement for a movement area management system, Korea specified that "[f]oreign firms should participate in a bid with local firms (leading or prime company) as consortium members or subcontractors."[515] The United States notes that Korea used this same language to limit the participation of foreign suppliers as prime contractors in procurements for radar and

---

[512] Second para. of the preamble to the GPA.

[513] Facilities Infrastructure Construction, New Airport Construction Corporation Announcement No. 98-68.

[514] 22.9 KV Electrical Wire Facilities Construction, New Airport Construction Corporation Announcement No. 98-71 (3 November 1998).

[515] Announcement of Bid for Movement Area Management System (MAMS) for Inchon International Airport (IIA), KOACA Publication 98-37 (16 June 1998).

communication systems[516], as well as for weather radar systems.[517] Finally, the United States argues that Korea prohibited foreign firms from bidding in a procurement unless they participated in a consortium with no less than two Korean firms.[518]

(a) Article III:1(a) of the GPA

4.462 **The United States argues** that Korea's domestic partnering requirements are inconsistent with the GPA's national treatment requirements contained in Article III:1(a) because they unfairly discriminate against foreign suppliers in favour of domestic suppliers.

4.463 The United States argues that Korea's domestic partnering requirements have provided less favourable competitive opportunities for foreign firms, in comparison with domestic firms. The United States contends, for instance, that in the procedures for "site preparation" and "electrical wire facilities," foreign suppliers were required to participate as joint bidders with local suppliers based in the Inchon area. The United States argues that this requirement accorded less favourable conditions to foreign firms in the procurement, since it became necessary for foreign firms to expend additional resources just to find and obtain partnering contracts with local suppliers. The United States contends that, moreover, for the foreign supplier, the potential profits from winning the tender were substantially reduced, since the foreign supplier would be obligated to share these profits and/or other benefits of the award with the local supplier. The United States further notes that, in contrast, local firms could bid alone, without being subjected to additional costs. The United States asserts that, as such, these requirements provide foreign suppliers with "less favourable treatment" than local suppliers within the meaning of GPA Article III:1(a).

4.464 The United States further argues that other domestic partnering requirements also provided less favourable competitive opportunities as between foreign and domestic suppliers. In the tendering procedures for "movement area systems," "radar and communications systems" and "weather radar systems," the United States asserts that Korea prohibited foreign suppliers from bidding as prime contractors, and further specified that local firms should be the "prime or leading company," with foreign suppliers permitted only to act as subcontractors or consortium members. The United States argues that this measure discriminated against foreign suppliers, because they could only participate if they were able to enter into a "partnership" arrangement with a domestic firm, not only to bid jointly, but to bid in a subordinate position. The United States argues that any potential profits for the foreign supplier must be shared with the domestic supplier (who, in this case as the prime contractor, would most likely exercise its control over the sharing of the profits). According to the United States, domestic suppliers, in contrast, could bid alone if they so choose, again without being subjected to additional costs or other disadvantages.

---

[516] Announcement of Bid for radars and ATC Communication System for Inchon International Airport, KOACA Publication 98-39 (18 June 1998).

[517] Announcement of Bid for Terminal Doppler Weather Radar for Inchon International Airport, KOACA Publication 98-66 (23 October 1998).

[518] Manufacture and Installation of IIA Passenger Boarding Bridge System, Project No. PMD1 (12 March 1998).

4.465 As a final example, the United States refers to another domestic partnering scheme in which foreign suppliers were obligated to bid with two or more domestic suppliers. The United States contends that domestic suppliers, on the other hand, were not forced to bid with foreign suppliers, let alone other domestic suppliers. The United States argues that this requirement again singled out foreign suppliers for less favourable competitive opportunities.

4.466 The United States argues that, for the foregoing reasons, it is clear that Korea's domestic partnering practices and procedures provide less favourable treatment to foreign suppliers than that accorded to domestic suppliers within the meaning of Article III:1(a) of the GPA.

(b) Article VIII first sentence of the GPA

4.467 **The United States argues** that qualification procedures set forth by Parties to the GPA must be consistent with the provisions of Article VIII and that Korea's domestic partnering requirements are all requirements within qualification procedures for procurements related to the IIA project. The United States contends that, however, since it has already been established that these requirements discriminate against foreign suppliers generally within the meaning of Article III:1(a) of the GPA, *a fortiori*, they also discriminate against foreign suppliers in violation of Article VIII, first sentence.

(c) Article VIII(b) of the GPA

4.468 **The United States argues** that Korea's domestic partnering requirements are inconsistent with Article VIII(b) of the GPA because, as conditions for participating in the tender procedures, they are not "essential" to a firm's "capability to fulfill the contract." The United States argues that, rather, it appears that these conditions were put in place to ensure that Korean suppliers would be able to benefit from and better participate in these valuable procurements.

4.469 The United States further argues that Korea's requirement that a foreign supplier bid as a joint contractor with a domestic supplier also cannot be deemed as "essential to ensure the firm's capability to fulfill the contract." The United States asserts that there is no legitimate rationale for concluding that all foreign suppliers would be incapable of performing the contract on their own. In the view of the United States, this too is simple protectionism. The United States asserts that if this were permitted, all GPA-covered procurements might eventually be subjected to such domestic partnering requirements, nullifying much of the benefit of the GPA.

4.470 The United States argues that, similarly, Korea in some procurements has permitted foreign suppliers to bid not as prime contractors, but only as subcontractors or consortium members (with a Korean supplier as the prime contractor). The United States further argues that there is no necessary basis for concluding that all foreign suppliers would be incapable of performing the contract as prime contractors. The United States contends that, therefore, it cannot legitimately be argued that these conditions are "essential to ensure the firm's capability to fulfill the contract."

4.471 Finally, the United States argues that Korea's requirement that foreign suppliers bid with two Korean suppliers is again simply protectionism. The United States contends that it cannot legitimately be argued that all foreign suppliers are incapable (acting individually or jointly) of fulfilling a contract, and that one Korean partner is not enough (i.e., for a foreign firm to fulfil the contract, the firm will need to partner with two Korean suppliers). The United States argues that as with the other requirements previously identified, this qualification requirement is imposed for the mere purpose of ensuring maximum domestic participation in procurements for the IIA project.

4. *Absence of Access to Challenge Procedures*

4.472 **The United States notes** that in 1995, Korea passed the *Act Relating to Contracts to Which the State is a Party.*[519] This Act established the "International Contract Dispute Mediation Committee" as the impartial and independent body that reviews domestic challenges to the procurement practices of GPA-covered entities.[520] The United States notes that Korea has indicated officially that this Committee is the impartial and independent body that will review challenges to the procurement practices of GPA-covered entities, which is meant to satisfy Korea's obligations under Article XX of the GPA.[521]

4.473 However, the United States argues that when suppliers and service providers protested certain procurement practices by KOACA, alleging inconsistencies with the GPA, the International Contract Dispute Mediation Committee has refused to consider such challenges on the grounds that KOACA is not "recognized as an entity covered by the government [sic] procurement agreement."[522]

4.474 The United States contends that, to date, Korea has yet to grant suppliers and service providers participating in procurements for the IIA construction project with access to non-discriminatory, timely, transparent, and effective domestic challenge procedures. Korea has failed to provide aggrieved foreign suppliers with access to the appropriate challenge procedures under Article XX.

4.475 Further, the United States argues that Korea has not otherwise provided suppliers and service providers of these procurements access to non-discriminatory, timely, transparent and effective domestic challenge procedures. In fact, KOACA's internal rules do not even contain dispute resolution procedures. Accordingly, no relief is allotted to foreign suppliers and service providers when an Inchon Airport procurement is conducted in a GPA-inconsistent manner. Thus, Korea is in violation of Article XX of the GPA.

5. *Korea's Response to the Violation Claim*

4.476 The Panel asked Korea whether it agreed with the United States' assertion that if the entities engaging in procurement for the IIA are "covered entities," such entities' IIA procurement practices would not be consistent with the Agreement on Gov-

---

[519] Law No. 4868, 5 January 1995.

[520] Ibid. Articles 28 and 29.

[521] GPA/12/Rev.1, Notification of National Implementing Legislation of the Republic of Korea, 9 June 1997.

[522] Report to Karen Ware, US Deputy Senior Foreign Commercial Service Officer to the Republic of Korea, containing remarks by Dr. Kim Jung-Min, Deputy Director, Government Procurement & Accounting Policy Division of MOFE on 18 November 1998.

ernment Procurement.[523] **In response, Korea states** that it has not taken a position on the assertions of the United States with regard to the consistency of Korea's procurement practices with the GPA, other than to note that the entities responsible for IIA procurement are not covered entities.[524]

D. Non-Violation Claim: Nullification or Impairment of Benefits

1. Details of the Non-Violation Claim

4.477 The **United States** argues that regardless of whether or not the measures referred to above violate the various articles of the GPA, they nevertheless nullify and impair any benefits accruing to the United States under the Agreement.

4.478 The United States argues that a successful determination of a non-violation nullification and impairment in the GPA requires the finding of three elements: (1) a concession was negotiated and exists; (2) a measure is applied that upsets the established competitive relationship; and (3) the measure could not have been reasonably anticipated at the time the concession was negotiated.[525]

4.479 The United States argues that given the inconsistency with the GPA of the procurement practices engaged in by the IIA authorities, elements (2) and (3) of the non-violation claim have already been met. The United States asserts that the only outstanding issue is the first element - that is, whether or not there is a concession.

4.480 The United States contends that, as a matter of judicial economy, it does not request a ruling on the non-violation claim if it is established that Korea has violated its obligations under the GPA. The United States also notes that a finding of non-violation nullification or impairment leads in the first instance to compensation and not necessarily to compliance. The United States contends that its interest in the dispute is first and foremost to assure Korea's compliance with its GPA obligations through the elimination of its GPA-inconsistent procurement practices.

4.481 **In response, Korea argues** that the burden placed upon the United States to support its non-violation claim under Article XXII:2 of the GPA is substantial. Korea notes that under Article 26:1(a) of the Understanding on Rules and Procedures Governing the Settlement of Disputes, "the complaining party shall present a detailed justification in support of any complaint relating to a measure which does not conflict with the relevant covered agreement."[526]

---

523 Panel's Question 20 following the First Substantive Meeting.

524 Korea's Answer to Question 20 from the Panel, dated 3 November 1999.

525 Report of the Working Party on *The Australian Subsidy on Ammonium Sulphate* (adopted on 3 April 1950), BISD II/188-196, para. 12; Panel Report on *Treatment by Germany of Imports of Sardines* (adopted on 31 October 1952), G/26, BISD 1S/53-59, para. 16; Panel Report on *European Economic Community - Production Aids Granted on Canned Peaches, Canned Pears, Canned Fruit Cocktail and Dried Grapes*, 20 February 1985 (unadopted), L/5778, para. 51; and Panel Report on *European Economic Community - Payments and Subsidies Paid to Processors and Producers of Oilseeds and Related Animal-Feed Proteins* (adopted on 25 January 1990), L/6627, BISD 37S/86, paras. 142-152.

526 *Understanding on Rules and Procedures Governing the Settlement of Disputes*, Article 26:1(a).

4.482 Korea refers to the Panel in *Japan - Film*[527] which noted three elements of a non-violation complaint incumbent upon the complainant to prove. Korea states that these elements are evident in the terms of Article XXII:2 of the GPA; namely, "(1) application of a measure by a WTO Member; (2) a benefit accruing under the relevant agreement; and (3) nullification of the benefit as the result of the application of the measure."[528]

4.483 Korea argues that the United States must demonstrate, by virtue of the requirement in Article XXII:2 that it identify a "benefit accruing" to it under the GPA, that it "reasonably expected" to obtain the benefit of GPA coverage for IIA procurement.[529] Korea further argues that "for expectations of a benefit to be legitimate, the challenged measures must not have been reasonably anticipated at the time the tariff concession was negotiated."[530] Korea asserts that this requirement is self-evident and quotes for support: "If the measures were anticipated, a Member could not have had a legitimate expectation of improved market access to the extent of the impairment caused by these measures."[531]

4.484 Korea also notes that the United States is correct that the first requirement referred to above in paragraph 4.478 - a concession - is very much at issue. Korea asserts that just what "concession" the United States made in exchange for the alleged inclusion of KAA among Korea's commitments is not clear. Korea states that it is aware of no evidence from the United States on this point. Korea also notes, as item (2) on the US list implies, that an "agreement" is necessary. Korea states that it understands that the essence of a non-violation is that some action of a party, after an agreement is concluded, which could not have been reasonably anticipated at the time of the agreement, nullifies or impairs a concession made by another party. According to Korea, the United States has not specified what agreement was made by the parties that was nullified or impaired by action taken by Korea after that agreement was entered into. Korea argues that it could not have been an agreement to include KAA (and KOACA and IIAC) in Korea's GPA coverage, for Korea never agreed to include KAA in any of its offers. Korea also states that in addition to the first point, the third is also very much in contention. Korea questions how the United States could reasonably anticipate that Korea would apply the GPA to procurements for the new airport without an agreement and a concession. In Korea's view, the whole premise of the United States' non-violation case rests on the elements it needs

---

527 Although the Panel in *Japan – Film, supra,* footnote 510, addressed a non-violation claim under Article XXIII:1(b) of the GATT 1994, there is no material difference between the language used in Article XXIII:1(b) of the GATT 1994 and Article XXII:2 of the GPA to enumerate the requirements for a non-violation complaint. The Panel's legal reasoning is, therefore, applicable in its entirety.

528 *Japan - Film, supra,* footnote 510, para. 10.41.

529 Ibid. para. 10.72. As further support for this principle, see *EEC - Oilseeds*, BISD 37S/86, 128-129 (paras. 147-148); *Operation of the Provisions of Article XVI*, BISD 10S/201, 209 (para. 28) (adopted on 21 November 1961); *Other Barriers to Trade*, BISD 3S/222, 224 (para. 13) (adopted on 3 March 1955); *Germany - Sardines*, BISD 1S/53, 58-59 (para. 16) (adopted on 31 October 1952); *Australian Subsidy on Ammonium Sulphate*, GATT/CP.4/39, BISD II/188, 193-194 (adopted on 3 April 1950).

530 *Japan - Film*, para. 10.76.

531 Ibid.

to prove for its violation claim: an agreement between the parties, which included a concession by the United States.

2. *Concession*

(a) 1991 Negotiations

4.485 **The United States argues** that during 1991 negotiations with Korea, the United States specifically accrued the benefit of all new airport construction projects under the coverage of the GPA. Further, the United States contends that even if the transfer of procurement authority as between the various IIA entities was reasonably anticipated by the United States, this fact is irrelevant to a determination of whether a concession was made.

4.486 For support of its argument that a concession was made, the United States notes that in July of 1991, Korea stated that the "New Airport Development Group under" MOCT and the "Office of Supply" are responsible for new airport construction projects. The United States further notes that in relation to the IIA project, Korea stated that the "basic plan" will be completed "by 1992 and the working plan by 1993," that Bechtel "is taking part in the basic plan project," and that the "procurement plan" is not yet "fixed because now the whole airport construction project is only in a basic planning stage." The United States notes that Korea is now arguing that when it said the "procurement plan has not been fixed," it actually meant "nothing concrete was fixed,"[532] or "nothing with regard to procurement was fixed."[533] The United States argues that, however, an entity is not a plan; the Office of Supply is not a procurement plan, it is a procuring entity.

4.487 Further, the United States argues that Korea has always made a distinction between an entity and a plan. The United States notes that Korea made such a distinction in attempting to explain what "procurement plan" meant. The United States quotes: "This included both the entities that might ultimately be responsible for procurement as well as the procurement plan itself."[534] The United States argues that if Korea had meant the "procurement plan" and the "entities that might ultimately be responsible for procurement," it would have said so in its July 1991 response. The United States notes that, instead, Korea only stated that the "procurement plan has not been fixed." The United States argues that Korea's plain language speaks for itself and questions how Korea's mention of "procurement plan" can refer to both the "procurement plan" and the "entities that might ultimately be responsible for procurement."

4.488 The United States also argues that Korea's claim that it had made no decision regarding "which entity would be responsible for IIA construction"[535] in July 1991 is inconsistent with Korea's actions in 1991. In support of this argument, the United States notes that it expressly held out MOCT and the Office of Supply as the responsible airport procurement entities, it included MOCT and the Office of Supply in its

---

532 Korea's Answer to Question 16 from the Panel, dated 3 November 1999.

533 Korea's Answer to Question 15 from the US, dated 3 November.

534 Korea's Answer to Question 16 from the Panel, dated 3 November 1999.

535 Korea's Answer to Question 3 from the Panel, dated 3 November 1999.

GPA schedule offer, and it conducted the procurement of IIA's basic plan through MOCT.[536]

4.489 Regarding the United States' interpretation of its July 1991 response, **Korea notes** that, in fact, the July 1991 response does not state that either MOCT or NADG were to be involved in procurement.[537] Moreover, Korea states that its July 1991 response was not a concessions offer, but merely a response to an inquiry. Even if it were such an offer, Korea argues, action by the Korean National Assembly in December 1991, designating KAA as the responsible entity for the IIA project, notified the United States of its position. The United States, moreover, admits that it had actual notice, and was even "surprised" by it.

4.490 **In response, the United States asserts** that this new argument by Korea is totally without basis. Korea's July 1991 response states that, "the new airport construction is being conducted by the New Airport Development Group under the Ministry of Transportation." The United States submits that any reasonable interpretation of "conducting the new airport construction" suggests "involvement" in the procurement process by MOCT. The United States further submits that, in fact, Korea itself admitted that MOCT solicited and awarded the first IIA procurement for the 1990-1991 basic plan.

4.491 With regard to the Office of Supply, **Korea states** that it does not consider that the interpretation suggested by the United States is reasonable and, therefore, does not consider that Korea's July 1991 response is reasonably susceptible to the interpretation suggested by the United States. Korea states that the qualification ("But at present ...") offered immediately after identification of the Office of Supply as the entity that would in principle, under the *Government Procurement Fund Act*, have undertaken IIA procurement had there even been any at the time, over 16 months before site preparation for the airport was to begin, made it unreasonable for any negotiator to conclude that the Office of Supply would, forever after, be the entity responsible for IIA procurement.[538]

4.492 **In response, the United States reiterates** that the phrase "But at present, the concrete procurement plan has not been fixed ..." refers only to the procurement plan and not the procurement entity.[539] The United States argues that, in addition, because MOCT was responsible for the first IIA procurement, *i.e.*, the 1990-1991 basic plan "by virtue of the *Government Procurement Fund Act*," the Office of Supply should also have been responsible for that procurement.[540]

4.493 The United States argues that, furthermore, it is wrong to imply that, based on its July 1991 representation, the United States concluded that "the Office of Supply would, forever after, be the entity responsible for IIA procurement." The United States contends that, rather, the United States reasonably expected that if Korea were to alter its position regarding an explicit representation made on paper during formal GPA negotiations, it would have explicitly informed the US trade negotiators of such

536 Korea's Answer to Question 16 from the Panel, dated 3 November 1999, and Korea's Answer to Question 5 from the US, dated 3 November 1999.

537 Korea's Answer to Question 2 from the Panel, dated 29 November 1999.

538 Korea's Answer to Question 2 from the Panel, dated 29 November 1999.

539 Second Written Submission of the United States, para. 61.

540 US Response to Korea's Answer to Question 2 from the Panel, dated 29 November 1999.

change. The United States contends that, moreover, a decision was taken by the Committee on Government Procurement that each signatory would notify changes to its annexes taking place between the signing of the GPA at Marrakesh and its entering into force.[541] The United States further states that if Korea were to change its position after the GPA came into force for it, Korea would be obligated to utilize Article XXIV:6 of the Agreement, the sole GPA provision that permits rectifications or modifications to a Party's annexes.[542]

4.494 **Korea states** that it has demonstrated that KAA, KOACA and IIAC, rather than the Office of Supply, have conducted the procurements for IIA.[543] Korea argues that since the Office of Supply has not in fact procured for the IIA, Korea's July 1991 response can speak only to the United States' expectations regarding the entities responsible for IIA procurement, purportedly held prior to the conclusion of negotiations for Korea's accession to the GPA.[544] Korea argues that to serve as the basis for a non-violation complaint, those expectations "must not have been reasonably anticipated at the time the tariff concession was negotiated."[545] Given the qualified nature of Korea's July 1991 response, followed by: the December 1991 amendments to the *Seoul Airport Act* appointing KAA as the entity responsible for the IIA project; correspondence between the United States and Korea regarding KAA's role in the IIA project[546]; and between Korea and major US airport authorities regarding KAA's role in the IIA project[547]; the successful participation of numerous US companies, closely consulted by the United States regarding Korea's offer[548] in KAA procurements for the IIA[549]; KAA's role as a separate "juristic" person[550]; the inclusion of airport authorities on Annex 3 rather than Annex 1 by the United States itself, Hong Kong, Israel, Japan, Aruba, Norway, Singapore, Switzerland and every member State of the European Communities; and the absence of KAA from any of the Annexes included in Korea's Appendix I, Korea argues that the United States' purported interpretation, even if reasonable in July 1991, was no longer reasonable after these developments,

541 See GPA/IC/M/2 at Annex 2, "Administration of Modifications to the Appendices to the Agreement on Government Procurement (1994) Prior to its Entry into Force, Other Than Rectifications of a Purely Formal Nature or Those Resulting from Negotiations Aimed at Expanding Coverage."

542 US Response to Korea's Answer to Question 2 from the Panel, dated 29 November 1999.

543 Exhibits Kor-19A through Kor-19D, Kor-48A through Kor-48N, Kor-57A through Kor-57E.

544 Korea's Answer to Question 2 from the Panel, dated 29 November 1999.

545 *Japan - Film, supra*, footnote 510, para. 10.76.

546 Letter from US Senator Slade Gorton to Mr. Wan-Sik Yook, Chairman, KAA, 6 October 1992; Letter from Council member of Seattle City Council to Mr. Wan-Sik Yook, Chairman, KAA, 22 September 1992; Letter from the Vice Chairman of KAA to Sung Yong Kim and J.A. Corbett, staff secretaries in the Economic Section of the US Embassy Seoul, 8 August 1992.

547 Exhibit Kor-34 (Port Authority of New York and New Jersey); Exhibit Kor-35 (Los Angeles Department of Airports); Exhibit Kor-36 (Denver (Stapleton) International Airport); Exhibit Kor-37 (Dallas/Fort Worth International Airport).

548 US First Written Submission, para. 92.

549 Exhibit Kor-23.

550 Notification of Act No. 3219, *Official Gazette*, 28 December 1979, p. 5892. Korea reiterates that KAA was established by the National Assembly pursuant to this Act. Article 3 states that KAA is a "juristic person."

well in advance of the conclusion of negotiations regarding Korea's concession, in December 1993.[551]

(b) Ambiguity Associated with July 1991 Response

4.495 **In response to a question from the Panel, Korea argues** that if Korea's July 1991 response is open to the interpretation the US now claims, Korea submits that the US interpretation is not the only possible interpretation, nor even the best possible interpretation. Korea further argues that the fact that the US interpretation is not the only possible interpretation is fatal to the US case.[552]

4.496 The **United States argues in response** that Korea newly attributes a "claim" to the United States that Korea's July 1991 response is open to more than one interpretation. The United States contends that Korea does not provide any citation as to where the United States allegedly made such a claim. The United States notes that, in fact, the United States has made statements directly to the contrary, which is consistent with the US view that Korea's July 1991 response to US questions concerning new airport construction projects was unequivocal and unambiguous.[553]

4.497 **Korea notes** that while the US was asking questions in its native language, Korea was responding in a foreign language. Korea notes further that ambiguity generally is in the eye of the reader or listener, not the writer or speaker. Korea states that those who communicate do not normally aim at ambiguity, and Korea certainly did not do so in this instance. Korea states that this July 1991 communication, which the US now finds is subject to more than one interpretation, concerned a subject that was apparently of crucial importance to the United States: the extent of Korea's GPA offer in relation to the new airport.[554]

4.498 **In response, the United States argues** that in making its argument, Korea appears to suggest that Korea is exempt from the normal rules of treaty interpretation, and of state responsibility, with respect to its GPA schedules and other official documents merely because those documents were translated from Korean to English. The United States asserts that this argument is specious and states that Korea has already agreed that its schedule to the GPA be "[a]uthentic in the English language only."[555] Indeed, all negotiating documents provided by Korea, including the *Government Organization Act of the Republic of Korea*, were provided in English. The United States contends that, moreover, when it has suited Korea, Korea has in many other instances argued for precise textual interpretations of translated Korean documents.[556]

4.499 **In response to a question from the Panel, Korea submits** that if the subject of Korea's GPA coverage was as important as the US suggests, and if the July 1991

---

[551] Korea's Answer to Question 2 from the Panel, dated 29 November 1999.

[552] Ibid.

[553] US Response to Korea's Answer to Question 2 from the Panel, dated 29 November 1999.

[554] Korea's Answer to Question 2 from the Panel, dated 29 November 1999.

[555] US Exhibit 45.

[556] US Response to Korea's Answer to Question 2 from the Panel, dated 29 November 1999, referring to Korea's Answer to Questions from the Panel, dated 29 November 1999, at p. 21 in which Korea argues that "Article 6 of the 1997 *Seoul Airport Act*, however, [was] not coincidentally titled 'Operator of New Airport Construction Project'."

communication was as imprecise as the US argues (in that it would support the US interpretation as well as Korea's) then Korea states that it is puzzling that the US did nothing to clear up the matter. Korea argues that a reasonable US reader of an allegedly imprecise communication concerning a crucial matter would have sought clarification, particularly when it knew that the language of the response was not the first language of the person who prepared it. Korea reiterates that no clarification was sought, and the US has submitted no evidence to the contrary.[557]

(c) Burden of Proof

4.500 **Korea refers** to the views of the Appellate Body in the *EC - LAN* case. Korea states that in that case, the panel concluded that it was the importing party - in the context of this case, Korea - that bore the responsibility for the clarity of its tariff schedule. Korea states that the Appellate Body disagreed. The Appellate Body said: "It is only normal that importing Members define their offers (and their ensuing obligations) in terms which suit their needs." "On the other hand," it continued, "exporting Members have to ensure that their corresponding rights are described in such a manner in the Schedules of importing Members that their export interests, as agreed in the negotiations, are guaranteed."[558] In other words, exporting Members have an obligation to ensure that their interests are guaranteed.[559]

4.501 Korea argues that the reasoning of the Appellate Body is equally applicable to this case. Korea states that it was entitled to define its GPA offer, and its ensuing obligations, in terms that suited its own needs. Korea further states that it was up to the United States to ensure that its interests were protected in this process; it was not up to Korea to do so.

4.502 Korea further argues that just what "concession" the United States made in exchange for the alleged inclusion of KAA among Korea's commitments is not clear. Korea asserts that there is no evidence on this point.

4.503 **In response, the United States argues that** Korea appears to suggest that it has no responsibility for the clarity of its GPA schedule. However, the United States argues that what the Appellate Body in *EC - LAN* made clear was that "[t]ariff negotiations are a process of reciprocal demands and concessions, of 'give and take'."[560]

4.504 The United States argues that, in addition, the *EC - LAN* dispute involved a situation in which "the detailed product composition of tariff commitments was never discussed in detail during the tariff negotiations" and the negotiators "relied on a continuation of the status quo."[561] The United States contends that, indeed, the factual record in *EC - LAN* confirms that the "detailed product composition of the tariff category" in question in that dispute was not discussed at all. The United States argues that, in contrast in this case, the United States specifically asked Korea during negotiations to "identify all Ministries that will be responsible for the procurement of goods and services related to new airport construction." The United States notes that

---

557 Korea's Answer to Question 2 from the Panel, dated 29 November 1999.

558 Appellate Body Report *EC – Computer Equipment, supra*, footnote 106, para. 109.

559 Korea's Answer to Question 2 of the Panel, dated 29 November 1999.

560 US Response to Korea's Answer to Question 1 from the Panel, dated 29 November 1999, referring to Appellate Body report on *EC – Computer Equipment, supra*, footnote 106, para. 109.

561 *EC – Computer Equipment, supra*, footnote 106, para. 91.

believing that the United States' question was emphasizing the IIA project, Korea responded that "[t]he new airport construction is being conducted by the New Airport Development Group under the Ministry of Transportation ... The responsible organization for procurement of goods and services relating to the new airport construction is the Office of Supply." The United States argues that, thus, it was through this question and response that the United States made sure "that [its] corresponding rights [were] described in such a manner in the Schedules of [Korea] that [its] interests, as agreed in the negotiations, [were] guaranteed."[562]

3. *Measure*

(a) Application of a Measure

4.505 **Korea argues** that the United States must demonstrate that the assignment to KAA of the responsibility for IIA procurement is a "measure" within the meaning of Article XXII:2 of the GPA. Korea argues that Article XXII:2 is written in the present tense. Korea notes that the Panel in *Japan - Film* stated that Article XXII:2, therefore, "contemplates nullification or impairment in the present tense," and "limits the non-violation remedy to measures that are currently being applied."[563]

4.506 Korea argues that since the measure granting KAA authority to undertake IIA procurement is no longer in effect, the United States' non-violation claim under Article XXII:2 must be rejected. Korea notes in this respect that the *Seoul Airport Act* was amended in August 1994 to shift responsibility for implementation of the IIA project from KAA to KOACA. Korea further notes that, similarly, Article 7(5-2) of the *Korea Airport Corporation Act*, which previously vested KAA with the authority to implement the IIA project, was deleted in August 1994.

4.507 Korea also argues that the transferral of responsibility from MOCT or Office of Supply in December 1991 to KAA which the United States claims undermined its legitimate expectations, occurred two years before the conclusion of the GPA negotiations, in December 1993, when Korea and other signatories submitted their final offers. Korea asserts that, as such, it must be presumed that the United States anticipated and in fact had knowledge of the event. It is the United States that bears the very significant burden of rebutting that presumption.

4.508 **In response, the United States argues** that the measures at issue in this dispute are the procurement practices and not, the United States argues as asserted by Korea, the transfer of procurement authority.

4.509 **Further, in response to a question from the Panel, Korea states** that KAA's authority over the IIA project was transferred to KOACA because it was determined that KAA's responsibilities for existing airports did not permit it to conduct the construction of the IIA efficiently. Korea notes in this respect that KAA is primarily focused upon the management of existing airport operations. Korea states that this may involve incidental repair and maintenance. Korea further notes that the only significant construction authority possessed by KAA was its responsibility, from

[562] US Response to Korea's Answer to Question 1 from the Panel, dated 29 November 1999, referring to *EC - LAN*, *supra*, footnote 106, para. 109.

[563] Panel Report, *Japan - Film*, *supra*, footnote 510, para. 10.57.

December 1991 to August 1994, for the IIA. Korea states that it believed that an entity devoted solely to the project was necessary given that KAA's existing portfolio made it difficult to balance its construction responsibilities for the IIA. As a result, responsibility for implementation of the basic plan for the IIA project and IIA procurement was transferred by the National Assembly to KOACA in August 1994. Korea notes that KAA continues to supervise the operation of existing airports, including construction and maintenance at those airports.[564]

(b) Measure Upsets Competitive Relationship

4.510 **The United States notes** that the situation in this dispute is analogous to a 1952 dispute, Treatment by Germany of Imports of Sardines, in which tariff reductions negotiated by Norway with Germany were later not honoured by Germany. The United States refers to the relevant panel report, which explains:

> "a nullification or an impairment of a benefit accruing to Norway directly or indirectly under the [GATT] ... would exist if the action of the German Government, which resulted in upsetting the competitive relationship between [products from Norway and other directly competitive products] could not reasonably have been anticipated by the Norwegian Government at the time it negotiated for tariff reductions on [its products]. The Panel concluded that the Government of Norway had reason to assume, during these negotiations that [the products from Norway] would not be less favourably treated than [other directly competitive products] and that this situation would not be modified by unilateral action of the German Government ...
>
> As the measures taken by the German Government have nullified the validity of the assumptions which governed the attitude of the Norwegian delegation [during negotiations] and substantially reduced the value of the concessions obtained by Norway, the Panel found that the Norwegian Government is justified in claiming that it had suffered an impairment of a benefit accruing to it under the General Agreement."[565]

4.511 The United States contends that, similarly, during Korea's GPA accession negotiations, the United States bargained for and received from Korea the coverage of all government entities responsible for the procurement of products and services related to new airport construction projects under Annex 1. According to the United States, Korea subsequently engaged in, and continues to engage in, measures in procurement that could not have reasonably been anticipated by the United States at the time the coverage of new airport construction was negotiated. More specifically, the United States argues that by applying GPA-inconsistent practices in the procurement of new airport construction projects, Korea upsets the established competitive relationship between US products, services and suppliers and Korean products, services and suppliers. The United States argues that these measures result in the upsetting of

[564] Korea's Answer to Question 18 from the Panel, dated 3 November 1999.

[565] GATT Panel Report *Treatment by Germany of Imports of Sardines* (adopted on 31 October 1952,) G/26, paras. 16-17.

the established competitive relationship between US products, services and suppliers and Korean products, services and suppliers in the IIA construction project, a competitive relationship worth potentially US$6 billion. On this basis, the United States argues that Korea is nullifying or impairing benefits accruing to the United States under the GPA.

4.512 **Korea argues** that the requirement that the measure at issue upset the competitive relationship created by the Agreement implies, that an "agreement" is necessary. Korea further argues that the essence of a non-violation claim is that some action of a party, after an agreement is concluded, which could not have been reasonably anticipated at the time of the agreement, nullifies or impairs a concession made by another party. Korea asserts that the United States has not specified what agreement was made by the parties that was nullified or impaired by action taken by Korea after that agreement was entered into. Korea further asserts that it could not have been an agreement to include KAA, KOACA and IIAC in Korea's GPA coverage given that Korea never agreed to include KAA in any of its offers.

4. *Reasonable Expectation of a Benefit*

(a) Relevance of "Reasonable Expectation of Benefit"

4.513 **Korea emphasizes** that whether or not the United States' expectations regarding Korea's GPA commitments are "reasonable" is entirely irrelevant to a "violation" complaint under the GPA. Korea notes that reference to a complainant's reasonable expectations in the context of a violation complaint "melds the legally-distinct bases for violation and non-violation complaints ... into one uniform cause of action, and is not in accordance with established GATT practice."[566] Korea asserts that the question whether expectations are reasonable or not is, therefore, relevant only in the context of a "non-violation" complaint, raised by the United States pursuant to Article XXII:2 of the GPA.

(b) Has there been a Reasonable Expectation of Benefit in this Case?

4.514 **Korea argues** that during the negotiation of the GPA, and specifically, during the period leading up to the submission by Korea of its final offer list for accession to the GPA, the United States was very much aware that KAA, rather than MOCT, Office of Supply or any other covered entity, was in fact responsible for IIA procurement. Korea further argues that the United States was aware of KAA's role as the entity responsible for IIA procurement years before Korea submitted its final offer for accession to the GPA, in December 1993. Korea notes in this respect that responsibility for IIA procurement was assigned to KAA two years before Korea's submission of its final offer for accession to the GPA on 15 December 1993, nearly two and one-half years before the conclusion of the Marrakesh Agreement on 15 April 1994, and six years before the effective date of the GPA, which for Korea was 1 January 1997.

[566] Appellate Body Report *EC - LAN*, *supra*, footnote 106, para. 80.

4.515 Korea further argues that during negotiations regarding Korea's accession to the GPA, the United States was aware of the existence and activities of Annex 1 entities undertaking "procurement for airports," whether related to new airport construction or work on existing airports. Specifically, Korea argues that the United States was aware that entities other than KAA - namely, the Regional Aviation Offices - existed, procured for Korean airports other than IIA and were included in Korea's offer.[567]

4.516 Korea states in this respect that the Korean cable report[568], the questions put to Korea by the United States in May 1991[569] and the May 1991 US Department of Commerce cable report[570] all note the United States' receipt of a February 1991 document titled "*Supplementary Explanation of the Note by the Republic of Korea dated 29 June 1990 relating to the Agreement on Government Procurement.*" Korea further notes that page 11 of this *Supplementary Explanation*, explaining Korea's initial offer, lists the Regional Aviation Offices or Bureaus as included within Korea's commitment of the Ministry of Transportation. Korea notes that it does not list KAA.[571]

4.517 Furthermore, Korea states that it has furnished proof of procurements undertaken by the Regional Aviation Offices both during the negotiations and up to the present.[572] Korea argues that it is not credible for the United States to claim, on the one hand, that it consulted carefully and extensively with US industry regarding Korean airport procurement and yet, on the other hand, that it had no idea about the entities undertaking that procurement.[573]

4.518 Korea also states that Korea's General Note 1(b) meant (and means), and what the United States reasonably expected it to mean at the conclusion of GPA negotiations with Korea, was that Annex 1 entities conducting procurements for airports existed (and exist) and that they are MOCT's Regional Aviation Offices. Korea states that during negotiations with Korea, the United States was aware of their existence, their identity, their procurement activity and their inclusion in Korea's offer. It was also aware that Korea did not include KAA in the February 1991 *Supplementary Explanation* as a procuring entity considered covered under Korea's offer by virtue of a relationship with the Ministry of Transportation.[574]

4.519 **In response, the United States** argues that Korea's GPA-inconsistent practices in the procurement of new airport construction projects could not have been reasonably anticipated by the United States at the time of the 1991 negotiations.

4.520 Further, the United States argues that it is completely irrelevant whether the United States knew that KAA was responsible for airport procurement or not. The United States argues that, rather, what is relevant is the fact that KAA is a subsidiary organization of MOCT. Given that it is a subsidiary organization of MOCT, and thus

---

567 Korea's Response to the US Answer to Question 17 from the Panel, dated 29 November 1999.
568 Exhibit Kor-118.
569 US Exhibit 4, Questions 9, 10, 11, 14, 15.
570 US Exhibit 2, p. 2.
571 Korea's Response to the US Answer to Question 17 from the Panel, dated 29 November 1999.
572 Exhibits Kor-61A through Kor-61J.
573 Korea's Response to the US Answer to Question 17 from the Panel, dated 29 November 1999.
574 Ibid.

covered under Annex 1 of the GPA, the United States could, therefore, not have reasonably anticipated the lack of GPA coverage for any of KAA's procurements.

4.521 Additionally, in response to a question from the Panel, the United States notes that its reasonable expectation relates not to KAA's status as a project operator, nor to the fact that KAA was operating under its own procurement regulations, but instead it relates to whether the United States reasonably expected new airport construction to be covered under Annex 1 of the GPA. The United States contends that this reasonable expectation did not change despite the shift of procurement authority to KAA, because KAA was (and is) a subordinate unit of MOCT, and a shift of procurement authority within MOCT was of no consequence, for Korea had already assured the United States that all of MOCT would be covered under Annex 1. The United States asserts that a transfer from one subordinate unit of MOCT to another subordinate unit of MOCT is no transfer at all. According to the United States, the procurement authority remained within MOCT.[575]

4.522 The United States contends that, moreover, the US reasonable expectation did not change because KAA was using different procurement regulations at the time. The United States further states that central government entities (including their subordinate units) are only required to come in line with GPA requirements after the GPA enters into force. According to the United States, it was reasonable to expect that Korea would bring KAA's practices into line with the GPA by the time the GPA entered into force for Korea, in January 1997.[576]

(c) Relevant Evidence Before Korea's Accession

(i) Negotiations and Communications

Korea's July 1991 Communication

4.523 **Korea argues** that assignment of responsibility for IIA procurement to what would become a non-covered entity should have been, and in fact was, reasonably anticipated by the United States during negotiations with Korea regarding its GPA commitments. In support of its argument, Korea states that in a 1 July 1991 response to a question from the United States regarding the IIA project, Korea stated that Office of Supply was to be the "responsible organization for procurement" for the IIA project. Immediately following that sentence, however, Korea expressly stated: "But at present, the concrete procurement plan has not been fixed because now the whole airport construction project is only in a basic planning stage." Korea asserts that it could not have made this qualification with greater clarity.

4.524 According to Korea, Korea argues that, furthermore, there would in July 1991 have existed some uncertainty concerning the entity responsible for IIA procurement was entirely reasonable. Korea notes in this respect that its response to the United States' inquiry was offered six months before the basic plan for IIA was completed, 16 months before site preparation for the IIA project was to begin, two and one-half years before Korea's submission of its final offer list, and nearly five years before ground-breaking for the IIA passenger terminal took place, on 23 May 1996. Korea

575 US Answer to Question 25(b) from the Panel, dated 3 November 1999.

576 Ibid.

states that given the express reservation in Korea's July 1991 response, and given that the IIA project was in the infancy of its planning stage when that response was given as stated in the July 1991 response, the United States was on notice that plans regarding the entities responsible for IIA procurement were not yet set. Procurement plans for the IIA project were simply not ready in July 1991, and Korea fully disclosed this fact to the United States.

4.525 **The United States contends in response** that Korea's argument is not persuasive because it fails to explain how the phrase, "procurement plan," can specifically be referring to "plans regarding the entities responsible for IIA procurement." The United States argues that "procurement plan," by its ordinary meaning, could only be referring to "the basic plan for the construction of IIA," which, consistent with Korea's own representation, was not yet fixed at the time of Korea's 1991 response. The United States contends that this basic plan provided for the "general direction of IIA construction, an outline of the construction plan, an estimated duration for the construction, and a financing plan for the project." The United States asserts that it did not provide for any change in entity coverage and it was not announced until 16 June 1992, whereas KAA became responsible for the procurement of airport construction in December 1991. The United States further asserts that if Korea had really wanted to provide "greater clarity," it would have said, "But at present, the procurement entity has not been fixed."

4.526 Further, the United States argues that, as for Korea's argument that the United States was placed on notice that "the entities responsible for IIA procurement were not yet set," the United States contends that Korea's representation that "the concrete procurement plan has not been fixed because now the whole airport construction project is only in a basic planning stage," referred only to the procurement "plan" and not to the procuring "entity." The United States notes that, furthermore, this condition directly followed plain statements referencing a "basic plan" and a "working plan" to be completed by 1992 and 1993, respectively, as well as a definitive representation regarding the role of MOCT and the Office of Supply as entities responsible for IIA construction. The United States concludes that, therefore, Korea's conditional statement could only be referring to the basic plan or the working plan, and not to the entities conducting the procurement.

4.527 The United States also states that it relied on Korea's representations in 1991, when Korea explicitly stated that the New Airport Development Group of MOCT and the Office of Supply are the only two entities responsible for procurements of new airport construction. The United States also states that it relied on Korea in subsequent years when Korea never again raised the issue of airport procurement.

4.528 **Korea responds** by arguing that even if Korea's July 1991 response did not alone effectively alert the United States to the possibility that IIA procurement responsibility might eventually fall to an entity other than the Office of Supply, there are numerous examples of constructive and actual notice that demonstrate that the United States was very much aware of KAA's role years before the conclusion of the GPA negotiations.

4.529 Korea states that those examples of constructive and actual notice include the following: In December 1991, Korea published in its *Official Gazette* notification of KAA's appointment to implement the IIA project, and the United States is charged with knowledge of this notice; during 1992, Korea and the United States exchanged correspondence regarding KAA's role as the entity responsible for the IIA project;

during the period 1992-1994, numerous US companies bid for and secured procurements conducted by KAA for the IIA project; during 1992, KAA broadcast its procurement role in the IIA project to airport and airport construction experts worldwide, including the Port Authority of New York and New Jersey, the Los Angles Department of Airports, the Denver (Stapleton) International Airport, and the Dallas/Fort Worth International Airport; press reports demonstrate that KAA was the entity in charge of IIA procurement; the United States was aware, by virtue of the publication in the *Official Gazette* of the *Korea Airport Corporation Act*, that KAA, like Korea's Annex 3 entities, is a separate "juristic" person; the United States was aware that its own airport authorities, as well as the airport authorities of nearly every GPA signatory, were included on Annex 3 rather than on Annex 1; in July 1998, the United States acknowledged that KOACA, is not covered, and the European Communities stated, in March 1993, that Korea's GPA proposal contained "no offer regarding airports."

4.530 According to Korea, therefore, during the period leading up to its submission of its final GPA offer, the United States was aware that KAA, rather than MOCT or the Office of Supply, was the entity responsible for IIA procurement. At the same time, Korea asserts that the United States was also aware that KAA was not listed on Korea's Annex 1.[577]

Korea's February 1991 Supplementary Explanation

4.531 **Korea argues** that the United States was aware that KAA did not feature on the list of subordinate bodies covered by virtue of Korea's offer of the Ministry of Transportation and also was well aware of the inclusion of other MOCT airport-procurement entities - that is, the Regional Aviation Offices - within Korea's offer of the Ministry of Transportation as an Annex 1 entity.[578]

4.532 Korea argues that procurements for construction at "other regional airports" are covered under Korea's Annex 1 not because they are covered projects, but because they are undertaken by covered entities - MOCT's Regional Aviation Offices or the Office of Supply on their behalf. Korea notes in this respect that responsibility for procurements for significant construction for these airports falls to the Regional Aviation Offices or the Office of Supply.[579]

4.533 Korea notes that the United States has claimed in these proceedings that it was not aware that entities other than KAA, KOACA and IIAC - namely, the Regional Aviation Offices and the Office of Supply - conduct procurements for "other regional airports" in Korea. Korea notes that the United States blames this lack of awareness on Korea, arguing that Korea should have disclosed the existence of the Regional Aviation Offices to the United States in its 1 July 1991 response and its response to other questions put to it by the United States in September 1998.[580]

4.534 Korea argues in response that the United States was in fact aware of the existence of the Regional Aviation Offices during negotiations with Korea regarding its

577 Korea's Second Written Submission, paras. 169-172.
578 Korea's Answer to Question 21 from the Panel, dated 29 November 1999.
579 Ibid.
580 Ibid.

accession to the GPA. Korea refers to a document, dated February 1991, and titled "*Supplementary Explanation of the Note by the Republic of Korea dated 29 June 1990 relating to the Agreement on Government Procurement,*" which lists on pages 6-14 all 47 Korean central government entities, along with their subordinate linear organizations, special local administrative organs and attached organs. Korea states that page 5 of the *Supplementary Explanation* notes that 35 of those 47 central governments were covered under Korea's June 1990 offer. Korea further notes that page 26 of the document describes the point of what eventually became Note 1 to Korea's Annex 1 - "to clarify the coverage of central government organs which come under 35 of [4]7 purchasing entities."[581]

4.535 Korea notes as an example, page 11 of the *Supplementary Explanation*, lists five bodies as covered by the inclusion of the Korean Ministry of Transportation, including the Regional Aviation Offices or Bureaus. Korea argues that this document confirms that Korea did intend to commit to coverage of procurements by the Regional Aviation Offices. Korea states that it is also noteworthy that KAA is not on this list included at pages 6-14 of the *Supplementary Explanation*, either as a body under the Ministry of Transportation, or as a central government entity in its own right.[582]

4.536 Korea argues that the United States received this document. Korea notes that this is evident from a Korean 25 February 1991 cable report indicating that the *Supplementary Explanation* was in fact delivered to and acknowledged as received by the United States.[583] Korea notes that, moreover, the United States' May 1991 questions to Korea include five citations to Korea's February 1991 *Supplementary Explanation.*[584] Korea also notes that the May 1991 US Department of Commerce cable report includes at least two references to the "ROKG's 2/91 *Supplementary Explanation*" or "the February *Supplementary Explanation.*"[585] Korea states that it is evident that the document was provided to the United States, scrutinized by the United States, and used as a starting point for questions put to Korea by the United States.[586]

4.537 Korea states that despite KAA's conspicuous absence from the list of MOCT airport-procurement entities included on page 11 of Korea's February 1991 *Supplementary Explanation*, despite the United States' purported interest in GPA negotiations with Korea, in the transportation sector generally and the "Airport Development Group" more specifically and despite the United States' awareness of KAA's role as the entity responsible for the IIA project, the United States never once, in the more than two and one-half years remaining in the GPA negotiations with Korea, asked where KAA fit into Korea's offer. Korea cannot be accorded responsibility for the United States' failure.[587]

---

581 Korea's Answer to Question 21 from the Panel, dated 29 November 1999. Korea notes that although p. 5 clearly states that 35 of the 47 total central government entities were covered by Korea's offer, p. 26 puts the number at "35 of 37"entities. The statement on p. 26 appears to be a typographical error, since the list on pp. 6-14 actually includes 47 entities.

582 Ibid.

583 Ibid.

584 Questions 9, 10, 11, 14, 15.

585 p. 2.

586 Korea's Answer to Question 21 from the Panel, dated 29 November 1999.

587 Ibid.

4.538 In support of its argument, Korea refers to an internal EC Commission note, dated 3 December 1993.[588] Korea states that this document refers to Korea's offer of coverage for "a number of major cities (Seoul, Pusang) [sic]" that "control their airports in co-operation with the Ministry of Transportation." MOCT's two Regional Aviation Offices are, again, the Seoul and the Pusan Regional Aviation Offices. Those are the airport procurement entities included in Korea's offer for Annex 1 GPA coverage of MOCT.[589]

4.539 **In response, the United States argues** that even though the February 1991 document lists all of the "subordinate linear organizations," "special local administrative organs," and "attached organs" of the Ministry of Transportation and the Ministry of Construction, when this document is compared with the 1994 and 1999 MOCT organizational charts[590], there are numerous discrepancies.[591]

4.540 The United States notes, for instance, that the General Affairs Division, the Planning and Management Office, the Construction Affairs Office, the Transportation Policy Office, the National Territory Planning Bureau, the Land Bureau, the Housing and Urban Affairs Bureau, the Surface Transportation Bureau, the Transportation Safety Bureau, the Civil Aviation Bureau, the Waterway Bureau, the Air Traffic Control Center and the Central Land Tribunal from the 1994 MOCT organizational chart are not listed in the February 1991 document. The United States contends that, yet it is uncontested that these entities are covered under Annex 1 of the GPA. In addition, the Construction Economy Bureau, the Technology and Safety Bureau, the Road Bureau and the Water Resources Bureau (entities from the 1999 MOCT organizational chart not found in the 1994 chart) are also not listed in the February 1991 document.[592]

4.541 The United States argues that, moreover, according to this February 1991 document, there are 24 District Construction Offices, five VOR-TAC Stations, and a Flight Inspection Office under the Ministries of Construction and Transportation, yet these entities cannot be found in either the 1994 or 1999 MOCT organizational charts. Similarly, the February 1991 document lists three Flood Control Offices, a National Construction Research Institute, a Central Equipment Management Office, and five Marine Accident Inquiry Offices. However, the organizational charts list five Flood Control Offices, and the 1999 chart excludes the National Construction Research Institute, a Central Equipment Management Office, and five Marine Accident Inquiry Offices (four of which have the exact same name on the 1994 chart). Finally, the United States notes that, in addition to KAA, the New Airport Development Group is not listed in the February 1991 document. Thus, it is not surprising that KAA is not listed in this document.[593]

4.542 The United States argues that what is clear is that the February 1991 document does not represent Korea's GPA commitments; it is not even Korea's final offer. The United States contends that as Korea itself has noted, it is merely "a starting

588 Attached as Annex V to the EC's Answer to Questions from the Panel, dated 3 November 1999.
589 Korea's Response to the EC's Answer to Question 1 from the Panel, dated 3 November 1999.
590 Exhibit Kor-111.
591 US Response to Korea's Answer to Question 21 from the Panel, dated 29 November 1999.
592 Ibid.
593 Ibid.

point for questions put to Korea by the United States." The United States contends that this makes sense, because subsequent to receiving this document, the United States in May 1991 asked Korea to "[p]lease identify all Ministries that will be responsible for the procurement of goods and services related to new airport construction." The United States notes that Korea responded in July 1991, "The new airport construction is being conducted by the New Airport Development Group under the Ministry of Transportation ... The responsible organization for procurement of goods and services relating to the new airport construction is the Office of Supply."[594]

4.543 The United States argues that it is also clear that whether a non-listed entity should be considered "attached/connected/affiliated" to a listed entity should not be determined by the listed entity's organizational chart, which is subject to unilateral alterations at any time, and was not considered as part of the GPA negotiations. The United States argues that following a textual analysis of the GPA, "control" is the only feasible, objective method in which one can determine whether a non-listed entity is "attached/connected/affiliated" to a listed entity, and therefore is covered under the GPA. The United States further argues that, in fact, at one point in its response, even Korea appears to embrace the "control" concept by claiming that it did not include KAA in the February 1991 document because it "did not consider KAA to be 'controlled' enough by MOCT to include it on the list of MOCT airport-procurement entities."[595]

Legislation

Act on the Promotion of a New Airport for Seoul Metropolitan Area Construction

4.544 **In response to a question from the Panel** as to why Korea did not refer to the 1991 enactments and amendments to IIA legislation in its July 1991 response, **Korea states** that pursuant to *Japan - Film*[596], the United States is charged with knowledge of the enactment of the *Seoul Airport Act*, and the significance thereof, from the date of its publication in the Official Gazette, which came not weeks or months before the conclusion of negotiations regarding Korea's GPA commitments, but instead more than two and one-half years before the conclusion of those negotiations.[597] Korea argues that by virtue of either the publication of the *Act* or otherwise, the United States was aware of the *Act* and its significance. Korea argues that, therefore, it was not incumbent upon Korea to provide an answer to a question that was not even asked of it, in circumstances where the United States had constructive and actual knowledge of the Act.[598]

4.545 Korea also notes that with the enactment of amendments to the *Seoul Airport Act* in December 1991, the National Assembly stated that MOCT would not be responsible for the IIA project and that that job would go to KAA. Korea states that the

[594] Ibid.

[595] Ibid.

[596] Korea's Answer to Question 9 from the Panel, dated 29 November 1999.

[597] Korea's Answer to Question 1 from the Panel, dated 29 November 1999, referring to *Japan - Film, supra*, footnote 510, para. 10.80.

[598] Korea's Answer to Question 1 from the Panel, dated 29 November 1999.

GPA significance of this fact is not found in the *Act* itself, but instead stems from the fact that KAA is not now and never was listed on any of the Annexes included in Korea's Appendix I.[599]

4.546 **In response, the United States argues** that this assertion is contradicted by the fact that no version of the *Seoul Airport Act* has ever stated that MOCT would not be responsible for the IIA project. The United States contends that, on the contrary, the *Seoul Airport Act* is filled with references to MOCT authority over the project operator and MOCT's role in the IIA project. The United States notes that, significantly, the December 1991 *Seoul Airport Act* amendments did not state that the job of responsibility over the IIA project would go to KAA. The United States notes that the December 1991 amendments merely added KAA to the list of potential project operators of the IIA project. The United States further contends that the December 1991 amendments did not alter Article 6(2) in any way, the provision which bestows upon MOCT authority to designate any project operator for the IIA project.[600]

4.547 The United States contends that, moreover, Korea's statement gives the impression that the National Assembly was responsible for designating KAA as the IIA project operator. The United States notes that, however, according to Korea, MOCT made the sole "internal decision" to designate KAA as project operator for the 1991-1994 portion of the IIA project. The United States notes further that MOCT then drafted and published the "draft legislation containing proposed amendments to the *Seoul Airport Act*." The United States further states that Korea submitted this draft legislation to the National Assembly, not because the National Assembly "assigned" KAA to this task, but because only the National Assembly can pass laws in Korea. The United States concludes that, thus, the National Assembly merely codified a decision made by MOCT, pursuant to the authority granted to MOCT in the *Seoul Airport Act*.[601]

4.548 **Korea states** that the appointment of KAA, in December 1991, as the entity responsible for IIA procurement occurred "prior to the conclusion of the tariff negotiations at issue." Korea further argues that there is "a presumption that the United States should be held to have anticipated those measures and it is for the United States to rebut that presumption."[602]

4.549 Korea reiterates that it is the United States that bears the considerable burden of rebutting this presumption. Korea need not demonstrate that the United States did not anticipate to secure coverage of the entities responsible for IIA procurement. To effectively rebut the presumption, it is for the United States to demonstrate, affirmatively, that it "reasonably expected" to obtain the benefit of GPA coverage for IIA procurement by virtue of Korea's inclusion of MOCT and the Office of Supply on its Annex 1 list.[603]

---

599 Korea's Answer to Question 5 from the Panel, dated 29 November 1999.

600 US Response to Korea's Answer to Question 5 from the Panel, dated 29 November 1999.

601 Ibid.

602 Panel Report, *Japan - Film, supra*, footnote 510 , para. 10.80.

603 *Ibid.* para. 10.72. As further support for this principle, see *EEC - Oilseeds*, BISD 37S/86, 128-129 (paras. 147-148); *Operation of the Provisions of Article XVI*, BISD 10S/201, 209 (para. 28) (adopted on 21 November 1961); *Other Barriers to Trade*, BISD 3S/222, 224 (para. 13) (adopted on 3 March 1955); *Germany - Sardines*, BISD 1S/53, 58-59 (para. 16) (adopted on 31 October 1952);

4.550 **In response, the United States argues** that Korea's argument is irrelevant to this case. The United States argues that it does not matter whether the United States had constructive or actual notice of the enactment of the *Seoul Airport Act*, for the significance of the *Act* is simply that it confirms MOCT's statutory authority and control over the IIA project.[604]

4.551 The United States reiterates that the *Seoul Airport Act* is replete with references to MOCT authority over the IIA project. The United States notes that, for example, Article 6 of the *Seoul Airport Act*, while listing a range of possible "operators" (which incidentally includes "state" and "local" governments), grants MOCT ultimate authority to select any entity to be the project operator for the IIA project. This is entirely consistent with the rights granted to MOCT under Article 94(2) of the *Aviation Act*.[605]

4.552 The United States contends that it is important to keep in mind that a "project operator" is distinct and separate from the entity that has ultimate authority over the project. The United States also states that it is important to remember that Korea itself reconfirmed that the Office of Supply and the Ministry of Transportation were responsible for the IIA airport development project when it responded to US questions in July 1991, two months after the enactment of the *Seoul Airport Act*.[606]

Aviation Act

4.553 **The United States notes** that the version of the *Aviation Act* granting statutory authority over airport development projects to MOCT, came into effect as a wholly amended Act on 14 December 1991. Accordingly, the United States argues that it was on notice from December 1991 onwards that MOCT retained statutory authority and control over all airport development projects in Korea, including the IIA project. In light of this, argues the United States, it felt confident that, from 1991 to the time when Korea submitted its final offer in December 1993 and signed the revised GPA at Marrakesh in 1994, MOCT was the proper entity to be covered under the GPA in order for the US to obtain non-discriminatory access to Korea's airport procurement market. The United States notes that to this day, the *Aviation Act* remains unaltered in providing MOCT the statutory authority over the IIA airport development project. The United States argues that this was one of the reasons why it was essential for the United States to negotiate MOCT's coverage under the GPA, and why the United States was not concerned about explicitly covering IIA project operators, which MOCT could change at will at any time (as evidenced by the shift of IIA responsibility from KAA to KOACA and IIAC over a span of eight years), but which would nevertheless remain covered under the GPA because of MOCT's ultimate control over the IIA project.[607]

Australian Subsidy on Ammonium Sulphate, GATT/CP.4/39, BISD II/188, 193-194 (adopted on 3 April 1950).

[604] US Response to Korea's Answer to Question 1 from the Panel, dated 29 November 1999.

[605] Ibid.

[606] Ibid.

[607] US Answer to Question 18 from the Panel, dated 29 November 1999.

4.554 **Korea argues in response** that the *Seoul Airport Act* replaces the *Aviation Act* for the purposes of the construction of the IIA.[608] Korea states that the United States, well beyond constructive knowledge of the *Seoul Airport Act*, had actual knowledge of that Act throughout and subsequent to negotiations with Korea regarding accession to the GPA. Korea asserts that the United States' awareness of the passage of the *Seoul Airport Act* and its understanding that the *Seoul Airport Act* rather than the *Aviation Act* regulates IIA construction is illustrated in the United States' First Written Submission, in which it cites 17 Articles from the *Seoul Airport Act* in support of its claims, and no Articles from the *Aviation Act.*[609]

4.555 Korea also argues that the United States' apparent assertion that its expectations regarding which entity would be responsible for IIA construction were formed by the *Aviation Act* presumes ignorance of the *Seoul Airport Act*. Korea argues that it is virtually impossible for one with knowledge of both Acts to have concluded that the question of responsibility for construction of the IIA was and is governed by the *Aviation Act*, rather than the *Seoul Airport Act.*[610] Korea states the purpose of the *Seoul Airport Act* alone - to "specify...the matters necessary for the speedy construction of a new airport in the Seoul Metropolitan area" - should have been enough to signal to any remotely observant reader that the *Seoul Airport Act* would regulate the IIA project.[611]

4.556 Korea also argues that the *Seoul Airport Act*, the *Korea Airport Corporation Act*, the *Korea Airport Construction Authority Act* and the *Law on Inchon International Airport Corporation* are the "other Acts" and "other laws" referred to in the *proviso* in Article 94(1) of the *Aviation Act* which allows an entity other than MOCT to implement IIA construction. Korea argues that the *proviso* in Article 94(1) was triggered on a number of occasions. Specifically, Korea notes that December 1991 amendments to the *Seoul Airport Act* and the *Korea Airport Corporation Act* appointed KAA as the entity responsible for the IIA project[612], August 1994 amendments to the *Seoul Airport Act* and the September 1994 enactment of the *Korea Airport Construction Authority Act* appointed KOACA to that role[613] and February 1999 amendments to the *Seoul Airport Act*, together with passage of the *Law on Inchon International Airport Corporation*, similarly appointed IIAC to perform this task.[614] Korea argues that the United States is charged with constructive knowledge - and

---

[608] Korea's Answer to Question 9 from the Panel, dated 29 November 1999.

[609] Ibid.

[610] Ibid.

[611] Ibid.

[612] 1991 *Seoul Airport Act*, Article 6(1). See also *Korea Airport Corporation Act*, Article 7(5-2) (assigning to KAA the task of "[n]ew airport construction projects as referred to subpara. 2 of Article 2 of the Act on the Promotion of New Airport Construction in Seoul Metropolitan Area.").

[613] 1997 *Seoul Airport Act*, Article 6(1). See also *Korea Airport Construction Authority Act*, Article 2 (defining project with which KOACA was charged as encompassing activities "stipulated in the subpara. 2, Article 2, '*Seoul Airport Act*'.").

[614] Korea's Answer to Question 9 from the Panel, dated 29 November 1999, referring to *Seoul Airport Act*, Article 6(1). See also *Law on Inchon International Airport Corporation*, Article 10(1)(1) (charging IIAC with responsibility for "[c]onstruction business of the Metropolitan New Airport (hereinafter referred to as Inchon International Airport) in accordance with the Article 2 of the promotional law on Metropolitan New Airport Construction.").

indeed has demonstrated actual knowledge - of the legislative events triggering the *proviso* of Article 94(1).[615]

4.557 **In response, the United States refers** to its arguments in paragraphs 4.111 and 4.114.

4.558 **Korea also submits** that it is not the *Seoul Airport Act* about which the United States was unaware at the time of Korea's 1991 response. Rather, Korea asserts that until its Second Written Submission in these proceedings, it was the *Aviation Act* about which the United States was unaware. Korea argues that any claim by the United States that the *Aviation Act* rather than the *Seoul Airport Act* formed the basis for its expectations regarding coverage of the entities responsible for IIA procurement is nothing more than a convenient post hoc rationalization. Korea states that this is totally apart from the fact that the *Aviation Act* was pre-empted by the *Seoul Airport Act*.[616]

Amendment of the GPA

4.559 Korea argues that the US and all of the Parties to the GPA negotiations knew that the Uruguay Round negotiators had dropped the control test and agreed to that. According to Korea, whatever their expectations might have been prior to rejection of the control test, reality changed in two crucial ways. First, as a matter of law, entities controlled by named entities, but not themselves named, no longer could be covered. Second, from that point forward it was no longer reasonable to believe that controlled entities, not themselves named, would in any way be covered. Korea argues that, thus, a non-violation claim based on control must fail.[617]

4.560 In response to the United States' control arguments, Korea also asserts that the "control" test was, according to the United States, "excluded" from the Uruguay Round GPA, and to the extent it was reinserted elsewhere, can be found in Annex 3. Korea states that whether the "control" test was excluded altogether, or reborn in Annex 3, the United States' purported expectation of coverage for KAA could not reasonably have been expected on the basis of any alleged "control" over it by MOCT. Korea argues that if the "control" test was excluded, any expectation of coverage based on "control" cannot be reasonable. Further, Korea argues that if the "control" test was reborn in Annex 3, then the United States could not have reasonably expected coverage for KAA without inclusion of KAA on Korea's Annex 3.[618]

Communications with the US Government

4.561 **In support of its argument** that the United States was aware that KAA, rather than MOCT, Office of Supply or any other covered entity, was in fact responsible for IIA procurement, **Korea refers** to a letter, dated 6 October 1992, from a US Senator to the Chairman of KAA, requesting consideration of a constituent company's bid for work on the IIA project.[619] Korea also refers to a letter, dated 22 Sep-

---

[615] Korea's Answer to Question 9 from the Panel, dated 29 November 1999.

[616] Korea's Answer to Question 1 from the Panel, dated 29 November 1999.

[617] Korea's Answer to Question 20 from the Panel, dated 29 November 1999.

[618] Korea's Response to US Answer to Question 16 from the Panel, dated 29 November 1999.

[619] Letter from US Senator Slade Gorton to Mr. Wan-Sik Yook, Chairman, KAA, 6 October 1992.

tember 1992, from the Seattle City Council to the Chairman of KAA regarding that same bid.[620] Korea then refers to a letter, dated 8 August 1992, from the Vice Chairman of KAA to (among others) Sung Yong Kim and J.A. Corbett, staff secretaries in the Economic Section of the US Embassy, Seoul, inviting them to attend KAA's International Symposium on Building Metropolitan Airport on 25 August 1992.[621] Korea notes that this letter states that KAA "is designated to construct a metropolitan airport, which shall become hub center of air transportation in east Asia." Finally, Korea states that it had also confirmed that the then-US Ambassador to Korea, the Honorable Donald Gregg, visited KAA during this period, and with other US officials accompanying him on the visit was fully briefed by KAA on the IIA project.

4.562 **In response, the United argues** that nothing in the correspondence cited suggests in any way that KAA would not be a covered entity under the GPA, or that the IIA project would not be covered under the GPA. The United States argues that, furthermore, none of the letters in question were to or by US trade negotiators. The United States asserts that, for example, it is obvious that a US Senator writing on behalf of a company in his State interested in participating in an IIA procurement and a Seattle City Council member writing on behalf of the same company do not represent the United States Government in GPA negotiating matters. The United States contends that by contrast, "responses to the United States' questions" during GPA negotiations by an "employee of the Ministry of Commerce," which were "review[ed] by his superiors in advance of the [July 1991] submission" unquestionably represented Korea's official position in such negotiations and the United States' action in relying on these responses, and assuming that they were made in good faith, was entirely reasonable.[622]

4.563 **Korea also argues** that, as was the case with KAA, the United States was and is aware of KOACA's role in IIA procurement. For support of this argument, Korea refers to a letter from the US Ambassador to Korea, addressed to the Chairman and President of KOACA, requesting consideration of a US company's bid for work on the IIA project.[623]

Communications with US Companies

4.564 In further support of its argument that the United States was aware that KAA was the IIA procuring entity, **Korea also states** that during KAA's tenure as operator of the IIA project, numerous US companies participated in and, in fact, successfully secured procurements conducted by KAA. Korea refers to a list of successful bids submitted by US companies to KAA during the period 1992-1994 to support this statement.[624] Korea argues that even if the United States had not had direct knowl-

---

[620] Letter from Council Member of Seattle City Council to Mr. Wan-Sik Yook, Chairman, KAA, 22 September 1992.

[621] Letter from the Vice Chairman of KAA to Sung Yong Kim and J.A. Corbett, staff secretaries in the Economic Section of the US Embassy Seoul, 8 August 1992.

[622] US Response to Korea's Answer to Question 2 from the Panel, dated 29 November 1999.

[623] Letter from US Ambassador Stephen Bosworth to Mr. Kang, Dong-Suk, Chairman & President, KOACA, dated 3 July 1998.

[624] The list includes successful bids made by US companies during the period 1992-1998. As will be addressed further below, another entity took over IIA procurement from KAA in August 1994.

edge of KAA's responsibility for the IIA project, were it intent on achieving coverage for IIA procurement it would have asked the numerous US firms actively and successfully bidding for the IIA project for some basic information regarding the entities that would need to be "covered" by Korea's GPA commitments to secure GPA coverage for the IIA project.

4.565 Korea also argues that, like the US Government, US firms[625] were aware that KOACA was the entity responsible for IIA procurement as was the case with KAA. For support of this argument, Korea refers to a list of successful bids submitted by US companies to KOACA during the period 1994-1998.[626]

Communications with Major Airports

4.566 **Korea also states** that, coincident with the negotiation of the GPA, KAA's responsibility for the IIA project was communicated to virtually every major airport construction expert and airport or aviation organization in the world. Korea refers to examples of correspondence, from the period 1991-1993, between KAA officials and the International Air Transport Association, the International Civil Aviation Organization, the International Union of Architects, the American Institute of Architects, the Airports Association Council International, the Civil Aviation Authority of Singapore, the Schiphol Airport Authority, the Frankfurt Airport Authority, the Port Authority of New York and New Jersey, the Los Angeles Department of Airports, the Denver (Stapleton) International Airport Office and the Dallas/Fort Worth International Airport. Correspondence between KAA and noted architects and architectural firms is also attached, including correspondence with I.M. Pei, Cesar Pelli & Associates, Richard Meier & Partners, Ricardo Bofill, Sir Norman Foster and Alco Rossi. Korea states that with all of these noted experts aware of KAA's role, it is difficult to imagine that the United States was not also itself aware of KAA's status as the entity responsible for IIA construction.[627]

Korea has also attached correspondence between KAA and US firms Greiner International Ltd. and Bechtel Aviation Services.

625 Korea refers to press releases by US firms, AT&T, dated 11 March 1997, and ARINC, dated 10 September 1998, announcing the conclusion of contracts with KOACA.

626 The list includes successful bids made by US companies during the period 1992-1998. Korea notes that KAA was responsible for procurement during the period December 1991 to September 1994.

627 Korea refers to KAA correspondence with the International Air Transport Association, the International Civil Aviation Organization, the International Union of Architects, the American Institute of Architects, the Airports Association Council International, the Civil Aviation Authority of Singapore, the Schiphol Airport Authority, the Frankfurt Airport Authority, the Port Authority of New York and New Jersey, the Los Angeles Department of Airports, the Denver (Stapleton) International Airport Office, the Dallas/Fort Worth International Airport, I.M. Pei, Cesar Pelli & Associates, Richard Meier & Partners, Ricardo Bofill, Sir Norman Foster and Alco Rossi.

EC's March 1993 Report and Other EC Communications

4.567 **Korea notes** that in March 1993, the European Communities stated that Korea's GPA proposal contained "no offer regarding airports."[628]

4.568 In response to a question from the Panel regarding a letter from the European Communities to the Korean Director of Multilateral Trade Affairs, dated 24 November 1993, which, according to Korea, allegedly indicates that Korea had offered to cover airports, Korea notes that although the letter presumes that a response was made by Korea, Korea has been unable to locate any reply to the European Communities' letter of 24 November 1993. Korea also notes that until Korea's 15 December 1993 final offer, which "for the first time" included General Note 1(b), the European Communities may have considered procurements by the Regional Aviation Offices to be part of Korea's offer. Korea notes these Offices are mentioned in Korea's February 1991 *Supplementary Explanation*.[629]

4.569 Korea notes that the November 1993 letter could of course mean that, in March 1993, the statement by a subdivision of the European Commission that Korea had made "no offer regarding airports" was inaccurate.[630] However, Korea argues that whatever its accuracy, this statement spoke to the European Communities' expectations at that time; it expected that Korea's offer would not include procurements by any entities responsible for airport procurement, including IIA procurement. Korea states that if those expectations changed with the European Communities' 24 November 1993 letter, available evidence, in the form of Korea's February 1991 *Supplementary Explanation*, suggest that the reference was to procurements by the Regional Aviation Offices. Korea states that no evidence provided by the European Communities suggests that the entities responsible for IIA procurement were to be included in Korea's Annex 1 offer.[631]

Reciprocal Derogations

4.570 **In response to a question from the Panel, the United States argues** that it interpreted the reciprocal airport derogations between the European Communities and Korea as an indication that Korea and the EC could not agree that each was offering "comparable and effective access [to their] relevant markets."[632] The United States further states that, moreover, it interpreted these derogations as a confirmation that Korea's GPA offer indeed included coverage of "new airport construction" under its Annex 1, consistent with Korea's July 1991 statement regarding the coverage of MOCT and the Office of Supply - as entities responsible for the IIA project under Annex 1. The United States contends that it was able to draw this conclusion because

---

628 Report from the Commission Concerning Negotiations Regarding Access to Third Countries' Markets in the Fields Covered by Directive 90/531/EEC (the Utilities Directive), COM (93) 80 final, 3 March 1993, p. 7.

629 Korea's Answer to Question 6 from the Panel, dated 29 November 1999.

630 Report from the Commission Concerning Negotiations Regarding Access to Third Countries' Markets in the Fields Covered by Directive 90/531/EEC (The Utilities Directive), COM (93) 80 final, 3 March 1993, p. 7.

631 Korea's Answer to Question 6 from the Panel, dated 29 November 1999.

632 See EC General Note 1 and Korea General Note 1 to Appendix I of the GPA.

Korea's country-specific derogation, which listed the EC and others, did not include the United States when carving out "procurement for airports by the entities listed in Annex 1."[633]

4.571 **Korea responds** that the reciprocal airport derogations between the European Communities and Korea, recorded for Korea's part in General Note 1(b) to its Appendix I, did not as the United States argues serve as "confirmation that Korea's GPA offer indeed included coverage of 'new airport construction' under its Annex 1."[634] Korea quotes the actual language of its General Note 1(b), which suggests simply that "procurement for airports by the entities listed in Annex 1" would be subject to GPA-consistent terms for US suppliers and service suppliers. According to Korea, there is no specification in General Note 1(b) of Annex 1 procurement by entities engaging in "*new* airport construction."

4.572 Korea then states that the United States was aware of Annex 1 entities - specifically, MOCT's Regional Aviation Offices - undertaking "procurement for airports," whether related to new airport construction or work on existing airports. Korea argues that the United States, therefore, knew that what Korea's General Note 1(b) meant (and means) was that Annex 1 entities conducting procurements for airports exist, and that they are MOCT's Regional Aviation Offices.

(ii) Conduct And Events

Availability of Government Organization Act

4.573 **Korea argues** that the United States knew, or should have known, that KAA was not included on Korea's Annex 1 by virtue of Note 1 thereto - that is, it knew, or should have known, that KAA was not a "subordinate linear organization," as prescribed by the Korean *Government Organization Act*. Korea states that that Act, including the list of "subordinate linear organizations" identified at Article 2(3) therein[635], was at the United States' disposal during negotiations with Korea regarding its commitments to the GPA.[636] KAA is not included in the list provided in Article 2(3) to the Act.

Failure to Enquire

4.574 **The United States argues** that the designation of KAA as IIA procurement operator came as a surprise to the United States, which had not been informed by Korea of this action. The United States asserts that, however, even assuming the United States was aware that KAA had been designated the procurement operator at that time, there would have been no need for the United States to take any specific action in response. The United States argues that as a subsidiary organization of MOCT, KAA remains covered under Annex 1 of the GPA because under a reading

[633] US Answer to Question 17 from the Panel, dated 29 November 1999.

[634] Korea's Comments on the United States' Answer to Question 17 from the Panel, dated 29 November 1999, *quoting* the United States' Answer to Question 17.

[635] *Government Organization Act*, Article 2(3).

[636] Reference to the *Government Organization Act* was included in Note 1, Annex 1 to Korea's initial GPA offer. Korea's Initial Offer to Accede to the Tokyo Round Agreement on Government Procurement, 25 June 1990.

of the plain text of Annex 1, (1) all subsidiary organizations of "central government entities" are automatically covered under Annex 1 unless otherwise specified and (2) KAA's procurements are, in fact, procurements by MOCT, pursuant to Article I of the GPA.

4.575 The United States argues that. moreover, the United States would not have taken any specific action in response to Korea's designation of KAA as project operator, because MOCT retains statutory authority under Korean law to carry out airport construction projects. The United States notes that the *Aviation Act* states that even though the Minister of Construction and Transportation can grant permission to another government entity to assume the role of project operator for a given project, "airport development projects shall be carried out by the Minister of Construction and Transportation.[637] The United States also notes that the *Aviation Act* defines "airport development projects" as "projects related to new construction, enlargement or improvement of airport facilities, executed under this Act."[638] The United States argues that, thus, because MOCT remained the entity responsible for carrying out airport development projects, there would be no reason for the United States to take any specific action following the designation of KAA as project operator.

4.576 Finally, the United States notes that documents provided by Korea indicate that even after KAA was designated by MOCT to be the project operator for the IIA project, KAA procurements were conducted by the Office of Supply - the entity responsible for procurement for Annex 1 entities and, as Korea's July 1991 responses indicate, the entity "responsible ... for procurement of goods and services relating to new airport construction. The United States also refers to its arguments in paragraph 4.520.

4.577 **In response, Korea argues** that in the two-year period between December 1991 when KAA's role in the IIA project was publicly announced and December 1993 when Korea submitted its final GPA offer, the United States did not once inquire whether or not KAA was included in Korea's offer. Korea further notes that the United States expressed surprise at the designation of KAA as the responsible IIA entity. Korea states that what is particularly unusual, in view of this surprise, is that at no time during the nearly two and one-half years between this designation and the signing of the GPA, did the United States ever note its surprise and ask where KAA appeared in Korea's Appendix I.

4.578 Korea further argues that even had the United States not been aware of the May 1991 enactment of the *Seoul Airport Act*, it has admitted that in December 1991, a full two years before the completion of negotiations for Korea's accession to the GPA, it was "surprised" at amendments to the *Seoul Airport Act* appointing KAA as the entity responsible for the IIA project.[639] Korea states that to be "surprised," it most certainly must actually have been aware of the *Act*, quite apart from the constructive knowledge with which it is charged. Korea argues that whether or not Korea expressly told the United States about the *Seoul Airport Act* in July 1991, therefore, the United States most certainly became aware of the *Act* and its implications in De-

637 *Aviation Act*, Article 1.

638 Ibid. Article 2:8.

639 US Answer to Question 23 from the Panel, dated 3 November 1999.

cember 1991 - a full two years before the completion of negotiations for Korea's accession to the GPA.[640]

4.579 **In response, the United States argues** that it is clear from the US comment regarding being surprised that the United States never indicated that it was surprised by Korea's action in 1991. The United States contends that this is pure conjecture by Korea; a plain reading of the second sentence confirms this. Indeed, to be surprised by Korea's action, the United States must have been aware of it. Yet the second sentence above begins, "even assuming the United States were aware ...," which indicates that the United States was not aware at the time, and therefore could not have been surprised at that time.[641]

4.580 **Korea also states** that given the massive effort to publicize KAA's role, no reasonable person would have supposed that a specific overture to the United States was necessary. Further, Korea asserts that given the apparent importance to the United States of attaining coverage for airport procurement entities, and given the absence of KAA from the terms of Korea's offer, the failure of the United States to seek clarification, at any time in the more than two-year period remaining in the GPA negotiations, is fatal to its claim.

4.581 Korea argues that, in these circumstances, the United States' failure to seek clarification can only mean one of two things: either it lost track of its objective, or it understood that it had not secured coverage of the entities responsible for IIA procurement.[642]

4.582 In either case, Korea states that it cannot be accorded responsibility for the United States' failure. Korea states that this does not indicate that Korea acted in bad faith and does not suggest that Korea employed a strategy of negotiation by stealth. Korea states that it is merely recognition that the United States' claim that it anticipated coverage of the entities responsible for IIA procurement was not reasonable.

4.583 Korea further argues that the United States cannot escape from this failure by arguing that it bargained in good faith for the coverage of the IIA project, without regard to which particular entity undertook procurements for the project. Korea observes in this respect that its Annex 1 commits "entities" rather than "projects." Korea argues that neither the United States nor any other party negotiated for coverage of projects under Korea's Annex 1. Korea notes that Annex 1, as opposed to other Korean Annexes, lists entities rather than projects.

4.584 **In response, the United States argues** that this assertion by Korea is contradicted by the very evidence provided in this dispute. The United States argues that during Korea's GPA accession negotiations, the United States specifically asked for "coverage of projects under Annex 1" by requesting Korea to identify "all Ministries that will be responsible for the procurement of goods and services related to new airport construction." The United States contends that Korea conceded that it under-

---

[640] Korea's Answer to Question 1 from the Panel, dated 29 November 1999.

[641] US Response to Korea's Answer to Question 1 from the Panel, dated 29 November 1999.

[642] Letter to Mr. Park, Sang-Kyun, Director, North American Trade Team, Korean Ministry of Foreign Affairs & Trade, from Karen Ware, Deputy Senior Commercial Officer, US Embassy Seoul, 6 July 1998, p. 2 ("During the period before KOACA formally is brought under the GPA, we propose that it agree to measures that would bring its procurement policies and practices de facto into conformity with the internationally-acceptable provisions of the GPA ...").

stood "that the United States' question was about the IIA project," and responded by giving "as much information as was available about what was at the time a fledgling project." The United States concludes that, thus, it is reasonable for the United States to expect that the new airport construction, *i.e.*, the Inchon airport development project, is covered under Korea's Annex 1 of the GPA. Indeed, the EC also considered it reasonable to expect coverage for the IIA project under the GPA.[643]

4.585 The United States contends that it would not have taken any specific action in response to Korea's designation of KAA as project operator, because MOCT retains statutory authority under Korean law to carry out airport construction projects. The United States notes that the *Aviation Act* of the Republic of Korea states that even though the Minister of Construction and Transportation can grant permission to another government entity to assume the role of project operator for a given project, "airport development projects shall be carried out by the Minister of Construction and Transportation."[644] The United States further notes that the *Aviation Act* defines "airport development projects" as "projects related to new construction, enlargement or improvement of airport facilities, executed under this Act."[645] The United States contends that, thus, because MOCT remained the entity responsible for carrying out airport development projects, there would be no reason for the United States to take any specific action following the designation of KAA as project operator.[646] The United States also notes that this version of the *Aviation Act* includes amendments through December 1997, and, therefore, also applied when KOACA was designated as the operator of the IIA construction project.[647]

4.586 Further, the United States notes that documents provided by Korea indicate that even after KAA was designated by MOCT to be the project operator for the Inchon Airport project, KAA procurements were conducted by the Office of Supply - the entity responsible for procurement for Annex 1 entities, and, as Korea's July 1991 responses indicate, the entity "responsible ... for procurement of goods and services relating to the new airport construction." The United States also asserts that Korea's exhibits show that the Office of Supply at times administered procurements for KAA and the Seoul and Pusan Regional Aviation Offices which Korea admits are covered under Korea's Annex 1 through MOCT's status as a central government entity, jointly on a single procurement notice. The United States asserts that this further reflects the fact that KAA procurement, like that of the Seoul and Pusan Regional Aviation Offices, is actually procurement by MOCT.[648] The United States also submits that if KAA had independent procurement authority, then presumably the Office of Supply would not have been issuing KAA procurement notices, let alone issuing them together with entities Korea agrees are covered under Annex 1 because of their relationship to MOCT.[649]

643 US Response to Korea's Answer to Question 4 from the Panel, dated 29 November 1999, referring to the European Communities' Answer to Question 5 from the Panel, dated 3 November 1999.
644 *Aviation Act*, Act. No. 4435, 14 December 1991, Articles 94-95.
645 Ibid. Article 2:8.
646 US Answer to Question 23 from the Panel, dated 3 November 1999.
647 US Answer to Question 26 from the Panel, dated 3 November 1999.
648 US Answer to Question 23 from the Panel, dated 3 November 1999.
649 US Answer to Question 26 from the Panel, dated 3 November 1999.

4.587 Further, in response to a question from the Panel, the United States notes that even assuming that US negotiators had been informed by private US companies or state and local aviation officials that KAA was now the operator of the project, it is unlikely that the United States would have requested clarification of the status of IIA procurements. In support of this argument, the United States notes it was not relevant that KAA was operating under its own procurement regulations. The United States argues that within a given "central government entity," subordinate entities often issue their own internal regulations that apply only to that entity. The United States notes that, for example, there are separate regulations that relate solely to the New Airport Development Group. The United States further notes that, moreover, the regulations of KAA (like all other subordinate units of covered central government agencies) would be required to come into conformity with the GPA only after the Agreement entered into force for Korea.[650] More specifically, the United States notes that these central government regulations did not come into existence until 1997 when Korea implemented the GPA, so the fact that KAA did not utilize the central government regulations for IIA procurement would not be of concern to the United States in 1991-1993.[651]

4.588 **In response, Korea notes** that it is not true that KAA's use of its own Contract Administration Regulations for IIA procurements during the period 1991-1994 was merely a result of the fact that "central government [procurement] regulations did not come into existence until 1997." Korea states that the government procurement regulations in effect during this period were included in the *Korean Budget and Accounting Act*. Korea notes that rather than being required to follow those rules, KAA drafted and adopted its own regulations.

4.589 Korea also notes that although it is true that the Office of Supply has procured for KAA, this does not mean that those procurements are covered by the GPA since Office of Supply procurements are only covered when made for entities listed on Annex 1. KAA is not, Korea asserts, included on Annex 1.[652] Korea also states that the Office of Supply has not in fact procured for the IIA[653], and that the procurements cited by the United States[654], were not for the IIA, which is exclusively the subject of the Panel's terms of reference.[655]

Failure to Inform

4.590 **The United States contends** that despite Korea's claim that "virtually every major airport construction expert and airport or aviation organization in the world"

---

650 US Answer to Question 25(a) from the Panel, dated 3 November 1999. The United States further notes that, in fact, the four primary enforcement decrees and regulations relating to the Act Relating to Contracts to Which a State is a Party—Korea's primary procurement law implementing its GPA commitments, entered into effect on 31 December 1996, one day before Korea's GPA commitments took effect.

651 US Answer to Question 26 from the Panel, dated 3 November 1999.

652 Korea's Statement for the Second Meeting of the Panel, para. 47.

653 Korea's Answer to Question 2 from the Panel, dated 29 November 1999.

654 Exhibits Kor-61D and Kor-61E.

655 Korea's Comments on the United States' Answer to Question 22 from the Panel, dated 29 November 1999.

was aware that MOCT shifted IIA procurement from the New Airport Development Group to KAA, Korea did not once inform its GPA negotiating partners of this supposed change in its negotiating position. The United States argues that Korea cannot expect to alter its concessions offer during international trade negotiations without directly and officially notifying the relevant government representatives involved.

4.591 The United States also states that it remains very concerned about Korea's assertions that if a country makes an express material representation to its negotiating partner, but then later it changes its mind, it is under no obligation to inform its negotiating partner, yet it can still expect its express representation to be no longer valid. The United States argues that by making express commitments which Korea should have expected its negotiating partners would rely on, and then refraining from informing them when it acted to change the status quo to which it had committed, Korea created a legitimate expectation among its GPA negotiating partners that its airport procurement was covered through its listing of MOCT and the Office of Supply.

4.592 **Korea argues in response** that the United States implicitly asserts that Korea altered its offer during negotiations without directly and officially notifying the United States and other concerned governments. Korea states that there are a number of reasons why this assertion is not applicable. First, it assumes that Korea's "concessions offer" was altered during negotiations. Korea notes that the only "evidence" put forward by the United States to support this argument is Korea's July 1991 response to the US inquiry. Korea argues that this is hardly a "concessions offer." According to Korea, this was a response to an inquiry.

4.593 Korea states that, second, even if the July 1991 response is deemed to be a "concessions offer," and even if it is interpreted as the United States would interpret it, Korea, through the formal designation of KAA as the responsible entity, by action of the National Assembly in December 1991, did notify the United States of its position. This was more than constructive notice. Korea asserts that the United States had actual notice and that the United States was even "surprised" by it.

(d) Evidence Following Korea's Accession

(i) The US July 1998 Communications

4.594 **Korea argues** that the United States was also aware of KOACA's role in IIA procurement. Korea argues that in a July 1998 letter from the US Embassy in Seoul to the Korean Ministry of Foreign Affairs & Trade, the United States acknowledged that KAA's successor for the IIA project, KOACA, was not covered.[656]

4.595 Korea notes that in the July 1998 letter, the United States proposed that "[d]uring the period before KOACA formally is brought under the GPA," Korea "agrees to measures that would bring its procurement policies and practices de facto

[656] Letter to Mr. Park, Sang-Kyun, Director, North American Trade Team, Korean Ministry of Foreign Affairs & Trade, from Karen Ware, Deputy Senior Commercial Officer, US Embassy Seoul, 6 July 1998, p. 2 ("During the period before KOACA formally is brought under the GPA, we propose that it agree to measures that would bring its procurement policies and practices de facto into conformity with the internationally-acceptable provisions of the GPA ...").

into conformity with the internationally-acceptable provisions of the GPA ..."[657] Korea argues that if KOACA is not yet "formally brought under the GPA," it is not a covered entity, thus necessitating the US request that KOACA bring its practices "de facto into conformity with the ... GPA." Korea further argues that had the United States considered that KOACA was a covered entity, it would surely not have requested de facto compliance with the GPA; it would have demanded *de jure* compliance.

(ii) MOCT's Website

4.596 **Korea notes** that the events to which the United States points to support its claimed expectations all date after the signing of the GPA. Korea states that this is particularly true of MOCT's website, which was not created until 1997. Korea argues that regardless of what claims MOCT makes on that website, those claims could in no way have influenced the United States three years earlier in April 1994, when the GPA was signed.

V. ARGUMENTS OF THIRD PARTIES (EUROPEAN COMMUNITIES)[658]

A. Entities Covered under Korea's Appendix I of the GPA

1. Interpretation of Appendix I and Notes

5.1 **The European Communities argues** that, in accordance with Article 18 of the *Vienna Convention on the Law of Treaties*, regard must be had to the common intentions of the Parties in determining the content and scope of their respective obligations under the GPA.

5.2 In support, the European Communities referred to the Appellate Body decision in the LAN case where it was stated that[659]:

> "The purpose of treaty interpretation under Article 31 of the Vienna Convention is to ascertain the common intentions of the parties. These common intentions cannot be ascertained on the basis of the subjective and unilaterally determined "expectations" of one of the parties to a treaty. Tariff concessions provided for in a Member's Schedule - the interpretation of which is at issue here - are reciprocal and result from a mutually-advantageous negotiation between importing and exporting Members."

5.3 The European Communities argues that the same reasoning, *mutatis mutandis*, should apply to this case.

---

[657] Letter to Mr. Park, Sang-Kyun, Director, North American Trade Team, Korean Ministry of Foreign Affairs & Trade, from Karen Ware, Deputy Senior Commercial Officer, US Embassy Seoul, 6 July 1998, p. 2.

[658] While Japan also reserved its rights as a Third Party to this dispute, it did not make any submissions for this case.

[659] Appellate Body Report, EC - *LAN*, *supra*, footnote 106, para. 84.

5.4 The European Communities further argues that the issue of what was the intention of Korea during the negotiations is legally irrelevant. According to the European Communities, the only matter that counts is how the common intention of the GPA Contracting Parties were expressed in the actual text of the agreement, having regard to the ordinary meaning of its terms in their context and the object and purpose of the Agreement.[660]

2. *Annex 1, Appendix I: the Scope of "Central Government Entities"*

(a) The Ordinary Meaning of "Central Government Entities"

5.5 **The European Communities believes** that the definition in Korea's GPA concession which includes the Ministry of Transport and Construction implies the inclusion of all entities hierarchically under that Ministry. The European Communities argues that the entities responsible for IIA's construction remained hierarchically subject to MOCT after 1991, and, further, were so on 15 April 1994.[661]

(b) The "Control" Test

5.6 **The European Communities argues** that the "control" test proposed by the United States to determine whether certain entities are covered by Annex 1 of the GPA is an incorrect yardstick in order to measure the extent of Korea's obligations under the GPA.

5.7 **The European Communities discusses**, by way of illustrative argument, the hypothetical case of procurement in the United States in similar circumstances to that which exist for the IIA project. Specifically, the European Communities considers, for example, the case of construction of a new North Dakota International Airport where the US Government transfers responsibility for the project to one of the authorities of a state which is not covered by the GPA. The European Communities states that, in such a case, the issue would not be, as the US suggests, whether that procurement is 'guided', 'supervised', 'inspected' or 'directed' by any covered entity. The European Communities further argues that, in fact, the relations between the federal government's covered entities and North Dakota's authorities would probably not correspond to those definitions.

5.8 The European Communities states that, in its view, the US would not be able to escape its obligations under the GPA which it undertook in 1994 by merely transferring responsibility to a non-covered entity in such a case. Rather, the United States would be obliged to duly notify the other GPA Contracting Parties of the transfer under Article XXIV:6 and to follow entirely the procedures laid down in that provision.

[660] EC's Answers to Panel's Questions, dated 29 November 1999, Preliminary Observations citing Article 31 of the *Vienna Convention*.

[661] EC's Answer to Question 5 from the Panel, dated 29 November 1999.

3. Annex 1, Appendix I: Note 1

(a) Ordinary Meaning of Note 1 to Annex 1

5.9 **The European Communities refers** to what it calls a "novel" interpretation by Korea of its Note 1 to Annex 1. The European Communities quotes the Korean argument as follows:

> "(...) Note 1 to Korea's Annex 1 provides the exclusive means by which to identify as Annex 1 covered entities those entities that, while not literally listed on Annex 1, are nonetheless considered Annex 1 covered entities by virtue of their relationships with entities listed on Annex 1. Under the ordinary meaning of Note 1 to Korea's Annex 1, the Panel is directed, exclusively, to the Government Organization Act of the Republic of Korea to determine whether particular entities not specifically included in Annex 1 are nonetheless considered covered entities by virtue of their status as subordinate linear organizations, special local administrative organs or attached organs."

5.10 The European Communities argues that the interpretation of Note 1 suggested by Korea does not correspond to its ordinary meaning. The European Communities asserts that according to the ordinary meaning and the syntax of the English language, the part of the sentence in Note 1 "as prescribed in the *Government Organization Act* of the Republic of Korea" can in fact only be a reference to the preceding words "attached organs" and not also to the earlier part - that is, "subordinate linear organizations" and to "local administrative organs." The European Communities further argues that, in fact, in order for this latter interpretation to apply, the text should have included a comma after the word "organ." However, the European Communities notes that the comma does not appear in the text.

5.11 The European Communities argues that the only correct reading of Note 1 is as follows: "The above central government entities include their subordinate linear organizations [like KAA, KOACA or IIAC]; special local administrative organs; and attached organs as prescribed in the *Government Organization Act* of the Republic of Korea."

5.12 The European Communities argues that this interpretation is confirmed by the text of Article 2(3) of the Korean *Government Organization Act* and by comments made by Korea:

> "(...) Article 2(3) [of the Government Organization Act of the Republic of Korea]- both in its current form and as it existed during the negotiations leading up to the submission by Korea of its final offer list for accession to the GPA - identifies not entities, but officials within a ministry's hierarchy."

5.13 The European Communities states that, thus, the words "as prescribed in the *Government Organization Act* of the Republic of Korea" logically cannot refer to "their subordinate linear organizations" since the Act identifies, according to Korea's own interpretation, officials, not organizations.

5.14 **In response, Korea states** that the European Communities arguments regarding interpretation of Article 2(3) of the *Government Organizations Act* are erroneous. Korea states that the modification of Note 1 offered by the European Communities, itself proves the point. Korea states that had it meant the reference to the *Government Organization Act* to modify only the term "attached organs," it would have used the semi-colons inserted by the European Communities after the terms "subordinate linear organizations" and "special local administrative organs." Korea notes that it did not do so.

5.15 Korea notes that, moreover, the fact that the rather unusual and unique English terms "subordinate linear organizations" and "special local administrative organs" are used and are specifically defined in the first three articles of the *Government Organization Act* is more than coincidence. Korea states that it confirms that the reference to the *Government Organization Act* in Note 1 is to modify those terms of art as well as the term "attached organs," defined in Article 4 of the *Government Organization Act*. Korea further states that all three of the terms in Note 1 to Korea's Annex 1 are defined "as prescribed in the *Government Organization Act* of the Republic of Korea." Korea concludes that no other reading of that language is sensible.

(b) Are the IIA Procuring Entities Subordinate Linear Organizations?

5.16 **The European Communities argues** that there is clear evidence indicating that KAA, KOACA and IIAC are "subsidiary organizations" within the meaning of the *Government Organization Act*.

5.17 The European Communities notes that at the time of the entry into force of the GPA, MOCT was in charge of aviation construction works.

5.18 The European Communities states that by Korea's own admission:

> KAA itself was established (under the name "Korea International Airports Authority") on 30 May 1980 as an independent public corporation pursuant to the International Airport Management Corporation Act, as enacted on 28 December 1979...[662]
>
> The chairman, deputy chairmen and auditor [of KAA] are [were] appointed by MOCT...[663] KAA is [was] subject to the 'direction and supervision' of the MOCT, which as stated in Article 28(1) of the Korea Airport Corporation Act permits MOCT to require KAA to submit to certain reporting and inspection requirements concerning activities of the Corporation. Specifically, pursuant to Article 28(2) of the Korea Airport Corporation Act, MOCT is to ensure that KAA officials do not commit 'unlawful or unreasonable acts.[664]

5.19 The European Communities argues that it follows that, at the time of the signature of the GPA, Korea itself admits that KAA was a "subordinate linear organization" within the meaning of the *Government Organization Act* (i.e., a subsidiary or subordinate body) of MOCT which had a very large degree of control over KAA. In the view of the European Communities, Korea's own statements confirms this. The European Communities also claim that the clear understanding of the entire business community and of all the other GPA Contracting Parties on 15 April 1994 was that MOCT was in fact running the entire Inchon Airport business and that KAA was nothing more than an articulation of such Ministries.

---

[662] Korea's First Written Submission, para. 23.
[663] Ibid. para. 24.
[664] Ibid. para. 25.

5.20 The European Communities concludes that KAA should be considered as "'attached/connected/affiliated' etc." to MOCT because of the control or decisive influence that the MOCT has over the KAA and, thus, over its procurement procedures. According to the European Communities, the KAA is, therefore, covered by the definition of "subordinate linear organizations" in Appendix I, Note 1 to Annex 1, of the Korean concession.[665]

4. *Appendix I: Note 1(b)*

5.21 The European Communities asserts that procurement for airports is covered by the original GPA Korean obligations. The European Communities argues that this is confirmed by the text of General Note 1(b) in Appendix I, which expressly subjects "procurement for airports by the entities listed in Annex 1" to a reciprocity clause *vis-à-vis* the European Communities and some other European Contracting Parties.

5.22 **In response, Korea notes** that in March 1993 the European Communities stated that Korea had made "no offer regarding airports." Korea states that the EC now asserts that this March 1993 statement was in reference to Korea's exclusion of the EC from airport procurement via General Note 1(b).[666] Korea further states that, however, this assertion follows acknowledgement by the European Communities that General Note 1(b) was added "for the first time" in Korea's third offer, dated 14 December 1993.[667] Korea argues that by its own chronology, the European Communities could not have known of Korea's General Note 1(b) until December 1993. In Korea's view, its statement concerning "no offer regarding airports" nine months earlier, in March, could not have referred to General Note 1(b). Korea states that, more importantly, the EC's statement in March 1993 that Korea made "no offer regarding airports" means all airports, which, according to Korea, includes the IIA. Korea argues that, whatever the accuracy of the EC statement in March 1993, it demonstrates that the EC did not expect coverage for all airports, including the IIA.

5.23 **In response to a question from the Panel, the European Communities argues** that during bilateral meetings between Korea and the European Communities in November and December 1993, Korea "declared" that airports were covered. In support of this argument, the European Communities produced a letter from the Commission of the European Communities to the Korean Ministry of Trade and Industry, dated 24 November 1993, which stated:

> "With regard to the inclusion of airports in your offer, you and your colleagues pointed out that generally they depend on the Ministry of Transportation, which is offered. I would be most grateful if you could provide me with some more detail about which airports are included in your offer by virtue of the inclusion of the Ministry of Transportation, or are otherwise included. Furthermore, if airports under the Ministry of Transportation are covered, does that imply that OSROK carries out their procurement on their behalf? Does that also apply to

---

665 EC's Answer to Question 7 from the Panel, dated 29 November 1999.

666 EC Answer to Question 4 from the Panel, dated 3 November 1999.

667 EC Answer to Question 3 (point 5) from the Panel, dated 3 November 1999.

ports which are under the authority of the Korea Maritime and Port Administration?"[668]

5.24 In responding to the Panel's question, the European Communities also refers to an internal Commission document, dated 3 December 1993, which stated:

> "Airports
> The Korean side has explained that a number of major cities (Seoul, Pusang), which are offered, control their airports in co-operation with the Ministry of Transportation. We have requested confirmation in writing."[669]

5.25 **Korea responds** that its February 1991 *Supplementary Explanation* indicates that the 24 November 1993 EC letter was referring to procurements by MOCT's Seoul and Pusan Regional Aviation Offices. Moreover, according to Korea, the 3 December 1993 internal EC note supports this conclusion. The 3 December 1993 note refers to Korea's offer of coverage for "a number of major cities (Seoul, Pusang) [sic]" that "control their airports in co-operation with the Ministry of Transportation." Korea notes that MOCT's two Regional Aviation Offices are in fact the Seoul and the Pusan Regional Aviation Offices, and that these two Offices are in fact covered under Korea's Annex 1 commitment to coverage of MOCT.[670]

5. *Amendments to the Appendix under Article XXIV:6*

(a) The Obligations Under Article XXIV:6

5.26 **The European Communities argues** that Korea attempted to modify its obligations under the GPA and in so doing, failed to comply with Article XXIV:6 of the GPA.

5.27 The European Communities argues that Article XXIV:6(a) of the GPA is expressly based on the principle of the maintenance of the balance of concessions. According to the European Communities, it corresponds, *mutatis mutandis*, to the fundamental provision of Article XXVIII GATT 1994[671] and is the expression in the GPA of the general principle of public international law codified in Article 26 of the *Vienna Convention on the Law of Treaties*.

5.28 The European Communities states that, according to Article XXIV:6 of the GPA, no GPA Contracting Party is allowed to alter in any way, either in form or in substance, its concessions as specified in the Appendices to the GPA, unless and until the procedures thereunder have been duly and entirely followed.

---

[668] Annex IV to EC Answers to Question 3 from the Panel, dated 3 November 1999.

[669] Annex V to EC Answers to Question 3 from the Panel, dated 3 November 1999.

[670] Korea's Response to the European Communities' Answer to Question 1 from the Panel, dated 29 November 1999.

[671] The European Communities refers in particular to Article XXVIII.2.

5.29 For support of its argument, the European Communities relies upon the following statement by the Appellate Body[672]:

> "The chapeau of Article 5.5 clearly states that the schedule in the body of that provision is mandatory. The word used in the chapeau is 'shall', not 'may'. There is no qualifying language, and there is no language that permits any method other than that set out in the schedule in Article 5.5 as a basis for the calculation of additional duties."

5.30 The European Communities states that in cases under both Article XXIV:6(a) and (b), a procedure is foreseen with ultimately the necessity of 'compensatory adjustments.' According to the European Communities, if the word 'shall' in either paragraph could be interpreted as anything less than a binding obligation, both paragraphs would become redundant. The European Communities states, in the words of the Appellate Body:

> "[o]ne of the corollaries of the 'general rule of interpretation' in the Vienna Convention is that interpretation must give meaning and effect to all the terms of the treaty. An interpreter is not free to adopt a reading that would result in reducing whole clauses or paragraphs of a treaty to redundancy or inutility."[673]

(b) Application of Article XXIV:6 to the Present Case

5.31 **The European Communities argues** that, notwithstanding these clear and indisputable obligations, Korea did not follow the procedures under Article XXIV:6.
5.32 The European Communities argues that Korea failed to notify the creation of KOACA, the alleged transfer of the authority for airport construction procurement to that entity, the alleged separation of that entity from the Ministry of Transport, and the transformation of KOACA into IIAC under Article XXIV:6.
5.33 The European Communities argues that Korea cannot claim now that KOACA and/or IIAC are not covered alleging *ex post* that they are separate from those covered in the original concession because it will automatically admit that it did not offer to the other GPA Contracting Parties, as it was unconditionally compelled, compensatory adjustments, with a view to maintaining a balance of rights and obligations and a comparable level of mutually agreed coverage.
5.34 In the view of the European Communities, the only relevant date that determines the point of reference for the implementation of Article XXIV:6 procedures is 15 April 1994 being the date of the official conclusion of the Uruguay Round and of signature of the GPA by all Contracting Parties, including Korea.
5.35 In support of its argument, the European Communities refers to Article 18 of the *Vienna Convention on the Law of Treaties* which states as follows:

> "[a] State is obliged to refrain from acts which would defeat the object and purpose of a treaty when:

---

[672] Appellate Body Report, *European Communities - Measures Affecting The Importation Of Certain Poultry Products* ("*EC – Poultry*"), WT/DS69/AB/R, adopted 23 July 1998, DSR 1998:V, 2031, para. 165.
[673] Panel Report, *US - Gasoline, supra*, footnote 105, at 21. See also Appellate Body Report, *Japan - Alcoholic Beverages II, supra*, footnote 105, at 106.

> (a) it has signed the treaty or has exchanged instruments constituting the treaty subject to ratification, acceptance or approval, until it shall have made its intention clear not to become a party to the treaty; or
>
> (b) it has expressed its consent to be bound by the treaty, pending the entry into force of the treaty and provided that such entry into force is not unduly delayed."

5.36 The European Communities refers to the Appellate Body decision in the LAN[674] case where it stated that:

> "A Schedule is made an integral part of the GATT 1994 by Article II:7 of the GATT 1994. Therefore, the concessions provided for in that Schedule are part of the terms of the treaty."

5.37 The European Communities argues that the same conclusion must be drawn from Article XXIV:12 of the GPA.

5.38 The European Communities further argues that the relevant date for Korean legislation and practice to be in conformity with the 1994 GPA was the date of entry into force of the 1994 GPA (for Korea: 1 January 1997), and thereafter. The European Communities states that Korea was, in its view, entitled to change its legislation before its entry into force, as long as it ensured that it complied from 1 January 1997 onwards with its obligations as they were undertaken on 15 April 1994.[675]

5.39 The European Communities argues that, as from 1 January 1997[676], pursuant to Article XXIV:6(a) and (b), Korea is unconditionally obliged to notify any change of its concessions as specified in the Appendices to the GPA - in particular Appendix I - that may have taken place since 15 April 1994. The European Communities notes further that if the modifications go beyond a mere formal correction of the text, it is unconditionally obliged to offer compensatory adjustment for those changes, with a view to maintaining a balance of rights and obligations and a comparable level of mutually agreed coverage provided in the GPA prior to the notification. The European Communities asserts that Korea clearly failed to do so.

5.40 **Korea responds** that its decision not to notify the "transfers of authority" for IIA procurement to and between KAA, KOACA and IIAC on the basis that those entities are not covered under the GPA does not constitute admission that "compensatory adjustments" were due to other GPA signatories. According to Korea, since neither KAA, KOACA nor IIAC are covered, "transfers" between them did not trigger the notification requirement of Article XXIV:6(a). Moreover, the "transfer" of IIA procurement authority to KAA took place in December 1991, at which time Korea was not bound by any GPA obligations, including those contained in Article XXIV:6(a).

(c) Shifting of an Entity from Annex 1 to Annex 3

5.41 **In response to a question from the Panel, the European Communities notes** that there is an explicit provision allowing for Korean National Railway Ad-

---

674 Appellate Body Report, *E C - Computer Equipment*, *supra*, footnote 106, para. 84.

675 EC's Answer to Question 5 from the Panel, dated 29 November 1999.

676 Date of application of the Agreement to Korea.

ministration (NRA) to be moved from Annex 1 to Annex 3 (once that it adopts the form of a public corporation) without any consultation and/or compensation.

5.42 The European Communities argues that this implies, *a contrario*, that, in the absence of a similar provision, a Party to the GPA can not even move an entity from one GPA Appendix I annex to another without following the appropriate consultation procedure. The European Communities asserts that this also implies, *a fortiori*, that a Party of the GPA cannot unilaterally remove an entity from all the annexes of the GPA without following the appropriate procedures (and offering adequate compensation) under Article XXIV:6 of the GPA.[677]

5.43 The European Communities states that, as a matter of fact, NRA was in a situation similar to that of KOACA, i.e., it simply changed its legal form but remained under government control. However, the European Communities goes on to state that (a) contrary to NRA, the GPA does not provide for an explicit exception applying to KOACA and (b) in any event, the solution adopted for NRA was not at all the exclusion of this entity from GPA coverage, but its transferral to another annex.[678]

VI. INTERIM REVIEW[679]

6.1 In letters dated 13 March 2000, the United States and Korea requested an interim review by the Panel of certain aspects of the Interim Report issued to the parties on 3 March 2000. The United States made several further comments regarding the Descriptive Part of the Report. Both parties requested review and amendments with respect to certain portions of the Findings. Neither party requested an Interim Review Meeting. On 24 March 2000, the United States requested that the Panel permit it to submit further comments regarding Korea's Interim Review comments. The Panel granted the request and, in the interests of fairness, also permitted Korea to make further comments, which Korea did on 29 March 2000.

6.2 Korea made several specific comments on a number of paragraphs which we will address below. However, Korea also submitted a covering letter noting that the Panel has appeared critical of Korea's actions with respect to events that occurred in mid to late-1991 regarding one of the questions submitted by the United States and Korea's response thereto. The facts are clear and we stand by our assessment of them.[680] We also find Korea's arguments in their covering letter misplaced. Korea appears to have mis-read the Findings.

6.3 First, we must note what we did not do in the Findings. We specifically did not make a finding that Korea acted in bad faith, or attempted to mislead or deceive the United States as Korea claims in its letter of 13 March 2000. We did not delve into the motivations of the Korean Government. We did not make a finding that the

677 EC's Answer to Question 1 from the Panel to Third Parties, dated 3 November 1999, p. 2.

678 Ibid.

679 Pursuant to Article 15.3 of the DSU, the findings of a panel report shall include a discussion of the arguments made at the interim review stage. Consequently, the following section entitled Interim Review is part of the Findings of this Panel Report.

680 See, among others, paras. 7.76-7.81, 7.104-7.110 and 7.121-7.122 and cross-references contained therein.

Korean Government was trying to conceal information from the United States. It is entirely possible that simple errors took place. We will add a footnote to paragraph 7.80 reiterating that we are not making a determination that Korea acted in bad faith. We will also make some minor modifications to the language in paragraphs 7.80 and 7.119 without altering the sense of our conclusions.

6.4 Second, we are concerned by the substantive comments made by Korea in this regard. The thrust of Korea's argument in their covering letter to their comments is that the answer provided to the United States in July 1991 was drafted by the Ministry of Commerce. Korea argues that the Korean Government is not a monolith and that the Ministry of Commerce should not be charged with knowledge about actions taken by the Ministry of Transportation when answering such questions. The impression given by Korea in its Interim Review comments is that the only piece of written and documented evidence before us of the negotiations between Korea and the United States[681] was the responsibility of a single individual in a single Ministry without actual or imputed knowledge of the subject-matter of the questions put to the Korean Government by the US Government. We do not find this at all compelling.

6.5 We note that this argument was previously made by Korea during the course of the proceedings and was fully taken into account by us in coming to our Findings. Furthermore, in our view, Korea is simply wrong in making such an argument. The Parties to the GPA did not expect incomplete or even possibly inaccurate answers from one portion of the Korean Government speaking only for itself. The answers *must* be on behalf of the whole of the Korean Government. Negotiations would be impossible otherwise. The Korean Government chose who was tasked with answering the questions and the Korean Government cannot avoid responsibility for the result. It cannot be a justifiable excuse for incomplete answers that an applicant for accession to the GPA gave responsibility to Ministry A to answer questions, but the projects and procurement responsibilities were really the concern of Ministry B and Ministry A was ignorant of the true situation when it provided answers. In our view, and as we stated in the Findings, there is an affirmative duty on the part of a Party or prospective Party to the GPA to answer such questions fully, comprehensively and on behalf of the whole government.[682] This conclusion is supported by the long es-

---

[681] In its covering letter for its Interim Review comments, Korea stated that it took a series of public actions that would have contradicted any implication that the United States was misled. Korea cites, among other things, "the preparation of communications to the European Communities clear enough to convince the EC that the entity responsible for IIA procurement was not covered by Korea's offer." Aside from repeating that we made no findings regarding Korea's motivations or intent, we recall our statement in para. 7.116 of the Findings that the United States is not charged with knowledge of bilateral communications between Korea and the European Communities. Furthermore, while we note that Korea is drawing a conclusion from the EC's response to Korea's communication of November or December 1993 that such communication was clear and convincing, we will refrain from agreeing with that characterization ourselves because Korea was unable to produce the document when requested.

[682] The Panel never dealt with a question of attributing information from one official to another. This is a construct of Korea's later taken up by the United States in its second Interim Review comments. The Panel's point is much more straightforward. In the context of negotiations, a communication from a Member government is considered to be on behalf of the government as a whole and cannot later be disavowed as the actions of a mere individual or Ministry.

tablished international law principles of State responsibility. The actions and even omissions of State organs acting in that capacity are attributable to the State as such and engage its responsibility under international law.[683]

6.6 One further anomaly of Korea's position is that it implies that other GPA Parties are charged with a higher degree of knowledge of Korean legislation than the Korean Government itself. Korea argues that the United States was charged with knowledge of its laws, including the *Seoul Airport Act* which came into effect on 31 May 1991, at least one month prior to Korea's response to the US questions.[684] On the other hand, Korea now strenuously argues that another Ministry of the Korean Government should not also be charged with such knowledge. This is a double standard we clearly do not accept.

6.7 Finally, we must also note our doubts about the position taken by Korea on this issue for purposes of this dispute. Korea asserts that the official at the Ministry of Commerce who answered the questions simply did not know about the actions underway at the Ministry of Transportation regarding the IIA project. However, aside from the fact that this supposedly ill-informed official replied to the US questions with 29 pages of extensive answers, as stated by Korea in its Interim Review comments of 13 March 2000, we note that the answer on the particular question at issue did provide some specific details. For example, it was stated that the New Airport Development Group was conducting airport construction. Even more specifically, the answer identified by name a US company taking part in the basic plan projects. It is not clear how such details could be known to the Ministry of Commerce officials who Korea now says were ignorant of the actions of the Ministry of Transportation. Had an inquiry into the motivations or lack thereof on the part of the Korean Government regarding the answer provided to the United States been relevant or probative, we would have followed up this issue in detail. We did not and we decline to do so now.

6.8 In making the above statements, we recall our determination that our inquiry in this matter could not stop with the events of 1991 and our Findings rest upon a weighing of all the facts of the dispute. Other than the addition noted in paragraph 6.3 above, we decline to make any of the changes requested by Korea in its covering letter to the Panel.

6.9 As noted, Korea made some specific technical comments on the Interim Report. We have made technical changes and corrections as requested in paragraphs 7.28, 7.33, 7.45, 7.66 (footnote 726), 7.110, 7.115, 7.120 and 7.125 (footnote 768).

6.10 With respect to paragraph 7.55, Korea states that it is its position that the "control" test contained in the Tokyo Round GPA was eliminated during the Uruguay

---

683 See the draft articles on State Responsibility drafted by the International Law Commission, Articles 5 and 6 and Commentary, *Yearbook of the International Law Commission* (1973), Vol. II, p. 173 *et seq*. See also *Corfu Channel Case*, 1949 ICJ Reports, p. 23; *US Diplomatic and Consular Staff in Tehran*, ICJ Reports 1980, pp. 30-31 and 33. These principles of attributability of actions of organs of the State must also function where it concerns communications of a State organ, particularly in the context of negotiations of a plurilateral agreement such as the GPA. Otherwise Parties to the GPA could not rely upon each other's communications, which ultimately could result in the breakdown of the treaty system itself.

684 Para. 4.544.

Round and that it was the United States that argued that the new annexes to the GPA made the test redundant. However, Korea did make the following statement in its Second Submission to the Panel:

> "If the United States "control" test were to prevail, Annex 3 would in such instances become redundant; entities listed on Annex 3 are subject to a degree of control by Annex 1 entities that would subject them, under the United States' test, to coverage under Annex 1."[685]

This statement implies the argument that the Panel attributed to Korea. However, we do note that it was made in the context of a broader argument made to rebut the US position. Therefore, we will clarify the language in paragraph 7.55.

6.11 With respect to paragraph 7.125, Korea requests that we add an additional reference to the parenthetical reference to evidence that the US Government and industry was aware of KAA's role in IIA procurement. Korea argues that we made such a reference in paragraph 7.115. We note that there is already a cross-reference in the previous sentence (by way of footnote 767) to paragraphs 7.104-7.116. Also, the use of the term "such as" indicates that the parenthetical phrase is illustrative and not comprehensive. Therefore, we see no need to expand the parenthetical phrase further.

6.12 With respect to the Factual Aspects section of the Report, the United States requests that paragraph 2.64 be further clarified to remove any possible implication that any version of the *Seoul Airport Act* designated KAA or its successors as the operators of the IIA project. It is the case that other laws made the specific designations, so we will change paragraph 2.64 accordingly.

6.13 With respect to paragraph 2.87, the United States requests that it would be appropriate to refer to the language of the original version of the *Korea Airport Corporation Act* when discussing the constitution of KAA.[686] We have made a change to clarify that the quoted provision is from the 1994 version of the Act.

6.14 With respect to paragraphs 2.95 and 2.113, the United States objects to including in this section a statement to the effect that KAA and KOACA employees and directors are not government employees. The United States considers this an unsubstantiated assertion made by Korea. Aside from the point that we do not have any reason to doubt this representation, we also note that, for example, Article 30 of the *Korean Airport Corporation Act* provides that KAA employees shall be considered government employees for specific limited purposes relating to certain criminal acts. The clear implication of this is that they are not considered government employees for all other purposes. Further, we note that the footnotes to paragraphs 2.95 and 2.113 clearly indicate that Korea's submissions are the source for these paragraphs. Thus, we think it is appropriate to leave these paragraphs as part of the Factual Aspects of the Panel's Report and in relevant portions of the Findings.

6.15 With respect to the Arguments of the Parties section, the United States asserts that this section represents an incomplete summary of arguments presented by the parties. We cannot agree with this assertion. All the arguments and rebuttals are fully

---

[685] Second Written Submission of Korea at para. 159.

[686] We note that the United States referred us to US Exhibit 20 for the 1979 version of the Act, but such version does not appear to be contained in that or any other exhibit.

reflected in the Report in essentially their original form.[687] We also arranged the parties' arguments under headings and in a sequence such that the arguments raised by the parties were addressed in the most logical and coherent way. In so doing, the Panel did its utmost to ensure that the context in which the arguments and rebuttals were raised by the parties was preserved. Additionally, the Panel sought to avoid unnecessary duplication of arguments. Since the parties often repeated arguments in their submissions, sometimes verbatim, we considered that it was sufficient to state those arguments in the most relevant section or sections and to include cross-references to those arguments in other sections where necessary. For example, this approach was adopted in relation to the additions proposed by the United States to paragraphs 4.232 and 4.239. In summary, in our view, the Descriptive Part of the Report contains a fair and accurate presentation of the parties' arguments and we cannot agree with the assertion by the United States that the Descriptive Part of the Report is skewed.

6.16 A further comment made by the United States is that this section of the Report separates textual arguments from supporting evidence which, according to the United States, results in the removal of such evidence from its context and its logical order. Again, we cannot agree with this comment. The United States argued, and the Panel agrees, that Articles 31 and 32 of the *Vienna Convention on the Law of Treaties* applies to this case. According to those Articles, regard must be had first to textual arguments in determining the meaning of Korea's Schedule. Supporting evidence in the form of preparatory work and the circumstances of the conclusion of the GPA should only be referred to in cases where a textual interpretation leads to a meaning that is ambiguous or obscure or would lead to a manifestly absurd result. Recourse also may be had to such materials to confirm the ordinary meaning of the text. Accordingly, the Panel believes that the separation of textual arguments from supporting non-textual evidence is appropriate. As an example, we note that this approach was adopted in relation to the addition proposed by the United States to paragraph 4.58. Finally, we note that we have made the amendments requested by the United States in relation to paragraph 4.45 but not in relation to paragraph 4.434 since the proposed amendment is already included in the next paragraph.

6.17 With respect to paragraph 7.17, the United States requests an amendment noting that control was but one aspect of the test it proposed. We recognize that the United States asserted more than just "control" and, indeed, we have throughout the Findings taken a very broad approach in our analysis as we explicitly stated in paragraph 7.57 and then followed-up fully in the subsections following that paragraph. What we are focusing on in paragraph 7.17 is the question of control which was the element most strongly emphasized by the United States. Then we proceeded to the broader examination. Thus, we think paragraph 7.17 is appropriate in context and decline to amend it.

---

[687] In this dispute, the United States recommended that the Panel dispense with the conventional Descriptive Part and append the parties' submissions to the Report. We indicated our willingness to adopt this approach as long as Korea agreed. In the event, Korea was unable to agree to such an approach and, therefore, we have undertaken the task to provide an extensive summary of the parties' arguments. It follows that we have not inserted the arguments verbatim in precisely the form originally submitted.

6.18 With respect to paragraph 7.18, the United States requests that we eliminate the portion of the first sentence concerning transfer of authority to KAA because the United States does not agree that any such transfer took place. We agree that the sentence should be amended to remove any implication that the United States agreed with such an interpretation of the *Seoul Airport Act*. The United States also requested several additions to its arguments. We will expand the reference to the US position, but recall that the full explanation of the US position is found in its submissions which are reflected in the Descriptive Part of this Report. The Findings are not the place to re-introduce such arguments in extensive detail.

6.19 With respect to paragraph 7.29, the United States requests that we amend the paragraph to reflect that MOCT has been directly responsible. If the United States means that MOCT was directly responsible throughout the period in question, obviously we disagree and decline to make the requested change. However, we will amend the paragraph to reflect that KAA, KOACA and IIAC have been responsible for the IIA project subsequent to enactment of the *Seoul Airport Act*.

6.20 With respect to paragraph 7.47, the United States requests that we include a number of other bureaus that were not included in the list provided in the portion of the *Supplementary Explanation* quoted in paragraph 7.46. However, our observation in paragraph 7.47 is limited to the subject of aviation bureaus and offices. This was significant in light of the fact that KAA was responsible for 10 regional airports. Such a significant element of Korea's offer surely would have been referenced in the *Supplementary Explanation*. Furthermore, we note that there was no evidence presented indicating that any party to the negotiations considered the 10 KAA-administered regional airports as part of Korea's offer. The evidence was to the contrary. We will amend paragraph 7.47 to clarify this point. We also will add a footnote to paragraph 7.61 in this regard.

6.21 With respect to paragraph 7.50, the United States requests we amend the paragraph to reflect that its arguments were not limited to "control". As noted above, we deal with the broader issues elsewhere and therefore decline to make the change requested by the United States.

6.22 With respect to paragraph 7.53, the United States requests that we drop any reference to the employment status of employees of KAA, KOACA and IIAC. The statements in this paragraph reflect our conclusions in this regard and we, therefore, decline to make the requested change.

6.23 With respect to paragraphs 7.60 and 7.61, the United States argues that the Panel has ignored evidence presented by the United States. This statement by the United States, of course, is incorrect. We fully considered all evidence presented by the parties. When we state our conclusions in the Findings, we summarize the evidence we found most persuasive without each time repeating all of the counter-arguments made by the party that disagrees with the conclusion. To do otherwise would render the Findings opaque and unreadable. Specifically, with regard to paragraph 7.60, the United States argues that KAA's by-laws are implemented upon approval of MOCT and that senior management appointments also are subject to such approval. We considered these matters and found them part of the oversight functions of MOCT.

6.24 The United States also reiterates its arguments about whether KAA's employees are properly considered government employees or not. We have explained our position elsewhere in this regard. Further, the United States argues implicitly that the non-governmental funding is minimal. In some years, it has been. However, KAA and its successors have provided other funds. The reference in footnote 720 in this regard was inaccurate and we have corrected it accordingly.

6.25 With respect to paragraph 7.61, the United States highlights again elements of what it considers "control" of KAA by MOCT. On these issues, as with others, we took into consideration the various aspects of control or authority between MOCT and KAA and its successors. We do not wish to imply that this was an easy factual assessment by any means. We weighed these and the other facts and, on balance, made our assessments as stated in the Findings. We have made a minor clarification of the language in paragraph 7.61, but otherwise, we decline to make the changes requested by the United States in this regard.

6.26 With respect to paragraph 7.63, the United States argues that: "it is inaccurate to portray the United States as relying 'heavily' on the Korean *Aviation Act* alone." We did not say that the United States relied on the *Aviation Act* "alone." If we had, we would not have used the term "heavily;" we would have used "exclusively" or a synonym for it. Our statement in paragraph 7.63 is accurate and we decline to change it.

6.27 We will change footnote 724 in paragraph 7.62 as requested by the United States to reflect the fact that Korea raised the question of the applicability of Article I:3 of the GPA.

6.28 With respect to paragraph 7.66, the United States argues that the Panel does not discuss the other cross-references between the *Aviation Act* and the *Seoul Airport Act*. We spent considerable time reviewing this question of cross-references and discussed in most detail the one that we felt of particular importance in light of the US arguments. We will amend the paragraph to note that we have taken into account the various cross-references before reaching our conclusions.

6.29 With respect to paragraph 7.67, the United States requests an amendment to reflect that the *Seoul Airport Act* does not relate to the relationship between KAA and MOCT but between MOCT and various other state, local or designated entities. KAA and its successors were designated later as entities to operate the project and, therefore, the Act does cover their relationship, even if it may cover others as well. We decline to make the change requested by the United States.

6.30 With respect to paragraphs 7.67 and 7.68, the United States requests that the Panel re-state further evidence that the United States argues that the relationship between MOCT and KAA beyond just oversight. As noted above, we have fully taken into account the references cited by the United States and have not found them, on balance, to be persuasive. We decline to make the changes requested by the United States in these paragraphs.

6.31 The United States requests several changes to paragraph 7.69. We agree that the reference to bid requests in the second sentence was more than a mere mention. We will amend the sentence accordingly. The United States requests we change the reference in the third sentence to the ratio of employees of KAA to MOCT rather than between IIAC and MOCT. We believe the reference to the current state of affairs is relevant and decline to change it. We requested information regarding the number of employees of IIAC but did not specifically request information on the number of employees of KAA in 1991. This is because KAA was an entity founded over 12 years earlier with responsibility for 10 regional airports. As such, it would have been impossible to separate the employees dedicated to the IIA project from those responsible for other activities of KAA. We also find it unlikely that KAA would have been an empty shell either given its other responsibilities. The US objects to our use of the term "empty shell" as a mis-characterization of its arguments concerning alleged Korean "shell games." The reference to an empty shell was ours and not related to the US point which was on another issue. We will make only the requested change to the first sentence of paragraph 7.69.

6.32 The United States objects to our reference to other bid documents in footnote 732 in paragraph 7.69 to the effect that they showed no relationship with MOCT. The United States argues that bid documents are not intended to show such relationships. However, that is precisely what the United States wished to establish with bid documents that indicated a role for MOCT or the Office of Supply. We were merely noting that of all the bid documents presented in evidence, the vast majority show no role for MOCT or the Office of Supply. We decline to make the change requested.

6.33 With respect to paragraph 7.70, the United States reminds the Panel of the references in the MOCT website to the role of NADG in the IIA project and argues that more than just oversight by MOCT was involved. We have acknowledged this evidence elsewhere and took it fully into consideration. We reiterate that it is not only not required, but would be counter-productive to recite every piece of evidence at every stage of the Findings.

6.34 With respect to paragraph 7.106, the United States argues that the date of the Korean response has not been established as 1 July 1991, only that Korea has asserted it. The relevance of the US point has not been established. In light of our extensive discussion about Korea's response and our views about its inadequacy, we do not think it would change our conclusions if the actual date was a week or two later. Therefore, we see no need to change our reference.

6.35 With respect to paragraph 7.115, the United States notes its strong objection to Korea's claim that the United States Government knew that KAA was in charge of the IIA project. However, the statement that the United States objects to is one of a list of factors considered by us as evidence of the wide knowledge of the fact that KAA was operating the IIA project and this reference was already qualified by noting that it was evidence submitted by Korea. We have amended paragraphs 7.115 and 7.119 to clarify the point.

6.36 The United States also claims that the only legally relevant officials with respect to knowledge of relevant factors are those within a particular government entity in a position to decide whether to go forward with the negotiated result. The United States has provided no legal support for this sweeping assertion.[688] While the US comment was directed at the issue of actual notice, it is difficult to see how it could have any legal relevance in a setting where constructive notice is sufficient.

6.37 With respect to paragraph 7.125, the United States requests that we qualify the statement by noting that at least one month of the four-month period was for verification. We agree that this is more accurate and will make the requested change.

---

[688] Indeed, the contrary would appear to be the case. See our discussion in para. 6.5 above, and the footnotes thereto.

6.38 We have corrected grammatical and typographical errors in paragraphs 7.4, 7.34, 7.46, 7.48, 7.61, 7.93 (footnote 751) and 7.100 and made a minor clarification in paragraph 7.48.

VII. FINDINGS

A. *Claims of the Parties*

7.1 The United States requested the Panel to make the following findings[689]: "That Ministry of Construction and Transportation ("MOCT") (including the New Airport Development Group ("NADG") under MOCT), the Korean Airport Authority ("KAA"), the Korean Airport Construction Authority ("KOACA"), and the Inchon International Airport Authority ("IIAC"), all of which are or have been in the past Korean Government entities involved in procurement for the Inchon International Airport ("IIA") project, are covered under Korea's Appendix I of the WTO Agreement on Government Procurement ("GPA") and:

(a) That by imposing bid deadlines for the receipt of tenders that are shorter than the GPA-required 40 days, Korea is in violation of Article XI:1(a) and XI:2(a) of the GPA.

(b) That by imposing qualification requirements specifying that an interested foreign supplier must have a licence that in turn requires that supplier to build or purchase manufacturing facilities in Korea, just so the supplier may be eligible to bid as a prime contractor, Korea is in violation of Articles III:1(a), VIII first sentence, and VIII(b) of the GPA.

(c) That by imposing domestic partnering requirements that force foreign firms to partner with, or act as subcontractors to, local Korean firms, just so the foreign firms may participate in tendering procedures, Korea is in violation of Articles III:1(a), VIII first sentence, and VIII(b) of the GPA.

(d) That by not establishing effective domestic procedures enabling foreign suppliers to challenge alleged breaches of the GPA for procurements related to the IIA project, Korea is in violation of Article XX of the GPA."

7.2 The United States also requested the Panel to make the following finding[690]: "That should the Panel determine that the above measures do not violate the GPA, the measures nevertheless nullify or impair benefits accruing to the United States under the GPA, pursuant to Article XXII:2 of the GPA."

7.3 Korea requested the Panel to reject the complaints to the United States on the basis of the following finding[691]:

---

[689] Para. 3.1.

[690] Para. 3.2.

"That the entities conducting procurement for the IIA are not covered entities under Korea's Appendix I of the GPA."

B. GPA Coverage of the Inchon International Airport Project

1. General

7.4 As discussed above, the United States has claimed that the procurement practices with respect to the IIA are not consistent with the provisions of the GPA. Specifically, the United States argues that the bid deadlines have been too short, there are improper qualification and local partnering requirements and there are not adequate challenge procedures. Korea has taken no position with respect to these allegations; rather, Korea argues that the entities responsible for IIA procurement are not covered by Korea's GPA commitments contained in Appendix I to the GPA and that, therefore, Korea is under no obligation to conduct IIA procurement in a manner consistent with the provisions of the GPA.

7.5 The question that we must address at the outset, therefore, is whether procurement for the IIA is covered by Korea's GPA commitments. Since Korea's final offer of concessions on 14 December 1993 and the Members' agreement to the WTO GPA and Korea's accession to it on 15 April 1994[692], three entities have been responsible for IIA procurement: KAA, KOACA and IIAC. It is undisputed between the parties that these three entities occupy similar situations, the transfer of authority between them being largely irrelevant to our analysis. Both parties agree that Korea has never utilized the procedures contained in GPA Article XXIV:6 for modification of its Schedules with respect to airport construction. The issue, therefore, is whether KAA was a covered entity[693] at the time that Korea concluded its accession negotiations. We will, however, also look at the activities of KOACA and IIAC, to the extent necessary, as well as the relationship of MOCT and the Office of Supply to the three entities, to see what impact, if any, that will have on our analysis.

7.6 Article I of the GPA provides as follows:

> "This Agreement applies to any law, regulation, procedure or practice regarding any procurement by an entity covered by this Agreement, as specified in Appendix I."

A footnote to Article I further provides that for each Party to the GPA, its Schedule is divided into five annexes covering different types of procuring entities. For our purposes, the most relevant annexes are: Annex 1 containing central government entities; Annex 2 containing sub-central government entities; and, Annex 3 containing other entities that procure in accordance with the provisions of the GPA. Generally, there are different procurement thresholds for each Annex.

7.7 The question arises as to how to interpret these Schedules in the event of a disagreement. In a recent dispute, the issue of the approach to take in interpreting

---

691 Para. 3.3.

692 The effective date of Korea's accession was 1 January 1997.

693 We note that the GPA does not use the term "covered entity" as such, rather it refers to entities covered by this Agreement. Both parties used the term "covered entity" as shorthand for this and we will continue in this manner as well.

Schedules under Article II of GATT 1994 was taken up by the Appellate Body. In particular, the Appellate Body addressed the question of whether and how to apply the normal rules of treaty interpretation contained in the *Vienna Convention* to the interpretation of the language contained in a Member's tariff schedule. In this dispute, *European Communities - Customs Classification of Certain Computer Equipment*, WT/DS62, WT/DS67, WT/DS68, ("*European Communities - Computer Equipment*"), the question involved the appropriate tariff treatment for certain electrical products such as local area network ("LAN") equipment. The United States claimed that the products should have been treated by the European Communities in its schedule as automatic data-processing machines. Some EC member States treated LAN equipment as telecommunications equipment. The panel found for the United States, among other things, on the basis that the United States had a legitimate expectation as to how the products would be treated.

7.8 The panel finding was reversed by the Appellate Body. In the Appellate Body's view, the panel had incorrectly based its findings on the unilateral and subjective expectations of the exporting party. Instead, the Appellate Body provided the following views:

> "Tariff concessions provided for in a Member's Schedule - the interpretation of which is at issue here - are reciprocal and result from a mutually-advantageous negotiation between importing and exporting Members. A Schedule is made an integral part of the GATT 1994 by Article II:7 of the GATT 1994. Therefore, the concessions provided for in that Schedule are part of the terms of the treaty. As such, the only rules which may be applied in interpreting the meaning of a concession are the general rules of treaty interpretation set out in the *Vienna Convention*."[694]

7.9 Like GATT Article II:7 which refers to the tariff Schedules as "integral" parts of the Agreement, Article XXIV:12 of the GPA states that: "The Notes, Appendices and Annexes to this Agreement constitute an integral part thereof." Thus, it follows that we should consider the Schedules appended to the GPA as treaty language. Accordingly, we will refer to the customary rules of interpretation of public international law as summarized in the *Vienna Convention* in order to interpret Korea's GPA Schedule.

7.10 Article 31 of the *Vienna Convention* reads as follows:

> "1. A treaty shall be interpreted in good faith in accordance with the ordinary meaning to be given to the terms of the treaty in their context and in light of its object and purpose.
>
> 2. The context for the purpose of a treaty interpretation shall comprise, in addition to the text, including its preamble and annexes:
>
> (a) any agreement relating to the treaty which was made between all the parties in connexion with the conclusion of the treaty;

[694] Appellate Body Report, *EC - LAN*, *supra*, footnote 106, para. 84. See also Appellate Body Report, *Canada - Dairy*, *supra*, footnote 208, para. 131.

(b) any instrument which was made by one or more parties in connexion with the conclusion of the treaty and accepted by the other parties as an instrument related to the treaty.

3. There shall be taken into account, together with the context:

(a) any subsequent agreement between the parties regarding the interpretation of the treaty or application of its provisions;

(b) any subsequent practice in application of the treaty which establishes the agreement of the parties regarding its interpretation;

(c) any relevant rules of international law applicable in the relations between the parties.

4. A special meaning shall be given to a term if it is established that the parties so intended."

7.11 Article 32 of the *Vienna Convention* provides guidance on supplementary means of interpretation. It reads as follows:

> "Recourse may be had to supplementary means of interpretation, including the preparatory work of the treaty and the circumstances of its conclusion, in order to confirm the meaning resulting from the application of Article 31, or to determine the meaning when the interpretation according to Article 31:
>
> (a) leaves the meaning ambiguous or obscure; or
>
> (b) leads to a result which is manifestly absurd or unreasonable."

7.12 The first step of the analysis, therefore, will be to examine Korea's Schedule and determine whether, within the ordinary meaning of the terms therein, the entity responsible for IIA procurement is covered. This will include a review of all relevant Annexes and Notes.

7.13 If the meaning is ambiguous or obscure, or would lead to a result which is manifestly absurd, then, in accordance with Article 32, recourse may be had to the preparatory work and the circumstances of the conclusion of the treaty. Such recourse could include reference to matters such as the questions asked of Korea by GPA members during the accession process and Korea's responses thereto. Reference to the negotiating history is also appropriate to confirm the Panel's understanding of the ordinary meaning of the terms in the treaty.

2. *Covered Entities under Korea's Annex 1*

(a) Arguments of the Parties

7.14 Listed in Annex 1 of Korea's Appendix I Schedule are, *inter alia*, the MOCT[695] and the Office of Supply. The Office of Supply is covered with respect to

[695] MOCT was formed in December 1994 through the merger of the Ministries of Construction and Transportation. Generally we will refer to the covered entity as MOCT for simplicity, recognizing that this may be anachronistic at points.

procurements made for entities listed in Annex 1. An important element in construing the coverage of Annex 1 is Note 1 to that Annex. It reads as follows:

> "The above central government entities include their subordinate linear organizations, special local administrative organs, and attached organs as prescribed in the Government Organization Act of the Republic of Korea."

7.15 The United States has argued that the interpretation of "central government entity" in Annex 1 includes branch offices and subsidiary organizations. According to the United States, proper treaty interpretation of this term must result in the inclusion of the subdivisions of listed entities and such subdivisions could include branch offices and subsidiary organizations or other such entities. The United States argues that this interpretation is wholly consistent with Note 1 because that Note states that Annex 1 entities "include" certain other organizations. "Include" is a broadening term, not a limiting one. Thus, the organizations described in Note 1 are in addition to the central government entities themselves. These other organizations include branch and subsidiary organizations.

7.16 The United States argues that NADG is a part of MOCT, or at least a branch or subsidiary organization of MOCT.[696] The United States further argues that, even though NADG has not been expressly listed in Korea's Schedule, it is nevertheless covered under the GPA by virtue of MOCT's listing. The United States argues that NADG is the organization responsible for IIA construction and that, therefore, the IIA is a project of a covered entity. Alternatively, the United States argues that KAA and its successors are branch offices or subsidiary organizations of MOCT and the IIA project would, therefore, also be covered under that line of analysis.

7.17 The United States urges the Panel to look closely at the element of "control" over the organizations in question, particularly in regard to the specific project in question and argues that given the degree of control exercised by MOCT over KAA and its successors, procurements by those entities are actually procurements by MOCT. The United States argues that, therefore, the GPA requirements apply to those procurements.

7.18 The United States points to the *Act on the Promotion of a New Airport for Seoul Metropolitan Area Construction* ("*Seoul Airport Act*") as evidence. Article 4(1) of that Act provides, among other things, that MOCT will establish a "master plan" for the IIA project. This plan is to include general direction of construction, outline of the construction plan, the construction period, a financing plan and other matters deemed necessary. The United States also refers to Article 7(1) which requires MOCT's approval of the project operator's "execution plan" and Article 12 which requires the project operator to submit reports to MOCT. Article 13 permits MOCT to cancel permission to operate or suspend or alter the work. Article 14 requires that the project operator permit MOCT inspection of its office and workplace and other places relevant to the new airport development project.

7.19 The United States also argues that the Korean *Aviation Act* is the controlling statutory authority for airport construction. Under Article 95 of the *Aviation Act*, KAA would have been a "project operator". The United States then refers to the nu-

[696] See paras. 4.13, 4.15 and 4.436.

merous provisions in the *Aviation Act* which require the project operator to work under the supervision of MOCT. The United States also refers to the obligation of the project operator to report to the MOCT under the *Seoul Airport Act*.

7.20 The United States further notes that General Note 1of Korea's Appendix reads as follows:

> "Korea will not extend the benefits of this Agreement
>
> (a) as regards the award of contracts by the National Railroad Administration,
>
> (b) as regards procurement for airports by the entities listed in Annex 1,
>
> (c) as regards procurement for urban transportation (including subways) by the entities listed in Annexes 1 and 2
>
> to suppliers and service providers of member States of the European Communities, Austria, Norway, Sweden, Finland and Switzerland, until such time as Korea has accepted that those countries give comparable and effective access for Korean undertakings to their relevant markets."

7.21 The United States argues that the reference to "procurement for airports" in paragraph (b) of the General Note confirms that there are, in fact, entities listed in Annex 1 of Korea's Schedule that are responsible for procurement for airports. The United States further argues that since MOCT, the NADG, KAA, KOACA and IIAC are the only entities Korea has held out as being responsible for procurements for airports, these are the entities that must be covered under Annex 1 for all countries not referred to in the General Note.

7.22 The United States points to MOCT's website which listed the NADG as responsible for IIA construction, along with other press and business group reports that also referred to MOCT or NADG responsibility for the IIA project. According to the United States, all of these factors showed that MOCT was in control of KAA and its successors, or, at the very least, was in control of the IIA project.

7.23 Korea responds that there is no textual basis for the US arguments about branch offices and subsidiary organizations. According to Korea, Note 1 to Annex 1 defines the scope of the coverage of central government entities under Annex 1. Korea argues that this is the most reasonable interpretation of the phrase "as prescribed in the *Government Organization Act*" that is contained in Note 1. In any event, Korea disagrees that KAA or its successors could be properly described as branch or subsidiary organizations of MOCT. While Korea disagrees that there was a "control" test contained in the WTO GPA, Korea also argues that KAA was independent both overall and with respect to the IIA project. This is because, among other things, KAA was established by law as an independent juristic entity; it authored and adopted its own by-laws; it had its own management and employees who were not government employees; it authored and adopted its own procurement rules distinct from the general government rules; it published bid announcements and requests for proposals of its own accord; it concluded contracts with successful bidders on its own behalf; and it funded portions of the IIA with its own monies.

7.24 Korea points out that Article 94(1) of the *Aviation Act* states that it is the controlling provision of law unless "otherwise provided by law." According to Korea, in this case, the *Seoul Airport Act* "otherwise provided by law." Therefore, the

Seoul Airport Act was the controlling law and it explicitly authorized an entity other than MOCT to have the responsibility for the IIA project. Korea acknowledges that there were elements of supervision by MOCT of the IIA project as it is an important national project. However, Korea argues, this sort of general oversight is very typical for projects that are closely linked to public welfare, safety and finance and ensures accountability. Korea argues that this sort of oversight does not involve the surrender of the supervised entity's status as a separate legal entity.

7.25 Korea further argues that the indicia of independence, as listed above, clearly indicated that KAA was an independent entity for purposes of coverage by the GPA. Korea notes that other entities such as KAA were typically Annex 3 entities both in Korea and in other GPA signatories, if the negotiators agreed to their coverage at all.

7.26 In regard to General Note 1(b), Korea responds that, in fact, procurement for some airports is conducted by covered Annex 1 entities. Specifically, the Seoul and Pusan Regional Airport Authorities are local administrative organs as provided in the *Government Organization Act* and are therefore covered by reason of Note 1 to Annex 1. Thus, there is nothing inconsistent about General Note 1(b) and Korea's position that KAA and its successors, and therefore the IIA project, are not covered.

7.27 With respect to MOCT's website, Korea argues that this was a product of MOCT's public relations department and was not a binding classification of responsibilities. Korea also argues that in July 1998, around the time the website evidence is cited, the US Commercial Officer in Seoul sent a letter to the Korean Government which implicitly acknowledged that KOACA was not a covered entity. The letter requested, among other things, that KOACA be considered de facto covered until actual GPA coverage took place.

7.28 The United States responds to this last point by providing a series of other US Government letters from this time-period, including some from more senior US officials, which the United States maintains made very clear the full and accurate position of the United States which was different from that of the above-mentioned Commercial Officer. In the US view, the July 1998 letter does not lead to the conclusion proposed by Korea, in any event, because in stating that there should be de facto coverage it did not imply that there was no *de jure* coverage.

(b) Evaluation of the Parties' Arguments

7.29 As noted in paragraph 7.5 above, three entities (KAA, KOACA and IIAC) have been directly responsible for IIA procurement following the designation of a project operator in December 1991.[697] In evaluating the parties arguments in regard to the claim of a violation of Korea's commitments under the GPA, there are two aspects which must be addressed. The first issue is the interpretation of Korea's Schedule of commitments. Is the entity conducting the procurement for the IIA project listed in the Annexes or the Notes thereto? This requires an interpretation of Annex 1 to Korea's Schedule and the Notes thereto, as well as other relevant portions of

[697] *Seoul Airport Act* as amended by Act No. 4436 (14 December 1991) Exhibit Kor-12; *Korea Airport Corporation Act* as amended by Act Nos. 4435 and 4436 (14 December 1991) Exhibit Kor-14.

the Schedule.[698] The second issue is whether there is some other test that we should apply to determine if the entity in question is covered by Korea's GPA commitments even if not listed. The United States has generally argued in this regard that the proper test should be whether the procuring entity is "controlled" by a listed entity. Korea has contested the validity of that proposed test. The question becomes whether there are some criteria exogenous to the lists and Notes in the Schedules that, when applied to an entity, would lead to the conclusion that its procurement should be covered by a GPA signatory's commitments.[699]

(i) Interpretation of Annex 1 of Korea's Schedule

7.30 A critical question we must first address is determining what is explicitly contained in Korea's Schedule. A preliminary issue is the status of Note 1 to Annex 1, in particular the extent to which Parties can qualify the coverage of listed entities through such Notes. In our view, Members determine, pursuant to negotiation, the scope of the coverage of their commitments as expressed in the Schedules. In this regard, we take note of the panel finding in *United States - Restrictions on Imports of Sugar* ("*United States - Sugar*") wherein the panel observed that Headnotes could be used to qualify the tariff concessions themselves.[700]

7.31 The implication of the Findings in *United States - Sugar* for the present case would be that a GPA signatory could use Notes to its Schedules to qualify the entity coverage itself. However, as will be discussed in subsequent sections, questions have been raised as to whether an entity not mentioned in a Schedule, either through an affirmative listing or an explicit exclusion, may still be covered due to the nature of its relationship with another entity which is covered.

7.32 Our first step, therefore, is to examine what entities are actually listed in Korea's Schedule. We note that MOCT is included in the list of central government entities. KAA and its successors are not listed either there or elsewhere.

7.33 Note 1 to Annex 1 states that the "central government entities include their subordinate linear organizations, special local administrative organs, and attached organs as prescribed in the *Government Organization Act* of the Republic of Korea." To begin with, we agree with Korea that the phrase "as prescribed in" means that the *Government Organization Act* defines the terms listed in the Note. The relevant definition of the verb prescribe is to: "limit, restrict, confine within bounds."[701] In our view, this concept of limiting or confining within bounds means that "prescribed" does provide definition to the preceding terms in Note 1. Indeed, one of the definitions of the verb "define" is to: "determine, *prescribe*, fix precisely, specify."[702] We think that the definitions of "prescribe" and "define" are so close as to make the words virtually synonymous. Thus, we will look to the cited Act for the definitions of the terms listed in Note 1.

---

698 See subsections (i) and (ii), below.

699 See subsection (iii), below.

700 Report of the Panel on *United States - Restrictions on Imports of Sugar*, adopted on 22 June 1989, (BISD 36S/331) at paras. 5.2-5.3 and 5.7.

701 *New Shorter Oxford English Dictionary*, (Clarendon Press, 1993) Vol. 2 at p. 2339.

702 Ibid., Vol. 1 at p. 618. (emphasis added)

7.34 Article 2(3) of the *Government Organization Act* states: "The subordinate linear organizations of the central administrative organs shall be Cha-Gwan (Vice-Minister), Cha-Jang (Deputy Administrator), Sil-Jang (Office Director) ..."[703] Thus, the subordinate linear organizations are defined as individual offices rather than organizations as such. In response to a question from the Panel, Korea states that this means that coverage would be with respect to areas of responsibility of those officials. We accept the explanation by Korea and, therefore, cannot agree with the US assertion that Article 2(3) of the *Government Organization Act* does not really provide a definition of "subordinate linear organizations." In our view, there is no doubt that Article 2(3) defines "subordinate linear organizations" by reference to the entities (ministries, divisions, units, etc.) which fall under the responsibility of one of these offices. It has not been argued that KAA falls within any of these offices. Therefore, we shall proceed on the basis that KAA is not a subordinate linear organization.

7.35 Article 3(1) provides that: "Each central administrative organ may have local administrative organs as prescribed by the Presidential Decree except those especially prescribed by laws, in case they are necessary for the implementation of the duties under its jurisdiction."[704] Examples of such organizations are the Seoul and Pusan Regional Airport Authorities. KAA and its successors are not considered local administrative organs.[705]

7.36 In addition, Article 4 of the Act provides as follows:

> "(Establishment of Attached Organs) In an administrative organ, there may be established by the Presidential Decree organizations for experiment, research, education and training, culture, medicine, manufacturing or advice, respectively, if necessary for the fulfilment [of] duties under its jurisdiction."[706]

There is no dispute that KAA is not an "attached organ" within the meaning of this definition.

7.37 As demonstrated above, KAA does not fall within the terms of Articles 2(3), 3(1) or 4 of the *Government Organization Act*. We, therefore, conclude that prima facie KAA does not fall within the terms of Note 1 to Annex 1 of Korea's Schedule. We note, however, that there are diverging views on whether this should be the end of the analysis of Korea's Schedule. Korea is of the view that it should be, while the United States urges us to interpret Note 1 (and, in particular, the word "include") in such a way as to permit us to look beyond Annex 1 itself.

703 Exhibit Kor-58. All translations of legislative materials have been provided by Korea.

704 Ibid.

705 Korea states that this is the case. The United states merely notes in response that the *Government Organization Act* does not identify the Seoul and Pusan Regional Aviation Offices as "special local administrative organs."

706 Ibid.

(ii) Further Evaluation of the Extent of Korea's Commitment

7.38 In effect, Korea argues for a narrow reading of the list in Annex 1 by using Note 1 as a definition. The implication of this is that because KAA and its successors are not prescribed in the *Government Organization Act*, they cannot be covered under Annex 1. On the other hand, the United States focuses on the term "include" and argues that Note 1 broadens the coverage beyond the central government entities listed in Annex 1 itself to also encompass additional entities described in the *Government Organization Act.*

7.39 A reference to Note 1 of Annex 2 (sub-central government entities) would tend to support the narrower interpretation. Note 1 to Annex 2 reads in relevant part as follows:

> "1. The above sub-central administrative government entities include their *subordinate organizations* under *direct control* and offices as prescribed in the Local Autonomy Law of the Republic of Korea."

7.40 There are two important observations to make in regard to this Note to Annex 2. First, there is a term "subordinate organizations" as opposed to "subordinate linear organizations." This would support an interpretation with respect to Note 1 to Annex 1 that subordinate linear organizations is a term of art and does not have a broader meaning inclusive of subordinate organizations (or, for that matter, "branch offices" or "subsidiary organizations"). Furthermore, it implies the negative that subordinate organizations in general are not meant to be included unless specifically stated as in Note 1 to Annex 2. We do note, however, that the translation from the original Korean may have added some ambiguity with respect to this issue.

7.41 The second observation is that when Korea wished to make reference to entities under direct control of the listed entities, it made the reference explicit. The absence of such a reference in Note 1 to Annex 1 implies that "direct control" is not a criteria there. This issue of control will be discussed further in subsection (iii), below.

7.42 However, we must note that the reading of Note 1 to Annex 1 as a definitional provision is that it implies a peculiar structure of the Annex 1 Schedule where one set of *organizations* is defined in terms of offices rather than entities. Another unusual aspect of Note 1 is that the comprehensiveness of the list of offices defining subordinate linear organizations could lead to a conclusion that the individual entities listed in Annex 1 are virtually without substance except as provided in the *Government Organization Act.* The problem raised by this observation is that the Note states that the central government entities in Annex 1 **include** subordinate linear organizations, local administrative organs and attached organs. We agree with the United States that the term "include" is normally not a limiting or defining term. The relevant definition of "include" is: "contain as *part* of a whole or as a subordinate element."[707]

7.43 In our view, this use of the term "include" along with the unusual use of a list of individuals to define subordinate linear organizations results in ambiguity regard-

[707] *New Shorter Oxford English Dictionary, supra.*, Vol. 1 at p. 1337.

ing the interpretation of Note 1 and therefore the meaning of the whole of Annex 1 including the Notes. While we will examine further the other aspects of Korea's Schedule and the relevant Notes, we find it helpful in accordance with paragraph (a) of Article 32 of the *Vienna Convention* to examine at this point the negotiating history of Korea's GPA accession to provide some clarity to Note 1. In this particular case, there is some very specific evidence in this regard which will assist in interpretation.[708]

7.44 Korea's original offer in 1990 provided for GPA coverage of 35 central government entities. In February 1991, Korea provided to the Tokyo Round Agreement signatories a *Supplementary Explanation of the Note by the Republic of Korea dated 29 June 1990 relating to the Agreement on Government Procurement.*[709] Section 3 of the *Supplementary Explanation* provided a "Clarification of Notes in Korea's Offer." Note 1 at that time was essentially the same as it appeared in Korea's Schedule. The clarification of Note 1 reads in relevant part:

> "o Note 1 is established to clarify the coverage of central government organs which come under 35 of 37[710] purchasing entities.
>
> o The meaning and categories of subordinate linear organizations, special local administrative organs and attached organs are prescribed in the Government Organization Act of the Republic of Korea as follows:
>
> - Subordinate linear organizations: office of the minister, vice-minister, assistant minister, director general, director, etc."[711]

7.45 This provides insight on two aspects of the interpretation of Note 1. First, the *Supplementary Explanation* by its terms was intended to *clarify* the coverage of central government organs. That is, it is a clarification of the scope of the list in Annex 1. Note 1 was not in itself intended as an extension of coverage to entities other than those listed in Annex 1. Secondly, the coverage based on offices is made explicit. This goes to the observation in paragraph 7.42 above, that Annex 1 is virtually without substance except as provided in the *Government Organization Act*. The answer is that this is precisely the case because, in fact, Note 1 defines the scope of the coverage by listing components of the central government entities themselves; it was not meant to denote something exterior to the central government entities as might be implied by the term "include."

7.46 The *Supplementary Explanation* also provided a list of central government entities which it described as the "total central government entities." With respect to the Ministry of Transportation, it provided as follows:

> "o Ministry of Transportation
>
> - Regional Aviation Bureaus (2)

---

708 We will return to the overall negotiating history of Korea's Schedule below.

709 Exhibit Kor-117.

710 Elsewhere in the *Supplementary Explanation* the figure of 35 out of 47 is given. Ibid. at p. 5. This may be a typographical error, but is not of relevance to our discussion.

711 Ibid. at p. 26.

- CHEJU Regional Aviation Office
- Flight Inspection Office of the Director-General - VOR-TAC Stations (5)
- Marine Accident Inquiry Offices"[712]

7.47 As noted above, Korea has maintained that the entities for which coverage is provided under Annex 1 of its Schedule are the Seoul and Pusan Regional Aviation offices. The reference to two Regional Aviation Bureaus in the *Supplementary Explanation* supports this assertion. This corresponds with the evidence arising later from the EC's inquiries of Korea in late 1993 which leads to the conclusion that the Regional Aviation Bureaus listed under the Ministry of Transport were the Seoul and Pusan Regional Airport Authorities which are included by Note 1 as local administrative organs. KAA is not included in the list contained in the *Supplementary Explanation*. We note that KAA was responsible for 10 regional airports (although apparently it was not itself localized in one region in its responsibilities and therefore was not "regional") and, as such, it would have been a major element of Korea's offer. In light of this, we find its omission from the list significant.

7.48 Thus, Note 1 provides a clarification of the scope of the coverage of the central government entities contained in the list in Annex 1. Obviously, even in light of this conclusion regarding the relationship between the list of entities in Annex 1 and the clarification in Note 1, the term "include" does nonetheless remain a part of Note 1. Also, while it is the case that the definitions of "subordinate linear organizations, local administrative organs, and attached organs" are virtually coterminous with the "central government entities" in Annex 1, there may be a gap. Based on the evidence before us, the office of the Minister is not included in the offices specified in the *Government Organization Act*, but it would evidently fall under the remit of the Ministry. This means, for example, that tasks or projects specifically designated by law or decree as the responsibility of the Minister are covered by the list in Annex 1, even though not "included" by virtue of the definition provided by the *Government Organization Act*. We note, in this regard, that NADG as an ad hoc task force is not contained in the definitions found in the *Government Organization Act*, but is assigned its tasks by regulations issued by the Minister of Construction and Transportation (paragraph 4.14). Thus, NADG would seem to be covered by the list in Annex 1 (as acknowledged by Korea), but not included by reason of Note 1. In contrast, KAA is not assigned its tasks by the Minister; is not listed in Annex 1; nor does Note 1 explicitly include KAA in coverage.

---

[712] Ibid. at p. 11. We also note that this piece of negotiating history also adds clarity to the meaning of General Note 1(b) and permits a consistent and coherent reading of Annex 1 in light of this General Note. We recall that the United States argued that General Note 1(b) did not make any sense if the IIA project was not covered because it would then refer to nothing at all and the treaty should not be read in a manner which renders any of it meaningless. However, the *Supplementary Explanation* confirms the meaning otherwise derived from a reading of the *Government Organization Act* as referred to in Note 1 to Annex 1. That is, Korea withheld coverage of airport procurement for the European Communities and certain other signatories, but this does not necessarily imply coverage of the IIA project under Note 1 of Annex 1. Rather, it implicitly refers to the regional airport authorities. We will discuss this further below in the context of the broader negotiating history of Korea's accession to the GPA.

7.49 Therefore, we next will examine whether the relationship between MOCT and KAA was such that KAA's procurement is covered (at least with respect to the IIA, if not more broadly) even though KAA is not explicitly included. As noted in paragraph 7.29 above, there is a remaining question as to whether there exists the possibility of the inclusion of certain procurements of an entity which is not listed, due to its relationship with a listed entity. These arguably are general issues which arise with respect to any Member's Schedule regardless of the structure and content of the Schedule and any qualifying Notes.

(iii) Evaluation of the Parties Arguments: The Issue of "Control"

7.50 The United States argues that KAA may be considered a part of MOCT because it is controlled, at least for the purposes of the IIA project, by MOCT. As noted in paragraph 7.29 above, a question is raised whether, regardless of what is specifically in a Schedule, an entity which is deemed "controlled" by a listed entity is also covered by the Member's GPA commitments?[713] If so, as a follow-on to this second question, does KAA fall within this category?

7.51 Korea has discussed this issue in a slightly different manner. Korea has argued that if we were to adopt the US proposed control test, it would cause a number of entities included within Korea's (and other Members') Annex 3 commitments to be put by operation of law under Annex 1 because such entities would arguably be under the "control" of Annex 1 entities. This is important because it would change the threshold levels negotiated with respect to the Annex 3 entities.

"Control" Generally

7.52 First, we must recall our observation made earlier in regard to Note 1 to Annex 2 of Korea's Schedule. Among other things, we observed that the term "direct control" arose in that Note as a means of describing the scope of the concessions in Annex 2. Arguably, because Korea used the term explicitly with respect to Annex 2, its absence in Note 1 to Annex 1 implies that it has no applicability to Annex 1. While this negative implication cannot be overlooked, we also recall that we are reviewing in this section the question of whether GPA coverage can result from the control relationship between two entities regardless of the Schedules and the way in which Parties seek to define them. Obviously, however, the more explicit the Schedule, the narrower the scope for any such coverage to exist.

7.53 The United States has referred us to the Appellate Body decision in *Canada - Measures Affecting the Importation of Milk and the Exportation of Dairy Products* ("*Canada - Dairy*") for guidance on the question of what constitutes "control" of an entity. However, the focus of that dispute was whether or not the Canadian milk marketing boards were "government agencies."[714] In our view, that is a different question than we are facing in the present dispute. While the employees of KAA,

---

[713] In our view, the US arguments regarding branch offices and subsidiary organizations, to the extent not already dealt with in the previous subsections, are subsumed within this general discussion regarding "control."

[714] Appellate Body Report, *Canada - Dairy, supra*, footnote 208, paras. 96-102.

KOACA and IIAC are not government employees (except for a "legal fiction" created by statute with respect to certain criminal actions), neither party has argued that these are not "government" agencies. We agree that they are. The question here is narrower. Are these "government" agencies actually a part of or an agent for *covered* government entities?

7.54 Indeed, the United States has acknowledged that there are different tests involved in answering these questions. There was considerable discussion regarding the implication we should draw, if any, from the exclusion in the current GPA of the relevant language contained in Article I of the Tokyo Round Agreement. That read:

> "Article I
>
> *Scope and Coverage*
>
> 1. This Agreement applies to:
>
> [...]
>
> (c) procurement by the entities under the direct or substantial control of Parties and other designated entities, with respect to their procurement procedures and practices. Until the review and further negotiations referred to in the Final Provisions, the coverage of this Agreement is specified by the lists of entities, and to the extent that rectifications, modifications or amendments may have been made, their successor entities, in Annex I."

7.55 Korea argued that the coverage of the current GPA now is defined exclusively by the Schedules and did not even arguably include another normative rule relating to direct control.[715] In response to a question from the Panel regarding the implications of the existence of this language for understanding the negotiations between the parties in 1991-1993, the United States answered that this language was irrelevant to the Panel's analysis of the US response to Korean legislation implemented in 1991. The United States went on to make the following statement:

> "With regard to the expansion of coverage to procurements by "entities under the direct or substantial control of Parties", the 1979 USITC report states that "[t]he broader language 'direct or substantial control' apparently is intended to encompass not only governmental units but quasi-governmental purchasing agents as well". In other words, this control reference is not related to the control of "central government entities" over their subdivisions. Instead it is referring to the control of Code parties (*i.e.*, the governments themselves) over their "quasi-governmental purchasing agents"."[716]

7.56 We agree with this statement both as to the nature of the language in Article I:1(c) of the Tokyo Round Agreement and the distinction between the two types of "control" questions. Article I:1(c) was referring to the broader question of whether an

[715] Korea referred to a United States International Trade Commission report with respect to the nature of the language in Article I:3 of the Tokyo Round Code. See Exhibit Kor-73.

[716] US Responses to Second Set of Panel Questions at p. 10.

entity was "governmental" or not rather than to the relationship between two "governmental" entities for purposes of the GPA. However, the panel and Appellate Body in *Canada - Dairy* also were referring to that broader question. Indeed, it seems to us that the GPA is virtually *sui generis* in this regard. It is an important question under the GATT/WTO Agreements as to whether an action is being taken by a "governmental" entity or a private person for the covered agreements are considered to apply to "governmental" action only. However, once it is determined that there are "governmental" measures at issue, it is not generally of legal relevance which "governmental" entity is applying the measures. But within the GPA this is a critical question. There are obligations on the part of certain government entities but not others.

7.57 There is no use of the term "direct control" or even "control" in the sense that the United States wishes to use it.[717] It has not been defined in this manner either in the context used in the Tokyo Round Agreement or elsewhere. We cannot agree with the overall US position that a "control" test should be read into the GPA. However, we also do not think that it is an entirely irrelevant question. We think the issue of "control" of one entity over another can be a relevant criterion among others for determining coverage of the GPA, as discussed below.

(iv) Evaluation of the Relationship of the Entities Concerned

7.58 As discussed above, we do believe that entities that are not listed in an Annex 1 to the GPA whether in the Annex list or through a Note to the Annex, can, nevertheless, be covered under the GPA. We believe that this flows from the fact that an overly narrow interpretation of "central government entity" may result in less coverage under Annex 1 than was intended by the signatories. On the other hand, an overly broad interpretation of the term may result in coverage of entities that were never intended to be covered by signatories.

7.59 In the present case, our view is that the relevant questions are: (1) Whether an entity (KAA, in this case) is essentially a part of a listed central government entity (MOCT) - in other words, are the entities, legally unified? and (2) Whether KAA and its successors have been acting on behalf of MOCT. The first test is appropriate because if entities that are essentially a part of, or legally unified with, listed central government entities are not considered covered, it could lead to great uncertainty as to what was actually covered because coverage would be dependent on the internal structure of an entity which may be unknown to the other negotiating parties. The second test is appropriate because procurements that are genuinely undertaken on behalf of a listed entity (as, for example, in the case where a principal/agent relationship[718] exists between the listed entity and another entity) should properly be covered under Annex 1 because they would be considered legally as procurements by MOCT.

[717] The term "control" does appear in Article XXIV:6(b), but it is referring there to privatization. That is, it is used in the same manner as per the analysis in *Canada - Dairy*, *supra*, footnote 208, for determining whether an entity is "governmental" or not rather than for examining the relationship between entities.

[718] The parties at various times referred to a concept of "agency." The term "agency" does not appear in the GPA, but could be used in a very general sense of one entity legally acting on behalf of another.

In our view, it would defeat the objectives of the GPA if an entity listed in a signatory's Schedule could escape the Agreement's disciplines by commissioning another agency of government, not itself listed in that signatory's Schedule, to procure on its behalf.

Are the Entities Legally Unified?

7.60 With respect to the first question, in our view, KAA is not legally unified with or a part of MOCT. There are a number of factors leading to this conclusion. Among them are: KAA was established by law as an independent juristic entity; it authored and adopted its own by-laws; it had its own management and employees who were not government employees[719]; it published bid announcements and requests for proposals of its own accord; it concluded contracts with successful bidders on its own behalf; and it funded portions[720] of the IIA project with its own monies.[721]

7.61 There are, nonetheless, some indicia of a relationship between MOCT and KAA and its successors. The senior members of KAA's board of directors are appointed by MOCT and the rest of the directors are appointed by these senior members. There are indicia of control, at least with respect to the IIA project, that indicate some level of oversight or monitoring of KAA by MOCT. We will discuss this in more detail below with respect to the second question, but, in our view, these levels of "control" relate to oversight or monitoring and not to the common identity of the entities. These sorts of relationships exist throughout the public sector. Without them, it would be difficult for governmental functions to be coordinated effectively. But not all such relationships lead to a finding that one entity is, in effect, a part of another entity. Certainly for purposes of the GPA, such a result would lead to a great deal of uncertainty in the coverage of the Schedules. The GPA has always been based on what is affirmatively included in Schedules[722] and extending the coverage further without clear indicia of effective unity between entities is not warranted by the structure and purpose of the GPA. On balance, we are persuaded by the indicia of independence of KAA and its successors and find that these entities are not a part of MOCT.[723]

---

[719] This, as noted above, is a different question from whether such employee status means KAA is not a "governmental" entity.

[720] See paras. 2.61, 2.101 and 2.130.

[721] Korea also argued that the fact that KAA authored and adopted its own procurement rules distinct from the general government rules indicated KAA's independence. We recognize that it is arguable that it is an indicia of independence that there was pre-existing authority for procurement regulations separate from the entity that KAA was asserted to be a part of. However, we also note that the question of separate and non-conforming procurement regulations is the core of the complaint in this regard and the inconsistency at issue should not generally be considered a justification for itself. Thus, this aspect of alleged independence is of sufficiently questionable probative value that we have not relied upon it.

[722] See USITC Report, Exhibit Kor-73.

[723] If KAA were to be considered a part of MOCT, then the 10 regional airports administered by KAA would also have been included in Annex 1 coverage. As noted in para. 7.47 above, even though the Panel requested that the parties (particularly the United States) address this issue, no evidence was presented that KAA's 10 regional airports were considered part of Korea's offer.

Legal responsibility for the IIA project

7.62 The second question is whether or not KAA and its successors were acting on behalf of MOCT, at least with respect to the IIA project. That is, was the IIA project really the legal responsibility of MOCT. In answering these questions, we must review the laws governing construction of the IIA.[724]

7.63 The United States relies heavily on the Korean *Aviation Act* for support for its position that MOCT has the legal responsibility for the IIA project. Paragraphs (1) and (2) of Article 94 read as follows:

> "(1) The airport development projects shall be carried out by the Minister of Construction and Transportation: *Provided*, that this shall not apply in case (of) provided otherwise [sic] by this Act or other Acts and subordinate statutes. (*emphasis in original*)
>
> (2) Any person other than the Minister of Construction and Transportation, who desires to operate the airport development projects, shall obtain the permission of the Minister of Construction and Transportation, under the conditions as prescribed by the Presidential Decree."[725]

7.64 Paragraph (3) of Article 94 provides that the land and airport facilities will revert to the State upon completion of the project. Article 95 then continues on with a statement of the requirements that the "project operator" as prescribed in Article 94 must fulfill regarding drawing up project plans and getting approval from the Minister before beginning work as provided in the Presidential Decree.

7.65 Korea has responded that the proviso in Article 94(1) means that the *Seoul Airport Act* is the ultimate controlling statute rather than the *Aviation Act*.

7.66 We agree with Korea's reading of these statutes. It seems clear to us that the *Aviation Act* provides for at least two methods of airport construction. One is by MOCT, in which case the whole of the *Aviation Act* applies. A second is by other entities as provided otherwise by law. The *Seoul Airport Act* is such a law.[726] The

---

[724] We note that Korea raised the question of the applicability of GPA Article I:3 to the present situation. This provision reads as follows:

> "Where entities, in the context of procurement covered under this Agreement, require enterprises not included in Appendix I to award contracts in accordance with particular requirements, Article III shall apply mutatis mutandis to such requirements."

This provision applies "in the context of procurement covered by this Agreement." This implies that it is already agreed that there is a covered entity with procurement under its responsibility. Here the question is whether the entity in question, KAA, is covered. The provision also refers to a covered entity requiring a particular *enterprise* to award contracts for a project. It is unclear what guidance this provides when reviewing the relationship of two entities. Thus, we do not think this provision provides guidance in the present situation.

[725] Exhibit Kor-115. The version of the law in effect in 1991 is included in Exhibit Kor-114 where Article 94(1) is phrased somewhat differently from the later version. The difference is not material to our purposes and it is unclear whether the difference is merely one of translation.

[726] *Seoul Airport Act*, Act No. 4383 (31 May 1991) as amended by Act No. 4436 (14 December 1991) Exhibit Kor-12; *Korea Airport Corporation Act* as amended by Act Nos. 4435 and 4436 (14 December 1991) Exhibit Kor-14.

United States argues[727] that the cross-reference to Article 95(1) of the *Aviation Act* in Article 8(1)16 of the *Seoul Airport Act* proves that the *Aviation Act* is still the controlling statutory authority. We do not think this aids the US case. Indeed, if anything, it would tend to support the opposite conclusion. Article 8(1)16 cross-references only the requirement in Article 95 of the *Aviation Act* regarding the submission of an operational plan by a project operator. Article 95(1) of the *Aviation Act* requires approval of an operational plan by MOCT; Article 7 of the *Seoul Airport Act* requires the project operator to draw up an "execution plan" for approval. Article 8(1)16 operates to create the presumption (legal fiction) that the Article 7(1) approval is equated with the approval given by Article 95(1) of the *Aviation Act*. One of the aspects that implies the contrary of the US assertion is the very limited cross-reference to Article 95(1) in the context of a series of cross-references in Article 96. These cross-references in Article 96 are made redundant by Article 8 of the *Seoul Airport Act*. As Korea has pointed out[728], the redundancies in these two Acts would not be necessary if, in fact, the *Aviation Act* were still the controlling statutory authority for the IIA project. Furthermore, we also note that Article 95(3) of the *Aviation Act* appears to make a distinction between operational plans made directly by MOCT and such plans merely approved by MOCT.[729]

7.67 The *Seoul Airport Act* has many provisions relating to the relationship between KAA and MOCT. These provisions, as noted in the previous paragraph, would be at the very least unnecessary if the *Aviation Act* were the controlling statutory authority. Moreover, Article 4 of the *Seoul Airport Act* provides for MOCT to draw up a master plan of the project including the *general direction* of construction, an *outline* of the construction plan, the construction period and a financing plan, as well as other matters deemed necessary by MOCT.[730] These issues of a general nature are not uncommon elements of a Ministry's oversight of a project but do not render the other entity its agent.

7.68 Article 6 of the *Seoul Airport Act* provides that the master plan shall be implemented by the state and local governments and by what was later designated as KAA. Article 7 then required KAA to develop an execution plan and have it approved by MOCT along with any alterations other than minor ones.[731] There obviously is a relationship of some degree between MOCT and KAA. MOCT has specific responsibilities of continued oversight. However, we are not persuaded that this oversight was such that KAA was acting as a mere agent of MOCT on a project that was still within the procurement responsibility of MOCT.

7.69 Importantly for purposes of analysis under the GPA, procurement appears to be the responsibility of KAA. The United States has provided examples of bid re-

---

727 Paras. 4.90-4.94, 4.101-4.104 and 4.114-4.116.

728 Paras. 4.95-4.100. See also paras. 4.86-4.89, 4.105-4.108 and 4.112-4.113.

729 While we consider the cross-reference discussed in the text the most salient for purposes of our Findings, we do note that the United States cited other cross-references. For example, the United States cited cross-references in Articles 2:1 and 2:2(a) of the *Seoul Airport Act* to definitions contained in the *Aviation Act*. We find such citations unpersuasive in support of the US point. It only makes sense that two statutes referring to aviation matters should operate from common definitions.

730 Exhibit Kor-12(a).

731 Ibid.

quests that identify MOCT or the Office of Supply, but we do not find these isolated instances that have been shown to us as sufficient evidence that MOCT is responsible for procurement for the IIA.[732] We note that the currently responsible entity, IIAC, has 557 employees and the NADG is staffed by 30 MOCT officials.[733] While we recognize that a smaller entity can utilize a larger agent, it does not appear that IIAC is a mere empty shell. We also take note of Korea's statement that MOCT has no role in IIA procurements.[734] We see no evidence that would cast doubt on this statement.

7.70 The United States has pointed out that the MOCT website states that NADG has responsibility for the IIA project. As discussed previously, we also take note of Korea's caution that a Ministry's website is not a legal document and that in this case it was prepared by the public relations department of MOCT which might have other motivations in describing the Ministry's business other than technical accuracy. There certainly is a role under Korean law for MOCT in the IIA project. It appears to be a role of oversight. We do not think oversight by one governmental entity of a project which has been delegated by law to another entity (which we have already found to be independent and not covered by GPA commitments) results in a conclusion that there is an agency relationship between them.

Conclusion

7.71 In our view, after reviewing the issues raised in this subsection, we return to our previous conclusion that the answer must be that Members generally may, pursuant to negotiations, decide which entities (and procurement covered by those entities) are included in their Schedules and in which Annex they will be included. The question of "control" or other indicia of affiliation is not an explicit provision of the GPA. Rather, it is a matter of interpretation for the content of the Schedules themselves. Therefore, the issue of whether a Party can use a Note to exclude an entity which would otherwise appear to be covered within the concession contained in a particular Annex is precisely the sort of issue appropriate for qualifications through Notes as found by the panel in *United States - Sugar*, as discussed in paragraphs 7.30-7.31, above.

7.72 We must also note, however, that this ability to define the scope of commitments is not absolute. The United States pointed out that procurement by NADG was unarguably covered by the GPA even though it was neither listed explicitly nor directly within the definition of a subordinate linear organization or otherwise in Note 1 to Annex 1. Korea responded that NADG was merely an ad hoc task force within MOCT. But this response of Korea somewhat avoids the challenge of this example. There can be something else beyond the strict confines of the language of the Schedule which must be examined. If a Party explicitly excludes an entity in a Note, that is conclusive. A Member may also affirmatively put entities in another Annex from an

---

732 US Exhibits 25, 75 and 76. We also note that several examples of such documents submitted by the United States to support the allegations of procurements inconsistent with the requirements of the GPA show no relationship with MOCT. See US Exhibits 34-43. See also Exhibit Kor-48 (A-N).

733 Para. 2.82.

734 Paras. 4.50, 4.69, 4.77 and 4.78. Exhibit Kor-116.

affiliated entity. But if the Schedule is completely silent on an entity, it may be necessary to look somewhat further to see if there is an affiliation of two entities such that they could be considered legally the same entity (which appears to be the case between MOCT and NADG) or one could be acting on behalf of another.

7.73 In this dispute, we cannot so far conclude from the language of Korea's Appendix I and the Notes contained therein that KAA and its successors as entities are covered by Korea's Schedule commitments or that the IIA project is somehow otherwise included. We must still note, however, the ambiguities in the wording of Note 1 to Annex 1 which were not fully resolved by a textual analysis and led us to refer already to one piece of the negotiating history of Korea's accession to the GPA. We, therefore, will complete our examination of the scope of Korea's Annex 1 through a more thorough discussion of the relevant aspects of negotiating history of Korea's accession to the GPA.

3. Negotiations for Korea's GPA Accession

7.74 As we noted above, Korea's Note 1 to Annex 1 leaves room for ambiguity. As an aid in interpreting Note 1 and Annex 1 we reviewed one particularly relevant piece of negotiating history. At that point we did not undertake a broader review of the negotiating history because it was a limited point we were examining and one piece of evidence was particularly relevant to its interpretation. Clearly, there are difficulties in interpreting the Schedule language, some aspects of which are ambiguous, and we wish to ensure that there are not other aspects of the negotiating history which might change the conclusions we reached with respect to Note 1. Also, the United States has specifically argued that the understanding of the parties at the time of the negotiations was that there was a concession with respect to the IIA project, regardless of which entity was responsible. Therefore, we consider it appropriate to engage in a further review of the overall negotiating history.

7.75 At the outset of our analysis of this issue, we must address some relevant issues relating to use of negotiating history which arose in the *European Communities - Computer Equipment* dispute. In that dispute, the Appellate Body specifically found that the standard of reasonable expectation or legitimate expectation existing with respect to non-violation cases had no role in reviewing negotiating history in order to aid in resolving the issues pertaining to a violation case. One of the reasons is that in a non-violation case the relevant question is what was the reasonable expectation of the complaining party. However, if it is necessary to go beyond the text in a violation case, the relevant question is to assess the objective evidence of the mutual understanding of the negotiating parties.[735] This involves not just the complaining and responding parties, but also involves possibly other parties to the negotiations. It is also important to note that there is a difference in perspectives of the reasonable expectations of one party as opposed to the mutual understanding of all the parties. The information available at the time of the negotiations may be available to some parties but not all. In other words, the evidence before the panel may be different in the two analyses and the weighting and probative value may also differ.

---

[735] Appellate Body Report, *EC - LAN*, *supra*, footnote 106, paras. 81-84, 93.

7.76 We start by noting again that Korea provided in February 1991 a *Supplementary Explanation* to its initial 1990 offer.[736] The United States then began bilateral negotiations with Korea regarding its accession bid on 22 April 1991. During the course of these negotiations, the United States put a series of questions to Korea regarding its offer.[737] Question 6 asked:

> "How does the Airport Development Group relate to the Ministry of Communications? Does Korea's offer of coverage of the Ministry of Communications include purchases for the Airport Development Group? Please identify all Ministries that will be responsible for the procurement of goods and services related to new airport construction."

7.77 In response, Korea answered:

> "The new airport construction is being conducted by the New Airport Development Group under the Ministry of Transportation. The new airport construction project is scheduled to be completed by 1997 after the completion of the basic plan by 1992 and the working plan by 1993. The US company, Bechtel, is taking part in the basic plan projects.
>
> The responsible organization for procurement of goods and services relating to the new airport construction is the Office of Supply. But at present, the concrete procurement plan has not been fixed because now the whole airport construction project is only in a basic planning stage."[738]

7.78 On 14 December 1993, Korea made its final offer. The final offer also introduced General Notes that applied to all the Annexes. General Note 1 provides:

> "Korea will not extend the benefit of this Agreement
>
> (a) as regards the award of contracts by National Railroad Administration,
>
> (b) as regards procurement for airports by the entities listed in Annex 1,
>
> (c) as regards procurement for urban transportation (including subways) by the entities listed in Annexes 1 and 2
>
> to the suppliers and service providers of member states of the European Community, Austria, Norway, Sweden, Finland and Switzerland, until such time as Korea has accepted that those countries give comparable and effective access for Korean undertakings to their relevant markets."

7.79 The European Communities had made an inquiry of Korea in late November 1993 as to the coverage of airports.[739] There apparently was no written response. However, an internal EC note does indicate that Korea responded that there was air-

---

736 See para. 7.44.
737 Paras. 2.51 and 4.328.
738 Paras. 2.52 and 4.330.
739 EC Response to First set of Panel Questions, Annex IV.

port coverage, but in parenthesis noted "Seoul, Pusan" as examples of the airports that would be covered. This implies that they are therefore the airports covered by reason of Note 1 to Annex 1. That is, this evidence is consistent with our conclusion reached in paragraph 7.47. There was no mention of KAA or the IIA project in the EC internal note.[740] Then the European Communities and several other countries introduced reservations excluding coverage of airports for Korea. Apparently, this is what prompted Korea's derogation quoted above in General Note 1(b) to Appendix I.

7.80 As will be discussed more fully in the following two sections, the Korean answer to the US question clearly was not as full and thorough a response as would normally be appropriate for GPA negotiations.[741] At the time Korea provided its answer it had already enacted legislation designating another entity (other than MOCT) as responsible for the IIA project. Further legislation to designate KAA as that entity was already in the planning stages. Korea has stated that it knew that the IIA project was the subject of the US inquiry.[742] The Korean answer can, at best, be described as inadequate.

7.81 Nonetheless, we do note that Korea's July 1991 answer to the US question was qualified by the reference to the fact that the procurement plans were not finalized. And this qualification was preceded by the linking word "but" which clearly means the previous statement should not have been taken as an absolute. We recognize that the "but" qualification refers to the procurement plan while the question and the previous portion of the answer refer to the responsible procuring entities. However, the Korean answer was sufficiently qualified so that it should have raised questions. And, importantly, the United States (we have no evidence that any Parties other than the United States were aware of this particular Korean response) had over two and a half years before reaching a final agreement during which time this ambiguity could have been cleared up. The European Communities and other negotiating parties did act in 1993 to clarify the coverage of airports and received answers that contribute to the overall picture that there was no mutual understanding of the parties that a covered entity was procuring for the IIA project. In fact, it seems that negotiating parties other than the United States were clear that the IIA project was not covered.[743] In light of the lapse of time and the actions of other Members, the United States should not have rested upon the conclusions they now tell this Panel they reached based on this qualified response from Korea in 1991.

7.82 In summary, with respect to the interpretation of the negotiating history of Korea's accession to the GPA, we recall our conclusion that this information clarifies that Note 1 to Annex 1 was meant to be definitional in nature and that the text of Korea's Schedule does not include coverage of KAA and its successors. In our view, the full negotiating history reflecting what the several parties to the negotiations un-

---

740 Ibid., Annex V.

741 The Panel notes that it has not made any finding at any point in this Report that Korea acted in bad faith during any portion of the negotiations for its accession to the GPA.

742 Para. 4.343.

743 The fact that the United States alone received an answer from Korea that may have resulted in a reasonable expectation on the US part of some different situation will be discussed below with respect to the non-violation claim.

derstood with respect to Korea's offer, confirms our conclusion that there was no mutual understanding on the coverage of KAA.

7.83 Therefore, we conclude that the IIA construction project was not covered as the entities engaged in procurement for the project are not covered entities within the meaning of Article I of the GPA. Furthermore, the kind of affiliation that we have concluded is necessary to render an unlisted entity subject to the GPA is not present in this case. Therefore, we do not need to proceed further and make specific findings with respect to the alleged inconsistencies of Korea's procurement practices in this regard.[744]

C. Allegation of Non-Violation Nullification or Impairment

1. General

(a) Asserted Basis of the Claim

7.84 We note at the outset that the basis for the non-violation claim that the United States has made in the context of this case is different from the basis that usually exists in relation to such claims.[745] In order to explain this difference clearly, it is necessary first to note the bases of a traditional non-violation claim.

7.85 The panel in *Japan - Measures Affecting Consumer Photographic Film and Paper* (WT/DS44) ("*Japan - Film*") summarized the traditional test for non-violation cases in the following manner:

> "The text of Article XXIII:1(b) establishes three elements that a complaining party must demonstrate in order to make out a cognizable claim under Article XXIII:1(b): (1) application of a measure by a WTO Member; (2) a benefit accruing under the relevant agreement; and (3) nullification or impairment of the benefit as the result of the application of the measure."[746]

To this we would add the notion that has been developed in all these cases that the nullification or impairment of the benefit as a result of the measure must be contrary to the reasonable expectations of the complaining party at the time of the agreement.

7.86 So, normal non-violation cases involve an examination as to whether there is: (1) an application of a measure by a WTO Member; (2) a benefit accruing under the relevant agreement; and (3) nullification or impairment of the benefit due to the application of the measure that could not have been reasonably expected by the exporting Member.

7.87 In this case, the United States has asserted that measures it claimed violated the GPA (that is, the imposition of inadequate bid-deadlines; the imposition of certain qualification requirements; the imposition of certain domestic partnering requirements; and the failure to establish effective domestic challenge procedures en-

[744] We note that had such Findings been required, Korea took no position in response to the US allegations and offered no evidence to refute that provided by the United States.

[745] The allegations made by the United States are pursuant to a portion of GPA Article XXII:2 which is equivalent to Article XXIII:1(b) of GATT 1994.

[746] Panel Report, *Japan - Film, supra*, footnote 510, para. 10.41, citing, *EEC - Oilseeds*, BISD 37S/86, paras. 142-152; *Australian Subsidy on Ammonium Sulphate*, BISD II/188, 192-193.

gaged in by KAA and its successors in relation to the IIA project) nullify or impair benefits accruing to the United States under the GPA, pursuant to Article XXII:2 of the GPA. A key difference between a traditional non-violation case and the present one would seem to be that, normally, the question of "reasonable expectation" is whether or not it was reasonably to be expected that the benefit under an existing concession would be impaired by the measures. However here, if there is to be a non-violation case, the question is whether or not there was a reasonable expectation of an entitlement to a benefit that had accrued pursuant to the *negotiation* rather than pursuant to a *concession*.

(b) Arguments of the Parties

7.88 The United States slightly re-arranges the test enunciated by the *Japan - Film* panel and proposes that a successful determination of a non-violation nullification and impairment in the GPA requires the finding of the following three elements: (1) a concession was negotiated and exists; (2) a measure is applied that upsets the established competitive relationship; and (3) the measure could not have been reasonably anticipated at the time the concession was negotiated.[747] The United States argues that of the three elements of a non-violation claim, the only outstanding issue in this case is the first element - that is, whether or not there is a concession.

7.89 The United States contends that, similarly, during Korea's GPA accession negotiations, the United States bargained for and received from Korea the coverage of all government entities responsible for the procurement of products and services related to new airport construction projects under Annex 1. According to the United States, Korea subsequently engaged in, and continues to engage in, measures in procurement that could not have reasonably been anticipated by the United States at the time the coverage of new airport construction was negotiated. The United States argues that these measures result in the upsetting of the established competitive relationship between US products, services, and suppliers and Korean products, services, and suppliers in the IIA construction project, a competitive relationship worth potentially US$6 billion. On this basis, the United States argues that Korea is nullifying or impairing benefits accruing to the United States under the GPA.

7.90 In response, Korea argues that the burden placed upon the United States to support its non-violation claim under Article XXII:2 of the GPA is substantial. Korea notes that under DSU Article 26:1(a), "the complaining party shall present a detailed justification in support of any complaint relating to a measure which does not conflict with the relevant covered agreement."

7.91 Korea argues that the United States must demonstrate, by virtue of the requirement in Article XXII:2 that it identify a "benefit accruing" to it under the GPA,

[747] The United States cites: Report of the Working Party on *The Australian Subsidy on Ammonium Sulphate* (adopted on 3 April 1950), BISD II/188-196, para. 12; Panel Report on *Treatment by Germany of Imports of Sardines* (adopted on 31 October 1952), G/26, BISD 1S/53-59, para. 16; Panel Report on *European Economic Community -Production Aids Granted on Canned Peaches, Canned Pears, Canned Fruit Cocktail and Dried Grapes*, 20 February 1985 (unadopted), L/5778, para. 51; and Panel Report on *European Economic Community - Payments and Subsidies Paid to Processors and Producers of Oilseeds and Related Animal-Feed Proteins* (adopted on 25 January 1990), L/6627, BISD 37S/86, paras. 142-152.

that it "reasonably expected" to obtain the benefit of GPA coverage for IIA procurement.[748] Korea further argues that "for expectations of a benefit to be legitimate, the challenged measures must not have been reasonably anticipated at the time the tariff concession was negotiated."[749] Korea asserts that this requirement is self-evident and quotes for support: "If the measures were anticipated, a Member could not have had a legitimate expectation of improved market access to the extent of the impairment caused by these measures."[750]

7.92 Korea argues that the requirement that the measure at issue has upset the competitive relationship created by the Agreement implies that an "agreement" is necessary. Korea further argues that the essence of a non-violation claim is that some action of a party, after an agreement is concluded, which could not have been reasonably anticipated at the time of the agreement, nullifies or impairs a concession made by another party. Korea asserts that the United States has not specified what agreement was made by the parties that was nullified or impaired by action taken by Korea after that agreement was entered into. Korea further asserts that it could not have been an agreement to include KAA and KOACA and IIAC in Korea's GPA coverage given that Korea never agreed to include these entities in any of its offers.

2. *Non-Violation Claims in the Context of Principles of Customary International Law*

7.93 In our view, the non-violation remedy as it has developed in GATT/WTO jurisprudence should not be viewed in isolation from general principles of customary international law. As noted above, the basic premise is that Members should not take actions, even those consistent with the letter of the treaty, which might serve to undermine the reasonable expectations of negotiating partners. This has traditionally arisen in the context of actions which might undermine the value of negotiated tariff concessions. In our view, this is a further development of the principle of *pacta sunt servanda* in the context of Article XXIII:1(b) of the GATT 1947 and disputes that arose thereunder, and subsequently in the WTO Agreements, particularly in Article 26 of the DSU. The principle of *pacta sunt servanda* is expressed in Article 26 of the *Vienna Convention*[751] in the following manner:

> "Every treaty in force is binding upon the parties to it and must be performed by them in good faith."

7.94 It seems clear that good faith performance has been agreed by the WTO Members to include subsequent actions which might nullify or impair the benefits reasonably expected to accrue to other parties to the negotiations in question. The

[748] Panel Report, *Japan – Film, supra*, footnote 510, para. 10.72. As further support for this principle, Korea cites *EEC - Oilseeds*, BISD 37S/86, 128-129 (paras. 147-148); *Operation of the Provisions of Article XVI*, BISD 10S/201, 209 (para. 28) (adopted on 21 November 1961); *Other Barriers to Trade*, BISD 3S/222, 224 (para. 13) (adopted on 3 March 1955); *Germany - Sardines*, BISD 1S/53, 58-59 (para. 16) (adopted on 31 October 1952); *Australian Subsidy on Ammonium Sulphate*, GATT/CP.4/39, BISD II/188, 193-194 (adopted on 3 April 1950).

[749] *Japan – Film, supra*, footnote 510, para. 10.76.

[750] Ibid.

[751] A reference to the rule of *pacta sunt servanda* also appears in the preamble to the Vienna Convention.

consistency of such an interpretation with the general principles of customary international law is confirmed by reference to the negotiating history of the *Vienna Convention*. According to the Report of the International Law Commission to the General Assembly, this issue was considered by the members negotiating the Convention in the following manner:

> "Some members felt that there would be advantage in also stating that a party must abstain from acts calculated to frustrate the object and purpose of the treaty. The Commission, however, considered that this was clearly implicit in the obligation to perform the treaty in good faith and preferred to state the *pacta sunt servanda* rule in as simple a form as possible."[752]

7.95 The non-violation doctrine goes further than just respect for the object and purpose of the treaty as expressed in its terminology. One must respect actual provisions (i.e., concessions) as far as their material effect on competitive opportunities is concerned. It is an extension of the good faith requirement in this sense.

7.96 We take note that Article 3.2 of the DSU requires that we seek within the context of a particular dispute to clarify the existing provisions of the WTO agreements in accordance with customary rules of interpretation of public international law.[753] However, the relationship of the WTO Agreements to customary international law is broader than this. Customary international law applies generally to the economic relations between the WTO Members. Such international law applies to the extent that the WTO treaty agreements do not "contract out" from it. To put it another way, to the extent there is no conflict or inconsistency, or an expression in a covered WTO agreement that implies differently, we are of the view that the customary rules of international law apply to the WTO treaties and to the process of treaty formation under the WTO.

7.97 As Korea has argued, non-violation is an exceptional concept within the WTO dispute settlement system. Article 26:1(a) of the DSU requires that:

> "[T]he complaining party shall present a detailed justification in support of any complaint relating to a measure which does not conflict with the relevant covered agreement."

7.98 As stated by the panel in *Japan - Film:*

> "Although the non-violation remedy is an important and accepted tool of WTO/GATT dispute settlement and has been "on the books" for almost 50 years, we note that there have been only eight cases in which panels or working parties have substantially considered Article XXIII:1(b) claims. This suggests that both the GATT contracting parties and WTO Members have approached the remedy with caution and, indeed, have treated it as an exceptional instrument of dispute settlement. We note in this regard that both the European Communi-

---

752 *Yearbook of the International Law Commission* (1966), Vol. II at p. 211.

753 We should also note that we can see no basis here for an *a contrario* implication that rules of international law other than rules of interpretation do not apply. The language of 3.2 in this regard applies to a specific problem that had arisen under the GATT to the effect that, among other things, reliance on negotiating history was being utilized in a manner arguably inconsistent with the requirements of the rules of treaty interpretation of customary international law.

> ties and the United States in the *EEC - Oilseeds* case, and the two parties in this case, have confirmed that the non-violation nullification or impairment remedy should be approached with caution and treated as an exceptional concept. The reason for this caution is straightforward. Members negotiate the rules that they agree to follow and only exceptionally would expect to be challenged for actions not in contravention of those rules."[754]

Despite this caution, however, the panel in *Japan - Film* was of the view that the non-violation remedy had an important role - that of protecting the reasonable expectations of competitive opportunities through negotiated concessions.

7.99 In our view, these observations by previous panels are entirely in line with the concept of *pacta sunt servanda*. The vast majority of actions taken by Members which are consistent with the letter of their treaty obligations will also be consistent with the spirit. However, upon occasion, it may be the case that some actions, while permissible under one set of rules (e.g., the Agreement on Subsidies and Countervailing Measures is a commonly referenced example of rules in this regard), are not consistent with the spirit of other commitments such as those in negotiated Schedules. That is, such actions deny the competitive opportunities which are the reasonably expected effect of such commitments. However, we must also note that, while the overall burden of proof is on the complainant, we do not mean to introduce here a new requirement that a complainant affirmatively prove actual bad faith on the part of another Member. It is fairly clear from the history of disputes prior to the conclusion of the Uruguay Round that such a requirement was never established and there is no evidence in the current treaty text that such a requirement was newly imposed. Rather, the affirmative proof should be that measures have been taken that frustrate the object and purpose of the treaty and the reasonably expected benefits that flow therefrom.

7.100 One of the issues that arises in this dispute is whether the concept of non-violation can arise in contexts other than the traditional approach represented by *pacta sunt servanda.* Can, for instance the question of error in treaty negotiation be addressed under Article 26 of the DSU and Article XXII:2 of the GPA? We see no reason why it cannot. Parties have an obligation to negotiate in good faith just as they must implement the treaty in good faith. It is clear to us (as discussed in paragraphs 7.110 and 7.121 below) that it is necessary that negotiations in the Agreement before us (the GPA) be conducted on a particularly open and forthcoming basis.

7.101 Thus, on the basis of the ample evidence provided by both parties to the dispute, we will review the claim of nullification or impairment raised by the United States within the framework of principles of international law which are generally applicable not only to performance of treaties but also to treaty negotiation.[755] To do

[754] Panel Report, *Japan – Film, supra*, footnote 510, para. 10.36.

[755] We note that DSU Article 7.1 requires that the relevant covered agreement be cited in the request for a panel and reflected in the terms of reference of a panel. That is not a bar to a broader analysis of the type we are following here, for the GPA would be the referenced covered agreement and, in our view, we are merely fully examining the issue of non-violation raised by the United States. We are merely doing it within the broader context of customary international law rather than limiting it to the traditional analysis that accords with the extended concept of *pacta sunt servanda*.

otherwise potentially would leave a gap in the applicability of the law generally to WTO disputes and we see no evidence in the language of the WTO Agreements that such a gap was intended. If the non-violation remedy were deemed not to provide a relief for such problems as have arisen in the present case regarding good faith and error in the negotiation of GPA commitments (and one might add, in tariff and services commitments under other WTO Agreements), then nothing could be done about them within the framework of the WTO dispute settlement mechanism if general rules of customary international law on good faith and error in treaty negotiations were ruled not to be applicable. As was argued above, that would not be in conformity with the normal relationship between international law and treaty law or with the WTO Agreements.

7.102 If non-violation represents an extension of the good faith requirements in the implementation of a treaty and can also be applied to good faith and error in negotiations under the GPA, and we think it can, then the special remedies for non-violation contained in DSU Article 26 should also be applied rather than the traditional remedies of treaty law which are not apposite to the situation of the GPA (see the discussion in footnote 769, below).

(a) The Traditional Approach: Extended *pacta sunt servanda*

7.103 Because the United States raised the non-violation issue in this dispute at least nominally under the traditional approach, we will examine the facts of the dispute in that context first. In our view, there is a slightly different cast to traditional non-violation claims with respect to the GPA than under previous GATT non-violation cases. Here the analysis would run as follows: (1) there was an agreed concession on entities; (2) resulting from that there was a reasonable expectation of enjoying competitive bidding opportunities; (3) an action which does not violate GPA rules is taken by the Member that made the concession, including the concessions on entities; and (4) resulting from that, the expected competitive bidding opportunities are not available and the benefits of the concession have been nullified and impaired.

7.104 In light of these elements, we will now turn to the facts of this case. In 1990, Korea made its initial offer of coverage when it requested accession to the Tokyo Round Agreement. In February 1991, Korea provided a *Supplementary Explanation*. As we discussed above, that February 1991 explanation noted airport coverage under the Ministry of Transportation.[756] It showed two unnamed regional airport authorities and one named airport entity. The IIA project was not mentioned nor was KAA. As we have also discussed above, the meaning of the proposed Note 1 to Annex 1 was clarified in a manner which clearly indicated it was intended as a guide to the scope of the coverage under Annex 1.

The purpose of the terms of reference is to properly identify the claims of the party and therefore the scope of a panel's review. We do not see any basis for arguing that the terms of reference are meant to *exclude* reference to the broader rules of customary international law in interpreting a claim properly before the Panel.

[756] See para. 7.44.

7.105 On 1 May 1991, the United States sent a series of questions to Korea including a question regarding coverage of airport construction. On 31 May 1991, the Korea National Assembly enacted the *Seoul Airport Act* which Korea has told the panel was the legal basis for the shift of authority away from MOCT. Otherwise the *Aviation Act* would have required that the Minister of Transportation build the facility. On 26 June 1991, the Ministry of Transportation began the preparatory legislative work that would result in KAA being designated in December 1991 as the responsible entity for the IIA project.

7.106 On 1 July 1991, Korea provided its response to the US questions. We will quote again at this point both the US question and Korea's answer because we think it is very important to review them in light of the facts described in the preceeding two paragraphs. The United States asked:

> "How does the Airport Development Group relate to the Ministry of Communications? Does Korea's offer of coverage of the Ministry of Communications include purchases for the Airport Development Group? Please identify all Ministries that will be responsible for the procurement of goods and services related to new airport construction."

In response, Korea answered:

> "The new airport construction is being conducted by the New Airport Development Group under the Ministry of Transportation. The new airport construction project is scheduled to be completed by 1997 after the completion of the basic plan by 1992 and the working plan by 1993. The US company, Bechtel, is taking part in the basic plan projects.
>
> The responsible organization for procurement of goods and services relating to the new airport construction is the Office of Supply. But at present, the concrete procurement plan has not been fixed because now the whole airport construction project is only in a basic planning stage."

7.107 Following this answer, on 10 July 1991, the MOT published a public notice of draft legislation containing proposed amendments to the *Seoul Airport Act.* Then extensive internal governmental consultations took place and, on 21 October 1991, the draft legislation was transferred to the National Assembly. It was adopted by the National Assembly on 20 November 1991 and signed by the President and published in the *Official Gazette* on 14 December 1991.

7.108 We find it very difficult to understand how Korea could have made the response that it did on 1 July 1991, state nothing else at that time or in the succeeding months and bring none of this to the attention of the United States. The enabling legislation was already passed on 31 May 1991 removing MOCT's direct authority for the project and this was at least one month before Korea provided its response to the question posed by the United States. Furthermore, at that time, plans were under way already to name a specific entity (KAA) as the entity responsible for the IIA. Yet Korea's response in July 1991 was that MOCT (through NADG) was currently responsible for the IIA project. Korea's answer was qualified by stating that procurement plans were not fixed, but much more than this was known by Korea at the time and should have been reported to the United States in the answer. Korea has offered no valid reason for why it did not do so.

7.109 We do not agree with Korea's argument that there is nothing to the GPA but the question of whether entities are covered. It is true that the Schedules are structured in terms of entities, but that is not the basis for the negotiations. Members do not negotiate to get coverage of entities as such. They do not bargain for names on a list. Rather, they negotiate to achieve coverage of the procurements which are the responsibility of the covered entities. As previous panels have noted, the object of negotiations on Schedule commitments is to achieve competitive opportunities and, in the context of the GPA, that comes with access to projects, not just a list of names of government entities.

7.110 In our view, an agreement such as the GPA requires full, timely and complete responses to questions. Negotiations for coverage of government procurement markets are difficult. Each market has its own characteristics which are fully understood only by the responding party. We recall how difficult it is to understand fully the structure of the Korean Government coverage pursuant to the *Government Organization Act* as an illustration of the difficulties in this regard. Korea has stated that in its view it had no obligation to try to guess what the United States was interested in and supply further information. However, Korea also stated that it did not mention in its answer the regional airport authorities that it had offered to include because it knew the United States was really interested in the IIA. Clearly the latter answer was correct. It was objectively clear what the US question was about. And Korea, knowing that, then had an obligation to make a full and frank response. The integrity of the negotiating system requires no less. In our view, Korea's actions fell short of the conduct expected of parties negotiating accession to the GPA.

7.111 However, having stated that Korea's answer was not satisfactory in various ways, that is not the end of our review of the facts. The next issue which we must address is the fact that Korea's answer to the US question was provided about two and a half years before submission of Korea's final offer and that responsibility for the IIA project was assigned to KAA two years before that 14 December 1993 offer. Indeed, the Agreement was not actually finalized until 15 April 1994. We note that in a previous dispute involving a tariff Schedule where there was an agreed concession, it was found possible to base a non-violation claim on measures taken prior to the close of negotiations that later impaired the benefits reasonably expected to accrue from the concessions. The panel in *Japan - Film* stated:

> "In the case of measures shown by Japan to have been introduced prior to the conclusion of the tariff negotiations at issue, it is our view that Japan has raised a presumption that the United States should be held to have anticipated those measures and it is for the United States to rebut that presumption. In this connection, it is our view that the United States is charged with knowledge of Japanese Government measures as of the date of their publication. We realize that knowledge of a measure's existence is not equivalent to understanding the impact of the measure on a specific product market. For example, a vague measure could be given substance through enforcement policies that are initially unexpected or later changed significantly. However, where the United States claims that it did not know of a measure's relevance to market access conditions in respect of film or paper, we

> would expect the United States to clearly demonstrate why initially it could not have reasonably anticipated the effect of an existing measure on the film or paper market and when it did realize the effect ... A simple statement that a Member's measures were so opaque and informal that their impact could not be assessed is not sufficient."[757]

7.112 In one situation that arose in that dispute, the United States showed that the relevant measure (a Cabinet Decision) was only published nine days before the conclusion of the Kennedy Round of negotiations. The panel made the following finding:

> "Because of the short time period between this particular measure's publication and the formal conclusion of the Kennedy Round, we consider it difficult to conclude that the United States should be charged with having anticipated the 1967 Cabinet Decision since it would be unrealistic to expect that the United States would have had an opportunity to reopen tariff negotiations on individual products in the last few days of a multilateral negotiating round."[758]

7.113 On the other hand, when the measure pre-dated the conclusion of the Round by a month and a half, the panel reached a different conclusion:

> "As we noted earlier, the United States is charged with knowledge of Japanese regulations on publication. Although we can conceive of circumstances where the exporting WTO Member may not reasonably be aware of the significance of a measure for or its potential disparate impact on imported products until some time after its publication, the United States has not demonstrated the existence of any such circumstance here."[759]

7.114 We recall that even though Korea's answer in July 1991 was almost two and a half years prior to Korea's final offer, it appears from evidence and statements from the parties that the Korean and US Governments had no further discussions on the subject. The United States has told us that they did not inquire further about that subject because they were reasonably convinced that they knew MOCT was covered and they believed that MOCT retained statutory authority under Korean law to carry out airport construction projects.

7.115 However, as pointed out by the panel in *Japan - Film* and quoted above, the United States is charged with knowledge of Korean legislation. The United States, therefore is presumed to have known of the *Seoul Airport Act* and the pieces of legislation enacted in December 1991 which actually put KAA in charge of the project. It is up to the United States to provide a persuasive explanation for why it did not know either about the legislation or the significance of it. Further, Korea has submitted evidence to show that US industry and Government had actual knowledge that KAA was in charge of the project.[760] Furthermore, while Korea's answer in July 1991 was not full and complete, it did contain a qualification. Over the course of about

757 Panel Report, *Japan - Film, supra*, footnote 510, para. 10.80.

758 Ibid. at para. 10.103.

759 Ibid. at para. 10.111.

760 See paras. 4.561, 4.563-4.566.

two and a half years, with knowledge that an entity other than MOCT was in charge of the project and in light of the qualification contained in the Korean answer upon which it was relying, at the very least, further inquiries should have been made by the United States.

7.116 Furthermore, the European Communities and several other Members did pursue the question of Korea's airport coverage. The United States is not charged with knowledge of the bilateral communications between these negotiating parties and Korea; however, more than that occurred here. The European Communities along with several other Members at some point in December 1993 added a derogation with respect to Korea's airport coverage in their GPA Schedules. Korea responded in kind with its derogation in its General Note 1(b). The United States certainly should have known from these circumstances that further clarifications from Korea were in order with respect to the US understanding of the Korean offer. We further note that the WTO GPA was not finalized until four months after Korea's final offer. At least one month of this period was to be used for verification with consultations to resolve the matter to follow if necessary.[761] We have seen no evidence that the United States made any effort to use this verification period to clarify the situation.

7.117 At this point, we will review the elements of a traditional non-violation case, applied in the context of the GPA, that we listed in paragraph 7.103 above, but we will do it in reverse order to illustrate a particular problem with this case. With respect to step four, the United States believes it has lost competitive opportunities on bidding for the IIA project. With respect to step three, the United States alleges that this is a result of actions taken by Korea. (However, these actions are identical to the actions alleged under the US violation complaint.) With respect to step two, the United States claims that it had reasonable expectations with respect to bidding opportunities on the IIA project (as discussed in paragraphs 7.104-7.107, above). But, with respect to step one, this was based on reasonable expectations derived from the negotiations, not from the concessions because we have found in section VII:B, above, that there were in fact no concessions given by Korea.

7.118 As discussed above, the United States bases its argument on the claim that it had a reasonable expectation that it had received a commitment with respect to a particular project, but the concessions themselves are based on covered entities. Thus, unlike traditional non-violation claims there is no actual Schedule commitment in this case.[762] If there were a commitment, the case would properly be a violation case because the measures cited by the United States as the basis for the non-violation nullification case (e.g., inadequate bid deadlines and insufficient challenge procedures) would, if they were substantiated, result in a violation. A traditional non-violation case could, therefore, not be sustained in this situation.

7.119 In sum, Korea's answer to the US question in July 1991 was insufficient. Members have a right to expect full and forthright answers to their questions sub-

[761] Minutes of the Meeting of the Committee on Government Procurement Held on 15 December 1993, Annex 1, GPR/M/50, 21 January 1994. US Exhibit 65.

[762] At best, the United States could argue that the relevant commitment was the coverage of MOCT. However, this does not really change the analysis, for we have already found that KAA was the responsible entity for IIA procurement and KAA was independent. It comes back again to the fact that the United States is arguing that it thought it had a commitment which it did not.

mitted during negotiations, particularly with respect to Schedules of affirmative commitments such as those appended to the GPA. However, Members must protect their own interests as well and in this case the United States did not do so. It had a significant amount of time to realize, particularly in light of the wide knowledge of KAA's role, that its understanding of the Korean answer was not accurate. Therefore, we find that, even if the principles of a traditional non-violation case were applicable in this situation the United States has failed to carry its burden of proof to establish that it had reasonable expectations that a benefit had accrued.

(b) Error in Treaty Formation

7.120 It is clear from the discussion above that the traditional claim of non-violation does not fit well with the situation existing in this dispute. Non-violation claims, as the doctrine has developed over the course of GATT and WTO disputes, have been based on nullification or impairment of benefits reasonably expected to flow from negotiated concessions. In this case, it was the negotiations which allegedly gave rise to the reasonable expectations rather than any concessions.

7.121 Therefore, we will continue with our analysis and first recall our finding that there is a particular duty of transparency and openness on the "offering" party in negotiations on concessions under the GPA. The negotiations between the Parties under the GPA do not benefit from a generally accepted framework such as the Harmonized System with respect to goods or even the Central Product Classification in services. The Annexes to the GPA which contain the entities whose procurement is covered by the Agreement are basically self-styled Schedules whose interpretation may require extensive knowledge of another country's procurement systems and governmental organization. Therefore, we believe that transparency and forthright provision of all relevant information are of the essence in negotiations on GPA Schedules.[763]

7.122 In our view, as discussed fully in the previous section, Korea's response to the US question was not as forthright as it should have been. Indeed, the response could be characterized as at best incomplete in light of existing Korean legislation and ongoing plans for further legislation. However, when addressing this problem, rather than asking whether there was a nullification or impairment of expectations arising from a concession, it might be better to inquire as to whether the United States was induced into error about a fact or situation which it assumed existed in the relation to the agreement being negotiated regarding Korea's accession to the GPA. In this case, it clearly appears that the United States was in error when it assumed that the IIA project was covered by the GPA as a result of the entity coverage offered by Korea.

7.123 Error in respect of a treaty is a concept that has developed in customary international law through the case law of the Permanent International Court of Justice[764] and of the International Court of Justice.[765] Although these cases are concerned primarily with the question in which circumstances of error *cannot* be advanced as a

[763] We do not imply by this para. or other similar portions of our Findings that parties to negotiations in other areas do not owe each other an obligation of transparency and openness.

[764] *Legal Status of Eastern Greenland* (1933) PCIJ, series A/B, No. 53, p. 22, at p. 71 and dissenting opinion of Judge Anzilotti, at pp. 91-92.

[765] Case concerning the *Temple of Preah Vihear*, ICJ Reports 1962, p. 6, at pp. 26-27.

reason for invalidating a treaty, it is implicitly accepted that error can be a ground for invalidating (part) of a treaty. The elements developed by the case law mentioned above have been codified by the International Law Commission in what became the *Vienna Convention on the Law of Treaties of 1969*. The relevant parts of Article 48 of the Convention read as follows:

> "Article 48
>
> *Error*
>
> 1. A State may invoke an error in a treaty as invalidating its consent to be bound by the treaty if the error related to a fact or situation which was assumed by that State to exist at the time when the treaty was concluded and formed an essential basis of its consent to be bound by the treaty.
> 2. Paragraph 1 shall not apply if the State in question contributed by its own conduct to the error or if the circumstances were such as to put that State on notice of a possible error."

Since this article has been derived largely from case law of the relevant jurisdiction, the PCIJ and the ICJ, there can be little doubt that it presently represents customary international law and we will apply it to the facts of this case.

7.124 As the Appellate Body has pointed out in *European Communities - Computer Equipment* and in *Canada - Dairy*, schedules are an integral part of a treaty. Hence negotiations about schedules, in this case GPA Annexes, are fundamentally treaty negotiations. In these treaty negotiations, we have noted that the United States believed that the IIA project was covered. As we have found in section VII:B of these Findings, that was not correct. The IIA project procurement was the responsibility of a non-covered entity. Hence the US error related to a fact or situation which was assumed by the US to exist at the time when the treaty was concluded. In our view, it also appears from the behaviour of the United States that this purported concession arguably formed an essential basis of its consent to be bound by the treaty as finally agreed. Hence the initial conditions for error under Article 48(1) of the *Vienna Convention* seem to us to be satisfied.

7.125 This raises the question of whether the exclusionary clause of the second paragraph of Article 48 can be overcome. Although we have indicated above that the duty to demonstrate good faith and transparency in GPA negotiations is particularly strong for the "offering" party, this does not relieve the other negotiating partners from their duty of diligence to verify these offers as best as they can.[766] Here again the facts already recounted in the previous sub-section[767] demonstrate that the United States has not properly discharged this burden. We do not think the evidence at all supports a finding that the United States has contributed by its own conduct to the error, but given the elements mentioned earlier (such as the two and a half year interval between Korea's answer to the US question and its final offer, the actions by the

[766] See Appellate Body Report *EC – Computer Equipment, supra*, footnote 106, paras. 109-110.

[767] See Paras. 7.104-7.116, above.

European Community in respect of Korea's offer[768], the subsequent four-month period, of which at least one month was explicitly designated for verification, etc.), we conclude that the circumstances were such as to put the United States on notice of a possible error. Hence the error should not have subsisted at the end of the two and a half year gap, at the moment the accession of Korea was "concluded." Therefore, the error was no longer "excusable" and only an excusable error can qualify as an error which may vitiate the consent to be bound by the agreement.

7.126 For these reasons, on balance, we are of the view that the US has not demonstrated error successfully as a basis for a claim of non-violation nullification or impairment of benefits.[769]

VIII. CONCLUSIONS

8.1 In light of our findings in Section VII, above, we conclude that the entities which have been conducting procurement for the IIA project are not covered entities under Korea's Appendix I of the GPA and are not otherwise covered by Korea's obligations under the GPA.

8.2 In light of our findings in Section VII, above, we conclude that the United States has not demonstrated that benefits reasonably expected to accrue under the GPA, or in the negotiations resulting in Korea's accession to the GPA, were nullified or impaired by measures taken by Korea (whether or not in conflict with the provisions of the GPA) within the meaning of Article XXII:2 of the GPA.

---

768 Note that the importance of the actions of a third State in avoiding error was already considered important in the case on the *Legal Status of Eastern Greenland*, loc. cit. PCIJ, p. 71 (the reaction of the US to the Danish request not to make any difficulties in the settlement of the Greenland question compared to the Norwegian reaction).

769 A finding of justifiable error in treaty formation might normally be expected to lead to the application of Article 65 of the *Vienna Convention*. However, Article 65 on the specific procedure for invoking invalidity of a treaty does not seem to belong to the provisions of the *Vienna Convention* which have become customary international law. See also the European Court of Justice in Case C-162/69 (Racke v. Hauptzollampt Mainz), 1998 ECR, I-3655, at point 59. The Article on separability (Article 44) raises the possibility that provisions may be separated, such as e.g. separate reciprocal concessions in schedules, if they do not form an essential basis for the consent of the other party of the treaty as a whole (though the fact or the circumstance to which the error related was an essential factor in the consent to be bound by the treaty (Art. 48(1)). We do not think that any of these provisions would be required with respect to non-violation under the WTO Agreements because Article 26 of the DSU clearly provides for the appropriate remedy.

ANNEX 1

WORLD TRADE ORGANIZATION

WT/DS163/4
11 May 1999
(99-2009)

Original: English

KOREA - MEASURES AFFECTING GOVERNMENT PROCUREMENT

Request for the Establishment of a Panel by the United States

The following communication, dated 11 May 1999, from the Permanent Mission of the United States to the Permanent Mission of the Republic of Korea and to the Chairman of the Dispute Settlement Body, is circulated in accordance with Article 6.2 of the DSU.

The Government of Korea is engaging in government procurement practices, in the construction of the new Inchon International Airport, that are inconsistent with Korea's obligations under the WTO Agreement on Government Procurement (GPA). These practices include:

- Qualification requirements: In order to be eligible to bid as a prime contractor, an interested supplier must have a license that in turn requires the supplier to have manufacturing facilities in Korea.
- Domestic partnering requirements: Foreign firms must partner with or act as subcontractors to local Korean firms in order to participate in tendering procedures.
- Absence of access to challenge procedures: The GPA requires that member countries provide effective procedures enabling suppliers to challenge alleged breaches of the GPA arising in the context of procurements. However, such procedures do not exist for Inchon International Airport and other airport construction procurements.
- Inadequate bid deadlines: There are impositions of deadlines for the receipt of tenders that are shorter than the GPA-required 40 days, such as when tendering procedures are cancelled without explanation and immediate re-bidding takes place with a shortened deadline for tendering.

On 16 February 1999, the United States Government requested consultations with the Government of Korea pursuant to Article 4 of the Understanding on Rules and Procedures Governing the Settlement of Disputes (DSU) and Article XXII of the

GPA with respect to the above measures. The United States and Korea held consultations in Geneva on 17 March 1999, but failed to settle the dispute.

During consultations, Korea asserted that the entities responsible for Inchon International Airport procurements are not within Korea's obligations under the GPA, and therefore not subject to the provisions of the GPA. The United States notes, however, that these entities are in fact within the scope of Korea's list of central government entities, as specified in Annex 1 of Korea's coverage of obligations in Appendix I of the GPA. The United States bargained in good faith for the coverage of all airport construction in Korea during negotiations for Korea's accession to the GPA; the United States' GPA commitments with respect to Korea and its acceptance of Korea as a party to the Agreement were based on a balance of rights and obligations that included this coverage. Korea's subsequent assertion that the entities responsible for the procurement of the Inchon International Airport are not covered by the GPA seriously disrupts this mutually-agreed balance.

Pursuant to Article I.1 of the GPA, Korea's obligations under the GPA apply in full with respect to government procurements for the Inchon International Airport. Consequently, the above measures are inconsistent with Articles III, VIII, XI, XVI and XX of the GPA. In addition, pursuant to Article XXII:2 of the GPA, whether or not these measures conflict with the provisions of the GPA, they nullify or impair benefits accruing to the United States under the GPA.

The United States continues to be interested in settling this dispute. However, in the absence of a settlement at this time, the United States, in order to preserve its rights, respectfully requests the establishment of a panel pursuant to Article XXII of the GPA, with standard terms of reference as set out in Article XXII.4 of the GPA. The United States further asks that this request for a panel be placed on the agenda for the next meeting of the Dispute Settlement Body, to be held on 26 May 1999.

UNITED STATES - SECTION 110(5) OF THE US COPYRIGHT ACT

Report of the Panel
WT/DS160/R

Adopted by the Dispute Settlement Body on 27 July 2000

TABLE OF CONTENTS

I. INTRODUCTION

1.1 On 26 January 1999, the European Communities and their member States (hereafter referred to as the European Communities) requested consultations with the United States under Article 4 of the Understanding on Rules and Procedures Governing the Settlement of Disputes ("DSU") and Article 64.1 of the Agreement on Trade-Related Aspects of Intellectual Property Rights ("TRIPS Agreement") regarding Section 110(5) of the United States Copyright Act as amended by the "Fairness in Music Licensing Act" enacted on 27 October 1998.[1]

1.2 The European Communities and the United States held consultations on 2 March 1999, but failed to reach a mutually satisfactory solution. On 15 April 1999, the European Communities requested the establishment of a panel under Article 6 of the DSU and Article 64.1 of the TRIPS Agreement.[2]

1.3 At its meeting on 26 May 1999, the Dispute Settlement Body ("DSB") established a panel in accordance with Article 6 of the DSU with the following standard terms of reference:

> "To examine, in the light of the relevant provisions of the covered agreements cited by the European Communities in document WT/DS160/5, the matter referred to the DSB by the European Communities in that document and to make such findings as will assist the DSB in making the recommendations or in giving the rulings provided for in those agreements."[3]

1.4 Australia, Brazil, Canada, Japan and Switzerland reserved their rights to participate in the panel proceedings as third parties.

1.5 On 27 July 1999, the European Communities made a request, with reference to Article 8.7 of the DSU, to the Director-in-charge to determine the composition of the Panel. On 6 August 1999, the Panel was composed as follows:

Chairperson:	Mrs. Carmen Luz Guarda
Members:	Mr. Arumugamangalam V. Ganesan
	Mr. Ian F. Sheppard

1.6 The Panel met with the parties on 8-9 November 1999 and 7 December 1999. It met with the third parties on 9 November 1999.

---

1 *See* document WT/DS160/1 (4 February 1999).

2 *See* document WT/DS160/5 (16 April 1999) reproduced in Annex 1 to this report.

3 *See* document WT/DS160/6 (6 August 1999) reproduced in Annex 2 to this report.

1.7 On 15 November, the Panel sent a letter to the International Bureau of the World Intellectual Property Organization (WIPO), that is responsible for the administration of the Berne Convention for the Protection of Literary and Artistic Works. In that letter, the Panel requested factual information on the provisions of the Paris Act of 1971 of that Convention ("Berne Convention (1971)"), incorporated into the TRIPS Agreement by its Article 9.1, relevant to the matter. The International Bureau of WIPO provided such information in a letter, dated 22 December 1999. The parties to the dispute provided comments on this information by means of letters, dated 12 January 2000.

1.8 The Panel submitted its interim report to the parties on 14 April 2000. The Panel submitted its final report to the parties on 5 May 2000.

II. FACTUAL ASPECTS

2.1 The dispute concerns Section 110(5) of the US Copyright Act of 1976[4], as amended by the Fairness in Music Licensing Act of 1998 ("the 1998 Amendment"),[5] which entered into force on 26 January 1999. The provisions of Section 110(5) place limitations on the exclusive rights provided to owners of copyright in Section 106 of the Copyright Act in respect of certain performances and displays.

2.2 The relevant parts of the current text of Section 106 read as follows:

> "§ 106. Exclusive rights in copyrighted works
>
> Subject to sections 107 through 120, the owner of copyright under this title has the exclusive rights to do and to authorize any of the following:
>
> ...
>
> (4) in the case of literary, musical, dramatic, and choreographic works, pantomimes, and motion pictures and other audiovisual works, to perform the copyrighted work publicly;
>
> (5) in the case of literary, musical, dramatic, and choreographic works, pantomimes, and pictorial, graphic, or sculptural works, including the individual images of a motion picture or other audiovisual work, to display the copyrighted work publicly; and
>
> ..."[6,7]

---

4 United States Copyright Act of 1976, Act of 19 October 1976, Pub.L. 94-553, 90 Stat. 2541 (as amended).

5 Fairness in Music Licensing Act of 27 October 1998, Pub.L. 105-298, 112 Stat. 2830, 105th Cong., 2nd Session (1998).

6 As contained in Exhibit US-15(b).

7 Section 101 of the US Copyright Act contains a number of definitions, of which the following are most relevant to the matter (as notified by the United States to the Council for TRIPS under Article 63.2 of the TRIPS Agreement, *see* WTO document IP/N/1/USA/1, dated 25 March 1996):

"To 'perform' a work means to recite, render, play, dance, or act it, either directly or by means of any device or process or, in the case of a motion picture or other audiovisual work, to show its images in any sequence or to make the sounds accompanying it audible."

"To perform or display a work 'publicly' means

(1) to perform or display it at a place open to the public or at any place where a substantial number of persons outside of a normal circle of a family and its social acquaintances is gathered; or

2.3 The relevant parts of the current text of Section 110(5) read as follows:[8]

"§ 110. Limitations on exclusive rights: Exemption of certain performances and displays

Notwithstanding the provisions of section 106, the following are not infringements of copyright:

...

(5)(A) except as provided in subparagraph (B), communication of a transmission embodying a performance or display of a work by the public reception of the transmission on a single receiving apparatus of a kind commonly used in private homes, unless -

(A) a direct charge is made to see or hear the transmission; or

(B) the transmission thus received is further transmitted to the public;

(B) communication by an establishment of a transmission or retransmission embodying a performance or display of a nondramatic musical work intended to be received by the general public, originated by a radio or television broadcast station licensed as such by the Federal Communications Commission, or, if an audiovisual transmission, by a cable system or satellite carrier, if—

(i) in the case of an establishment other than a food service or drinking establishment, either the establishment in which the communication occurs has less than 2,000 gross square feet of space (excluding space used for customer parking and for no other purpose), or the establishment in which the communication occurs has 2,000 or more gross square feet of space (excluding space used for customer parking and for no other purpose) and—

(I) if the performance is by audio means only, the performance is communicated by means of a total of not more than 6 loudspeakers, of which not more than 4 loudspeakers are located in any 1 room or adjoining outdoor space; or

(II) if the performance or display is by audiovisual means, any visual portion of the performance or display is communicated by means of a total of not more than 4 audiovisual devices, of which not more than 1 audiovisual device is located in any 1 room, and no such audiovisual device has a diagonal screen size greater than 55 inches, and any audio portion of the performance or display is communicated by means of a total of not more than 6 loudspeakers, of which not

---

(2) to transmit or otherwise communicate a performance or display of the work to a place specified by clause (1) or to the public, by means of any device or process, whether the members of the public capable of receiving the performance or display receive it in the same place or in separate places and at the same time or at different times."

"To 'transmit' a performance or display is to communicate it by any device or process whereby images or sounds are received beyond the place from which they are sent."

[8] As contained in Exhibit US-15(a). There is no official US Government consolidated text of the amended Section 110(5).

more than 4 loudspeakers are located in any 1 room or adjoining outdoor space;

(ii) in the case of a food service or drinking establishment, either the establishment in which the communication occurs has less than 3,750 gross square feet of space (excluding space used for customer parking and for no other purpose), or the establishment in which the communication occurs has 3,750 gross square feet of space or more (excluding space used for customer parking and for no other purpose) and—

(I) if the performance is by audio means only, the performance is communicated by means of a total of not more than 6 loudspeakers, of which not more than 4 loudspeakers are located in any 1 room or adjoining outdoor space; or

(II) if the performance or display is by audiovisual means, any visual portion of the performance or display is communicated by means of a total of not more than 4 audiovisual devices, of which not more than one audiovisual device is located in any 1 room, and no such audiovisual device has a diagonal screen size greater than 55 inches, and any audio portion of the performance or display is communicated by means of a total of not more than 6 loudspeakers, of which not more than 4 loudspeakers are located in any 1 room or adjoining outdoor space;

(iii) no direct charge is made to see or hear the transmission or retransmission;

(iv) the transmission or retransmission is not further transmitted beyond the establishment where it is received; and

(v) the transmission or retransmission is licensed by the copyright owner of the work so publicly performed or displayed; and

..."[9]

2.4 Subparagraph (A) of Section 110(5) essentially reproduces the text of the original "homestyle" exemption contained in Section 110(5) of the Copyright Act of

[9] Section 205 of the Fairness in Music Licensing Act amended Section 110 of the Copyright Act of 1976 by inserting a number of definitions thereto that relate to the new Section 110(5)(B), including the following:

"An 'establishment' is a store, shop, or any similar place of business open to the general public for the primary purpose of selling goods or services in which the majority of the gross square feet of space that is nonresidential is used for that purpose, and in which nondramatic musical works are performed publicly."

"A 'food service or drinking establishment' is a restaurant, inn, bar, tavern, or any other similar place of business in which the public or patrons assemble for the primary purpose of being served food or drink, in which the majority of the gross square feet of space that is nonresidential is used for that purpose, and in which nondramatic musical works are performed publicly."

"The 'gross square feet of space' of an establishment means the entire interior space of that establishment, and any adjoining outdoor space used to serve patrons, whether on a seasonal basis or otherwise."

1976. When Section 110(5) was amended in 1998, the homestyle exemption was moved to a new subparagraph (A) and the words "except as provided in subparagraph (B)" were added to the beginning of the text.

2.5 A House Report (1976) accompanying the Copyright Act of 1976 explained that in its original form Section 110(5) "applies to performances and displays of all types of works, and its purpose is to exempt from copyright liability anyone who merely turns on, in a public place, an ordinary radio or television receiving apparatus of a kind commonly sold to members of the public for private use". "The basic rationale of this clause is that the secondary use of the transmission by turning on an ordinary receiver in public is so remote and minimal that no further liability should be imposed." "[The clause] would impose liability where the proprietor has a commercial 'sound system' installed or converts a standard home receiving apparatus (by augmenting it with sophisticated or extensive amplification equipment) into the equivalent of a commercial sound system."[10] A subsequent Conference Report (1976) elaborated on the rationale by noting that the intent was to exempt a small commercial establishment "which was not of sufficient size to justify, as a practical matter, a subscription to a commercial background music service".[11]

2.6 The factors to consider in applying the exemption are largely based on the facts of a case decided by the United States Supreme Court immediately prior to the passage of the 1976 Copyright Act. In *Aiken*,[12] the Court held that an owner of a small fast food restaurant was not liable for playing music by means of a radio with outlets to four speakers in the ceiling; the size of the shop was 1,055 square feet (98 m^2), of which 620 square feet (56 m^2) were open to the public. The House Report (1976) describes the factual situation in *Aiken* as representing the "outer limit of the exemption" contained in the original Section 110(5). This exemption became known as the "homestyle" exemption.

2.7 As indicated in the first quotation in the preceding paragraph, the homestyle exemption was originally intended to apply to performances of all types of works. However, given that the present subparagraph (B) applies to "a performance or display of a nondramatic musical work", the parties agree, by way of an *a contrario* interpretation, that the effect of the introductory phrase "except as provided in subparagraph (B)", that was added to the text in subparagraph (A), is that it narrows

---

[10] These quotations are from the Report of the House Committee on the Judiciary, H.R. Rep. No. 94-1476, 94th Congress, 2nd Session 87 (1976), as reproduced in Exhibit US-1. The Report adds that "[f]actors to consider in particular cases would include the size, physical arrangement, and noise level of the areas within the establishment where the transmissions are made audible or visible, and the extent to which the receiving apparatus is altered or augmented for the purpose of improving the aural or visual quality of the performance".

[11] Conference Report of the House Committee on the Judiciary, Subcommittee on Courts and Intellectual Property, H.R. Rep. No. 94-1733, 94th Congress., 2nd Session 75 (1976), as reproduced in Exhibit US-2.

In their first written submissions, the European Communities and the United States expressed their views on the background and subsequent application of the original homestyle exemption.

[12] *Twentieth Century Music Corp. v. Aiken*, 422 U.S. 151 (1975).

down the application of subparagraph (A) to works other than "nondramatic musical works".[13]

2.8 The Panel notes that it is the common understanding of the parties that the expression "nondramatic musical works" in subparagraph (B) excludes from its application the communication of music that is part of an opera, operetta, musical or other similar dramatic work when performed in a dramatic context. All other musical works are covered by that expression, including individual songs taken from dramatic works when performed outside of any dramatic context. Subparagraph (B) would, therefore, apply for example to an individual song taken from a musical and played on the radio. Consequently, the operation of subparagraph (A) is limited to such musical works as are not covered by subparagraph (B), for example a communication of a broadcast of a dramatic rendition of the music written for an opera.[14]

2.9 The 1998 Amendment has added a new subparagraph (B) to Section 110(5), to which we, for the sake of brevity, hereinafter refer to as a "business" exemption. It exempts, under certain conditions, communication by an establishment of a transmission or retransmission embodying a performance or display of a nondramatic musical work intended to be received by the general public, originated by a radio or television broadcast station licensed as such by the Federal Communications Commission, or, if an audiovisual transmission, by a cable system or satellite carrier.

2.10 The beneficiaries of the business exemption are divided into two categories: establishments other than food service or drinking establishments ("retail establishments"), and food service and drinking establishments. In each category, establishments under a certain size limit are exempted, regardless of the type of equipment they use. The size limits are 2,000 gross square feet (186 m^2) for retail establishments and 3,750 gross square feet (348 m^2) for restaurants.

2.11 In its study of November 1995[15] prepared for the Senate Judiciary Committee, the Congressional Research Service ("CRS") estimated that 16 per cent of eating establishments, 13.5 per cent of drinking establishments and 18 per cent of retail establishments were below the area of the restaurant ran by Mr. Aiken, i.e. 1,055 square feet.[16] Furthermore, the CRS estimated that 65.2 per cent of eating establishments and 71.8 per cent of drinking establishments would have fallen at that time under a 3,500 square feet limit, and that 27 per cent of retail establishments would have fallen under a 1,500 square feet limit.

2.12 In 1999, Dun & Bradstreet, Inc. ("D&B") was requested on behalf of the American Society of Composers, Authors and Publishers (ASCAP) to update the CRS study based on 1998 data and the criteria in the 1998 Amendment. In this study, the D&B estimated that 70 per cent of eating establishments and 73 per cent of

---

13 *See* the second written submissions by the United States (para. 3) and the European Communities (para. 7).

14 The notion "nondramatic musical work" was introduced to Section 110(5) with the 1998 Amendment. However, this notion is also used in the Copyright Act of 1976 in a number of other limitations to the public performance right (Section 110(2), (3), (4), (6) and (7)), and certain provisions concerning the making of phonorecords (Section 115), juxeboxes (Section 116) and non-commercial broadcasting (Section 118), all of which apply to nondramatic musical works, but not to dramatic works.

15 As reproduced in Exhibit EC-16.

16 The *Aiken* case is explained in para. 2.6 above.

drinking establishments fell under the 3,750 square feet limit, and that 45 per cent of retail establishments fell under the 2,000 square feet limit.[17]

2.13 The studies conducted by the National Restaurant Association (NRA) concerning its membership indicate that 36 per cent of table service restaurant members (those with sit-down waiter service) and 95 per cent of quick service restaurant members are less than 3,750 square feet.[18,19]

2.14 If the size of an establishment is above the limits referred to in paragraph 2.10 above (there is no maximum size), the exemption applies provided that the establishment does not exceed the limits set for the equipment used. The limits on equipment are different as regards, on the one hand, audio performances, and, on the other hand, audiovisual performances and displays. The rules concerning equipment limitations are the same for both retail establishments and restaurants above the respective size limits.

2.15 The types of transmissions covered by both subparagraphs (A) and (B) of Section 110(5) include original broadcasts over the air or by satellite, rebroadcasts by terrestrial means or by satellite, cable retransmissions of original broadcasts, and original cable transmissions or other transmissions by wire.[20] The provisions do not distinguish between analog and digital transmissions.

2.16 Section 110(5) does not apply to the use of recorded music, such as CDs or cassette tapes, or to live performances of music.

2.17 Holders of copyright in musical works (composers, lyricists and music publishers) normally entrust the licensing of nondramatic public performance of their works to collective management organizations ("CMOs" or performing rights organizations). The three main CMOs in the United States in this area are ASCAP, the Broadcast Music, Inc. (BMI) and SESAC, Inc. CMOs license the public performance of musical works to users of music, such as retail establishments and restaurants, on behalf of the individual right holders they represent, collect licence fees from such users, and distribute revenues as royalties to the respective right holders. They normally enter into reciprocal arrangements with the CMOs of other countries to license the works of the right holders represented by them. Revenues are distributed to individual right holders through the CMOs that represent the right holders in question. The above-mentioned three US CMOs license nondramatic public performances of musical works, including nondramatic renditions of "dramatic" musical works.

---

[17] *See* para. 49 of the first written submission by the EC. The EC observers that the percentage figures referred to in paras. 2.11 and 2.12 do not take account of other exempted establishments such as hotels, financial services outlets, estate property brokers, and other types of service providers.

[18] *See* the response from the US to question 9 from the Panel and confidential exhibit US-18.

[19] The relevance of the percentage figures referred to in paras. 2.11 and 2.13 for the case at hand, as well as other factual information and estimations concerning the number of establishments licenced by collective management organizations and the revenues collected by them provided by the parties will be discussed in section VI of this report. For complete information, please see the attached submissions by the parties.

[20] *See* the response of the US to question 5 from the Panel.

III. FINDINGS AND RECOMMENDATIONS REQUESTED BY THE PARTIES

3.1 The European Communities alleges that the exemptions provided in subparagraphs (A) and (B) of Section 110(5) of the US Copyright Act are in violation of the United States' obligations under the TRIPS Agreement. In particular, it alleges that these US measures are incompatible with Article 9.1 of the TRIPS Agreement together with Articles 11(1)(ii) and 11*bis*(1)(iii) of the Berne Convention (1971) and that they cannot be justified under any express or implied exception or limitation permissible under the Berne Convention (1971) or the TRIPS Agreement. In the view of the EC, these measures cause prejudice to the legitimate rights of copyright owners, thus nullifying and impairing the rights of the European Communities.
3.2 The European Communities requests the Panel to find that the United States has violated its obligations under Article 9.1 of the TRIPS Agreement together with Articles 11*bis*(1)(iii) and 11(1)(ii) of the Berne Convention (1971) and to recommend that the United States bring its domestic legislation into conformity with its obligations under the TRIPS Agreement.
3.3 The United States contends that Section 110(5) of the US Copyright Act is fully consistent with its obligations under the TRIPS Agreement. The Agreement, incorporating the substantive provisions of the Berne Convention (1971), allows Members to place minor limitations on the exclusive rights of copyright owners. Article 13 of the TRIPS Agreement provides the standard by which to judge the appropriateness of such limitations or exceptions. The exemptions embodied in Section 110(5) fall within the Article 13 standard.
3.4 The United States requests the Panel to find that both subparagraphs (A) and (B) of Section 110(5) of the US Copyright Act meet the standard of Article 13 of the TRIPS Agreement and the substantive obligations of the Berne Convention (1971). Accordingly, the United States requests the Panel to dismiss the claims of the European Communities in this dispute.

IV. ARGUMENTS OF THE PARTIES AND THE THIRD PARTIES AND FACTUAL INFORMATION PROVIDED BY THE INTERNATIONAL BUREAU OF WIPO

4.1 The arguments of the parties and the third parties are set out in their submissions to the Panel (see Attachment 1 for the European Communities, Attachment 2 for the United States and Attachment 3 for the third parties). The letter from the Chair of the Panel to the Director General of WIPO and the response thereto by the Director General of WIPO are reproduced in Attachment 4. [21]

---

21 Exhibits attached to the submissions and annexes to the letter from the Director General of WIPO are not reproduced in this report.

V. INTERIM REVIEW

5.1 On 26 April 2000, the European Communities and the United States requested the Panel to review, in accordance with Article 15.2 of the DSU, precise aspects of the interim report that had been issued to the parties on 14 April 2000. Neither the European Communities nor the United States requested that a further meeting of the Panel with the parties be held. In a letter, dated 1 May 2000, the United States made observations on some of the EC comments.

5.2 The European Communities made some editorial comments and requested some clarifications to the Panel's reasoning:

(a) The European Communities deemed section III on "findings and recommendations requested by the parties" and subsection VI.A on "claims" overlapping. We considered that it was useful to reflect the parties' main claims in both sections.

(b) In subsection VI.B on "preliminary issue", the European Communities suggested shortening the Panel's reasoning on its treatment of a letter from a law firm representing ASCAP to the United States Trade Representative that was copied to it. We made an editorial adjustment to the wording of paragraph 6.8.

(c) As proposed by the European Communities, we deleted the last sentence of paragraph 6.27 of the interim report.

(d) With regard to an EC comment on the last sentence of paragraph 6.41, we considered it useful to note that Article 30 of the Vienna Convention on the relation between successive treaties on the same subject-matter was not relevant to the case at hand.

(e) We were of the view that it was not necessary to rephrase our statement in paragraph 6.93 that the minor exceptions doctrine is *primarily* concerned with *de minimis* use.

(f) As suggested by the European Communities, we agreed to refer to the Dun & Bradstreet study prepared in 1999 based on data from 1998 as the 1999 D&B study.

(g) As regards the second sentence of paragraph 6.140, the European Communities stressed that it had consistently referred to the *Claire's Boutique* and *Edison Bros.* cases as evidence that the homestyle exemption is not narrowly confined but had been applied to huge nationally operating corporations. We clarified the sentence by indicating that it expresses *our* understanding of the EC argumentation.

(h) The European Communities requested us to clarify our reasoning in paragraph 6.214. We deemed the reasoning to be sufficiently clear.

(i) We did not agree to change our finding in paragraph 7.1(a), as suggested by the European Communities, by adding, after the words "subparagraph (A) of Section 110(5) of the US Copyright Act", the words "which covers exclusively dramatic musical works".

5.3 The United States mainly made comments of an editorial and factual nature:

(a) We accepted certain editorial suggestions and made minor clerical changes in paragraphs 6.97, 6.205 and 6.260 of the findings.

(b) We agreed, as requested by the United States, to refer to exhibits US-17 and US-18 as "confidential exhibits", given that the United States had obtained them in confidence.

(c) Furthermore, as proposed by the United States, we deleted a reference in footnote 127, inserted specific factual information from its responses to questions in footnote 173 and added updated information in footnote 188.

VI. FINDINGS

A. Claims

6.1 As mentioned above, the European Communities alleges that the exemptions provided in subparagraphs (A) and (B) of Section 110(5) of the US Copyright Act are in violation of the United States' obligations under the TRIPS Agreement, and requests the Panel to find that the United States has violated its obligations under Article 9.1 of the TRIPS Agreement together with Articles 11*bis*(1)(iii) and 11(1)(ii) of the Berne Convention (1971) and to recommend that the United States bring its domestic legislation into conformity with its obligations under the TRIPS Agreement.

6.2 The United States contends that Section 110(5) of the US Copyright Act is fully consistent with its obligations under the TRIPS Agreement, and requests the Panel to find that both subparagraphs (A) and (B) of Section 110(5) of the US Copyright Act meet the standard of Article 13 of the TRIPS Agreement and the substantive obligations of the Berne Convention (1971). Accordingly, the United States requests the Panel to dismiss the claims of the European Communities in this dispute.

B. Preliminary Issue

6.3 Before examining the substantive aspects of this dispute, we discuss how we treat a letter from a law firm representing ASCAP to the United States Trade Representative ("USTR") that was copied to the Panel.

6.4 By means of a letter addressed to a law firm representing ASCAP, dated 16 November 1999,[22] the USTR requested information from ASCAP in relation to questions 9-11 from the Panel to the United States, which were reproduced in the letter.[23] The law firm responded to the USTR by means of a letter, dated 3 December 1999. It forwarded a copy of this letter, addressed to the USTR, to the Panel. The Panel received this copy on 8 December 1999. The Panel transmitted the letter forthwith to both parties and invited them to comment on it if they so wished.

6.5 In a letter, dated 17 December 1999, the United States, *inter alia*, distanced itself from positions expressed in the letter by that law firm and emphasized that in its view the letter was of little probative value for the Panel because it provided essentially no factual data not already provided by either party. But the United States

---

[22] Exhibit US-19(a). The USTR sent a similar letter to the BMI, Exhibit US-19(b).

[23] These questions and the responses thereto by the United States are contained in Attachment 2.3 to the report.

supported in general the right of private parties to make their views known to WTO dispute settlement panels.

6.6 In a letter, dated 12 January 2000, the European Communities stated that it did not have substantive comments on the letter. While it appreciated ASCAP's contribution to the current case, it considered that the letter did not add any new element to what was already submitted by the parties. In referring to the Appellate Body's interpretation of Article 13 of the DSU in its report in the dispute *United States - Import Prohibition of Certain Shrimp and Shrimp Products*,[24] the European Communities also remarked that in its view, the authority of panels is limited to the consideration of factual information and technical advice by individuals or bodies alien to the dispute and thus did not include the possibility for a panel to accept any legal argument or legal interpretation from such individuals or bodies.

6.7 According to Article 13 of the DSU, "each panel shall have the right to seek information and technical advice from any individual or body which it deems appropriate. ...". We recall that in the *United States - Shrimps* dispute the Appellate Body reasoned with respect to the treatment by a panel of non-requested information that the "authority to seek information is not properly equated with a prohibition on accepting information which has been submitted without having been requested by a panel. A panel has discretionary authority to accept and consider or to reject information and advice submitted to it, whether requested by a panel or not. ...".[25]

6.8 In this dispute, we do not reject outright the information contained in the letter from the law firm representing ASCAP to the USTR that was copied to the Panel. We recall that the Appellate Body has recognized the authority of panels to accept non-requested information. However, we share the view expressed by the parties that this letter essentially duplicates information already submitted by the parties. We also emphasize that the letter was not addressed to the Panel but only copied to it. Therefore, while not having refused the copy of the letter, we have not relied on it for our reasoning or our findings.

C. *Burden of Proof*

6.9 Before turning to the substantive aspects of this dispute, we also discuss the issue of burden of proof.

6.10 We note that the United States does not dispute that subparagraphs (A) and (B) of Section 110(5) implicate Articles 11 and 11*bis* of the Berne Convention (1971) as incorporated into the TRIPS Agreement. But we also recall the US statement that the question of whether these subparagraphs are consistent with those Articles cannot be determined without looking both to the scope of the rights that they afford and to the exceptions which are permitted to those rights. In the view of the United States, only if subparagraphs (A) and (B) of Section 110(5) do not fall within the confines of the relevant exceptions under the TRIPS Agreement, will a finding of inconsistency be possible.[26]

---

24 Appellate Body Report, *United States - Import Prohibition on Certain Shrimp and Shrimp Products*, WT/DS58/AB/R, adopted 6 November 1998, DSR 1998:VII, 2755, paras. 99-110.

25 Ibid., para. 108.

26 Response to question 2 from the Panel to the United States at the first substantive meeting.

6.11 We further recall the European Communities' contention that it merely needs to establish an inconsistency of Section 110(5) with any provision of the TRIPS Agreement (including those of the Berne Convention (1971) incorporated into it). Once such inconsistency is established by the complainant (or admitted by the respondent), in the view of the European Communities, the burden rests on the United States to invoke and prove the applicability of an exception.[27]

6.12 Recalling the principles set out in the Appellate Body report on *United States - Shirts and Blouses*,[28] we note that the burden of proof rests upon the party, whether complaining or defending, who asserts the affirmative of a particular claim or defence. If that party adduces evidence sufficient to raise a presumption that what is claimed is true, the burden then shifts to the other party, who will fail unless it adduces sufficient evidence to rebut the presumption.

6.13 Consistent with past WTO dispute settlement practice,[29] we consider that the European Communities bears the burden of establishing a *prima facie* violation of the basic rights that have been provided under the copyright provisions of the TRIPS Agreement, including its provisions that have been incorporated by reference from the Berne Convention (1971). By the same token, once the European Communities has succeeded in doing so, the burden rests with the United States to establish that any exception or limitation is applicable and that the conditions, if any, for invoking such exception are fulfilled.

6.14 The same rules apply where the existence of a specific fact is alleged. We note that a party who asserts a fact, whether the claimant or the respondent, is responsible for providing proof thereof. It is for the party alleging the fact to prove its existence. It is then for the other party to submit evidence to the contrary if it challenges the existence of that fact.

6.15 While a duty rests on all parties to produce evidence and to cooperate in presenting evidence to the Panel, this is an issue that has to be distinguished from the question of who bears the ultimate burden of proof for establishing a claim or a defence.

6.16 Thus we conclude that it is for the European Communities to present a *prima facie* case that Section 110(5)(A) and (B) of the US Copyright Act is inconsistent with the provisions of the TRIPS Agreement (including those of the Berne Convention (1971) incorporated into it). Should the European Communities fail in estab-

---

[27] First written submission by the European Communities, para. 74; the second written submission by the European Communities, para. 34.

[28] In *United States - Shirts and Blouses*, the Appellate Body stated:

"... the party who asserts a fact, whether the claimant or the respondent, is responsible for providing proof thereof. Also, it is a generally-accepted canon of evidence in civil law, common law and, in fact, most jurisdictions, that the burden of proof rests upon the party, whether complaining or defending, who asserts the affirmative of a particular claim or defence. If that party adduces evidence sufficient to raise a presumption that what is claimed is true, the burden then shifts to the other party, who will fail unless it adduces sufficient evidence to rebut the presumption." (Footnotes omitted). *See* the Appellate Body Report, *United States - Measure Affecting Woven Wool Shirts and Blouses from India*, WT/DS33/AB/R, adopted 23 May 1997, DSR 1997:I, 323 at 334.

[29] Appellate Body Report *United States - Standards for Reformulated and Conventional Gasoline*, WT/DS2/AB/R, adopted 20 May 1996, DSR 1996:I, 3 at 21; Appellate Body Report *United States - Shirts and Blouses from India, supra*, footnote 28, at 334.

lishing such violation, it goes without saying that the United States would not have to invoke any justification or exception. However, we also consider that the burden of proving that any exception or limitation is applicable and that any relevant conditions are met falls on the United States as the party bearing the ultimate burden of proof for invoking exceptions.[30] In view of the statements made by both parties at the first substantive meeting to the Panel, it is our understanding that the parties do not disagree with our interpretation concerning the allocation of the burden of proof as described above.

D. Substantive Aspects of the Dispute

1. General Considerations about the Exclusive Rights Concerned and Limitations Thereto

(a) Exclusive Rights Implicated by the EC Claims

6.17 Articles 9-13 of Section 1 of Part II of the TRIPS Agreement entitled "Copyright and Related Rights" deal with the substantive standards of copyright protection. Article 9.1 of the TRIPS Agreement obliges WTO Members to comply with Articles 1-21 of the Berne Convention (1971) (with the exception of Article 6*bis* on moral rights and the rights derived therefrom) and the Appendix thereto.[31] The European Communities alleges that subparagraphs (A) and (B) of Section 110(5) are inconsistent primarily with Article 11*bis*(1)(iii) but also with Article 11(1)(ii) of the Berne Convention (1971) as incorporated into the TRIPS Agreement.

6.18 We note that through their incorporation, the substantive rules of the Berne Convention (1971), including the provisions of its Articles 11*bis*(1)(iii) and 11(1)(ii), have become part of the TRIPS Agreement and as provisions of that Agreement have to be read as applying to WTO Members.

(i) Article 11*bis* of the Berne Convention (1971)

6.19 The provision of particular relevance for this dispute is Article 11*bis*(1)(iii).[32] Article 11*bis*(1) provides:

> "Authors of literary and artistic works shall enjoy the exclusive right of authorizing:
>
> (i) the broadcasting of their works or the communication thereof to the public by any other means of wireless diffusion of signs, sounds or images;

---

30 Appellate Body Report, *US - Gasoline*, *supra*, footnote 29, at 21.

31 Article 9.1 of the TRIPS Agreement: "Members shall comply with Articles 1 through 21 of the Berne Convention (1971) and the Appendix thereto. However, Members shall not have rights or obligations under this Agreement in respect of the rights conferred under Articles 6*bis* of that Convention or the rights derived therefrom."

32 Article 11*bis* was introduced into the Berne Convention at the occasion of the Rome Revision (1928) and further elaborated by the Brussels Revision (1948) in the light of technological developments.

(ii) any communication to the public by wire or by re-broadcasting of the broadcast of the work, when this communication is made by an organization other than the original one;

(iii) the public communication by loudspeaker or any other analogous instrument transmitting, by signs, sounds or images, the broadcast of the work."

6.20 In the light of Article 2 of the Berne Convention (1971), "artistic" works in the meaning of Article 11*bis*(1) include nondramatic and other musical works. Each of the subparagraphs of Article 11*bis*(1) confers a separate exclusive right; exploitation of a work in a manner covered by any of these subparagraphs requires an authorization by the right holder. For example, the communication to the public of a broadcast creates an additional audience and the right holder is given control over, and may expect remuneration from, this new public performance of his or her work.

6.21 The right provided under subparagraph (i) of Article 11*bis*(1) is to authorize the broadcasting of a work and the communication thereof to the public by any other means of wireless diffusion of signs, sounds or images. It applies to both radio and television broadcasts. Subparagraph (ii) concerns the subsequent use of this emission; the authors' exclusive right covers any communication to the public by wire or by rebroadcasting of the broadcast of the work, when the communication is made by an organization other than the original one.

6.22 Subparagraph (iii) provides an exclusive right to authorize the public communication of the broadcast of the work by loudspeaker, on a television screen, or by other similar means. Such communication involves a new public performance of a work contained in a broadcast, which requires a licence from the right holder.[33] For the purposes of this dispute, the claims raised by the European Communities under Article 11*bis*(1) are limited to subparagraph (iii).[34]

(ii) Article 11 of the Berne Convention (1971)

6.23 Of relevance to this dispute are also the exclusive rights conferred by Article 11(1)(ii) of the Berne Convention (1971). Article 11(1) provides:

---

[33] The Guide to the Berne Convention, published by WIPO in 1978 ("Guide to the Berne Convention") gives the following explanation on the situation covered by Article 11*bis*(1)(iii): "This case is becoming more common. In places where people gather (cafés, restaurants, tea-rooms, hotels, large shops, trains, aircraft, etc.) the practice is growing of providing broadcast programmes. ... The question is whether the licence given by the author to the broadcasting station covers, in addition, all the use made of the broadcast, which may or many not be for commercial ends. ... The Convention's answer is 'no'. Just as, in the case of a relay of a broadcast by wire, an additional audience is created (para. (1)(ii)), so, in this case, too, the work is made perceptible to listeners (and perhaps to viewers) other than those contemplated by the author when his permission was given. Although, by definition, the number of people receiving a broadcast cannot be ascertained with any certainty, the author thinks of his licence to broadcast as covering only the direct audience receiving the signal within the family circle. Once this reception is done in order to entertain a wider circle, often for profit, an additional section of the public is enabled to enjoy the work and it ceases to be merely a matter of broadcasting. The author is given control over this new public performance of his work." *See* Guide to the Berne Convention, paras. 11*bis*.11 and 11*bis*.12, p.68-69.

[34] EC reply to question 8 of Panel; Paras. 41-46 of the EC oral statement at the first panel meeting; Paras. 61-72 of the EC first written submission.

"Authors of dramatic, dramatico-musical and musical works shall enjoy the exclusive right of authorizing:

(i) the public performance of their works, including such public performance by any means or process;

(ii) any communication to the public of the performance of their works."

6.24 As in the case of Article 11*bis*(1) of the Berne Convention (1971), which concerns broadcasting to the public and communication of a broadcast to the public, the exclusive rights conferred by Article 11 cover *public* performance; private performance does not require authorization. Public performance includes performance by any means or process, such as performance by means of recordings (e.g., CDs, cassettes and videos).[35] It also includes communication to the public of a performance of the work. The claims raised by the European Communities under Article 11(1) of the Berne Convention (1971) are limited to its subparagraph (ii).

6.25 Regarding the relationship between Articles 11 and 11*bis*, we note that the rights conferred in Article 11(1)(ii) concern the communication to the public of performances of works in general. Article 11*bis*(1)(iii) is a specific rule conferring exclusive rights concerning the public communication by loudspeaker or any other analogous instrument transmitting, by signs, sounds or images, the broadcast of a work.

6.26 As set out in section III above, the European Communities raises claims against Section 110(5) primarily under Article 11*bis*(1)(iii), which covers the communication to the public of a broadcast which has been transmitted at some point by hertzian waves. But the EC claims also relate to Article 11(1)(ii) to the extent that a communication to the public concerns situations where the entire transmission has been by wire.

6.27 We share the understanding of the parties that a communication to the public by loudspeaker of a performance of a work transmitted by means other than hertzian waves is covered by the exclusive rights conferred by Article 11(1) of the Berne Convention (1971).[36] Moreover, we note that both parties consider that it is the third exclusive right under Article 11*bis*(1)(iii) - i.e., the author's right to authorize the public communication of a broadcast of a work by loudspeaker or any other analogous instrument - which is primarily concerned in this dispute. But we also note that there is no disagreement between the parties that both subparagraphs (A) and (B) of

---

[35] However, public performance by means of cinematographic works is separately covered in Article 14(1)(ii) of the Berne Convention. Public performance of a literary work or communication to the public of the recitation is covered by Article 11*ter* of the Berne Convention.

[36] In this respect we recall the explanation given in the Guide to the Berne Convention: "The communication to the public of a performance of the work ... covers all public communication except broadcasting which is dealt with in Article 11*bis*. For example, a broadcasting organisation broadcasts a chamber concert - Article 11*bis* applies. But if it or some other body diffuses the music by landline to subscribers, this is a matter for Article 11." Guide to the Berne Convention, para. 11.5, p. 65.

Section 110(5) implicate both Articles 11*bis*(1)(iii) and 11(1)(ii) - albeit to a varying extent.[37]

6.28 Both provisions, i.e., Articles 11*bis*(1)(iii) and 11(1)(ii) of the Berne Convention (1971) are implicated only if there is a *public* element to the broadcasting or communication operation. We note that it is undisputed between the parties that playing radio or television music by establishments covered by Section 110(5) involves a communication that is available to the *public* in the sense of Articles 11*bis*(1)(iii) and 11(1)(ii) of the Berne Convention (1971). We share this view of the parties.[38]

6.29 As noted above, the United States acknowledges that subparagraphs (A) and (B) of Section 110(5) implicate Articles 11*bis*(1)(iii) and 11(1)(ii) of the Berne Convention (1971). Consequently, the core question before this Panel is which of the exceptions under the TRIPS Agreement invoked are relevant to this dispute and whether the conditions for their invocation are met so as to justify the exemptions under subparagraphs (A) and (B) of Section 110(5) of the US Copyright Act.

(b) Limitations and Exceptions

(i) Introduction

6.30 A major issue in this dispute is the interpretation and application to the facts of this case of Article 13 of the TRIPS Agreement. The US defense is firmly based upon it. The United States submits that the Article clarifies and articulates the "minor exceptions" doctrine applicable under certain provisions of the Berne Convention (1971) and incorporated into the TRIPS Agreement. But the determination of the dispute raises other questions, for instance questions concerning the relationship between Article 13 and the "minor exceptions" doctrine developed in relation to Articles 11 and 11*bis*(1) and (2) of the Berne Convention (1971) and incorporated into the TRIPS Agreement by Article 9.1 thereof. So although the US case rests on Article 13, the determination of the questions at issue between the parties involves considerations beyond those that arise from the mere application of Article 13 to the facts of this case.

6.31 Article 13 of the TRIPS Agreement, entitled "Limitations and Exceptions", is the general exception clause applicable to exclusive rights of the holders of copyright. It provides:

---

[37] EC reply to question 8 of Panel; Paras. 41-46 of the EC oral statement at the first panel meeting; Paras. 61-72 of the EC first written submission; US response to question 2 by the Panel to the United States. The United States emphasizes, however, that it may not be found in violation of Articles 11 and/or 11*bis* if subparagraphs (A) and (b) of Section 110(5) meet the requirements of relevant exceptions or limitations under the TRIPS Agreement.

[38] We note that Section 101 of the US Copyright Act contains the following definition: "To perform or display a work 'publicly' means

(1) to perform or display it at a place open to the public or at any place where a substantial number of persons outside of a normal circle of a family and its social acquaintances is gathered; or

(2) to transmit or otherwise communicate a performance or display of the work to a place specified by clause (1) or to the public, by means of any device or process, whether the members of the public are capable of receiving the performance or display receive it in the same place or in separate places and at the same time or at different times."

"Members shall confine limitations or exceptions to exclusive rights to certain special cases which do not conflict with a normal exploitation of the work and do not unreasonably prejudice the legitimate interests of the right holder."

6.32 We discuss the scope of Article 13 of the TRIPS Agreement in subsection (iv) of this section (paragraphs 6.71ff). In the second part of this report (paragraphs 6.97ff), we will apply the three conditions contained in that Article to subparagraphs (A) and (B) of Section 110(5) of the US Copyright Act.

(ii) Summary of the Arguments Raised by the Parties

6.33 The United States submits that the TRIPS Agreement, incorporating the substantive provisions of the Berne Convention (1971), allows Members to place minor limitations on the exclusive rights of copyright owners. Article 13 of the TRIPS Agreement provides the standard by which to judge the appropriateness of such limitations or exceptions. The exemptions embodied in Section 110(5) fall within the Article 13 standard.

6.34 The principal EC argument concerning Article 13 is that it only applies to exclusive rights newly introduced under the TRIPS Agreement and that the rights conferred under Articles 1-21 of the Berne Convention (1971) as incorporated into the TRIPS Agreement can be derogated from only on the grounds of pre-existing exceptions applicable under the Berne Convention (1971). In the EC view, its position is supported by Article 2.2 of the TRIPS Agreement and Article 20 of the Berne Convention (1971), which it interprets as a prohibition on any derogation from existing standards of protection under the Berne Convention (1971).

6.35 In the US view, Article 13 applies to all copyright-related provisions of the TRIPS Agreement, including the articles of the Berne Convention (1971) incorporated into it. As far as Articles 11*bis*(1) and 11(1) of the Berne Convention (1971) as incorporated into the TRIPS Agreement are concerned, the US view is that Article 13 clarifies and articulates the scope of the so-called "minor exceptions" doctrine,[39] which applies to the exclusive rights provided under those Articles. Thus, the United States argues that Article 13 provides the standard by which the permissibility of limitations or "minor exceptions" from exclusive rights in question has to be judged.

6.36 In the alternative to its argument referred to in paragraph 6.34 above, the European Communities contends that even if Article 13 of the TRIPS Agreement was considered to be applicable to the exclusive rights provided under the Berne provisions incorporated into the TRIPS Agreement, its role would be to confine the scope of the pre-existing limitations and exceptions provided in those Berne provisions. The European Communities concedes that the minor exceptions doctrine has been referred to in the discussions during the diplomatic conferences for the revision of the Berne Convention held in Brussels in 1948[40] and Stockholm in 1967,[41] but considers its precise scope and legal status under the Berne Convention as unclear. In

---

[39] See explanation in paras. 6.45ff below.

[40] Brussels Diplomatic Conference for the Revision of the Berne Convention, 5 to 26 June 1948.

[41] Intellectual Property Conference of Stockholm, 11 June to 14 July 1967.

its view, the scope of limitations allowed under the minor exceptions doctrine is limited to public performance of works for religious ceremonies, military bands and the needs of child and adult education. It adds that such uses are characterized by their non-commercial character. The European Communities also argues that the minor exceptions doctrine was intended to "grandfather" only pre-existing exceptions that existed in national legislation prior to the Stockholm Diplomatic Conference of 1967, regardless of when a particular country acceded to the Berne Convention.[42]

6.37 The United States submits that the minor exceptions doctrine constitutes a subsequent practice of the Berne Union members in the meaning of Article 31(3)(b) of the Vienna Convention on the Law of Treaties ("Vienna Convention"). In the US view, it is not limited to the specific examples mentioned in the reports of the Brussels and Stockholm diplomatic conferences. There is no requirement that exempt uses be non-commercial. Moreover, the minor exceptions doctrine is not limited to pre-existing exceptions in force prior to 1967 or any other date.[43]

6.38 As far as the exclusive rights conferred by Article 11*bis*(1) are concerned, the European Communities takes the position that neither the minor exceptions doctrine nor Article 13 can be applied in isolation from the requirement to provide an equitable remuneration set forth in Article 11*bis*(2) of the Berne Convention (1971). In its view, an exception to the exclusive rights in question must provide, as a minimum, equitable remuneration to the right holder, in addition to meeting the three conditions of Article 13. In its view, an equitable remuneration can be provided through means other than compulsory licensing[44] and thus the scope of application of Article 11*bis*(2) covers all exceptions to the exclusive rights conferred by Article 11*bis*(1). The European Communities also refers to the extensive argumentation supporting this interpretation as developed in Australia's third party submission.[45]

6.39 The United States responds that there is a basic distinction between exceptions to exclusive rights and compulsory licences. Article 11*bis*(2) merely authorizes a country to substitute a compulsory licence, or its equivalent, for an exclusive right under Article 11*bis*(1). Neither the negotiating history of the Berne Convention nor the subsequent writings of commentators support the view that 11*bis*(2) authorizes outright exceptions to Article 11*bis*, or represents a standard against which to judge such exceptions. Consequently, Article 11*bis*(2) is not related to the minor exceptions doctrine, and does not bear upon the scope of exceptions permissible under that doctrine.[46]

---

42 *See, inter alia*, the second written submission by the European Communities, paras. 16, 17, 22, 23, 27 and 28.

43 *See* the second written submission by the United States, paras. 16-22.

44 The European Communities notes that "[i]t would appear that a country could set minimum or precise levels of royalties to be paid for the different uses protected under Article 11*bis* of the Berne Convention. Another way to provide for equitable remuneration could be the introduction of a levy system for the audio/TV equipment purchased by the establishment being allowed to play copyrighted works without authorisations, whereby the proceeds from such a levy system is distributed to the right holders". *See* EC response to question 12 from the Panel to the European Communities.

45 The written submission of Australia, paras. 2.8-2.14, 3.7-3.14, 4.3 and 4.8.

46 Paras. 23 and 24 of the US second written submission; *see* also US response to question 6 from the Panel to both parties.

6.40 In the following, we first examine the legal status and scope of the minor exceptions doctrine under the TRIPS Agreement, and then the applicability of Article 13 to the rights provided under the provisions of the Berne Convention (1971), in particular to its Articles 11*bis*(1) and 11(1), as incorporated into the TRIPS Agreement. We then consider the relevance of Article 11*bis*(2) of the Berne Convention (1971) for this case.

6.41 In examining these issues, the question that arises is how the conditions for invoking exceptions provided under the Berne Convention (1971), in particular under the minor exceptions doctrine and Article 11*bis*(2), and the conditions for invoking Article 13 of the TRIPS Agreement interrelate. We note that Article 30 of the Vienna Convention[47] on the application of successive treaties is not relevant in this respect, because all provisions of the TRIPS Agreement - including the incorporated Articles 1-21 of the Berne Convention (1971) - entered into force at the same point in time.

(iii) The Minor Exceptions Doctrine

6.42 As we noted above, the US view is that Article 13 of the TRIPS Agreement clarifies and articulates the scope of the minor exceptions doctrine, which is applicable under the TRIPS Agreement. Before considering the applicability of Article 13 to Articles 11*bis*(1)(iii) and 11(1)(ii) of the Berne Convention (1971) as incorporated into the TRIPS Agreement, we will first examine whether the minor exceptions doctrine applies under the TRIPS Agreement. This examination involves a two-step analysis. As the first step, we analyse to what extent this doctrine forms part of the Berne Convention *acquis*; in doing so, we will also consider the different views of the parties as to the scope of the doctrine. The second step is to analyse whether that doctrine, if we were to find that it applies under certain Articles of the Berne Convention (1971), has been incorporated into the TRIPS Agreement, by virtue of Article 9.1 of that Agreement, together with Articles 1-21 of the Berne Convention (1971).

General rules of interpretation

6.43 As frequently referred to by WTO panels and the Appellate Body, the fundamental rules of treaty interpretation are Article 31[48] "General rule of interpretation" and Article 32 "Supplementary means of interpretation" of the Vienna Convention.

---

[47] The relevant parts of Article 30 of the Vienna Convention on the Law of Treaties provide: "...

2. When a treaty specifies that it is subject to, or that it is not to be considered as incompatible with, an earlier or later treaty, the provisions of that other treaty prevail.

3. When all parties to the earlier treaty are parties also to the later treaty but the earlier treaty is not terminated or suspended in operation under article 59, the earlier treaty applies only to the extent that its provisions are compatible with those of the later treaty.

4. When the parties to the later treaty do not include all the parties to the earlier one:

(a) as between States parties to both treaties the same rule applies in para. 3;

(b) as between a State party to both treaties and a State party to only one of the treaties, the treaty to which both States are parties governs their mutual rights and obligations. ..."

[48] "A treaty shall be interpreted in good faith in accordance with the ordinary meaning to be given the terms of the treaty in their context and in the light of its object and purpose."

We note that, pursuant to Article 31(1) of the Vienna Convention, we have to interpret in good faith the provisions within our terms of reference in accordance with the ordinary meaning to be given to the terms of the treaty in their context and in the light of its object and purpose. We have already addressed the terms of these Articles. But our task does not end with that. The ordinary meaning has to be given to the terms of a treaty in their context and in the light of its object and purpose.[49]

6.44 In that respect, we note that Article 31(2) of the Vienna Convention provides that:

> "The context for the purpose of the interpretation of a treaty shall comprise, in addition to the text, including its preamble and annexes:
>
> (a) any agreement relating to the treaty which was made between all the parties in connexion with the conclusion of the treaty; ..."[50]

6.45 The International Law Commission explains in its commentary on the final set of draft articles on the law of treaties that this provision is based on the principle that a unilateral document cannot be regarded as forming part of the context unless not only was it made in connection with the conclusion of the treaty, but its relation to the treaty was accepted by the other parties.[51] "On the other hand, the fact that these two classes of documents are recognized in paragraph 2 as forming part of the 'context' does not mean that they are necessarily to be considered as an integral part of the treaty. Whether they are an actual part of the treaty depends on the intention of the parties in each case."[52] It is essential that the agreement or instrument should be related to the treaty. It must be concerned with the substance of the treaty and clarify certain concepts in the treaty or limit its field of application.[53] It must equally be drawn up on the occasion of the conclusion of the treaty.[54] Any agreement or instrument fulfilling these criteria will form part of the "context" of the treaty and will thus

[49] Reading treaty terms in their context requires that the text of the treaty must of course be read as a whole. One cannot simply concentrate on a para., an article, a section, a chapter or a part. (Cf. Ian Sinclair, The Vienna Convention on the Law of Treaties (2nd ed.), Manchester (1984), p. 127.). *See* also: Competence of Assembly regarding admission to the United Nations, Advisory Opinion, I.C.J. Reports 1950, p. 8; Arbitral Award of 31 July 1989, Judgment, I.C.J. Reports 1991, p. 69; Polish Postal Service in Danzig, P.I.C.J. Series B, No. 11, p. 39. Yasseen notes that "[d]'autres dispositions plus ou moins éloignées risquent d'apporter une exception à la disposition qu'il s'agit d'interpréter ou de poser une condition à la mise en oeuvre de cette disposition". *See* Yasseen, L'interprétation des traités d'aprés la Convention de Vienne sur le Droit des Traités, 151 Recueil des Cours (1976-III), p. 34.

[50] Subpara. (b) of Article 31(2) provides that the context for the purpose of the interpretation of a treaty also comprises: "any instrument which was made by one or more parties in connexion with the conclusion of the treaty and accepted by the other parties as an instrument related to the treaty".

[51] Sinclair, op.cit. p. 129.

[52] Yearbook of the International Law Commission (1966-II), p. 221.

[53] Yasseen, L'interprétation des traités d'aprés la Convention de Vienne sur le Droit des Traités, op.cit., p. 37; cited by Sinclair, op.cit., p.129.

[54] "Il y a ici une certaine notion de contemporanéité, l'un ou l'autre peut être concomitant à cette conclusion, mais il peut la précéder ou la suivre sans s'en éloigner trop. Cette condition est justifée par l'idée même du contexte." See: Yasseen, op.cit., para. 16, p. 38.

not be treated as part of the preparatory works but rather as an element in the general rule of interpretation.[55]

6.46 Also uncontested interpretations given at a conference, e.g., by a chairman of a drafting committee, may constitute an "agreement" forming part of the "context".[56] However, interpretative or explanatory statements by members of a drafting committee in their personal capacity should be considered, if at all, simply as part of the preparatory works. We recall in this respect that, according to Article 32 of the Vienna Convention, preparatory works of a treaty are relevant as supplementary means of interpretation, together with the circumstances of its conclusion, *inter alia,* in order to confirm the meaning resulting from the application of Article 31 of that Convention.

The legal status of the minor exceptions doctrine under the Berne Convention

6.47 We will now apply these fundamental rules of interpretation to the provisions of the Berne Convention (1971) within our terms of reference, with a view to ascertaining the legal status of the minor exceptions doctrine in relation to Articles 11*bis*(1) and 11(1) of that Convention.

6.48 We note that, in addition to the explicit provisions on permissible limitations and exceptions to the exclusive rights embodied in the text of the Berne Convention (1971), the reports of successive revision conferences of that Convention refer to "implied exceptions" allowing member countries to provide limitations and exceptions to certain rights. The so-called "minor reservations" or "minor exceptions" doctrine is being referred to in respect of the right of public performance and certain other exclusive rights.[57] Under that doctrine, Berne Union members may provide minor exceptions to the rights provided, *inter alia*, under Articles 11*bis* and 11 of the Berne Convention (1971).[58]

---

[55] Sinclair, op.cit. 129. Sinclair mentions the example of the Council of Europe, where governmental experts charged with the task of negotiating and formulating an international convention of a particular topic, draw up, in parallel with the text of the convention, an explanatory report which sets out the framework within which and the background against which the convention has been drawn up, and which then goes on to furnish an article by article commentary on the text. The explanatory report is agreed upon unanimously by the governmental experts responsible for drawing up the text of the convention and it is adopted simultaneously with the text of the convention.

[56] "De plus, la procédure de certaines conférences générales permet, sans adoption de résolution formelle, de discerner un accord qui fait partie du contexte. Des explications concernant une disposition pourront être données, avant le vote de cette disposition, par une personne chargée par la conférence d'une certaine fonction. Le président du comité de rédaction peut, en tant que tel, être appelée à préciser le sens d'une disposition telle qu'elle est adoptée par ce comité. Si la déclaration n'a pas été contredite ou moins pas sérieusement, et si la disposition ainsi clarifiée est acceptée par un vote à la majorité requise, il est possible de soutenir que cette acceptation s'étend à ladite déclaration, qui peut ainsi être considérée comme la base d'un accord faisant partie du contexte. Tout se ramène ici à une question de preuve susceptible d'être élucidée par les circonstances qui ont entouré l'adoption de la disposition dont il s'agit." *See*: Yasseen, op.cit., para. 20, p. 39.

[57] The other main category of implied exceptions are understood to apply to the use of translations of literary works.

[58] The doctrine refers to (i) public performance and (ii) communication thereof to the public in the meaning of Article 11(1)(i-ii) as well as to (i) broadcasting by wireless diffusion, (ii) communication

6.49 This possibility, available to all Berne Union members, to provide exceptions to certain exclusive rights is most often referred to as "minor reservations" doctrine. However, this terminology is somewhat misleading in the sense that this possibility does not constitute a reservation within the meaning of Articles 19-23 of Section 2 on "Reservations" of the Vienna Convention. Specific rules apply to the members of the Berne Union under Article 30 of the Berne Convention (1971) for making reservations under that Convention. It should also be noted that WTO Members are forbidden to make reservations under Article 72 of the TRIPS Agreement[59] without the consent of the other Members. No reservation has been made on this basis under the TRIPS Agreement on this or any other matter.[60] For the sake of clarity, we therefore use hereinafter the term "minor exceptions" doctrine.

6.50 With respect to public performance of works, until 1948 only a national treatment obligation was provided for under the Berne Convention. Subparagraphs (i) and (ii) of Article 11 of that Convention originated in the Brussels Act of 1948. Their wording remained essentially unchanged in the Stockholm Act of 1967 and the Paris Act of 1971. No specific exception clause applicable to this right was added to the text of the Convention. However, when the general right of public performance was embodied for the first time in Article 11 of the Brussels Act, a statement was included in the General Report of the Brussels Conference referring to the minor exceptions doctrine.

6.51 The provisions currently contained in Article 11*bis*(1)(i) and 11*bis*(2) were first introduced into the Berne Convention at the Rome Conference of 1928, but subsequently modified. Subparagraphs (ii) and (iii) of Article 11*bis*(1) were added to the Convention at the Brussels Conference of 1948. In discussing subparagraphs (ii) and (iii) of Article 11*bis*(1), the General Report of the Brussels Conference states that the minor exceptions doctrine applies also to the exclusive rights under Article 11*bis*.

6.52 More specifically, it was proposed at the Brussels Conference of 1948 that a general provision be inserted into the Berne Convention under which it would be permissible for States parties to the Convention to retain various minor exceptions that already existed in their national laws. However, the proposal was not adopted by the Conference due to a concern that such a general provision could encourage the widening of existing minor exceptions or the introduction of additional minor exceptions in national laws. But the Conference did not question the very existence and maintenance of minor exceptions in national laws as such. In the context of the discussions on Article 11, it was agreed that rather than dealing with this matter in the

---

of the broadcast to the public by wire or re-broadcasting, and (iii) public communication by loudspeaker etc. of the broadcast in the meaning of Article 11*bis*(1). The minor exceptions doctrine also has been referred to in the context of Articles 11*ter*, 13 and 14 of the Berne Convention. *See* the Berne Convention for the Protection of Literary and Artistic Works from 1886 to 1986, published by the International Bureau of WIPO (1986), published by the International Bureau of WIPO in 1986 ("Berne Convention Centenary"), pp. 203 and 204. *See* also Ricketson, Sam: The Berne Convention for the Protection of Literary and Artistic Works: 1886-1986, Centre for Commercial Law Studies, Queen Mary College, London (1987), pp. 532-537ff.

[59] Article 72 of the TRIPS Agreement: "Reservations may not be entered in respect of any of the provisions of this Agreement without the consent of the other Members."

[60] Article XVI:5 of the Agreement Establishing the WTO reaffirms Article 72 of the TRIPS Agreement.

text of the Convention itself, a statement concerning the possibility to provide minor exceptions in national law would be included into the General Report.[61]

6.53 When ascertaining the legal status of the minor exceptions doctrine, it is important to note that the General Report states that the Rapporteur-General had been "*entrusted with making an express mention* of the possibility available to national legislation to make what is commonly called minor reservations".[62] We believe that the choice of these words reflects an agreement within the meaning of Article 31(2)(a) of the Vienna Convention between the Berne Union members at the Brussels Conference to retain the possibility of providing minor exceptions in national law. We arrive at this conclusion for the following reasons. First, the introduction of Articles 11*bis*(1)(iii) and 11(1)(ii) occurred simultaneously with the adoption of the General Report expressly mentioning the minor exceptions doctrine. Second, this doctrine is closely related to the substance of the amendment of the Berne Convention in that it limits the scope of the exclusive rights introduced by Articles 11*bis*(1)(iii) and 11(1)(ii) of the Berne Convention. Third, an "agreement" between all the parties exists because, on the one hand, the Rapporteur-General is being "entrusted to expressly mention" minor exceptions and, on the other hand, the General Report of the Brussels Conference reflecting this express mentioning was formally adopted by the Berne Union members. We therefore conclude that an agreement within the meaning of Article 31(2)(a) of the Vienna Convention between all the parties on the possibility to provide minor exceptions was made in connection with the conclusion of a revision of the Convention introducing additional exclusive rights, including those contained in Articles 11*bis*(1)(iii) and 11(1)(ii), to which these limitations were to apply, and that this agreement is relevant as context for interpreting these Articles.[63]

6.54 As pointed out above, the wording of Articles 11*bis* and 11 remained essentially the same at the Diplomatic Conferences in Stockholm (1967) and Paris (1971) where the General Reports were also formally adopted by the Berne Union members. The reports of the Stockholm Conference reconfirm our conclusion concerning the existence of an agreement on minor exceptions. The report of the Main Committee I[64] refers to the existence of an agreement between the Berne Union members that

---

61 The relevant part of the General Report of the Brussels Diplomatic Conference reads as follows:

"Your Rapporteur-General has been entrusted with making an express mention of the possibility available to national legislation to make what are commonly called minor reservations. The Delegates of Norway, Sweden, Denmark, and Finland, the Delegate of Switzerland and the Delegate of Hungary, have all mentioned these limited exceptions allowed for religious ceremonies, military bands and the needs of the child and adult education. These exceptional measures apply to articles 11*bis*, 11*ter*, 13 and 14. You will understand that these references are just lightly pencilled in here, in order to avoid damaging the principles of the right." *See* Annex XII.1 to the letter from the Director General of WIPO to the Chair of the Panel. The statement is also reproduced in the Berne Convention Centenary, op.cit., p. 181.

62 This is not merely a statement by a chair of a drafting group made in his/her personal capacity.

63 If there were no possibility for "minor exceptions" from Articles 11*bis* and 11, no *de minimis* exemptions in national law whatsoever, allowing the use of the rights conferred by these Articles without remuneration, could be justified under any provision of the Berne Convention.

64 The relevant parts of the Report of the Work of Main Committee I (Substantive Provisions of the Berne Convention: Articles 1 to 20) read as follows:

minor exceptions are permitted, *inter alia*, in respect of Articles 11 and 11*bis* of the Berne Convention.[65]

6.55 Furthermore, we recall that Article 31(3) of the Vienna Convention provides that together with the context (a) any subsequent agreement, (b) subsequent practice,[66] or (c) any relevant rules of international law applicable between the parties, shall be taken into account for the purposes of interpretation. We note that the parties and third parties have brought to our attention several examples from various countries of limitations in national laws based on the minor exceptions doctrine.[67] In our

"209. In the General Report of the Brussels Conference, the Rapporteur was instructed to refer explicitly, in connection with Article 11, to the possibility of what it had been agreed to call 'the minor reservations' of national legislation. Some delegates had referred to the exceptions permitted in respect of religious ceremonies, performances by military bands, and the requirements of education and popularization. The exceptions also apply to articles 11*bis*, 11*ter*, 13 and 14. The Rapporteur ended by saying that these allusions were given lightly without invalidating the principle in the right.

210. It seems that it was not the intention of the Committee to prevent States from maintaining in their national legislation provisions based on the declaration contained in the General Report of the Brussels Conference."

See the Berne Convention Centenary, p. 204. For a more complete review of the history of the minor exceptions doctrine and other implied exceptions under the Berne Convention, *see* e.g. Ricketson, The Berne Convention, op. cit., pp. 532 f.

65 While we note that this statement in the reports of the Stockholm Conference of 1967 confirms the agreement on the possibility of providing minor exceptions to certain exclusive rights at the Brussels Conference of 1948, we feel that there is no need to determine whether it constitutes a separate or renewed agreement at the Stockholm Conference within the meaning of Article 31(2) of the Vienna Convention. For the purposes of our examination of Articles 11*bis*(i)(iii) and 11(1)(ii), such an agreement would be relevant only to the extent that these Articles had been modified or amended at the Stockholm Conference.

66 In *Japan - Alcoholic Beverages*, the Appellate Body described subsequent practice within the meaning of Article 31(3)(b) of the Vienna Convention: "... Generally, in international law, the essence of subsequent practice in interpreting a treaty has been recognised as a 'concordant, common and consistent' sequence of acts or pronouncements which is sufficient to establish a discernible pattern implying the agreement of the parties regarding its interpretation. An isolated act is generally not sufficient to establish subsequent practice; it is a sequence of acts establishing the agreement of the parties that is relevant." (Footnotes omitted). *See* Appellate Body Report, *Japan - Taxes on Alcoholic Beverages* ("*Japan – Alcoholic Beverages II*"), WT/DS8,10,11/AB/R, adopted 1 November 1996, DSR 1996:I, 97 at 105.

67 For example, Australia exempts public performance by wireless apparatus at premises of, *inter alia*, hotels or guest houses. Belgium exempts a work's communication to the public in a place accessible to the public where the aim of the communication is not the work itself, and exempts the performance of a work during a public examination where the purpose is the assessment of the performer. Finland exempts public performance in connection with religious services and education. Finland and Denmark provide for exceptions where a work's performance is not the main feature of the event, provided that no fee is charged and the event is not for profit. New Zealand exempts public performance of musical works at educational establishments. The Philippines exempts public performances for charitable and educational purposes. A similar exception applies in India, where also performances at amateur clubs or societies are exempted. Canadian law provides for exceptions with respect to different exclusive rights for educational, religious or charitable purposes, and also at conventions and fairs. South Africa exempts public performances in the context of demonstrations of radio or television receivers and recording equipment by dealers of or clients for such equipment. (*See* US response to question 16 by the Panel to the United States.) Brazil allows free use of works in commercial establishments for the purpose of demonstration to customers in establishments that

view, state practice as reflected in the national copyright laws of Berne Union members before and after 1948, 1967 and 1971, as well as of WTO Members before and after the date that the TRIPS Agreement became applicable to them, confirms our conclusion about the minor exceptions doctrine.[68]

The scope of the minor exceptions doctrine

6.56 Apart from the legal status of the minor exceptions doctrine under the Berne Convention, the parties disagree also on the scope of the doctrine. In the US view, the defining element of the minor exceptions doctrine is that a limitation or exception must be minimal in nature to be permissible. The possibility of providing minor exceptions is not limited to the examples provided in the records of the Brussels and Stockholm Conferences cited above. In contrast, the European Communities argues that the examples given in the Brussels and Stockholm records are exhaustive. It submits that the minor exceptions doctrine is confined to limitations or exceptions of exclusively non-commercial character. It also emphasizes that the records of the Stockholm Conference describe the minor exceptions doctrine as a means to allow countries to "maintain" existing national exceptions. It infers from the above quoted statement in the records of the Stockholm Conference that the minor exceptions doctrine is capable of excusing only those exceptions or limitations which existed in the national legislation of a country prior to 1967, when the Stockholm Conference took place.[69] The United States rejects this "grandfathering" theory and the interpretation that the lists of examples found in the records of the Diplomatic Conferences are exhaustive.

6.57 The General Report of the Brussels Conference of 1948 refers to "religious ceremonies, military bands and the needs of the child and adult education" as examples of situations in respect of which minor exceptions may be provided. The Main Committee I Report of the Stockholm Conference of 1967 refers also to "popularization" as one example.[70] When these references are read in their proper context, it is evident that the given examples are of an illustrative character.[71] We also note that the examples given in the reports of the Brussels and Stockholm Conferences are not identical. Furthermore, the examples are given in the context of Article 11(1) of the Berne Convention, but the reports clarify that minor exceptions can also be provided to the exclusive rights conferred under Articles 11*bis*, 11*ter*, 13 and 14, without giving any specific examples. It is also evident that existing minor exceptions vary be-

---

market equipment that makes such use possible. (*See* the response by Brazil to question 1 from the Panel to the third parties.)

[68] By enunciating these examples of state practice we do not wish to express a view on whether these are sufficient to constitute 'subsequent practice' within the meaning of Article 31(3)(b) of the Vienna Convention. *See* description by the Appellate Body in its report on *Japan - Alcoholic Beverages II, supra*, footnote 66, at 105.

[69] Response to question 11 from the Panel to the European Communities.

[70] *See* the citations in footnote 64 above.

[71] For example, in their preparatory work for the Brussels Conference, the Belgian Government and BIRPI took the view that it would be impossible to list all of the pre-existing exceptions exhaustively in the Convention as they were too varied. Documents de la Conférence Réunie a Bruxelles du 5 au 26 juin 1948, published by BIRPI in 1951, p. 255.

tween different countries. The information presented to us on state practice in respect of minor exceptions in different countries is illustrative of that fact.[72] Furthermore, the academic literature supports the view that these examples of uses in respect of which minor exceptions could be provided are not intended to be exhaustive.[73]

6.58 We note that some of the above-mentioned examples (e.g., religious ceremonies, military bands) typically involve minimal uses which are not carried out for profit. With respect to other examples (e.g., adult and child education and popularization), however an exclusively non-commercial nature of potentially exempted uses is less clear. On the basis of the information provided to us, we are not in a position to determine that the minor exceptions doctrine justifies only exclusively non-commercial use of works and that it may under no circumstances justify exceptions to uses with a more than negligible economic impact on copyright holders. On the other hand, non-commercial uses of works, e.g., in adult and child education, may reach a level that has a major economic impact on the right holder. At any rate, in our view, a non-commercial character of the use in question is not determinative provided that the exception contained in national law is indeed *minor*.[74]

6.59 As regards the coverage of the minor exceptions doctrine in temporal respect, we cannot share the European Communities' view that the coverage was "frozen" in 1967.[75] In our view, the use of the term "*maintain*" in the Stockholm records[76] is not sufficient evidence to substantiate the interpretation that countries could justify under the minor exceptions doctrine only those limitations which were in force in their national legislation prior to the year when that Conference was held.

The legal status of the minor exceptions doctrine under the TRIPS Agreement

6.60 Having concluded that the minor exceptions doctrine forms part of the "context" of, at least, Articles 11*bis* and 11 of the Berne Convention (1971) by virtue of an agreement within the meaning of Article 31(2)(a) of the Vienna Convention, which was made between the Berne Union members in connection with the conclusion of the respective amendments to that Convention, we next address the second step of our analysis outlined above. This second step deals with the question whether or not the minor exceptions doctrine has been incorporated into the TRIPS Agree-

---

72 *See* footnote 67 above.

73 Ricketson notes that "[t]he examples of uses given in the records of the Brussels and Stockholm Conferences are in no way an exhaustive list or determinative of which particular exceptions will be justified". *See* Ricketson, Berne Convention, op.cit., p. 536.

74 In the literature, it has been argued that such exceptions to the rights protected under the relevant provisions of the Berne Convention must be concerned with minimal use, or use without significance to the author. *See* Ricketson, Berne Convention, op.cit., p. 532-535.

75 As regards the year 1967 as a suggested cut-off date, we note that the substantive provisions of the Stockholm Act of 1967 have never entered into force. Its substantive provisions were later incorporated into the Paris Act of 1971, which entered into force on 10 October 1974.

76 Para. 210 of the Main Committee I Report of the Stockholm Conference uses the term "maintain". However, the original statement in the General Report of the Brussels Conference of 1948, to which the Stockholm records refer, uses the expression "the possibility available to national legislation to make what are commonly called minor reservations".

ment, by virtue of its Article 9.1[77], together with Articles 1-21 of the Berne Convention (1971) as part of the Berne *acquis*.

6.61 We note that the express wording of Article 9.1 of the TRIPS Agreement neither establishes nor excludes such incorporation into the Agreement of the minor exceptions doctrine as it applies to Articles 11, 11*bis*, 11*ter*, 13 and 14 of the Berne Convention (1971).[78]

6.62 We have shown above that the minor exceptions doctrine forms part of the context, within the meaning of Article 31(2)(a) of the Vienna Convention, of at least Articles 11 and 11*bis* of the Berne Convention (1971). There is no indication in the wording of the TRIPS Agreement that Articles 11 and 11*bis* have been incorporated into the TRIPS Agreement by its Article 9.1 without bringing with them the possibility of providing minor exceptions to the respective exclusive rights. If that incorporation should have covered only the text of Articles 1-21 of the Berne Convention (1971), but not the entire Berne *acquis* relating to these articles, Article 9.1 of the TRIPS Agreement would have explicitly so provided.[79]

6.63 Thus we conclude that, in the absence of any express exclusion in Article 9.1 of the TRIPS Agreement, the incorporation of Articles 11 and 11*bis* of the Berne Convention (1971) into the Agreement includes the entire *acquis* of these provisions, including the possibility of providing minor exceptions to the respective exclusive rights.

6.64 We find confirmation of our interpretation in certain references to the minor exceptions doctrine in the documentation from the GATT Uruguay Round negotiations on the TRIPS Agreement.[80] A TRIPS Negotiating Group document[81] reproduces a document that was prepared by the International Bureau of the WIPO following a decision taken by the Negotiating Group, on 3 March 1988, inviting the Bureau "to prepare a factual document to facilitate an understanding of the existence, scope and form of generally internationally accepted and applied standards/norms for

---

77 Article 9.1 of the TRIPS Agreement provides: "Members shall comply with Articles 1 through 21 of the Berne Convention (1971) and the Appendix thereto. However, Members shall not have rights or obligations under this Agreement in respect of the rights conferred under Article 6*bis* of the Convention or of the rights derived therefrom."

78 While Article 9.1 does not mention the minor exceptions doctrine, it does not exclude the possibility that this doctrine was incorporated into the TRIPS Agreement as part of the Berne *acquis* together with the above-mentioned provisions to which it applies under the Berne Convention (1971).

79 In this respect, we refer to the treatment of moral rights under the TRIPS Agreement. Article 9.1 explicitly excludes Members' rights and obligations in respect of the rights conferred under Article 6*bis* of the Berne Convention (1971) and of the rights derived therefrom.

80 We recall that, according to Article 32 of the Vienna Convention, "recourse may be had to supplementary means of interpretation, including the preparatory works of the treaty and the circumstances of its conclusion, in order to confirm the meaning resulting from the application of Article 31 ...". We see no need to determine whether the GATT Uruguay Round documentation constitutes "preparatory works " or relate to the "circumstances of ... [the] conclusion" of the TRIPS Agreement as annexed to the Agreement Establishing the WTO.

81 MTN.GNG/NG11/W/24/Rev.1 of 15 September 1988.

the protection of intellectual property".[82] The Section on the "Scope of Rights" contains the following text on the minor exceptions doctrine:[83]

> "In addition to the limitations explicitly mentioned in the text of the Convention, there is one more possibility for certain exceptions about which there was express agreement at various revision conferences, namely the possibility of minor exceptions to the right of public performance (a concept which is close to the notion of 'fair use' or 'fair dealing'; see item (iii), below)."

6.65 Another TRIPS Negotiating Group document[84] mentions the minor exceptions doctrine as forming part of existing international standards. We are not aware of any record in the Uruguay Round documentation of any country participating in the negotiations challenging or questioning the minor exceptions doctrine being part of the Berne *acquis* on which the TRIPS Agreement was to be built.[85]

6.66 In the area of copyright, the Berne Convention and the TRIPS Agreement form the overall framework for multilateral protection. Most WTO Members are also parties to the Berne Convention. We recall that it is a general principle of interpretation to adopt the meaning that reconciles the texts of different treaties and avoids a conflict between them. Accordingly, one should avoid interpreting the TRIPS Agreement to mean something different than the Berne Convention except where this is explicitly provided for. This principle is in conformity with the public international law presumption against conflicts, which has been applied by WTO panels and the Appellate Body in a number of cases.[86] We believe that our interpretation of the legal

---

[82] See GATT document MTN.GNG/NG11/6, paras. 39 and 40 and Annex.

[83] Ibid. p. 22.

[84] MTN.GNG/NG11/W/32/Rev.2 of 2 February 1990 contains synoptic tables of proposals tabled in the Group. It contains the first specific proposals on the rights to be conferred and on the permissible limitations, exceptions and compulsory licensing in the area of copyright. The first column in each table sets out the provisions of the international treaties existing at that time corresponding to the proposals made. The Secretariat prepared the content of this column drawing on the above-mentioned document prepared by the International Bureau of WIPO. In the first column of para. 5 on limitations, the Secretariat reproduced, in its rendering of the existing international standards, the above-mentioned information provided by WIPO on minor exceptions doctrine. *Ibid.* p. 32.

[85] We find a further confirmation of our interpretation in the negotiating history of Article 9.1 of the TRIPS Agreement. Earlier drafts of that Article referred merely to "the substantive provisions" of the Berne Convention (1971), indicating that the intention was to embody the overall Berne *acquis* rather than just the literal wording of the individual articles. During the negotiations a preference was expressed for identifying these substantive provisions. As a result, these provisions where identified in the final version of the Article as "Articles 1 through 21 of the Berne Convention (1971) and the Appendix thereto". It appears that this was done for the sake of clarity, and there is no indication in the records that there was an intention to change the aim of embodying the overall Berne *acquis*.

[86] Appellate Body Report, *Canada - Certain Measures Concerning Periodicals* ("*Canada - Periodicals*"), WT/DS31/AB/R, adopted 30 July 1997, DSR 1999:I, 449 at 465. Appellate Body Report *European communities - Regime for the Importation, Sale and Distribution of Bananas*, ("*EC - Bananas III*"), WT/DS27/AB/R, adopted 25 September 1997, DSR 1997:II, 591, paras. 219-222.

In *Guatemala - Cement*, the Appellate Body when discussing the possibility of conflicts between the provisions of the Anti-dumping Agreement and the DSU, stated: "A special or additional provision should only be found to *prevail* over a provision of the DSU in a situation where adherence to the one provision will lead to a violation of the other provision, that is, in the case of a *conflict* between them." *See* Appellate Body Report *Guatemala - Antidumping Investigation Regarding Port-*

status of the minor exceptions doctrine under the TRIPS Agreement is consistent with these general principles.

Subsequent developments

6.67 The United States argues that Article 10 of the WIPO Copyright Treaty ("WCT"), adopted at a Diplomatic Conference on 20 December 1996 organized under the auspices of WIPO, reflects the standard set forth in Article 13 of the TRIPS Agreement. Paragraph (1) of that Article provides a standard for permissible limitations and exceptions to the rights granted to authors under the WCT, while paragraph (2) extends this standard to the application of the provisions of the Berne Convention (1971).[87] In the view of the United States, it becomes clear from the Agreed Statement concerning Article 10 of the WCT that the signatories of the WCT, which include the European Communities and its member States and the United States, commonly recognized the minor exceptions doctrine.[88] In support of its view, the United States also points out that Article 10 of the WCT is based on Article 12 of the Basic Proposal for the 1996 Diplomatic Conference.[89] The commentary in the Basic Proposal explains that the TRIPS Agreement already enunciates the standard of that Article for limitations and exceptions in Article 13 of the TRIPS Agreement, and further states that "[n]o limitation, not even those that belong in the category of minor reservations, may exceed the limits set by the three-steps test".

land Cement from Mexico, WT/DS60/AB/R, adopted 25 November 1998, DSR 1998:IX, 3767, para. 65.

In *Indonesia - Autos*, the panel noted: "... we recall first that in public international law there is a presumption against conflict. This presumption is especially relevant in the WTO context since all WTO agreements, including GATT 1994 which was modified by Understandings when judged necessary, were negotiated at the same time, by the same Members and in the same forum. In this context we recall the principle of effective interpretation pursuant to which all provisions of a treaty (and in the WTO system all agreements) must be given meaning, using the ordinary meaning of words." (footnotes omitted). *See* Panel Report *Indonesia - Certain Measures Affecting the Automobile Industry* ("*Indonesia - Autos*"), WT/DS/54/R, WT/DS55/R, WT/DS59/R and WT/DS64/R, adopted 23 July 1998, DSR 1998;VI, 2201, para. 14.28.

87 Article 10 of the WCT provides:

"1. Contracting Parties may, in their national legislation, provide for limitations of or exceptions to the rights granted to authors of literary and artistic works under this Treaty in certain special cases that do not conflict with a normal exploitation of the work and do not unreasonably prejudice the legitimate interests of the author.

2. Contracting Parties shall, when applying the Berne Convention, confine any limitations of or exceptions to rights provided for therein to certain special cases that do not conflict with a normal exploitation of the work and do not unreasonably prejudice the legitimate interests of the author."

88 Agreed Statement concerning Article 10 of the WCT reads as follows: "It is understood that the provisions of Article 10 permit Contracting Parties to carry forward and appropriately extend into the digital environment *limitations and exceptions in their national laws which have been considered acceptable under the Berne Convention*. Similarly these provisions should be understood to permit Contracting Parties *to devise new exceptions and limitations that are appropriate in the digital network environment*." (emphasis added).

89 Response to question 14 from the Panel to the United States.

6.68 The European Communities argues that the WCT has to date been ratified by only a small number of contracting parties and has not yet reached the threshold of thirty ratifications necessary for its entry into force.

6.69 We note that the subsequent developments just mentioned do not constitute a subsequent treaty on the same subject-matter within the meaning of Article 30, or subsequent agreements on the interpretation of a treaty, or subsequent practice within the meaning of Article 31(3). Thus such subsequent developments may be of rather limited relevance in the light of the general rules of interpretation as embodied in the Vienna Convention. However, in our view, the wording of the WCT, and in particular of the Agreed Statement thereto, nonetheless supports, as far as the Berne Convention is concerned, that the Berne Union members are permitted to provide minor exceptions to the rights provided under Articles 11 and 11*bis* of the Paris Act of 1971, and certain other rights. It appears that the objective was not to disallow the provision of such minor exceptions by WCT parties, but rather to make their application subject to the "three step test" contained in Article 10(2) of the WCT.

6.70 In paragraph 6.66 we discussed the need to interpret the Berne Convention and the TRIPS Agreement in a way that reconciles the texts of these two treaties and avoids a conflict between them, given that they form the overall framework for multilateral copyright protection. The same principle should also apply to the relationship between the TRIPS Agreement and the WCT. The WCT is designed to be compatible with this framework, incorporating or using much of the language of the Berne Convention and the TRIPS Agreement.[90] The WCT was unanimously concluded at a diplomatic conference organized under the auspices of WIPO in December 1996, one year after the WTO Agreement entered into force, in which 127 countries participated. Most of these countries were also participants in the TRIPS negotiations and are Members of the WTO.[91] For these reasons, it is relevant to seek contextual guidance also in the WCT when developing interpretations that avoid conflicts within this overall framework, except where these treaties explicitly contain different obligations.

(iv) The Scope of Article 13 of the TRIPS Agreement

6.71 As earlier mentioned, at the heart of the US case is Article 13 of the TRIPS Agreement. The United States submits that it clarifies and articulates the scope of the minor exceptions doctrine, which is applicable under the TRIPS Agreement. Having considered the legal status of the minor exceptions doctrine under the TRIPS Agreement, we will later examine the applicability of Article 13 to Articles 11*bis*(1) and 11(1) of the Berne Convention (1971) as incorporated into the TRIPS Agreement.[92]

---

90 Article 10 of the WCT addresses the WCT's relation to the Berne Convention, but there is no direct connection between the WCT and the TRIPS Agreement. Article 1 of the WCT provides that "[t]his Treaty shall not have any connection with the treaties other than the Berne Convention, nor shall it prejudice any rights and obligations under any other treaties".

91 As of 1 March 1999, 13 countries had ratified the WCT. It has 51 signatories, including the European Communities and its member States.

92 *See* the chapter "The three criteria test under Article 13 of the TRIPS Agreement", beginning with para. 6.97 of this report.

6.72 The language used in Article 13 of the TRIPS Agreement[93] has its origins in the similar language used in Article 9(2) of the Berne Convention (1971),[94] although the latter only applies in the case of the reproduction right.[95]

6.73 A general right of reproduction was not recognized under the Berne Convention until the Stockholm Act of 1967. The main difficulty in the preparation of this amendment was to find an appropriate formula which would allow exceptions to that right. In adopting the present text of Article 9(2) of the Berne Convention, the Main Committee I of the Stockholm Diplomatic Conference (1967) gave the following guidance on its interpretation:

> "The Committee also adopted a proposal by the Drafting Committee that the second condition should be placed before the first, as this would afford a more logical order for the interpretation of the rule. If it is considered that reproduction conflicts with the normal exploitation of the work, reproduction is not permitted at all. If it is considered that reproduction does not conflict with the normal exploitation of the work, the next step would be to consider whether it does not unreasonably prejudice the legitimate interests of the author. Only if such is not the case would it be possible in certain special cases to introduce a compulsory license, or to provide for use without payment. A practical example may be photocopying for various purposes. If it consists of producing a very large number of copies, it may not be permitted, as it conflicts with a normal exploitation of the work. If it implies a rather large number of copies for use in industrial undertakings, it may not unreasonably prejudice the legitimate interests of the author, provided that, according to national legislation, an equitable remuneration is paid. If a small number of copies is made, photocopying may be permitted without payment, particularly for individual or scientific use."[96]

6.74 Apart from the difference in the use of the terms "permit" and "confine",[97] the main difference between Article 9(2) of the Berne Convention (1971) and Article 13

---

93 Article 13 of the TRIPS Agreement provides:

"Members shall confine limitations or exceptions to exclusive rights to certain special cases which do not conflict with a normal exploitation of the work and do not unreasonably prejudice the legitimate interests of the right holder."

94 Article 9(2) of the Berne Convention (1971) provides:

"It shall be a matter for legislation in the countries of the Union to permit the reproduction of such works in certain special cases, provided that such reproduction does not conflict with a normal exploitation of the work and does not unreasonably prejudice the legitimate interests of the author."

95 The preparatory works to Article 9(2) of the Berne Convention may be illustrative of how the language used was originally intended to be understood. While Article 9(2) may form part of the context of Article 13, preparatory works and negotiating history would, of course, be relevant primarily in the framework Article 32 of the Vienna Convention, e.g., for purposes of confirming an interpretation developed consistent with Article 31 of the Vienna Convention.

96 Records of the Intellectual Property Conference of Stockholm. June 11 to July 14, 1967. Report on the Work of Main Committee I (Substantive Provisions of the Berne Convention: Articles 1 to 20). As reproduced in the Berne Convention Centenary, p. 197.

97 Article 9(2) of the Berne Convention (1971) provides that "[i]t shall be a matter for legislation in the countries of the Union to permit the reproduction", while Article 13 of the TRIPS Agreement provides that "Members shall confine limitations and exceptions to exclusive rights".

of the TRIPS Agreement is that the former applies only to the reproduction right. The wording of Article 13 does not contain an express limitation in terms of the categories of rights under copyright to which it may apply. It states that limitations or exceptions to exclusive rights can only be made if three conditions are met: (1) the limitations or exceptions are confined to certain special cases; (2) they do not conflict with a normal exploitation of the work; and (3) they do not unreasonably prejudice the legitimate interests of the right holder. As both parties agree, these three conditions apply cumulatively; a limitation or an exception is consistent with Article 13 only if it fulfils each of the three conditions.

6.75 The European Communities argues that Article 13 of the TRIPS Agreement applies only to those rights that were added to the TRIPS Agreement, and, therefore, it does not apply to those provisions of the Berne Convention (1971), including its Articles 11(1) and 11*bis*(1), that were incorporated into the TRIPS Agreement by reference.[98]

6.76 In the view of the European Communities, Article 20 of the Berne Convention (1971) speaks against the interpretation of Article 13 as providing a basis for exceptions to the Berne rights incorporated into the TRIPS Agreement, because Article 20 of the Convention only allows "countries of the Berne Union to enter into special agreements among themselves, insofar as such agreements grant to authors more extensive rights than those granted by the (Berne) Convention".[99] In other words, the European Communities contends that parties to the Berne Convention cannot agree in another treaty to reduce the Berne Convention level of protection.

6.77 Furthermore, the European Communities adds that Article 20 of the Berne Convention (1971) is mirrored in the TRIPS Agreement by Article 2(2), which reads as follows:

> "Nothing in Parts I to IV of this Agreement shall derogate from existing obligations that Members may have to each other under the Paris Convention, the Berne Convention, the Rome Convention and the Treaty on Intellectual Property in Respect of Integrated Circuits."

6.78 In the alternative to its principal argument, the European Communities contends that, even if Article 13 of the TRIPS Agreement were given a role in the context of exceptions to exclusive rights under the Berne Convention (1971), a principle should be respected according to which the objective of the TRIPS Agreement is to reduce or eliminate existing exceptions, rather than to grant new or extend existing ones. The European Communities refers to the difference in the wording between Article 13 ("Members *shall confine* limitations or exceptions") and Articles 17, 26(2) and 30 of the TRIPS Agreement ("Members *may provide* limited exceptions").[100] We recall, however, that under its principal argument the European Communities takes

---

[98] *See* EC response to question 10 from the Panel to the European Communities.

[99] The complete text of Article 20 of the Berne Convention (1971) reads:

"The Governments of the countries of the Union reserve the right to enter into special agreements among themselves, in so far as such agreements grant to authors more extensive rights than those granted by the Convention, or contain other provisions not contrary to this Convention. The provisions of existing agreements which satisfy these conditions shall remain applicable."

[100] Para. 27 of the second written submission by the European Communities.

the view that Article 13 provides exceptions to new rights, rather than reduce the scope of any existing limitations.

6.79 The United States contends that "[t]he text of Article 13 is straightforward and applies to 'limitations or exceptions to exclusive rights'. Not *some* limitations, not limitations to *some* exclusive rights".[101] The United States adds that the application of Article 13 of the TRIPS Agreement to the rights provided under Article 11(1) and 11*bis*(1) of the Berne Convention (1971) does not derogate from the obligations under the Berne Convention in violation of Article 2.2 of the TRIPS Agreement or Article 20 of the Berne Convention, because Article 13 of the TRIPS Agreement articulates the standard applicable to minor exceptions under the Berne Convention (1971) as far as these Articles are concerned.

6.80 In our view, neither the express wording nor the context of Article 13 or any other provision of the TRIPS Agreement supports the interpretation that the scope of application of Article 13 is limited to the exclusive rights newly introduced under the TRIPS Agreement.

6.81 The application of Article 13 of the TRIPS Agreement to the rights provided under Articles 11(1) and 11*bis*(1) of the Berne Convention (1971) as incorporated into the TRIPS Agreement need not lead to different standards from those applicable under the Berne Convention (1971), given that we have established that the possibility of providing minor exceptions forms part of the context of these articles. Taking into account this contextual guidance, we will examine the scope for permissible minor exceptions to the exclusive rights in question by applying the conditions of Article 13 of the TRIPS Agreement.

6.82 In regard to the argument of the European Communities that the US interpretation of Article 13 is incompatible with Article 20 of the Berne Convention (1971) and Article 2.2 of the TRIPS Agreement because it treats Article 13 of the TRIPS Agreement as providing a basis for exceptions that would be inconsistent with those permitted under the Berne Convention (1971), we note that the United States is not arguing this but rather that Article 13 clarifies and articulates the standards applicable to minor exceptions under the Berne Convention (1971). Since the EC arguments in relation to these provisions would only be relevant if a finding that would involve inconsistency with the Berne Convention (1971) were being advocated, we do not feel it is necessary to examine them further.

(v) Article 11*bis*(2) of the Berne Convention (1971) as Incorporated into the TRIPS Agreement

6.83 Article 11*bis*(2) of the Berne Convention (1971) as incorporated into the TRIPS Agreement relates to the exclusive rights conferred under Article 11*bis*(1), including the communication to the public of a broadcast in the meaning of its subparagraph (iii). It reads as follows:

> "It shall be a matter for legislation in the countries of the Union to determine the conditions under which the rights mentioned in the preceding paragraph may be exercised, but these conditions shall apply

[101] Para. 4 of the oral statement of the United States at the second meeting with the Panel.

only in the countries where they have been prescribed. They shall not in any circumstances be prejudicial to the moral rights of the author, nor to his right to obtain equitable remuneration which, in the absence of agreement, shall be fixed by competent authority."

6.84 This provision was inserted into the Rome Act of 1928, when the right of broadcasting was first introduced. At the Brussels Conference of 1948, its scope was extended to cover the additional rights recognized by Article 11*bis*(1), including the rights under Article 11*bis*(1)(iii). Article 11*bis*(2) does not apply to the rights provided under Article 11(1). The reference to "conditions" is usually understood to allow countries to substitute, for the author's exclusive right, a system of compulsory licences,[102] or determine other conditions provided that they are not prejudicial to the right holder's right to obtain an equitable remuneration.[103]

6.85 The European Communities argues that any exception to the rights contained in Article 11*bis*(1) of the Berne Convention (1971) as incorporated into the TRIPS Agreement would have to provide for an equitable remuneration to the right holder; this is not the case under Section 110(5) of the US Copyright Act. In this respect, the European Communities refers to the extensive argumentation supporting this interpretation as developed in Australia's third party submission.[104]

6.86 The United States contends that Article 11*bis*(2) has no bearing on Section 110(5); Article 11*bis*(2) merely authorizes a country to substitute a compulsory licence, or its equivalent, for an exclusive right under Article 11*bis*. The United States adds that Article 11*bis*(2) is not related to the minor exceptions doctrine, and does not bear upon the scope of exceptions permissible under that doctrine as it applies under Article 11*bis*.

6.87 We believe that Article 11*bis*(2) of the Berne Convention (1971) and Article 13 cover different situations. On the one hand, Article 11*bis*(2) authorizes Members to determine conditions under which the rights conferred by Article 11*bis*(1)(i-iii) may be exercised. The imposition of such conditions may completely replace the free exercise of the exclusive right of authorizing the use of the rights embodied in subparagraphs (i-iii) provided that equitable remuneration and the author's moral rights are not prejudiced. However, unlike Article 13 of the TRIPS Agreement, Article 11*bis*(2) of the Berne Convention (1971) would not in any case justify use free of charge.

6.88 On the other hand, it is sufficient that a limitation or an exception to the exclusive rights provided under Article 11*bis*(1) of the Berne Convention (1971) as incorporated into the TRIPS Agreement meets the three conditions contained in its Article 13 to be permissible. If these three conditions are met, a government may choose between different options for limiting the right in question, including use free

---

102 *See* e.g. the Guide to the Berne Convention, op.cit., para. 11*bis*.15, p. 70.

103 The European Communities notes that "[i]t would appear that a country could set minimum or precise levels of royalties to be paid for the different uses protected under Article 11*bis* of the Berne Convention. Another way to provide for equitable remuneration could be the introduction of a levy system for the audio/TV equipment purchased by the establishment being allowed to play copyrighted works without authorisations, whereby the proceeds from such a levy system is distributed to the right holders." *See* EC response to question 12 from the Panel to the European Communities.

104 The written submission of Australia, paras. 2.8-2.14, 3.7-3.14, 4.3 and 4.8.

of charge and without an authorization by the right holder. This is not in conflict with any of the paragraphs of Article 11*bis* because use free of any charge may be permitted for minor exceptions by virtue of the minor exceptions doctrine which applies, *inter alia*, also to Article 11*bis*.

6.89 As regards situations that would not meet the above-mentioned three conditions, a government may not justify an exception, including one involving use free of charge, by Article 13 of the TRIPS Agreement. However, also in these situations Article 11*bis*(2) of the Berne Convention (1971) as incorporated into the TRIPS Agreement would nonetheless allow Members to substitute, for an exclusive right, a compulsory licence, or determine other conditions provided that they were not prejudicial to the right holder's right to obtain an equitable remuneration.

6.90 We believe that our interpretation gives meaning and effect to Article 11*bis*(2), the minor exceptions doctrine as it applies to Article 11*bis*, and Article 13. However, in our view, under the interpretation suggested by the European Communities this would not be the case, e.g., in the following situations. If any *de minimis* exception from rights conferred by Article 11*bis*(1)(i-iii) were subject to the requirement to provide equitable remuneration within the meaning of Article 11*bis*(2), no exemption whatsoever from the rights recognized by Article 11*bis*(1) could permit use free of charge even if the three criteria of Article 13 were met. As a result, narrow exceptions or limitations would be subject to the three conditions of Article 13 in addition to the requirement to provide equitable remuneration. At the same time, broader exceptions or limitations which do not comply with the criteria of Article 13 could arguably still be justified under Article 11*bis*(2) as long as the conditions imposed ensure, *inter alia*, equitable remuneration. Such an interpretation could render Article 13 somewhat redundant because narrow exceptions would be subject to all the requirements of Article 13 and Article 11*bis*(2) on a cumulative basis, while for broader exceptions compliance with Article 11*bis*(2) could suffice. Both situations would lead to the result that any use free of charge would not be permissible. These examples are illustrative of situations where the terms and conditions of Article 13, Article 11*bis*(2) and the minor exceptions doctrine would not be given full meaning and effect.

6.91 In our view, Section 110(5) of the US Copyright Act contains exceptions that allow use of protected works without an authorization by the right holder and without charge. Whether these exceptions meet the United States' obligations under the TRIPS Agreement has to be examined by applying Article 13 of the TRIPS Agreement. Article 11*bis*(2) of the Berne Convention (1971) as incorporated into the TRIPS Agreement is not relevant for the case at hand; the United States has not provided a right in respect of the uses covered by the present Section 110(5), the exercise of which would have been subjected to conditions determined in its legislation.

(vi) Summary of Limitations and Exceptions

6.92 In the light of the foregoing analysis, we conclude that the context of Articles 11 and 11*bis* of the Berne Convention (1971) comprises, within the meaning of Article 31(2)(a) of the Vienna Convention, the possibility of providing minor exceptions to the exclusive rights in question. This minor exceptions doctrine has been incorporated into the TRIPS Agreement, by virtue of its Article 9.1, together with these provisions of the Berne Convention (1971). Therefore, the doctrine is relevant as forming part of the context of Articles 11(1)(ii) and 11*bis*(1)(iii) of the Berne Convention (1971) as incorporated into the TRIPS Agreement.

6.93 As regards the scope of permissible limitations and exceptions under the minor exceptions doctrine, we conclude that the doctrine is primarily concerned with *de minimis* use, but that otherwise its application is not limited to the examples contained in the reports of the Berne Convention revision conferences held in Brussels and Stockholm, to exclusively non-commercial uses or to exceptions in national legislation that existed prior to 1967. However, we note that the reports of the Brussels and Stockholm Conferences are inconclusive about the precise scope of exceptions that can be provided in national legislation.

6.94 We conclude that Article 13 of the TRIPS Agreement applies to Articles 11*bis*(1)(iii) and 11(1)(ii) of the Berne Convention (1971) as incorporated into the TRIPS Agreement, given that neither the express wording nor the context of Article 13 or any other provision of the TRIPS Agreement supports the interpretation that the scope of application of Article 13 is limited to the exclusive rights newly introduced under the TRIPS Agreement.

6.95 We also conclude that Article 11*bis*(2) of the Berne Convention (1971) as incorporated into the TRIPS Agreement allows Members to substitute a compulsory licence for an exclusive right under Article 11*bis*(1), or determine other conditions provided that they are not prejudicial to the right holder's right to obtain an equitable remuneration. Article 11*bis*(2) is not relevant for the case at hand, because the United States has not provided a right in respect of the uses covered by the present Section 110(5), the exercise of which would have been subjected to conditions determined in its legislation.

6.96 We now proceed to applying the three conditions contained in Article 13 of the TRIPS Agreement to the exemptions contained in Section 110(5) of the US Copyright Act in relation to Articles 11*bis*(1)(iii) and 11(1)(ii) of the Berne Convention (1971) as incorporated into the TRIPS Agreement.

2. *The Three Criteria Test under Article 13 of the TRIPS Agreement*

(a) General Introduction

6.97 Article 13 of the TRIPS Agreement requires that limitations and exceptions to exclusive rights (1) be confined to certain special cases, (2) do not conflict with a normal exploitation of the work, and (3) do not unreasonably prejudice the legitimate interests of the right holder.[105] The principle of effective treaty interpretation requires us to give a distinct meaning to each of the three conditions and to avoid a reading that could reduce any of the conditions to "redundancy or inutility".[106] The three con-

---

[105] *See* the text of the Article in para. 6.31 and in footnote 93 above. As we noted in para. 6.72 above, the wording of Article 13 derives largely from Article 9(2) of the Berne Convention (1971) which applies, however, to reproduction rights only. Given the similarity of the wording, we consider that the preparatory works of Article 9(2) of the Berne Convention and its application in practice may be of contextual relevance in interpreting Article 13 of the TRIPS Agreement.

[106] Appellate Body Report *United States - Standards for Reformulated and Conventional Gasoline*, *supra*, footnote 29, at 21.

ditions apply on a cumulative basis, each being a separate and independent requirement that must be satisfied. Failure to comply with any one of the three conditions results in the Article 13 exception being disallowed. Both parties agree on the cumulative nature of the three conditions. The Panel shares their view. It may be noted at the outset that Article 13 cannot have more than a narrow or limited operation. Its tenor, consistent as it is with the provisions of Article 9(2) of the Berne Convention (1971), discloses that it was not intended to provide for exceptions or limitations except for those of a limited nature. The narrow sphere of its operation will emerge from our discussion and application of its provisions in the paragraphs which follow.

6.98 In the following, we will first explore the interpretation of the first condition of Article 13 in general terms in the light of the arguments made by the parties. We will then examine, in turn, subparagraphs (B) and (A) of Section 110(5) of the US Copyright Act of 1976, as amended by the Fairness in Music Licensing Act of 1998, that contain, respectively, the business and homestyle exemptions. We will discuss the business exemption of subparagraph (B) first because most of the arguments raised by the parties focus on it. After that, we will similarly explore the interpretation of the second and third conditions and apply them to subparagraphs (B) and (A) of Section 110(5).

6.99 The parties have largely relied on similar factual information in substantiating their legal arguments under each of the three conditions of Article 13. We are called upon to evaluate this information from different angles under the three conditions, which call for different requirements for justifying exceptions or limitations. We will look at the defined and limited scope of the exemptions at issue under the first condition, and focus on the degree of conflict with normal exploitation of works under the second condition. In relation to the third condition, we will examine the extent of prejudice caused to the legitimate interests of the right holder in the light of the information submitted by the parties.

6.100 In providing such factual information, the United States has focused on describing the immediate and direct impact on copyright holders caused by the introduction of the exemptions into its law; this can be characterized as the *actual* effects of the exemptions. The United States argues that while both actual losses and potential losses may be relevant to the analysis, the key is a realistic appraisal of the conditions that prevail in the market; the only way to avoid the danger of arbitrariness is to base the analysis on realistic market conditions.[107]

6.101 The European Communities emphasizes the importance of taking into account the way that the exemptions affect the right holders' opportunities to exercise their exclusive rights as well as the indirect impact of the exemptions; this can be characterized as the *potential* effects of the exemptions. We will address below the question to what extent we should focus on the actual impact on the right holder and to what extent we should also take into account the potential impact.

[107] US second oral statement, para. 18.

(b) "Certain Special Cases"

(i) General Interpretative Analysis

6.102 In invoking the exception of Article 13, as an articulation and clarification of the minor exceptions doctrine, the United States claims that both subparagraphs (A) and (B) of Section 110(5) meet the standard of being confined to "certain special cases".

6.103 The United States submits that the fact that the TRIPS Agreement does not elaborate on the criteria for a case to be considered "special" provides Members flexibility to determine for themselves whether a particular case represents an appropriate basis for an exception.[108] But it acknowledges that the essence of the first condition is that the exceptions be well-defined and of limited application.[109]

6.104 In the view of the European Communities, an exception has to be well-defined and narrow in scope to meet the requirements under the first condition. In the EC's view, in the case at hand, such significant numbers of establishments are excepted from the duty to pay fees for the use of exclusive rights under subparagraph (A) and (B) of Section 110(5) that the exemptions contained therein constitute a rule rather than an exception.[110]

6.105 The European Communities argues that, in the light of the wording of the first condition in Article 9(2) of the Berne Convention (1971), which forms part of the context of Article 13, an exemption should serve a "special purpose". For the European Communities, in the case of Section 110(5), no such special public policy or other exceptional circumstance exists that would make it inappropriate or impossible to enforce the exclusive rights conferred by Articles 11 and 11*bis* of the Berne Convention (1971). In the EC view, the subparagraphs of Section 110(5) do not pursue legitimate public policy objectives.

6.106 In the US view, if the purpose of an exception is relevant at all, the TRIPS Agreement only requires that an exception has a specific policy objective. It does not impose any requirement as to the legitimacy of the policy objectives that a particular country might consider special in the light of its own history and national priorities.

6.107 We start our analysis of the first condition of Article 13 by referring to the ordinary meaning of the terms in their context and in the light of its object and purpose. It appears that the notions of "exceptions" and "limitations" in the introductory words of Article 13 overlap in part in the sense that an "exception" refers to a derogation from an exclusive right provided under national legislation in some respect, while a "limitation" refers to a reduction of such right to a certain extent.

6.108 The ordinary meaning of "certain" is "known and particularised, but not explicitly identified", "determined, fixed, not variable; definitive, precise, exact".[111] In other words, this term means that, under the first condition, an exception or limitation in national legislation must be clearly defined. However, there is no need to identify explicitly each and every possible situation to which the exception could

---

108 US first written submission, para. 24.

109 US second written submission, para. 29.

110 EC first oral statement, para. 66ff and second written submission, para. 31.

111 The New Shorter Oxford English Dictionary ("Oxford English Dictionary"), Oxford (1993), p. 364.

apply, provided that the scope of the exception is known and particularised. This guarantees a sufficient degree of legal certainty.

6.109 We also have to give full effect to the ordinary meaning of the second word of the first condition. The term "special" connotes "having an individual or limited application or purpose", "containing details; precise, specific", "exceptional in quality or degree; unusual; out of the ordinary" or "distinctive in some way".[112] This term means that more is needed than a clear definition in order to meet the standard of the first condition. In addition, an exception or limitation must be limited in its field of application or exceptional in its scope. In other words, an exception or limitation should be narrow in quantitative as well as a qualitative sense. This suggests a narrow scope as well as an exceptional or distinctive objective. To put this aspect of the first condition into the context of the second condition ("no conflict with a normal exploitation"), an exception or limitation should be the opposite of a non-special, i.e., a normal case.

6.110 The ordinary meaning of the term "case" refers to an "occurrence", "circumstance" or "event" or "fact".[113] For example, in the context of the dispute at hand, the "case" could be described in terms of beneficiaries of the exceptions, equipment used, types of works or by other factors.

6.111 As regards the parties' arguments on whether the public policy purpose of an exception is relevant, we believe that the term "certain special cases" should not lightly be equated with "special purpose".[114] It is difficult to reconcile the wording of Article 13 with the proposition that an exception or limitation must be justified in terms of a legitimate public policy purpose in order to fulfill the first condition of the Article. We also recall in this respect that in interpreting other WTO rules, such as the national treatment clauses of the GATT and the GATS, the Appellate Body has rejected interpretative tests which were based on the subjective aim or objective pursued by national legislation.[115]

6.112 In our view, the first condition of Article 13 requires that a limitation or exception in national legislation should be clearly defined and should be narrow in its scope and reach. On the other hand, a limitation or exception may be compatible with the first condition even if it pursues a special purpose whose underlying legitimacy in

[112] Oxford English Dictionary, p. 2971.

[113] Oxford English Dictionary, p. 345.

[114] We note that the term "special purpose" has been referred to in interpreting the largely similarly worded Article 9(2) of the Berne Convention (1971). *See* Ricketson, The Berne Convention, op.cit., p. 482. We are ready to take into account "teachings of the most highly qualified publicists of the various nations" as a "subsidiary source for the determination of law". We refer to this phrase in the sense of Article 38(d) of the Statute of the International Court of Justice which refers to such "teachings" (or, in French "la doctrine") as "subsidiary means for the determination of law." But we are cautious to use the interpretation of a term developed in the context of an exception for the reproduction right for interpreting the same terms in the context of a largely similarly worded exception for other exclusive rights conferred by copyrights.

[115] *See* Appellate Body Report *Japan - Alcoholic Beverages*, *supra*, footnote 66, at 101. 19-23, for the rejection of the so-called "aims and effects" test in the context of the national treatment clause of Article III of GATT 1994. *See* also the Appellate Body Report, *EC - Bananas III*, *supra*, footnote 86, paras. 241, 243, 246, for the rejection of the "aims-and-effects" test in the context of the national treatment clause of Article XVII of GATS.

a normative sense cannot be discerned. The wording of Article 13's first condition does not imply passing a judgment on the legitimacy of the exceptions in dispute. However, public policy purposes stated by law-makers when enacting a limitation or exception may be useful from a factual perspective for making inferences about the scope of a limitation or exception or the clarity of its definition.

6.113 In the case at hand, in order to determine whether subparagraphs (B) and (A) of Section 110(5) are confined to "certain special cases", we first examine whether the exceptions have been clearly defined. Second, we ascertain whether the exemptions are narrow in scope, *inter alia*, with respect to their reach. In that respect, we take into account what percentage of eating and drinking establishments and retail establishments may benefit from the business exemption under subparagraph (B), and in turn what percentage of establishments may take advantage of the homestyle exemption under subparagraph (A). On a subsidiary basis, we consider whether it is possible to draw inferences about the reach of the business and homestyle exemptions from the stated policy purposes underlying these exemptions according to the statements made during the US legislative process.[116]

(ii) The Business Exemption of Subparagraph (B)

6.114 As noted above, the United States argues that the essence of the first condition of Article 13 of the TRIPS Agreement is that exceptions be well-defined and of limited application. It claims that the business exemption of subparagraph (B) meets the requirements of the first condition of Article 13, because it is clearly defined in Section 110(5) of the US Copyright Act by square footage and equipment limitations.[117]

6.115 In the US view, if at all the purpose of an exception is relevant, the first condition only requires that the exception has a specific policy objective, but it does not impose any requirements on the policy objectives that a particular country might consider special in the light of its own history and national priorities. As regards the business exemption, the United States claims that the specific policy objective pursued by this exemption is fostering small businesses and preventing abusive tactics by CMOs.[118]

6.116 The European Communities contends that the business exemption is too broad in its scope to pass as a "certain special case", given the large number of establishments which potentially may benefit from it. For the European Communities, it is irrelevant that the size of establishments and the type of equipment are clearly defined, when the broad scope of the business exemption turns an exception into the rule.

6.117 It appears that the European Communities does not dispute the fact that subparagraph (B) is clearly defined in respect of the size limits of establishments and the

---

[116] We discuss the business exemption of subparagraph (B) first because most of the arguments raised by the parties focus on this exception. In turn, we then examine the homestyle exemption in its current form as contained in subparagraph (A).

[117] US second written submission, para. 29.

[118] *Ibid.*

type of equipment that may be used by establishments above the applicable limits.[119] The primary bone of contention between the parties is whether the business exemption, given its scope and reach, can be considered as a "special" case within the meaning of the first condition of Article 13.

6.118 The Congressional Research Service ("CRS") estimated in 1995 the percentage of the US eating and drinking establishments and retail establishments that would have fallen at that time below the size limits of 3,500 square feet and 1,500 square feet respectively. Its study found that:

(d) 65.2 per cent of all eating establishments;

(e) 71.8 per cent of all drinking establishments; and

(f) 27 per cent of all retail establishments

would have fallen below these size limits.[120]

6.119 The United States confirms these figures as far as eating and drinking establishments are concerned.[121]

6.120 We note that this study was made in 1995 using the size limit of 3,500 square feet for eating and drinking establishments, and the size limit of 1,500 square feet for retail establishments, while the size limits under subparagraph (B) now are 3,750 square feet for eating and drinking establishments and 2,000 square feet for retail establishments. Therefore, in our view, it is safe to assume that the actual percentage of establishments which may fall within the finally enacted business exemption in the Fairness in Music Licensing Act of 1998 is higher than the above percentages.

6.121 The United States has also submitted estimates by the National Restaurant Association (NRA) concerning its membership.[122] According to these estimates, 36 per cent of its table service restaurant members (i.e., those with sit-down waiter service) are of a size less than 3,750 square feet, and approximately 95 per cent of its fast-food restaurant members are of a size less than 3,750 square feet.[123] We are not able to fully reconcile the 1995 CRS estimates with those of the NRA because we have not been provided with information on how representative the NRA membership is of all restaurants in the United States, and on the proportion of table-service restaurants in relation to fast-food restaurants among its membership. Therefore, we limit ourselves to stating that the NRA figures do not seem to contradict the estimates of the CRS study of 1995.

---

[119] We recall that the beneficiaries of the business exemption are divided into two categories: establishments other than food service or drinking establishments ("retail establishments"), and food service and drinking establishments. In each category, establishments under certain size limit (2,000 and 3,750 square feet, respectively) are exempted regardless of the type of equipment they use. If the size of an establishment is above the applicable limit, the exemption applies provided that the establishment does not exceed the limits set for the equipment used. For details, *see* paras. 2.10 and 2.14 of Section II on Factual Aspects of this Report.

[120] *See* also para. 2.11 above.

[121] Exhibit US-16.

[122] US reply to question 9 by the Panel to the United States and confidential exhibit US-18.

[123] *See* also para. 2.13 above.

6.122 In 1999, Dun & Bradstreet, Inc. ("D&B") was requested by ASCAP to update the 1995 CRS study based on 1998 data and the criteria in the 1998 Amendment.[124] The European Communities explains that the methodology used by the D&B in 1998/1999 was identical to the methodology used in the analysis which the D&B prepared in 1995 for the CRS during the legislative process that eventually led to the adoption of the Fairness in Music Licensing Act. The D&B study of 1999[125] concludes that approximately 73 per cent of all drinking, 70 per cent of all eating, and 45 per cent of all retail establishments in the United States are entitled under subparagraph (B), without any limitation regarding equipment, to play music from radio and television on their business premises without the consent of the right holders.[126]

6.123 We note that while the United States does not confirm the figures of the 1999 D&B study, it has used them, for the sake of argument, as a basis for its calculations on possible losses suffered by EC right holders as a result of the subparagraph (B) exemption.[127]

6.124 In view of the vagueness of the explanation available to us of the methodology used for the 1999 D&B study,[128] we are not in a position to recalculate exactly the results and trends of this study. But it appears that the results of the 1999 D&B study are largely consistent with the results and trends of the 1995 CRS study.

6.125 Referring to these studies, the European Communities points out that these 70 per cent of eating and drinking establishments and 45 per cent of retail establish-

---

124 *See* also para. 2.12 and Exhibit EC-7. According to the European Communities, the 1998/1999 D&B's "Dun's Market Identifying Market Profile" is a database of more than 6.5 million US businesses, based on square footage. The European Communities explains that the figures of the D&B studies comprise bars, restaurants, tea-rooms, snackbars, etc. and retail stores. However, other sectors, e.g. hotels, financial service outlets, estate property brokers, other types of service providers, in which a number of establishments are likely to be exempted as well, were not taken into account.

125 According to the information submitted by the European Communities, the number of establishments contained in the D&B database in 1998 were as follows:

(a) 7,819 drinking establishments of a square footage below 3,750 square feet which amounts to 73 per cent of all US drinking establishments filed in the D&B database;

(b) 51,385 eating establishments of a square footage below 3,750 square feet which amounts to 70 per cent of all US eating establishments filed in the D&B database;

(c) 65,589 retail establishments of a square footage below 2,000 square feet or 45 per cent of all US retail establishments filed in the D&B database.

In addition, D&B estimated the total figures as follows:

(a) 49,061 drinking establishments of a square footage below 3,750 square feet which amounts to 85 per cent of all US drinking establishments filed in the D&B database;

(b) 192,692 eating establishments of a square footage below 3,750 square feet which amounts to 68 per cent of all US eating establishments filed in the D&B database;

(c) 281,406 retail establishments of a square footage below 2,000 square feet or 42 per cent of all US retail establishments filed in the D&B database. *See* Exhibit EC-7.

126 The European Communities calculates that the number of eating, drinking and retail establishments that fall below the size limits of subpara. (B), compared to the number of establishments that fall below the size of the restaurant that was operated by Mr. *Aiken*, has increased by 437 per cent, 540 per cent, and 250 per cent, respectively. While we do not wish to accept or reject the particular percentage figures of these estimates, we note that there is a magnitude of difference in the coverage between the original homestyle exemption and the new business exemption.

127 US second submission, paras. 33-48.

128 Exhibit EC-7.

ments are all potential users of the business exemption, because they can at any time, without permission of the right holders, begin to play amplified music broadcasts.[129]

6.126 The United States contends that even if 70 per cent of all eating and drinking establishments and 45 per cent of all retail establishments are implicated by the size limits under subparagraph (B) after the 1998 Amendment, many of these establishments would have to be subtracted for various reasons. These include (i) establishments that do not play music at all; (ii) those that would turn off the music if they became liable to pay fees; (iii) those that play music from sources other than the radio or television, such as tapes, CDs, jukeboxes or live performances; (iv) establishments that were not licensed prior to the enactment of the business exemption in 1998; (v) establishments that would take advantage of group licensing arrangements such as the one between the NLBA and the CMOs.[130]

6.127 We agree with the European Communities that it is the scope in respect of potential users that is relevant for determining whether the coverage of the exemption is sufficiently limited to qualify as a "certain *special* case". While it is true, as the United States argues, that some establishments might turn off the radio or television if they had to pay fees, other establishments which have not previously played music might do the opposite, because under the business exemption the use of music is free. Some establishments that have used recorded music may decide to switch to broadcast music in order to avoid paying licensing fees. It is clear that, in examining the exemption, we have to also consider its impact on the use of other substitutable sources of music. Consequently, we do not consider the US calculations of establishments to be deducted from the CRS or D&B estimates as relevant for ascertaining the potential scope of the business exemption in relation to the first condition of Article 13.

6.128 We refer to our discussion concerning the third condition of Article 13, in which context we will examine in more detail the relevance of the US arguments concerning the five types of subtractions that would need to be made from the above percentage figures, and the exemption's likely effects on the licensing of other sources of music.[131] In that context, we will also address the US argument that many establishments were not licensed before the enactment of the business exemption and that many establishments covered by subparagraph (B) would be likely subscribers to the group licensing agreement between the NLBA and the CMOs.

6.129 The United States does not appear to make a distinction between, on the one hand, the eating and drinking or retail establishments whose size is within the applicable limits of subparagraph (B), and, on the other hand, larger establishments that may still use music for free if they comply with the applicable equipment limitations

---

[129] Cf. the discussion on actual and potential effects in paras. 184ff below.

[130] We discuss the US calculations under the third condition of Article 13 in the subsection entitled "The alternative calculations by the parties of losses suffered by right holders" in paras. 6.252ff below.

[131] These include, e.g., CDs, tapes, jukeboxes or live music. Music played on radio and television is probably more interchangeable with recorded music than with live music performance. However, the fact that there is a different degree of elasticity of substitution does not mean that the effect of substitution between different sources of music is negligible.

(e.g., concerning loudspeakers per room or screen size).[132] We have not been provided with information concerning the absolute numbers or the proportion of these larger establishments qualifying under the business exemption. Suffice it to say that the percentage of all US eating, drinking and retail establishments that may fall within the coverage of subparagraph (B) could be even higher than the above figures or estimates suggest.

6.130 The United States further notes that the prohibitions against charging admission fees and retransmission in indent (iii) and (iv) of subparagraph (B) limit the field of application of the business exemption. The European Communities contends that these prohibitions have no potential whatsoever to limit the impact of the exemption. We have not been presented with information on whether these prohibitions significantly reduce the number of establishments that could otherwise qualify for the exemption. In view of this fact, we recall our general considerations about the allocation of the ultimate burden of proof for invoking exceptions.

6.131 We note that, according to its preparatory works, Article 11*bis*(iii) of the Berne Convention (1971) was intended to provide right holders with a right to authorize the use of their works in the types of establishments covered by the exemption contained in Section 110(5)(B). Specifically, the preparatory works for the 1948 Brussels Conference indicate that the establishments that were intended to be covered were places "above all, where people meet: in the cinema, in restaurants, in tea rooms, railway carriages ...". The preparatory works also refer to places such as factories, shops and offices.[133] We fail to see how a law that exempts a major part of the users that were specifically intended to be covered by the provisions of Article 11*bis*(1)(iii) could be considered as a *special* case in the sense of the first condition of Article 13 of the TRIPS Agreement.

6.132 We are aware that eating, drinking and retail establishments are not the only potential users of music covered by the exclusive rights conferred under Articles 11*bis*(1)(iii) and 11(1)(ii) of the Berne Convention (1971). The United States has mentioned, *inter alia*, conventions, fairs and sporting events as other potential users of performances of works in the meaning of the above Articles. However, we believe that these examples of other potential users do not detract from the fact that eating, drinking and retail establishments are among the major groups of potential users of the works in the ways that are covered by the above-mentioned Articles.

6.133 The factual information presented to us indicates that a substantial majority of eating and drinking establishments and close to half of retail establishments are covered by the exemption contained in subparagraph (B) of Section 110(5) of the US Copyright Act. Therefore, we conclude that the exemption does not qualify as a "certain special case" in the meaning of the first condition of Article 13.

6.134 The European Communities warns that the potential coverage of both exemptions contained in Section 110(5) could become even larger because subparagraphs (A) and (B) could arguably exempt the transmission of musical works over

[132] *See* Section II on Factual Aspects, para. 2.14.

[133] Documents de la Conférence Réunie a Bruxelles du 5 au 26 juin 1948, published by BIRPI in 1951, p. 266. In discussing this provision, the Guide to the Berne Convention refers to "cafés, restaurants, tea-rooms, hotels, large shops, trains, aircraft, etc.", op.cit., para. 11*bis*.11, p. 68. (For a more complete quote *see* footnote 33 above).

the Internet. Given that we have found that the business exemption does not meet the first condition of Article 13 regardless of whether it potentially implicates transmission of works over the Internet, we see no need to address this question in the context of subparagraph (B). However, we will take up this question when we examine the homestyle exemption of subparagraph (A) in relation to the first condition of Article 13.

(iii) The Homestyle Exemption of Subparagraph (A)

6.135 We examine now whether the homestyle exemption in subparagraph (A), in the form in which it is currently in force in the United States, is a "certain special case" in the meaning of the first condition of Article 13 of the TRIPS Agreement.

6.136 The United States submits that the exemption of subparagraph (A) is confined to "certain special cases", because its scope is limited to the use involving a "homestyle" receiving apparatus. In the US view, in the amended version of 1998 as well, this is a well-defined fact-specific standard. The essentially identical description of the homestyle exemption in the original Section 110(5) of 1976 was sufficiently clear and narrow for US courts to reasonably and consistently apply the exception - including square footage limitation since the *Aiken* case - in a number of individual decisions. For the United States, the fact that judges have weighed the various factors slightly differently in making their individual decisions is simply a typical feature of a common-law system.

6.137 The European Communities contends that the criteria of the homestyle exemption in subparagraph (A) are ambiguously worded because the expression "a single receiving apparatus of a kind commonly used in private homes" is in itself imprecise and a "moving target" due to technological development. Also the variety of approaches and factors used by US courts in applying the original version of the homestyle exemption are proof for the European Communities that the wording of subparagraph (A) of Section 110(5) is vague and open-ended.

Beneficiaries of the homestyle exemption

6.138 The wording of the amended version of Section 110(5)(A) is essentially identical to the wording of Section 110(5) in its previous version of 1976, apart from the introductory phrase "except as provided in subparagraph (B)". Therefore, we consider that the practice as reflected in the judgements rendered by US courts after 1976 concerning the original homestyle exemption may be regarded as factually indicative of the reach of the homestyle exemption even after the 1998 Amendment.

6.139 We recall that in *Twentieth Century Music Corp. v. Aiken*,[134] the Court held that an owner of a small fast food restaurant was not liable for playing music by means of a radio with outlets to four speakers in the ceiling. The size of the shop was 1,055 square feet ($98m^2$), of which 620 square feet ($56m^2$) were open to the public. In the evolution of case law, subsequent to the inclusion of the original homestyle exemption in the Copyright Act of 1976 in reaction to the *Aiken* judgement, US

[134] *See* para. 2.6 of the section on factual aspects above.

courts have considered a number of factors to determine whether a shop or restaurant could benefit from the exemption.[135] These factors have included: (i) physical size of an establishment in terms of square footage (in comparison to the size of the *Aiken* restaurant); (ii) extent to which the receiving apparatus was to be considered as one commonly used in private homes; (iii) distance between the receiver and the speakers; (iv) number of speakers; (v) whether the speakers were free-standing or built into the ceiling; (vi) whether, depending on its revenue, the establishment was of a type that would normally subscribe to a background music service; (vii) noise level of the areas within the establishment where the transmissions were made audible or visible; and (viii) configuration of the installation. In some federal circuits, US courts have focused primarily on the plain language of the homestyle exemption that refers to "a single receiving apparatus of a kind commonly used in private homes".

6.140 The European Communities emphasizes that in some US court cases large chain store corporations were found to be exempted provided that each branch shop met the criteria of the exemption, e.g., in respect of the size of the establishment and the equipment used by it, regardless of the ownership and the economic size or corporate structure of the chain store corporation.[136] It is our understanding that the European Communities does not argue that the ability of a corporate chain to pay or the number of individual stores in joint ownership or under the control of the chain store corporation should be a decisive factor for refusing to grant the exemption to a particular branch store. However, the European Communities cautions that these US court decisions are illustrative of a judicial trend towards broadening the homestyle exemption of 1976 in recent years.

6.141 The United States responds that, in applying Section 110(5) of the Copyright Act of 1976, only three US court judgements have found that a defendant was entitled to take advantage of the exemption. It also contends that only two US court judgements (*Claire's Boutiques* and *Edison Bros.*[137]) dealt with the applicability of the exemption to particular branch shops of chain stores.

6.142 We note that the parties have submitted quantitative information on the coverage of subparagraph (A) with respect to eating, drinking and other establishments. The 1995 CRS study found that:

(a) 16 per cent of all US eating establishments;

(b) 13.5 per cent of all US drinking establishments; and

(c) 18 per cent of all US retail establishments

were as big as or smaller than the *Aiken* restaurant (1,055 square feet of total space), and could thus benefit from the homestyle exemption. These figures are not disputed

[135] According to the European Communities, US Courts have never favourably applied the homestyle exemption to an eating or drinking establishment of more than 1,500 square feet of total space, nor to establishments using more than four loudspeakers.

[136] Broadcast Music, Inc. v. Claire's Boutiques Inc., US Court of Appeals for the Seventh Circuit, N° 91-1232. 11 December 1991. *See* Exhibit EC-6.

[137] Broadcast Music, Inc. v. Edison Bros. Stores Inc., US Court of Appeals for the Eight Circuit, N° 91-2115, 13 January 1992. *See* Exhibit EC-5.

between the parties. The United States expressly confirms these figures as far as eating and drinking establishments are concerned.[138]

6.143 We believe that from a quantitative perspective the reach of subparagraph (A) in respect of potential users is limited to a comparably small percentage of all eating, drinking and retail establishments in the United States.

6.144 We are mindful of the above-mentioned EC argument alleging a judicial trend towards broadening the homestyle exemption of 1976 in recent years. We cannot exclude the possibility that in the future US courts could establish precedents that would lead to the expansion of the scope of the currently applicable homestyle exemption as regards covered establishments. But we also note that since 1976 US courts have in the vast majority of cases applied the homestyle exemption in a sufficiently consistent and clearly delineated manner. Given the sufficiently consistent and narrow application practice of the homestyle exemption of 1976, we see no need to hypothesise whether at some point in the future US case law might lead to a *de facto* expansion of the homestyle exemption of 1998.

Homestyle equipment

6.145 We note that what is referred to as homestyle equipment (i.e., "a single receiving apparatus of a kind commonly used in private homes") might vary between different countries, is subject to changing consumer preferences in a given country, and may evolve as a result of technological development. We thus agree in principle with the European Communities that the homestyle equipment that was used in US households in 1976 (when the original homestyle exemption was enacted) is not necessarily identical to the equipment used in 1998 (when US copyright legislation was amended) or at a future point in time. However, we recall that the term "*certain* special case" connotes "known and particularised, but not explicitly identified". In our view, the term "homestyle equipment" expresses the degree of clarity in definition required under Article 13's first condition. In our view, a Member is not required to identify homestyle equipment in terms of exceedingly detailed technical specifications in order to meet the standard of clarity set by the first condition. While we recognize that homestyle equipment may become technologically more sophisticated over time, we see no need to enter into speculations about potential future developments in the homestyle equipment market. At any rate, we recall that our factual determinations are invariably limited to what currently is being perceived as homestyle equipment in the US market.

Musical works covered by subparagraph (A)

6.146 We have noted[139] the common view of the parties that the addition of the introductory phrase "except as provided in subparagraph (B)" to the homestyle exemption in the 1998 Amendment should be understood by way of an *a contrario* argument as limiting the coverage of the exemption to works other than "non-

---

[138] US reply to question 9(a) by the Panel to the United States and a letter from the NRA of 18 November 1999, confidential exhibit US-18.

[139] *See* para. 2.7.

dramatic" musical works.[140] As regards musical works, the currently applicable version of the homestyle exemption is thus understood to apply to the communication of music that is part of an opera, operetta, musical or other similar dramatic work when performed in a dramatic context. All other musical works are covered by the expression "nondramatic" musical works, including individual songs taken from dramatic works when performed outside any dramatic context. Subparagraph (B) would, therefore, apply for example to an individual song taken from a musical and played on the radio. Consequently, given the common view of the parties, the operation of subparagraph (A) is limited to such musical works as are not covered by subparagraph (B), for example a communication of a broadcast of a dramatic rendition of the music written for an opera, operetta, musical or other similar works.

6.147 While taking this position on the interpretation of subparagraph (A), the European Communities has, however, cautioned that US courts might read a broader coverage into subparagraph (A) at a future point in time.[141] In view of the common understanding of the parties in the current dispute, and given the EC responses to our questions about the scope of its claims, we see no need to speculate whether in the future subparagraph (A) could be interpreted by US courts to cover musical works other than those considered as "dramatic".

6.148 In practice, this means that most if not virtually all music played on the radio or television is covered by subparagraph (B). Subparagraph (A) covers, in accordance with the common understanding of the parties, dramatic renditions of operas, operettas, musicals and other similar dramatic works. We consider that limiting the application of subparagraph (A) to the public communication of transmissions embodying such works, gives its provisions a quite narrow scope of application in practice.

Internet transmissions

6.149 As we noted in paragraph 2.15 above, the types of transmissions covered by both subparagraphs of Section 110(5) include original broadcasts over the air or by satellite, rebroadcasts by terrestrial means or by satellite, cable retransmissions of original broadcasts, and original cable transmissions or other transmissions by wire. The provisions do not distinguish between analog and digital transmissions.

6.150 The European Communities presumes that, given its open-ended wording, subparagraph (A) may apply to the public communication of musical works transmitted using new technologies such as computer networks (e.g., the Internet), the importance of which increases from day to day.[142]

6.151 The United States emphasizes that, in general, neither subparagraph of Section 110(5) exempts communication over a digital network. In its view, the transmission of works over a computer network involves numerous incidents of reproduction

[140] *See* the second written submission by the United States (para. 3) and the second written submission by the European Communities and their member States (para. 7).

[141] Second written submission by the European Communities and their Member States, para. 8.

[142] For example, an FCC-licensed radio (or TV) broadcaster parallels its over-the-air transmissions on the Internet (as an audio back-up to his web-site). These programmes are received by a PC connected with a number of loudspeakers in a bar or other establishment meeting all the conditions set out in Section 110(5) of the US Copyright Act.

and could also implicate distribution rights. Therefore, Internet users would have to seek a licence for the reproduction and possibly for the distribution of works. The United States further developed its argumentation by adding that it was unclear whether the performance aspect of an Internet transmission would be covered by either subparagraph of Section 110(5).[143] It stated, however, that if an FCC-licensed broadcaster itself streams its signals over the Internet, the performance aspect of the broadcast might fall within the exemption.

6.152 Whether or not an establishment would need an authorization for the reproduction or distribution of musical works, in the situations envisaged under Section 110(5), does not in our view detract from the fact that an authorization is required for the exploitation of protected works in respect of the exclusive rights protected under Articles 11(1)(ii) or 11*bis*(1)(iii) of the Berne Convention (1971).

6.153 In the light of the parties' arguments, we cannot exclude the possibility that the homestyle exemption might apply to the communication to the public of works transmitted over the Internet. But we also note that, based on the information provided to us by the parties, there seems to be no experience to date of the application of the homestyle exemption in its original or amended form to the transmission of "dramatic" musical works over the Internet. In these circumstances, we cannot see how potential repercussions in the future could affect our conclusions concerning subparagraph (A) at this point in time in relation to the first condition of Article 13 of the TRIPS Agreement. But we also do not wish to exclude the possibility that in the future new technologies might create new ways of distributing dramatic renditions of "dramatic" musical works that might have implications for the assessment of subparagraph (A) as a "certain special case" in the meaning of the first condition of Article 13.

Other considerations

6.154 The European Communities contends that neither subparagraph of Section 110(5) discloses a "valid" public policy or other exceptional circumstance that makes it inappropriate or impossible to enforce the exclusive rights conferred.

6.155 A US Congress House Report explained Section 110(5) of the Copyright Act of 1976: "The basic rationale of this clause is that secondary use of the transmission by turning on an ordinary receiver in public is so remote and minimal that no further liability should be imposed". "[The clause] would impose liability where the proprietor has a commercial 'sound system' installed or converts a standard home receiving apparatus ... into the equivalent of a commercial sound system."[144] A subsequent Conference Report elaborated on the rationale by noting that the intent was to exempt a small commercial establishment "which was not of sufficient size to justify, as a practical matter, a subscription to a commercial background music service".[145]

---

[143] US reply to question 6(a) by the Panel to the United States.

[144] Report of the House Committee on the Judiciary, H.R. Rep. No. 94-1476, 94th Congress, 2nd Session 87 (1976), Exhibit US-1. *See* section on Factual Aspects, para. 2.5.

[145] Conference Report of the House Committee on the Judiciary, Subcommittee on Courts and Intellectual Property, H.R. Rep. No. 94-1733, 9th Congress, 2nd Session 75 (1976), Exhibit US-2. *See* also footnote 11 to para. 2.5 above.

6.156 The United States further explains that the policy purpose justifying subparagraph (A) is the protection of small "mom and pop" businesses which "play an important role in the American social fabric" because they "offer economic opportunities for women, minorities, immigrants and welfare recipients for entering the economic and social mainstream".

6.157 We recall our considerations above that we reject the idea that the first condition of Article 13 requires us to pass a value judgement on the legitimacy of an exception or limitation. However, we also observed that stated public policy purposes could be of subsidiary relevance for drawing inferences about the scope of an exemption and the clarity of its definition. In our view, the statements from the legislative history indicate an intention of establishing an exception with a narrow scope.

6.158 Finally, we recall our conclusion that the context of Articles 11 and 11*bis* of the Berne Convention (1971) as incorporated into the TRIPS Agreement allows for the possibility of providing minor exceptions to the exclusive rights in question; i.e. the intention was to allow exceptions as long as they are *de minimis* in scope.

6.159 Taking into account the specific limits imposed in subparagraph (A) and its legislative history, as well as in its considerably narrow application in the subsequent court practice on the beneficiaries of the exemption, permissible equipment and categories of works, we are of the view that the homestyle exemption in subparagraph (A) of Section 110(5) as amended in 1998 is well-defined and limited in its scope and reach. We, therefore, conclude that the exemption is confined to certain special cases within the meaning of the first condition of Article 13 of the TRIPS Agreement.

(iv) Need to Examine the Other two Conditions

6.160 Having concluded that subparagraph (B) of Section 110(5) does not comply with the first condition of Article 13 of the TRIPS Agreement, we could, therefore, conclude that the business exemption does not satisfy the requirements of Article 13, given that its three conditions are cumulative. Thus it would appear that subparagraph (B) is in violation of Articles 11*bis*(1)(iii) and 11(1)(ii) of the Berne Convention (1971), as incorporated into the TRIPS Agreement by reference in Article 9.1, and not justified by Article 13. Nevertheless, we continue our analysis of the other conditions of Article 13 in relation to subparagraph (B) for the reasons discussed below.

6.161 Given our conclusion that subparagraph (A) of Section 110(5) does comply with the first condition of Article 13 of the TRIPS Agreement, it is necessary for us to examine subparagraph (A) also in relation to the subsequent conditions of the Article. We note that the two subparagraphs are closely related and their respective fields of operation overlap in respects other than the categories of works covered. In the light of this, we consider, in performing our task to examine the matter referred to the DSB and to make such findings as will assist the DSB in making recommendations or in giving rulings,[146] it is appropriate to address the several other fundamental

[146] *See* Article 7 of the DSU.

arguments made by the parties with respect to subparagraph (B) that relate to its consistency with the other two conditions of Article 13 of the TRIPS Agreement.[147]

6.162 In continuing our analysis of the second and third conditions of Article 13 with respect to the business exemption in subparagraph (B), we note the statements of the Appellate Body on "judicial economy" in the dispute on *United States - Shirts and Blouses*.[148] In a subsequent dispute on *Australia - Measures Affecting the Importation of Salmon*, the Appellate Body focuses on the need for panels to address all claims and/or measures necessary to secure a positive solution to a dispute and adds that providing only a partial resolution of the matter at issue would be false judicial economy.[149] It is in the spirit of the Appellate Body's statements in *Australia - Salmon* that we will continue our analysis of the business exemption in relation to the other conditions of Article 13. We now proceed to examine the compatibility of subparagraph (A), as well as of subparagraph (B), with the other two conditions of Article 13 of the TRIPS Agreement.

(c) "Not Conflict with a Normal Exploitation of the Work"

(i) General Interpretative Analysis

6.163 The United States claims that both subparagraphs (A) and (B) of Section 110(5) do "not conflict with a normal exploitation of the work" in the meaning of the second condition of Article 13 of the TRIPS Agreement. The European Communities contests that. We will first address the interpretation of this second condition of Article 13 in general, and then examine the business and homestyle exemptions in turn.

---

147 A GATT panel has held that a finding of violation does not necessarily preclude the panel's consideration of other legal claims where correction of the violation will not necessarily eliminate the basis of the complainant's other legal claims. *See* Panel Report *European Economic Community - Payments and Subsidies Paid to Processors and Producers of Oilseeds and Related Animal-Feed Proteins*, adopted on 25 January 1990, BISD 37S/86, 126, para. 142.

148 In *United States - Shirts and Blouses*, the Appellate Body stated:

"Nothing in this provision or in previous GATT practice *requires* a panel to examine *all* legal claims made by the complaining party. Previous GATT 1947 and WTO panels have frequently addressed only those issues that such panels considered necessary for the resolution of the matter between the parties, and have declined to decide other issues. Thus, if a panel found that a measure was inconsistent with a particular provision of the GATT 1947, it generally did not go on to examine whether the measure was also inconsistent with other GATT provisions that a complaining party may have argued were violated. ...". (Footnotes omitted). *See* Appellate Body Report *United States - Measures Affecting Imports of Woven Wool Shirts and Blouses*, WT/DS33/AB/R, adopted 23 May 1997, *supra*, footnote 28, at 339.

149 In *Australia - Salmon*, the Appellate Body stated:

"The principle of judicial economy has to be applied keeping in mind the aim of the dispute settlement system. This aim is to resolve the matter at issue and "to secure a positive solution to a dispute". To provide only a partial resolution of the matter at issue would be false judicial economy. A panel has to address those claims on which a finding is necessary in order to enable the DSB to make sufficiently precise recommendations and rulings so as to allow for prompt compliance by a Member with those recommendations and rulings "in order to ensure effective resolution of disputes to the benefit of all Members." (Footnotes omitted). *See* the Appellate Body Report *Australia - Measures Affecting the Importation of Salmon* ("*Australia – Salmon*"), WT/DS18/AB/R, adopted 6 November 1998, DSR 1998:VIII, 3327, para. 223.

6.164 In interpreting the second condition of Article 13, we first need to define what "exploitation" of a "work" means. More importantly, we have to determine what constitutes a "normal" exploitation, with which a derogation is not supposed to "conflict".

6.165 The ordinary meaning of the term "exploit" connotes "making use of" or "utilising for one's own ends".[150] We believe that "exploitation" of musical works thus refers to the activity by which copyright owners employ the exclusive rights conferred on them to extract economic value from their rights to those works.

6.166 We note that the ordinary meaning of the term "normal" can be defined as "constituting or conforming to a type or standard; regular, usual, typical, ordinary, conventional ...".[151] In our opinion, these definitions appear to reflect two connotations: the first one appears to be of an empirical nature, i.e., what is regular, usual, typical or ordinary. The other one reflects a somewhat more normative, if not dynamic, approach, i.e., conforming to a type or standard. We do not feel compelled to pass a judgment on which one of these connotations could be more relevant. Based on Article 31 of the Vienna Convention, we will attempt to develop a harmonious interpretation which gives meaning and effect to both connotations of "normal".

6.167 If "normal" exploitation were equated with full use of all exclusive rights conferred by copyrights, the exception clause of Article 13 would be left devoid of meaning. Therefore, "normal" exploitation clearly means something less than full use of an exclusive right.[152]

6.168 In the US view, it is necessary to look to the ways in which an author might reasonably be expected to exploit his work in the normal course of events, when one determines what constitutes a normal exploitation. In this respect, it is relevant that Article 13 does not refer to particular specific rights but to "the work" as a whole. This implies that, in examining an exception under the second condition, consideration should be given to the scope of the exception *vis-à-vis* the panoply of all the rights holders' exclusive rights, as well as *vis-à-vis* the exclusive right to which it

---

[150] Oxford English Dictionary, p. 888.

[151] Oxford English Dictionary, p. 1940.

[152] In the context of exceptions to reproduction rights under Article 9(2) of the Berne Convention (1971) - whose second condition is worded largely identically to the second condition of Article 13 of the TRIPS Agreement - the Main Committee I of the Stockholm Diplomatic Conference (1967) stated:

"If it is considered that reproduction conflicts with the normal exploitation of the work, reproduction is not permitted at all. If it is considered that reproduction does not conflict with the normal exploitation of the work, the next step would be to consider whether it does not unreasonably prejudice the legitimate interests of the author. Only if such is not the case would it be possible in certain special cases to introduce a compulsory licence, or to provide for use without payment. A practical example may be photocopying for various purposes. If it consists of producing a very large number of copies, it may not be permitted, as it conflicts with a normal exploitation of the work. If it implies a rather large number of copies for use in industrial undertakings, it may not unreasonably prejudice the legitimate interests of the author, provided that, according to national legislation, an equitable remuneration is paid. If a small number of copies is made, photocopying may be permitted without payment, particularly for individual or scientific use." *See* the Records of the Intellectual Property Conference of Stockholm, 11 June - 14 July 1967. Report on the Work of the Main Committee I (Substantive Provisions of the Berne Convention: Articles 1- 20. As reproduced in the Berne Convention Centenary, p. 197.

applies. In its view, the most important forms of exploitation of musical works, namely, "primary" performance and broadcasting, are not affected by either subparagraph of Section 110(5). The business and homestyle exemptions only affect what the United States considers "secondary" uses of broadcasts, and that too, subject to size and equipment limitations. In the US view, right holders normally obtain the main part of their remuneration from "primary" uses and only a minor part from "secondary" uses.

6.169 The European Communities rejects the idea that there could be a hierarchical order between "important" and "unimportant" rights under the TRIPS Agreement. For the European Communities, there are no "secondary" rights and the exclusive rights provided for in Articles 11*bis*(1)(iii) and 11(1)(ii) of the Berne Convention (1971) are all equally important separate rights.[153]

6.170 The United States itself clarifies that it does not imply that a legal hierarchy exists between different exclusive rights conferred under Articles 11, 11*bis* or any other provision of the Berne Convention (1971) and that a country cannot completely eliminate an exclusive right even if that right be economically unimportant. But it takes the view that when a possible conflict with a normal exploitation of the work is analysed, it is relevant whether the exception applies to one or several exclusive rights. Similarly, the degree to which the exception affects a particular exclusive right is also relevant for the analysis of the second condition of Article 13.

6.171 It is true, as the United States points out, that Article 13 refers to a normal exploitation of "the work." However, the TRIPS Agreement and the Berne Convention provide exclusive rights in relation to the work. These exclusive rights are the legal means by which exploitation of the work, i.e., the commercial activity for extracting economic value from the rights to the work, can be carried out. The parties do not in principle question that the term "works" should be understood as referring to the "exclusive rights" in those works.[154] In our view, Article 13's second condition does not explicitly refer *pars pro toto* to exclusive rights concerning a "work" given that the TRIPS Agreement (or the Berne Convention (1971) as incorporated into it) confers a considerable number of exclusive rights to all of which the exception clause of Article 13 may apply. Therefore, we believe that the "work" in Article 13's second condition means all the exclusive rights relating to it.

6.172 While we agree with the United States that the degree to which an exception affects a particular right is relevant for our analysis under the second condition, we emphasize that a possible conflict with a normal exploitation of a particular exclusive right cannot be counter-balanced or justified by the mere fact of the absence of a conflict with a normal exploitation of another exclusive right (or the absence of any exception altogether with respect to that right), even if the exploitation of the latter right would generate more income.

6.173 We agree with the European Communities that whether a limitation or an exception conflicts with a normal exploitation of a work should be judged for each exclusive right individually. We recall that this dispute primarily concerns the exclu-

---

153 See also the written submission of Australia, para. 3.8.

154 These rights include, *inter alia*, the rights of public performance and broadcasting as well as the right of communication to the public in the meanings of Articles 11*bis*(1)(iii) and 11(1)(ii) of the Berne Convention (1971).

sive right under Article 11*bis*(1)(iii) of the Berne Convention (1971) as incorporated into the TRIPS Agreement, but also the exclusive right under Article 11(1)(ii). In our view, normal exploitation would presuppose the possibility for right holders to exercise separately all three exclusive rights guaranteed under the three subparagraphs of Article 11*bis*(1), as well as the rights conferred by other provisions, such as Article 11, of the Berne Convention (1971). If it were permissible to limit by a statutory exemption the exploitation of the right conferred by the third subparagraph of Article 11*bis*(1) simply because, in practice, the exploitation of the rights conferred by the first and second subparagraphs of Article 11*bis*(1) would generate the lion's share of royalty revenue, the "normal exploitation" of each of the three rights conferred separately under Article 11*bis*(1) would be undermined.[155]

6.174 An individual analysis of the second condition for each exclusive right conferred by copyright is in line with the GATT/WTO dispute settlement practice. One panel found that GATT non-discrimination clauses do not permit balancing more favourable treatment under some procedure against a less favourable treatment under others.[156] As another panel put it, an element of more favourable treatment would only be relevant if it would always accompany and offset an element of differential treatment causing less favourable treatment.[157] While these cases involved the GATT

[155] Moreover, we need to keep in mind that the exclusive rights conferred by different subparagraphs of Articles 11*bis* and 11 need not necessarily be in the possession of one and the same right holder. An author or performer may choose not to license the use of a particular exclusive right but to sell and transfer it to another natural or juridical person. If it were permissible to justify the interference into one exclusive right with the fact that another exclusive right generates more revenue, certain right holders might be deprived of their right to obtain royalties simply because the exclusive right held by another right holder is more profitable.

Our view that exclusive rights need to be analysed separately for the purposes of the second condition is also corroborated by the licensing practices between CMOs and broadcasting organizations in the United States and the European Communities. These practices do not appear to take into account the potential additional audience created by means of a further communication by loudspeaker of a broadcast of a work within the meaning of Article 11*bis*(1)(iii), i.e. no fees are collected from broadcasters for the additional audiences. *See* EC and US responses to question 4 by the Panel to both parties.

[156] The Panel on *European Communities - Regime for the Importation, Sale and Distribution of Bananas* ,WT/DS27/ECU, DSR 1997:III, 1085, WT/DS27/GTM, WT/DS27/HND, DSR 1997:II, 695, WT/DS27/MEX, DSR 1997:II, 803, WT/DS/27/USA, DSR 1997:II, 943, adopted 25 September 1997, para. 7.239 and footnote 446 referred to the Panel on *United States - Denial of Most-favoured Nation Treatment as to Non-rubber Footwear from Brazil:*

"Article I:1 does not permit balancing more favourable treatment under some procedure against a less favourable treatment under others. If such balancing were accepted, it would entitle a contracting party to derogate from the most-favourable nation obligation in one case, in respect of one contracting party, on the ground that it accords more favourable treatment in some other case in respect of another contracting party. In the view of the Panel, such an interpretation of the most-favoured nation obligation of Article I:1 would defeat the very purpose underlying the unconditionality of that obligation." (Adopted on 19 June 1992, BISD 39S/128, 151, para. 6.10).

[157] The Panel on *EC - Bananas III* also referred to the Panel on *United States - Section 337 of the Tariff Act of 1930* for the principle that "an element of more favourable treatment would only be relevant if it would always accompany and offset an element of differential treatment causing less favourable treatment". (Adopted on 7 November 1989, BISD 36S/345, 388, para. 5.16).

See also Panel Report *United States - Measures Affecting the Importation, Internal Sale and Use of Tobacco*, adopted 4 October 1994, BISD 41S/131, 169, para. 98.

non-discrimination clauses, we believe that the general principle embodied therein is *mutatis mutandis* relevant to the issue at hand.

6.175 We also note that the amplification of broadcast music will occur in establishments such as bars, restaurants and retail stores for the commercial benefit of the owner of the establishment.[158] Both parties agree on the commercial nature of playing music even when customers are not directly charged for it. It may be that the amount yielded from any royalty payable as a consequence of this exploitation of the work will not be very great if one looks at the matter in the context of single establishments. But it is the accumulation of establishments which counts. It must be remembered that a copyright owner is entitled to exploit each of the rights for which a treaty, and the national legislation implementing that treaty, provides. If a copyright owner is entitled to a royalty for music broadcast over the radio, why should the copyright owner be deprived of remuneration which would otherwise be earned, when a significant number of radio broadcasts are amplified to customers of a variety of commercial establishments no doubt for the benefit of the businesses being conducted in those establishments. We also note that although, in a sense, the amplification which is involved is additional to and separate from the broadcast of a work, it is tied to the broadcast. The amplification cannot occur unless there is a broadcast. If an operator of an establishment plays recorded music, there is no legislative exception to the copyright owners' rights in that regard. But the amplification of a broadcast adds to the broadcast itself because it ensures that a wider audience will hear it. Clearly Article 11*bis*(iii) contemplates the use which is in question here by conferring rights on copyright owners in respect of the amplification of broadcasts.

6.176 That leaves us with the question of how to determine whether a particular use constitutes a normal exploitation of the exclusive rights provided under Articles 11*bis*(1)(iii) and 11(1)(ii) of the Berne Convention (1971). In academic literature, one approach that has been suggested would be to rely on "the ways in which an author might reasonably be expected to exploit his work in the normal course of events".[159]

6.177 The main thrust of the US argumentation is that, for judging "normal exploitation", Article 13's second condition implies an economic analysis of the degree of "market displacement" in terms of foregone collection of remuneration by right owners caused by the free use of works due to the exemption at issue.[160] In the US view, the essential question to ask is whether there are areas of the market in which the copyright owner would ordinarily expect to exploit the work, but which are not available for exploitation because of this exemption. Under this test, uses from which an owner would not ordinarily expect to receive compensation are not part of the normal exploitation.

6.178 In our view, this test seems to reflect the empirical or quantitative aspect of the connotation of "normal", the meaning of "regular, usual, typical or ordinary". We can, therefore, accept this US approach, but only for the empirical or quantitative

[158] We note that US court cases and the legislative history of Section 110(5) suggest that restaurants and other establishments play music in order to attract customers with a view to enhance turnover and profit. (*See* Press Release by the NLBA, Exhibit US-7.)

[159] Ricketson, The Berne Convention, op.cit., p. 483.

[160] US reply to question 17 by the Panel to both parties.

side of the connotation. We have to give meaning and effect also to the second aspect of the connotation, the meaning of "conforming to a type or standard". We described this aspect of normalcy as reflecting a more normative approach to defining normal exploitation, that includes, *inter alia*, a dynamic element capable of taking into account technological and market developments. The question then arises how this normative aspect of "normal" exploitation could be given meaning in relation to the exploitation of musical works.

6.179 In this respect, we find persuasive guidance in the suggestion by a study group, composed of representatives of the Swedish Government and the United International Bureaux for the Protection of Intellectual Property ("BIRPI"), which was set up to prepare for the Revision Conference at Stockholm in 1967 ("Swedish/BIRPI Study Group"). In relation to the reproduction right, this Group suggested to allow countries:

> "[to] limit the recognition and the exercising of that right, for specified purposes and *on the condition that these purposes should not enter into economic competition with these works*" in the sense that "*all forms of exploiting a work, which have, or are likely to acquire, considerable economic or practical importance, must be reserved to the authors.*"[161] (emphasis added).

6.180 Thus it appears that one way of measuring the normative connotation of normal exploitation is to consider, in addition to those forms of exploitation that currently generate significant or tangible revenue, those forms of exploitation which, with a certain degree of likelihood and plausibility, could acquire considerable economic or practical importance.

6.181 In contrast, exceptions or limitations would be presumed not to conflict with a normal exploitation of works if they are confined to a scope or degree that does not enter into economic competition with non-exempted uses. In this respect, the suggestions of the Swedish/BIRPI Study Group are useful:

> "In this connection, the Study Group observed that, on the one hand, it was obvious that *all forms of exploiting a work which had, or were likely to acquire, considerable economic or practical importance must in principle be reserved to the authors*; exceptions that might restrict the possibilities open to the authors in these respects were unacceptable. On the other hand, it should not be forgotten that *domestic laws already contained a series of exceptions in favour of various public and cultural interests* and that it would be vain to suppose that countries would be ready at this stage to abolish these exceptions to any appreciable extent."[162] (emphasis added).

6.182 We recall that the European Communities proposes to measure the impact of exceptions by using a benchmark according to which, at least, all those forms of use of works that create an economic benefit for the user should be considered as normal exploitation of works. We can accept that the assessment of normal exploitation of

---

[161] Document S/1: Berne Convention; Proposals for Revising the Substantive Copyright Provisions (Articles 1-20). Prepared by the Government of Sweden with the assistance of BIPRI, p. 42.

[162] *Ibid.*, p. 41.

works, from an empirical or quantitative perspective, requires an economic analysis of the commercial use of the exclusive rights conferred by the copyrights in those works. However, in our view, not every use of a work, which in principle is covered by the scope of exclusive rights and involves commercial gain, necessarily conflicts with a normal exploitation of that work. If this were the case, hardly any exception or limitation could pass the test of the second condition and Article 13 might be left devoid of meaning, because normal exploitation would be equated with full use of exclusive rights.

6.183 We believe that an exception or limitation to an exclusive right in domestic legislation rises to the level of a conflict with a normal exploitation of the work (i.e., the copyright or rather the whole bundle of exclusive rights conferred by the ownership of the copyright), if uses, that in principle are covered by that right but exempted under the exception or limitation, enter into economic competition with the ways that right holders normally extract economic value from that right to the work (i.e., the copyright) and thereby deprive them of significant or tangible commercial gains.

6.184 In developing a benchmark for defining the normative connotation of normal exploitation, we recall the European Communities' emphasis on the potential impact of an exception rather than on its actual effect on the market at a given point in time, given that, in its view, it is the potential effect that determines the market conditions.

6.185 We note that a consideration of both actual and potential effects when assessing the permissibility of the exemptions would be consistent with similar concepts and interpretation standards as developed in the past GATT/WTO dispute settlement practice. For example, proof of actual trade effects has not been considered an indispensable prerequisite for a finding of inconsistency with the national treatment clause of Article III of GATT where there was a potentiality of adverse effects on competitive opportunities and equal competitive conditions for foreign products (in comparison to like domestic products).[163] We wish to express our caution in in-

[163] The Working Party Report on *Brazilian Internal Taxes* noted in the context of the GATT national treatment clause that "the absence of imports from contracting parties during any period of time that might be selected for examination would not necessarily be an indication that they had no interest in exports of the product affected by the tax, since their potentialities as exporters, given national treatment, should be taken into account. These members of the working party therefore took the view that the provision of ... Article III ... were equally applicable whether imports from other contracting parties were substantial, small or non-existent." *See* Report of the Working Party on *Brazilian Internal Taxes*, adopted 30 June 1949, BISD II/181, 185.

The statement that proof of actual trade effects was not an indispensable prerequisite for a finding of GATT-inconsistency was followed by a number of subsequent panels, *inter alia*, in the dispute on *United States - Taxes on Petroleum and Certain Imported Substances*, adopted on 17 June 1987, BISD 34S/136, 158, para. 5.1.9. *See* also Panel Report *United States - Measures Affecting Alcoholic and Malt Beverages*, adopted 19 June 1992, BISD 39S/206, 270/271, para. 5.6; Panel Report *United States - Measures Affecting the Importation, Internal Sale and Use of Tobacco*, adopted 4 October 1994, BISD 41S/131, 169, para. 98.

These and other panels, including in *Italian Discrimination Against Imported Agricultural Machinery* (adopted on 23 October 1958, BISD 7S/60, 64, para. 12) and in *Canada - Administration of the Foreign Investment Review Act* (adopted on 7 February 1984, BISD 30S/140, 159-161, paras. 5.8-5.10), interpreted the national treatment standard, which prohibits *de jure* as well as *de facto* discrimination, as protecting the equality in competitive opportunities and as prohibiting any laws or

terpreting provisions of the TRIPS Agreement in the light of concepts that have been developed in GATT dispute settlement practice. But we also recall that, e.g., in the dispute *EC - Bananas III*, the panel and the Appellate Body introduced concepts, as developed in dispute settlement practice under Article III of GATT, into the national treatment clause of Article XVII of GATS whose wording is based on the GATT national treatment clause and interpretations developed in GATT dispute settlement practice.[164] Given that the agreements covered by the WTO form a single, integrated legal system, we deem it appropriate to develop interpretations of the legal protection conferred on intellectual property right holders under the TRIPS Agreement which are not incompatible with the treatment conferred to products under the GATT, or in respect of services and service suppliers under the GATS, in the light of pertinent dispute settlement practice.

6.186 Therefore, in respect of the exclusive rights related to musical works, we consider that normal exploitation of such works is not only affected by those who actually use them without an authorization by the right holders due to an exception or limitation, but also by those who may be induced by it to do so at any time without having to obtain a licence from the right holders or the CMOs representing them. Thus we need to take into account those whose use of musical works is free as a result of the exemptions, and also those who may choose to start using broadcast music once its use becomes free of charge.

6.187 We base our appraisal of the actual and potential effects on the commercial and technological conditions that prevail in the market currently or in the near future.[165] What is a normal exploitation in the market-place may evolve as a result of technological developments or changing consumer preferences. Thus, while we do not wish to speculate on future developments, we need to consider the actual and

regulations which might adversely modify conditions of competition between foreign and like domestic products.

Panels dealing with the prohibition of quantitative restrictions or prohibitions similarly found that Article XI of GATT protected conditions of competition and that an import restriction was prohibited regardless of whether it actually impeded imports. *See* Panel Report *EEC - Payments and Subsidies to Processors and Producers of Oilseeds and Related Animal Feed Proteins*, adopted on 25 January 1990, BISD 37S/86, 130, para. 150. *See* also Panel Report *Japanese Measures on Imports of Leather*, adopted on 15/16 May 1984, BISD 31S/94, 113, para. 55.

In the dispute *Japan - Taxes on Alcoholic, supra,* footnote 66, at 109, the Appellate Body upheld the concepts of equality of competitive conditions and equal competitive relationship between foreign and like domestic products. In the dispute *Korea - Taxes on Alcoholic Beverages,* WT/DS75,84/AB/R, adopted 17 February 1999, DSR 1999:I, 3, paras. 125-131, the Appellate Body confirmed the absence of a trade effects test under the national treatment clause and the principle that Article III of GATT protects expectations as to competitive opportunities.

[164] Para. 2 of Article XVII of GATS draws on the interpretation developed by a GATT panel with respect to Article III:4 of GATT. *See* Panel Report *United States - Section 337 of the Tariff Act of 1930*, adopted on 7 November 1989, BISD 36S/345, 386, para. 5.11.

Para. 3 of Article XVII of GATS draws on the interpretation developed in the Panel Report *Italian Discrimination of Imported Agricultural Machinery,* adopted on 23 October 1958, BISD 7S/60, 63, para. 12.

[165] Appellate Body Report *Korea - Taxes on Alcoholic Beverages*, *supra*, footnote 163, paras. 125-131. *See* also Report of the Working Party on *Brazilian Internal Taxes*, adopted 30 June 1949, BISD II/181, 185. Panel Report *United States - Taxes on Petroleum and Certain Imported Substances*, adopted on 17 June 1987, BISD 34S/136, 158, para. 5.19.

potential effects of the exemptions in question in the current market and technological environment.

6.188 We do acknowledge that the extent of exercise or non-exercise of exclusive rights by right holders at a given point in time is of great relevance for assessing what is the normal exploitation with respect to a particular exclusive right in a particular market. However, in certain circumstances, current licensing practices may not provide a sufficient guideline for assessing the potential impact of an exception or limitation on normal exploitation. For example, where a particular use of works is not covered by the exclusive rights conferred in the law of a jurisdiction, the fact that the right holders do not license such use in that jurisdiction cannot be considered indicative of what constitutes normal exploitation. The same would be true in a situation where, due to lack of effective or affordable means of enforcement, right holders may not find it worthwhile or practical to exercise their rights.

6.189 Both parties are of the view that the "normalcy" of a form of exploitation should be analysed primarily by reference to the market of the WTO Member whose measure is in dispute, i.e., the US market in this dispute. The European Communities is also of the view that comparative references to other countries with a similar level of socio-economic development could be relevant to corroborate or contradict data from the country primarily concerned.[166] We note that while the WTO Members are free to choose the method of implementation, the minimum standards of protection are the same for all of them.[167] In the present case it is enough for our purposes to take account of the specific conditions applying in the US market in assessing whether the measure in question conflicts with a normal exploitation in that market, or whether the measure meets the other conditions of Article 13.

(ii) The Business Exemption of Subparagraph (B)

6.190 The United States contends that the business exemption does not conflict with a normal exploitation of works for a number of reasons. First, in view of the great number of small eating, drinking and retail establishments, individual right holders or their CMOs face considerable administrative difficulties in licensing all these establishments. Given that the market to which the business exemption applies was never significantly exploited by the CMOs, the US Congress merely codified the *status quo* of the CMOs' licensing practices. Second, a significant portion of the establishments exempted by the new business exemption had already been exempted under the old homestyle exemption. Thus owners of copyrights in nondramatic musical works had no expectation of receiving fees from the small eating, drinking or retail establishments covered by the latter exemption. Third, even if subparagraph (B) had not been enacted, many of the establishments eligible for that exemption would have been able to avail themselves of an almost identical exemption under the group licensing agreement between the NLBA and ASCAP, the BMI and SESAC ("US CMOs"). For these reasons, the United States assumes that, even before the 1998

---

[166] EC and US responses to question 14 by the Panel to both parties.

[167] In this regard, the United States refers to Article 1.1 of the TRIPS Agreement, which provides that Members "shall be free to determine the appropriate method of implementing the provisions of this Agreement".

Amendment, right holders would not have normally expected to obtain fees from these establishments. The United States believes that the number of establishments, that would not have been entitled to take advantage of the original homestyle exemption of 1976 or the NLBA agreement and thus were newly exempted under subparagraph (B), is small. Viewed against the panoply of exploitative uses available to copyright owners under US copyright law,[168] in the US view, the residual limitation on some secondary uses of broadcast works does not rise to the level of a conflict with normal exploitation.

6.191 The European Communities responds that administrative difficulties in licensing a great number of small establishments do not excuse the very absence of the right, because there can be enforcement of only such rights as are recognized by law. It also points out that the use of recorded music is not covered by the exemptions. Arguing that this differentiation is difficult to justify, it contends that, to the extent the licensing of a great number of establishments meets insurmountable difficulties, then such difficulties should occur independently of the medium used. It also notes that the EC CMOs are successfully licensing a great number of small businesses without encountering insurmountable obstacles, whereas the US CMOs due to the lack of legal protection have not developed the necessary administrative structure to licence small establishments.

6.192 In response to a question from the Panel, the United States clarifies that it does not argue that administrative difficulties in licensing small establishments are more severe with respect to broadcast music as opposed to CDs or live music. Part of the rationale for this distinction is rather an historical one.[169]

6.193 In relation to its statement that the market to which the business exemption applies was never significantly exploited by the CMOs, the United States submitted information concerning the number and percentage of establishments that were licensed in the past by the CMOs.[170] The United States explains that, in considering the original homestyle exemption of Section 110(5), the US Congress found that, prior to 1976, the majority of beneficiaries of the then contemplated exemption were not licensed.[171] As regards the situation between the entry into force of the 1976 Copyright Act and the 1998 Amendment, the United States refers to the information provided by the NRA.[172] Based on the US Census Bureau data for 1996 and a number of its own studies, the NRA estimates that 16 per cent of table service restaurants and 5 per cent of fast food restaurants were licensed by the CMOs at that time in the United States. According to the NRA estimates based on the Census Bureau data, there was approximately the same number of table service and fast food restaurants in the United States.[173] Averaging these percentage figures, the United States concludes that approximately 10.5 per cent of restaurants were licensed by the CMOs.

---

[168] Exhibit US-14.

[169] US response to question 7 from the Panel to the United States.

[170] US response to question 10 from the Panel to the United States.

[171] House Report (1976), Exhibit US-1.

[172] Letter, dated 18 November 1999, from the NRA to the USTR. Confidential exhibit US-18.

[173] Based on the Census Bureau data, the NRA estimates that there were 183,253 table service restaurants and 185,891 quick-service restaurants in the United States. Based on this data and a number of its own surveys, it estimates that 16% (28,000-31,000) table service restaurants and 5%

6.194 In this context, the United States refers to the testimony of the President of ASCAP before the US Congress in 1997.[174] Based on the total number of ASCAP restaurants licensees[175] and the total number of restaurants estimated by the NRA on the basis of the Census Bureau data,[176] the United States estimates that ASCAP did not license more than 19 per cent of restaurants at that time. This, in its view, also indicates a relatively low level of licensing of such establishments.

6.195 We recall that, in its study of November 1995,[177] the CRS estimated that the size of 16 per cent of eating establishments 13.5 per cent of drinking establishments and 18 per cent of retail establishments did not exceed at that time the size of the *Aiken* restaurant, i.e. 1,055 square feet. These establishments could benefit from the exemption under the original Section 110(5), subject to equipment limitations. The United States gives two estimates of the number of licensed restaurants at that time: on the one hand, 10.5 per cent of restaurants were licensed by the CMOs,[178] and, on the other hand, 19 per cent of restaurants were licensed by ASCAP.[179] The United States also estimates that 74 per cent of all restaurants play some kind of music.[180]

6.196 Even when we deduct the share of the restaurants that were potentially exempted under the original homestyle exemption, we can agree with the United States that these figures indicate a relatively low level of licensing of restaurants likely to play music. However, as we noted above, whether or not the CMOs fully exercise their right to authorize the use of particular exclusive rights, or choose to collect remuneration for particular uses, or from particular users can, in our view, not necessarily be fully indicative of "normal exploitation" of exclusive rights. In considering whether the 1998 Amendment conflicts with normal exploitation, the fact that it does not generally change the licensing practices in relation to those establishments that were already exempted under the old homestyle exemption is not relevant; it is evident that due to the pre-existing homestyle exemption such establishments could not be licensed. Below, we will address separately, whether the homestyle exemption as contained in the amended Section 110(5) conflicts with normal exploitation.

6.197 The restaurants that were licensed by the CMOs before the 1998 Amendment were presumably mostly restaurants which were above the *Aiken* size limits (or did not meet the equipment limits for smaller restaurants). The two US estimates of the share of licensed restaurants (10.5 and 19 per cent) read together with the US estimate of the share of restaurants that play some kind of music (74 per cent) imply that

---

(8,000-10,000) quick service restaurants were licensed in the same period by CMOs. *See* US response to question 10(b) from the Panel to the United States.

174 Written statement by the President of ASCAP, Ms. Marilyn Bergman, dated 31 July 1997, to the Subcommittee on Courts and Intellectual Property, House Judiciary Committee. Exhibit US-20.

175 In her testimony before Congress in 1997, the President of ASCAP stated that "the total number of ASCAP restaurant licensees does not exceed 70,000". Exhibit US-20, p. 177. In her testimony, she also complained that "[t]here exists a massive non-compliance problem by tens of thousands of restaurants". Exhibit US 20, p. 175.

176 The NRA estimated on the basis of the Census Bureau data that there were a total of 369 144 table and quick-service restaurants in the United States. Confidential exhibit US-18.

177 *See* para. 2.11.

178 US response to question 10(b) by the Panel to the United States, para. 1.

179 US response to question 10(b) by the Panel to the United States, para. 2.

180 US response to question 11(b) by the Panel to the United States.

many restaurants, that were above the *Aiken* size limits and that were likely to play music, appear not to have been licensed. This tends to indicate that amongst similar users some paid licence fees while others did not. We have not been provided with any evidence that it would be considered normal to expect remuneration from some but not other similarly situated users.

6.198 We do not find the argument compelling, according to which an exception that codifies an existing practice by the CMOs of not licensing certain users should be presumed not to conflict with normal exploitation, as it would not affect right holders' current expectations to be remunerated. In our understanding, this would equate "normal exploitation" with "normal remuneration" practices existing at a certain point in time in a given market or jurisdiction. If such exceptions were permissible *per se*, any current state and degree of exercise of an exclusive right by right holders could effectively be "frozen". In our view, such argumentation could be abused as a justification of any exception or limitation since right holders could never reasonably expect remuneration for uses which are not covered by exclusive rights provided in national legislation. Logically, no conflict with normal exploitation could be construed. The same would apply where a low level of exercise of an exclusive right would be due to lack of effective or affordable means of enforcement of that right. In other words, the licensing practices of the CMOs in a given market at a given time do not define the minimum standards of protection under the TRIPS Agreement that have to be provided under national legislation.

6.199 The United States draws attention to a proposal by the US CMOs to amend Section 110(5).[181] In 1995, the CMOs set forth a substitute text for the bill[182] that was pending in Congress at that time. The CMO proposal suggested a square footage limit of 1,250 square feet and specific equipment limitations of no more than four loudspeakers and two television screens not greater than 44 inches. With respect to other matters, the CMOs said in their proposal that it was possible and desirable to leave them for a negotiated settlement with user associations.[183] The CMO proposal represented a modest expansion of the original homestyle exemption.[184]

6.200 There may be a variety of reasons and motivations why CMOs, coalitions of small businesses or other interest groups make legislative proposals to a national parliament. Certain proposals might form part of a larger package deal with elements that are more or less favourable for particular groups involved in the process. It is not our task to second-guess such motivations or bargaining strategies. Our terms of reference are limited to examining the consistency of the currently applicable Section 110(5), which was eventually enacted, with the substantive standards of the TRIPS Agreement. In carrying out our mandate, we have to interpret the phrase "not conflict with a normal exploitation" on the basis of the criteria of Article 31 of the Vienna Convention and examine subparagraph (B) in the light of an objective standard. Therefore, we do not consider the legislative proposal by the US CMOs as relevant for interpreting the second condition of Article 13. A proposal made during

181 US first written submission, para. 11.

182 H.R. 789, Exhibit US-4.

183 Letter of 24 July 1995 to the Honourable Carlos Moorhead from ASCAP, BMI, Inc. and SESAC, Inc., Exhibit US-5.

184 US first written submission, para. 11.

the legislative proceedings by the CMOs cannot be held against them nor be used to determine treaty obligations.

6.201 The United States also submits that, in the absence of a legislative solution at that time, the US CMOs signed a private group licensing agreement with the NLBA in October 1995 ("NLBA Agreement"). The CMOs offered to extend the agreement to the National Restaurant Association (NRA) and other members of the coalition advocating an extension of the exemption in the law. The agreement exempts establishments affiliated with the NLBA from paying licensing fees for the performance of music by the radio or television, if the establishment is smaller than 3,500 square feet, or bigger and complies with certain limitations on equipment. The United States emphasizes that the scope of the exemptions in this voluntarily negotiated group licensing agreement is largely identical to the legislation that, three years later, in 1998, became the Fairness in Music Licensing Act.[185]

6.202 The European Communities contends that the CMOs tried to negotiate such group licensing agreements in order to prevent even less favourable legislation from being enacted. The European Communities compares this to a situation where a right owner will be more inclined to grant a contractual licence on relatively unfavourable terms in a country where it is easy to obtain a compulsory licence than in a country where it is difficult to obtain a compulsory licence. Furthermore, in its view, the US reference to private agreements is circular in nature. It is only after the legislator has established a legal framework that private economic operators can start to act within this framework. In other words, only when a law stipulates a public performance right can parties usefully agree on a licensing contract. Where a law contemplates free use, there is no reason for a licensing contract as there is no right to license in the first place.

6.203 We note that the United States was not in a position to provide a copy of the NLBA Agreement to the Panel, because the NLBA considered it to contain business proprietary information.[186] Therefore, in considering the relevance of the NLBA Agreement for the issues at hand, we have had to rely on other indirect information provided to us by the parties.

6.204 While we recognize similarities between the terms of the NLBA Agreement and the provisions of the finally passed version of the business exemption in subparagraph (B), we also notice differences. The NLBA Agreement appears to be a comprehensive performing rights licensing package, the terms of which go beyond the issues addressed in the business exemption as it was then pending or later enacted. For example, the agreement is administered by the NBLA against a small portion of the collected licence fees. Small establishments qualifying for an exemption under the agreement have to apply for an "exemption licence" from the NLBA for a fee of US$30 per year. Thus, the agreement can be characterized as a form of exercise of exclusive rights by the grant of "exemption licences" to small eating and drinking establishments against the payment of a small flat-rate fee.[187] Furthermore,

---

[185] For details, *see* US first written submission, paras. 12 and 13.

[186] *See* US response to the question 1(c) from the Panel to the United States.

[187] In comparison, we note that the Australian Performing Rights Association grants complimentary licences to certain small establishments. *See* Australia's response to question 2 by the Panel to the third parties.

under the agreement, the CMOs and the NLBA commit themselves to work together to provide value-added packages for those who choose the group agreement. In announcing the agreement, the NBLA strongly urged its members to acquire a licence under the agreement.[188] This course of action by the NLBA was likely to induce a larger number of restaurants to voluntarily subscribe to the group licence than concerted efforts by the CMOs to license individual restaurants.[189]

6.205 It is one thing to have a practice such as the NLBA Agreement. Right holders do not need to exploit their rights, or they may do so for a nominal fee or no fee. It is another thing to pass legislation preventing the exercise of a right, which a country is obliged, under a treaty binding it, to afford to the nationals of the other parties to the treaty. Individual or group licensing arrangements result from negotiations between parties, not from governmental imposition. They may, subject to the terms agreed between the parties, be extended, modified or terminated at will. While the NLBA arrangement may evolve in response to market developments affecting the normal exploitation of works, the statutory business exemption cannot evolve similarly since it prevents the market from developing or distorts it. We note that Article 13, including its second condition, sets forth an objective test for permissible exceptions to exclusive rights. In assessing whether a statutory exemption meets that test, a comparison between its provisions and the terms and conditions of a group licensing arrangement such as the one between the NLBA and the US CMOs is not pertinent.

6.206 We recall that a substantial majority of eating and drinking establishments and close to half of retail establishments are eligible to benefit from the business exemption. This constitutes a major potential source of royalties for the exercise of the exclusive rights contained in Articles 11(1)*bis*(iii) and 11(1)(ii) of the Berne Convention (1971), as demonstrated by the figures of the D&B studies referred to under our analysis of the first condition of Article 13.

6.207 We recall that subparagraph (B) of Section 110(5) exempts communication to the public of radio and television broadcasts, while the playing of musical works from CDs and tapes (or live music) is not covered by it. Given that we have not been provided with reasons other than historical ones for this distinction, we see no logical

[188] The information above is based on the NLBA News, April 1997, Exhibit US-6, and "Music Licensing Agreement with ASCAP, BMI & SESAC for NLBA members; NLBA announces the deal of the century", Exhibit US-7. According to the United States, the fee for an exemption licence is currently US$50.

[189] We cannot exclude the possibility that terms of the NLBA Agreement could have been influenced by the Bill pending in the US Congress at the time when the agreement was concluded. However, we believe it is irrelevant for the purposes of our examination of Article 13's second condition whether, as noted by the United States, ASCAP praised the private group licensing agreement and called it a fair compromise, stating that it would benefit small businesses while ensuring that the rights of rights holders would be protected. Likewise, it is irrelevant for the purposes of our examination of that condition whether, as noted by the European Communities, ASCAP and the BMI condemned the Fairness in Music Licensing Act of 1998 in a press release at the occasion of its passage by US Congress. (The EC refers to a joint press release by ASCAP and BMI, Exhibit EC-14: "With this music licensing legislation, which seizes the private property of copyright owners, the US Government has severely penalised American songwriters, composers and publishers ... The earnings of songwriters, composers and publishers have been reduced by tens of millions of dollars annually.") We note that right holders or their CMOs are not prevented from enforcing their rights because of legislative proposals or comments thereon made by them.

reason to differentiate between broadcast and recorded music when assessing what is a normal use of musical works.

6.208 It is true, as the United States notes, that many of these establishments might not play music at all, or play recorded or live music. According to NLBA surveys,[190] among its member establishments 26 per cent use CDs or tapes, 18 per cent rely on background music services, 37 per cent have live music performances, while 28 per cent play radio music.[191] The United States estimates that overall approximately 74 per cent of US restaurants play music from various sources. The United States provided estimates also by the NRA concerning its membership on the percentage of restaurants that play the radio or use the television; these figures are not reproduced here, given that this information was provided to the United States in confidence.[192] From this data, the United States assumes that no more than 44 per cent of licensing fees can be attributed to radio music.[193]

6.209 We note that the parties agree that the administrative challenges for the CMOs related to the licensing of a great number of small eating, drinking and retail establishments do not differ depending on the medium used for playing music. We believe that the differentiation between different types of media may induce operators of establishments covered by subparagraph (B) to switch from recorded or live music, which is subject to the payment of a fee, to music played on the radio or television, which is free of charge. This may also create an incentive to reduce the licensing fees for recorded music so that users would not switch to broadcast music.

6.210 Right holders of musical works would expect to be in a position to authorize the use of broadcasts of radio and television music by many of the establishments covered by the exemption and, as appropriate, receive compensation for the use of their works. Consequently, we cannot but conclude that an exemption of such scope as subparagraph (B) conflicts with the "normal exploitation" of the work in relation to the exclusive rights conferred by Articles 11*bis*(1)(iii) and 11(1)(ii) of the Berne Convention (1971).

6.211 In the light of these considerations, we conclude that the business exemption embodied in subparagraph (B) conflicts with a normal exploitation of the work within the meaning of the second condition of Article 13.

(iii) The Homestyle Exemption of Subparagraph (A)

6.212 The United States argues that the homestyle exemption, even before non-dramatic musical works were removed from its scope through the 1998 Amendment, was limited to the establishments that were not large enough to justify a subscription

[190] US response to question 11(b) by the panel to the United States.
[191] Letter from NLBA of 18 November 1999, confidential exhibit US-17.
[192] We find that the designation as confidential of such statistical information does not assist us in discharging of our responsibility to make findings that will best enable the DSB to perform its dispute settlement functions. However, given our findings on the compatibility of the business exemption with the second condition of Article 13, including our considerations on substitution effects between various sources of music, the information in question is not essential for our findings.
[193] US response to question 11(b) by the panel to the United States.

to a commercial background music service.[194] As noted in the House Report (1976), the United States Congress intended that this exemption would merely codify the licensing practices already in effect. The original homestyle exemption of 1976 was intended to affect only those establishments that were not likely otherwise to enter into a licence, or would not have been licensed under the practices at that time. The United States contends that subparagraph (A) of the amended Section 110(5) does not conflict with the expectation of right holders concerning the normal exploitation of their works.

6.213 As regards the permissible equipment, we note that, according to the House Report (1976), the purpose of the exemption in its original form was to exempt from copyright liability "anyone who merely turns on, in a public place, an ordinary radio or television receiving apparatus of a kind commonly sold to members of the public for private use". "[The clause] would impose liability where the proprietor has a commercial 'sound system' installed or converts a standard home receiving apparatus (by augmenting it with sophisticated or extensive amplification equipment) into the equivalent of a commercial sound system."[195] We also recall the rationale behind the homestyle exemption as expressed in the legislative history relating to its original version: "The basic rationale of this clause is that the secondary use of the transmission by turning on an ordinary receiver in public is so remote and minimal that no further liability should be imposed."[196]

6.214 In other words, the provision is intended to define the borderline between two situations: a situation where one listens to the radio or watches the television - this is clearly not covered by the scope of copyright and, hence, outside normal exploitation of works - and a situation where one uses appropriate equipment to cause a new public performance of music contained in a broadcast or other transmission. This borderline is defined by laying emphasis on "turning on an ordinary receiver", albeit that members of the public might also hear the transmission.

6.215 As regards the beneficiaries of the homestyle exemption, we note that its legislative history reveals the intention that the exemption should affect only those establishments that were not likely otherwise to enter into a licence, or would not have been licensed under the practices at that time. As pointed out above, according to the 1995 CRS study, the number of establishments that were as big or smaller than the *Aiken* restaurant and could benefit from the homestyle exemption is limited to a

[194] US Congress Conference Report (1976), Exhibit US-2, referred to in para. 2.5 above.

[195] These quotations are from the Report of the House Committee on the Judiciary, H.R. Rep. No. 94-1476, 94th Congress, 2nd Session 87 (1976), as reproduced in Exhibit US-1. The Report adds that "[f]actors to consider in particular cases would include the size, physical arrangement, and noise level of the areas within the establishment where the transmissions are made audible or visible, and the extent to which the receiving apparatus is altered or augmented for the purpose of improving the aural or visual quality of the performance". The factors to consider in applying the exemption are largely based on the facts of a case decided by the United States Supreme Court immediately prior to the passage of the 1976 Copyright Act, *Twentieth Century Music Corp. v. Aiken*, 422 U.S. 151 (1975). In *Aiken*, the Court held that an owner of a small fast food restaurant was not liable for playing music by means of a radio with outlets to four speakers in the ceiling; the size of the shop was 1,055 square feet (98 m^2), of which 620 square feet (56 m^2) were open to the public. The Report describes the factual situation in *Aiken* as representing the "outer limit of the exemption".

[196] See the House Report (1976), Exhibit US-1, referred to in para. 2.5 above.

comparatively small percentage of all eating, drinking and retail establishments in the United States.[197]

6.216 The United States argues that the homestyle exemption of 1998 is even less capable of being in conflict with normal exploitation of works because its scope is now limited to works other than nondramatic musical works. While a collective licensing mechanism for nondramatic musical works exists in the United States, there is no such mechanism for "dramatic" musical works and there is little or no direct licensing by individual right holders of the establishments in question. Therefore, in the US view, authors might not reasonably expect to exploit "dramatic" musical works in the normal course of events through licensing public performances or communications thereof to the establishments that may invoke subparagraph (A).

6.217 We recall that it is the common understanding of the parties that the operation of subparagraph (A) is limited, as regards musical works, to the public communication of transmissions embodying dramatic renditions of "dramatic" musical works, such as operas, operettas, musicals and other similar dramatic works. Consequently, performances of, e.g., individual songs from a dramatic musical work outside a dramatic context would constitute a rendition of a nondramatic work and fall within the purview of subparagraph (B).

6.218 It is our understanding that the parties agree that the right holders do not normally license or attempt to license the public communication of transmissions embodying dramatic renditions of "dramatic" musical works in the sense of Article 11*bis*(1)(iii) and/or 11(1)(ii). We have not been provided with information about any existing licensing practices concerning the communication to the public of broadcasts of performances of dramatic works (e.g., operas, operettas, musicals) by eating, drinking or retail establishments in the United States or any other country. In this respect, we fail to see how the homestyle exemption, as limited to works other than nondramatic musical works in its revised form, could acquire economic or practical importance of any considerable dimension for the right holders of musical works.

6.219 Therefore, we conclude that the homestyle exemption contained in subparagraph (A) of Section 110(5) does not conflict with a normal exploitation of works within the meaning of the second condition of Article 13.

(d) "Not Unreasonably Prejudice the Legitimate Interests of the Right Holder"

(i) General Interpretative Analysis

6.220 The United States defines "prejudice [to] the legitimate interests of the right holder" in terms of the economic impact caused by subparagraphs (A) and (B) of Section 110(5). In the US view, while the second condition of Article 13 of the TRIPS Agreement looks to the degree of market displacement caused by a limitation or exception, the "unreasonable prejudice" standard measures how much the right holder is harmed by the effects of the exception. Given that any exception to exclu-

[197] More specifically, the 1995 CRS study found that 16 per cent of all US eating establishments, 13.5 per cent of all US drinking establishments and 18 per cent of all US retail establishments were as big or smaller than the *Aiken* restaurant (1,055 square feet of total space). See above paras. 2.11 and 6.142.

sive rights may technically result in some degree of prejudice to the right holder, the key question is whether that prejudice is unreasonable.[198]

6.221 The European Communities submits that the legitimate interests of a right holder consist in being able to prevent all instances of a certain use of his or her work protected by a specific exclusive right undertaken by a third party without his or her consent. The legitimate interests include, at a minimum, all commercial uses by a third party of the right holder's exclusive rights. For the European Communities, both empirical and normative elements are relevant for the examination of the third condition of Article 13. In practice, economic prejudice to right holders should be assessed primarily on the basis of the economic effects in the country applying the exception. In the EC's view, it is sufficient to demonstrate the potentiality to prejudice; it is not necessary to quantify the actual financial losses suffered by the right holders concerned.

6.222 We note that the analysis of the third condition of Article 13 of the TRIPS Agreement implies several steps. First, one has to define what are the "interests" of right holders at stake and which attributes make them "legitimate". Then, it is necessary to develop an interpretation of the term "prejudice" and what amount of it reaches a level that should be considered "unreasonable".

6.223 The ordinary meaning of the term "interests"[199] may encompass a legal right or title to a property or to use or benefit of a property (including intellectual property). It may also refer to a concern about a potential detriment or advantage, and more generally to something that is of some importance to a natural or legal person. Accordingly, the notion of "interests" is not necessarily limited to actual or potential economic advantage or detriment.

6.224 The term "legitimate" has the meanings of

> "(a) conformable to, sanctioned or authorized by, law or principle; lawful; justifiable; proper;
>
> (b) normal, regular, conformable to a recognized standard type."

Thus, the term relates to lawfulness from a legal positivist perspective, but it has also the connotation of legitimacy from a more normative perspective, in the context of calling for the protection of interests that are justifiable in the light of the objectives that underlie the protection of exclusive rights.

6.225 We note that the ordinary meaning of "prejudice" connotes damage, harm or injury.[200] "Not unreasonable" connotes a slightly stricter threshold than "reasonable". The latter term means "proportionate", "within the limits of reason, not greatly less or

---

[198] Guide to the Berne Convention, op.cit., pp. 55-56, para. 9.8.

[199] Further meanings: "The fact or relation of having a share or concern in, or a right to, something, especially by law; a right or title, especially to a (share in) property or a use or benefit relating to property", "a financial share or stake in something;", "a thing which is to the advantage of someone, a benefit, an advantage", "the relation of being involved or concerned as regards potential detriment or advantage", "a thing that is of some importance to a person, company, state etc."; Oxford English Dictionary, p. 1393.

[200] "Harm, damage or injury to a person or that results from a judgement or action, especially one in which his/her rights are disregarded." Oxford English Dictionary, p. 2333.

more than might be thought likely or appropriate", or "of a fair, average or considerable amount or size".[201]

6.226 Given that the parties do not question the "legitimacy" of the interest of right holders to exercise their rights for economic gain, the crucial question becomes which degree or level of "prejudice" may be considered as "unreasonable". Before dealing with the question of what amount or which kind of prejudice reaches a level beyond reasonable, we need to find a way to measure or quantify legitimate interests.

6.227 In our view, one - albeit incomplete and thus conservative - way of looking at legitimate interests is the economic value of the exclusive rights conferred by copyright on their holders. It is possible to estimate in economic terms the value of exercising, e.g., by licensing, such rights. That is not to say that legitimate interests are necessarily limited to this economic value.[202]

6.228 In examining the second condition of Article 13, we have addressed the US argument that the prejudice to right holders caused by the exemptions at hand are minimal because they already receive royalties from broadcasting stations. We concluded that each exclusive right conferred by copyright, *inter alia*, under each subparagraph of Articles 11*bis* and 11 of the Berne Convention (1971), has to be considered separately for the purpose of examining whether a possible conflict with a "normal exploitation" exists.[203]

6.229 The crucial question is which degree or level of "prejudice" may be considered as "unreasonable",[204] given that, under the third condition, a certain amount of

---

[201] Oxford English Dictionary, p. 2496.

[202] Panel Report *Canada - Patent Protection of Pharmaceutical Products* ("*Canada – Pharmaceutical Patents*"), WT/DS114/R, adopted 7 April 2000, DSR 2000:V, 2295, paras. 7.60ff. We note, however, the difference in wording between Articles 13 and 30 of the TRIPS Agreement. The latter also refers to "taking account of the legitimate interests of third parties".

[203] We also recall from our examination of Article 13's second condition that we were not presented with evidence of licensing arrangements between CMOs and broadcasting organizations, concerning mainly the exclusive rights of Article 11*bis*(1)(i) or (ii), that would make allowance for the additional communication to the public in the meaning of Article 11*bis*(1)(iii) by, e.g., the categories of establishments covered by the subparagraphs of Section 110(5). We believe that we have to analyse whether the exemptions in question cause unreasonable prejudice to the legitimate interests of right holders similarly in respect of each exclusive right. Our view is confirmed by the fact that, as we pointed out when examining the second condition of Article 13, particular exclusive rights conferred by the subparagraphs of Articles 11 and 11*bis* in relation to one and the same work may be held by different persons. *See* EC and US replies to question 4 from the Panel to both parties.

[204] The term used in the French version of the Berne Convention is "*injustifié*". According to Article 37(1)(c) of the Berne Convention, both the English and the French text of the Convention are equally authentic, but "in case of differences of opinion on the interpretation of the various texts, the French text shall prevail".

However, Article 37 of the Berne Convention has not been incorporated into the TRIPS Agreement. To the extent that Articles 1-21 of the Berne Convention have been incorporated into the TRIPS Agreement by virtue of its Article 9.1, the general rule of Article XVI of the Agreement Establishing the WTO applies, i.e., that the English, French and Spanish versions of the covered agreements are equally authentic.

Article 33 of the Vienna Convention on the Law of Treaties stipulates that treaties which are authentic in several languages should be interpreted harmoniously, i.e., presuming that expressions in the treaty have the same meaning in all authentic languages.

"prejudice" has to be presumed justified as "not unreasonable".[205] In our view, prejudice to the legitimate interests of right holders reaches an unreasonable level if an exception or limitation causes or has the potential to cause an unreasonable loss of income to the copyright owner.

Legitimate interests of right holders of EC, US and third-country origin

6.230 We note the EC argument that, in respect of all conditions of Article 13, the effect on all right holders from all WTO Members must be taken into account. For the European Communities, the specific impact on EC right holders is not at issue at this stage of the dispute settlement process, but could become relevant only in the context of Article 22 of the DSU concerning compensation or the suspension of concessions or other obligations equivalent to nullification or impairment suffered. The United States has limited its estimations of the economic impact of subparagraph (B) to the actual losses caused by it to the EC right holders.

6.231 This raises the question who may enforce the legitimate interests of right holders of various WTO Members in panel proceedings within the WTO dispute settlement system.[206] In *EC - Bananas III*, the Appellate Body agreed with the panel that no DSU provision contains a requirement that a complaining party show its legal interest as a prerequisite for requesting a panel.[207] This rejection of a "legal interest" requirement does not necessarily imply that, in the context of the third condition of Article 13, prejudice to the legitimate interests of right holders other than EC right holders should be relevant. But we cannot find any indication in the express wording

---

[205] In respect of what could be the dividing line between "unreasonable" and "not unreasonable" prejudice, we consider the explanation of the Guide to the Berne Convention to be of persuasive value. It states in the context of the third condition of Article 9(2) of the Berne Convention, which is worded almost identically to Article 13 of the TRIPS Agreement but refers to exceptions to the reproduction right:

"Note that it is not a question of prejudice or no: all copying is damaging to some degree ...". The para. goes on to discuss whether photocopying "prejudices the circulation of the review", whether it "might seriously cut in on its sales" and says that "[i]n cases where there would be serious loss of profit for the copyright owner, the law should provide him with some compensation (a system of compulsory licensing with equitable remuneration)." *See* the Guide to the Berne Convention, para. 9.8.pp. 55-56. We do not believe that in this respect the benchmark has to be substantially different for reproduction rights, performance rights or broadcasting rights in the meanings of Articles 9, 11 or 11*bis* of the Berne Convention (1971).

[206] In addressing the question of effects on right holders from the European Communities, the United States and other WTO Members, we note that Article 1.3 of the TRIPS Agreement provides that "Members shall accord the treatment provided for in this Agreement to the nationals of other Members. ...". For the purposes of this dispute, this provision means that the United States is required to observe the obligations of the TRIPS Agreement with respect to nationals of all other WTO Members including, but not limited to, EC nationals.

[207] Appellate Body Report, *EC - Bananas III*, *supra*, footnote 86, para. 132. The Appellate Body also agreed with the panel's statement that "with the increased interdependence of the global economy, ... Members have greater stake in enforcing WTO rules than in the past since any deviation from the negotiated balance of rights and obligations is more likely than ever to affect them, directly or indirectly." *See* para. 136, citing from the Panel Reports on *EC - Bananas III*, *supra*, footnote 105, para. 7.50.

of the third condition of Article 13 that the assessment of whether the prejudice caused by an exception or limitation to the legitimate interests of the right holder is of an unreasonable level should be limited to the right holders of the Member that brings forth the complaint. For such a limitation to exist, the third condition of Article 13 would have to refer exclusively to the right holders who are nationals of the complaining party, not to "the right holder" as such.

6.232 We also refer to the explanation on the difference between the panel and Appellate Body proceedings and the enforcement process within the WTO dispute settlement system given by the Arbitrators, acting pursuant to Article 22.6 of the DSU, in the US/EC arbitration on the suspension of concessions in *Bananas III*.[208] An assessment of the impact of a WTO-inconsistent measure on an individual Member in terms of nullification or impairment is relevant under Article 22.6 of the DSU when compensation or suspension of concessions or other obligations has to be estimated in equivalence to the nullification or impairment suffered from a WTO-inconsistent measure which has not been brought into WTO-compliance within a reasonable period of time.

6.233 In this case, both parties have provided estimations on the market share of music of EC right holders. The European Communities submits that at least 25 per cent of all music played in the United States belongs to EC copyright owners. This figure is based on an industry estimate according to which the United Kingdom performing artists had a 23 per cent share of the US record sales in 1988. The European Communities appears to imply that this figure concerning United Kingdom performing artists would be indicative of the share due to EC composers and other copyright holders of the royalties collected for the amplification of music transmissions. The European Communities adds that another way to estimate EC authors' market share is to look at the royalty distributions by the US CMOs. The European Communities gives a figure, provided by ASCAP for 1998, indicating what percentage of its total distributions were paid to EC right holders; this figure is not reproduced here, given that the figure was given to the European Communities in confidence.[209]

---

[208] The Arbitrators explained: "The *presumption* of nullification or impairment in the case of an infringement of a GATT provision as set forth by Article 3.8 of the DSU cannot in and of itself be taken simultaneously as *evidence* proving a particular level of nullification or impairment allegedly suffered by a Member requesting authorization to suspend concessions under Article 22 of the DSU at a much later stage of the WTO dispute settlement system. The review of the level of nullification or impairment by Arbitrators from the objective benchmark foreseen by Article 22 of the DSU, is a separate process that is independent from the finding of infringements of WTO rules by a panel or the Appellate Body. As a result, a Member's potential interests in trade in goods or services and its interest in a determination of rights and obligations under the WTO Agreements are each sufficient to establish a right to pursue a WTO dispute settlement proceeding. However, a Member's legal interest in compliance by other Members does not, in our view, automatically imply that it is entitled to obtain authorization to suspend concessions under Article 22 of the DSU." *See* the Decision by the Arbitrators on *EC - Regime for the Importation, Sale and Distribution of Bananas - Recourse to Arbitration by the European Communities under Article 22.6 of the DSU* ("*EC – Bananas III (US) (Article 22.6 – EC)*"), WT/DS27/ARB, adopted 19 April 1999, DSR 1999:II, 725, para. 6.10.

[209] EC Response to question 5 from the Panel to the European Communities. Again we find that the EC's designation as confidential of such information does not assist us in discharging our responsibility to make findings that will best enable the DSB to perform its dispute settlement functions. However, given that our assessment of whether the prejudice caused by the exemptions of Section

6.234 The United States disagrees with the EC's implication that 25 per cent of royalties collected in the United States are due to EC right holders. According to the United States, a 1998 internal EC analysis of the economic effect of the homestyle exemption on EC right holders estimated that just 6.2 per cent of ASCAP revenues were distributed to all foreign CMOs, and that just 5.6 per cent of BMI revenues were due to all foreign CMOs.[210] Obviously, the percentage payable to the EC collecting societies would be significantly less than these figures for total payments to all foreign CMOs.[211]

6.235 We take note of these estimations, which are illustrative of the market conditions. However, given our considerations above, our assessment of whether the prejudice, caused by the exemptions contained in Section 110(5), to the legitimate interests of the right holder is of an unreasonable level is not limited to the right holders of the European Communities.

Summary of the general interpretative analysis

6.236 We will now examine subparagraphs (B) and (A) of Section 110(5) in the light of these general considerations. What is at stake in our examination of the third condition of Article 13 of the TRIPS Agreement is whether the prejudice caused by the exemptions to the legitimate interests of the right holder is of an unreasonable level. We will consider the information on market conditions provided by the parties taking into account, to the extent feasible, the actual as well as the potential prejudice caused by the exemptions, as a prerequisite for determining whether the extent or degree of prejudice is of an unreasonable level. In these respects, we recall our consideration above that taking account of actual as well as potential effects is consistent with past GATT/WTO dispute settlement practice.[212]

(ii) The Business Exemption of Subparagraph (B)

6.237 The European Communities focuses on an analysis of the potential economic effects of subparagraph (B) on the legitimate interests of right holders. It argues that the unreasonableness of the prejudice caused to the right holder becomes fully apparent when 73 per cent of all drinking establishments, 70 per cent of all eating establishments and 45 per cent of all retail establishments are unconditionally covered by the business exemption, while the rest of the establishments may also be exempted under conditions which are easy to meet. In its view, the denial of protection has been turned into the rule and protection of the exclusive right has become the exception.[213]

110(5) to the legitimate interests of the right holder is of an unreasonable level is not exclusively limited to EC right holders, the exact figure is not essential for our findings.

210 The United States refers to the Examination Procedure Regarding the Licensing of Music Works in the United States of America. European Commission, 23 February 1998. *See* US second written submission, para. 34.

211 US response to question 12 from the Panel to the United States.

212 *See* para. 6.185 and footnotes 163-165 above.

213 *See* paras. 2.11-2.13, 6.118-6.122 and 6.142 above for more detailed discussions on the estimations of the establishments exempted by subparagraphs (A) and (B) of Section 110(5).

6.238 The United States does not focus on questioning the correctness of these figures that indicate the percentage of US eating, drinking and retail establishments that fall within the size limits of subparagraph (B). Taking these figures as a starting-point for alternative calculations, the United States, however, contends that they are not useful for estimating the economic impact or prejudice caused by subparagraph (B) to right holders, because they fail to account for many relevant factors that determine whether a right holder would be economically prejudiced at all by the business exemption. In order to obtain a reasonable estimate of the number of establishments from which copyright owners have truly lost revenue as a result of the business exemption, the United States subtracts from these figures those establishments that:

(i) do not play music at all;

(ii) rely on music from some source other than radio or TV (such as tapes, CDs, commercial background music services, jukeboxes, or live music);

(iii) were not licensed prior to the passage of the 1998 amendment and which the CMOs would not be able to license anyway;

(iv) would take advantage of the NLBA agreement, whose terms are practically identical to subparagraph (B), if the statutory exemption were not available; and

(v) would prefer to simply turn off the music rather than pay the fees demanded by the CMOs.

The United States concedes that it is impossible to estimate these figures, but assumes that there is ample reason to believe that they represent a substantial number of establishments.

6.239 We examine the relevance of these factors, beginning with the first, second and the fifth factors, and then the third and fourth factors. In this context, we recall that, while both parties have to adduce evidence supporting their legal and factual arguments, it is the United States that bears the ultimate burden of proof that Section 110(5) meets all three conditions of Article 13 of the TRIPS Agreement.

No music or music from another source

6.240 In detailing its first, second and fifth reduction factor, the United States provides estimates on the percentages of restaurants that use various sources of music, which we have summarized in paragraph 6.208 above. We agree that it is possible that some establishments that currently play broadcast music might decide to stop doing so, if they were required to pay fees to CMOs representing right holders in the absence of an exemption. But it is also evident that establishments that currently play recorded music may at any time decide to switch to music broadcast over the air or transmitted by cable in order to avoid paying licensing fees. Also, some establishments that do not play any music at all may start to use broadcast music, given that the only cost would be that of acquiring a sound system. Similarly, if amplified broadcast music would not be free of charge due to subparagraph (B) of Section 110(5), operators of establishments covered by that provision that currently use such broadcast music might switch to recorded music, to commercial background music services or to live music performances. Furthermore, an exemption that makes the use of music from one source free of charge is likely to affect, not only the number of establishments that opt for sources of music that require the payment of a licensing fee, but also the price for which the protected sources of music can be licensed.

6.241 It appears that the use of recorded music or commercial background music services can be easily replaced by the amplification of music transmitted over the air or by cable. Digital broadcasts and cable transmissions are increasing the supply of different types of music transmissions. The fact that one source of music is free of charge while another triggers copyright liability may have a significant impact on which source of music the operators of establishments choose, and on how much they are willing to pay for protected music. Therefore, in addition to the right holders' loss of revenue from the users that were newly exempted under subparagraph (B) of Section 110(5), the business exemption is also likely to reduce the amount of income that may be generated from restaurants and retail establishments for the use of recorded music or commercial background music services.

6.242 Although these considerations do not render irrelevant the statistics and estimations on the numbers and percentages of establishments that may play music from different sources or no music at all, it is clear that such statistics and estimations have to be considered with the *caveat* that, although they may reflect realities at a given point in time, they do not take into account the substitution between various sources of music that is likely to take place in the longer term.

Establishments not licensed before the 1998 Amendment and the NLBA Agreement

6.243 As to its third reduction factor, the United States submitted information concerning past licensing practices of establishments covered by Section 110(5). As regards the situation before the 1976 Copyright Act, the United States notes that, in considering the original homestyle exemption of Section 110(5), the US Congress found that prior to 1976 the majority of beneficiaries of the then contemplated exemption were not licensed. As regards the situation between the entry into force of the 1976 Copyright Act and the 1998 Amendment, the United States gives two estimates, one according to which approximately 10.5 per cent of restaurants were licensed by the CMOs, and second according to which ASCAP licensed 19 per cent of restaurants at that time. In its view, these figures indicate a relatively low level of licensing of establishments. We also recall the November 1995 estimate by the CRS that 16 per cent of eating establishments, 13.5 per cent of drinking establishments and 18 per cent of retail establishments were at that time below the size of the *Aiken* restaurant, i.e. 1,055 square feet.[214] In addition, the United States estimates that 74 per cent of all restaurants play some kind of music.[215]

6.244 Based on these statistics about past licensing practices and ASCAP's revenue collection, the United States submits that the likely impact of the amended Section

214 We note that the size of 1,055 of square feet is not contained in the original or revised text of the homestyle exemption but derives from the *Aiken* judgement. *See* para. 2.6 above.

215 The above figures are discussed in more detail in the context of our examination of the second condition of Article 13 in paras. 6.208 and US reply to question 11(b) by the Panel to the United States.

110(5) on the revenues collected earlier by the CMOs from such establishments is likely to be minimal.[216] ASCAP collects 14 per cent of its total revenues from general licensees, including eating, drinking and retail establishments. Much of this revenue is from the public performance of live or recorded music, rather than broadcast music. Based on the data provided by the NLBA and NRA, the United States estimates that radio music accounts for a maximum of 28-44 per cent of revenues from eating and drinking establishments; this 28-44 per cent of 14 per cent is equivalent to 3.9-6.2 per cent of total revenues. The United States reduces this figure further because not all restaurants and bars are eligible for the Section 110(5) exemptions. The United States adds that, even using the EC figure indicating that 70 per cent of all US restaurants are exempted under subparagraph (B), it appears that the exemption for radio music will have a maximum effect on revenues of 2.7-4.3 per cent.

6.245 The EC's main contention against the reduction factors applied by the United States to its estimates of potential prejudice is that actual distributions to right holders, past licensing practices and revenue collected or foregone by the CMOs in the past or at present are not representative of the potential economic effect of subparagraph (B), because collection practices of the CMOs are a function of the legal protection of the relevant exclusive rights.

6.246 More specifically, the European Communities points out that the long-standing exceptions to copyright protection (i.e., prior to 1976, the *Aiken* decision, the passage of the homestyle exemption of the 1976 Copyright Act, subsequent court decisions in *Claire's Boutique* and *Edison Bros.*[217]) render the actual royalty collection practices of the CMOs in the past unrepresentative for measuring losses to right holders. In the EC view, this assessment is corroborated by the fact that, since the 1995 group licensing agreement between the US CMOs and the NLBA entered into force, no licensing fees have been collected from exempted establishments with a square footage below 3,500. These include 65 per cent of all eating and 72 per cent of all drinking establishments.[218]

6.247 We recall our conclusion that in the application of the three conditions of Article 13 to an exemption in national law, both actual and potential effects of that exception are relevant. As regards the third condition in particular, we note that if only actual losses were taken into account, it might be possible to justify the introduction of a new exception to an exclusive right irrespective of its scope in situations where the right in question was newly introduced, right holders did not previously have effective or affordable means of enforcing that right, or that right was not exercised because the right holders had not yet built the necessary collective management structure required for such exercise. While under such circumstances the introduction of a new exception might not cause immediate additional loss of income to the right holder, he or she could never build up expectations to earn income from the exercise of the right in question. We believe that such an interpretation, if it became the norm,

[216] US reply to question 11(d) by the Panel to the United States.

[217] Broadcast Music, Inc. v. Claire's Boutiques Inc., US Court of Appeals for the Seventh Circuit, N° 91-1232, 11 December 1991. *See* Exhibit EC-6. Broadcast Music, Inc. v. Edison Bros. Stores Inc., US Court of Appeals for the Eight Circuit, N° 91-2115, 13 January 1992. *See* Exhibit EC-5.

[218] *See* EC first oral statement, para. 37.

could undermine the scope and binding effect of the minimum standards of intellectual property rights protection embodied in the TRIPS Agreement.[219]

6.248 We recall our consideration, in relation to the second condition of Article 13, of the relatively low level of licensing, before the 1998 Amendment, of restaurants above the *Aiken* size limits that were likely to play music. We concluded that, without further evidence, the fact that some similarly situated users were licensed, while others were not, could not be taken as an indication of normal exploitation. As regards the third condition of Article 13, we have not been provided with any persuasive arguments why the legitimate interests of the right holder would differ in respect of those similarly situated users that are currently licensed and those that are not; neither have we been given any persuasive explanation why some of these users were licensed and others not.

6.249 Therefore, in considering the prejudice to the legitimate interests of right holders caused by the business exemption, we have to take into account not only the actual loss of income from those restaurants that were licensed by the CMOs at the time that the exemption become effective, but also the loss of potential revenue from other restaurants of similar size likely to play music that were not licensed at that point.

6.250 As to the fourth US reduction factor, we note that we have already addressed the US argument about the similarity between the 1998 Amendment and the group licensing agreement reached between the CMOs and the NLBA in 1995 in our discussion of the second condition of Article 13. In that context, we noted that a private agreement constitutes a form of exercising exclusive rights and is by no means determinative for assessing the compliance of an exemption provided for in national law pursuant to international treaty obligations.[220]

Summary of the relevance of the above factors

6.251 Consequently, we caution against attributing too much relevance to the factors proposed by the United States for reducing the EC figures intended to indicate the potential prejudice in relation to eating, drinking or retail establishments, and, accordingly, for the determination of the level of prejudice caused by the business exemption to the legitimate interests of right holders. At the same time, we recognize the difficulty of quantifying the economic value of potential prejudice. Most of the factual information on the current US licensing market provided by the parties relates to the immediate actual losses to the right holders; in particular, both parties have provided us with detailed calculations of the loss of income to the right holders resulting from the 1998 Amendment. Keeping in mind our conclusion that such figures cannot alone be determinative for the assessment of the level of prejudice suffered by right holders, we will now examine these calculations.

---

[219] In comparison, we recall that in relation to the second condition, we noted that a low level of licensing cannot be determinative of normal exploitation to the extent that it results from lack of legal protection or of effective or affordable means of enforcement.

[220] *See* paras. 6.204-6.205 above.

The alternative calculations by the parties of losses suffered by right holders

6.252 The United States estimates that the maximum annual loss to EC right holders of distributions from the largest US collecting society, ASCAP, as a result of the Section 110(5) exemption, is in the range of $294,113 to $586,332. Applying the same analysis, it estimates that the loss from the second largest society, BMI, is $122,000. In its calculation of ASCAP's distributions, the United States takes as a starting-point the total royalties paid to EC right holders by ASCAP. Second, it reduces the amount attributable to general licensing (i.e. licensing of commercial background music services, and a wide variety of licensees, including conventions and sports arenas, as well as restaurants, bars and retail establishments). Third, it makes a deduction to account for licensing revenue from general licensees that do not meet the statutory definition of an "establishment". Fourth, it deducts from the general licensing revenue the portion that is due to music from sources other than radio or television (e.g., tapes, CDs, commercial background music services, jukeboxes, live performances); and fifth, it reduces this amount to account for licensing revenue from general licensing of eating, drinking or retail establishments which play the radio but do not meet the size and equipment limitations of subparagraph (B) and thus do not qualify for the business exemption. The complete calculation and the US comments thereon can be found in the second written submission and in the second oral statement of the United States.[221]

6.253 The European Communities estimates that the annual loss to all right holders amounts to $53.65 million. The EC calculation takes as the starting-point the number of establishments that may qualify for the exception. Second, the European Communities makes a reduction from that number using the US hypotheses that 30.5 per cent of all eating and drinking establishments with a surface area below 3,750 square feet actually play music from the radio. Third, it applies to the remaining establishments the appropriate licensing fees selected from the licensing schedules of ASCAP[222] and BMI.[223] The complete calculation and related comments can be found in paragraphs 39-45 of the second oral statement by the European Communities, which is reproduced in Attachment 1.6 to this report.[224]

---

[221] *See* US second written submission, paras. 33-48, and US second oral statement, paras. 29-42, reproduced in Attachments 2.5 and 2.6 to this report.

[222] *See* excerpt in Exhibit EC-26.

[223] *See* excerpt in Exhibit EC-27.

[224] In response to question 4 from the Panel to the European Communities requesting information or estimations on the revenues collected by the EC collecting societies, the European Communities was only able to provide information in regard to the Irish Music Rights Organisation (IMRO). As Ireland represents approximately one per cent of the EC population, the European Communities suggests to multiply the Irish figures by hundred in order to obtain an estimate for the EC CMOs in their entirety.

We recall our view that our analysis should focus primarily on the US market, but that information from other countries might be useful for a comparative analysis of the US market. We regret that the European Communities and its member States were not in a position to provide us with more meaningful data. We do not believe that information from a single EC member State which would have to be extrapolated with a multiplier of 100 for the entire EC territory can be useful for the task before us.

6.254 Overall, we consider that neither estimate is devoid of relevance for the purposes of estimating whether prejudice caused by subparagraph (B) to the legitimate interests of right holders amounts to a level that could be deemed unreasonable. The difference between the results of these two calculations can, to an extent, be explained by differences in the starting points and the parameters used for the calculations. The calculations use also a number of similar assumptions. We highlight below some of these differences and similarities.

6.255 The US estimate can be characterized as a "top-down" approach, which takes as its starting-point ASCAP's and the BMI's average total distributions of domestic income for the years 1996-1998. We recall that the United States estimates that only 10.5-19 per cent of restaurants were licensed at that time. Hence, this calculation based on the pre-existing collection does not take into account the potential income from establishments that were already covered at that time by the old homestyle exemption or from the larger restaurants that used music but were not licensed at that time.

6.256 The EC calculation can, in turn, be characterized as a "bottom-up" approach. It takes as its starting point the total number of restaurants and retail establishments that fall under the size limits of the exemption; then it applies to those establishments the lowest ASCAP and BMI licence fees, assuming a 100 per cent compliance rate among the establishments concerned.

6.257 The EC calculation covers all right holders, while the US calculation covers only the EC right holders' share. The United States estimates that this share is between 5 and 13.7 per cent of ASCAP's distributions of domestic income, and 8.15 per cent of the BMI's distributions.

6.258 Both calculations make a number of reductions from the above starting points based on estimations. In the absence of more detailed information from ASCAP, the United States estimates that 50 per cent of ASCAP's general licensing revenue is derived from the establishments covered by the business exemption. Based on the NRA and NLBA surveys, the United States estimates that 30.5 per cent of the establishments covered by the exemption play radio; the European Communities also uses this figure. Averaging the NRA estimations of the percentage of restaurants that meet the size limits, and the D&B study on the equivalent percentage of retail establishments, the United States estimates that 52.1 per cent of all establishments fall below the size limits of the business exemption.

6.259 Neither calculation takes into account the distributions of the third US CMO, SESAC, or music played on the television. The calculations do not attempt to estimate the losses from establishments above the size limits of subparagraph (B) of Section 110(5), which however comply with the respective equipment limitations. It appears that neither party assumes that these factors would essentially change the outcome of their estimations.

6.260 We note that both calculations include many estimations and assumptions. The fact that neither party was in a position to provide more direct information on the revenues collected from the establishments affected by the business exemption does not facilitate the estimation of the immediate effect of the exemption in terms of annual losses to the right holders.

6.261 One of the major differences between the calculations is that the US calculation takes into account the loss of income only from those establishments that were not already exempted under the old homestyle exemption and were actually paying licence fees. Given our considerations on the potential impact of the exemption, we are of the view that the loss of potential income from other users of music is also relevant.

6.262 In addition, the United States indicates a number of reasons why it considers that its five-step calculation is conservative. It assumes that 30.5 per cent of the licensing revenue is attributable to radio-playing, because 30.5 per cent of establishments play the radio, although these establishments might play music from multiple sources. Furthermore, the United States assumes that the 65.5 per cent of restaurants and the 45 per cent of retail establishments that meet the square footage limits account for 65 per cent or 45 per cent of the losses to right holders; but it adds that the small establishments that qualify for the exemptions are likely to represent a smaller proportion of the licensing revenue. The United States does not argue that these considerations would change the outcome of its estimation to an essential degree.

6.263 The United States also submits that its calculation does not take into account steps that ASCAP and the BMI might take to minimize any impact of the 1998 Amendment (e.g., focusing licensing resources exclusively on larger stores that generally pay larger fees, or by charging more for the playing of music from CDs and tapes). In the US view, the analysis should also take into account the limited resources of the CMOs and the small percentage of the market actually licensed by the CMOs. In the light of the certainty provided by the precise limitations of the business exemption contained in subparagraph (B), the CMOs can now efficiently redirect their licensing resources toward those establishments not eligible for the business exemption, and thus compensate for any minor prejudice they might suffer. The United States refers to an ASCAP statement of its intent to "reverse the effects" of the 1998 Amendment by redirecting its licensing resources toward establishments not covered by subparagraph (B) as well as by generating additional income by encouraging the use of live and recorded music, for which there is no exemption.[225]

6.264 In our view, this line of argument is irrelevant for the issue before us, i.e., whether subparagraph (B) complies with Article 13's third condition. If we were to find that subparagraph (B) does not meet the conditions for invoking the exception of Article 13, there is no rule in WTO law compelling another Member or private parties affected by a Member's WTO-inconsistent measure to take steps to remedy any actual, or reduce the potential, nullification or impairment caused.

6.265 We recall that the ultimate burden of proof concerning whether all of the conditions of Article 13 are met lies with the United States as the Member invoking the exception. In the light of our analysis of the prejudice caused by the exemption, including its actual and potential effects, we are of the view that the United States has not demonstrated that the business exemption does not unreasonably prejudice the legitimate interests of the right holder.

6.266 Accordingly, we conclude that the business exemption of subparagraph (B) of Section 110(5) does not meet the requirements of the third condition of Article 13 of the TRIPS Agreement.

---

225 "A critical element of our plan will be to aggressively license those eligible establishments that have withheld royalty payment and to promote the value of live and mechanical music to a large number of newly targeted establishments." *See* ASCAP, Playback, October-November-December 1998, p. 2, Exhibit US-13.

(iii) The Homestyle Exemption of Subparagraph (A)

6.267 The United States submits that the economic effect of the original homestyle exemption of Section 110(5) of 1976 was minimal. Its intent was to exempt from liability small shop and restaurant owners whose establishments would not have justified a commercial licence. Given that such establishments are not a significant licensing market, they could not be significant sources of revenue for right holders. Where no licences would be sought or issued in the absence of an exception, there was literally no economic detriment to the right holder from an explicit exception. Exempted establishments with small square footage and elementary sound equipment are the least likely to be aggressively licensed by the CMOs and licensing fees for these establishments would likely be the lowest in the range.[226] Given their size and that the playing of music is often incidental to their services, these establishments are among those most likely simply to turn off the radio if pressed to pay licensing fees. The 1998 Amendment has only decreased the economic relevance of the exemption by reducing its scope to "dramatic" musical works. Therefore, in the US view, the homestyle exemption as contained in subparagraph (A) of Section 110(5) does not prejudice the legitimate interests of the right holder.

6.268 The European Communities responds that the vast body of case law on the pre-1998 homestyle exemption makes it clear that very significant economic interests were at stake. Already under the *Aiken* scenario,[227] a considerable number of US establishments were covered by the exemption. According to the European Communities,[228] the *Aiken* surface limitations were doubled by US Courts before the 1998 Amendment.[229]

6.269 We recall our discussion concerning the legislative history of the original homestyle exemption in connection with the first and second conditions of Article 13. In particular, as regards the beneficiaries of the exemption, the Conference Report (1976) elaborated on the rationale of the exemption by noting that the intent was to exempt a small commercial establishment "which was not of sufficient size to justify, as a practical matter, a subscription to a commercial background music serv-

---

[226] *See* Judiciary Committee Hearing, letter from Marilyn Bergman, ASCAP President and Chairman of the Board, pp. 175-186. *See* US first written submission, para. 34.

[227] According to the 1995 CRS study, 13.5 per cent, 16 per cent and 18 per cent of all US drinking, eating and retail establishments were covered by the exemption. *See* paras. 2.11 and 6.142 above.

[228] The European Communities initially raised its concerns that if the Courts might after the 1998 Amendment use in subparagraph (A), the surface categories set out in subparagraph (B), the coverage of subparagraph (A) is likely to be similar or even identical to the coverage of subparagraph (B) and that, in practical terms, this means that at least one half of all US service establishments are likely to be covered by the subparagraph (A) exemption. Given that the European Communities has not further substantiated this hypothetical about future jurisprudence, we abstain from addressing this argument any further.

[229] *See* EC first oral statement, para. 74. The European Communities also notes that, while it is irrelevant for the question of unreasonable prejudice to look at the degree of aggressiveness of licensing activities by CMOs, the US assertion that the establishments exempted under subparagraph (A) are least likely to be aggressively licensed by the CMOs is in contradiction with the US statement that the CMOs have used harassment and abusive tactics in the licensing practice.

ice".[230] We also recall the estimations on the percentages of establishments covered by the exemption.[231] Moreover, the exemption was applicable to such establishments only if they use homestyle equipment. The House Report (1976) noted that "[the clause] would impose liability where the proprietor has a commercial 'sound system' installed or converts a standard home receiving apparatus (by augmenting it with sophisticated or extensive amplification equipment) into the equivalent of a commercial sound system."[232] In this respect, we refer to our discussion on permissible equipment as well as the applicability of the exemption to Internet transmissions in connection with the first and second conditions of Article 13.

6.270 Furthermore, we recall the common understanding of the parties that the operation of the homestyle exemption as contained in the 1998 Amendment has been limited, as regards musical works, to the public communication of transmissions embodying dramatic renditions of "dramatic" musical works (such as operas, operettas, musicals and other similar dramatic works). We have not been presented with evidence suggesting that right holders would have licensed or attempted to license the public communication, within the meaning of Article 11(1)(ii) or 11*bis*(1)(iii) of the Berne Convention (1971), of broadcasts of performances embodying dramatic renditions of "dramatic" musical works either before the enactment of the original homestyle exemption or after the 1998 Amendment. We also fail to see how communications to the public of renditions of entire dramatic works could acquire such economic or practical importance that it could cause unreasonable prejudice to the legitimate interests of right holders.

6.271 We note that playing music by the small establishments covered by the exemption by means of homestyle apparatus has never been a significant source of revenue collection for CMOs. We recall our view[233] that, for the purposes of assessing unreasonable prejudice to the legitimate interests of right holders, potential losses of right holders, too, are relevant. However, we have not been presented with persuasive information suggesting that such potential effects of significant economic or practical importance could occur that they would give rise to an unreasonable level of prejudice to legitimate interests of right holders. In particular, as regards the exemption as amended in 1998 to exclude from its scope nondramatic musical works, the European Communities has not explicitly claimed that the exemption would currently cause any prejudice to right holders.

6.272 In the light of the considerations above, we conclude that the homestyle exemption contained in subparagraph (A) of Section 110(5) does not cause unreasonable prejudice to the legitimate interests of the right holders within the meaning of the third condition of Article 13.

---

[230] Conference Report of the House Committee on the Judiciary, Subcommittee on Courts and Intellectual Property, H.R. Rep. No. 94-1733, 94th Congress., 2nd Session 75 (1976), as reproduced in Exhibit US-2.

[231] *See* paras. 2.11 and 6.142 above.

[232] Report of the House Committee on the Judiciary, H.R. Rep. No. 94-1476, 94th Congress, 2nd Session 87 (1976), as reproduced in Exhibit US-1.

[233] *See* para. 6.185, footnotes 163-165 and para. 6.237 above.

VII. CONCLUSIONS AND RECOMMENDATIONS

7.1 In the light of the findings in paragraphs 6.92-6.95, 6.133, 6.159, 6.211, 6.219, 6.266 and 6.272 above, the Panel concludes that:

(a) Subparagraph (A) of Section 110(5) of the US Copyright Act meets the requirements of Article 13 of the TRIPS Agreement and is thus consistent with Articles 11*bis*(1)(iii) and 11(1)(ii) of the Berne Convention (1971) as incorporated into the TRIPS Agreement by Article 9.1 of that Agreement.

(b) Subparagraph (B) of Section 110(5) of the US Copyright Act does not meet the requirements of Article 13 of the TRIPS Agreement and is thus inconsistent with Articles 11*bis*(1)(iii) and 11(1)(ii) of the Berne Convention (1971) as incorporated into the TRIPS Agreement by Article 9.1 of that Agreement.

7.2 The Panel *recommends* that the Dispute Settlement Body request the United States to bring subparagraph (B) of Section 110(5) into conformity with its obligations under the TRIPS Agreement.

ANNEX I

(WT/DS160/5 of 16 April 1999)

UNITED STATES - SECTION 110(5) OF US COPYRIGHT ACT

Request for the Establishment of a Panel by the European Communities and their Member States

The following communication, dated 15 April 1999, from the Permanent Delegation of the European Commission to the Chairman of the Dispute Settlement Body, is circulated pursuant to Article 6.2 of the DSU.

My authorities have asked me to submit the following request on behalf of the European Communities and their Members States for consideration at the next meeting of the Dispute Settlement Body.

Section 110(5) of the United States Copyright Act, as amended by the "Fairness in Music Licensing Act" enacted on 27 October 1998, exempts, under certain conditions, the communication or transmission embodying a performance or display of a work by the public reception of the transmission on a single receiving apparatus of a kind commonly used in private homes (sub-paragraph A) and, also under certain conditions, communication by an establishment of a transmission or retransmission embodying a performance or display of a non dramatic musical work intended to be received by the general public (subparagraph B) from obtaining an authorisation to do so by the respective right holder. In practice this means that Section 110(5) of the US Copyright Act permits under certain circumstances, the playing of radio and television music in public places (such as bars, shops, restaurants etc.) without the payment of a royalty fee.

However, Article (9)1 of the WTO Agreement on Trade-Related Aspects of Intellectual Property Rights contained in Annex 1C to the Agreement Establishing the World Trade Organization (hereafter the "TRIPS Agreement") obliges WTO Members to comply with Articles 1 to 21 of the Berne Convention for the Protection of Literary and Artistic Works (hereafter the "Berne Convention").

Article 11*bis*(1) of the Berne Convention, as revised by the Paris Act of 1971 grants the authors of literary and artistic works, including musical works, the exclusive right of authorising not only the broadcasting and other wireless communication of their works, but also the public communication of a broadcast of their works by loudspeaker or any other analogous instrument. Article 11(1) of the same Convention grants the authors of musical works the exclusive right of authorising the public performance of their works, including such public performance by any means or process, and any communication to the public of the performance of their works.

As a consequence of the above, Section 110(5) of the United States Copyright Act appears to be inconsistent with the United States' obligations under the TRIPS Agreement, including, but not limited to, Article 9(1) of the TRIPS Agreement.

In a communication dated 26 January 1999 (WT/DS160/1-IP/D/16) the European Communities and their Member States requested consultations with the United States of America pursuant to Article 4 of the Understanding on Rules and Procedures Governing the Settlement of Disputes contained in Annex 2 of the WTO Agreement (hereafter "the DSU"). Such consultations, which were held on 2 March 1999 in Geneva, have allowed a better understanding of the respective positions, but have not led to a satisfactory resolution of the dispute.

Accordingly, the European Communities and their Member States request the establishment of a panel pursuant to Article 6 of the DSU and Article 64:1 of the TRIPS Agreement to examine the matter in the light of the relevant provisions of the TRIPS Agreement and to find that the United States of America fails to conform to the obligations contained in the TRIPS Agreement, including, but not limited to, Article 9(1) of the TRIPS Agreement, and thereby nullifies or impairs the benefits accruing directly or indirectly to the European Communities and their Member States under the TRIPS Agreement.

The European Communities and their Member States request that the panel be established with the standard terms of reference as provided for in Article 7 of the DSU.

ANNEX II

(WT/DS160/6 of 6 August 1999)

UNITED STATES - SECTION 110(5) OF THE US COPYRIGHT ACT

Constitution of the Panel Established at the Request of the European Communities

Note by the Secretariat

1. At its meeting on 26 May 1999, the DSB established a panel pursuant to the request by the European Communities (WT/DS160/5), in accordance with Article 6 of the DSU (WT/DSB/M/62).

2. At that meeting, the parties to the dispute agreed that the Panel should have standard terms of reference. The terms of reference are the following:

> "To examine, in light of the relevant provisions of the covered agreements cited by the European Communities in document WT/DS160/5, the matter referred to the DSB by the European Communities in that document and to make such findings as will assist the DSB in making the recommendations or in giving the rulings provided for in those agreements."

3. On 27 July 1999, the European Communities made a request, with reference to paragraph 7 of Article 8 of the DSU, to the Director-in-charge to determine of the composition of the Panel. Paragraph 7 of Article 8 provides:

> "If there is no agreement on the panelists within 20 days after the date of the establishment of a panel, at the request of either party, the Director-General, in consultation with the Chairman of the DSB and the Chairman of the relevant Council or Committee, shall determine the composition of the panel by appointing the panelists whom the Director-General considers most appropriate in accordance with any relevant special or additional rules or procedures of the covered agreement or covered agreements which are at issue in the dispute, after consulting with the parties to the dispute. The Chairman of the DSB shall inform the Members of the composition of the panel thus formed no later than 10 days after the date the Chairman receives such a request."

4. On 6 August 1999, the Director-in-charge composed the Panel as follows:

Chairperson:	Carmen Luz Guarda
Members:	Arumugamangalam V. Ganesan
	Ian F. Sheppard

5. Brazil, Australia, Canada, Japan and Switzerland reserved their rights as third parties to the dispute.

ATTACHMENT 1.1

FIRST WRITTEN SUBMISSION OF THE EUROPEAN COMMUNITIES AND THEIR MEMBER STATES

(5 October 1999)

TABLE OF CONTENTS

I. INTRODUCTION

1. The European Communities and their member States (hereinafter EC/MS) bring this complaint against the United States of America (US) because they consider that certain aspects of the US legislation relating to the protection of copyrighted works are incompatible with the US' obligations stemming from the WTO Agreement on Trade-Related Aspects of Intellectual Property Rights (TRIPS).

2. While Section 106 Copyright Act gives the right holder of a copyrighted work the exclusive right to reproduce the work, prepare derivative works, distribute copies of the work and to perform the copyrighted work publicly, Section 110(5) Copyright Act provides for two exemptions from copyright protection, which in simple terms can be summarised as follows:

- Under Subsection A, anybody is allowed to perform in his business premises for the enjoyment of customers under certain conditions, without the consent of the copyright holder, copyrighted works other than nondramatic compositions such as plays, operas or musicals from radio or television (TV) transmissions;
- Under Subsection B, anybody is allowed to perform in his business premises for the enjoyment of customers, "nondramatic music" by communicating radio or TV transmissions without the consent of the copyright owner in cases where a certain surface is not exceeded without any practical limitation or above that surface limit by respecting certain conditions as to the number of loudspeakers used.

3. In the view of the EC/MS these US measures are in violation of the US' obligations under the WTO-TRIPS Agreement. In particular, the US measures are incompatible with Article 9(1) TRIPS together with Articles 11(1) and 11*bis*(1) of the Berne Convention and cannot be justified under any express or implied exception or limitation permissible under the Berne Convention or under TRIPS. These measures cause prejudice to the legitimate rights of copyright owners, thus nullifying and impairing the rights of the EC/MS.

4. The EC/MS would also like to mention that several senior US government officials, which have testified before the US Congress during the legislative process which led to the present version of Section 110(5) Copyright Act, have expressed the view that the extension of the scope of this provision would violate the US' obligations under TRIPS and the Berne Convention.[1,2,3]

---

[1] The Register of Copyrights stated on 17 July 1997 in Congress (copy of the entire statement on international aspects attached - *Exhibit EC-11*) that: "*The Copyright Office believes that several of the expanded exemptions, if passed in their current form, would lead to claims by other countries that the United States was in violation of its obligations under the Berne Convention for the Protection of Literary and Artistic Works, incorporated into the Agreement on Trade-Related Aspects of Intellectual Property Rights ("TRIPS") of the Uruguay Round of GATT*".

[2] At the same occasions, the Assistant Secretary of Commerce and Commissioner of Patents and Trademarks stated that: "*Our trading partners are likely to allege that several of the changes to the copyright law proposed in Section 2 of the proposed bill may be inconsistent with our obligations under the Berne Convention and the Agreement on Trade-Related Aspects of Intellectual Property Rights ("the TRIPS Agreement") administered by the World Trade Organisation. If H.R. 789 is enacted, and we undermine the rights of copyright owners of musical works to perform their works*

5. The EC/MS' economic interests in this matter are significant. According to a study to which the EC/MS will refer to under Part IV, approximately 70% of all drinking and eating establishments and 45% of all retail establishments in the US can play without limitation radio or TV music without the consent of the copyright owner. This demonstrates clearly the potential of Section 110(5) Copyright Act to cause very significant losses of licensing income.

II. PROCEDURAL HISTORY

6. The so-called "homestyle exemption", which textually corresponds to the present subsection A of Section 110(5) Copyright Act, was already contained in the Copyright Act of 1976 which entered into force on 1 January 1978. Subsection B was added to the Copyright Act in October 1998 by the "Fairness in Music Licensing Act". The practical result of the latter amendment consists in a significant extension of the scope of the exemption from copyright protection as compared to the previous "homestyle" exemption.

7. The US notified their laws and regulations governing the protection of intellectual property rights (IPRs) to the TRIPS Council[4] on the basis of Article 63(2) TRIPS and the relevant guidelines[5] adopted by the TRIPS Council. At its meeting of July 1996, the US copyright legislation, together with the copyright legislation of other industrialised WTO Members, was subject to a review carried out in the TRIPS Council in which the EC/MS *inter alia* asked a number of questions to the US concerning copyright protection in the area of copyrighted works to which the US replied in writing.[6]

8. On the bilateral level the EC/MS raised their concerns by means of several diplomatic demarches at various levels, including the political level. Unfortunately, it proved impossible to make any progress to resolve the issues in this way.

9. By a communication dated 26 January 1999[7], the EC/MS requested consultations pursuant to Article 4 DSU and Article 64 TRIPS in conjunction with Article XXII GATT 1994.

10. By communications dated 11 and 12 February 1999 Australia[8] and Canada[9] expressed their desire to join the consultations pursuant to Article 4 (11) DSU. By a

in public, in particular at a restaurant or bar as envisioned by Section 2(a) and at the establishments covered by Section 2(c), we are seriously concerned that they will claim that we are in violation of our international commitments under both the Berne Convention and the TRIPS Agreement, the latter of which contains a similar right under Article 14(3)" (copy of the entire statement on international aspects attached - *Exhibit EC-12*).

3 For the sake of accuracy, it has to be mentioned that the statements referred to under point 4 have been made on the basis of an earlier proposal (H.R. 789 attached as *Exhibit EC-13*) which provided for slightly wider exception than the one contained in the present Section 110(5) Copyright Act.

4 WTO Doc. IP/N/1/USA/C/1 and 2.

5 WTO Doc. IP/C/M/7.

6 WTO Doc. IP/Q/USA/1.

7 WTO Doc. WT/DS/160/1.

8 WTO Doc. WT/DS/160/4.

9 WTO Doc. WT/DS/160/2.

communication dated 15 February 1999, Switzerland[10] did likewise. All three requests were accepted by the US.[11]

11. Consultations between the EC/MS and the US were held in Geneva on 2 March 1999. Canada participated in these consultations. Prior to the consultations, the EC/MS submitted to the US a number of written questions, to most of which the US replied orally. These consultations did not, however, lead to a satisfactory resolution of the matter.

12. By a communication dated 15 April 1999[12], the EC/MS requested the establishment of a Panel pursuant to Article 64(1) TRIPS and Articles 4(7) and 6(1) DSU. The US refused the establishment of a Panel at the meeting of the DSB on 28 April 1999. At the DSB meeting held on 26 May 1999, the Panel was established.

13. The terms of reference of the Panel are the following:

> "To examine in light of the relevant provisions of the covered agreements cited by the European Communities in document WT/DS 160/5 the matter referred to the DSB by the EC/MS in that document and to make such findings as will assist the DSB in making the recommendations or in giving the rulings provided for in those agreements."[13]

14. Five WTO Members have notified under Article 10(2) DSU their interest in the matter before the panel. These third parties are Australia, Brazil, Canada, Japan and Switzerland.[14]

III. PROTECTION OF COPYRIGHTED WORKS AND THE EXCEPTIONS THERETO UNDER THE US COPYRIGHT ACT

1. Historical Background: Section 110(5) Copyright Act before the 1998 AMENdment ("the Homestyle Exemption")

15. Under Section 106 Copyright Act (1976), the right holder of a work has the exclusive right to reproduce the work, prepare derivative works and distribute copies of the work. Under Section 106(4) of said Act, the owner of copyright has also the exclusive right *"to perform the copyrighted work publicly"*.

16. In order fully to understand the exemptions contained in the present version of Section 110(5), it is essential to consider its previous version. Prior to 1999, Section 110(5) only consisted of the current Subsection A (minus the words "*except as provided in subparagraph (B)*"). Subsection B was added to the statute in October 1998 by the "Fairness in Music Licensing Act". The 1976 version of Section 110(5) was generally referred to as "the homestyle exemption". It reads as follows:

> *"Notwithstanding the provisions of Section 106, the following are not infringements of copyright:*

---

[10] WTO Doc. WT/DS/160/3.

[11] Note from the Permanent Mission of the United States to the WTO dated 31 March 1999.

[12] WTO Doc. WT/DS/160/5.

[13] WTO Doc. WT/DS/160/6.

[14] WTO Doc. WT/DS/160/6.

(5) communication or transmission embodying a performance or display of a work by the public reception of the transmission on a single receiving apparatus of a kind commonly used in private homes, unless:

(a) a direct charge is made to see or hear the transmission, or

(b) the transmission thus received is further retransmitted to the public."

17. In broad terms, the homestyle exemption covered the use of a "homestyle" radio or TV in a shop, a bar, a restaurant or any other place frequented by the public. The exemption did *not* apply to venues playing tapes, CD's or other mechanical music.

18. The *ratio legis* of the homestyle exemption goes back to the 1975 US Supreme Court case *Twentieth Century Music Corp. v. Aiken..*[15] Mr Aiken was the owner of a small fast-food restaurant who operated a radio with outlets to four speakers in the ceiling. This installation received the transmission of various radio stations which included protected musical works. At that time it was believed that the 1931 *Jewell-Lasalle* Supreme Court ruling[16] meant that a business establishment had to obtain a licence to pick up a broadcast and in order to legally communicate it to the public. However, Mr Aiken had no licence from the right holders of the copyrighted works that were broadcast through the radio on his premises. The Supreme Court exempted Aiken from liability under the 1909 Copyright Act (which is the predecessor of the 1976 Act), as, according to the Court, what he was doing could not be considered as *"performing"* within the meaning of said Act.[17]

19. However, in the Copyright Act (1976), the new definition of *"perform"* clearly covered what Mr Aiken had been doing. In order to keep the "Aiken" activities permissible without the consent of the right holder, a specific provision has been inserted into the Copyright Act to provide users with an exemption from copyright liability.

20. In order to qualify for the exemption, the transmission must be received on *"a single receiving apparatus of a kind commonly used in private homes"*. The benefit of the exemption is lost if a direct charge is made to see or hear the transmission or if the transmission is retransmitted to the public.

21. An important question arises as to what is to be considered *"a single receiving apparatus of a kind commonly used in private homes"*. Technology is under constant evolution and the "household radio" technology of the 70's has been superseded several times, having as a practical effect that the scope of the homestyle exemption has continuously been extended.

---

15 Twentieth Century Music Corp. v. Aiken, 422 U.S. 151 (1975) (*Exhibit EC-1*).

16 Buck v. Jewell-Lasalle Realty Co. 283 U.S. 191 (1931).

17 Under Section 101 US Copyright Act to *perform* a work means *"to recite, render, play, dance or act it, either directly or by means of any device or process"*, while to *transmit* a performance or *display* it is *"to communicate it by any device or process whereby images or sounds are received beyond the place from which they are sent"*.

22. Although it is clear that, in practice, the homestyle exemption has applied in the past and continues to apply at present primarily to radio and TV broadcasts, and satellite and cable TV, the wording of Section 110(5) Copyright Act (1976) appears in view of the EC/MS to be also applicable to a wider range of transmissions, including computer networks and the internet.[18]

23. The scope of Section 110(5) (in its "homestyle" version) has evolved over the years. At the time of the adoption of the Copyright Act (1976), the intention of the US Congress appeared to be that the scope of the exemption should be narrow and apply only to small commercial establishments "where mom is behind the counter and dad does the cashier".[19] However, the Congressional intent was rather ambiguous, as indicated by the following passage: that *"(i)t applies to performances and displays of all types of works, and its purpose is to exempt from copyright liability anyone who merely turns on, in a public place, an ordinary radio or TV (...)".*[20]

24. According to the statements by the US authorities made in connection with this case, US Courts have also interpreted this provision narrowly: if the receiving equipment and loudspeakers were too sophisticated and powerful, the exemption would not apply.[21] In fact, when looking closely at the vast litigation on Section 110(5) Copyright Act (1976), one does not come to the same conclusion. In these 20 years of litigation, two periods can be distinguished.

25. Until the early 90's, the main elements that Courts took into consideration in this respect were:[22]

- the physical size of the establishment (in terms of square footage, e.g. by comparing with the size of Aiken's[23] restaurant);
- the economic significance of the establishment;
- the number of speakers;
- whether the speakers were free standing or built into the ceiling;
- whether, depending on its revenue, the establishment was of a type that would normally subscribe to a background music service;
- the noise level of the areas within the establishment where the transmissions were made audible;

---

18 We will come back to this issue when discussing Article 110(5)(B) Copyright Act below.

19 Compare also reply by the US administration to questions by Canada and the EC/MS within the TRIPS Council, 30 October 1996, WTO Doc. IP/Q/USA/1 at p. 12 with a reference to H.R. Rep. N°1476, 94th Congress, 2nd Session 87 (1976) (*Exhibit EC-2*) *"The basic rationale of this clause is that the secondary use of the transmission by turning on an ordinary receiver in public is so remote and minimal that no further liability should be imposed. (...). [T]he Committee considers [the particular fact situation of Aiken] to represent the outer limit of the exemption, and believes that the line should be drawn at this point. Thus the clause would exempt small commercial establishments whose proprietors merely bring onto their premises standard radio or TV equipment and turn it on for their customers' enjoyment, but it would impose liability where the proprietor has a commercial sound system installed or converts a standard home receiving apparatus (...) into the equivalent of a commercial sound system".*

20 See H.R. Rep. N° 1476, 94th Congress, 2nd Session 86 (1976) (*Exhibit EC-3*).

21 Reply by the US authorities to questions by Canada and the EU within the TRIPS Council, 30 October 1996, WTO Doc. IP/Q/USA/1 at p. 12.

22 A non-exhaustive list of relevant Court cases applying the Section 110(5) exemption is attached as *Exhibit EC-4*.

23 See under footnote 15 above.

- the extent to which the receiving apparatus was to be considered as one commonly used in private homes; and
- the configuration of the installation.

As a result of the ambiguous statutory language of Section 110(5) Copyright Act (1976), the selective use of these criteria during a decade of litigation has given rise to a certain degree of inconsistency of the case law.[24]

26. In recent years, rather than to look at the legislative history of Section 110(5) Copyright Act (1976) and the intention of the legislator, Courts started to focus more on the plain text of the homestyle exemption, resulting in a broader interpretation of the exemption. As a result of this, large chain store corporations were found to be exempt from applying for a licence and paying a licence fee. *Edison*[25] and *Claire's Boutiques*[26] are illustrative decisions which were taken by two different Federal Appeal Courts one month from each other.

27. The core question in both cases was whether in the case of a large nationwide company, with annual revenues of several hundred million dollars and with a large number of outlets, each outlet using a single receiver of a kind commonly used in private homes, Section 110(5) Copyright Act (1976) was still applicable.[27] In both cases the Courts' answers were in the affirmative. According to the Courts, the only relevant factors in assessing the applicability of the exemption are the quantity and the quality of the receiving apparatus used in a particular premise. The physical size of the establishment qualifying for the exemption, the ownership and/or the corporate structure of the establishment or any other factor considered in previous case law were declared irrelevant with regard to the application of the homestyle exemption.

---

[24] It appears from the analysis of US case law on the homestyle exemption that, although surface was not the only criterion used for the application, no Court has ever favourably applied it to an eating or drinking establishment with more than 1500 square feet of total space (the Aiken restaurant was 1,055 square feet). In the same vein, the homestyle exemption does not appear to have been applied by Courts to establishments using more than 4 speakers.

[25] BMI v. Edison Bros. Stores Inc., US Court of Appeals for the Eight Circuit, N° 91-2115, January 13, (*Exhibit EC-5*). In the early 80's, Edison Brothers, an important chain retail store, reached an understanding with a major US collecting society (BMI) on a "radio policy" designed to exempt its more than 1500 stores from copyright liability. The terms of the arrangement were as follows: (a) only two speakers may be attached to a radio receiver, (b) the speakers must be placed within 15 feet of the receiver, (c) speakers that are built into walls must not be used, only portable speakers are allowed, (d) only the radio may be played, no tapes or records. In order to comply with this policy, Edison Brothers made a considerable investment. In 1988, BMI adopted a new policy concluding that the exemption of Section 110(5) could never apply to chain stores, no matter what kind of equipment was used. However, Edison Brothers successfully challenged this interpretation before Court. This has led an important number of large chain stores to adapt their music installation in order to benefit from the exemption. Some of these chains even cancelled their subscription to background music from other sources than radio.

[26] BMI v. Claire's Boutiques Inc., US Court of Appeals for the Seventh Circuit, N° 91-1232, December 11, 1991 (*Exhibit EC-6*). This case also opposed right holders and a chain store corporation, the factual and legal situation was similar to the Edison case.

[27] Both in Edison and Claire's Boutiques, each store was fully owned and centrally managed by Edison Inc. and Claire's Boutique Inc. No franchising system was applied. The Claire's Boutique Stores had an individual surface between 861 and 2,000 square feet. Edison stores had an individual surface per outlet between 800 and 1,200 square feet.

28. In the early nineties, a coalition of business associations started active lobbying of Congress members in order to secure both a clarification of Section 110(5) and a widening of its scope. The coalition's efforts rapidly bore fruit. As from 1995 several bills were introduced in the US House of Representatives and in the US Senate aimed at significantly extending the scope of the homestyle exemption.
29. On 6 and 7 October 1998, a bill, entitled Fairness in Music Licensing Act , was adopted by, respectively, the US House of Representatives and the US Senate. The bill consisted of adding a new Subsection B to Section 110(5) of the US Copyright Act, while the wording of the homestyle exemption remains unchanged under Subsection A. It was signed by the President on 27 October 1998, and entered into force on 26 January 1999.

2. *Current Scope and Application of Section 110(5) of the US Copyright Act*

30. Section 110(5) now contains two distinct exemptions: the so-called "homestyle exemption" under Subsection A modified as to the kind of works covered and a new exemption under Subsection B (sometimes referred to as the "business exemption").

(a) Subsection A

31. The exact meaning and scope of the "homestyle" exemption, now under Subsection A of Section 110(5), after the adding of Subsection B to the statute, and preceded by the expression *"except as provided for in subparagraph (B)"*, appears to be as follows.

While Section 110(5) Copyright Act applied to all kinds of copyrighted works before the 1998 amendment, apparently, Section 110(5)(A) Copyright Act is now intended to exclude from its scope "nondramatic musical works" and continues to apply to all other types of works, including e.g. plays, sketches, operas, operettas, musicals, because Section 110(5)(A) Copyright Act refers to "works" in general, while the scope of Subsection B is expressly limited to "nondramatic musical works".
32. What has been said on Section 110(5) Copyright Act (1976) above continues to apply to subsection A of the current Section 110(5) Copyright Act with the proviso that the scope of this provision has apparently been limited by excluding nondramatic musical works which are now dealt with in Section 110(5)(B) Copyright Act. However, given that the limitations on the size of the establishment have been greatly relaxed in subsection B, it is doubtful whether Courts will uphold the limit on the size of the establishment, which they have set in the case law on Section 110(5) Copyright Act (1976).[28]

(b) Subsection B

33. Subsection B of Section 110(5) Copyright Act reads as follows:

[28] Compare footnote 22.

"Notwithstanding the provisions of Section 106, the following are not infringements of copyright:

(B) communication by an establishment of a transmission or retransmission embodying a performance or display of a nondramatic musical work intended to be received by the general public, originated by a radio or TV broadcast station licensed as such by the Federal Communications Commission, or, if an audiovisual transmission, by a cable system or satellite carrier, if -

(i) in the case of an establishment other than a food service or drinking establishment, either the establishment in which the communication occurs had less than 2,000 gross square feet of space (excluding space used for customer parking and for no other purpose), or the establishment in which the communication occurs has 2,000 or more gross square feet of space (excluding space used for customer parking and for no other purpose) and -

(I) if the performance is by audio means only, the performance is communicated by means of a total of not more than 6 loudspeakers of which not more than 4 loudspeakers are located in any 1 room or adjoining outdoor space; or

(II) if the performance or display is by audiovisual means, any visual portion of the performance or display is communicated by means of a total of not more than 4 audiovisual devices, of which not more than 1 audiovisual device is located in any 1 room, and no such audiovisual device has a diagonal screen size greater than 55 inches, and any audio portion of the performance or display is communicated by means of a total of not more than 6 loudspeakers, of which not more than 4 loudspeakers are located in any 1 room or adjoining outdoor space;

(ii) in the case of a food service or drinking establishment in which the communication occurs has less than 3,750 gross square feet of space (excluding space used for customer parking and for no other purpose), or the establishment in which the communication occurs has 3,750 gross square feet of space or more (excluding space used for customer parking and for no other purpose) and

(I) if the performance is by audio means only, the performance is communicated by means of a total of not more than 6 loudspeakers of which not more than 4 loudspeakers are located in any 1 room or adjoining outdoor space; or

(II) if the performance or display is by audiovisual means, any visual portion of the performance or display is communicated by means of a total of not more than 4 audiovisual devices, of which not more than one audiovisual device is located in any 1 room, and no such audiovisual device has a

diagonal screen size greater than 55 inches, and any audio portion of the performance or display is communicated by means of a total of not more than 6 loudspeakers, of which not more than 4 loudspeakers are located in any 1 room or adjoining outdoor space ;

(iii) no direct charge is made to see or hear the transmission or retransmission;

(iv) the transmission or retransmission is not further transmitted beyond the establishment where it is received; and

(v) the transmission or retransmission is licensed by the copyright owner of the work so publicly performed or displayed."

(ba) Exempted Uses

34. The exemption contained in Section 110(5)(B) Copyright Act covers transmissions or retransmissions embodying a performance[29] or display[30] of a nondramatic musical work intended to be received by the general public, originated from a radio or TV broadcast station licensed as such by the Federal Communications Commission. This basically covers a situation which appears similar to the one covered by the homestyle exemption, *i.e.* establishments which are open to the public may play radio or TV on their premises for the enjoyment of their customers without the consent of the right owners.

35. A last difference is that Subsection B does not apply to "works" in general but only to "nondramatic musical works", *i.e.* songs, and not to operas, operettas, musicals.

36. While the former "homestyle exemption" and the present Subsection A limit the exemption to the use of a single receiving apparatus commonly used in private homes, this condition is completely absent in Subsection B for cases where the establishment does not exceed a certain size. For all larger establishments the "homestyle" requirement has been replaced by much less stringent conditions in relation to the audio or TV equipment which can be used.

37. Moreover, *retransmissions* which were not expressly exempted under Section 110(5) Copyright Act (1976) are now expressly exempted. Under the US Copyright Act, to "transmit" a program means "to communicate it by any device or process whereby images or sounds are received beyond the place where they are sent".[31] Consequently, to "retransmit" a program means to further transmit a transmission, as is for example the case with cable TV operators, who receive TV signals and retransmit them to their subscribers, or with satellites, which receive the earth-to-satellite signals and retransmit them to the earth.

---

[29] Under Section 101 Copyright Act to perform a work means to recite, render, play, dance or act, either directly or by means of any device or process.

[30] Under Section 110 Copyright Act to display a work means to show a copy of it either directly or indirectly by means of any device.

[31] Section 101 Copyright Act.

38. Most TV programmes in the US are transmitted either by over-the-air broadcast or by cable or satellite. Therefore, the express inclusion of this transmission mode makes TV programmes fully subject to the exceptions in all forms of transmission.

39. It is presumed that Section 110(5)(B) Copyright Act applies in a case of public communication of musical works involving new technologies such as computer networks (e.g. Internet) in view of the wording of this provision. This transmission mode, the importance of which increases from day to day, is now subject to the exemption from copyright protection.[32]

(bb) Exempted Users

40. For the application of the exemption to *the establishments other than food service or drinking establishments*, the following conditions apply:

- if the establishment has less than 2,000 gross square feet (= 186 square meters), the exemption applies *without any further condition*, i.e. any audio equipment also of a professional character and any number of loudspeakers can be used;
- if the establishment has more than 2,000 gross square feet of space, the exemption applies under the following conditions:
    - if the performance is by audio means only, it may be communicated by means of a maximum of 6 loudspeakers, of which not more than 4 may be located in any one room;
    - if the performance or display is by audiovisual means:
        - any visual portion of the performance may be communicated by a maximum of 4 audiovisual devices, of which not more than one may be located in any one room. Moreover such devices should not have a diagonal screen size larger than 55 inches;
        - any audio portion of the performance may be communicated by a maximum of 6 loudspeakers, of which not more than 4 may be located in any one room.

41. For *food service or drinking establishments*[33], the following even more generous conditions apply:

- if the establishment has less than 3,750 gross square feet (= 348 square meters) of space (excluding parking space) *the exemption applies without condi-*

---

[32] The following example is mentioned as an illustration of a situation in which this becomes relevant: an FCC-licensed radio (or TV) broadcaster parallels its over-the-air transmissions on the internet (as an audio back-up to his web-site). These programmes are received by a PC connected with a number of loudspeakers in a bar or other establishment meeting all the conditions set out in Section 110(5)(B) Copyright Act.

[33] Which are defined in Section 101 Copyright Act amended by Section 205 of the Fairness in Music Licensing Act as: "*restaurant, inn, bar, tavern or any other similar place of business in which the public or patrons assemble for the primary purpose of being served food or drink, in which the majority of the gross square feet of space that is non-residential is used for that purpose, and in which nondramatic musical works are performed publicly*".

tions, i.e. any kind of audio(-visual) equipment, including professional equipment and any number of loudspeakers may be used;

- if the establishment has more than 3,750 gross square feet of space, the exemption applies under the following conditions:
  - if the performance is by audio means only, it may be communicated by means of a maximum of 6 loudspeakers, of which not more than 4 may be located in any one room;
  - if the performance or display is by audiovisual means:
    - any visual portion of the performance may be communicated by a maximum of 4 audiovisual devices, of which not more than one may be located in any one room. Moreover such devices should not have a diagonal screen size larger than 55 inches;
    - any audio portion of the performance may be communicated by a maximum of 6 loudspeakers, of which not more than 4 may be located in any one room.

42. The exemption applies to "*establishments*" which are now defined by Section 101 of the US Copyright Act (upon amendment by Section 205 of the Fairness in Music Licensing Act) as "*a store, shop or any similar place of business open to the general public for the primary purpose of selling goods or services in which the majority of the gross square feet of space that is non-residential is used for that purpose and in which nondramatic musical works are performed publicly*". This definition also reconfirms the findings of the two Circuit Courts referred to above[34] in relation to Section 110(5) Copyright Act (1976) that in order to meet the copyright exception each individual store, shop or place of business has to be looked at individually, it being irrelevant if a company operates several thousand such places of business all over the US.

(bc) General Conditions

43. *No direct charge must be made to the public to see or hear the transmission or retransmission.* This condition also applies to the homestyle exemption. However, this condition has no potential whatsoever to limit the exception, because the operator of the establishment remains completely free to amortise the acquisition and operating costs of the audio(-visual) equipment by charging his customers for the goods and services sold accordingly.

44. *The transmission or retransmission may not be further transmitted beyond the establishment where it is received.* Further transmission or retransmission would of course imply that a new audience is reached, and would thus be a further communication to the public. Thus also this condition has in practice no potential to limit the exception in any meaningful manner.

45. *The transmission or retransmission must be licensed by the copyright owner of the work performed.* This means that the original broadcaster must be properly licensed by the right holder. Given that virtually all radio or TV stations in the Unites

---

[34] Compare footnotes 25 and 26.

States are licensed by performing rights organisations, this condition is also unlikely to have any practical effect to limit the scope of the exemption.

(c) Summary

46. The exemptions from copyright protection contained in Article 110(5) Copyright Act can be summarised as follows:

As far as copyrighted works excluding nondramatic musical works are concerned, anybody in the US can play such works from radio or TV on his business premises for the enjoyment of his customers without the consent of the copyright owner. The only condition in the law which has the potential to somewhat reduce the benefit of the exception from applying to all business premises in the US, consists in requiring that a single apparatus of a kind commonly found in private homes be used, without defining in the law what is meant by this. The other conditions are unlikely to have any limiting effect in practice.

47. *As to nondramatic musical works*, anybody can play such works originating from radio or TV in his establishment for the enjoyment of his customers without the consent of the copyright holder. In case the establishment being below a certain size (3,750 square feet for restaurants and bars and 2,000 square feet for all other establishments), no further conditions apply with a potential to limit the number of exempted establishments. In case the premises exceed these size limits, there exist some rather generous limitations in relation mainly to the number of loudspeakers which can be used. In any event, the use of professional equipment is perfectly permissible.

IV. QUANTITATIVE EFFECTS ON COPYRIGHT OWNERS

48. In order to illustrate the scope of the exception, as far as the establishments referred to under Section 110(5)(B) Copyright Act are concerned, *and on which no limitations as to the audio(-visual) equipment used exist*, the following figures are instructive.

49. On the basis of a 1998 Dun & Bradstreet's "Dun's Market Identifiers Market Profile"[35,36], which is a data base containing information, *inter alia* on square footage, of more than 6,5 million US businesses, the following can be said:

In 1998, the following number of establishments were contained in the D&B database (this was also the approach by the CRS in 1995), while the total figures as estimated by D&B are given in brackets:

- 7,819 (49,061) drinking establishments of a square footage below 3,750 square feet (= 73 % (85 %) of all US drinking establishments filed in the D&B database);

[35] Further explanations and the data provided by Dun & Bradstreet are contained in Dun's Market Identifiers Market Profiles (*Exhibit EC-7*).

[36] The 1995 figures of this data base were used by the US Congress Research Service to establish in 1996 the number of establishments in certain size categories to be covered by the new law.

- 51,385 (192,692) eating establishments of a square footage below 3,750 square feet (= 70 % (68 %)of all US eating establishments filed in the D&B database);
- 65,589 (281,406) retail establishments of a square footage below 2,000 square feet (=45 % (42 %) of all US retail establishments filed in the D&B database).

50. These figures comprise bars, restaurants, tea-rooms, snackbars, etc. and retail stores. However, other sectors in which a number of establishments are likely to be exempted as well were not taken into account (for example: hotels, financial service outlets, estate property brokers, other types of service providers).

51. To put the results of these data otherwise approximately 70% of all drinking and eating establishments in the US and 45% of all retail establishments in the US are entitled under Section 110(5) Copyright Act, without any limitation, to play music from the radio and TV on their business premises for the enjoyment of their customers without the consent of the copyright owners thus depriving the latter of a significant source of licensing income.

52. All other - larger - establishments are of course benefiting from the exception under Section 110(5)(B) Copyright Act, if they meet the very lenient conditions as to the number of permissible loudspeakers.

V. INCOMPATIBILITY OF THE US LEGISLATION WITH ITS OBLIGATIONS UNDER THE WTO AGREEMENT ON TRADE-RELATED ASPECTS OF INTELLECTUAL PROPERTY RIGHTS

1. Short Negotiating History of the TRIPS Agreement[37]

53. At the Ministerial Conference which launched the Uruguay Round of Multilateral Trade Negotiations at Punta del Este, Uruguay in September 1986, TRIPS was included into the negotiation agenda as one of the so-called new topics. Multilateral rulemaking in the IPR area had been so far dominated by the World Intellectual Property Organisation (WIPO) which administers or co-administers practically all important conventions in this area. There existed at the outset different views between industrialised countries, who wished to achieve a comprehensive coverage of all intellectual property rights and developing countries (LDCs) who wanted to limit work to a Code against trade in counterfeit goods.

54. During the negotiating process the view of those who pursued a comprehensive approach prevailed. This had as a consequence that practically all existing IPRs were included in TRIPS. To start with the principles of national treatment and most favoured nation treatment (the latter being a novelty in the area of IPRs) were stipulated. The most important WIPO conventions (the Paris Convention covering industrial property rights and the Berne Convention covering copyright as well as the Washington Treaty for the protection of semiconductor topographies) were included by reference, also to make these conventions subject to an efficient dispute settlement system. Furthermore extensive rules for the enforcement of the substantive IPR

---

[37] For a detailed report of the negotiating history of TRIPS see Gervais, The TRIPS Agreement: Drafting History and Analysis, London 1998, pp 3-28.

standards were provided, which constituted an absolute novelty for international IPR rulemaking.

55. The so-called Dunkel text on TRIPS of December 1991 became almost verbatim part of the Final Act adopted at the Marrakech Ministerial Conference in April 1994 which successfully concluded the Uruguay Round Negotiations. The provisions of TRIPS became fully applicable to non-developing country Members of the WTO from 1 January 1996 (Article 65(1) TRIPS).

2. *Copyright Protection under TRIPS*

56. The substantive provisions for the protection of copyright (including related rights) are contained in Section 1 of Part II, i.e. Articles 9-14 of the TRIPS Agreement. Article 9 stipulates the principle that WTO Members have to comply with the substantive provisions of the Berne Convention (its Articles 1 to 21) and reiterates the basic principle of copyright protection, i.e. protection extends only to expressions and not to ideas, methods of operation or mathematical concepts.

57. Article 12 of the Agreement provides minimum standards for the term of protection of copyrighted works. The term of protection for many works is the life of the author plus 50 years.

58. Article 9(2) of the Berne Convention bans the imposition of limitations on, or exceptions to, the reproduction right except in special cases when such limits or exceptions do not conflict with a normal exploitation of the work and do not unreasonably prejudice the legitimate interests of the right holder. Article 13 TRIPS, which has also to be read together with Article 20 Berne Convention, makes this provision also applicable to all other exclusive rights in copyright and related rights, thus narrowly circumscribing the limitations and exceptions that WTO member countries may impose.

3. *Section 110(5) Copyright Act in the light of Article 9(1) TRIPS together with Article 11bis (1) and 11(1) Berne Convention*

59. For ease of presentation, both Subsections of Section 110(5) Copyright Act will be dealt with together for the legal analysis.

(a) Article 9(1) TRIPS

60. This provision reads:

> *"Members shall comply with Articles 1 through 21 of the Berne Convention and the Appendix thereto..."*

This provision has as a consequence that the obligations contained in Articles 1 through 21 of the Berne Convention have become part of the obligations under TRIPS and are fully subject to the WTO dispute settlement system[38,39]

---

[38] Compare Gervais, The TRIPS Agreement, Drafting History and Analysis, 1998, at p. 72.

[39] See also Message from the President of the Unites States transmitting the Uruguay Round Trade Agreements, texts of Agreements Implementing Bill, Statement of Administrative Action and Required Supporting Statements, 103[d] Congress, 2[d] Session, House Document 103-316, Vol. 1, p. 981, September 1994 (*Exhibit EC-8*).

(b) Article 11*bis* (1) Berne Convention

61. The provision which is of particular relevance for the case at hand is Article 11*bis*(1) Berne Convention which reads:

> *"(1) Authors of literary and artistic works shall enjoy the exclusive right of authorising:*
>
> *(i) the broadcasting of their works or the communication thereof to the public by any other means of wireless diffusion of signs, sounds or images;*
>
> *(ii) any communication to the public by wire or by rebroadcasting of the broadcast of the work, when this communication is made by an organization other that the original one;*
>
> *(iii) the public communication by loudspeaker or any analogous instrument transmitting, by signs, sounds or images, the broadcast of the work."*

62. Article 11*bis* was introduced into the Berne Convention at the occasion of the Rome Revision (1928), and further elaborated by the Brussels Revision (1948) in a period where public communication by loudspeakers, radio etc. had become a very important means of communication. Such a means of communication was clearly similar to the public performance of a work, except that it increased the potential audience.

63. Each of the uses described in Article 11*bis*(1)(i) to (iii) Berne Convention is to be considered as a separate use, which requires a separate authorisation for each such use by the owner of the copyright.[40] It is Article 11*bis*(1)(iii) Berne Convention which is the relevant provision for the case of hand.

64. There can be no doubt that communications to the public not only emanating from radio broadcasts but also from TV are covered by Article 11*bis* Berne Convention.[41] There can also be no doubt that under Article 2 Berne Convention[42] that *musi-*

---

[40] The underlying reasoning for this is explained in WIPO, Guide to the Berne Convention, 1978, at pp 68-69: *"The question is whether the licence given by the author to the broadcasting station covers, in addition, all the use made of the broadcast, which may or may not be for commercial ends.*

11bis.12. The Convention's answer is " no ". Just as, in the case of a relay of a broadcast by wire, an additional audience is created (para. (1)(ii)), so, in this case too, the work is made perceptible to listeners (and perhaps viewers) other than those contemplated by the author when his permission was given. Although, by definition, the number of people receiving a broadcast cannot be ascertained with any certainty, the author thinking his license to broadcast as covering only the direct audience receiving the signal within the family circle. Once this reception is done in order to entertain a wider circle, often for profit, an additional section of the public is enabled to enjoy the work and it ceases to be merely a matter of broadcasting. The author is given control over this new public performance of his work.

11bis.13. Music has already been used as an example, but the right clearly covers all other works as well-plays, operettas, lectures and other oral works. Nor is it confined to entertainment; instruction is no less important. What matters is whether the work which has been broadcast is then publicly communicated by loudspeaker or by some analogous instrument e.g., a television screen.

11bis.14. Note that the three parts of this right are not mutually exclusive but cumulative, and come into play in all the cases foreseen by the Convention."

[41] Compare OMPI / WIPO, Guide to the Berne Convention, 1978, p. 66 (*Exhibit EC-9*).

cal works, dramatic, dramatic-musical or other musical works qualify *as literary and artistic works*. Thus it can be concluded that the works for which Section 110(5) Copyright Act (in both alternatives) denies protection, are protected works under Articles 11*bis* and 2 Berne Convention.

65. While the term *public communication*[43] has not been defined in the Berne Convention, the Programme for the Brussels Revision[44] provides some guidance as to what is meant by public communication:

> *"...above all where people meet in the cinema, in restaurants, in tea rooms..."*

66. While Subsection A of Section 110(5) Copyright Act refers expressly to *"...performance or display of a work by the public reception..."*, also the communication of a musical work in an establishment to its customers as described in Subsection B of Section 110(5) Copyright Act constitutes a public communication in the sense of Article 11*bis*(1) Berne Convention.[45]

67. Under Article 11*bis*(1) Berne Convention, the public communication has to be "by loudspeaker or any other analogous instrument". In this context, it is irrelevant whether the loudspeakers are incorporated in the radio or TV set or other apparatus (including for example a computer) or if they are separate. It is obvious that the communication to the public envisaged in Section 110(5) Copyright Act covers the case that the musical works are played over loudspeakers to the customers of the businesses. In any event, music transmitted over radio or TV can only be made audible by means of some sort of loudspeaker.

68. By denying copyright protection to musical works (in Subsection A to copyrighted works other than nondramatic musical works) when they are received via radio or TV by hertzian waves and subsequently played on business premises for the enjoyment of customers, the US is not granting the protection which it is obliged to grant under Article 9(1) TRIPS together with Article 11*bis*(1)(iii) Berne Convention.

(c) Article 11(1) Berne Convention

69. This provision reads:

> *"(1) Authors of <u>dramatic, dramatico-musical and musical works</u> shall enjoy the exclusive right of authorizing :*
>
> *(i) ...*
>
> *(ii) any communication to the public of the performance of their works."*

---

42 Compare OMPI / WIPO, Guide to the Berne Convention, 1978, p. 14 (*Exhibit EC-10*).

43 The term "communication to the public" is synonymous.

44 Comments in Programme for the Brussels Conference: Documents 1948, at pp 266 et seq.

45 Both acts are also clearly covered by the definition given by US domestic law under Section 101 Copyright Act, which defines public performance or display of a work as: *"(...)To perform or display a work publicly means: (1) to perform or display at a place open to the public or at any place where a substantial number of persons outside of a normal circle of family and its social acquaintances is gathered; or (2) to transmit or otherwise communicate a performance or display the work to a place specified by clause (1) or to the public by means of any device or process, whether the members of the public capable of receiving the performance or display receive it in the same place or in separate places and at the same time or at different times(...)."*.

70. While Article 11*bis*(1)(iii) Berne Convention necessitates that the musical work has been transmitted by hertzian waves at some point during its way to the reception apparatus, Article 11(1)(ii) Berne Convention covers the case when the entire transmission was by wire.[46]

71. The considerations put forward above under Article 11*bis* Berne Convention as to *works* and *communication to the public* apply *mutatis mutandis* to Article 11(1) Berne Convention.

72. It can, therefore, be said that the playing of music or other copyrighted works from radio and TV on the business premises for the enjoyment of customers as described in Section 110(5) Copyright Act constitutes acts which are protected by Article 11(1)(ii) Berne Convention if the entire radio or TV transmission is by wire. By denying such protection, the US is violating its obligations under Article 9(1) TRIPS together with Article 11(1)(ii) Berne Convention.

4. *Permissible Exceptions to Copyright Protection*

73. While the US have at some point in time disputed that a "homestyle radio" is a "loudspeaker or other analogous instrument" in the sense of Article 11*bis*(1)(iii) Berne Convention, they have subsequently exclusively relied on assertions that Section 110(5) Copyright Act would be permissible under exception clauses contained in the Berne Convention and TRIPS. The US have in particular referred to so-called "minor exceptions" under the Berne Convention, to Articles 9(2) and 11*bis*(2) Berne Convention and Article 13 TRIPS.

74. The EC/MS would like to observe that the burden to invoke and prove the applicability of an exception fall on the party invoking the exception. This standard is in accord with the Appellate Body reports in United States - Standards for Reformulated and Conventional Gasoline[47] and United States - Measures Affecting Woven Wool Shirts and Blouses from India.[48]

75. In this situation, the EC/MS would like to say that in their view, none of the exceptions to copyright protection contained in the TRIPS Agreement and the Berne Convention can excuse - totally or in part - the exceptions contained in Section 110(5) Copyright Act. The EC/MS will comment in more detail on this issue in light of arguments which the US might wish to submit in this context to the Panel.

---

[46] See the unequivocal language in WIPO, Guide to the Berne Convention, 1978, at p. 65 which reads: *"the communication to the public of a performance of the work. It covers all public communication except broadcasting which is dealt with in Article 11bis. For example, a broadcasting organisation broadcasts a chamber concert. Article 11bis applies. But if it or some other body diffuses the music by landline to subscribers, this is a matter for Article 11".*

[47] Appellate Body Report *United States – Standards for Reformulated and Conventional Gasoline*, WT/DS2/AB/R, adopted 20 May 1996, DSR 1996:I, 3, at 21.

[48] Appellate Body Report, *United States - Measures Affecting Woven Wool Shirts and Blouses from India*, WT/DS33/AB/R, adopted 23 May 1997, DSR 1997:I, 323, at 335.

5. *Nullification and Impairment*

76. Under Article 64(1)TRIPS, Article XXIII GATT and Article 3(8)DSU, the violation of the US' obligations under the TRIPS Agreement are considered prima facie to constitute a case of nullification or impairment.

VI. CONCLUSION

77. The EC/MS therefore respectfully request the Panel to find that the US has violated its obligations under Article 9(1) TRIPS together with Articles 11*bis*(1)(iii) and 11(1)(ii) Berne Convention and should bring its domestic legislation into conformity with its obligations under the TRIPS Agreement.

ATTACHMENT 1.2

ORAL STATEMENT OF THE EUROPEAN COMMUNITIES AND THEIR MEMBER STATES AT THE FIRST MEETING WITH THE PANEL

(8 and 9 November 1999)

I. INTRODUCTION

1. The European Community (EC) and its Member States (MS) first of all would like to thank you Ms Chairperson and Members of the Panel for taking on this case in anticipation of the time and effort which you will devote to it. These thanks are extended also to the Members of the Secretariat who assist this Panel in its task.

2. This is the fourth panel on TRIPS and the first one on copyright issues. The findings of this Panel are likely to be of significant importance for the implementation by Members of issues namely in relation to the section on copyright of the TRIPS Agreement and the interrelationship between TRIPS and the Berne Convention.

3. We set out our understanding of the facts of this case and our arguments in the first written submission dated 5 October 1999 in which it is explained why we consider that certain aspects of the US' legislation relating to the protection of copyrighted works are incompatible with the US' obligations stemming from the WTO Agreement on Trade-Related Aspects of Intellectual Property Rights (TRIPS). We will refrain today from repeating all facts and arguments made in the written submission, but will rather concentrate on what we consider to be the pivotal facts and arguments. We will also comment provisionally on the First Written Submission of US of 26 October 1999 and Third Party submissions. The EC/MS will of course reply in full to the US and Third Party Submissions in our rebuttal submission.

4. To put it in telegraphic style, the particular situation under US copyright law, which is the object of the EC/MS' complaint, presents itself as follows:

While Section 106 Copyright Act gives the right holder of a copyrighted work the exclusive right to reproduce the work, prepare derivative works, distribute copies of the work and to perform the copyrighted work publicly, Section 110(5) Copyright Act provides for two exemptions from copyright protection, which in simple terms can be summarised as follows:

- under Subsection B, anybody is allowed to perform in his business premises for the enjoyment of customers "nondramatic music" by communicating radio or television (TV) transmissions without the consent of the copyright owner in cases where a certain surface is not exceeded without any practical limitation or above that surface limit by respecting certain conditions as to the number of loudspeakers used;
- under Subsection A, anybody is allowed to perform in his business premises for the enjoyment of customers without the consent of the copyright holder, any other copyrighted works such as plays, operas or musicals from radio or TV transmissions under the condition, in particular, that the equipment used can be considered "homestyle".

5. In the view of the EC/MS these US' measures are in violation of the US' obligations under the WTO-TRIPS Agreement. In particular, the US' measures are incompatible with Article 9(1) TRIPS together with Articles 11(1) and 11*bis*(1) of the Berne Convention and cannot be justified under any express or implied exception or limitation permissible under the Berne Convention or under TRIPS. These measures cause prejudice to the legitimate rights of European copyright owners, thus nullifying and impairing the rights of the EC/MS.

6. The EC/MS' economic interests in this matter are significant. According to a study to which the EC/MS will refer to in more detail, approximately 70% of all drinking and eating establishments and 45% of all retail establishments in the US can play without limitation radio or TV music without the consent of the copyright owner. This demonstrates clearly the potential of Section 110(5) Copyright Act to cause very significant losses of licensing income.

II. PROTECTION OF COPYRIGHTED WORKS AND THE EXCEPTIONS THERETO UNDER THE US COPYRIGHT ACT

1. Historical Background: Section 110(5) Copyright Act before the 1998 Amendment ("the Homestyle Exemption")

7. Under Section 106 Copyright Act (1976), the right holder of a work has the exclusive right to reproduce the work, prepare derivative works and distribute copies of the work. Under Section 106(4) of said Act, the owner of copyright has also the exclusive right *"to perform the copyrighted work publicly"*.

8. In order fully to understand the exemptions contained in the present version of Section 110(5), it is helpful to consider its previous version. Prior to 1999 Section 110(5) only consisted of the current Subsection A. Subsection B was added to the statute in October 1998 by the "Fairness in Music Licensing Act". The 1976 version of Section 110(5) was generally referred to as "the homestyle exemption". In broad terms, the homestyle exemption covered the use of a "homestyle" radio or TV in a shop, a bar, a restaurant or any other place frequented by the public. The exemption did *not* apply to the playing of tapes, CD's or other mechanical music.

9. The *ratio legis* of the homestyle exemption goes back to the 1975 US Supreme Court case *Twentieth Century Music Corp. v. Aiken* (full text in Exhibit EC-1). Mr Aiken was the owner of a small fast-food restaurant who operated a radio. This installation received the transmission of various radio stations which included protected musical works. At that time it was believed that a business establishment had to obtain a licence to pick up a broadcast and in order to legally communicate it to the public, but Mr Aiken had no licence from the right holders of the copyrighted works that were broadcast through the radio on his premises. The Supreme Court exempted Aiken from liability under the 1909 Copyright Act (which is the predecessor of the 1976 Act), as, according to the Court, what he was doing could not be considered as *"performing"* within the meaning of said Act.

10. However, in the Copyright Act (1976), the new definition of *"perform"* clearly covered what Mr Aiken had been doing. In order to keep the "Aiken" activities permissible without the consent of the right holder, a specific provision has been inserted into the Copyright Act to provide users with an exemption from copyright liability.

11. The scope of Section 110(5) (in its "homestyle" version) has evolved over the years. At the time of the adoption of the Copyright Act (1976), the intention of the US Congress appeared to be that the scope of the exemption should be narrow and apply only to small commercial establishments "where mom is behind the counter and dad does the cashier". However, the Congressional intent was not altogether clear (a good example of the ambiguity of the legislator's intent can be seen in the Congressional record which we have submitted as Exhibit EC-3).

12. While the US claim repeatedly that US Courts have interpreted this provision narrowly, in fact, when looking closely at the vast litigation on Section 110(5) Copyright Act (1976), one does not come to the same conclusion. In these 20 years of litigation, two periods can be distinguished.

13. Until the early 90's, the main elements that Courts took into consideration in this respect were:

- the physical size of the establishment;
- the economic significance of the establishment;
- the number of speakers;
- whether the speakers were free standing or built into the ceiling;
- the extent to which the receiving apparatus was to be considered as one commonly used in private homes.

As a result of the ambiguous statutory language of Section 110(5) Copyright Act (1976), Courts selectively focused on various criteria or different sets of criteria, what has lead to a certain degree of inconsistency of the case law.

14. In recent years, rather than to look at the legislative history of Section 110(5) Copyright Act (1976), Courts started to focus more on the plain text of the homestyle exemption, resulting in a broader interpretation of the exemption. As a result of this, large chain store corporations were found to be exempt from applying for a licence and paying a licence fee. *Edison* and *Claire's Boutiques* are illustrative decisions which were taken by two different Federal Appeal Courts one month from each other.

15. The core question in both cases was whether in the case of a large nationwide company, with annual revenues of several hundred million dollars and with a large number of outlets, each outlet using a single receiver of a kind commonly used in private homes, Section 110(5) Copyright Act (1976) was still applicable. In both cases the Courts' answers were in the affirmative. According to the Courts, the only relevant factors in assessing the applicability of the exemption are the quantity and the quality of the receiving apparatus used in a particular premise. The physical size of the establishment qualifying for the exemption, the ownership and/or the corporate structure of the establishment or any other factor considered in previous case law were declared irrelevant with regard to the application of the homestyle exemption.

16. The EC/MS do not see a contradiction between these two appellate decisions and the two appellate decisions cited by the US in its first written submission under point 7, because the relevant business surfaces in the two cases cited by the US were significantly larger than in the Edison and Claire's Boutiques cases (in the Sailor Music case, the average surface was 3,500 square feet, while in Edison and Claire's Boutiques, the surfaces were 800 - 1,200 square feet and 900 - 2,000 square feet respectively).

17. In the early nineties, a coalition of business associations started active lobbying of Congress members in order to secure a widening of the scope of Section

110(5). The coalition's efforts rapidly bore fruit. As from 1995 several bills were introduced in the US House of Representatives and in the US Senate aimed at significantly extending the scope of the homestyle exemption.

18. In October 1998, a bill, entitled Fairness in Music Licensing Act, was adopted by the Congress, signed by the President and entered into force on 26 January 1999.

2. *Current Scope and Application of Section 110(5) of the US Copyright Act*

19. Section 110(5) now contains two distinct exemptions: the so-called "homestyle exemption" under Subsection A modified as to the kind of works covered and a new exemption under Subsection B (sometimes referred to as the "business exemption").

20. The exact meaning and scope of the "homestyle" exemption, now under Subsection A of Section 110(5), after the adding of Subsection B to the statute, and preceded by the expression *"except as provided for in subparagraph (B)"*, appears to be as follows.

While Section 110(5) Copyright Act applied to all kinds of copyrighted works before the 1998 amendment, apparently, Section 110(5)(A) Copyright Act is now intended to exclude from its scope "nondramatic musical works" and continues to apply to all other types of works, including e.g. plays, sketches, operas, operettas, musicals, because Section 110(5)(A) Copyright Act refers to "works" in general, while the scope of Subsection B is expressly limited to "nondramatic musical works".

While the EC/MS are pleased to learn that this interpretation is shared by the US (point 9 first written submission), we would nevertheless remark that this interpretation may not the one necessarily followed by all US Courts. There might be Courts which do not draw the *a contrario* conclusion and apply the exemption contained in Section 110(5)(A) Copyright Act to any sort of literary and artistic work.

Exempted Uses

21. The exemption contained in Section 110(5)(B) Copyright Act covers transmissions or retransmissions embodying a performance or display of a nondramatic musical work intended to be received by the general public, originated from a radio or TV broadcast station licensed as such by the Federal Communications Commission. This basically covers a situation which appears similar to the one covered by the homestyle exemption, *i.e.* establishments which are open to the public may play radio or TV on their premises for the enjoyment of their customers without the consent of the right owners.

22. A last difference is that Subsection B does not apply to "works" in general but only to "nondramatic musical works", *i.e.* popular music, and not to operas, operettas, musicals.

23. While the former "homestyle exemption" and the present Subsection A limit the exemption to the use of a single receiving apparatus commonly used in private homes, this condition is completely absent in Subsection B for cases where the establishment does not exceed a certain size. For all larger establishments the "homestyle" requirement has been replaced by much less stringent conditions in relation to the audio or TV equipment which can be used; in practical terms, it limits

the number of loudspeakers to six. Moreover, communications to the public from *retransmissions* which were not expressly exempted under Section 110(5) Copyright Act (1976) are now expressly exempted.

24. Most TV programmes in the US are transmitted either by over-the-air broadcast or by cable or satellite. Therefore, the express inclusion of this transmission mode makes TV programmes fully subject to the exceptions in all forms of transmission.

25. It is presumed that Section 110(5)(B) Copyright Act applies in a case of public communication of musical works involving new technologies such as computer networks (e.g. Internet) in view of the wording of this provision. This transmission mode, the importance of which increases from day to day, is now subject to the exemption from copyright protection. The following example is mentioned as an illustration of a situation in which this becomes relevant: an FCC-licensed radio (or TV) broadcaster parallels its over-the-air transmissions on the internet (as an audio backup to his web-site). These programmes are received by a PC connected with a number of loudspeakers in a bar or other establishment meeting all the conditions set out in Section 110(5)(B) Copyright Act. While the EC/MS appreciate that communications over a digital network also involve the reproduction right and distribution right, we are not concerned with these rights in this case.

In this case, we are exclusively concerned with the communication to the public right and nothing in the US first written submission supports in our view the US' assertion (point 16 first written submission) that communications to the public of works where a computer serves as the receiving and amplifying apparatus would not be covered by the exemptions contained in Section 110(5) Copyright Act.

Exempted Users

26. The legislator has made a distinction between food service and drinking establishments on the one hand and other establishments on the other. For the application of the exemption to *the establishments other than food service or drinking establishments*, the following conditions apply:

- if the establishment has less than 2,000 gross square feet (= 186 square meters), the exemption applies *without any further condition*, i.e. any audio equipment also of a professional character and any number of loudspeakers can be used;
- if the establishment has more than 2,000 gross square feet of space, the exemption applies under the following conditions:
    - if the performance is by audio means only, it may be communicated by means of a maximum of 6 loudspeakers, of which not more than 4 may be located in any one room;
    - if the performance or display is by audiovisual means:
        - any visual portion of the performance may be communicated by a maximum of 4 audiovisual devices, of which not more than one may be located in any one room. Moreover such devices should not have a diagonal screen size larger than 55 inches;

- any audio portion of the performance may be communicated by a maximum of 6 loudspeakers, of which not more than 4 may be located in any one room.

27. For *food service or drinking establishments*, the following even more generous conditions apply:

- if the establishment has *less than 3,750 gross square feet* (= 348 square meters) of space *the exemption applies without conditions*, i.e. any kind of audio(-visual) equipment, including professional equipment and any number of loudspeakers may be used;
- if the establishment has *more than 3,750 gross square feet* of space, the exemption applies under the following conditions:
  - if the performance is by audio means only, it may be communicated by means of a maximum of 6 loudspeakers, of which not more than 4 may be located in any one room;
  - if the performance or display is by audiovisual means:
    - any visual portion of the performance may be communicated by a maximum of 4 audiovisual devices, of which not more than one may be located in any one room. Moreover such devices should not have a diagonal screen size larger than 55 inches;
    - any audio portion of the performance may be communicated by a maximum of 6 loudspeakers, of which not more than 4 may be located in any one room.

28. The exemption applies to "*establishments*" which are now defined by Section 101 of the US Copyright Act (upon amendment by Section 205 of the Fairness in Music Licensing Act) as "*a store, shop or any similar place of business open to the general public for the primary purpose of selling goods or services in which the majority of the gross square feet of space that is non-residential is used for that purpose and in which nondramatic musical works are performed publicly*".

Summary

29. The exemptions from copyright protection contained in Article 110(5) Copyright Act can be summarised as follows: *As far as copyrighted works excluding nondramatic musical works are concerned* (this is Subsection A of Section 110(5) Copyright Act), anybody in the US can play such works from radio or TV on his business premises for the enjoyment of his customers without the consent of the copyright owner. The only condition in the law which has the potential to somewhat reduce the benefit of the exception from applying to all business premises in the US, consists in requiring that a single apparatus of a kind commonly found in private homes be used, without defining in the law what is meant by this. The other conditions are unlikely to have any limiting effect in practice.

30. *As to nondramatic musical works* (this is Subsection B of Section 110(5) Copyright Act), anybody can play such works originating from radio or TV in his establishment for the enjoyment of his customers without the consent of the copyright holder. In case the establishment being below a certain size (3,750 square feet for restaurants and bars and 2,000 square feet for all other establishments), no further conditions apply with a potential to limit the number of exempted establishments. In

case the premises exceeding these size limits, there exist only limitations as to the number of loudspeakers which can be used. In any event, the use of professional equipment is perfectly permissible.

III. QUANTITATIVE EFFECTS ON COPYRIGHT OWNERS

31. In order to illustrate the scope of the exception, as far as the establishments referred to under Section 110(5)(B) Copyright Act are concerned, *and on which no limitations as to the audio(-visual) equipment used exist*, the following figures are instructive.

32. In 1999, the Dun & Bradstreet Corp. has prepared a quantitative analysis in order to find out how many businesses in the US fall below the surface thresholds established by Section 110(5) Copyright Act, thus escaping copyright liability. The methodology used by Dun & Bradstreet was identical to the methodology used in an analysis it had prepared in 1995 for the US Congressional Research Service during the legislative process of what eventually became the Fairness in Music Licensing Act.

33. The analysis is based on 1998 figures using Dun & Bradstreet's database comprising more than 6.5 million businesses all over the US.

The result of the analysis is that:

- 73% of all US drinking establishments have a surface of below 3,750 square feet;
- 70% of all US eating establishments have a surface below 3,750 square feet; and
- 45% of all US retail establishments have a surface below 2,000 square feet.

34. These figures comprise bars, restaurants, tearooms, snackbars, etc. and retail stores. However, other sectors in which a number of establishments are likely to be unconditionally exempted as well were not taken into account (for example: hotels, financial service outlets, estate property brokers, other types of service providers).

35. To put the results of these data otherwise, approximately 70 % of all drinking and eating establishments in the US and 45 % of all retail establishments in the US are entitled under Section 110(5) Copyright Act, without any limitation, to play music from radio and TV on their business premises for the enjoyment of their customers without the consent of the copyright owners thus depriving the latter of any potential source of licensing income for this use of his work. *All other - larger - establishments* are of course benefiting from the exception under Section 110(5)(B) Copyright Act, if they meet the very lenient conditions as to the number of permissible loudspeakers.

36. Dun & Bradstreet had prepared alternative figures based on its own estimations rather than on actual answers received to its questionnaires to which we have also referred in our First Written Submission. Given that the results of both analyses are very similar, we do not intend to repeat the figures here.

37. For comparison purposes the figures which have been prepared by Dun & Bradstreet in 1995 on behalf of the US Congress, the results were as follows:

- the first scenario used the assumption that premises being unconditionally exempted from copyright liability not exceed the surface of the Aiken establishment which was 1,055 square feet:
    - 16 % of all US eating establishments,

- 13.5 % of all US drinking establishments, and
- 18 % of all US retail establishments.

fall below this surface threshold, thus benefiting from the unconditional exemption.

- the second scenario was based on the alternative assumption that the unconditional copyright exemption would apply to eating and drinking establishments with a surface below 3,500 square feet and retail establishments below 1,500 square feet:
  - 65 % of all US eating establishments,
  - 72 % of all US drinking establishments, and
  - 27 % of all US retail establishments.

  fall below this alternative surface threshold, thus benefiting from the unconditional exemption.

38. These figures do not only corroborate the figures of the 1999 Dun & Bradstreet analysis but also demonstrate very clearly the very significant increase of the scope of the exemption under the 1976 Copyright Act in comparison to today's exception. The scope for eating establishment has seen an increase by 437%, for drinking establishments by 540% and for retail establishments by 250%. We will come back to these figures and explain why they are of relevance to this case later on.

IV. INCOMPATIBILITY OF THE US LEGISLATION WITH ITS OBLIGATIONS UNDER THE WTO AGREEMENT ON TRADE-RELATED ASPECTS OF INTELLECTUAL PROPERTY RIGHTS

1. Section 110(5) Copyright Act in the Light of Article 9(1) TRIPS together with Articles 11bis(1) and 11(1) Berne Convention

39. Given that the distinction between both Subsections of Section 110(5) Copyright Act may not be entirely clear, these Subsections will be taken together for the legal analysis.

Article 9(1) TRIPS

40. This provision reads:

> *"Members shall comply with Articles 1 through 21 of the Berne Convention and the Appendix thereto..."*

This provision has as a consequence that the obligations contained in Articles 1 through 21 of the Berne Convention have become part of the obligations under TRIPS and violations of these provisions are fully subject to the WTO dispute settlement system.

Article 11bis(1) Berne Convention

41. The provision which is of particular relevance for the case at hand is Article 11*bis*(1) Berne Convention which reads:

> *"(1) Authors of literary and artistic works shall enjoy the exclusive right of authorising:*

- *(i) the broadcasting of their works or the communication thereof to the public by any other means of wireless diffusion of signs, sounds or images;*
- *(ii) any communication to the public by wire or by rebroadcasting of the broadcast of the work, when this communication is made by an organisation other that the original one;*
- *(iii) the public communication by loudspeaker or any analogous instrument transmitting, by signs, sounds or images, the broadcast of the work."*

42. Article 11*bis* was introduced into the Berne Convention at the occasion of the Rome Revision (1928), and further elaborated by the Brussels Revision (1948) in a period where public communication by loudspeakers, radio etc. had become a very important means of communication. Such a means of communication was considered to be clearly similar to the public performance of a work, except that it increased the potential audience.

43. Each of the uses described in Article 11*bis*(1)(i) to (iii) Berne Convention is to be considered as a separate use, which requires a separate authorisation for each such use by the owner of the copyright. It is Article 11*bis*(1)(iii) Berne Convention which is the pertinent provision for the case of hand.

Article 11(1) Berne Convention

44. While Article 11*bis*(1)(iii) Berne Convention necessitates that the musical work has been transmitted by hertzian waves at some point during its way to the reception apparatus, Article 11(1)(ii) Berne Convention covers the case when the entire transmission was by wire.

2. *Compatibility of Section 110(5) Copyright Act with Articles 11bis(1)(iii) 11(1)(ii) Berne Convention*

45. Given that the US appear to concede that Section 110(5) Copyright Act is at variance with Articles 11*bis*(1) and 11(1) Berne Convention (point 17 first written submission), we will limit our presentation of the analysis today to the following remarks and refer to the systematic presentation of the legal analysis on Articles 11*bis*(1)(iii) and 11(1)(ii) Berne Convention to our first written submission. By denying copyright protection to works when they are received via radio or TV by hertzian waves and subsequently played on business premises for the enjoyment of customers, the US are not granting the protection which it is obliged to grant under Article 9(1) TRIPS together with Article 11*bis*(1)(iii) Berne Convention.

46. The considerations put forward under Article 11*bis* Berne Convention apply *mutatis mutandis* to Article 11(1) Berne Convention. It can, therefore, be said that the playing of music or other copyrighted works from radio or TV on the business premises for the enjoyment of customers as described in Section 110(5) Copyright Act constitutes acts which are protected by Article 11(1)(ii) Berne Convention if the entire radio or TV transmission is by wire. By denying such protection, the US are violating its obligations under Article 9(1) TRIPS together with Article 11(1)(ii) Berne Convention.

3. *Permissible Exceptions to Copyright Protection*

47. The EC/MS would like to observe that the burden to invoke and prove the applicability of an exception falls on the party invoking the exception. This standard is in accord with the Appellate Body reports in United States - Standards for Reformulated and Conventional Gasoline and United States - Measures Affecting Woven Wool Shirts and Blouses from India.

4. *The Exceptions to Copyright Protection under TRIPS and the Berne Convention*

48. The US point out in point 18 of their first written submission that:

> "The Berne Convention permits members to make "minor reservations" to the exclusive rights guaranteed by Berne, including limitations to the public performances right in Article 11 and 11*bis* TRIPS. Article 13 articulates the standard by which the permissibility of these limitations to exclusive rights must be judged."

The EC/MS would disagree with this statement.

49. The Berne Convention allows certain exceptions to the specific exclusive rights conferred. Article 9(2) Berne Convention allows exceptions to the reproduction right and Articles 10 and 10*bis* Berne Convention define precisely certain possible free uses of otherwise protected works.

50. As to the public performance and communication to the public right contained in Article 11 Berne Convention, no exceptions or limitations are foreseen in the Berne Convention.

51. As to the exclusive rights covered by Article 11*bis* Berne Convention, a certain "fine tuning" facility is provided in paragraph two which reads:

> *"It shall be a matter for legislation in the countries of the Union to determine the conditions under which the rights mentioned in the preceding paragraph may be exercised, but these conditions shall apply only in the countries where they have been prescribed. <u>They shall not in any circumstances be prejudicial</u> to the moral rights of the author, nor to his right <u>to obtain equitable remuneration</u> which, in the absence of agreement, shall be fixed by competent authority."*

While "countries of the Union" are given the freedom to determine conditions for the exercise of the rights, this freedom is limited by the minimum requirement that a copyright owner obtains as a minimum equitable remuneration. Section 110(5) Copyright Act fails to provide such equitable remuneration.

52. It is true that some discussion in WIPO on so-called "minor reservations" have taken place during the Brussels and Stockholm Conferences, but the precise scope of Berne rights, subject to such minor reservations, has never been fully clarified. In any event, such minor reservations would be limited to public performances of works for religious ceremonies, military bands and the needs of the child and adult education. All these uses are characterised by their non-commercial character and it is obvious that the uses contemplated in Section 110(5) Copyright Act do not meet this requirement.

53. As an intermediate result, it can be said that the Berne Convention does not contain an express or implied provision which would justify the exceptions contained in Section 110(5) Copyright Act.

54. While the US would appear to agree up to this point, it expresses the view that Article 13 TRIPS provides an exception clause which, if its threefold conditions are met, can permit exceptions to the exclusive rights conferred by Articles 11 and 11*bis* of the Berne Convention. The EC/MS disagree with this interpretation of Article 13 TRIPS.

55. First of all, Article 20 Berne Convention clearly speaks against the US' interpretation of Article 13 TRIPS because it only allows "countries of the (Berne) Union to enter into special agreements among themselves, in so far as such agreements grant to authors more extensive rights than those granted by the (Berne) Convention". In other words, the Berne Convention countries cannot agree in another treaty to reduce the Berne Convention level of protection. The US interpretation of Article 13 TRIPS would exactly have the effect to reduce the Berne Convention level of protection.

56. Article 20 Berne Convention is mirrored in the TRIPS Agreement by Article 2(2), which stipulates that:

> *"Nothing in Parts I to IV of this Agreement shall derogate from existing obligations that Members may have to each other under the ..., the Berne Convention".*

57. Furthermore, the US' interpretation of Article 13 TRIPS would lead to the absurd result that TRIPS would diminish the level of protection contained in the pre-existing Berne Convention. The opposite is true; both the EC/MS and the US fought vigorously and in the end successfully to increase the pre-existing levels of protection through TRIPS.

58. Even if Article 13 TRIPS were considered to be applicable to Articles 11 or 11*bis* Berne Convention, as far as the latter is concerned any permissible exception or limitation would at least have to give the author an equitable remuneration (Article 11*bis*(2) last sentence Berne Convention) what Section 110(5) Copyright Act fails to do. This view appears to be fully shared by Australia (see points 2.10 and 5.2 of its Third Party Submission).

59. In any event, the three criteria set out in Article 13 TRIPS are not met by Article 110(5) Copyright Act, neither as far as Subsection A nor Subsection B is concerned.

60. Before analysing the three conditions contained in Article 13 TRIPS, a few more systemic remarks on the US argumentation on this issue appears to be necessary.

61. The US give at several places in their first written submission (e.g. points 28, 29) the impression that the exclusive rights contained in the Berne Convention and TRIPS would form a hierarchical order with "important" rights and "unimportant" rights, and refers to the public performance rights contained in Articles 11(1)(ii) and 11*bis*(1)(iii) Berne Convention as "secondary" rights. The EC/MS disagree with this view. Each and every exclusive right stipulated in the Berne Convention and TRIPS are equally important separate rights, which have to be looked at on the basis of theirs respective merits. The relative importance to an individual copyright owner will vary according to the kind of work involved and the way in which he manages his works.

62. From this, it follows that contrary to what the US appear to suggest under points 28 and 29 of their first written submission, it is not possible to argue under Article 13 TRIPS that by increasing the level of protection in relation to one specific exclusive right, it can be justified to reduce the protection of another exclusive right below minimum standard. In other words, one cannot justify a below standard protection for the public performance rights by an above standard protection of the reproduction right. Also Australia underlines in its Third Party Submission (see, for example, point 3.8) that the different exclusive rights granted to a copyright owner have to be looked at separately.

63. Furthermore the US also refer at several instances to agreements between private operators or their associations and associations representing copyright owners (e.g. point 12 first written submission) and claim that these private agreements were similar to what was finally codified by Section 110(5) Copyright Act. While the US have not made available the agreement to which reference has been made, the appreciation of the two leading US collecting societies has been expressed in unambiguous terms in a joint press release by BMI and ASCAP on the day following the passage of the Fairness in Music Licensing Act by Congress of which I will cite only a few passages (the text of the entire press release will be submitted as Exhibit EC-8).

> *"With this music licensing legislation, which seizes the private property of copyright owners, the United States Government has severely penalised American songwriters, composers and publishers... The earnings of songwriters, composers and publishers have been reduced by tens of millions of dollars annually."*

More importantly, the US' argument to refer to private agreements in order to justify provisions of a statute is of a circular nature. It is the task of the law to set the legal framework and to grant certain rights. It is only *after* the legislator has established this legal framework that the private economic operators can start to act within this framework. Only if the law stipulates a public performance right can the parties usefully agree on a licensing contract. For uses which are free such as the ones contemplated in Section 110(5) Copyright Act there is no object for a licensing contract because there is no right to be licensed in the first place. In its Third Party Submission, Australia points rightly out that the right to obtain remuneration has to be distinguished from a situation in which the right owner elects not to pursue his entitlement (see points 3.12 and 3.13).

64. The US are also making reference to the inherent administrative difficulties to license a great number of small establishments. Logically speaking, questions of enforcement of a right cannot be used to excuse its very existence. One can only enforce a right if it is recognised by the law. European collecting societies are successfully licensing great numbers of also small businesses and do apparently not encounter insurmountable obstacles. In the US, it would appear that if indeed the collecting societies were to encounter administrative difficulties, this is because collection societies in the US have never developed the necessary administrative structure to licence small establishments due to a lack of legal protection for extended periods of time in the US. The US' argument is further flawed by the fact that Section 110(5) denies protection to copyrighted works emanating from the radio and TV. The playing of copyrighted works from CDs and tapes is not covered by the exceptions. In

other words the operators of establishments have to obtain licences to play music from CDs or tapes, but they can play music from the radio or TV without a license. This differentiation is difficult to justify. Either the licensing of a great number of establishments meets insurmountable difficulties, then it should meet these difficulties independently of the medium used or it does not.

65. Let's now look more specifically at the three conditions to make limitations or exceptions to exclusive rights under Article 13 TRIPS permissible:

- They have to be confined to certain special cases;
- They may not conflict with a normal exploitation of the work; and
- They may not unreasonably prejudice the legitimate interests of the right holder.

These three conditions have to be met cumulatively.

66. When the US claim that Section 110(5) Copyright Act confines the exclusion from copyright protection to "certain special cases" (pages 13-14 first written submission) [49], this would appear to the EC/MS rather to be a claim that the exceptions are well defined in the sense of legal certainty. However, nothing is said about what makes the playing of music from the radio and TV for the enjoyment of customers "special" as compared to other cases. One of the questions coming immediately to one's mind is why is the playing of music from the radio or TV "special" as compared to music played from CDs or cassettes. The remark by Australia in its Third Party Submission (see point 5.5) that "... Section 110(5) Copyright Act appears to provide a blanket exemption for such establishments rather than dealing with special cases" comes to the same conclusion.

67. Furthermore, the fact that very significant numbers of establishments are covered by the exception demonstrates that the exemption rather constitutes the rule than the exception in a situation in which one half to more than two thirds of all US establishments are covered by the exception.

68. As to Section 110(5)(A) Copyright Act, the reference to "homestyle receiving apparatus" is in itself so imprecise that it does not even create any legal certainty leave alone precisely defining a "special case" in the sense of Article 13 TRIPS.

The notion of homestyle receiving apparatus is a moving target that is subject to the developments of technology. Today's audio sets which are purchased by ordinary private customers to be played in their homes may have several hundred Watts of output capable of servicing many times the surface involved in the historic Aiken case.

69. The limitations or exceptions may not conflict with the normal exploitation of the work. As pointed out above, this analysis has to be carried out on the basis of each exclusive right individually.

70. Articles 11(1)(ii) and 11*bis*(1)(iii) Berne Convention create an exclusive right for a copyright owner to grant permission for the public performance of his work. While it is difficult to establish with precision what kind of performance to the public would not form part of the normal exploitation of the exclusive public performance rights, it appears in the view of the EC/MS safe to say that at least all uses which create an economic benefit to the users of the works are comprised in the nor-

[49] See paras. 24-26.

mal exploitation. The ample case law and the legislative history of Section 110(5) Copyright Act make it utterly clear that playing music on the commercial establishment is not an event which happens incidentally, but is a deliberate commercial act to attract customers and to make their stay on the premises of the establishment more enjoyable with the ultimate objective to enhance turnover and profit. This latter aspect is expressly recognised by the NLBA in a News release referred to by the US in their Exhibit US-7. In view of the EC/MS, there can be no doubt that the normal exploitation of the exclusive right concerned includes these commercial activities. This view is also shared by Australia in its Third Party Submission (points 5.6 and 5.7).

71. These arguments apply to both Subsections of Section 110(5) Copyright Act. The author of dramatic musical works, like the author of popular music both expect that their exclusive rights not be disregarded at least for such activities which are carried out by others for commercial gain. The US is offering no evidence whatsoever to support its assertion that owners of dramatic musical works do not expect any benefit from the rights curtailed by Section 110(5) Copyright Act (point 31 first written submission). Also the argument that "Congress intended that this exception would merely codify the licensing practice already in effect..." has to be refuted as circular. Only if there is a right, there can be a licence.

72. The exception may not unreasonably prejudice the legitimate interests of the right holder. The legitimate interest of the right holder consists in being able to prevent all instances of a certain use of his work protected by a specific exclusive right done by a third party without his consent. Clearly, these legitimate interests include as a minimum all the commercial uses by a third party of his exclusive rights. By creating exceptions contained in Section 110(5) Copyright Act, these legitimate interests are diminished, thus prejudiced. This view is shared by Australia in its Third Party Submission point 5.10.

73. While it is difficult to draw the precise line between reasonable and unreasonable prejudice, in view of the EC/MS both exceptions contained in Section 110(5) Copyright Act cause unreasonable prejudice to the owner of the exclusive right concerned.

74. While the US claim that the economic effect of Section 110(5) Copyright Act was minimal, even before the passage of the 1998 Amendment, no evidence whatsoever is offered to support this assertion. To the contrary, the vast body of case law on the pre-1998 homestyle exemptions makes it clear that very significant economic interests were at stake. This is further corroborated by the long and acrimonious legislative debate on the 1998 Amendment. Already under the Aiken scenario the 1995 CRS study showed that 13.5%, 16 and 18% of all US drinking, eating and retail establishments were covered by the exemption. Given that the Aiken surface had been doubled by the Courts before the 1998 Amendment and given that the Courts might after the 1998 Amendment use in Subsection A, the surface categories set out in Subsection B, the coverage of Subsection A is likely to be similar or even identical to the coverage of Subsection B. In practical terms, this means that at least one half of all US service establishments are likely to be covered by the Subsection A exemption. While it is irrelevant for the question of unreasonable prejudice to look at the degree of aggressiveness of licensing activities by the collecting societies, the US' assertion that the establishments exempted under Subsection A ... are the least likely to be aggressively licensed by the PROs... (point 34 first written submission) is in

contradiction with the US' statement (point 10 first written submission) that the PROs have used harassment and abusive tactics in the licensing practice.

75. As to Section 110(5)(B) Copyright Act, the unreasonableness of the prejudice flowing to the rightholder becomes fully apparent when 73% of all drinking establishments, 70% of all eating establishments and 45% of all retail establishments are unconditionally covered by the exception and the rest of establishments may additionally be exempted under lenient conditions. In this situation, the denial of protection has been elevated to being the rule and protection of the right has become the exception.

76. In relation to the analyses prepared by Dun & Bradstreet one branch of the US government may consider them "meaningless by themselves" the fact of the matter is that the 1995 analysis has been commissioned by the US Congress, because some meaningful insight into the effects of the size of an exemption was expected. The 1998 analysis is but a re-run of the 1995 analyses based on 1998 figures. In view of the EC/MS, it is irrelevant to quantify the actual financial losses suffered by the rightholders concerned. It is sufficient to demonstrate the potential of the prejudice suffered.

77. As to the criticism by the US that the EC has made no attempt to address the effects of these exceptions on its rightholders, it is sufficient to say that at least 25 % of all music played in the US belong to EC copyright owners.

78. To sum-up our legal argumentation, Ms Chairperson, Members of the Panel, let me point out the following:

In the view of the EC/MS, which is apparently shared by the US, Section 110(5) Copyright Act is at variance with Article 9(1)TRIPS together with Articles 11(1)(ii) and 11*bis*(1)(iii) Berne Convention.

79. The EC/MS do not agree with the US defence that the exception stipulated in Section 110(5) Copyright Act can be justified under Article 13 TRIPS. In view of the EC/MS Article 13 TRIPS is not applicable to Articles 11 and 11*bis* Berne Convention because both Article 20 Berne Convention and Article 2(2) TRIPS do not allow that TRIPS extends the scope of exceptions allowable under Berne. In any event, no exception to Article 11*bis* Berne Convention could ignore the requirement stipulated in Article 11*bis*(2) last sentence Berne Convention which requires as the bottom line that the rightholder receive equitable remuneration. Such equitable remuneration is not foreseen in Section 110(5) Copyright Act.

80. Finally, even if Article 13 TRIPS would be applicable to Articles 11 or 11*bis* Berne Convention none of its three conditions, which have to be met cumulatively, would be met by either alternative contained in Section 110(5) Copyright Act. Of course, based on WTO precedents, the US bear the full burden of proof to establish that Article 13 TRIPS would be applicable and all its conditions be met.

5. *Nullification and Impairment*

81. Under Article 64(1) TRIPS, Article XXIII GATT and Article 3(8)DSU, the violation of the US' obligations under the TRIPS Agreement are considered prima facie to constitute a case of nullification or impairment.

V. CONCLUSION

82. The EC/MS therefore respectfully request the Panel to find that the US have violated their obligations under Article 9(1) TRIPS together with Articles 11*bis*(1)(iii) and 11(1)(ii) Berne Convention and should bring their domestic legislation into conformity with their obligations under the TRIPS Agreement. Of course, the EC/MS would be pleased to reply to any question the Panel might have. The written version of this statement will be made available during the course of tomorrow at the latest.

ATTACHMENT 1.3

RESPONSES OF THE EUROPEAN COMMUNITIES AND THEIR MEMBER STATES TO WRITTEN QUESTIONS FROM THE PANEL - FIRST MEETING

(19 November 1999)

I. REPLIES TO QUESTIONS FROM THE PANEL TO THE EUROPEAN COMMUNTIES AND THEIR MEMBER STATES

Legislation in the EC

Q.1 What types of minor exceptions apply to the public performance of works in the EC law or the laws of the EC member States, and in particular whether any limitations apply to food service and drinking establishments and establishments other than food service and drinking establishments (below referred to as "other establishments").

See reply under question 2.

Q.2 Is the communication to the public of music contained in broadcasts or played from sound recordings or live performances subject to exclusive rights or right of remuneration in the EC law or the laws of the EC member States, and are the rights in respect of such uses of music exercised by the right holders or by their collective management organizations?

While the Panel uses here and in other instances the term "minor exception", the EC/MS would like to note that this term is not a term of art neither under the Berne Convention nor under TRIPS. We will refer to "exceptions" where referring to Article 13 TRIPS or express exceptions under the Berne Convention and to "minor reservations" where referring to the concept which has been addressed at the Brussels and Stockholm Diplomatic Conferences of the Berne Union.

There exists no EC law, which addresses directly the question of exceptions to public performance of works; this matter is exclusively dealt with in the domestic laws of Member States. Given the very short time available to prepare these replies, it was not possible to collect this information.

Questions on exceptions to exclusive rights have been asked to the EC/MS in the context of the review of the implementation by WTO Members and replies have been provided to the TRIPS Council in 1996. These replies have been reproduced in documents IP/Q/name of WTO Member/1.

According to the information of which we dispose, it appears safe to say that none of the Member States of the EC has an exception to copyright protection identical or similar to Section 110(5) US Copyright Act. Upon express request, the Irish Music Rights Organisation (Imro), whose complaint to the EC is historically at the origin of this dispute settlement case, has confirmed that it and other Collecting Societies in the MS of the EC are actively and systematically enforcing the rights stipulated by Articles 11*bis*(1)(iii) and 11(1)(ii) Berne Convention, and that this activity generates significant amounts of income (1.2 million IR£ for 1998 for Ireland alone; of this amount 0.86 million IR£ accrues to bars, night-clubs, guesthouses, hair & beauty salons, hotels, restaurants, retail shops and stores), which is distributed to the right holders.

Impact on the market

Q.3 Please provide information on the estimated losses to the EC right holders resulting from the exemptions contained in Section 110(5), if possible divided between Subsections (A) and (B) of that paragraph.

It is very difficult to establish precise figures for losses suffered by EC right holders from the operation of Section 110(5) Copyright Act. But in view of the EC/MS, it is not our task to demonstrate such precise figures.

However, in view of having an order of magnitude of losses which European owners of copyrighted works are likely to suffer, the EC/MS would like to refer the Panel to the order of losses for all right holders, which the two major US Collecting Societies have estimated, when the old coverage of the "homestyle exemption" was enlarged by the Fairness in Music Licensing Act in 1998, to represent an amount of "tens of millions of dollars" per year (see Exhibit produced during first substantive meeting and now reproduced as Exhibit EC-14).

The losses to be allocated to EC right holders are the part of these "tens of millions of dollars" proportionate to the EC authors' market share for which we have given estimates in our reply to question 5 below.

This analysis would suggest that the losses suffered by EC authors are, in any event, in the sphere of millions of dollars per year.

Q.4 Please provide any available information or estimations on the revenues collected by the EC collecting societies, in particular:

(a) The total revenues from the licensing of public performance of music divided between the major categories of uses, including:

(i) broadcasting and rebroadcasting within the meaning of Article 11*bis*(1)(i) and (ii) of the Berne Convention,

(ii) public communication within the meaning of Article 11*bis*(1)(iii), and

(iii) other rights, including those referred to under Article 11(1) of the Berne Convention;

(b) As regards the revenues collected from food serving and drinking establishments and other establishments, what is the breakdown as between royalties for the public performance of broadcast music and the public performance of music from other sources;

(c) Breakdown of these revenues between various sources of revenue, in particular the percentage of the revenues collected from small business establishments (e.g. of the type covered by Section 110(5)).

Information or estimations of the revenues collected by all Collecting Societies in the EU in relation to the licensing of the public performance of music under the categories mentioned in this question are not available to EC/MS.

It should be noted by the Panel that the Collecting Societies in the EU do not necessarily categorise the revenues they collect in respect of the licensing of the public performance of music by reference to the Articles, paragraphs and sub-paragraphs of the Berne Convention or by reference to the categories mentioned in subsections (b) and (c) of this question.

However, the EC/MS have been able to obtain illustrative information in respect of one EU Member State from the Irish Music Rights Organisation (Imro). Imro is a Collecting Society, which licenses and collects revenue in respect of the public performance of music in Ireland. If one were to extrapolate the quantitative data for Ireland to the level of the EC, Ireland representing roughly one hundredth of the EC's population (3.6 million for Ireland; 370 million for the EC), the Irish figures would have to be multiplied with a factor of 100.

(a) (i) In its financial year, which ended on 31 December 1998, Imro collected revenues in respect of broadcasting and rebroadcasting of music (approximating to the rights provided for in Article 11*bis*(1)(i) and (ii) Berne Convention amounting to IR£ 3,634,594 (Euro 4,614,982).

(ii) In the same financial year, Imro collected revenues from the licensing of the public performance of music by means of radio and TV (approximating to the right provided for in Article 11*bis*(1)(iii)) in the amount of IR£ 1,242,210 (Euro 1,577,281).

(iii) In the same financial year, Imro collected revenue from the licensing of all public performances of music in the amount of IR£ 6,237,676 (Euro 7,920,214). This does not include the revenue collected in respect of the licensing of broadcasting and rebroadcasting (approximating to Article 11*bis*(1)(i) and (ii)) mentioned at subsection (a) above. Excluding the radio and TV public performance revenue, Imro collected IR£ 4,995,466 (Euro 6,342,933) in respect of the licensing of all other public performances of music (including those referred to under Article 11(1) Berne Convention).

(b) As indicated above, during its most recent financial year, Imro collected revenues in the amount of IR£ 1,242,210 (Euro 1,577,281) in respect of the public performance of broadcast music from food serving and drinking establishments and other establishments. In that same financial year, Imro collected revenues in the amount of IR£ 6,237,676 (Euro 7,920,214) in respect of the public performances of music from all sources (including the public performance of broadcast music) in food serving and drinking establishments and other establishments.

(c) Imro estimates that it collected revenue from the licensing of the public performance of music by means of radio and TV in small business establishments amounting to approximately IR£ 861,098 (Euro 1,093,369) during its most recent financial year. The categories of establishment mentioned in the Section 110(5) Copyright Act are not the basis used by Imro in identifying revenue from "*small business establishments*". However, in identifying the revenue from small business establishments, Imro has included the revenue collected from retail shops, bars, nightclubs, guesthouses, hotels, restaurants, hair and beauty salons. The revenue collected from these small business establishments for the licensing of the public performance of music by means of radio and TV represented 13.8 % of the public performance revenue collected by Imro in that year.

Q.5 In view of paragraph 77 of your oral statement at the first substantive meeting that 25 per cent of all music played in the US belongs to EC right holders, please provide information about what amount of revenue is transferred from the US CMOs to the EC CMOs for the last three years for which data are available. What is the proportion of this transferred revenue in relation to the total revenues collected by EC CMOs?

An assessment of the market share of European authors for copyrighted works, which are communicated via radio and TV to the public, is a very difficult task, and the best one can achieve is an estimate. It has to be recalled that a typical musical work has not only a significant number of holders of copyrights and neighbouring rights (song writers, text writers, singers, musicians, producers, publishers, broadcasters, etc) but also the category of authors typically comprises more than one.

Moreover, statistics on record sales are apparently not organised in function of the origin of the right holder of a given work, but rather in function of the origin of the producer. The Frank Sinatra song "My way", for instance, was written by a French composer. Part of this song's licensing income accrues to an EC right holder. The record with the Frank Sinatra version was however produced in the US. Sales of that record will therefore not be categorised as "sales of a French record".

The figure of 25% used in point 77 of our oral statement is based on estimate provided to the EC by the industry, which used published data which suggested for 1988 a 23% "market share" of United Kingdom performing artists in relation to sales of recorded music in the US. This of course requires two additional assumptions to be relevant for the communication to the public, the first being that the presence of performing artist is proportionate to the presence of authors of texts or music; and secondly, that there exists a proportionality between the sale of recorded music to the incidence of communication to the public via radio or TV.

Another way to estimate European authors' "market share" is by looking at the ratio of distributions received from US Collecting Societies. The figures, which we have received from ASCAP (see Exhibit EC-15) for 1998 indicate that EC right holders receive x% of total distributions.[1]

---

1 This information has been provided to the EC in confidence.

The EC/MS would point out that both figures suggest that EC authors represent a significant "market share" of the US market for the communication to the public by radio or TV.

Q.6 Please provide a copy of the full study by Dun & Bradstreet referred to in EC Exhibit 7. Please comment on the US observations contained in paragraph 37 of its submission, especially with regard to deductions to be made from the relevant numbers?

The EC/MS have made available - as part of Exhibit EC-7 - copy of a document prepared by Dun & Bradstreet in which the results of its 1999 analysis on the basis of 1998 data are shown. We attach - as requested by the Panel - our entire documentation concerning the Dun & Bradstreet analysis (see Exhibit EC-16).

The 1999 - as well as the 1995 - analysis of the impact of Section 110(5) address the *potential* impact of the exceptions. The US in point 37 of their first written submission makes an attempt to transform the data of potential impact to information on *actual impact.*

In view of EC/MS, it is the potential impact, which is relevant for the analysis of Article 13 TRIPS, and not actual impact, which is extremely difficult if not impossible to establish with a sufficient degree of certainty. It would appear that the US Congress in 1995 also considered it more instructive to ask for data on potential impact than on actual impact.

Q.7 Please provide any market information concerning other countries that you would consider relevant for the case at hand.

The EC/MS do not dispose of market data concerning other countries.

International treaty obligations

Q.8 Please explain which individual exclusive rights under which specific provisions of Articles 11(1) and 11*bis*(1) of the Berne Convention are affected to what extent by which specific provision of Subsection (A) and/or (B) of Section 110(5)?

As pointed out in points 61-72 of our first written submission, and reconfirmed in points 41-46 of our oral statement at the first meeting with the Panel, it is the view of the EC/MS - which is apparently shared by the US, Australia and Switzerland - that both Subsections of Section 110(5) Copyright Act are at variance with Article 11*bis*(1)(iii) and Article 11(1)(ii) Berne Convention.

Both provisions of the Berne Convention cover the same exclusive right, i.e. the communication to the public of a protected work. The distinction being drawn between the two provisions relate to the way (i.e. hertzian waves for Article 11*bis* and through cable for Article 11) in which the works reach the place where they are eventually played to the public (see also the citation from the guide to the Berne Convention cited in footnote 46 of our first written submission). Both Subsections of Section 110(5) allow the playing of music for the enjoyment of customers.

Q.9 Is the potential scope of application rather than the existing actual impact of Section 110(5)(A) and (B) relevant for the examination of its consistency

with Article 11*bis*(1) or Article 11(1) of the Berne Convention, as the case may be, or for assessing whether Section 110(5) meets the requirements of Article 13 of the TRIPS Agreement, in particular its second and third conditions?

In the view of the EC/MS, Section 110(5) is incompatible with Articles 11*bis* and 11 Berne Convention simply because an exclusive right is denied, which according to both Parties is the case. The dichotomy between potential scope and actual impact is, in the view of the EC/MS, of relevance for the three conditions contained in Article 13 TRIPS. This would of course require that Article 13 TRIPS be applicable as an exception to Articles 11*bis* and 11 Berne Convention, something that the EC/MS have repeatedly denied (see also reply to question 11 below).

In the view of the EC/MS, it is the potential impact, which is of primary importance to assess the conditions contained in Article 13 TRIPS. Seen from the right owner, his exclusive right is not only menaced by those who actually perform the acts prohibited by the exclusive right but also by all those who are free to decide to do so at any time and without having to inform him or his Collecting Society of their intentions.

It is the potential, which is created which sets the market conditions. This argument can also be illustrated by reference to another field of IPR. In the patent area, long and acrimonious discussions took place in the Uruguay Round negotiations on TRIPS in relation to compulsory licenses, which generated eventually the disciplines contained in Articles 27(1) and 31 TRIPS.

In the review of the TRIPS implementation by WTO Members which was carried out during 1996-1997, it became apparent that very few and in several case no single compulsory licence has been granted over an extended period of time by a great number of countries reviewed, despite the fact that practically all these countries had provisions on their statute books which allowed the grant of compulsory licences. Also here, the impact of compulsory licences cannot be reasonably measured by the mere number of licenses granted in a given period of time, but can only be fully appreciated by the impact of the possibility to grant compulsory licences on the market place as such. In a country in which it is relatively easy to obtain a compulsory licence, a right owner will be more inclined to grant a contractual licence on more disadvantages terms than if the system makes it more difficult to obtain a compulsory licence.

Q.10 Could the EC further explain the legal basis for its interpretation that the exception of Article 13 of the TRIPS Agreement applies only to those copyrights which were introduced by the TRIPS Agreement in addition to those protected in Article 1 - 21 of the Berne Convention? Does this conflict with the argument that the three conditions of Article 13 of the TRIPS Agreement can apply in addition to any requirements under exceptions embodied in the Berne Convention?

The TRIPS Agreement has been negotiated, at least from the perspective of the EC/MS, to improve the level of protection of IPRs as compared to the pre-existing situation. Given that the Berne Convention already contained a system of well-defined exceptions to specific rights, there existed no need to define a general exception for all rights covered by Section 1 Part II of TRIPS. If the latter had been the objective, exceptions would have been created for Berne rights, going beyond those contained in the Berne Convention before TRIPS. Such a result would clearly be incompatible with Article 20 Berne Convention and Article 2(2) TRIPS.

The EC/MS negotiating position is well reflected in MTN.GNG/NG11/W/68 (Exhibit EC-17). The proposed text on the draft TRIPS Article on limitations and exceptions (Article 8 of the proposal) allowed Members to provide for limitations, exceptions and reservations in relation to certain related rights as permitted by the Rome Convention. It did not, however, allow to provide for limitations and exceptions to Berne rights. It is interesting to note that the US had apparently the same objective when stating in their submission to the negotiating group (doc. MTN.GNG/NG11/W/14/Rev.1, Exhibit EC-18) that *"Any limitation and exceptions to exclusive economic rights shall be permitted only to the extent allowed and in full conformity with the requirements of the Berne Convention (1971)"*.

The argument that the three conditions of Article 13 TRIPS can apply in addition to any requirement under exceptions embodied in the Berne Convention, is made under the alternative hypotheses that Article 13 TRIPS is applicable to Articles 11*bis* and 11 Berne Convention.

Q.11 What is the legal basis for the EC view that the "minor reservations" doctrine under the Berne Convention justifies only pre-existing exceptions? Does this "grandfathering" of exceptions relate to exceptions existing prior to the conclusion of the Berne Convention, prior to the revision or amendment of certain articles (e.g., Article 9(2) in 1967 or Article 11*bis* in 1928/1948), prior the date of entry into force of the Berne Convention for a particular country entering the Union, or prior to the entry into force of the TRIPS Agreement?

Discussions in the Berne Union on the issue of "minor reservations" were never conclusive. However, one can conclude from several sources that it was intended to preserve or as the Panel puts it to "grandfather" pre-existing "minor reservations". The WIPO Guide to the Berne Convention under point 11.6 states that:

> *"It is in relation to this Article that the question of the "minor reservations" arises... At Stockholm (1967), it was agreed that the Convention did not stop member countries from preserving (emphasis added) their law on exceptions which come under this heading of "minor reservations."*

Furthermore, the Report of the Stockholm Conference (1967) (as cited in Ricketson, The Berne Convention at p. 535 - attached as Exhibit EC-11) states:

> *"210. It seems that it was not the intention of the Committee to prevent States from maintaining (emphasis added) in their national legislation provisions based on the declaration contained in the General Report of the Brussels Conference."*

The intent not to admit new "minor reservations" is confirmed by the fact that the Brussels Conference decided against the adoption of a general provision because this could "positively incite those nations which had not, to this time, recognised such exceptions to incorporate them in their laws" (Ricketson, The Berne Convention: 1886-1986, at pp. 533 and 536).

As to the timing aspect, the benefits of the "minor reservations" doctrine should only accrue to those national legislations which have been on the statute books on or before 1967. The EC/MS would argue that countries acceding to the Berne Convention after 1967 are either completely prevented from "grandfathering" under the "minor reservations" doctrine or can only "grandfather" their pre-1967 exceptions (of course if all the other conditions are also met). To argue otherwise would give "newcomers" more rights than to established Members.

This logic has also been followed in a TRIPS grandfather provision Article 24(4) where the relevant timeframe is identical for establishment Members and newcomers. The entry into force of TRIPS would appear to be an irrelevant point in time for the "minor reservations" doctrine.

Q.12 Since under Article 11*bis*(2) equitable remuneration has to be paid, are there ways to provide such equitable remuneration other than through compulsory licensing?

It would appear that a country could set minimum or precise levels of royalties to be paid for the different uses protected under Article 11*bis* Berne Convention. Another way to provide for equitable remuneration could be the introduction of a levy system for the audio/TV equipment purchased by the establishment being allowed to play copyrighted works without authorisations, whereby the proceeds from such a levy system are distributed to the right holders.

II. REPLIES OF THE EUROPEAN COMMUNITIES AND THEIR MEMBER STATES TO QUESTIONS FROM THE PANEL ADDRESSED TO BOTH PARTIES

Q.1 Please explain the extent to which the case law concerning Section 110(5) cited in your respective submissions is relevant for the purposes of interpreting the present subsection (A) of that paragraph.

The caselaw is first of all relevant to appreciate the development of the exceptions contained in Section 110(5) Copyright Act (1976) to the Fairness in Music Licensing Act (1998). As far as Section 110(5)(A) is concerned, the caselaw would appear to remain relevant for all the elements of the exception which have remained unchanged under the new law.

Categories of works

Q.2 The Panel understands that the text of the original Section 110(5) is identical to that of the present subsection (A) minus the words "except as provided in subparagraph (B)". The preparatory work reproduced in exhibits EC-3 and US-1 (H.R. Rep. No. 94-1476 (1976)) explains that the provision "applies to performances and displays of all types of works". Paragraph 31 of the EC submission and paragraph 9 of the US submission (and certain other paragraphs) contain an interpretation according to which this text, as contained in subsection (A), is intended to exclude from its scope "nondramatic musical works". Please clarify your interpretation of the text of this provision, on the one hand, as part of the original paragraph, and, on the other hand, as part of subsection A, and,

to the extent that, in your view, the text should be understood differently in these two contexts. Explain why.

While we consider that Section 110(5) has to be looked at as an entity, we have pointed out our understanding of a possible dividing line between Section 110(5)(A) and (B) as far as the respective coverage of copyrighted works is concerned, both in our first written submission (see points 31 and 32) and in our oral statement (see point 20). In the latter, we have also referred to the possibility of diverging interpretations by US Courts.

Q.3 What is the definition of the term "nondramatic musical work" in the context of Section 110(5)? What types of musical works are either included in or excluded from the application of the provisions of that Section, and which types of copyright holders are affected by the provisions of Subsections (A) and (B)? Does it also cover communication to the public of live music performances? For example, would the performance of, e.g., one song from a musical, constitute a performance of a "dramatic" or of a "nondramatic" musical work? Is it still a "dramatic" work if a song from a musical is performed separately and by another artist? To what extent the notion of "nondramatic musical work" corresponds or is intended to correspond with the notion of "small musical rights" applied in the practice of CMOs?

Given that neither the Berne Convention nor TRIPS provide for such a distinction, we would expect that the US points out this distinction existing in its statute, while we reserve our right to comment on such explanations.

Licensing practice

Q.4 Paragraph 4 of the US oral statement at the first substantive meeting states that Section 110(5) is limited to only certain secondary uses of broadcasts of public performances, for which the right holder has already been compensated for the primary performance. In which way, if any, do licensing arrangements between collective management organisations (CMOs) and broadcasting organisations in the US or the EC take into account the potential additional audience created by means of further communication by loudspeaker etc. of broadcasts to the public within the meaning of Article 11*bis*(1)(iii) of the Berne Convention?

The EC/MS would like to reiterate that in their view, each exclusive right has to be looked at separately. Therefore, for each use, an express authorisation of the right holder has to be granted. While it would - from a purely legal point of view - be possible that the broadcaster also obtains - and pays for - a license for "downstream" users of his broadcast (third party beneficiary licence), the EC/MS are not aware of the existence of such a practice in the US for the uses concerned in this case.

Interpretation of treaty obligations

Q.5 What is the legal nature of materials including "General Reports" of Diplomatic Conferences of the Berne Convention countries in light of Article 31

of the Vienna Convention on the Law of Treaties (VCLT)? Are they "subsequent agreements on the interpretation or application" in the meaning of Article 31(3)(a), "subsequent practice" in the meaning of Article 31(3)(b), "rules of international law applicable between the parties" in the meaning of Article 31(3)(c), or a "special meaning ... given to a term if its established that the parties so intended"?

Materials such as the "General Reports" of Diplomatic Conferences of the Berne Convention would appear to be in the nature of negotiating history. They therefore could constitute "preparatory works" of the Convention within the meaning of Article 32 VCLT. Since, the EC/MS do not consider that an interpretation of the "ordinary meaning" of the relevant provisions of Articles 11 and 11*bis* Berne Convention as incorporated into TRIPS according to Article 31(1) VCLT leads to a result which is manifestly absurd or unreasonable, they do not consider that there is any scope for relying on the General Reports as "preparatory works" for the purpose of determining the meaning of these provisions of the Berne Convention.

The relevant parts of the General Reports may constitute or be evidence of an agreement or instrument on the interpretation or application of the Berne Convention of the kinds described in Article 31(3) VCLT. The obvious difficulty with this suggestion is that there is no language whatsoever in Articles 11 and 11*bis* Berne Convention capable to be *interpreted* as allowing "minor reservations" or as having a special meaning to the same effect.

A further possibility, which may be easier to reconcile with the text of the Berne Convention, is to consider that the "agreement" between the parties in 1967 was to *modify* the Berne Convention so as to allow what has been referred to in the diplomatic conferences as "minor reservations". This option however encounters difficulties because the Berne Convention contains specific provisions and procedures for amendment in its Article 27. This makes it difficult to argue that an amendment was effected in a General Report of the diplomatic conference.

Another possibility, which the EC would mention is that the statements about minor reservations in the General Reports could constitute genuine "reservations" to the treaty, expressed by certain parties and accepted by the other parties through their approval of the General Reports. This approach suffers from a similar difficulty to the "amending agreement" theory since the Berne Convention provides for reservations in its Article 28 and requires them to be expressed in the instrument of ratification (see also Articles 19-21 VCLT) .

The question of whether they constitute customary international law is discussed under reply to question 8 below. However, the EC/MS consider that for the present case it is not necessary to resolve the issue of the legal nature of the "minor reservations" doctrine. The *content* of the "minor reservations" is such that they cannot excuse the US measures subject of this dispute, whatever their legal nature.

The origin of the "minor reservations" is considered to be the General Report of the Brussels Conference (1948) in which it is stated that:

> *"Your Rapporteur-General has been entrusted with making an express mention of the possibility available to national legislation to make what are commonly called minor reservations. The Delegates of Norway, Sweden, Denmark, and Finland, the*

Delegate of Switzerland and the Delegate of Hungary, have all mentioned these limited exceptions allowed for religious ceremonies, military bands and the needs of the child and adult education. These exceptional measures apply to Articles 11bis, 11ter, 13 and 14. You will understand that these references are just lightly pencilled in here, in order to avoid damaging the principles of the right."[2]

Its existence is considered to be confirmed by General Report of the Stockholm Conference (1967):

> *"In the General Report of the Brussels Conference, the Rapporteur was instructed to refer explicitly, in connection with Article 11, to the possibility of what it had been agreed to call 'the minor reservations' of national legislation. Some delegates had referred to the exceptions permitted in respect of religious ceremonies, performances by military bands, and the requirements of education and popularisation. The exceptions also apply to articles 11bis, 11ter, 13 and 14. The Rapporteur ended by saying that these allusions were given lightly without invalidating the principle in the right.*
>
> *It seems that it was not the intention of the Committee to prevent States from maintaining in their national legislation provisions based on the declaration contained in the General Report of the Brussels Conference."*[3]

Whatever the legal nature of the principle set out in these texts, the EC/MS consider that there was a clear intention to limit the "minor reservations" to:

- non-commercial uses described in the General Reports: religious ceremonies, performances by military bands, and the requirements of child and adult education;
- such exceptions existing in the legislation of the MS of the Berne Union at the time the conferences took place (1967 at the latest), i.e. to grandfather pre-existing practices. This appears expressly from the use of the terms "maintain" and "preserve" and the clear intention not to undermine (or "invalidate the principle of") the right by allowing the creation of new exceptions expressed in the Brussels General Report (*supra*).

Since both the US "homestyle" and "business" exemptions are clearly far removed from "religious ceremonies", "military bonds" and "the requirements of child or adult education" but are of an obvious commercial nature and cover a wide proportion of business establishments and because the "homestyle exemption" in original formulation was only introduced in 1976/78 (and the "business exemption"

2 The Berne Convention for the Protection of Literary and Artistic Works from 1886 to 1986,WIPO, Geneva, 1986, page 181.

3 Records of the Intellectual Property Conference of Stockholm WIPO, Geneva, 1971, paras. 209-210, page 1166.

in the "Fairness in Music Licensing Act" has only been introduced in 1998) it would appear that they cannot in any event benefit from the "minor reservations" doctrine.

Q.6 In your view, what is the relationship between Article 13 of the TRIPS Agreement and Article 11*bis*(2) of the Berne Convention? Does Article 13 of the TRIPS Agreement prevail over the exception in Article 11*bis*(2) with respect to the exclusive rights conferred by Article 11*bis*(1)(i-iii) of the Berne Convention in the sense that when the three conditions of Article 13 are met, no requirement to pay equitable remuneration arises? Do the requirements of Article 11*bis*(2) of the Berne Convention prevail as a *lex specialis* over the requirements of Article 13 of the TRIPS Agreement, in the sense that if equitable remuneration is paid, there is no need to comply with the three-conditions test under Article 13? Do the requirements of Article 13 and Article 11*bis*(2) apply on a cumulative basis in the sense that, on the one hand, even if the three-condition test of Article 13 is fulfilled, there is an additional, fourth requirement to pay equitable remuneration, and on the other hand, even if equitable remuneration is paid consistently with Article 11*bis*(2), is it necessary to comply in addition with the three conditions of Article 13? Please explain.

As pointed out in our presentation at the oral hearing, the EC/MS are of the view that Article 13 TRIPS is not applicable as an exception to exclusive rights contained in the Berne Convention (see points 54-58; please compare also reply given to question 10 by the Panel to the EC/MS). If one were to apply Article 13 TRIPS to the Berne rights the relationship between Article 13 TRIPS and Article 11*bis*(2) Berne Convention becomes relevant. In view of the EC/MS, it would appear that in any event the equitable remuneration requirement constitutes a condition *sine qua non* for the grant of exceptions to the rights stipulated by Article 11*bis*(1) Berne Convention.

Q.7 In your view, to what extent has the Berne Convention become part of customary international law, and if so, in particular which part of the Articles 1-21 of the Berne Convention?

In view of the EC/MS, the Berne Convention is *not* part of customary international law. Customary international law is "constant and uniform usage, accepted as law".[4] It cannot be lightly inferred that a treaty provision has become customary international law.[5] The Berne Convention is not universally accepted and those countries that have accepted it have accepted different versions. The EC/MS do not therefore believe that it is possible to speak of a "constant and uniform usage". They also do not see how the principles set out in it can be considered as having been "accepted as law" independently of its provisions.

Q.8 Has the "minor exceptions" doctrine under the Berne Convention, and especially in the context of Articles 11*bis*(1) and 11(1) of the Berne Convention, acquired the status of customary international law? What is the legal signifi-

4 *Asylum Case: Columbia v Peru* (1950) ICJ Rep p266.

5 *North Sea Continental Shelf Cases* (1969) ICJ Rep p3.

cance of the "minor exceptions" doctrine under the Berne Convention in the light of subparagraph (3)(a-c) or paragraph (4) of Article 31 of the VCLT or in the light of Article 32 of the VCLT? Has the "minor exceptions" doctrine or any other implied exceptions been incorporated, by virtue of Article 9.1 of the TRIPS Agreement, together with Articles 1-21 of the Berne Convention into the TRIPS Agreement? Please explain.

As explained in the reply given to question 5, the EC/MS do not consider the Berne Convention to be part of customary international law. For the EC/MS it follows that the "minor reservations" doctrine is unlikely to form part of customary international law. One particular difficulty arises out of their exceptional character, which would prevent them becoming "constant and uniform usage, accepted as law".

The EC/MS would not exclude that the "minor reservations" doctrine has, by virtue of Article 9(1) TRIPS, whatever its legal significance may be, become part to the TRIPS Agreement. The EC/MS do not understand what the Panel intends by reference to "other implied exceptions".

With regard to Article 31(4) VCLT, the EC/MS do not see what term in Articles 11 and 11*bis* Berne Convention the "minor reservations" doctrine could give a special meaning to.

Q.9 What else other than religious ceremonies, performances by military bands, charitable concerts or requirements of education does the "minor reservations" doctrine cover? Does it only cover non-commercial uses? Was this doctrine be conceived of only with respect to Article 11 of the Berne Convention, or was it also extended to Article 11*bis*(1)(iii) of the Berne Convention, given that these articles concern different types of rights? What such instances of implied exceptions could be relevant for this dispute?

The General Report of the Brussels Conference (1948), which refers to the "minor reservations" doctrine in relation to Article 11 Berne Convention, mentions an exhaustive list of circumstances where the doctrine may apply. These circumstances were limited to religious ceremonies, military bands and child/adult education.

From these circumstances, it can - in view of the EC/MS - be concluded that "minor reservations" cannot apply to commercial activities. This view is also supported by a reference to the minutes of the Brussels Conference where it is made clear that *"these limitations should have a restricted character and that, in particular, it did not suffice that the performance, representation or recitation was 'without the aim or profit' for it to escape the exclusive right of the author"* (see Ricketson, *The Berne Convention: 1886-1986*, at p. 536).

Q.10 In order to meet the first condition of Article 13 of the TRIPS Agreement ("certain special cases"), is it enough if the limitation or exception is defined in great precision?

The criterion "certain special cases" requires that these cases have to be singled out for their particularities from the totality of cases covered by an individual right.

"Special" means "out of the ordinary". Therefore this notion has a qualitative element. Special cases have to be distinguished from the non-special, i.e. normal cases. In other words, a rule-exception distinction has to be drawn.

There is also a quantitative element involved, whereby the ratio between "certain special cases" and the normal cases can under no circumstances exceed a *de minimis* threshold.

Q.11 Under the second condition of Article 13, in which respect, if at all, is a normal exploitation of the "work" the same as a normal exploitation of "exclusive rights" relating to that work?

In the view of the EC/MS, the analysis has to be done in relation to a specific exclusive right. Thus the normal exploitation of the work under Article 13 TRIPS is the normal exploitation of this very exclusive right in relation to a given work.

By arguing otherwise, entire exclusive rights could be done away with under Article 13 TRIPS if only the "core" rights would be maintained.

This latter approach would be clearly at variance with the very foundation of the Berne Convention, which establishes a sophisticated system of different exclusive rights with different fine tuning mechanisms.

Q.12 To what extent is it appropriate in evaluating the compliance of a law with the conditions of Article 13 of the TRIPS Agreement based on looking at the current market situation in a given country?

The EC/MS do not fully understand what is meant by "current market situation in a given country".

It would appear clear to us that the three conditions contained in Article 13 TRIPS have to be analysed for the territory of a given country, here the US, given that the protection of intellectual property rights is based on the principle of territoriality.

Q.13 To what extent subsequent technological and market developments (e.g., new means of transmission of or increased use of background music or television) are relevant for the interpretation of the conditions under Article 13 of the TRIPS Agreement?

It would also appear that this analysis has to be based on the socio-economic environment existing in the country concerned. We have however repeatedly pointed out that in our view, the economic effects of an exception have to be assessed as to its *potential* effect. See also our reply to question 9 to the EC/MS above.

Q.14 Is it justified to define the three conditions exclusively by reference to a particular market, or is a comparative analysis of licensing practices in other Members with similar economic conditions warranted?

While it would appear, also in the light of the reply to question 12 above, that the three conditions referred to in Article 13 TRIPS have to be analysed by reference to the situation in the WTO Member concerned, data from other Members at a similar level of socio-economic development can be useful to corroborate or contradict original data in the country concerned or to provide data which is for practical reasons unavailable in the Member concerned.

Q.15 Under the third condition of Article 13, should the concepts of "unreasonable prejudice" and "legitimate interests" be defined based on existing, legally guaranteed entitlements, or do these concepts also connote an aspect of normative concern of right holders? In the latter case, what could be the normative concern at issue? In addition to an empirical analysis of prejudice to legitimate interests, how could such a normative element be taken into account in defining the threshold of the third condition of Article 13?

It is not quite clear to the EC/MS what is meant by "normative concern". As also pointed out in the reply to question 18 below, the EC/MS consider that both normative and empirical elements have to be taken into consideration under Article 13 TRIPS and that empirical elements can have an impact on normative questions. We would also refer to the example given in the reply to question 18 below.

Q.16 What is the extent of "reasonable" prejudice to the legitimate interests of rights holders that is permissible under the third condition of Article 13?

All three conditions referred to in Article 13 TRIPS are intended to make sure that the exception-rule situation not be reversed. The reasonable prejudice has to be compared within the unreasonable prejudice. While, as we have pointed out earlier (see points 73 et seq. of our oral statement), it may be difficult to draw an exact line between reasonable / unreasonable prejudice, there can be no doubt in view of the EC/MS that the prejudice caused by an exception which covers 45 to more than 70 % of establishments can under no circumstance be considered reasonable because it reverses the rule-exception situation.

Q.17 With a view to giving distinct meaning to the second and the third condition of Article 13, in which respect does an extent, degree or form of interference with exclusive rights below the threshold of "conflict with normal exploitation" differ from an extent, degree or form of interference with exclusive rights that exceeds the threshold of a reasonable prejudice to the interests of the right holder? In other words, how does a permissible degree of prejudice under the third condition relate to "normal exploitation" under the second condition of Article 13?

The EC/MS agree that the second and third conditions of Article 13 TRIPS are distinct conditions, which must be applied cumulatively.

First, the requirement that an exception or limitation does not conflict with normal exploitation of the work would appear to call for a more normative or qualitative approach than the third requirement. This appears from the comparison of the word "conflict" (in the sense of "interfere with" or "not be consistent with") with the term "unreasonably prejudice".

Second, "normal exploitation of the work" requirement differs from the "legitimate interests of the right holder" in a number of ways. Exploitation, which is not "normal", may still be a "legitimate interest" of the right holder. Also, "exploitation" refers to the ways in which an author may obtain a *reward* from an exclusive right in his work, whereas his "interests" may cover other matters than financial interests in the exploitation of the particular right in question, such as his interest in an acknowledgement of his work or information about its use.

As a result of the excessive coverage of situations by Section 110(5) (see also the results of the Dun & Bradstreet analysis to which we have referred repeatedly), there can be no doubt in view of the EC/MS that neither of the latter two conditions of Article 13 TRIPS are met.

Q.18 Should quantitative empirical or normative approaches be used in defining the three conditions of Article 13?

In view of the EC/MS, both quantitative and normative elements have to be used for the interpretation. There are also instances in which quantitative data can influence a normative assessment like in the situation where it is established from quantitative data that the exception covers more than one half of all situations, thus reversing the rule-exception principle which underlies Article 13 TRIPS.

ATTACHMENT 1.4

RESPONSES OF THE EUROPEAN COMMUNITIES AND THEIR MEMBER STATES TO WRITTEN QUESTIONS FROM THE UNITED STATES - FIRST MEETING

(19 November 1999)

Q.1 Does the EC have any factual support for its assertion that European music represents 25 % of all music played in the US?

Please see reply to question 5 asked by the Panel to the EC/MS.

Q.2 On what facts does the EC base its assertion that establishments in the US have "adapted their music installation" or have cancelled contracts for commercial music services in the wake of the Claire's Boutiques and Edison Bros. decisions?

It clearly appears from the complaint for Declaratory Judgement and the Motion of Plaintiff for summary judgement in the case Edison Brothers Stores Inc. v. Broadcast Music Inc. (Edison case) (see Exhibits EC-19 and EC-20) that Edison adapted the music equipment in its stores in order to benefit from the homestyle exemption. This is referred to as the "Edison radio policy" which was initially agreed with BMI until it revoked its agreement (which gave rise to the Edison proceedings).

In its *amicus curiae* brief submitted to the Court of Appeals in the Claire's Boutiques proceedings (see Exhibit EC-21), ASCAP declared that it believed that *"this decision* (i.e. the District Court's decision), *if not reversed, will result in a very substantial reduction in license fees from owners of establishments who use music by means of radios and loudspeaker systems and from background music licensees, many of whose subscribers will cancel their subscriptions and substitute radio music".*

Q.3 Does the EC contend that no exceptions to the public performance are permissible to Berne Article 11 rights?

As pointed out in the reply to question 11 by the Panel to the EC/MS, the discussions in WIPO on the "minor reservations" doctrine have concentrated on Article 11 Berne Convention. In view of the EC/MS, Section 110(5) under no circumstances would qualify as a "minor reservation" as addressed in WIPO even if the "doctrine" were applicable to Article 11 Berne Convention.

Q.4 Does the EC contend that the "minor reservations" doctrine does not permit any exceptions other than those that existed in Member countries at the time of accession to the Berne Convention?

Please see reply to question 11 by the Panel to the EC/MS.

Q.5 Please list and describe any exemptions in copyright laws or neighbouring rights laws of EC/MS to the public performance right, and provide the dates of enactment of such exemptions.

The US are referred to the replies given by the EC/MS in the context of the TRIPS review on copyright and related rights which has been carried out during the first semester of 1996 in the TRIPS Council, for which the WTO Secretariat has established an extensive documentation. Furthermore, we would like to draw the attention of the US to the fact that all laws and regulations relevant for the implementation of the TRIPS Agreement have been notified to the TRIPS Council in the manner provided therein.

Q.6 Out of the 70% of all eating and drinking establishments and 45% of all retail establishments that the EC alleges are impacted by the 1998 Amendment, does the EC have any factual data regarding:

- **how many of these establishments play music at all?**
- **how many of these establishments play radio music as opposed to recorded music?**

All percentage figures given in the Dun & Bradstreet analyses, including of course the basis of 100%, are potential users. The exempted potential users are free to benefit from the possibility offered by Section 110(5) at will at any point in time and without any notification to the right holders or their collecting societies. Therefore, the EC/MS would consider that the question of *"how many establishments actually play music from the radio or recorded at a given point in time?"* is of secondary importance and factually difficult to establish.

Q.7 On what facts does the EC base its assertion that EC right holders have lost or will lose revenue as a result of Section 110(5)(B). What is the estimated amount of the losses or projected losses?

As appears from the joint press release by BMI and ASCAP on the day after the adoption by Congress of the Fairness in Music Licensing Act (see Exhibit EC-14), the total losses from these measures to right holders amount to "tens of millions of dollars per year". The losses suffered by EC right holders will be an amount proportionate to their share in the US market for which we have submitted an estimate in reply to question 5 of the Panel to the EC/MS.

Q.8 Have EC right holders ever received any revenue from secondary performances in US establishments of works other than nondramatic musical works? If so, please provide factual support. If the EC alleges that its right holders have lost or will lose revenue as a result of Section 110(5)(A), please provide supporting data and the estimated amount of such losses.

The EC assumes that the US means by the phrase "*secondary performances*" (a term unknown in the Berne Convention and TRIPS) the performances over which authors enjoy exclusive rights under Articles 11*bis*(1)(iii) and 11(1)(ii) Berne Convention.

In the time available, it has not been possible for the EC/MS to consult with all the Collecting Societies in the EU on this question. However, the EC/MS have received information relating to this question from the Irish Music Rights Organisation (Imro), the Collecting Society which administers the public performance right in music for most of the music right holders resident in Ireland. Imro has confirmed that, on behalf of its Members, who are right holders in the public performance right in dramatic musical works, it entrusts the collection of revenue in the US in respect of public performance in those works to the US Collecting Societies, subject only to the exclusion of the performance of those works on stage or in similar circumstances. Imro specifically confirms that it entrusts to the US Collecting Societies the collection of revenues deriving from the broadcasting and rebroadcasting of those dramatic musical works in the US (approximating to the right provided for in Article 11*bis*(1)(i) and (ii) Berne Convention) and from the public performance of broadcasts of those dramatic musical works in the US (approximating to the right provided for in Article 11*bis*(1)(iii) Berne Convention).

Q.9 Given that the EC's assertion that exceptions to exclusive rights under Berne Article 11*bis* must be assessed in the light of Article 11*bis*(2), how would the EC evaluate the permissibility of Section 110(5), which implicates two separate exclusive rights, only one of which is subject to a right of equitable remuneration?

If an exception from copyright liability is provided for in a national law of a WTO Member, which concerns several exclusive rights for which different conditions apply, these different conditions have to be met cumulatively.

Q.10 Does the EC contend that under no circumstances may an exemption for any commercial purpose be permissible to the Berne Article 11 and 11*bis* rights?

The EC/MS are of the view that the "minor reservations" doctrine does not allow exceptions for a commercial use of the right. See also reply to question 9 from the Panel to both Parties. We would, however, not exclude that an exception for commercial purposes could, if properly formulated, meet the requirements set out in Article 11*bis*(2) Berne Convention.

ATTACHMENT 1.5

SECOND WRITTEN SUBMISSION OF THE EUROPEAN COMMUNITIES AND THEIR MEMBER STATES

(24 November 1999)

TABLE OF CONTENTS

I. INTRODUCTION

1. In the light of the extensive number of questions, to which the Parties and Third Parties have replied recently, and because of the often quite detailed discussions held at the first substantive meeting with the Panel on 8-9 November 1999, the EC/MS will take this opportunity to present their case in a systematic way and highlight the remaining conflictual issues.

II. FACTUAL ELEMENTS

2. A large number of factual elements have been clarified in the process up to now. In view of the EC/MS, there remain certain important factual elements, which require further clarification.

1. Economic Significance for the Author of Musical Works of the Communication to the Public Rights as Compared to the Other Exclusive Rights Enjoyed by the Author

3. The principal aim of copyright is to compensate authors for their creative efforts and investment. Thus, through appropriate licensing arrangements authors are able to control and to be adequately remunerated for each protected use of their intellectual property.

4. Yet, in the last decades, certain uses have become more important in commercial terms than others. In particular, according to some US commentators, "the right of public performance has become the most important legal right, providing the largest single source of income, for most composers, lyricists and music publishers".[1]

5. The magnitude of the commercial value of the right of public performance, or communication to the public, for authors, whether considered on its own or in comparison to reproduction rights, is significant and confirmed by the figures published annually by collecting societies. For instance, in Belgium, where a single collecting society is responsible for the collection of all rights related to musical works (thus making a comparison more immediate), the total revenues distributed to authors in 1998 for performance rights amounted to BEF 867 mio (Euro 21 mio), while in the first semester of the same year the amount distributed for mechanical reproduction rights was only BEF 324 mio (Euro 8 mio). This means that about 60 % of all authors' income came from the right of communication to the public.[2]

6. This illustrates well the consequent scale, in quantitative terms, of the loss that exemptions similar to those provided under Section 110(5) Copyright Act cause for authors. Following our domestic example, in Europe revenues distributed for TV and radio broadcast in small establishments open to the public represent between 26 % and 10 % of the total public performance revenues. Consequently, exemptions similar to those at issue in the present case would diminish the overall income that authors receive from their work in an order of 15 to 6 %. These figures and proportions make it utterly clear that the exclusive rights stipulated by Articles 11*bis*(1)(iii) and 11(1)(ii) Berne Convention are not some secondary, ancillary rights worth little or nothing in reality, but constitute very significant exclusive rights not only in absolute terms but also when compared with the other exclusive rights guaranteed by the Berne Convention and TRIPS.

2. Interplay and Separation between Subsections A and B Contained in Section 110(5) Copyright Act

7. Both Parties interpret Section 110(5) Copyright Act - by way of an *a contrario* argument from Subsection B - to mean that Subsection A applies to all sorts of literary and artistic works with the exception of nondramatic musical works.

8. While this interpretation has been put forward by both Parties, it is however uncertain that US Courts would invariably share this interpretation. The risk that a

---

1 B. Korman and I. F. Koenigsberg, "Performing rights in music and performing rights societies", in *33 Journal of Copyright Society,* 1986, pp 332 et seq. (Attached as Exhibit EC-22).

2 See Exhibit EC-23.

US Court might rely textually on Subsection A entails the danger that it would apply the exception contained in Subsection A to all literary and artistic works, including nondramatic musical works.

9. In this context, another element merits clarification. During the first meeting with the Panel on 8-9 November 1999, the US, upon a question from the Panel, made some explanatory remarks on the definition of nondramatic musical works. It explained that a dramatic musical work would be definitively categorised as such at the moment of the creation of the work. This would have the consequence that an aria from an opera or a song from a musical work would continue to be considered as a dramatic musical work, even if played individually.

10. According to the information available to the EC/MS, this does not correctly reflect the situation under US' law and practice. The categorisation of a work as dramatical / nondramatical depends on the circumstances of the performance of the work. This means that a song from a dramatic musical work played on its own, outside the dramatic work, will be considered as a nondramatic work. Furthermore, it is important to note that all the music originating from a dramatic musical work, but being performed as nondramatic works, is part of the repertoire licensed in the US by ASCAP and BMI.[3] This does not mean that right holders of dramatic works do not get any remuneration for the public performance of their works. In the US, the communication to the public of dramatic works is licensed directly by the right holder, without ASCAP and BMI acting as intermediaries.

11. These serious difficulties to clearly separate both Subsections constitute a further argument to treat both Subsections as an entity, where the common objective consists in allowing the widespread use of literary and artistic works in a vast variety of establishments for the enjoyment of customers, if the works have been received by radio or TV.

3. Internet

12. While the EC/MS have already in their first written submission drawn the Panel's attention to the fact that Section 110(5) Copyright Act is likely to also apply to cases involving certain communications via the Internet,[4] the US have, in particular by referring to other exclusive rights, which are not the object of this case, tried to exclude or minimise this danger.[5] The EC/MS are pleased to see in the US' reply to question 6 by the Panel to the US that the US do no more exclude this possibility. In any event, there can be no doubt that Section 110(5) Copyright Act fully applies where a computer is used as a receiving device for radio or TV broadcasts.

4. Third country Practices

13. While the EC/MS were not able in the short time since the US' replies were received, to verify the accuracy of the reply on third country practices given on question 16 by the Panel to the US, it is remarkable, albeit not surprising that not a single

---

3 See citation in footnote 1 above.
4 See point 39.
5 See point 16.

country mentioned allows an exception to copyright protection for situations comparable to Section 110(5) Copyright Act. It is also noteworthy that a certain number of countries (Brazil, India, the Philippines and South Africa) do not yet have to comply with the copyright section of Part II of TRIPS because they benefit from additional transitional periods under Article 65(2) TRIPS and their domestic legislation has not yet been subject to TRIPS review.

5. *US Practices*

14. It is worth noting that examples of exceptions, which are similar to the third country practices indicated by the US, do exist also in the US copyright law outside Section 110(5) Copyright Act. These are in particular provided in Section 110(1) to (4) Copyright Act and are not under dispute in this case.

III. LEGAL ELEMENTS

1. *Article 9(1) TRIPS Together with Articles 11bis(1)(iii) and 11(1)(ii) Berne Convention*

15. While the drafting of the submissions is not identical, the Parties appear to agree that Section 110(5) Copyright Act creates exceptions to the exclusive rights stipulated in the provisions referred to above. The divergence of views relates to the issue of if and to what extent these exceptions can be justified by other provisions of the Berne Convention or TRIPS.

2. *"Minor Reservations" Doctrine*

16. At the occasion of two diplomatic conferences of the Berne Union, some discussion took place on the issue of "minor reservations", which is reflected in the General Reports of both diplomatic conferences.

(a) Legal Character

17. As we have pointed out in our reply to question 5 of the Panel to the EC/MS and US, it is unclear what legal standing the "minor reservations" doctrine has. For the reasons pointed out, these General Reports of diplomatic conferences can, in principle, be used under Article 31(3) VCLT to interpret the Berne Convention, however there is no language in Articles 11*bis* and 11 Berne Convention being susceptible of being interpreted in a "minor reservations" way.

18. The option that the "minor reservations" doctrine constitutes customary international law, by which the text of the Berne Convention has been modified, has been discarded by both Parties.[6]

19. A further option is that the General Reports constitute evidence of an agreement between the Berne Union Members to modify the Berne Convention accordingly. Not only is the language used in the General Report of the Brussels Conference (1948): "You will understand these references are *just lightly pencilled* in (em-

---

6 See replies to question 8 by the Panel to both Parties.

phasis added)"[7], not supportive of such an approach, but also Article 27 Berne Convention would create a serious obstacle to such an interpretation.

20. Finally, the option of considering that the relevant language in the General Reports constitutes genuine reservations, encounters similar obstacles as the "agreement approach" because Article 28 Berne Convention prescribes procedures for invoking reservations which have not been followed in the case before us.

(b) Scope and Timing

21. Eventually, the EC/MS consider that these difficult legal questions can remain unresolved in the case before us, because the exceptions provided for in Section 110(5) Copyright Act go, in many aspects, significantly beyond what the "minor reservations" doctrine would have allowed.

22. As far as the scope of "minor reservations" is concerned, only three instances for exceptions have been mentioned in the General Reports, which were religious ceremonies, playing of military bands, child and adult education. There can be no doubt and, as it appears, nobody has argued so far that the exceptions created by Section 110(5) Copyright Act fit under any of the three headings or are comparable with any one of them.

23. Furthermore, there exists clear textual evidence that the "minor reservations" doctrine was intended to "grandfather" the practices referred to in the preceding paragraph, existing on or prior to the Diplomatic Conference in 1967. At that time the US did not have any such exception clause, and the US only became a Berne Union Member in 1989.

24. To recapitulate, whatever the legal status of the "minor reservations" doctrine, Section 110(5) Copyright Act would clearly not be covered by its scope nor by its "grandfathering" aspect. In other words, no exception under the Berne Convention excuses Section 110(5) Copyright Act.

3. Article 13 TRIPS

25. While both Parties agree apparently to the principle, which is clearly set out in Article 2(2) TRIPS and Article 20 Berne Convention, that the TRIPS Agreement was intended to increase the level of protection of intellectual property rights, the US argue that Section 110(5) Copyright Act could be justified under Article 13 TRIPS.

26. The application of Article 13 TRIPS to the rights contained in Article 11*bis*(1) Berne Convention, has also to be seen in relation to Article 11*bis*(2) Berne Convention, which stipulates a specific exception clause for the rights contained in Article 11*bis*(1) Berne Convention. This means that any exception would, as a minimum, have to provide for the equitable remuneration to be granted to the right holder. This is not the case under Section 110(5) Copyright Act. The EC/MS are of the view that Article 11*bis*(2) Berne Convention applies to all exceptions and limitations to Article 11*bis*(1) Berne Convention. There is no language whatsoever to support the US' view that Article 11*bis*(2) Berne Convention only applies to compulsory licences. The language in the title of Article 11*bis* Berne Convention is irrelevant

7 See citation contained in reply to question 5 by the Panel to both Parties.

given that it is not based on a negotiated text but on a draft done by the International Bureau of WIPO.[8]

27. The EC/MS have consistently argued that Article 13 TRIPS, for a multitude of reasons, does not apply to Articles 11*bis*(1) and 11(1) Berne Convention. Even if one were to give to Article 13 TRIPS a role in the context of exceptions to exclusive rights under Berne Convention, one would have to respect the principle that TRIPS rather than to grant new or extend existing exceptions, has as objective to reduce or eliminate existing exceptions. Also the language of Article 13 TRIPS itself says that:

> "Members *shall confine* (emphasis added) their limitations or exceptions... "

This language is in remarkable contrast to the language used in all other TRIPS exception clauses, i.e. Articles 17, 26(2) and 30 TRIPS, which provide that:

> "Members *may provide* (emphasis added) limited exceptions ..."

(a) Scope

28. On the assumption that Article 13 TRIPS was intended to contain existing exceptions under the Berne Convention, it would have been necessary for the US to point out precisely the extent of the pre-existing exceptions to Articles 11*bis* and 11 Berne Convention. The "minor reservations" doctrine as pointed out above, has addressed pre-existing situations of religious ceremonies, playing of music by military bands and child and adult education, and would, under no hypothesis, have covered Section 110(5) Copyright Act, leave alone gone beyond, so that Article 13 TRIPS could serve any "confining" job.

29. The EC/MS do not understand the relevance of the US' arguments in relation to the WIPO Copyright Treaty (WCT) and the WIPO Performances and Phonograms Treaty (WPPT), which were adopted by a Diplomatic Conference in December 1996. These treaties (signatories 51 WCT, 50 WPPT) have to date only been ratified by a small number of contracting Parties (9 WCT - 7 WPPT; the EC/MS have not yet ratified) and have not reached the threshold of thirty ratifications necessary for entry into force. It is difficult to imagine that such treaties, which are still in a *nasciturus* state, can add or subtract anything to / from obligations under the TRIPS Agreement which has been in force since 1995 and by which more than 130 WTO Members are bound.

(b) Conditions of Article 13 TRIPS

30. Even if one were to argue that Article 13 TRIPS creates new exceptions also to existing rights under the Berne Convention, a situation which would of course be irreconcilable with the argument that TRIPS is intended to improve the level of IPR protection and thus Article 13 TRIPS to reduce or eliminate existing exceptions, the effects of Section 110(5) Copyright Act are such that none of the three conditions set out in Article 13 TRIPS would be met.

[8] See footnote 1 to Article 1 Berne Convention.

31. As to "certain special cases", the EC/MS have pointed out[9] why we think that Section 110(5) Copyright Act does not meet this requirement. From a plausibility point of view, it appears obvious that an exemption, which covers from 45% to more than 70% of all existing establishments, does not represent "certain special cases" but reverses the rule-exception relationship.

32. In relation to the second and third conditions, the EC/MS have indicated their view in reply to questions 11 and 12 from the Panel to both Parties and in our oral statement of the first meeting with the Panel on 8-9 November 1999.[10] The EC/MS continue to believe that the analysis has to be based on an assessment in relation to the exclusive right concerned, given the sophisticated distinction of individual exclusive rights under the Berne Convention. To argue otherwise would entail the risk that entire exclusive rights can be disregarded as long as the core economic right remains protected; a situation, which also the US would consider as not being contemplated by Article 13 TRIPS.[11]

33. The EC/MS cannot follow the argumentation of the US in reply to question 18 by the Panel, in which they put forward the idea that the analysis has to be based on both aspects, i.e. individual exclusive right and whole work. While one can indeed imagine a cumulative test, the test will be failed if only one of its constituent element fails. In other words, if the test is not met on the basis of the individual exclusive right, the entire test is not met and it is irrelevant of how the analysis for the entire work turns out.

34. Finally, the EC/MS would like to reiterate that according to well-established WTO jurisprudence[12], it is the task of the US to prove that the exceptions invoked are applicable and their conditions fully met.

IV. CONCLUSION

35. Under Article 64(1) TRIPS, Article XXIII GATT and Article 3(8) DSU, the violation to the US' obligations under the TRIPS Agreement are considered prima facie to constitute a case of nullification or impairment.

36. The EC/MS therefore respectfully request the Panel to find that the US have violated their obligations under Article 9(1) TRIPS together with Articles 11*bis*(1)(ii) and 11(1)(ii) Berne Convention and should bring their domestic legislation into conformity with their obligations under the TRIPS Agreement.

---

[9] See reply to question 10 by the Panel to both Parties and points 66 to 68 of our oral statement at the first meeting with the Panel.

[10] See points 69 to 71.

[11] See US reply to question 18 from the Panel to the US.

[12] See reference under point 47 of our oral presentation at the first meeting with the Panel.

ATTACHMENT 1.6

ORAL STATEMENT OF THE EUROPEAN COMMUNITIES AND THEIR MEMBER STATES AT THE SECOND MEETING WITH THE PANEL

(7 & 8 December 1999)

TABLE OF CONTENTS

I. INTRODUCTION

This is the second hearing in this case and thus the last opportunity for the Parties to present their facts and arguments as a whole to you.

The EC/MS will present its case in the light of the facts and arguments made available by the Parties and third Parties. Wherever necessary, we will also comment on the US' replies to questions from the Panel and the EC/MS and on the US' rebuttal statement dated 24 November 1999.

II. FACTUAL ELEMENTS

1. It would appear to the EC/MS that the coverage of Section 110(5) Copyright Act has by now been largely clarified by the Parties with the exception of the question of the interplay and separation between Subsections A and B and the applicability to the IT world and Internet.

2. As to the first issue, the plain text of Subsection A would suggest that all copyright works, which are susceptible to be communicated to the public by loud-speaker, are covered. Subsection B defines its coverage as nondramatic musical works. While it appears possible to draw an *a contrario* argument from Subsection B with the result that Subsection A does not apply to nondramatic musical works, it is far from certain that US Courts would consistently follow this *a contrario* argument.

When the US mention (point 4 of their rebuttal statement) that there exists *" ... consistent jurisprudence of US Courts interpreting the homestyle exemption... "*, the EC/MS would like to remark that there exists not a single US Court decision to date, which interprets the scope of Section 110(5)(A) Copyright Act.

3. Also, the distinction between dramatic and nondramatic musical works remains unresolved. While the US have pointed out at the first meeting upon a question from the Panel that the distinction is made definitively when the work is created, the EC/MS have put forward in their rebuttal statement that, according to US literature, the dividing line is not a permanent one, but depends on the circumstances of the performance. In other words, this would suggest that an individual aria from an opera or a song from a musical played on the radio or TV are to be considered as nondramatic, which in turn has important repercussions for the licensing practice.

4. While the EC/MS appreciate that in the IT world other exclusive rights than the ones covered by Section 110(5) Copyright Act are relevant for communications to the public, no argument has been put forward by the US, that the exemptions contained in Section 110(5) Copyright Act do not apply in the digital context.

III. LEGAL ELEMENTS

5. While the language used by the US differs, it would appear that the US agree in essence with the EC/MS.

Section 110(5) Copyright Act is inconsistent with Article 9(1) TRIPS together with Articles 11*bis*(1)(iii) and 11(1)(ii) Berne Convention unless the US can demonstrate that their measure is covered by an exception provision.

6. The US argue that Article 13 TRIPS allows the exceptions to Articles 11*bis*(1) and 11(1) Berne Convention, which are contained in Section 110(5) Copyright Act.

In view of the EC/MS, the exemptions contained in Section 110(5) Copyright Act cannot be justified under any kind of argumentation in relation to Article 13 TRIPS.

7. The EC/MS have pointed out in detail why in their view, Article 13 TRIPS is not applicable to the Berne rights, which have been incorporated into TRIPS by reference. The plain text, the negotiating history and the object and purpose of TRIPS militate for this result.

8. However, even if one were to argue that Article 13 TRIPS may play a role in the context of exceptions to Berne rights, the exceptions contained in Section 110(5) Copyright Act cannot be justified.

9. It would appear that the US agree that one of the major objectives of the TRIPS Agreement consists in increasing the level of IPR protection as compared to the level of protection prevailing under the pre-existing WIPO Conventions. This in turn means for Article 13 TRIPS that - if it were applicable to Articles 11*bis*(1) and

11(1) Berne Convention - its objective would have to consist in limiting any wider pre-existing Berne exceptions.

10. While the Berne Convention provides for a number of exceptions such as Articles 9(2), 10, 10*bis*, there exists no exception provision to Article 11 Berne Convention and Article 11*bis* Berne Convention has a specific exception provision in its paragraph 2, which provides that - as a minimum - the right holder has to be granted equitable remuneration. The US themselves do not claim that Section 110(5) Copyright Act can be justified by Article 11*bis*(2) Berne Convention.

1. "Minor Reservations" Doctrine

11. In this situation, the US claim the benefit of the "minor reservations" doctrine, which, in the US view, has been further clarified and articulated by TRIPS Article 13 (see point 2 of the rebuttal statement).

12. Discussions have indeed taken place on so-called minor reservations at the occasion of two diplomatic conferences of the Berne Union in 1948 and 1967. We have considered in detail the possible legal character of the references to "minor reservations" in the General Reports of these diplomatic conferences in our reply to question 5 by the Panel to the EC/MS. We have concluded that the legal significance of the "minor reservations" doctrine under public international law is doubtful.

13. The US claim that the "minor reservations" doctrine constitutes "subsequent practice" in the sense of Article 31(3)(b)VCLT. However, such "subsequent practice" is a tool, among others, to interpret provisions of treaty language, which need interpretation. In the case at hand, it is utterly clear that Article 11 Berne Convention does not contain an exception provision and Article 11*bis* Berne Convention contains an exception provision whose conditions are not met by Section 110(5) Copyright Act. Thus no need exists to interpret the plain language any further.

(a) Scope of the "Minor Reservations" Doctrine

14. The list of alleged exception provisions, which is contained in Exhibit US-22, merely states figures of Articles without even specifying the statute to which these articles belong, and without any explanation as to their context. This does not contribute anything to establishing "subsequent practice", and even less so to determining the scope of the "minor reservations" doctrine. The US have referred also to the "minor reservations" doctrine in relation to exceptions provided for in 10 countries Members of the Berne Union (the Berne Union is presently composed of more than 130 Members). All these exceptions are characterised by their non-commercial character and mostly reflect the exceptions, which also exist in the US copyright law, notably in Section 110, paragraphs (1) to (4) Copyright Act. These situations are not the ones covered by Section 110, paragraph (5) Copyright Act.

15. All this leads us to the conclusion that it is difficult to give any legal status to the "minor reservations" doctrine. As we have pointed out repeatedly, there is fortunately no need to decide this thorny issue in the case before the Panel, because the exceptions contained in Section 110(5) Copyright Act do under no circumstance meet the requirements on scope and timing as referred to in the General Reports.

16. The only instances, which were mentioned in the discussions on "minor reservations" at the two diplomatic conferences were military bands, religious services and child and adult education. Obviously, Section 110(5) Copyright Act is not lim-

ited to any of these categories. But even if one were to argue that these three instances were only illustrative, their common features consist in being for non-commercial activities and for a well-defined social purpose. Given that Section 110(5) Copyright Act is directly intended to serve commercial interests by the use of the copyright works in commercial establishments for the enjoyment of customers with the objective to enhance turnover and profit neither of these common characteristics can be found in Section 110(5) Copyright Act.

17. The US argument that the underlying policy consideration for Section 110(5) Copyright Act consists in fostering small businesses is spurious at best. First of all, it has to be remembered that copyright owners themselves are in their vast majority "small businesses" and second as is well evidenced in the Claire's Boutique case (see Exhibit EC-6) the homestyle exemption applies to big corporations. Claire's Boutique Inc. had a yearly turnover in the vicinity of 200 million dollars and net earnings in excess of 13 million dollars.

(b) The "Minor Reservations" Doctrine as a Grandfathering Device

18. As to the aspect of timing for the adoption of minor exceptions, we maintain our view that the citations from the General Reports make it utterly clear that the "minor reservations" doctrine was intended to "grandfather" existing practices and not as an invitation to Berne Union Members to subsequently adopt such "minor reservations".

19. Also as to the application of grandfather provisions to newcomers to a convention, our arguments remain. There is no reason to treat newcomers any better than established Members, by allowing them to reduce the level of obligations at a time when an established Member would no more be allowed to do so. This approach is perfectly neutral as to the level of development of a country Member or candidate to an international convention.

20. The case of the Berne Convention represents indeed a good illustration of the non-discriminatory effects of this approach in a situation in which the vast majority of developing countries were already a Member of the Berne Union at the moment the US joined. Furthermore, TRIPS has taken exactly this approach for its grandfather provisions (see Articles 4(d) and 24(4) TRIPS).

(c) Tunis Model Law on Copyright

21. A further argument to support our view that the "minor reservations" doctrine under no circumstances covers the situations contemplated by Section 110(5) Copyright Act, can be drawn from the "Tunis Model Law on Copyright", which has been adopted in 1976 (i.e. after the last reference to "minor reservations" at the diplomatic conference in 1967). This model law was intended to provide the legislators in developing countries with guidance on how to draft a copyright statute in compliance with the Berne Convention (for more details, see the description contained in WIPO, Background Reading Material on Intellectual Property, 1988 at pp. 255-257, Exhibit EC-24).

This model law *"provides for a fairly wide variety of limitations to copyright: both free uses and non-voluntary licenses"* but none of these limitations resembles even remotely the exemptions contained in Section 110(5) Copyright Act. The text of the Tunis Model Law referred to is reproduced in our written text.

Free uses according to the Model Law include:

(a) use of a work for one's own personal and private requirement;

(b) quotations compatible with fair practice and to the extent not exceeding that justified by the purpose;

(c) the use of a work for illustration in publications, broadcast or sound or visual recordings for teaching, provided that such use is again compatible with fair practice and that the source and the name of the author are mentioned by the user;

(d) the reproduction in the press or communication to the public of articles on current economic, political or religious topics published in newspapers or periodicals and broadcast works of the same character, provided that the source is indicated by the user and such uses were not expressly prohibited when the work was originally made accessible;

(e) the use of a work that can be seen or heard in the course of a current event for reporting on that event;

(f) the reproduction of works of art and architecture in a film or television broadcast, if their use is incidental or if the said work is located in a public place;

(g) the reprographic reproduction of protected work, when it is made by public libraries, non-commercial documentation centres, scientific institutions and educational establishments, provided that the number of copies made is limited to the needs of their activities and the reproduction does not unreasonably prejudice the legitimate interest of the author;

(h) the reproduction in the press or communication to the public of political speeches, speeches delivered during legal proceedings, or any lecture or sermon delivered in public, etc, provided that the use is exclusively for the purpose of current information and does not mean publishing a collection of such works.

(d) WCT and WPPT

22. Finally, the US rely on the WIPO Copyright Treaty (WCT) and WIPO Performances and Phonograms Treaty (WPPT) in order to suggest that some wide undefined exceptions must exist under the Berne Convention.

23. We have already pointed out in the rebuttal statement that given the *nasciturus* status of these treaties, which are not even in force and not yet ratified by the EC/MS, whatever they stipulate cannot reduce the level of protection of Berne or TRIPS, or create new exceptions which have not previously existed under Berne or TRIPS.

But also from a substantive point of view nothing in the text of Article 10 WCT suggests that new exceptions would have been contemplated. While Article 10(1) WCT creates limitations and exceptions to new exclusive rights being created by the WCT, Article 10(2) addresses the cases in which the WCT makes Berne rights applicable to the digital network environment, which was not covered under Berne Convention previously.

24. This is in contrast with the case before us, where Section 110(5) Copyright Act is at variance with Articles 11*bis* and 11 Berne Convention whose scope has not been modified by TRIPS.

25. The arguments put forward in relation to Article 10 WCT apply *mutatis mutandis* to Article 16 WPPT.

26. All in all, it can be said that there exists no exception or limitation provision - express or implied - under the Berne Convention which could justify the exemptions contained in Section 110(5) Copyright Act, leave alone an exception or limitation provision which when "narrowed down" by Article 13 TRIPS could justify Section 110(5) Copyright Act.

2. *Article 13 TRIPS*

27. In the hypothesis that the Panel should consider that Article 13 TRIPS is of relevance for the assessment of Section 110(5) Copyright Act, we now apply the three steps test provided for in Article 13 TRIPS to Section 110(5) Copyright Act.

(a) Certain Special Cases

28. We have pointed out repeatedly why we consider that the exemptions contained in Section 110(5) Copyright Act do not constitute "certain special cases". We do not intend to repeat the reasons here, but think it is sufficient to say that exceptions which unconditionally exempt 45 to more than 70% of all retail, drinking and eating establishments from copyright liability for playing of copyright works from the radio or TV and exempting the remainder of such establishment under generous conditions cannot be considered as certain special cases, such exemptions are rather a reversal of the rule-exception principle.

(b) Conflict with the Normal Exploitation

29. Here again we have pointed out in detail the reasons why we consider that the exemptions created by Section 110(5) Copyright Act (see for example our replies to questions 11 and 12 from the Panel to both Parties) do conflict with the normal exploitation. We would limit ourselves to mention here again the sheer size of the exception, which covers huge proportions of entire business sectors unconditionally and thus, conflict with the normal exploitations of the public performance rights.

(c) Unreasonable Prejudice to the Legitimate Interests of the Right Holders

30. We do not intend to repeat all the arguments we have made in support of our view that the exemptions contained in Section 110(5) Copyright Act do indeed unreasonably prejudice the legitimate interests of the right holders, but we would like to concentrate on the new quantitative guestimates made in this context by the US in its rebuttal statement (points 33 et seq.).

31. We agree as pointed out in our reply to question 12 by the Panel to both Parties that the economic prejudice to the right holder has to be assessed primarily on the basis of the economic effects in the country, which provides the exceptions. As

we have said earlier, and as the US themselves put forward during the negotiations of the TRIPS exceptions' clause (see US submissions to the negotiating group doc. MTN.GNG/NG 11/W/14/Rev. 1, Exhibit EC-18, and Article 6 in doc. MTN.GNG/NG 11/W/70, Exhibit EC-25), we are of the view that it is more appropriate to look at the potential impact (as opposed to the actual impact) because it can be established with a higher degree of certainty and is less subject to unforeseen changes.

32. We have provided an analysis on the potential economic effects of Section 110(5) Copyright Act, which has never been challenged in a substantiated manner by the US. This analysis demonstrates that 73% of all drinking establishments, 70% of all eating establishments and 45% of all retail establishments in the US are unconditionally exempted by Section 110(5) Copyright Act and all remaining such establishments are exempted if a condition essentially on the number of loudspeakers is met. In our view, these results make it utterly clear that the exemptions stipulated in Section 110(5) Copyright Act do constitute an unreasonable prejudice to the legitimate interest of the right holder.

(i) US Guestimate of Losses

33. In its rebuttal submission, the US have made an attempt to minimize the prejudice on the basis of guestimated actual losses based on historic distributions by one single collecting society (ASCAP).

In view of the EC/MS, this approach is fundamentally flawed for a number of reasons:

34. The distributions from collecting societies to right holders are a function of their collections on the market and the collections on the market in turn are a function of the legal protection of the relevant exclusive rights.

In the US, the rights referred to in Articles 11*bis*(1)(iii) and 11(1)(ii) Berne Convention were not at all protected until 1976 (see the US Supreme Court Decision in Aiken, Exhibit EC-1). While these exclusive rights were protected in general from 1976, the "homestyle" exemption was introduced at the same time by the previous version of Section 110(5) Copyright Act.

This exemption already excluded a wide range of commercial uses (see for example the situations in the Claire's Boutique and Edison cases, Exhibits EC-6 and EC-5 respectively), thus seriously reducing the number of businesses subject to a need to obtain a license.

35. Furthermore, the fact that the National Licensed Beverage Association (NLBA) has, according to the US, concluded in 1995 an agreement with the US collecting societies, which excludes all establishments below 3,500 square feet from copyright liability and under certain conditions excludes larger establishments from such liability (see first written submission by the US points 12-14) lead to a situation in which, for the eating and drinking establishments which are members of the NLBA, no licensing fees have been collected since the entry into force of this agreement.

36. Just as a reminder, the figures given in the US Congress sponsored Dun & Bradstreet Analysis (see oral statement by the EC/MS at the first hearing, point 37) show that the unconditional exemption of eating and drinking establishments with

less than 3,500 square feet cover 65% and 72% of all such establishments respectively.

37. Also the use of a figure of losses, which is attributable to EC right holders only in the context of establishing the prejudice under Article 13 TRIPS misinterprets Article 13 TRIPS.

For all conditions referred to in Article 13 TRIPS, the effect on all right holders, US right holders, EC right holders and right holders from other countries, have to be taken together. The specific impact on EC right holders is perfectly irrelevant at this stage. It only becomes relevant in the context of Article 22 DSU.

38. A further shortcoming in the US quantitative guestimate consists in the fact that, while there exist three collecting societies for the collection of the proceeds for the rights concerned in this case, the US only provide figures for one of them.

(ii) Alternative Bottom-Up Approach

39. While we have repeatedly argued that it is the potential impact rather than the actual impact, which should be applied to an analysis under Article 13 TRIPS, the EC/MS consider that the following bottom-up approach gives at least some plausible indications of the order of actual losses suffered by right holders as a consequence of the operation of Section 110(5) Copyright Act.

40. In the database run by Dun & Bradstreet (see Exhibit EC-16), the figures for 1998 show for the entire US:

- 49,061 drinking establishments, and
- 192,692 eating establishments,

with a square footage of below 3,750 square feet and

- 281,406 retail establishments with a square footage of below 2,000 square feet.

These figures are likely to be lower that the actual number of establishments when compared to the figures for eating establishments on the basis of the US Census Bureau data for 1996 (see Exhibit US-18) from which a figure of 240,000 eating establishments below 3,750 square feet resorts.

41. As a second step, we would agree with the US that not all these establishments would actually play music from the radio or TV on their premises for the enjoyment of their customers.

The US offer in their rebuttal submission (see point 39) the hypotheses that 30.5% of all eating and drinking establishments with a surface below 3,750 square feet, actually play music from the radio in their establishments.

While this assumption has not been motivated by the US, we will use this hypothesis for this analysis and apply it equally to retail establishments.

This process demonstrates that:

- 14,700 drinking establishments,
- 57,800 eating establishments, and
- 84,400 retail establishments,

which all fall below the 3,750/2,000 square feet threshold actually play music from the radio on their premises without having to pay for a license. This analysis disregards the playing of music from TV.

42. As a subsequent step, the appropriate licensing fee for playing music from the radio in the relevant establishments, has to be selected from the licensing schedules of ASCAP (an excerpt is provided as Exhibit EC-26) and BMI (an excerpt is provided as Exhibit EC-27).

Given that ASCAP and BMI represent different repertories, licenses have to be sought from both in order to play the radio in the business establishments.

The lowest ASCAP and BMI licensing fees for eating and drinking establishments add up to an amount of 410 US$ per year. This can also be compared to the fee schedule contained in Exhibit US-7, which effectively mentions yearly licensing fees of 455 US$ for establishments smaller than 1,500 square feet, 869 US$ for establishments between 1,500/2,500 square feet and 1,265 US$ for establishments between 2,500/3,500 square feet.

For retail establishments, the lowest fee categories of BMI and ASCAP add up to 283.50 US$ per year.

43. When applying the respective rate to the number of establishments playing music from the radio in their establishments, one arrives at the amount of lost revenue by BMI and ASCAP as a consequence of the operation of Section 110(5) Copyright Act.

For eating and drinking establishments, the lost revenues amount to 29.725 mio US$ and for retail establishments, lost revenues amount to 23.93 mio US$ which adds up to a total of 53.65 mio US$.

44. These are the losses in relation to all right holders, US right holders, EC right holders and right holders from third countries. This analysis also confirms the claim made by BMI and ASCAP in their press release on the day following passage of the Fairness in Music Licensing Act (see Exhibit EC-14) when they state that:

> *"The earnings of song writers, composers and publishers have been reduced by tens of millions of dollars annually"*

45. This excursion into the sphere of estimated actual losses suffered by copyright owners from the operation of Section 110(5) Copyright Act confirms the analysis based on potential losses presented earlier and does in the view of the EC/MS clearly indicate that the exceptions provided for in Section 110(5) Copyright Act do unreasonably prejudice the legitimate interests of the copyright owner and thus also the third condition contained in Article 13 TRIPS cannot be met.

IV. CONCLUSION

46. The EC/MS therefore respectfully request the Panel to find that the US have violated their obligations under Article 9(1) TRIPS together with Articles 11*bis*(1)(iii) and 11(1)(ii) Berne Convention and should bring their domestic legislation into conformity with their obligations under the TRIPS Agreement.

Of course, the EC/MS would be pleased to reply to any further question the Panel might have. As to the replies provided by WIPO, the EC/MS reserve their right to comment after having had the possibility to carefully look at them.

ATTACHMENT 1.7

COMMENTS FROM THE EUROPEAN COMMUNITIES AND THEIR MEMBER STATES ON THE LETTER FROM THE DIRECTOR GENERAL OF WIPO TO THE CHAIR OF THE PANEL[1]

(12 January 2000)

1. The European Communities and their Member States (EC/MS) would like to express through you their appreciation to the International Bureau of WIPO for its work done to reply to the Panel's three questions.

2. As to the substance of the replies given, we note that no evidence in relation to the existence and scope under the Berne Convention of any exception or limitation including the so-called "minor reservations" doctrine, which would be susceptible of justifying the exemptions contained in Section 110(5) US Copyright Act, is contained in WIPO's replies and annexes.

3. In view of the EC/MS, this confirms our conclusion already expressed in point 26 of our presentation at the second substantive meeting that:

> *"All in all, it can be said that there exists no exception or limitation provision - express or implied - under the Berne Convention which could justify the exemptions contained in Section 110(5) Copyright Act, leave alone an exception or limitation provision which when "narrowed down" by Article 13 TRIPs could justify Section 110(5) Copyright Act."*

4. The EC/MS trust that they will be invited to comment on any substantive remarks that may be made by the US based on the WIPO reply and annexes.

---

[1] This submission by the EC contained also comments on a letter from a law firm representing ASCAP to the USTR that was copied to the Panel. This part of the submission is not reproduced here; neither is the letter in question nor the US comments on it reproduced in the attachments to this report. *See* section VI.B of the report.

ATTACHMENT 2.1

FIRST WRITTEN SUBMISSION OF THE UNITED STATES

(26 October 1999)

TABLE OF CONTENTS

I. INTRODUCTION

1. Section 110(5) of the United States Copyright Act of 1976[1] is fully consistent with the United States' obligations under the Agreement on Trade-Related Aspects of Intellectual Property Rights (the "TRIPS Agreement" or "TRIPS"). The TRIPS Agreement, incorporating the substantive provisions of the Berne Convention on Literary and Artistic Works (1971) ("Berne Convention"), allows Members to place minor limitations on the exclusive rights of copyright owners. Article 13 of TRIPS provides a standard by which to judge the appropriateness of such limitations or exceptions. The exemptions embodied in Section 110(5) fall within the Article 13 standard: they are special cases which do not conflict with a normal exploitation of the work and they do not unreasonably prejudice the legitimate interests of the right holder.

II. FACTUAL BACKGROUND

2. The United States has one of the strongest systems of intellectual property protection in the world. Under the U.S. copyright system, copyright holders are

[1] United States Copyright Act of 1976, Act of Oct. 19, 1976, Pub. L. 94-553, 90 Stat. 2541(as amended).

granted a "bundle" of exclusive rights. Specifically, Section 106 of the Copyright Act grants to right holders the exclusive right to do and authorize:

(i) the reproduction of a copyrighted work;

(ii) the preparation of derivative works based upon the copyrighted work;

(iii) the distribution of copies of the copyrighted work to the public;

(iv) in the case of literary, musical, dramatic, and choreographic works, pantomimes, and motion pictures and other audiovisual works, to perform the copyrighted work publicly;

(v) in the case of literary, musical, dramatic, and choreographic works, pantomimes, and pictorial, graphic, or sculptural works, the right to display the copyrighted work publicly; and

(vi) in the case of sound recordings, to perform the copyrighted work publicly by means of a digital audio transmission.

3. Section 110 of the Copyright Act provides for several limited exceptions to one of these exclusive rights - the public performance right. The exemptions in Section 110 include exceptions to the performance right for certain educational, charitable and religious uses, as well as the provisions challenged by the EC in this proceeding, Section 110(5)(A) and (B).

A. *Section 110(5)(A)*

4. Section 110(5)(A) constituted the entire Section 110(5) exemption for the 22 years prior to the passage of the Fairness in Music Licensing Act of 1998 ("the 1998 Amendment").[2] Section 110(5)(A) exempts public performances communicated by means of "homestyle" receiving equipment, subject to certain additional limitations, and provides as follows.[3]

> Notwithstanding the provisions of section 106, the following are not infringements of copyright:
>
> (5) communication of a transmission embodying a performance or display of a work by the public reception of the transmission on a single receiving apparatus of a kind commonly used in private homes, unless -
>
> (A) direct charge is made to see or hear the transmission; or
>
> (B) the transmission thus received is further transmitted to the public.

5. In establishing the "homestyle" exemption in 1976, Congress intended to exempt from copyright liability small stores and restaurants whose owners merely turned on an ordinary radio or television set while they worked. As explained in the House Report accompanying the 1976 revision of the Copyright Act,

---

2 The 1998 Amendment added a new subsection (B) to Section 110(5). Consequently, the previous Section 110(5) was redesignated Section 110(5)(A). Fairness in Music Licensing Act of Oct. 27, 1998, P.L. 105-298, 112 Stat. 2830, 105th Cong. 2nd Sess. (1998).

3 Section 110(5), both (A) and (B), also exempt the display right. Because that right has little or no economic relevance to copyright owners in musical works, it is not discussed here.

> [T]he clause would exempt small commercial establishments whose proprietors merely bring onto their premises standard radio or television equipment and turn it on for their customers' enjoyment, but it would impose liability where the proprietor has a commercial 'sound system' installed or converts a standard home receiving apparatus (by augmenting it with sophisticated or extensive amplification equipment) into the equivalent of a commercial sound system.[4]

According to the House Report, factors to consider in particular cases would include the size, physical arrangement, and noise level of the areas within the establishment where the transmissions were made, and the extent to which the receiving apparatus was altered or augmented for the purpose of improving the quality of the performance.[5] The Conference Report elaborates on the rationale for the exemption, noting that it would be justified in situations where the defendant was a small commercial establishment and "not of sufficient size to justify, as a practical matter, a subscription to a commercial background music service".[6]

6. By its nature, the licensing of thousands of individual restaurants and retail establishments is a difficult and resource-intensive process.[7] Naturally, there is a point at which the potential licensing revenue does not justify the administrative burden of the licensing process. The licensing process is especially difficult with respect to smaller establishments that might benefit from the homestyle exception. Congress expected the homestyle exemption to have a limited economic effect because it essentially codified the licensing practices of the performing rights organizations ("PROs") with respect to such establishments. As observed in the House Report on the homestyle exception, "in the vast majority of cases no royalties are collected today, and the exemption should be made explicit in the statute".[8]

7. In the almost two and one-half decades since the homestyle exemption was enacted, U.S. courts have applied the exception narrowly and in a manner consistent with Congress's intent. Of the forty decisions reported under Section 110(5) (now

---

4 Report of the House Committee on the Judiciary, H.R. Rep. No. 94-1476, 94th Cong., 2nd Sess. 87 (1976) (hereinafter " House Report") (the relevant page is annexed hereto as exhibit US-1).

5 Ibid. The factors to consider in applying the exemption are largely based on the facts of a case decided by the United States Supreme Court immediately prior to the passage of the 1976 Copyright Act, *Twentieth Century Music Corp. v. Aiken*, 422 U.S. 151 (1975). In *Aiken*, the Court held that an owner of a small fast food restaurant was not liable for playing music in a 1,055 square-foot shop that had only four speakers and a radio. The House Report describes the fact situation in *Aiken* as representing the "outer limit" of the homestyle exemption. Ibid.; *see also* exhibit EC-1.

6 Conference Report of the House Committee on the Judiciary, Subcommittee on Courts and Intellectual Property, H.R. Rep. No. 94-1733, 94th Cong., 2nd Sess. 75 (1976) (hereinafter "Conference Report") (annexed as exhibit US-2).

7 *See* Music Licensing in Restaurants and Retail and Other Establishments, Hearing before the House of Representatives, Subcommittee on Courts and Intellectual Property, Committee on the Judiciary (July 17, 1997) (hereinafter "Judiciary Committee Hearing") (testimony of Patrick Collins, SESAC, at 109-110). Due to the length of the Judiciary Committee Hearing transcript, we are not annexing this document, however, the transcript is available on the internet at: http://commdocs.house.gov/committees/judiciary/hju43667.000/ hju43667_0.htm.

8 House Report, at 86 (exhibit US-1).

Section 110(5)(A)), only three courts have found that the defendant was entitled to take advantage of the exception. In reaching their conclusions, courts have generally engaged in a highly fact-specific analysis, taking into account the factors cited in the text and legislative history of Section 110(5)(A). For example, in *Sailor Music v. Gap Stores, Inc.*, the Court of Appeals for the Second Circuit found that a chain store was not entitled to the homestyle exception because it used four to seven speakers recessed in the ceilings of its stores, and in the court's words, "was of sufficient size to justify, as a practical matter, a subscription to a commercial background music service".[9] Similarly, in *Broadcast Music, Inc. v. United States Shoe Corp.*, the Court of Appeals for the Ninth Circuit followed *Gap Stores* in denying the applicability of the homestyle exemption to a chain of retail stores. The Court expressly relied on the fact that the size and nature of the Defendant's operation justified the use of a commercial background music system.[10]

8. Two courts have given relatively greater weight to equipment, rather than other factors, in applying the homestyle exception. These two courts did not consider corporate revenues or ownership structure, but rather focused on the fact that the chain stores at issue had extremely limited stereo equipment. In *Broadcast Music, Inc. v. Claire's Boutiques*, for example, the "receiving apparatus" at issue retailed at $129.95, had just five watts of power, and was able to drive only two speakers, each of which measured 7 inches x 5 inches x 4 inches (approximately 18 x 13 x 10 cm). The Court then went on to conduct a stringent analysis of the stereo system, requiring the Defendant to prove that each of the components of the system was "home-type," and also that the components were configured in a manner commonly found in a home.[11] Similarly, in *Broadcast Music, Inc. v. Edison Brothers* , the court was persuaded that the exemption applied where it found that the company used only "low grade radio-only" receivers, with no more than two portable speakers placed within 15 feet (4.6m) of the receiver.[12]

---

[9] *Sailor Music v. Gap Stores, Inc.*, 668 F.2d 84 (2d Cir. 1981), *cert. denied*, 456 U.S. 945 (1982) ("*Gap Stores*") (the cases interpreting section 110(5)(A) are annexed as exhibit US-3 in alphabetical order).

[10] *Broadcast Music, Inc. v. United States Shoe Corp.*, 678 F.2d 816 (9th Cir. 1982). *See also Red Cloud Music Co. v. Schneegarten, Inc.*, 27 U.S.P.Q.2d 1219 (C.D. Cal. 1992) (following the *United States Shoe* decision). Other courts across the country have also applied this type of nuanced analysis of equipment and establishment size and revenues in finding that the homestyle exception did not apply. *E.g.*, *Hickory Grove Music v. Andrews*, 749 F. Supp. 1031 (D. Mont. 1990) (restaurant with 1,192 square feet using radio and recessed speaker system did not qualify for section 110(5) exemption); *Little Mole Music v. Mavar's Supermarket*, 12 U.S.P.Q.2d 1209 (N.D. Ohio 1988) (chain of supermarkets did not qualify for 110(5) exemption based on use of six to ten ceiling speakers and physical size); *Merrill v. Bill Miller's Bar-B-Q Enters.*, 688 F. Supp. 1172 (W.D. Tex. 1988) (chain of restaurants did not qualify for 110(5) because equipment was not homestyle, physical size was 1000 - 1500 sq. feet and annual revenues justified a commercial subscription service).

[11] *Broadcast Music Inc. v. Claire's Boutiques*, 949 F.2d 1482, 1493 (7th Cir. 1991).

[12] *Broadcast Music Inc. v. Edison Bros. Stores, Inc.*, *supra*. The EC makes the unsubstantiated statement in its submission that, as a result of this case, chain stores have adapted their music installation to qualify for the exemption or even canceled their subscription to music services. EC Submission, p. 9 note 25. The EC offers no support or citations whatsoever for these statements, and the U.S. is not aware of any cases in which this scenario actually occurred.

9. Taken as a whole, the substantial body of case law under Section 110(5)(A) demonstrates its limited nature and careful application by the courts. In addition, however, it is important to recognize that the 1998 Amendment dramatically limited the homestyle exception even further. As the EC acknowledges, Section 110(5)(A) no longer covers nondramatic musical works at all. Rather, it covers only other types of works, such as plays and operas. No licensing mechanism currently exists for right holders to collect royalties on a collective basis for secondary performances of these other types of works in establishments. As a practical matter, no royalties are collected for these secondary performances, and thus the statutory exemption for homestyle receiving equipment has no effect on this market.

B. Section 110(5)(B)

10. In the mid-1990s, in response to complaints from different sectors of the small business community of various abuses by the PROs,[13] Congress undertook consideration of a proposed expansion of the homestyle exemption advocated by a coalition of business associations (the "coalition"). The proposal put forward by the coalition was much broader than that which was eventually passed into law, and called for a complete exemption for the performance of nondramatic musical works, regardless of the type of establishment, size of establishment or equipment used to broadcast the work. It also would have permitted further retransmission beyond where the transmission was received. The only limitations were that no admission fee could be charged, and that the transmission must be properly licensed.[14]

11. At that time, the PROs also proposed amendments to Section 110(5) that they believed "accurately reflect[ed] uses by small commercial establishments in the mar-

[13] Specifically, there was widespread complaint from small business owners about harassment and abusive tactics by the PROs in the licensing process. *See generally*, Judiciary Committee Hearing, statement of Bruce A. Lehman, the Assistant Secretary of Commerce and Commissioner of Patents and Trademarks, at 42, statement of Pete Madland on behalf of the Tavern League of Wisconsin at 220, and testimony of Peter Kilgore on behalf of the National Restaurant Association at 235-236.

[14] The coalition's proposal was reflected in H.R. 789, the Fairness in Music Licensing Act of 1997, by Representative James Sensenbrenner, annexed hereto as exhibit US-4. This proposal, *not* the provisions at issue in this case, were the basis of the testimony by the Register of Copyright, Marybeth Peters, and Bruce Lehman, that is cited by the EC in its submission. EC first submission, para. 4. While the EC cites the portion of Ms. Peters' statements relating to this much broader exemption that was not enacted into law, they neglect to mention her statement on Section 110(5)(A). With respect to Section 110(5)(A), Ms. Peters noted that an ad hoc committee had investigated 110(5) in the context of U.S. accession to the Berne Convention and stated: "I strongly believe that the existing section 110(5) is fine, given what is required by the Berne Convention, and may be similar to exemptions that you see in a few other countries." Judiciary Committee Hearing at 46. Furthermore, the EC mischaracterizes the statements by Ms. Peters and Mr. Lehman concerning the TRIPS-compatibility of the coalition proposal. Even a cursory reading of the quoted statements reveals that Ms. Peters and Mr. Lehman actually expressed the belief that the proposed amendments would lead to *claims by other countries* that the United States was in violation of its obligations - an unsurprising view since the EC had already complained about the TRIPS-consistency of the homestyle exemption, and had initiated a formal investigation of the provision at the time the statements were made. *See also* exhibits EC-11 and EC-12.

ketplace".[15] The PROs' proposal, in addition to suggesting a square footage limit of 1,250 sq. ft. (116.2 sq. m.), also advocated specific equipment limitations of no more than four loudspeakers and two TV screens not greater than 44 inches (1.1m).[16] Notably, the scope of the exemption advocated by the PROs in this initial proposal was broader than the courts' interpretation of the existing homestyle exemption, and thus represented a modest expansion of the exemption.

12. In October of 1995, the National Licensed Beverage Association ("NLBA"), which had been one of the initial proponents of an amendment to Section 110(5) and an important member of the coalition, settled its differences with the PROs and signed a private group licensing agreement. This agreement applied to most of the NLBA's wide membership, and was also available to any eating, drinking or retail establishment licensed to sell alcohol for on-premise consumption.[17] It exempts establishments affiliated with the NLBA from paying licensing fees for the performance of music by radio or television if:

(i) the establishment is smaller than 3,500 sq. ft. [325.28 m. sq.], or,

(ii) the establishment is 3,500 sq. ft. or larger and no more than 6 radio and/or TV speakers are used, with no more than 4 in any one room; and no more than 3 TVs of a screen size smaller than 55 inches [1.4 m.] are used, with no more than 2 TVs in any one room; and

(iii) no direct charge was made to see or hear the transmission and there was no retransmission.[18]

13. The NLBA agreement also provided reduced licensing rates for music performances by other means, such as mechanical music, live performances, establishment-owned jukeboxes and radio and TV performances not qualifying for the exemption.[19] The largest U.S. PRO, the American Society of Composers, Authors and Publishers (ASCAP), praised the agreement, calling it a "fair compromise",[20] and stating that it would benefit small businesses while ensuring that the rights of "songwriters, composers and music publishers will remain protected".[21] Again, it is notable that the scope of the exemption in this voluntarily negotiated agreement is almost identical to the legislation that, three years later, in 1998, became the Fairness in Music Licensing Act. Moreover, at the time that the agreement was concluded with the NLBA, the PROs offered to extend the same proposal to the National Restaurant

---

15 Letter of July 24, 1995 to The Honorable Carlos Moorhead from ASCAP, BMI, Inc. and SESAC, Inc., (annexed hereto as exhibit US-5).

16 Ibid. at 5-6.

17 Any establishment that is a member of the NLBA can take advantage of the terms of the agreement and establishments which are not members of NLBA can, by joining the NLBA, also avail themselves of the agreement. To be a member of the NLBA, an establishment must sell alcohol on its premises, a condition that applies to all bars and taverns, as well as a very large number of restaurants.

18 NLBA News, April 1997 (annexed hereto as exhibit US-6).

19 Ibid.; *see also* Music Licensing Agreement with ASCAP, BMI & SESAC for NLBA Members, 2-3 (attached as exhibit US-7).

20 ASCAP *Playback*, February 1996 (annexed as exhibit US-8).

21 ASCAP *Playback*, December 1995 (annexed as exhibit US-9).

Association and other members of the business coalition, but, at that time, it was rejected.[22]

14. In October 1998, after extended negotiations between the PROs and the coalition, Congress passed legislation amending Section 110(5), with terms very similar to the NLBA agreement. The 1998 amendment revised Section 110(5) to add subsection (B), which applies exclusively to nondramatic musical works. The new subsection (B) exempts secondary performances of nondramatic musical works based on defined criteria of square footage and/or equipment, subject to three additional limitations. It provides in full as follows:

> (5)(B) communication by an establishment of a transmission or retransmission embodying a performance or display of a nondramatic musical work intended to be received by the general public originated by radio or television broadcast station licensed as such by the Federal Communications Commission, or, if an audiovisual transmission, by a cable system or satellite carrier, if:
>
> (i) in the case of an establishment other than a food service or drinking establishment, either the establishment in which the communication occurs has less than 2,000 gross square feet of space (185.9 m. sq.) (excluding space used for customer parking and for no other purpose) and:
>
>> (I) if the performance is by audio means only, the performance is communicated by means of a total of not more than 6 loudspeakers, of which not more than 4 loudspeakers are located in any 1 room or adjoining outdoor space; or
>>
>> (II) if the performance or display is by audiovisual means, any visual portion of the performance or display is communicated by means of a total of not more than 4 audiovisual devices, of which not more than 1 audiovisual device is located in any 1 room, and no such audiovisual device has a diagonal screen size greater than 55 inches, and any audio portion of the performance or display is communicated by means of a total of not more than 6 loudspeakers, of which not more than 4 loudspeakers are located in any 1 room or adjoining outdoor space;
>
> (ii) in the case of a food service or drinking establishment, either the establishment in which the communication occurs has less than 3,750 gross square feet of space (348.5 m. sq.) (excluding space used for customer parking and for no other purpose), or the establishment in which the communication

[22] Judiciary Committee Hearing (testimony of Wayland Holyfield, on behalf of ASCAP at 75). The NRA did not accept the offer, however, because of their view that its standards were more appropriately reflected in legislation, rather than a private commercial agreement.

occurs has 3,750 gross square feet of space or more (excluding space used for customer parking and for no other purpose) and:

(I) if the performance is by audio means only, the performance is communicated by means of a total of not more than 6 loudspeakers, of which not more than 4 loudspeakers are located in any 1 room or adjoining outdoor space; or

(II) if the performance or display is by audiovisual means, any visual portion of the performance or display is communicated by means of a total of not more than 4 audiovisual devices, of which not more than one audiovisual device is located in any 1 room, and no such audiovisual device has a diagonal screen size greater than 55 inches, and any audio portion of the performance or display is communicated by means of a total of not more than 6 loudspeakers, of which not more than 4 loudspeakers are located in any 1 room or adjoining outdoor space;

(iii) no direct charge is made to see or hear the transmission or retransmission;

(iv) the transmission or retransmission is not further transmitted beyond the establishment where it is received; and

(v) the transmission or retransmission is licensed by the copyright owner of the work so publicly performed or displayed.[23]

15. This legislation was part of a larger bill in which the term of protection for copyright was extended by twenty years, giving copyright owners substantially more protection than that required by international agreements.

16. Contrary to the assertions of the EC, Section 110(5)(B) does not apply to the communication of works over the Internet.[24] In fact, neither Section 110(5)(A) or Section 110(5)(B) exempts communications over a digital network. Such communications, by the very nature of the technological process of transmission, involve numerous incidences of reproduction, and could implicate the distribution right as well. When a work is transmitted to a distant location over a computer network, temporary RAM copies are made in the computers through which it passes, by virtue of the technological process of transmission.[25] This is an essential function of the way that digital information is transported over a digital network. The Section 110(5) exemp-

---

[23] P.L. 105-298, Section 202 (annexed as exhibit US-10).

[24] EC first submission, para. 39.

[25] The US courts have consistently held that RAM copies implicate the copyright holder's reproduction right. *See, e.g., MAI Sys. Corp. v. Peak Computer, Inc.*, 991 F.2d 511 (9th Cir. 1993), *cert. dismissed*, 114 S.Ct. 671 (1994); *Stenograph L.L.C. v. Bossard Assocs.*, 144 F.3d 96, 101-02 (D.C.Cir. 1998) (these cases are annexed as exhibit US-11). This conclusion was codified in Title III of the Digital Millennium Copyright Act at section 301.

tions, both (A) and (B), only apply to the performance right, and do not affect copyright holders' exclusive reproduction and distribution rights. Therefore, even under Section 110(5) as amended, establishment owners generally must still seek a license for the reproduction and possibly distribution rights implicated by Internet transmissions.

III. LEGAL ANALYSIS

17. The EC devotes almost its entire legal argument to arguing that Articles 11 and 11*bis* of the Berne Convention are implicated by the Section 110(5) exemptions. This issue is not in dispute. The relevant issue in this case is not whether Berne rights are implicated, but whether the provisions at issue are permissible exceptions under the standard of TRIPS Article 13. In its submission, the EC does not substantively address this central issue at all.

18. TRIPS Article 9(1) incorporates Articles 1 through 21 of the Berne Convention. The Berne Convention permits members to make "minor reservations" to the exclusive rights guaranteed by Berne, including limitations to the public performance right in Article 11 and 11*bis.*[26] TRIPS Article 13 articulates the standard by which the permissibility of these limitations to exclusive rights must be judged. This standard is based on the language in Berne Article 9(2),[27] which pertains to exceptions to the reproduction right, and provides: "It shall be a matter for legislation in the countries of the Union to permit the reproduction of such works in certain special cases, provided that such reproduction does not conflict with a normal exploitation of the work and does not unreasonably prejudice the legitimate interests of the author."

19. Article 13 of the TRIPS Agreement provides that "Members shall confine limitations and exceptions to exclusive rights to certain special cases which do not conflict with a normal exploitation of the work and do not unreasonably prejudice the legitimate interests of the right holder." This provision must be interpreted in accordance with the principles of treaty interpretation set out in Article 31 of the *Vienna Convention,* which provides in relevant part that "A treaty shall be interpreted in good faith in accordance with the ordinary meaning to be given to the terms of the treaty in their context and in the light of its object and purpose.[28]

20. The text of Article 13 plainly establishes cumulative requirements for exceptions to exclusive rights. Any exception must apply only to certain special cases, cannot conflict with a normal exploitation of the work, and, in addition, cannot cause unreasonable prejudice to the legitimate interests of the right holder.

21. The context of Article 13 includes other exceptions in the TRIPS Agreement that provide WTO members a certain amount of flexibility in implementing the relevant provisions of the Agreement. Articles 17, 26 and 30 contain language very similar to Article 13 and apply this exception to trademarks, industrial designs and

---

[26] World Intellectual Property Organization, *Guide to the Berne Convention for the Protection of Artistic and Literary Works (Paris Act 1971)* 103 (1978) ("WIPO Guide to the Berne Convention").

[27] *See also* Gervais, The TRIPS Agreement: Drafting History and Analysis, §2.72, 90 (1998).

[28] Appellate Body Report, *India - Patent Protection for Pharmaceutical and Agricultural Chemical Products*, WT/DS50/AB/R, adopted 16 January 1998, DSR 1998:I, 9 (citing Vienna Convention, done at Vienna, 23 May 1969, 1155 U.N.T.S. 221; 8 *International Legal Materials* 679 (1969)).

patents, respectively. Article 1.1 of TRIPS also emphasizes flexibility, and provides that "Members shall be free to determine the appropriate method of implementing the provisions of this Agreement within their own legal system and practice".

22. The object and purpose of Article 13, as reflected in its text, are to allow certain exceptions to the exclusive rights conferred by a copyright. The object and purpose should be considered in light of the "Objectives" of the Agreement, set forth in Article 7, which provides that the provisions of the Agreement are designed to result in mutual advantages to producers and users, and contribute to a balance of rights and obligations.

23. Each of the criteria in Article 13 of the TRIPS Agreement must be interpreted in light of these principles. Under such an analysis, the exceptions in Section 110(5)(A) and (B) satisfy Article 13 because they are confined to special cases which do not conflict with normal exploitation and do not unreasonably prejudice the legitimate interests of copyright holders.

A. Section 110(5) Applies to Certain Special Cases

24. As a preliminary matter, Section 110(5) is confined to "certain special cases." The TRIPS Agreement does not elaborate on the criteria for a case to be considered "special," and WTO Members have flexibility to determine for themselves whether a particular case represents an appropriate basis for an exception to exclusive rights. The limiting adjectives "certain" and "special" in Article 13 do indicate that exceptions should be "clearly delineated," rather than vague and open ended.[29]

25. Section 110(5)(A) is confined to certain special cases - *i.e.*, those involving use of a "homestyle" receiving apparatus. This is a fact-specific standard, but nonetheless one that is well-defined. Courts have considered the various factors articulated in the text and legislative history of the provision in determining whether a given establishment meets the Section 110(5)(A) standard. Although judges may have weighed the various factors differently in making their individual decisions, these cases reflect the reasonable and consistent application of a fact-specific standard in a common-law system.

26. Section 110(5)(B) is also confined to certain special cases, and defines with great precision the establishments that are entitled to benefit from the exception. The size and equipment limitations in the law are unambiguous, and can be applied with ease.

B. Section 110(5) Does Not Conflict with Normal Exploitation

27. There is no normative definition in TRIPS as to what constitutes the "normal exploitation" of a copyrighted work. The normal exploitation of a work, however, can and must necessarily include permissible exceptions to an author's exclusive rights - it is for the purpose of allowing those exceptions that Article 13 was included in the TRIPS Agreement. Limitations and exceptions to exclusive rights by definition deprive a copyright owner of potential compensation for certain uses of his or her work. If every time a copyright owner was deprived of any potential compensation,

[29] Gervais at 90.

such deprivation constituted a conflict with normal exploitation, then Article 13 would have no meaning.

28. To determine what constitutes normal exploitation, the Panel must look at all "the ways in which an author might reasonably be expected to exploit his work in the normal course of events".[30] Under U.S. copyright law, the copyright owner of a musical work has a broad range of exclusive rights. Those most important to such right holders include the right to reproduce their work in copies and phonorecords, the right to distribute and sell those copies and phonorecords, and the right to perform their music publicly.[31] Section 110(5) is an exception to only the public performance right.

29. With respect to the public performance right, by far the most significant area of exploitation for the copyright owner is the primary performance of the work. The compensation paid by broadcasters for the right to broadcast the musical work is particularly important. Royalties from broadcasting and live performance are the principal means by which copyright owners in nondramatic musical works receive compensation for the public performance of their works. Section 110(5) does not affect a copyright owner's right to be compensated for these types of exploitation. Rather, it affects only secondary uses of broadcasts. Moreover, it does not exempt all secondary performances, but only those in establishments that use homestyle receiving equipment, or meet the square footage and other criteria in the statute. Finally, even in those establishments exempted by Section 110(5), owners must still pay licensing fees for the use of recorded music, on CD or cassette tapes, and for live performances of music.

30. Furthermore, as noted by Professor Ricketson, a use does not conflict with normal exploitation if the copyright owner would not otherwise expect to collect a fee from that use.[32] It is important to emphasize that the issue in this dispute is the scope of normal exploitation in the United States. Thus, even though a use may technically fall within the exclusive rights of the copyright owner, it may not normally be capable of being exploited within a particular market or jurisdiction. With respect to the homestyle exemption in Section 110(5)(A), even *before* nondramatic musical works were removed from its scope by the passage of the 1998 Amendment, it was limited to establishments that were not large enough to justify a subscription to a commercial background music service.[33] As noted in the House Report, Congress intended that this exception would merely codify the licensing practices already in effect by the right holders and their licensing organizations.[34] Congress's intent and scope has been followed by the courts, as discussed above. Since 110(5)(A) only affected establishments that were not likely otherwise to enter into a license, or

---

30 Sam Ricketson, *The Berne Convention for the Protection of Literary and Artistic Works: 1886-1986*, 483 (Kluwer 1987). This language refers to the use of the phrase "normal exploitation" in the context of Berne Art. 9(2).

31 This includes the right to broadcast their work found in Berne Art. 11*bis*.

32 Ricketson, at 483 (an example of uses that would not conflict with normal exploitation is "uses for which [the copyright owner] would not ordinarily expect to receive a fee - even though they fall strictly within the scope of his [exclusive] right").

33 Conference Report, 75 (exhibit US-2).

34 House Report, 86 (exhibit US-1).

would not have been licensed under the practices at that time, it did not conflict with the expectations of right holders concerning the normal exploitation of their works.

31. Now that Section 110(5)(A) excludes nondramatic musical works (*e.g.*, songs commonly played on the radio rather than as part of a larger dramatic performance such as an opera) from its scope, it is even more clear that it does not conflict with the normal exploitation of copyrighted works. For nondramatic musical works, there is, at least, a collective licensing mechanism (the PROs) that generates *some* revenue from secondary performances. For the remaining works covered by the exemption, such as operas, plays, and musicals, there is no such system for the collective licensing of secondary performances, and little or no direct licensing by right holders to retail, eating or drinking establishments. Owners of copyright in these works do not and have never expected direct revenue from secondary performances in such establishments. In other words, licensing this aspect of the performance right is not a part of how an author "might reasonably [] expect[] to exploit his work in the normal course of events.[35]

32. In the case of Section 110(5)(B), a significant portion of the establishments exempted by that section had already been exempted, for almost a quarter of a century, by the homestyle exception. Owners of copyrights in nondramatic musical works had no expectation of receiving a fee from these establishments. Moreover, even if Section 110(5)(B) had not been passed, many of the establishments now eligible for that exemption would have been able to avail themselves of the nearly identical exemption under the NLBA agreement voluntarily concluded by the PROs. Thus, even prior to the passage of the 1998 Amendment, copyright owners would not normally expect a fee from these establishments either. In the final analysis, a small number of establishments may not have been entitled to take advantage of either the homestyle exemption or the NLBA agreement; and thus were newly exempted under Section 110(5)(B). However, when viewed against the panoply of exploitative uses available to a copyright owner under the U.S. Copyright Act, this minor limitation on some secondary uses on broadcasts to the public simply does not rise to the level of a conflict with normal exploitation.

C. Section 110(5) Does Not Unreasonably Prejudice the Legitimate Interests of the Right Holder

33. While the "conflict with normal exploitation" standard of TRIPS Article 13 looks to the amount of market displacement caused by a limitation or exception, the "unreasonable prejudice" standard measures how much the right holder is harmed by the effects of the exception. It is important to recognize that the issue in this analysis is not whether the right holder's interests are prejudiced. Given that any exception to exclusive rights may technically result in some degree of prejudice to the right holder, the key question is whether that prejudice is unreasonable.[36]

[35] Ricketson, 483. This language refers to the use of the phrase "normal exploitation" in the context of Berne Art. 9(2).

[36] WIPO Guide to the Berne Convention at 55-56.

1. Section 110(5)(A)

34. The economic effect of Section 110(5)(A) was minimal even before the passage of the 1998 Amendment, and thus caused no unreasonable prejudice to any legitimate interests of EC right holders. Returning again to the fundamental intent of the provision, it was to exempt from liability small shop and restaurant owners whose establishments, for a variety of reasons, would not have justified a commercial license. In general, where no such licenses would have been sought or issued in the absence of an exception, there is literally no economic detriment to the right holder from an explicit exception.[37] The establishments exempted by Section 110(5)(A), with small square footage and elementary sound equipment, are the least likely to be aggressively licensed by the PROs and licensing fees for these establishments would likely be the lowest in the range.[38] Furthermore, given their size and that the playing of music is often incidental to their services, these establishments are among those most likely simply to turn off the radio if pressed to pay licensing fees.

35. With the passage of the 1998 Amendment, and the removal of nondramatic musical works from the scope of Section 110(5)(A), this section has been limited even further and ceased to have any real economic relevance. As described above, there is, for all practical purposes, no substantial licensing market for secondary performances in retail, eating or drinking establishments for works now covered by Section 110(5)(A). In other words, these establishments are not and could not be significant sources of revenue for right holders. Therefore, this exception does not prejudice the legitimate interests of these right holders.

36. Perhaps most probative of this issue, the EC has not made any attempt, in its submission, to address the effect of this exception on its right holders. Nowhere in its submission are there any concrete allegations as to the prejudice the EC believes it suffers as a result of Section 110(5)(A).

2. Section 110(5)(B)

37. In the section of its submission entitled "Quantitative effects on copyright owners," the EC provides no information about the quantitative effects on copyright owners of Section 110(5)(B). Instead, the EC provides the Panel with a few statistics - meaningless by themselves - concerning the square footage of certain drinking, eating and retail establishments in the United States. For several reasons, these numbers do not serve as a useful basis for estimating the economic impact of Section 110(5)(B) on right holders. They fail to account for the majority of the relevant factors that determine whether a right holder would be economically prejudiced at all by the exemption in Section 110(5)(B). Even assuming for the sake of argument the accuracy of the figures cited by the EC, in order to obtain a reasonable estimate of the number of establishments from which copyright owners have truly lost revenue as a result of the FMLA, one would have to:

- subtract from those gross totals the sizable number of establishments that do not play music;

---

[37] *See supra* para. 6 (discussion of licensing practice).

[38] *See* Judiciary Committee Hearing, letter from Marilyn Bergman, ASCAP President and Chairman of the Board, at 175-186.

- subtract from that number the establishments that rely on music from some source other than radio or TV (such as tapes, CDs, jukeboxes, or live music);
- subtract again for the number that were not licensed prior to the passage of the FMLA and which the PROs would not be able to license anyway regardless of the exemption;
- subtract once more for the establishments that would simply take advantage of the NLBA agreement practically identical to Section 110(5)(B) if the statutory exemption were not available; and,
- finally, subtract again for the establishments that would prefer to simply turn off the music rather than pay the fees demanded by the PROs.

While these figures are impossible to estimate with scientific precision, there is ample reason to believe that they represent substantial numbers of establishments. Even a realistic figure of the number of establishments from which copyright owners have lost revenue, however, would not present a true figure of economic harm to EC right holders. Whatever revenues could be collected from these smaller establishments would then have to be reduced again by the portion due to right holders in the EC, as opposed to all other right holders.

38. The EC makes no attempt to take these factors into account but rather merely asserts that copyright owners have been deprived of a significant source of income. Without providing any support for this assertion, the EC has not presented a *prima facie* case that any prejudice suffered by EC right holders is unreasonable within the meaning of Article 13 of the TRIPS Agreement.

39. In light of the history of the 1998 Amendment, and the close similarity between that legislation and the voluntary agreement reached between the PROs and the NLBA in 1995, the EC's claim that copyright holders are suffering unreasonable prejudice is even more tenuous. As previously discussed, the PROs voluntarily concluded the agreement with the NLBA that exempts almost the same establishments. Far from alleging unreasonableness, the PROs hailed this agreement as a "fair" deal that "protected" their members' rights. Marilyn Bergman, President and Chairman of ASCAP, explained in ASCAP's 1996 Annual Report, "We are proud to have reached a resolution with the NLBA and it is a good one for both of our organizations".[39]

40. Finally, the analysis of unreasonable prejudice must also take into account the limited resources of the PROs and the small percentage of the market actually licensed by the PROs. In light of the certainty provided by the precise limitations of the Section 110(5)(B) exemption, the PROs can now efficiently redirect their licensing resources toward those establishments not eligible for the Section 110(5)(B) exemption, and thus compensate for any minor prejudice they might suffer. In fact, the largest PRO has already stated its intent to do exactly this, as well as generate additional income by encouraging live and recorded music, for which there is no exemption. Even before the 1998 Amendment went into effect, ASCAP outlined its plan to "reverse the effects" of the legislation: "A critical element of our plan will be to *aggressively license those eligible establishments that have withheld royalty payment*

[39] Marilyn Bergman, *Safeguarding the Creative Community*, ASCAP Annual Report, 1 (1996) (annexed as exhibit US-12).

and to promote the value of live and mechanical music to a large number of newly targeted establishments."[40]

IV. CONCLUSION

41. For all of these reasons, the Panel should find that both Section 110(5)(A) and Section 110(5)(B) of the U.S. Copyright Act meet the standards of Article 13 of the TRIPS Agreement and the substantive obligations of the Berne Convention. Both provisions are limited to certain special cases, and do not conflict with a normal exploitation of the work, nor cause unreasonable prejudice to the legitimate interests of EC right holders. Accordingly, this Panel should dismiss the claims of the EC in this dispute.

[40] ASCAP, *Playback*, October-November-December 1998, at 2 (emphasis added) (annexed as exhibit US-13).

ATTACHMENT 2.2

ORAL STATEMENT OF THE UNITED STATES AT THE FIRST MEETING WITH THE PANEL

(8 November 1999)

I. INTRODUCTION

1. Good morning, Madame Chair and members of the Panel. We are pleased to have this opportunity to appear before you to present the arguments of the United States in defense of the Section 110(5) music licensing exemptions. We welcome any questions you may have, and we look forward to responding to them.

2. The United States has one of the strongest systems of intellectual property protection in the world. In fact, the 1998 music licensing amendment was part of a larger bill in which the term of protection for copyright was extended by twenty years, giving copyright owners substantially more protection than that required by international agreements. To help the Panel focus on the real issue in this dispute, we have provided you a chart, exhibit US-14, which outlines the scope of the exemptions in the relevant context.

II. BACKGROUND OF SECTION 110(5) EXEMPTIONS

3. Turning to exhibit US-14, we see that the U. S. copyright system grants a bundle of exclusive rights to right holders. Specifically, right holders are granted the exclusive right to do and authorize: (1) the reproduction of their work in copies and phonorecords, (2) the distribution and sale of those copies and phonorecords, (3) the adaptation, translation, arrangement or other transformation of their work, (4) the public performance of their work, (5) the display of their work, and (6) with respect to sound recordings, the public performance by means of a digital audio transmission. Of these rights, the most important to a right holder in musical works are the reproduction, distribution and public performance nights.

4. Section 110(5) effectively limits only one of these exclusive nights - the public performance right. Moreover, Section 110(5) has no effect on the most significant area of public performance exploitation for a copyright owner - the primary performance of his or her work (for example, broadcasting of works over the television and radio). Rather, the exception is limited to only certain secondary uses of broadcasts of public performances, for which the right holder has already been compensated for the primary performance.

5. The EC grossly exaggerates the scope of Section 110(5). It is important to remember that there are two exceptions contained in Section 110(5): the Section 110(5)(A) homestyle exemption (which has been narrowed), and Section 110(5)(B), which was added by the 1998 amendment. Almost all of the EC's allegations are based on speculation regarding the impact of the 1998 Amendment, which created Section 110(5)(B).

6. With respect to the homestyle exemption, the EC acknowledges that its scope has been limited by the 1998 Amendment's removal of nondramatic musical works from its purview. However, the EC attempts to distort the standing body of caselaw developed by U.S. courts over more than twenty years regarding the scope of the homestyle exemption.

7. As we demonstrated in our first submission, in the almost two and one-half decades since the homestyle exemption was enacted, U.S. courts have applied the exception narrowly and in a manner consistent with the text of the statute and with Congress's stated intent. Of the forty decisions reported under Section 110(5) (the homestyle exemption), only three courts have found that the defendant was entitled to take advantage of the exception. Of those three cases, only two courts, in *Claire's Boutiques* and in *Edison Bros.,* found that chain stores qualified for the exemption. In both cases the deciding factor was the limited and unsophisticated homestyle-type equipment used in the stores. For example, in *Edison Bros.,* the stores used only a *radio-only* receivers with two portable speakers placed within 15 feet of the receiver. These two cases are not "illustrative" as the EC has claimed this morning and in their submission. They are the only cases finding that a chain store qualified for the exemption.

8. The mid-1990s brought a call for relief from small businesses against what they viewed as abusive collecting tactics and harassment by the collecting societies. Over the next several years, a broad expansion of the homestyle exemption was advocated by a diverse coalition of businesses. In response, the collecting societies proposed legislation exempting establishments based on size and equipment. Indeed, the legislation that ultimately became Section 110(5)(B) last year, after intensive negotiations with the business coalition and the collecting societies, was remarkably similar to the agreement the collecting societies voluntarily negotiated with the National Licensed Beverage Association three years earlier. At that time, ASCAP, the largest U.S. collecting society, praised the NLBA agreement, calling it a "fair compromise."

III. SECTION 110(5) MEETS ARTICLE 13'S STANDARD

9. As we noted in our first submission, the relevant issue in this case is not whether Berne Convention rights are implicated, but whether the provisions at issue are permissible exceptions under the TRIPS articulation, in Article 13, of the Berne "minor reservations" standard. TRIPS Article 13 articulates the standard by which the permissibility of limitations (or "minor reservations") to exclusive rights must be judged. Indeed, TRIPS Article 13 is based on the Berne standard for exceptions to the exclusive reproduction right, Berne Article 9(2).

10. In considering, the scope of Berne Convention rights such as those at issue in this case, it is important to remember the basic distinction that exists in copyright law between exceptions to exclusive rights and compulsory licenses. Sections 110(5)(A) and (B) are exceptions to an exclusive right. By contrast, with respect to certain rights, Berne permits countries to provide a compulsory license in lieu of an exclusive right. With a compulsory license, an author is deprived of the right to authorize or prohibit use of the work, provided that compensation is provided. Exceptions and compulsory licenses are subject to different standards of review under Berne. Excep-

tions to exclusive rights are generally subject to the doctrine of "minor reservations." Compulsory licenses are subject to the standard of equitable remuneration, such as articulated in Article 11*bis*(2). For this reason, Article 11*bis*(2) is not relevant to the Panel's consideration of Sections 110(5)(A) and (B).

11. The central issue for the Panel then, is to determine whether, in accordance with TRIPS Article 13, Section 110(5) exempts from copyright infringement "special cases which do not conflict with a normal exploitation of the work and do not unreasonably prejudice the legitimate interests of the right holder".

12. As a preliminary matter, Section 110(5) is confined to "certain special cases". The TRIPS Agreement does not elaborate on the criteria for a case to be considered "special", and WTO Members have flexibility to determine for themselves whether a particular case represents an appropriate basis for an exception to exclusive rights. The limiting adjectives "certain" and "special" in Article 13 do indicate that exceptions should be "clearly delineated", rather than vague and open ended.

13. The homestyle exemption is confined to certain special cases - that is, those involving use of a "homestyle" receiving apparatus in small businesses which would not generally pay for a commercial license. This is a fact-specific standard, but nonetheless one that is well-defined. Courts have considered the various factors articulated in the text and legislative history of the provision in determining whether a given establishment meets the homestyle exemption standard. Although judges may have weighed the various factors differently in making their individual decisions, these cases reflect the reasonable and consistent application of a fact-specific standard in a common-law system.

14. The 1998 Amendment is also confined to certain special cases, and defines with great precision the establishments that are entitled to benefit from the exception. The size and equipment limitations in the law are unambiguous, and can be applied with ease. The legislative history of the 1998 Amendment demonstrates Congress's view that the straightforward square footage criteria would curtail overreaching and abusive tactics by the collecting societies.

IV. NORMAL EXPLOITATION

15. The two central assessments therefore, are whether Section 110(5) conflicts with normal exploitation and unreasonably prejudices the legitimate interests of the copyright holder. First, limitations and exceptions to exclusive rights by definition deprive a copyright owner of potential compensation for certain uses of his or her work. If every time a copyright owner was deprived of any potential compensation, such deprivation constituted a conflict with normal exploitation, then Article 13 would have no meaning.

16. To determine what constitutes normal exploitation, the Panel must look to the ways in which an author might reasonably be expected to exploit his work in the normal course of events. As outlined in exhibit US-14, under U.S. copyright law, the copyright owner of a musical work has a broad range of exclusive rights. Section 110(5) is an exception to only one of the three most important exclusive rights - the public performance right. Of the uses protected by this public performance right, Section 110(5) affects only certain secondary uses, and does not affect the most significant area of public performance exploitation for the copyright owner, the primary

performance of the work. Moreover, even in those establishments exempted by Section 110(5), owners must still pay licensing fees for the use of recorded music, on CD or cassette tapes, and for live performances of music.

17. As we emphasized in our submission, the relevant market to assess the scope of normal exploitation in this dispute is that of the United States. Thus, even though a use may technically fall within the exclusive rights of the copyright owner, it may not normally be capable of being exploited within a particular market or jurisdiction. With respect to the homestyle exemption, even before nondramatic musical works were removed from its scope by the passage of the 1998 Amendment, it was limited to establishments that were not large enough to justify a subscription to a commercial background music service.

18. Indeed, this exception merely codified the licensing practices already in effect by the right holders and their licensing organizations. Since the homestyle exemption only affected establishments that were not likely otherwise to enter into a license, or would not have been licensed under the practices at that time, it did not conflict with the expectations of right holders concerning the normal exploitation of their works.

19. Now that the homestyle exemption excludes nondramatic musical works *(e.g.*, songs commonly played on the radio rather than as part of a larger dramatic performance such as an opera) from its scope, it is even more clear that it does not conflict with the normal exploitation of copyrighted works. For nondramatic musical works (such as pop, jazz or rock songs), there is, at least, a collective licensing mechanism (the collecting societies) that generates *some* revenue from secondary performances. For the remaining works covered by the homestyle exemption, such as operas, plays, and musicals, there is no such system for the collective licensing of secondary performances, and little or no direct licensing by right holders to retail, eating or drinking establishments. Owners of copyright in these works do not and have never expected direct revenue from secondary performances in such establishments.

20. In the case of the 1998 Amendment, a significant portion of the establishments exempted by that section had already been exempted, for almost a quarter of a century, by the homestyle exception. Owners of copyrights in nondramatic musical works had no expectation of receiving a fee from these establishments. Moreover, even if the 1998 Amendment had not been passed, many of the establishments now eligible for that exemption would have been able to avail themselves of the nearly identical exemption under the NLBA agreement voluntarily concluded by the collecting societies. We would note that both the NLBA agreement and the 1998 Amendment are based on square footage, as well as equipment. In the NLBA agreement, the square footage requirement is 3,500 square feet, and in the 1998 Agreement it is 3,750 square feet, a difference of only 250 square feet. Thus, even prior to the passage of the 1998 Amendment, copyright owners would not normally have expected a fee from these establishments either.

21. In the final analysis, a small number of establishments may not have been entitled to take advantage of either the homestyle exemption or the NLBA agreement; and thus were newly exempted under the 1998 Amendment. However, given that copyright owners did not expect to receive compensation from most of the uses exempted by the statute, this minor limitation on some secondary uses on broadcasts to the public simply does not rise to the level of a conflict with normal exploitation. Therefore, the Section 110(5) exemptions do not conflict with normal exploitation.

V. UNREASONABLE PREJUDICE

22. The "unreasonable prejudice" standard measures how much the right holder is harmed by the effects of the exception. It is important to recognize that the issue in this analysis is not whether the right holder's interests are prejudiced. Any exception to exclusive rights may technically result in some degree of prejudice to the right holder. The key question is whether that prejudice is unreasonable.

23. The economic effect of the homestyle exemption was minimal even before the passage of the 1998 Amendment, and thus caused no unreasonable prejudice to any legitimate interests of EC right holders. Returning again to the fundamental intent of the provision, it was to exempt from liability small shop and restaurant owners whose establishments did not justify a commercial license. Rather, the homestyle exemption merely codified then existing licensing practices. In general, where no such licenses would have been sought or issued in the absence of an exception, there is literally no economic detriment to the right holder from an explicit exception. As noted by ASCAP, the establishments exempted by the homestyle exemption, with small square footage and elementary sound equipment, are the least likely to be aggressively licensed by the collecting societies and licensing fees for these establishments would likely be the lowest in the range. (ASCAP's letter introduced at the Judiciary Committee Hearings). Furthermore, given their size and that the playing of music is often incidental to their services, these establishments are among those most likely simply to turn off the radio if pressed to pay licensing fees.

24. With the passage of the 1998 Amendment, and the removal of nondramatic musical works from the scope of the homestyle exemption, this section has been limited even further and ceased to have any real economic relevance. As we have demonstrated, there is, for all practical purposes, no substantial licensing market for secondary performances in retail, eating or drinking establishments for the limited category of works now covered by the homestyle exemption (dramatic works such as operas). In other words, these establishments are not and could not be significant sources of revenue for right holders. Therefore, this exception does not prejudice the legitimate interests of these right holders.

25. In the section of its submission entitled "Quantitative effects on copyright owners," and here again today, the EC provides the Panel with a few statistics - meaningless by themselves - concerning the square footage of certain drinking, eating and retail establishments in the United States, intended to show the dramatic effect of the 1998 Amendment. For several reasons, however, these numbers are not relevant. They certainly do not serve as a useful basis for estimating the economic impact of the 1998 Amendment on right holders. They fail to account for the majority of the relevant factors that determine whether a right holder would be economically prejudiced at all by the exemption in the 1998 Amendment. Even assuming for the sake of argument the accuracy of the figures cited by the EC, in order to obtain a reasonable estimate of the number of establishments from which copyright owners have truly lost revenue as a result of the 1998 Amendment, one would have to:

- subtract from those gross totals the sizable number of establishments that do not play music;
- subtract from that number the establishments that rely on music from some source other than radio or TV (such as tapes, CDs, jukeboxes, or live music);

- subtract again for the number that were not licensed prior to the passage of the 1998 Amendment and which the collecting societies would not be able to license anyway regardless of the exemption;
- subtract once more for the establishments that would simply take advantage of the NLBA agreement practically identical to the 1998 Amendment if the statutory exemption were not available; and,
- finally, subtract again for the establishments that would prefer to simply turn off the music rather than pay the fees demanded by the collecting, societies.

While these figures are impossible to estimate with scientific precision, there is ample reason to believe that they represent substantial numbers of establishments.

26. Even a realistic estimate of the number of establishments from which copyright owners have lost revenue, however, would not present a true picture of economic harm to EC right holders. Whatever revenues could be collected from these smaller establishments would then have to be reduced again by the portion due to right holders in the EC, as opposed to all other right holders.

27. The EC makes no attempt to take these factors into account but rather merely asserts that copyright owners have been deprived of a significant source of income. Without providing any support for this assertion, the EC has not presented *prima facie* case that any prejudice suffered by EC right holders is unreasonable within the meaning of Article 13 of the TRIPS Agreement.

28. In light of the history of the 1998 Amendment, and the close similarity between that legislation and the voluntary agreement reached between the collecting societies and the NLBA in 1995, the EC's claim that copyright holders are suffering unreasonable prejudice is even more tenuous. As previously discussed, the collecting societies voluntarily concluded the agreement with the NLBA that exempts almost the same establishments. Far from alleging unreasonableness, the collecting societies hailed this agreement as a "fair" deal that "protected" their members' rights.

29. Finally, the analysis of unreasonable prejudice must also take into account the limited resources of the collecting societies and the small percentage of the market they actually license. For example, the revenues generated by ASCAP from general licensing average 14% of overall revenues. This 14% includes significant sources of revenues that are unaffected by Section 110 (5). In addition to radio music played in establishments, it includes use of music at large gatherings such as conventions and in establishments such as circuses, theme parks, shopping malls, sports events and roller and ice rinks. It also includes revenues from certain live performances and from recorded music (CDs, records and tapes). Therefore, any revenue loss to the collecting societies as a result of Section 110(5) is necessarily a small fraction of the 14% of total revenues.

30. In light of the certainty provided by the precise limitations of the 1998 Amendment, the collecting societies can now efficiently redirect their licensing resources toward those establishments not eligible for the Section 110(5)(B) exemption, and thus compensate for any minor prejudice they might suffer. In fact, ASCAP has already stated its intent to do exactly this, as well as generate additional income by encouraging live and recorded music, for which there is no exemption. As noted in our first submission, even before the 1998 Amendment went into effect, ASCAP outlined its plan to "reverse the effects" of the legislation.

31. We believe that a thorough analysis of all the issues will lead you to conclude that both the homestyle exemption and the 1998 Amendment are fully consistent with the TRIPS Agreement. Thank you.

ATTACHMENT 2.3

RESPONSES OF THE UNITED STATES TO WRITTEN QUESTIONS FROM THE PANEL - FIRST MEETING

(19 November 1999)

I. REPLIES TO QUESTIONS FROM THE PANEL TO THE UNITED STATES

Q.1 Please provide:

(a) a consolidated version of the current text of Section 110(5) of the US Copyright Act together with the current text of Section 106;

(b) a copy of the study by the US Congressional Research Service on the impact of the proposed legislation referred to in paragraph 5.3 of the Australian submission;

(c) if possible, a copy of the full text of the group licensing agreement between the US collective management organizations (CMOs) and the National Licensed Beverage Association (NLBA) referred to in your submission.

(a) There is no official U.S. Government text consolidating Section 110(5). We are providing the Panel with a copy of a commercial service's consolidated Section 110(5), as well as the current text of Section 106 at exhibit US-15.

(b) It is our understanding that the CRS "study" referred to by Australia involved only the preparation of a couple of estimates, resulting in the one chart attached at exhibit US-16.

(c) We have been advised by the NLBA that its Agreement with the collecting societies contains a strict nondisclosure provision, and cannot be released. However, we have attached an NLBA circular, as well as a letter from the organization, both of which provide an overview of its main terms. (*See* exhibit US-17.)

Exceptions and limitations

Q.2 In paragraph 17 of its first submission, the US states - with respect to the EC allegations that Section 110(5) of the US Copyright Act violates Articles 11 and/or Article 11*bis* of the Berne Convention in combination with Article 9.1 of the TRIPS Agreement - "this issue is not in dispute" and that the dispute centres around the exceptions and limitations in Article 13 of the TRIPS Agreement. Could the US clarify whether it accepts that Section 110(5)(A)(B) in its revised form is not consistent with Articles 11 and/or 11*bis* of the Berne Convention read in combination with Article 9.1 of the TRIPS Agreement, but that it claims that Section 110(5) is fully justified by the exceptions and limitations provided in Article 13 of the TRIPS Agreement?

The U.S. does not dispute that Section 110(5)(A) and (B) implicate Articles 11 and 11*bis* of the Berne Convention. That is to say, it affects rights that are protected under those Articles. The question of whether Section 110(5) is consistent with those Articles cannot be determined, however, without looking both to the scope of the rights that they afford, and to the exceptions which are permitted to those rights. Only if Section 110(5) does not fall within the exceptions permitted to Articles 11 and 11*bis* will it be inconsistent with them.

The U.S. does not claim that TRIPS Article 13 permits exceptions or limitations that would not be allowed by the Berne Convention, with respect to Berne rights. The U.S. does claim that Section 110(5) is justified under the minor reservations doctrine. TRIPS Article 13 is relevant because it provides an explicit test under which a minor reservation must be evaluated. TRIPS Article 13 is a mechanism for evaluating what would, and what would not, be permissible under Berne. (For further discussion of this issue, please see U.S. Response to Panel Question 14.)

Categories of works

Q.3 Section 110(5)(B) applies to "performance or display of a nondramatic musical work". What was the objective of excluding works other than nondramatic musical works from the scope of application of Subsection (B)? When is "display" of a nondramatic musical work relevant? To what extent does Subsection (B) apply to categories other than musical works, in particular to audiovisual works?

Nondramatic works were the focus of Subsection (B) for two related reasons. First, the impetus for the enactment of Subsection (B) was complaints from business owners about the licensing tactics of the PROs. Since PROs do not license dramatic musical works, there were no complaints about the licensing of such works, and thus there was no reason to address these works in the amendment. Furthermore, in as much as the PROs do not license them, there is effectively no licensing of secondary performances of dramatic musical works in establishments affected by the exemption. To our knowledge, individual right holders do not license these types of secondary performances. Without any licensing taking place in this field, there was no need for Section 110(5)(B) to include such works.

A display of a nondramatic musical work is almost never relevant. The only occasion in which it would conceivably arise would be an audiovisual transmission in which sheet music was held up to the camera. It should also be noted that the display right, while present in U.S. law, is not required by the Berne Convention.

Subsection (B) does not to apply to any categories of works other than nondramatic musical works. The application of this provision to works other than nondramatic musical works, and in particular audiovisual works, turns on the construction of the word "embodying". Subsection (B) exempts only the performances of nondramatic musical works which occur in the process of an audiovisual transmission. While the establishment owner would not be required to pay a license fee for the performance of music during television programs, he or she would still be required to pay the copyright owners of the other works performed, such as cinematographic works. In practice, however, there is no licensing of the secondary performances of other types of works, including audiovisual works, to bars, restaurants and retail establishments.

Establishments covered

Q.4 Under Subsection 110(5)(B) of the U.S. Copyright Act, if (I) an establishment other than a food service or drinking establishment has less than 2,000 gross square feet of space or (ii) a food service or drinking establishment has less than 3,750 gross square feet of space, and if it wants to play nondramatic musical works, can it use any professional equipment or can it use only a homestyle-type equipment described in Subsection 110(5)(A)?

If an establishment falls within the 2,000/3,750 square footage limit, the equipment limitations of Subsection (A) do not apply.

Rights affected

Q.5 What types of transmissions are covered by Section 110(5)(A) and (B), in particular:

(a) Please specify separately in respect of Subsection (A) and (B) whether they cover:

(i) original broadcasts over the air;

Both Subsections A and B would cover if the broadcasts originated from a radio or TV station licensed by the FCC.

(ii) original satellite broadcasting;

Both Subsections A and B would cover.

(iii) rebroadcasting by terrestrial means or by satellite;

Both Subsections A and B would cover.

(iv) cable retransmission of original broadcast;

Both Subsections A and B would cover.

(v) original cable transmission or other transmission by wire.

Both Subsections A and B would cover.

(b) In the above-mentioned cases, is there a difference between the treatment of audio and audiovisual transmissions?

Generally, there is no difference in treatment except in regard to the technical aspects of the receiving devices.

(c) What are the objectives and implications of the specific reference to audiovisual transmissions by a cable system or satellite carrier in Subsection (B)? What situations are intended to be either included or excluded?

Because cable systems and satellite carriers are not licensed as "radio or television station licensed as such" by the FCC, they were specifically included in Subsection (B). This makes application of the provision uniform and predictable, applying to most audiovisual transmissions without distinctions between originating source.

(d) Does Subsection (A) apply to transmissions regardless of whether they are intended to be received by the general public (cf. the wording of Subsection (B))?

Under Subsection (A), the performance must be by "the *public* reception of the transmission on a single receiving apparatus ...". If the reception was not public, then Subsection (A) would not apply. For both sections, if transmissions are not received by the public, then they would not implicate the author's exclusive rights under Berne Article 11 and 11*bis*. For example, if the radio were playing in a person's car, or in the private back office of a restaurant, there would be no exercise of the public performance right.

As the Panel notes, for Subsection (B), there is the added requirement that the transmission must have been *intended* to be received by the general public. Presumably this would exclude from the exemption transmissions intended for a more select audience, such as music subscription or on-demand services. There is no such requirement in Subsection (A). For all practical purposes, however, this limitation is implicit in Subsection (A), since homestyle devices are not likely to be capable of receiving other types of transmissions than those intended for the public.

Q.6(a) Are Internet transmissions covered by Section 110(5)(A) and (B)?

Internet transmissions would generally not be covered by Sections 110(5)(A) or (B) because those sections apply only to the public performance right. See answer to sub-question (b) below. It is unclear whether the performance aspect of an internet transmission would be covered by either Section 110(5)(A) or (B). Under Subsection (A), the courts have not determined whether a computer would be considered a "single receiving apparatus of a type commonly used in homes", although it should be observed that computers differ in many ways from the stereo and radio receivers contemplated by the legislative history of the homestyle exception and the case law of Section 110(5)(A). In the case of Subsection (B), most Internet transmissions will not originate from television or radio stations licensed as such by the FCC, nor will they be AV transmissions by satellite or cable systems. However, if an FCC-licensed broadcaster itself streams its signal on the Internet, the performance aspect of the broadcast might fall within Subsection (B).

(b) **Paragraph 16 of the US submission says that "establishment owners generally must still seek a licence for the reproduction and possibly distribution rights implicated by Internet transmission". Please explain to what extent reproductions are created by a person who listens to a radio transmission "streamed" over the Internet and whether an authorization is required for such reproductions, as well as under what circumstances a person who receives radio transmissions "streamed" over the Internet would violate the distribution right. Please clarify whether any small stores or restaurants covered by Section 110(5) have acquired a reproduction or distribution licence for communicating by a loudspeaker music streamed over the Internet, and from whom such licences have been or could be obtained.**

Temporary reproductions are created by *all* transmissions that traverse a computer network. This a technical requirement of sending digital information - the information is sent from one computer, and goes through numerous other computer servers before it reaches its final destination. Each one of the computer servers through which the information passes makes a copy of that information in the process of passing it on. Under U.S. law, these copies implicate an author's reproduction right.

The process of creating temporary reproductions occurs whether or not a transmission is "streaming". The term "streaming" means only that a reproduction of the entire work may not be created on the recipient's computer. Reproductions still occur as the information is transmitted across the network.

The distribution right could be implicated by copies of the work, or parts of the work, being deposited on the recipient's computers. This occurs with many streaming technologies, in which portions of the streamed work are "cached" on the recipient's computer as a backup or buffer to the portion being performed or displayed on-screen.

The United States has no information regarding whether or how business owners have obtained or could obtain licenses for the practices described above. The idea of a business owner performing broadcast works over a computer for the benefit of his or her patrons is still a novel one, with which we have no experience.

Even in the event that such forms of reception become more widely used, it is important to note that the owner of an establishment would receive no greater, or broader, ability to play music than he receives from his radio. In consultations prior to this Panel, the EC voiced concerns that this Subsection would apply to a variety of new music services that could become available over the Internet, such as on-demand music. However, since the Subsection is limited to transmissions "intended to be received by the general public," a restaurant or small business owner would only have access to the same broadcasts he or she could get over a common radio or TV. Access to those same broadcasts over a computer, and only to those originating from the relatively small number of licensed radio stations, pose no additional threat to copyright owners.

(c) **Assuming that a food service or drinking or other establishment would be required to acquire a reproduction and/or distribution licence for the**

public performance of music transmitted over the Internet, would this affect the scope to which it would be permissible to provide limitations to the public performance right in the law?

Yes, the requirement to obtain a license for the reproduction and/or distribution of music performed over the internet could affect the scope of permissible exceptions to the public performance right. Although it is difficult to answer this question without any licensing experience in this area, it appears that right holders could take into account in their licensing practices for reproduction/distribution any diminished revenues for performances. The exception from the public performance right might then cause right holders no economic prejudice whatsoever. Moreover, right holders could simply withheld authorization of the reproduction or distribution in any instance in which they wished to prevent an unauthorized public performance.

Q.7 What is the purpose for exempting under Section 110(5) communications to the public of music broadcasts but not of music from tapes or CDs or live music? In which respect are administrative difficulties with licensing thousands of small establishments for playing broadcasts more difficult to surmount than those arising in the context of collecting royalties for playing tapes or CDs or live music?

The United States does not argue that administrative difficulties in licensing small establishments are more severe with respect to broadcasts as opposed to CDs or live music. Part of the rationale for this distinction is a historical one. In the *Aiken* decision, the Supreme Court decided that a radio broadcast was not a public performance. When Congress overruled the rationale, though not the result of *Aiken*, in the 1976 Copyright Act by declaring that playing the radio was a public performance, it created an exemption to the exclusive right of public performance based on the fact pattern of the *Aiken* case (ie., a small establishment of approximately 1055 square feet with limited receiving equipment). The equitable consideration that the copyright owner had already been compensated once is reflected in the legislative history of both Sections 110(5)(A) and (B). Congress thus determined to encourage small business by creating the exception, but at the same time limited the scope of that exemption to broadcasts.

Governmental proceedings to set or adjust royalties

Q.8 Please clarify the purpose of a new paragraph added to Section 110 concerning the impact of the exemptions provided under paragraph (5) on any administrative, judicial, or other governmental proceedings to set or adjust royalties, in particular whether the intention is that the exemptions can or cannot be reflected in the royalties payable to right holders for broadcasting or other transmissions.

Our understanding is that this paragraph was drafted by the collecting societies to ensure that the exemption in Section 110(5)(B) would not be taken into consideration in any proceeding to determine the amount of royalties each of the right holders should be paid by the collecting societies. One can surmise that the provision was the result of a business decision on the part of the collecting societies that the passage of Section 110(5) should not affect the distribution of their royalty payments to right holders.

Impact on the market

Q.9 Please provide any available information or estimations on the actual or potential beneficiaries of the exemption in Section 110(5), in particular:

(a) Percentage of food service or drinking establishments and establishments other than food service and drinking establishments (below other establishments) that benefitted from the original "homestyle" exemption;

In 1996, the Congressional Research Service estimated that based on the square footage guidelines of the *Aiken* case (1,055 square feet), approximately 16% of eating establishments and 13.5% of drinking establishments, were eligible for the homestyle exemption. Combined with the estimate from the National Restaurant Association that approximately x% of restaurants use the radio (and x% use the television)[1], the result is that less than 5% of restaurants and drinking establishments might have been eligible for the original homestyle exemption with respect to radio music and less than 3% with respect to television usage. Exhibit US-18 (Letter from the National Restaurant Association, 18 November 1999).

(b) Percentage of food service or drinking establishments and other establishments that fall under the relevant size limits of Subsection (B) (3,750 square feet and 2,000 square feet respectively);

The National Restaurant Association (NRA) estimates that 36% percent of table service restaurants in the United States (those with sit-down waiter service) are less than 3,750 square feet, and approximately 95% of fast-food restaurants are less than 3,750 square feet. Exhibit US-18. In 1996, the Congressional Research Service conducted an analysis of a legislative proposal from ASCAP and BMI that would have exempted restaurants under 3,500 square feet. CRS estimated that 65.2% of restaurants would fall under this size limit and 71.8% of drinking establishments. Exhibit US- 16. The United States has not been able to obtain information regarding the number of retail establishments that may fall under 2,000 square feet.

(c) Percentage of such establishments either below or above the limit that are likely to be exempted when other factors, in particular the limits on equipment, are taken into account.

The United States has no access to data regarding the establishments likely to be exempted by Section 110(5)(B) based on equipment usage.

1 Confidential Exhibit US-18.

Q.10 Please provide information on the licensing practices of the three US CMOs in regard to public performance of music by food service and drinking establishments and other establishments, in particular:

The United States is pleased to provide the following information in response to the Panel's questions numbered 10, 11 and 12. We would like to note that, as we mentioned at the first meeting with the Panel, in preparation for this case we requested information from the largest U.S. collecting societies (ASCAP and BMI) regarding their licensing practices, but that information was not provided. In response to the Panel's questions, we have renewed and reiterated these requests to the collecting societies. If they are responsive, we may be able to provide the Panel with additional information in the future. See Exhibit US-19.

(a) **The percentage of such establishments in which broadcast music was licensed before the 1976 Copyright Act;**

The United States does not have detailed information regarding the pre-1976 period; however, in the House Report cited in the U.S. First Submission, (Exhibit US-1), Congress found that the majority of beneficiaries of the homestyle exemption were not licensed.

(b) **The percentage of such establishments in which broadcast music was licensed since the entry into force of the 1976 Copyright Act until the entry into force of the Fairness in Music Licensing Act (for the last three years for which data are available);**

According to surveys conducted by the National Restaurant Association in 1996-1997, 16% of table service establishments and 5% of fast food establishments in the United States were licensed before the 1998 Amendment. According to Census Bureau Data, in 1996 there were approximately the same number of table service and fast food restaurants in the United States. (Confidential Exhibit US-18, NRA letter reporting estimates based on Census Bureau figures of 183,253 table service restaurants in the United States and 185,891 quick-service restaurants). Thus, averaging 16% and 5%, it appears that approximately 10.5% percent of restaurants were licensed in the United States.

Information from ASCAP, the largest collecting society also indicates the relatively low level of licensing of establishments. In her testimony before Congress in 1997, Marilyn Bergman, the President of ASCAP stated that "the total number of ASCAP restaurant licensees does not exceed 70,000." Exhibit US-20, page 177. The Census Bureau figures cited above indicate that there are approximately 368,044 total restaurants (table and quick-service) in the United States. Thus, it appears that even the largest U.S. collecting society, ASCAP, estimates that it licenses no more than 19% of the restaurants in the United States.

(c) **To what extent collecting societies license the use by such establishments of music other than broadcast music (such as live music and music performed by means of sound recordings or jukeboxes) (for the last three years for which data are available).**

The United States has no data regarding the extent to which the collecting societies attempt to collect from establishments under 3750 or 2000 square feet for the use of live music, recorded music or jukeboxes.

Q.11 Please provide any available information or estimations on the revenues collected by the US collecting societies (for the last three years for which data are available), in particular:

(a) **The total revenues from the licensing of public performance of music divided between the major categories of uses, including (a) broadcasting and retransmission within the meaning of Article 11*bis*(1)(I) and (ii) of the Berne Convention (b) public communication within the meaning of Article 11*bis*(1)(iii) and (c) other rights, including those under Article 11(1) of the Berne Convention;**

ASCAP's annual reports for 1995-1997, attached as exhibit US-21, indicate that the revenues from broadcasting are by far its most significant source of revenue.

Revenues from the licensing of public performances of music by television broadcast amounted to 32%-33% of ASCAP's annual revenues in 1995, 1996 and 1997. Revenues from radio broadcasts amounted to 25%-26% of ASCAP annual revenues in each of those same years. The actual revenue figures are as follows (in millions):

	1995	*1996*	*1997*
Radio	$110	$120	$124.7
TV	$141.8	$158.4	$155.2
Total revenue	$436.8	$482.6	$482.1

Precise figures on the amount of revenues from public communication by loudspeaker are not available. The only available statistics are ASCAP's receipts for so-called "general and background licensing", which include all licensing revenues from food, drinking and retail establishments, as well as from licensees such as conventions, circuses, theme parks and sports events. It must be remembered that these general figures include *all* licensing revenues from such establishments, including revenues from the playing of recorded music and live bands. For this reason, these figures do not represent the potential loss of revenue from the Section 110(5)(A) or (B) exemptions, but most certainly represent an upper bound on those losses. For each of the years 1995, 1996 and 1997, general licensing revenue amounted to approximately 14% of ASCAP's total revenue.

	1995	*1996*	*1997*
General licensing	$63.2	$66.2	$67.3

The other sources of revenue reported by ASCAP in each of the three years include revenues from symphonies and concerts (1%), revenues from foreign collecting societies (25%-26%), and interest and member dues (1%).

(b) As regards the revenues collected from food service and drinking establishments and other establishments, what is the breakdown as between royalties for the public performance of broadcast music and the public performance of music from other sources;

As described above, in ASCAP's case, total revenues from food service, drinking and other establishments is less than 14% of total revenues for the years 1995-97. The United States does not have access to data itemizing ASCAP's general licensing revenues by broadcast music and music from other sources.

Surveys conducted by the NLBA, however, indicate that the use of recorded music from CDs and tapes (26% in member establishments) or background music services (18%) is very significant in its members establishments, and approximately as prevalent as the use of radio music (28%). The same survey showed that the public performance of live music (37%) was even more prevalent than the use of radio music. See Letter from NLBA (November 18, 1999) Exhibit US-17. Given that many establishments play music from several different sources, these percentage figures do not represent the percentage of total royalties collected for the use of music from each of these sources. For example, the percentage of royalties collected for the use of radio music is almost certainly less than 28% because many establishments that play radio music also play music from other sources.

The United States estimates that approximately 74% of all restaurants play some kind of music. From this data, as well as confidential NRA estimates, it can safely be assumed that no more than 44% of licensing fees from restaurants can be attributed to radio music.

(c) Breakdown of these revenues between various sources of revenue, in particular the percentage of the revenues collected from food serving and drinking establishments and other establishments; to the extent possible, please break down these figures between food service and drinking establishment and other establishments that fall below and above the respective size limits provided for in Subsection (B);

To the extent that this information is available, it has been provided in the answer to question 10 and sub-questions (a) and (b), above.

(d) What is the likely impact of the amended Section 110(5) on the revenues collected earlier from such establishments.

The effect of the amended Section 110(5) on the revenues of the collecting societies is likely to be minimal. ASCAP collects just 14% of its total revenues from general licensees, including eating, drinking and retail establishments. Much of this revenue is for the public performance of live or recorded music, rather than broadcast music. Based on the data provided by the NLBA and other sources, it can be conservatively estimated that radio music accounts for a maximum of 28% to 44% of revenues from eating and drinking establishments. 28%-44% of 14% is equivalent to 3.9% - 6.2% of total revenues. In addition, this figure must be reduced further, since all restaurants and bars are not eligible for the Section 110(5) exemptions. Even using the EC's figure that 70% of all U.S. restaurants would be exempt under Section 110(5)(B), it appears that the exception for radio music will have a maximum effect on revenues of *2.7% - 4.3%*.

Q.12 Can the US confirm the EC statement in paragraph 77 of its oral statement at the first substantive meeting that at least 25 per cent of all music played in the US belongs to EC copyright owners? If not, could the US give alternative estimates?

The United States does not agree with the EC statement. In particular, we cannot agree with the EC's implication that 25% of royalties collected in the United States are due to EC right holders. In fact, the United States is surprised by the EC's statement, given that a 1998 internal EC analysis of the economic effect of the homestyle exception on EC right holders estimated that just 6.2% of ASCAP revenues were distributed to all foreign collecting societies, and that just 5.6% of BMI revenues were due to all foreign collecting societies. Obviously, the percentage payable to EC collecting societies would be significantly less than these figures for total payments to all foreign collecting societies. European Commission, Examination Procedure Regarding the Licensing of Music Works in the United States of America (23 Feb. 1998).

Q.13 Please provide any market information concerning other countries that you would consider relevant to the case at hand.

Market conditions in the United States are the most relevant to the case at hand and thus the United States does not believe that market information concerning other countries is necessary to the resolution of this case. Right holders' legitimate expectations regarding the exploitation of their work in a particular market must be guided by the conditions in that market.

International treaty obligations

Q.14 Could the US explain how, absent express wording to that effect in the TRIPS Agreement, Article 13 of the TRIPS Agreement "constitutes the articulation" of the "minor reservation" doctrine under the Berne Convention? Does the US claim that Article 13 of the TRIPS Agreement can be invoked on its own or only through the "minor reservation" doctrine under the Berne Convention?

During the negotiation of Article 13 in TRIPS, the question posed by the Panel was discussed at length, and there were differing views regarding the need for Article 13. Eventually, the position that prevailed recognized that practically every country had small exceptions to exclusive rights under Berne, either through statutory law, case law or practice, and that the inclusion of Article 13 was an effective way to measure the appropriateness of such exceptions.

In the draft of the TRIPS text from July 23, 1990 (W/76), this statement is made regarding Article 13: "In respect of the rights provided for at point 3, the limitations and exemptions, including compulsory licensing, recognized under the Berne

Convention(1971) shall also apply *mutatis mutandis*". Furthermore, a prominent scholar, and author of a book on the negotiating history of TRIPS comments:

> The interpretation of [Article 13] is possible only in the light of Article 2(2) and 9(1) of the Agreement and, by incorporation, Article 20 of the Berne Convention. Hence, Article 13 does not create new exceptions, even though when read separately from these other provisions, one would be tempted to say that it allows countries to create new compulsory licenses. ... Yet this line of argument must fail. Introducing *new* compulsory licenses would in almost all cases violate the Berne Convention. *Article 13 allows a dispute settlement panel to review exceptions, including the so called "small exceptions", to ensure that they pass the test. . .* [Quotes report from the Brussels Conference mentioning minor reservations applicable to Article 11, 11*bis*, 11*ter*, 13 and 14.] *When these exceptions are invoked, they may from now on be submitted to the general test of Article 13. . .* (emphasis added).
>
> *D. Gervais, The TRIPS Agreement: Drafting History and Analysis, 89-80 (1998).*

Importantly, this interpretation is also confirmed by the language and history of subsequent treaty affirming Berne rights. The WIPO Copyright Treaty (WCT) and the WIPO Performances and Phonograms Treaty (WPPT) were adopted by the WIPO Diplomatic Conference on December 20, 1996, at Geneva. The WCT requires compliance with the substantive rights of Berne (WCT, Article 1(4)), and includes language very similar to Article 13 of TRIPS. Furthermore, the WCT specifically provides that it is a "special agreement within the meaning of Article 20 of the Berne Convention". WCT, Article 1(1). With respect to both the WCT (in Article 10) and the WPPT (in Article 16), it was believed important to incorporate the same standard for judging limitations and exceptions as already applied in the TRIPS Agreement and the Berne Convention.

The WCT explicitly clarifies the application of the standard set forth in TRIPS Article 13 to existing provisions of the Berne Convention as well as the rights established in the new Treaty. Article 10(1) of the WCT provides that:

> (1) Contracting Parties may, in their national legislation, provide for limitations of or exceptions to the rights granted to authors of literary and artistic works under this Treaty in certain special cases that do not conflict with a normal exploitation of the work and do not unreasonably prejudice the legitimate interests of the author.

Article 10(2) clarifies that this standard also applies in respect of the implementation of any limitations on or exceptions to any rights under the Berne Convention:

> (2) Contracting Parties shall, when applying the Berne Convention, confine any limitations of or exceptions to rights provided for therein to certain special cases that do not conflict

> with a normal exploitation of the work and do not unreasonably prejudice the legitimate interests of the author.

The Agreed Statement concerning Article 10 of the WCT further buttresses this view:

> It is understood that the provisions of Article 10 permit Contracting Parties to carry forward and appropriately extend into the digital environment limitations and exceptions in their national laws which have been considered acceptable under the Berne Convention. Similarly these provisions should be understood to permit Contracting Parties to devise new exceptions and limitations that are appropriate in the digital network environment.
>
> It is also understood that Article 10 neither reduces nor extends the scope of applicability of the limitations and exceptions permitted by the Berne Convention.

If no minor exceptions or limitations were permitted under Berne, there would be no reason for Article 10(2) of the WCT or the cited provision of the Agreed Statement.

Article 10 of the WCT reflects the same text included as Article 12 in the Basic Proposal for the 1996 Diplomatic Conference (CRNR/DC/4). The commentary on the Basic Proposal is enlightening. After observing that the TRIPS Agreement already enunciated this standard for permissible limitations and exceptions to rights, it states that "[n]o limitations, not even those that belong in the category of minor reservations, may exceed the limits set by the three step test".

The EC and the U.S. are signatories of both the WCT and the WPPT.

Q.15 In the light of Article 2.2 of the TRIPS Agreement and Article 20 of the Berne Convention, can Article 13 of the TRIPS Agreement derogate from the requirement under Article 11*bis*(2) of the Berne Convention to provide "equitable remuneration"?

Article 13, as explained above, in no way derogates from the protection afforded under the Berne Convention and consequently is entirely consistent with TRIPS Article 2.2 and Berne Article 20. In fact, Article 13 strengthens the protection under the Berne Convention, by providing explicit criteria to judge exceptions where none existed before.

In particular as applied to Article 11*bis*(2), Article 13 does not derogate from the right to equitable remuneration. Minor exceptions apply in respect of many of the rights under Berne, explicitly including Article 11 and 11*bis*. Should a party choose to implement a compulsory licensing regime under Article 11*bis*(2), as opposed to having a small exception to that right, such a system must provide for equitable remuneration. The U.S. compulsory licensing regime, for example, as it applies to secondary retransmissions of broadcast signals by cable systems clearly falls within, and complies with, this provision. (For further discussion of this issue, please see US Response to Panel Question 6 to US and EC.).

Q.16 Are there exceptions similar to the US Section 110(5)(A) or (B), or examples of "minor reservation" exceptions in the copyright laws of other countries?

There are numerous exceptions similar to U.S. Section 110(5)(A) and (B), and examples of minor reservation exceptions, in the copyright laws of other countries. Although the United States has not been able, in the time provided, to review the copyright laws of all other WTO or Berne Members, even a limited review of the copyright laws of a handful of WTO members reveals a number of exceptions to the public performance right, including a number in EC Member States.

For example, the Australian copyright law provides a number of exceptions to the public performance right. Section 46 provides an exemption for public performances by wireless apparatus or by a record "at premises where persons reside or sleep, as part of the amenities provided exclusively for residents or inmates of the premises or for those residents or inmates and their guests". *Copyright Act 1968 (amended 1994), Section 46.* The commercial nature of this exemption is notable, as it applies to hotels and guest houses. Parliament of Australia, Standing Committee on Legal and Constitutional Affairs, "Don't Stop the Music!: a report on the inquiry into copyright, music and small business", 29 (May1998) (available at *www.aph.gov.au/house/committee/laca/ reports/copyrigh/index.htm.* Australia also exempts public performances for educational purposes. *Id., Section 28.*

Under the Belgian copyright law, Section 22, an author "may not prohibit ... communication to the public of a work shown in a place accessible to the public where the aim of the [ ] communication to the public is not the work itself". *Law on Copyright and Neighboring Rights 1994 (amended 1995), Art. 22(1).* Belgium also has an exception for the "free performance of a work during a public examination where the purpose of the performance is not the work itself, but assessment of the performer ..." *Id.*

Under the Copyright Law of Finland, "A published work may also be publicly performed in events where the performance of such works is not the main feature, provided that no admission fee is charged and the event is not arranged for profit". *Copyright Act (amended 1997) Law 446/ 1995, Art. 21.* The same law also contains an exemption for public performances "in connection with religious services and education". *Id.* Denmark also provides an exception for public performances of non-dramatic works on radio or television "on occasions when the performance of such works is not the main feature of the event, provided that no admission fee is charged and the event is not for profit". *Act on Copyright 1995, Sec. 21.*

New Zealand exempts public performances of musical works at educational establishments. *Copyright Act 1994, Section 47.* The Philippines excepts public performances for educational and charitable purposes. *Intellectual Property Code of the Philippines, Sec. 184* (1997). India, in addition to educational exemptions, also exempts "the performance of a literary, dramatic or musical work by an amateur club or society, if the performance is given to a non-paying audience ..." *India Copyright Act 1957 (amended 1994), Sections 52(l), 52(I).*

Canada provides a number of exceptions to the public performance right. *Copyright Act 1994 (amended 1997).* It provides several exceptions for educational purposes, *see Sections 2 9.4 & 29.5*, and for performances "at any agricultural or agricultural-industrial exhibition or fair," *Section 32.2(2)*, as well as a blanket exception for any public performance of a musical work - whether live or by "communication signal" - by a religious organization or institution, education institution, charitable or fraternal organization in furtherance of a religious educational or charitable object. *Section 32.2.(3).* The later section specifically provides that under such circumstances, no such organization "shall be held liable to pay *any* compensation". *(Emphasis added.)*

South African law provides that "the copyright in a literary or musical work shall not be infringed by the use thereof in a *bona fide* demonstration of radio or television receivers or any type of recording equipment or playback equipment to a client by a dealer in such equipment. *Copyright Act of 1978 (amended May 1995).*

Finally, the United States references Brazil's letter to the Panel of 17 November 1999, in which Ambassador Amorim noted that Brazilian copyright law contains exceptions in the sense of the minor reservations doctrine.

Q.17 Precisely how do you justify the submission that the provisions of Section 110(5)(A) and (B) constitute a special case within the meaning of Article 13 of the TRIPS Agreement?

Article 13 requires that exceptions be limited to certain special cases. The Oxford Dictionary defines "certain" as "determined; fixed" and "definite". *The New Shorter Oxford Dictionary* (ed. Lesley Brown), 364 (1993). The word "special" is defined as "exceptional", "distinguished from others of the kind by a particular quality or feature; distinctive in some way", "appointed or employed for a particular purpose or occasion", "having an individual or limited application or purpose", and "containing details, precise, specific". *Id.* at 2971. These definitions contain a significant degree of overlap, and the key criterion that emerges from the requirement that exceptions be limited to "certain, special" cases is that the exception be both well-defined and of limited application. One report of the TRIPS negotiating history explains as follows: "When these exceptions are invoked, they may from now on be submitted to the general test of Article 13, which should be interpreted on the basis of Article 9(2) of the Berne Convention. The two tests contained in that Article are cumulative. In addition, any exception must be clearly delineated so as to apply only to "certain special cases". *Gervais, at 90.*

The negotiating history of Berne Article 9(2) reinforces this view. The original text proposed for Article 9(2) listed three areas of permissible exceptions, the third of which was "certain *particular* cases, provided (I) that reproduction is not contrary to the legitimate interests of the author, and (ii) that it does not conflict with a normal exploitation of the work". The Conference decided, however, that a more general formula for exceptions was preferable, and instead of the three areas of exceptions, adopted a proposal of the United Kingdom to modify the text to allow exceptions "in certain special cases" that met the two conditions. WIPO, *Records of the Stockholm Conference*, 1144-46, paras. 78, 81, & 86 (1967). The WIPO Guide to the Berne Convention also supports the idea that the phrase "certain special cases" in Article 9(2) is not intended as a separate threshold requirement for exceptions, and does not discuss the imposition of any limitation on the purposes for which an exception can be made. *WIPO - Guide to the Berne Convention,* 55, para. 9.6 (focusing exclusively on the "two" conditions that limit the power to make exceptions: conflict with normal exploitation and unreasonable prejudice).

Thus, the concept of "special" need not include the concept of the purpose of the exception. To the extent that the purpose of an exception is relevant under TRIPS Article 13, it is only necessary that the exception have a particular purpose. By itself, the term "special" does not convey any priority of purpose, or preference for one purpose over another.

Moreover, in considering whether an exception constitutes a "special case," it is critical that a WTO Panel not judge the desirability of a country's public policy rationale for an exception. In an organization as diverse as the WTO, a Panel should not determine the acceptability of a Member's public policy objectives. There is no support in the TRIPS Agreement for a Panel to determine acceptable policy rationales for exceptions under Article 13 of TRIPS. The purpose for which countries may make exceptions to exclusive rights is not the central focus of Article 13; rather, it is tangentially relevant, if at all. It is the scope of the exception and its effect on right holders that is key.

As discussed in the U.S. first submission, paragraphs 24-26, the exceptions in Sections 110(5)(A) and (B) of the U.S. Copyright Law are well-defined and limited to particular circumstances. Section 110(5)(A) is limited to cases involving use of a homestyle receiving apparatus, and Section 110(5)(B) is confined to cases involving establishments meeting its clear size and equipment requirements.

Moreover, important public policy concerns underlie both Sections 110(5)(A) and (B). With respect to 110(5)(A), the record is clear that Congress was concerned with small "mom and pop" businesses. Small businesses play a particularly important role in the American social fabric. They foster local values and innovation and experimentation in the economy. Small businesses also create a disproportionately greater number of economic opportunities for women, minorities, immigrants, and those formerly on public assistance, and thus are an essential mechanism by which millions enter the economic and social mainstream. *The State of Small Business: Report of the President*, (U.S. GPO: Washington) 3 (1998).

Important public policy concerns also support the exception in Section 110(5)(B). With respect to many of the businesses exempted, the same concerns relating to the social importance of small businesses apply. *E.g.*, Congressional Record (Oct. 7, 1998); Letter from Representative James Sensenbrenner, Jr. to Members of Congress, *"Key small business vote next week"* (Mar. 20, 1998). In addition, the legislative history of this provision is replete with concern over abuses of the PROs. By exempting small businesses, many of whom the collecting societies had already agreed to exempt in the context of the NLBA Agreement, Congress believed that it was resolving the issue of abusive licensing practices without causing any unreasonable prejudice to right holders.

Q.18 Does Article 13 of the TRIPS Agreement permit the balancing of revenues generated or likely to accrue under individual exclusive rights, *inter alia*, for purposes of determining "normal exploitation" of works, and/or "unreasonable prejudice to legitimate interests of rights holders", or is it necessary to consider each individual exclusive right separately?

This question, like question 19, appears to assume that the Panel must *either* consider each right separately *or* consider all rights together. On the contrary, both paradigms are relevant. Exceptions should be considered in the context of all the exclusive rights granted to the right holder, as well as the context of the particular right to which the exception applies.

Exceptions can take many forms. Some exceptions might represent a great intrusion on one particular exclusive right, and no intrusion on any other exclusive right. Other exceptions might represent a lesser degree of intrusion on several exclusive rights. Both kinds of exceptions might violate the TRIPS Agreement, and the analytical framework of Article 13 must take both situations into account.

Thus, a Panel considering an exception should consider the scope of the exception *vis-à-vis* the scope of all the right holders' exclusive rights, as well as the scope of the exception *vis-à-vis* the exclusive right to which it applies. Whether an exception applies to one exclusive right or several is relevant in the analysis of conflict with normal exploitation and unreasonable prejudice. Similarly, the degree to which an exception affects a particular exclusive right is also relevant to that analysis. Whether any particular exception is determined to conflict with normal exploitation or cause unreasonable prejudice is ultimately a highly fact-specific inquiry that will turn on the precise circumstances of the exception and the market at issue.

The text of Article 13 supports this broad analysis. Article 13 requires that exceptions be limited to cases that do not conflict with a normal exploitation of the "work", not a normal exploitation of the particular right affected. If the drafters had meant to limit the analysis to the exclusive right to which an exception applied, the provision could easily have referenced the "normal exploitation of such exclusive rights". It is also significant that Article 13 also references unreasonable prejudice to the "legitimate interests of the right holder" without any limiting language regarding their legitimate interests in a particular right.

The fact that an exception must be evaluated in the overall context of the rights granted by a country does not imply that a country could completely eliminate an exclusive right if that right were economically unimportant. TRIPS established minimum standards. The exclusive rights set forth in Articles 1-21 of the Berne Convention (minus 6*bis*) and in Part I, Section 1 of TRIPS must be provided. Moreover, Article 13 references "limitations or exceptions" to exclusive rights. The abolition of an exclusive right is not equivalent to a limitation to such right. So long as the exclusive right is provided, however, the relative economic importance of that exclusive right would be a relevant factor in the Article 13 analysis.

Actual revenues from exclusive rights are also important in the Article 13 analysis. Marketplace realities guide the expectations of benefit of copyright owners. In determining the scope of normal exploitation, and unreasonable prejudice it is highly appropriate to look at marketplace realities. The concepts of normal exploitation and unreasonable prejudice cannot be determined in the abstract.

Q.19 In considering criteria for determining "normal exploitation" and/or "unreasonable prejudice to legitimate interests of rights holders" under Article 13 of the TRIPS Agreement, is it necessary to consider each individual exclusive right separately?

See answer to Question 18, above.

Q.20 Could the US further explain how the provision of Article 11*bis*(2) of the Berne Convention could amount to a greater degree of derogation from sub-

stantive copyright law than an exception under Article 13 of the TRIPS Agreement?

This question could also be phrased: "How could a right of remuneration under Article 11*bis*(2) of the Berne Convention amount to a greater degree of derogation from exclusive rights than an exception under the minor reservations doctrine applicable to Article 11*bis*?" As discussed above, Article 13 does not "provide" exceptions that are not already provided for by Berne, it merely furnishes a standard under which they can be judged.

Generally speaking, a compulsory license may be much broader, and may abrogate more rights, than an exception. The minor reservation doctrine, applied to Article 11*bis,* would only allow narrow and reasonable exceptions to a right holder's rights. Should a country choose to substitute a right of remuneration for the exclusive right under Article 11*bis*, rather than creating a narrow exception targeted to address a particular problem, it could result in a far greater diminution of revenues. A compulsory license under 11*bis*(2) potentially could abrogate all of a right holder's rights under Article 11*bis* - including his right to license his work to radio stations, television stations, and cable systems. Especially in the context of certain audiovisual works, which receive virtually all their revenue through this mechanism, it can be seen how broad this abrogation would be. Furthermore, although the right holder would still be entitled to some compensation for use of the work, he cannot set the price of that compensation himself. It will most likely be set by an administrative or quasi-governmental entity, which could determine that the work is worth far less than the right holder himself believes, or could get in a free market.

In contrast, under the minor reservations doctrine, outright exceptions to the Berne rights must be narrow, and cannot conflict with normal exploitation or prejudice a right holder's legitimate interests in the work. Exceptions which pass this test will likely be narrower and have less impact on the right holder than the licenses authorized by Article 11*bis*(2).

In sum, under Article 11*bis*(2), a country can put any condition on a right holder's rights, provided that he is not deprived of equitable remuneration, which he does not even have the authority to determine himself. In contrast, under the minor reservations doctrine, as judged through TRIPS Article 13, countries can only create narrow exceptions which have a reasonable effect.

Q.21 Does the US protect broadcasting rights through the performance rights protected in Section 106 of the US Copyright Act?

Assuming that by "broadcasting rights" the Panel is referring to the right of broadcasting of the copyright owner under Article 11*bis* (as opposed to broadcasters' rights in the programming that they produce), the simple answer is yes.

Broadcasting is only one means by which a work may be publicly performed. The copyright owner generally has the exclusive right under U.S. copyright law to authorize or prohibit that broadcast. The right of public performance in Section 106 of the U.S. Copyright Act includes the broadcasting right in Berne Article 11*bis* as well as other types of public performances.

II. REPLIES OF THE UNITED STATES TO QUESTIONS FROM THE PANEL ADDRESSED TO BOTH PARTIES

Q.1 Please explain the extent to which the case law concerning Section 110(5) cited in your respective submissions is relevant for the purposes of interpreting the present subsection (A) of that paragraph.

The United States believes that the case law is relevant because Section 110(5) was TRIPS consistent even before non-dramatic musical works were excluded from its scope. Moreover, the case law also provides guidance as to the bounds of the exception with respect to works other than non-dramatic musical works.

Categories of works

Q.2 The Panel understands that the text of the original Section 110(5) is identical to that of the present subsection (A) minus the words "except as provided for in subparagraph (B)". The preparatory work reproduced in exhibits EC-3 and US-1 (H.R. Rep. No. 94-1476 (1976)) explains that the provision "applies to performances and displays of all types of works". Paragraph 31 of the EC submission and paragraph 9 of the US submission (and certain other paragraphs) contain an interpretation according to which this text, as contained in subsection (A), is intended to exclude from its scope "nondramatic musical works". Please clarify your interpretation of the text of this provision, on the one hand, as part of the original paragraph, and, on the other hand, as part of subsection A, and, to the extent that, in your view, the text should be understood differently in these two contexts. Explain why.

With respect to the original (homestyle) exemption, the precursor to subsection A, as noted, the intent was to exempt the public performance of all types of work, within the other limitations of the exemption. The 1998 Amendment narrowed the scope of the homestyle exemption. Subsection B refers to "nondramatic musical works" and the scope of subsection A is specifically limited to whatever is not detailed in subsection B. *See also* U.S. Response to Panel Question 3 to the U.S. Thus, given that nondramatic musical works are covered under Subsection B, they are not included within Subsection A. The United States observes that on this particular question of fact - the scope of Section 110(5) - there is no dispute between the parties to the case.

Q.3 What is the definition of the term "nondramatic musical work" in the context of Section 110(5)? What types of musical works are either included in or excluded from the application of the provisions of that Section, and which types of copyright holders are affected by the provisions of Subsections (A) and (B)? Does it also cover communication to the public of live music performances? For example, would the performance of, e.g., one song from a musical, constitute a performance of a "dramatic" or of a "nondramatic" musical work? Is it still a "dramatic" work if a song from a musical is performed separately and by another artist? To what extent the notion of "nondramatic musical work" corre-

sponds or is intended to correspond with the notion of "small musical rights" applied in the practice of CMOs?

The term "nondramatic musical work" is not defined in Section 110(5). However, as we have discussed, nondramatic musical works are typically those not accompanied by a dramatic performance, such as a play or opera. Nondramatic music represents most of the music played in the United States since it encompasses pop, rock, jazz, and ethnic music. The United States wishes to clarify our preliminary answer at the first meeting of the Panel with the Parties, and note our understanding that the PROs do license nondramatic renditions of dramatic musical works.

Licensing practice

Q.4 Paragraph 4 of the US oral statement at the first substantive meeting states that Section 110(5) is limited to only certain secondary uses of broadcasts of public performances, for which the right holder has already been compensated for the primary performance. In which way, if any, do licensing arrangements between collective management organisations (CMOs) and broadcasting organizations in the US or the EC take into account the potential additional audience created by means of further communication by loudspeaker etc. of broadcasts to the public within the meaning of Article 11*bis*(1)(iii) of the Berne Convention?

The United States does not assert that licensing arrangements between broadcast organizations and the collecting societies include royalties for secondary performances by the receiving public. In assessing the economic impact of Section 110(5), however, and specifically the extent of prejudice to a copyright owner, the Panel should take note that the copyright owner has already been compensated once for the broadcast or radio transmission of a particular public performance.

Interpretation of treaty obligations

Q.5 What is the legal nature of materials including "General Reports" of Diplomatic Conferences of the Berne Convention countries in light of Article 31 of the Vienna Convention on the Law of Treaties (VCLT)? Are they " subsequent agreements on the interpretation or application" in the meaning of Article 31(3)(a), "subsequent practice" in the meaning of Article 31(3)(b), "rules of international law applicable between the parties" in the meaning of Article 31(3)(c), or a "special meaning ... given to a term if its established that the parties so intended"?

The General Reports of Diplomatic Conferences of the Berne Convention countries may, depending on the context, be considered to be preparatory work for revisions to the Berne Convention, or evidence of the circumstances surrounding the adoption of the text of the revisions to the Berne Convention; thus they would be analyzed under Article 32 of the Vienna Convention. They are not "agreements on the interpretation or application" of the Berne Convention, they do not represent a widespread "subsequent practice" of the parties to the Convention, and they do not as such constitute "rules of international law applicable between the parties." Thus they do not fall within any of the categories listed as Article 31(3)(a), (b) or (c).

Q.6 In your view, what is the relationship between Article 13 of the TRIPS Agreement and Article 11*bis*(2) of the Berne Convention? Does Article 13 of the TRIPS Agreement prevail over the exception in Article 11*bis*(2) with respect to the exclusive rights conferred by Article 11*bis*(1)(I-iii) of the Berne Convention in the sense that when the three conditions of Article 13 are met, no requirement to pay equitable remuneration arises? Do the requirements of Article 11*bis*(2) of the Berne Convention prevail as a *lex specialis* over the requirements of Article 13 of the TRIPS Agreement, in the sense that if equitable remuneration is paid, there is no need to comply with the three-conditions test under Article 13? Do the requirements of Article 13 and Article 11*bis*(2) apply on a cumulative basis in the sense that, on the one hand, even if the three-condition test of Article 13 is fulfilled, there is an additional, fourth requirement to pay equitable remuneration, and on the other hand, even if equitable remuneration is paid consistently with Article 11*bis*(2), is it necessary to comply in addition with the three conditions of Article 13? Please explain.

As a fundamental matter, it must be clarified that the "equitable remuneration" language of Article 11*bis*(2) only applies to, and indeed is a shorthand for, compulsory licenses. Article 11*bis*(2) allows a country to put any conditions on a right holder's broadcasting rights, provided that they do not deprive the right holder of equitable remuneration. This is a compulsory license. Compulsory licenses may be much broader than an exception, and are a different mechanism for limiting rights than the minor reservations doctrine.

Article 11*bis*(2) is consistently described as a provision authorizing compulsory licenses:

> - "Long discussions - in the subcommittee as in the General Committee - was caused by para. 2 [of Article 11*bis*] which enables Union countries to introduce obligatory licenses in favor of the radio." (*Report on The Brussels Conference for the Revision of the Berne Convention*, Dr. Alfred Baum, Zurich, 1948.)
>
> - "This provision [Article 11*bis*(2)] allows member countries to substitute, for the author's exclusive right, a system of compulsory licenses." (WIPO Guide to the Berne Convention, 70.)
>
> - "The reference to "conditions" in article 11*bis*(2) is usually taken to refer to the imposition of compulsory licenses, but the form of these licenses is left to national legislation to determine."
>
> *(S. Ricketson, The Berne Convention for the protection of literary and artistic works: 1886-1986, 525 (1987)).*

Notably, the minor reservations doctrine, discussed at length in the negotiating history of Berne and in subsequent treatises, is never linked in any way to compulsory licenses or to Article 11*bis*(2). In the General Report at the Brussels Conference (1948), Marcel Plaisant explicitly discusses the applicability of minor reservations to Article 11*bis*: "These exceptional measures apply to Articles 11*bis*, 11*ter*, 13 and 14". (Quoted in Ricketson, p. 534.) The right to remuneration provision in Article 11*bis*(2) was already in the Convention at that time. If the drafting committee had intended that minor reservations should be subject to some additional requirement with respect only to Article 11*bis*, it surely would have mentioned that fact in the Report. Likewise, in the WIPO Guide to the Berne Convention, Article 11*bis*(2) is discussed on page 70 under the heading "Compulsory Licenses". The minor reservation doctrine, is discussed on page 65: "It is in relation to Article 11 that the question of the 'minor reservations' arises. ... It was agreed at Brussels that these exceptions (which apply also to Articles 11*bis*, 11*ter*, 13 and 14) were valid". No mention is made of Article 11*bis*(2), and there is no indication that it relates to the minor reservations doctrine.

Q.7 In your view, to what extent has the Berne Convention become part of customary international law, and if so, in particular which part of the Articles 1-21 of the Berne Convention?

The United States is continuing to consult internally regarding the issues raised by this question, as well as the following one. For this reason, the following views must be considered preliminary, and we may elaborate further in our Second Submission to the Panel.

The United States does not consider that the Berne Convention has become part of customary international law. In the view of the United States, there is not the required degree of consistency and uniformity of practice, nor do non-signatories States view the obligations of the Berne Convention as sufficiently obligatory, to consider it part of customary international law. First negotiated in 1886, the Berne Convention has been revised five times with two additions since that time. The current text is that of the Paris revision of 1971. Many countries are not party to the Berne Convention, do not comply with its provisions, or have not accepted some of the latter revisions of the Convention. The United States acceded to the Berne Convention only in 1989 when it passed domestic legislation to conform its law to Berne requirements. Berne Convention Implementation Act of 1988, H.R. Rep. No. 100-609, 100th Cong., 2d Sess. (1988).

Q.8 Has the "minor exceptions" doctrine under the Berne Convention, and especially in the context of Articles 11*bis*(1) and 11(1) of the Berne Convention, acquired the status of customary international law? What is the legal significance of the "minor exceptions" doctrine under the Berne Convention in the light of subparagraphs (3)(a-c) or paragraph (4) of Article 31 of the VCLT or in the light of Article 32 of the VCLT? Has the "minor exceptions" doctrine or any other implied exceptions been incorporated, by virtue of Article 9.1 of the TRIPS Agreement, together with Articles 1-21 of the Berne Convention into the TRIPS Agreement? Please explain.

The "minor exceptions" doctrine under the Berne Convention has not acquired the status of customary international law. The doctrine under the Berne Convention constitutes subsequent practice of Berne Members under Vienna Convention Article 31(3)(b). See U.S. Response to Panel Question 16 to the U.S. regarding minor exceptions in the laws of other Berne members. The minor exceptions doctrine is also explicitly referenced in the preparatory work of the Berne Convention, which constitutes a supplementary means of interpretation under Article 32 of the Vienna Convention. See U.S. response to Panel Question 14 to the U.S.

The "minor exceptions" doctrine has been incorporated into TRIPS by the specific articulation in Article 13 of the standard by which to judge such minor exceptions. See U.S. response to Panel Questions 14 and 15 to the U.S. The 1996 WIPO Copyright Treaty also confirms that Berne countries intended to allow minor exceptions to Berne rights. See U.S. response to Panel Question 14 to the U.S.

Q.9 What else other than religious ceremonies, performances by military bands, charitable concerts or requirements of education does the "minor reservations" doctrine cover? Does it only cover non-commercial uses? Was this doctrine be conceived of only with respect to Article 11 of the Berne Convention, or was it also extended to Article 11*bis*(1)(iii) of the Berne Convention, given that these Articles concern different types of rights? What such instances of implied exceptions could be relevant for this dispute?

Minor reservations cover exceptions that meet the standard now articulated in TRIPS Article 13. The doctrine is not limited to the specific examples cited by some countries in the negotiating history, and subsequent practice of many countries demonstrates the applicability of the doctrine to a wide variety of types of exceptions. As set forth in the negotiating history, the doctrine was intended to extend to Article 11*bis*.

Q.10 In order to meet the first condition of Article 13 of the TRIPS Agreement ("certain special cases"), is it enough if the limitation or exception is defined in great precision?

See our response to Question 17 of the Panel's questions to the United States.

Q.11 Under the second condition of Article 13, in which respect, if at all, is a normal exploitation of the "work" the same as a normal exploitation of "exclusive rights" relating to that work?

See our response to Question 18 of the Panel's questions to the United States.

Q.12 To what extent is it appropriate in evaluating the compliance of a law with the conditions of Article 13 of the TRIPS Agreement based on looking at the current market situation in a given country?

The current situation in a given country is extremely important in that it determines the bounds of normalcy in that market and sheds light on the reasonableness of any prejudice suffered by right holders. A contrary approach - evaluating the TRIPS Article 13 criteria by reference to hypothetical future or potential market situations - would be unworkable, and finds no support in the TRIPS Agreement. That is not to say that the evolution of market conditions is irrelevant. It is possible that exceptions justifiable under Article 13 at one point in time may become unacceptably broad with the passage of time and changes in the market. It is also possible that an exception that fails to meet the Article 13 criteria at a certain time may in fact meet those criteria as market conditions evolve.

It seems highly speculative to attempt to determine whether the conditions of Article 13 are met with respect to any potential market situation. One could also hypothesize changes in the market that would affect the degree of prejudice caused by an exception to exclusive rights. The WTO dispute settlement system is not based on such speculation. To look at anything other than the current market situation would be tantamount to reading into TRIPS a requirement that exceptions avoid *any potential* conflict with normal exploitation of a work and avoid even the *possibility* of unreasonable prejudice to the right holder. The plain text of Article 13, however, provides that exceptions must be evaluated by the extent to which they "do" not conflict with a normal exploitation and "do" not cause unreasonable prejudice.

Q.13 To what extent subsequent technological and market developments (e.g. new means of transmission of or increased use of background music or television) are relevant for the interpretation of the conditions under Article 13 of the TRIPS Agreement?

Technological and market developments are relevant to the interpretation of the conditions under Article 13 of TRIPS to the extent that they relate to a particular case at a particular time. The Article 13 analysis should be based on the current state of technology and market development, as opposed to speculation about future possibilities. See U.S. Response to Question 10, above.

Q.14 Is it justified to define the three conditions exclusively by reference to a particular market, or is a comparative analysis of licensing practices in other Members with similar economic conditions warranted?

TRIPS Article 1.1 provides guidance on this question, and provides that WTO Members are "free to determine the appropriate method of implementing the provisions of this Agreement within their own legal system and practice". This provision would mean little if the reasonableness of a country's exceptions were determined in part by foreign right holders' licensing practices in other Members. Similarly, Article 5(2) of Berne provides that "apart from the provisions of this Convention, the extent of protection, as well as the means of redress afforded to the author to protect his rights, shall be governed exclusively by the laws of the country where protection is claimed." The spirit of this provision is that, except where Berne specifically provides otherwise, countries are free to determine the content of their own national laws regarding the extent of copyright protection.

A Member's national market is the most important determinant of normalcy and reasonableness with regard to that Member. It cannot be assumed that right holders have identical interests in various WTO Members, even where similar economic conditions prevail. There is no support in the TRIPS Agreement for requiring that any exception to exclusive rights be justified not only by reference to the prejudice it might cause to right holders' in the market that it would affect, but also by reference to the prejudice it would cause in theory if it were imposed in a completely separate market.

A comparative analysis of other WTO Members is particularly inappropriate with respect to the issue of "certain, special cases." Local history and tradition may play a major role in determining whether a particular country considers a case sufficiently special to warrant an exception to an exclusive right. TRIPS certainly does not require that other Members share the same social values.

Q.15 Under the third condition of Article 13, should the concepts of "unreasonable prejudice" and "legitimate interests" be defined based on existing, legally guaranteed entitlements, or do these concepts also connote an aspect of normative concern of right holders? In the latter case, what could be the normative concern at issue? In addition to an empirical analysis of prejudice to legitimate interests, how could such a normative element be taken into account in defining the threshold of the third condition of Article 13?

Existing, legally guaranteed entitlements to an exclusive right are one factor in defining the concepts of unreasonable prejudice and legitimate interests. Existing entitlements determine the benefits that a right holder might legally expect from his work, and thus provide helpful guidance in evaluating prejudice to the right holder's interests. In addition, the concepts of unreasonable prejudice and legitimate interests do also connote an aspect of normative concern to right holders.

Q.16 What is the extent of "reasonable" prejudice to the legitimate interests of rights holders that is permissible under the third condition of Article 13?

The extent of prejudice that may be deemed reasonable under TRIPS Article 13 must be determined on the facts and circumstances of each case, and cannot be established in the abstract due to the myriad potential factors that may influence the inquiry in any particular instance. To determine whether prejudice is unreasonable, the Panel should undertake a fact-intensive inquiry into the extent of the prejudice suffered by right holders subject to an exception, and then must ultimately balance these facts to reach a conclusion based on reason, rather than on a *per se* notion of the permissible degree of prejudice.

Q.17 With a view to giving distinct meaning to the second and the third condition of Article 13, in which respect does an extent, degree or form of interference with exclusive rights below the threshold of "conflict with normal exploitation" differ from an extent, degree or form of interference with exclusive rights that exceeds the threshold of a reasonable prejudice to the interests of the right holder? In other words, how does a permissible degree of prejudice under the third condition relate to "normal exploitation" under the second condition of Article 13?

The normal exploitation element of Article 13 looks to the amount of market displacement caused by the exception or limitation at issue. In other words, are there areas of the market in which the copyright owners would expect to exploit his or her work which are not now available to be exploited because of this exemption? Note that it is only the *normal* exploitation that is at issue - uses from which an owner would not expect to receive compensation are not part of normal exploitation. In contrast, the legitimate interest element of Article 13 looks at the amount of harm that is caused to the owner, economic or otherwise, by whatever provision is in dispute. Although these two elements may overlap, they are not coextensive. One could imagine a situation in which a large part of the market was displaced, but, because it was not a particularly profitable market and the right holder lost very little money, there was not unreasonable prejudice of the owners' interests. Likewise, one could imagine a situation in which relatively little of the market was displaced, but, because those few uses were so lucrative, the owner's legitimate interests would be unreasonably prejudiced.

Q.18 Should quantitative empirical or normative approaches be used in defining the three conditions of Article 13?

A quantitative empirical approach is the most appropriate approach to the Article 13 conditions. The grant of an exclusive right compensates the author for his initiative and creativity and for his investment and risk in producing the work. Exceptions should neither unreasonably prejudice the right holders' economic rewards, nor should not undermine the incentive to create. Without an empirical analysis of the actual effect of an exception on the market, it is not possible to determine the extent to which a right holder is actually prejudiced and the reasonableness of that prejudice. For example, the fact that a right holder has not collected royalties from a particular market for decades is at least a relevant factor bearing on the reasonableness of an exception applicable to that particular market.

The context, object and purpose of Article 13 are also relevant to this discussion. The TRIPS Agreement is a trade agreement, and its purpose was to "reduce distortions and impediments to international trade". TRIPS, preamble. The Agreement was negotiated against the backdrop of a wide variety of national systems, and was intended to contribute to "the mutual advantage of producers and users" and "a balance of rights and obligations". As mentioned above, the drafters also intended that Members would have flexibility in implementing the Agreement within the context of "their own legal system and practice". These guiding principles support the position that the analysis of the conditions of Article 13 must be grounded in local market realities, and in the actual practice and experience of right holders and users in the country concerned.

ATTACHMENT 2.4

RESPONSES OF THE UNITED STATES TO WRITTEN QUESTIONS FROM THE EUROPEAN COMMUNITIES AND THEIR MEMBER STATES - FIRST MEETING

(19 November 1999)

Q.1 Does the US agree that Section 110(5) US Copyright Act would be inconsistent with Article 11*bis*(1)(iii) Berne Convention if it were not for the minor reservations doctrine? If not why not?

The US agrees that *any* exception to the exclusive right under Article 11*bis*(1)(iii) would be inconsistent with the Berne Convention if it were not for the minor reservations doctrine. If there were no minor reservations doctrine, then no exceptions would be permitted to the exclusive rights under either Berne Article 11 or Berne Article 11*bis*. This would mean that exceptions for marching bands, religious services or school activities, found in many European Union member states' laws as well as those of other WTO Members, would all be inconsistent with the Berne Convention. For further discussion of this and related issues, see US response to Panel Questions to the United States and the European Communities, numbers 8 and 9.

Q.2 Would the US in particular confirm that it does not consider that Section 110(5) can be justified under Article 11*bis*(2) Berne Convention?

The U.S. confirms that it does not consider that any exception to an exclusive right can be justified under Berne Article 11*bis*(2). That provision does not speak to whether exceptions to an exclusive right are permissible, but merely authorizes a country to substitute a compulsory license for that exclusive right. Only compulsory licenses can be evaluated under Article 11*bis*(2). For further discussion of this and related issues, see US response to Panel Question 6 to the United States and the European Communities.

Q.3 The US seems to concede that TRIPS does not diminish any rights available under the Berne Convention. Would the US not therefore agree that Article 13 TRIPS, rather than being considered as an exemption in its own right, can only be considered as a further limitation of any possibility to maintain limitations, reservations or exceptions that may be contained in the Berne Convention?

No. Article 13 is not a further limitation on the possibility of providing exceptions to exclusive rights under Berne; rather, it articulates the standard by which implied exceptions to Berne should be evaluated.

Q.4 Does the US agree that the purpose of minor reservations under the Berne Convention is to allow Parties to maintain existing minor exceptions when acceding to the Berne Convention?

No. The U.S. does not agree with this statement. Although the negotiating history of Berne may contain some references to countries' desire not to encourage exceptions (and thus the minor reservations doctrine was kept implicit, rather than specified in the text of the Convention), a general desire to minimize exceptions is not equivalent to an intent to prohibit them.

Q.5 Where in the negotiating history of TRIPS does the US find a basis for its contention that Article 13 TRIPS was designed to "articulate" the minor reservations under the Berne Convention? Does the US consider that the possibility of "minor reservations" can apply to all rights guaranteed under the Berne Convention?

See U.S. response to Question 14 from the Panel to the United States.

Q.6 In paragraph 32 of its First Written Submission the US seeks to justify the "business exemption" by saying that it adds only a "small number of establishments" to those benefiting from the pre-existing homestyle exemption. Would the US please provide an estimate of this additional "small number of establishments"? If the US Congress were to further increase the thresholds, would the US then seek to justify the new version under Article 13 TRIPS by arguing that most of the establishments covered by the newly-formulated exemption were exempted under the pre-existing version?

See U.S. Response to Panel Questions 9-10 to the United States for the data available to the United States. The United States will not speculate concerning the hypothetical sub-question posed in the above question.

Q.7 What percentage of establishments would have to be excluded from protection under Article 110(5) US Copyright Act before it ceased to qualify for exemption under Article 13 TRIPS according to the US?

See U.S. Response to Question 16 from the Panel to the United States and the European Communities.

Q.8 Could the US please explain why the playing of copyrighted works originating from radio or TV broadcasts may be excluded from protection and not the playing of copyrighted works directly from tapes or cassettes?

See U.S. Response to Question 7 from the Panel to the United States.

Q.9 Could the US please provide a copy of the NLBA licence which it claims at paragraph 13 of its First Written Submission is based on similar criteria to those used in Section 110(5)?

See U.S. response to Panel Question 1 to the United States and exhibit US-16.

Q.10 In paragraph 4 of its Oral Statement, the US states that the Article 110(5) "exception is limited to only certain secondary uses of broadcasts of public performances, for which the right holder has already been compensated for the primary performance." Does the US really consider that payment of a royalty for the "primary performance" may be considered to also compensate for "secondary uses"?

See U.S. response to Panel Question 4 to the United States and the European Communities.

Q.11 Please explain why you consider the other exception provisions of TRIPS (Articles 17, 26(2) and 30) to be relevant context for the interpretation of Article 13 and what consequences you draw? What is the relative importance of these other provisions of TRIPS and the exceptions, reservations or limitations allowed under the Berne Convention as context for the interpretation of Article 13?

Under Article 31 of the Vienna Convention, other provisions of a treaty are part of the context for the purpose of interpreting a particular provision. In considering the interpretation of Article 13 of TRIPS, it would be inappropriate not to consider three other similarly worded provisions governing exceptions in the Agreement. Generally under TRIPS, the permissibility of exceptions is determined by similar (though not identical) standards in relation to copyrights, patents, industrial designs as well as trademarks. These exceptions reinforce the principle that the TRIPS Agreement was intended to balance the interests of producers and users of intellectual property. There is no basis in the negotiating history of TRIPS to assume that WTO Members used similar wording, but nevertheless intended to permit exceptions of radically differing scope, with respect to different types of intellectual property rights.

Moreover, Articles 30 and 31 reinforce the point made in U.S. Response to Panel Question 6 to the United States, in that they reflect the clear distinction in intellectual property between exceptions (for which equitable remuneration is not required) and compulsory licenses (for which equitable remuneration is required).

ATTACHMENT 2.5

SECOND WRITTEN SUBMISSION OF THE UNITED STATES

(24 November 1999)

TABLE OF CONTENTS

I. INTRODUCTION

1. In this case, the Panel is faced with two important questions under the TRIPS Agreement. First, the Panel must decide on the proper standard to evaluate an exception to an exclusive right under the Berne Convention that has been challenged under the provisions of the TRIPS Agreement. Second, the Panel must apply that standard to the case at hand to determine whether the exception is permissible under Berne and TRIPS. The proper determination to both of these questions leads to the conclusion that Section 110(5)(A) and (B) of the U.S. Copyright Law are permissible under the Berne Convention and the TRIPS Agreement.

2. The minor reservations doctrine is well-founded in the history and practice of the Berne Convention, and should be applied to exceptions to the Berne rights at issue here — Article 11 and 11*bis* rights. That doctrine, however, has been clarified and further articulated by TRIPS Article 13, which is the standard by which such exceptions are to be judged. The Article 13 test should be used by the Panel as the means to judge the permissibility of Section 110(5) under Berne. The exemptions in Section 110(5) fall within the Article 13 standard: they are special cases which do not conflict with a normal exploitation of the work and they do not unreasonably prejudice the legitimate interests of the right holder.

II. FACTUAL ISSUES

3. As an initial matter, several factual issues relating to Section 110(5)(A) require clarification. First, the United States emphasizes that there is no factual dispute before the Panel regarding the works covered under the current Section 110(5)(A), and the text of the provision itself is unambiguous. Both parties *agree* that the homestyle exemption was substantially narrowed by the removal of nondramatic

musical works from its spectrum, and that the exemption now applies only to works other than nondramatic musical works.[1]

4. Although it has failed to provide any evidence of prejudice to EC right holders as a result of Section 110(5)(A), the EC has nevertheless made unsupported factual assertions regarding the scope of this provision. The scope of Section 110(5) is a question of fact to be established before this Panel, as it is an accepted principle of international law that municipal law is a fact to be proven before an international tribunal.[2] Despite the plain language of Section 110(5)(A) regarding the requirement of homestyle receiving equipment, the EC asks the Panel to consider that at some point in the future, U.S. courts might expand that exemption by applying the square footage and size requirements of Section 110(5)(B) to subsection (A).[3] The Panel should give no weight to the EC's speculative and unsupported assertion that U.S. courts might begin to ignore the text of Section 110(5)(A) in the future. The consistent jurisprudence of U.S. courts interpreting the homestyle exemption is dispositive evidence of the scope of this law.[4]

5. The EC also argues that two particular cases, *Edison Bros.* and *Claire's Boutiques*, are "illustrative" of a judicial trend toward broadening the homestyle exemption.[5] Far than being illustrative, however, these two cases are the *only* decisions allowing chain stores to take advantage of the homestyle exception. Furthermore, as explained in the U.S. first submission, these cases are consistent with the body of U.S. case law under Section 110(5), in that they involved the use of extremely limited receiving equipment.

6. With respect to Section 110(5)(B), the EC again wrongly asserts that the prohibitions against charging admission fees and retransmission "have no potential whatsoever to limit the exception."[6] As a factual matter, the prohibitions do limit the scope of both subsections. There is a market for paid events at restaurants in the United States - for example, sporting events. If restaurants charged a fee for entrance, it would change the nature of a customer's visit to a restaurant, signifying that the main reason for the visit was to attend an event, not necessarily to eat. This requirement thus limits the impact of the exemption.

---

[1] EC Oral Statement, para. 20.

[2] See Appellate Body Report, *India - Patent Protection for Pharmaceutical and Agricultural Chemical Products* ("*India Mailbox*"), WT/DS50/AB/R, adopted 16 January 1998, DSR 1998:I, 9, paras. 65-66.

[3] EC first submission, para. 32.

[4] See Judge Lauterpacht, Case Concerning the Guardianship of an Infant [1958], ICJ Rep., Sep. Op., at 91 (It is settled practice among States that international judicial bodies should accept, and treat as binding, questions of municipal law and practice decided by competent municipal courts); Case Concerning the Payment of Various Serbian Loans Issued in France [1929], PCIJ Rep., Series A, No. 20, at 46; Case Concerning Certain German Interests in Polish Upper Silesia [1926], PCIJ Rep., Series A, No. 7, at 19; Case Concerning the Payment in Gold of Brazilian Federal Loans Contracted in France [1929], PCIJ Rep., Series A, No. 21, at 124-25 (The PCIJ attached controlling weight to the manner in which French courts had interpreted French legislation). See also India - Mailbox, para. 65.

[5] EC first submission, paras. 26-27, EC Oral Statement, para. 12-16.

[6] EC first submission, paras. 43-44.

III. TRIPS ARTICLE 13 IS THE APPLICABLE STANDARD FOR EVALUATING EXCEPTIONS

7. Given that this case was initiated under the WTO TRIPS Agreement, the text of that Agreement should be the starting-point for the Panel's legal analysis regarding the exceptions in Section 110(5) of the U.S. Copyright Law. In this case, the plain language of Article 13 indicates that it is the appropriate standard by which to judge exceptions to exclusive rights such as Section 110(5). This interpretation of Article 13 is confirmed by the recently-concluded WIPO Copyright Treaty ("WCT"), as well as the negotiating history of the TRIPS Agreement.

8. The EC argues that TRIPS Article 13 should not apply to this case because Article 13 would then represent a derogation from the protection afforded by the Berne Convention, in violation of TRIPS Article 2.2 and Berne Article 20. On the contrary, however, this result does not derogate from Berne because TRIPS Article 13 articulates the standard applicable to minor reservations under Berne. According to the EC, Berne either does not permit exceptions to Articles 11 and 11*bis* at all, or, if it does permit such exceptions, then Section 110(5) does not fall within those permitted exceptions because it is commercial in nature and enacted after 1967. These arguments fail, however, because neither of these factors is determinative in deciding whether an exception falls within the minor reservations doctrine under the Berne Convention.

A. *Plain Language of Article 13*

9. The text of Article 13 is straight-forward and applies to "limitations or exceptions to exclusive rights". In light of this plain language, the Panel should be particularly reluctant to adopt an interpretation of Article 13 that makes it somehow inapplicable to a "limitation or exception" to an exclusive right. The EC's position conflicts with the text of Article 13, in that the EC argues that Article 13 is not applicable to limitations and exceptions to the particular exclusive rights in TRIPS that have been incorporated from the Berne Convention.

10. The general rule of treaty interpretation in the WTO is that "a treaty shall be interpreted in good faith in accordance with the ordinary meaning to be given to the terms of the treaty in their context and in the light of its object and purpose".[7] A corollary to the general rule of interpretation is that the interpretation must give meaning and effect to all terms of a treaty, and not adopt a reading that would reduce or nullify a provision.[8] These rules govern a Panel's interpretation of TRIPS.[9] As we discussed extensively in the U.S. first submission and Statement at the first meeting of the Panel with the Parties, Article 13 articulates the standard for exceptions within

---

[7] Vienna Convention on the Law of Treaties, Article 31(1). See Appellate Body Report, United States - Standards for Reformulated and Conventional Gasoline, WT/DS2/AB/R, adopted 20 May 1996, DSR 1996:I, 3, at 15; India - Mailbox, *supra*, footnote 2, paras. 43 and 44.

[8] United States - Reformulated Gas, *supra*, footnote 7 at 21; India - Mailbox , *supra*, footnote 2, para. 46.

[9] See India - Mailbox, *supra*, footnote 2, paras. 43, 46.

the context of the TRIPS Agreement and the Berne Convention as incorporated into TRIPS.[10]

B. *WIPO Copyright Treaty*

11. The WCT represents further evidence of the applicability of the standard articulated in Article 13 to exclusive rights provided under the Berne Convention. As articulated in the U.S. Response to Panel Question 14 to the United States, the WCT was adopted by consensus in 1996 by the WIPO Diplomatic Conference. The overwhelming majority of Berne members (99 out of 119) and WTO members (94 out of 128) participated in the Diplomatic Conference.[11] Like TRIPS, the WCT is an Agreement explicitly designed to provide a higher level of protection than that provided under Berne. Article 1 of the WCT provides that it is a "Special Agreement" within the meaning of Berne Article 20, provides that it does not derogate from existing obligations under Berne, and also explicitly requires compliance with Articles 1-21 and the Appendix of the Berne Convention.[12]

12. The preamble of the WCT states that the Parties recognized "the need to introduce new international rules and clarify the interpretation of certain existing rules".[13] Article 10(2) of the WCT is an example of a clarifying interpretation of Berne, and provides: "Contracting Parties shall, *when applying the Berne Conven-*

---

[10] Neil W. Netanel, *The Digital Agenda of the World Intellectual Property Organization: The Impact of the WIPO Copyright Treaty on TRIPS Dispute Settlement*, 37 Va. J. Int'l L. 441, 460 (Winter 1997) ("Article 13 to applies to all exclusive rights"); Laurence R. Helfer, *Adjudicating Copyright Claims Under the TRIPS Agreement: The Case for a European Human Rights Analogy* , 39 Harv. Int'l Law J. 357, 380 (Spring 1998) ("On its face, article 13 applies to all copyright limitations and exceptions, both those added by TRIPS and those incorporated by Berne, and it overrides the more expansive limitations and exceptions set forth in other Berne articles."); Ruth L. Gana, *Prospects for Developing Countries Under The TRIPS Agreement*, 29 Vand. J. Transnat'l L. 735, 760 ((1996) (noting that the Article 13 standard "extends to all rights covered by the TRIPS Agreement, not just the reproductive right."); Pamela Samuelson, *The Digital Agenda of the World Intellectual Property Organization: The U.S. Digital Agenda at WIPO*, 37 Va. J. Int'l L. 369, 403 (Winter 1997) ("[at the time of the WCT], it is true that the universalization of Article 9(2)'s three-step test had already become an international norm by the adoption of Article 13 of the TRIPS Agreement").

[11] For a complete listing of states participating in the Geneva conference, see List of Participants, WIPO Doc. CRNR/DC/INF.2 at *www.wipo.org/eng/dipconf).*

[12] Article 1 of the WCT is entitled "Relation to the Berne Convention", and provides as follows:

> (1) This Treaty is a *special agreement within the meaning of Article 20* of the Berne Convention for the Protection of Literary and Artistic Works, as regard Contracting Parties that are countries of the Union established by that Convention. This Treaty shall not have any connection with treatises other than the Berne Convention, nor shall it prejudice any rights and obligations under any other treaties.
>
> (2) Nothing in this Treaty shall derogate from existing obligations that Contracting Parties have to each other under the Berne Convention for the Protection of Literary and Artistic Works.
>
> (3) Hereinafter, "Berne Convention" shall refer to the Paris Act of July 24, 1971, of the Berne Convention for the Protection of Literary and Artistic Works.
>
> (4) *Contracting Parties shall comply with Article 1 to 21 and the Appendix of the Berne Convention.*

[13] WCT, preamble.

tion, confine any limitations or exceptions to rights provided for therein to certain special cases that do not conflict with a normal exploitation of the work and do not unreasonably prejudice the legitimate interests of the author." (Emphasis added.) Thus, under the WCT, exceptions permissible under Berne are those that meet the same standard set out in TRIPS Article 13. On the other hand, under the EC's interpretation of TRIPS Article 13 - that it cannot represent the standard governing exceptions to Berne rights because TRIPS would then represent a derogation of rights provided under Berne - the WCT must represent a derogation of rights provided under Berne, a conclusion flatly at odds with Article 1 of the WCT.

C. Negotiating History of the TRIPS Agreement

13. The negotiating history of the TRIPS Agreement further supports our conclusion that Article 13 applies to Berne rights. As explained by one commentator: "Article 13 allows a dispute settlement panel to review exceptions, including the so called 'small exceptions', to ensure that they pass the test. ... When these exceptions are invoked, they may from now on be submitted to the general test of Article 13".[14] The United States has already elaborated on the negotiating history of TRIPS in its Response to the Panel Question 14 to the United States and in its first submission.

14. In its Response to Question 10 from the Panel, the EC has cited its opening position in the TRIPS negotiations as evidence of the non-applicability of Article 13 to Berne rights. During the TRIPS negotiations, the EC had taken the position that the exceptions article in TRIPS should not apply to Berne rights, but rather should apply only to so-called "Berne-plus" rights set forth in particular provisions of TRIPS.[15] The contrast between the EC negotiating position and the final text of Article 13, the application of which is not limited to specified exclusive rights, demonstrates that if WTO Members had intended Article 13 to apply only to certain exclusive rights under TRIPS, they would have specified that result. Rather, Article 13 was phrased generally, does not indicate any sort of limited application, and was intended to apply to *all* exclusive rights.

D. Relationship with the Berne Convention

15. The U.S. view that Article 13 sets forth the standard governing all exceptions or limitations to exclusive rights is consistent with the context of Article 13, including TRIPS Article 2.2. It does not imply that TRIPS reduced the level of protection below the level permissible under Berne. Even though not explicitly stated, the Berne Convention permits minor exceptions to the exclusive rights provided for therein. As acknowledged by the EC in its response to Panel Question 11 to the EC, and Panel Question 5 to the US and EC, the minor reservation doctrine is well-established under Berne.[16]

---

[14] D. Gervais, The TRIPS Agreement: Drafting History and Analysis, 89-80 (1998).

[15] Exhibit EC-17 ("Contracting parties may, in relation to the rights conferred by a Articles 4, 5, 6, and 7 provide for limitations, exceptions and reservations as permitted by the Rome Convention ...").

[16] The responses of the EC now assert that the existence of the minor reservations doctrine "is considered to be confirmed" by the General Report of the Stockholm Conference (1967) and that the EC "would not exclude that the 'minor reservations' doctrine has, by virtue of the Article 9(1) TRIPS,

16. Minor exceptions to the public performance right appear in the copyright laws of very many, if not virtually all, Berne members. Under Article 31 of the Vienna Convention, subsequent practice is to be "taken into account, together with the context" in interpreting treaty text.[17] Subsequent practice is important, according to the International Law Commission, because it "constitutes objective evidence of the understanding of the parties as to the meaning of the treaty.[18] According to the Appellate Body, subsequent practice under Article 31(3)(b) includes practice that is "concordant, common, and consistent".[19] Although the United States has not been able to review the copyright laws of all Berne members, a large number of exceptions were cited in our response to Panel Question 16 to the United States. Additional countries that permit exceptions to the public performance right are cited in Exhibit US-22. This widespread practice of allowing minor exceptions to this particular Berne right illustrates its common acceptance among Berne members.

17. Relevant negotiating history of the Berne Convention has already been reviewed in this proceeding, and also clearly establishes the permissibility of minor reservations under Berne. Under Article 32 of the Vienna Convention, preparatory work of a treaty may be used to confirm the meaning of the text and context or to clarify ambiguities. The negotiating history regarding minor exceptions confirms that Berne members intended that exceptions be allowed to the exclusive rights provided in Articles 11 and 11*bis*.

18. Contrary to the EC's assertions, minor reservations under Berne are not limited to either: (a) the specific noncommercial uses listed in the General Reports - "religious ceremonies, performances by military bands and the requirements of child and adult education"; or (b) exceptions existing in the legislation of the member states of the Berne Union in 1967, at the latest.

19. First, there is no requirement that exempt uses be noncommercial. Although, as a general rule, noncommercial uses may be less prejudicial to right holders than commercial ones, this is not an absolute rule. Even the uses discussed in the General Reports are not necessarily noncommercial; for example, there are many educational institutions or training programs that are run for profit. Several of the public performance exceptions in EC member state laws exempt educational activities without specifying that the educational institution must be nonprofit. Exemptions in the laws of certain third parties to this dispute are also applicable to commercial uses. These include the Australian law that exempts secondary performances in hotels and guest houses, and the Canadian law that exempts performances at agricultural fairs and exhibitions.[20] These exceptions demonstrate that the commercial nature of a use cannot be dispositive.

---

whatever its legal significance may be, become part to [sic] the TRIPS Agreement." EC Response to Panel Question 5 and 8 to the US and EC.

[17] Vienna Convention, Article 31(3).

[18] Yearbook of the International Law Commission, Vol. II, p. 221 (1966).

[19] Appellate Body Report, *Japan - Taxes on Alcoholic Beverages* ("*Japan - Alcoholic Beverages II*"), WT/DS8/AB/R, WT/DS10/AB/R, WT/DS11/AB/R, adopted 1 November 1996, DSR 1996:I, 97, at 106.

[20] See U.S. response to Panel Question 16 to the Panel.

20. Furthermore, the discussion of the minor reservations doctrine in the General Reports precludes the notion that the doctrine was limited to the exceptions specifically mentioned in those Reports. The General Reports only list several traditional exceptions to the public performance right of Article 11, such as military bands and religious ceremonies. However, the Reports also make certain to note that the minor reservation doctrine is *also* applicable to Article 11*bis*, 13 and 14, but do not provide any examples of permissible exceptions to those rights.[21] It must have been intended that the doctrine apply to exceptions not specifically listed in the Reports, otherwise that language would have no meaning.

21. Second, the EC's argument that the exceptions allowable under the minor reservations doctrine must be frozen in 1967 fails for a number of reasons. Notably, it is explicitly contradicted by the language in the Agreed Statement concerning Article 10 of the WCT, which states "It is understood that the provisions of Article 10 permit Contracting Parties to carry forward and appropriately extend into the digital environment limitations and exceptions in their national laws which have been considered acceptable under the Berne Convention." If the exceptions permissible under Berne were frozen in 1967, then this language would effectively contradict Article 1 of the WCT, which states that nothing in the Treaty shall derogate from the protection afforded under Berne.

22. Construing the minor reservation doctrine to apply only to exceptions in existence in 1967 also creates unfair results in regard to developing countries, and renders the Berne Convention less applicable in the modern world. Many developing countries that are now members of Berne had no copyright law at all, or only a rudimentary one, in 1967. If the EC's argument that countries can only "grandfather their pre-1967 exceptions" when acceding to Berne is accepted, then most developing countries will not be allowed to have any exceptions at all. In addition, the flexibility of the principles of copyright protection represented in Berne would be drastically undermined were they not allowed to respond to changes and developments in technology as well as practice. As provided in the WCT, countries must be able to appropriately extend and adapt exceptions to fit the realities of a changing world. The EC's interpretation of Berne, freezing it in 1967, would deprive it of much relevance in today's intellectual property environment.

E. Significance of Berne Article 11bis(2)

23. We note that there has also been some discussion, in third party submissions and in the questions from the Panel, about the relevance of Article 11*bis*(2) to the permissibility of Section 110(5). We reiterate our position, more fully articulated in the U.S. Response to Panel Question 6 to the US and EC, that Article 11*bis*(2) has no bearing on Section 110(5). Article 11*bis*(2) merely authorizes a country to *substitute* a compulsory license, or its equivalent, for an exclusive right under Article 11*bis*. Neither the negotiating history of Berne, nor the subsequent writings of commentators support the view that 11*bis*(2) authorizes outright exceptions to Article 11*bis*, or

[21] Records of the Intellectual Property Conference of Stockholm, WIPO, Geneva, 1971, paras. 209-210, p. 1166.

represents a standard against which to judge such exceptions.[22] Simply put, Article 11*bis*(2) is not related to the minor reservations doctrine, and does not bear upon the scope of exceptions permissible under that doctrine.[23]

24. Indeed, interpreting Article 11*bis*(2) to apply to exceptions as well as compulsory licenses leads to illogical and impractical results. For example, where an exception implicates several rights, such as Section 110(5), only one of which is subject to a right of equitable remuneration, it would be practically impossible to divide the exception into the different rights affected and then apply different standards to each right.

F. Conclusion

25. In conclusion, as the plain meaning of the provision suggests, Article 13 articulates the standard by which to determine the permissibility of "exceptions or limitations" to exclusive rights. By contrast, the EC interpretation of Article 13 is at odds with the text of that provision, as well as its negotiating history, and is not consistent with the WCT. Furthermore, minor exceptions to exclusive rights under Articles 11 and 11*bis* have always been permitted under the Berne Convention, and have not been limited to any particular purpose or date of enactment. TRIPS Article 13 articulates the standard governing such minor reservations, and thus is the appropriate focal point of the legal analysis in the case.

IV. SECTION 110(5) MEETS ARTICLE 13 CRITERIA

26. Sections 110(5)(A) and (B) are consistent with the principles of the minor reservations doctrine, and satisfy the TRIPS Article 13 standard. Section 110(5) applies to certain special cases, does not conflict with the normal exploitation of the work and does not unreasonably prejudice the legitimate interests of the right holder.

A. Interpreting the Article 13 Criteria

27. Interpretation of the TRIPS Article 13 criteria requires a fact-intensive analysis by the Panel that takes into account all the circumstances of an individual case. Article 13 is intended to be a flexible mechanism to evaluate numerous different exceptions in many different contexts and legal systems. It does not impose any "per-se" rules with respect to any of the criteria in the Article. Rather, the permissibility of

---

[22] The negotiating history of the TRIPS Agreement also supports the distinction between compulsory licenses and outright exceptions. Of interest is a late version of Article 13 which included a separate provision on rights of equitable remuneration, providing: "Any compulsory license (or any restriction of exclusive rights to a right of remuneration) shall provide mechanisms to ensure prompt payment and remittance of royalties." Status of Work in the Negotiating Group: Prepared by the chairman, No. 2341 (1 October 1990).

[23] The EC implicitly acknowledges the lack of a relationship between 11*bis*(2) and the minor reservations doctrine in its response to Question 12 of the Panel to the EC, in which the Panel asks the EC to provide examples of ways to provide "equitable remuneration" under 11*bis*(2) other than compulsory licensing. In response, the EC posits several mechanisms, such as royalty schemes and levy systems, that are the functional equivalent of compulsory licenses.

exceptions under TRIPS Article 13 must necessarily be determined on a case-by-case basis.

28. In such an analysis, the market of the country imposing the exception is the most relevant. The United States and the EC are apparently in agreement regarding this issue.[24] Moreover, while both actual market conditions as well as potential market may be relevant to the analysis under Article 13, actual conditions are of primary importance. An analysis based on assumptions about a potential market is necessarily less reliable and subject to speculation. The EC, for example, argues that the Panel should consider the alleged 70% of exempt restaurants as the potential market for its right holders - even though there is no possibility that all such restaurants actually play radio music and would be licensed by ASCAP or BMI. The only way to avoid the danger of arbitrariness is to accord the greatest weight to actual existing market conditions.

B. Section 110(5)(A) and (B) Apply to Certain, Special Cases

29. As discussed in the U.S. Response to Panel Question 17 to the U.S., both Section 110(5)(A) and (B) represent exceptions that apply in certain special cases. The essence of this requirement is that exceptions be well-defined and of limited application. Both Sections 110(5)(A) and (B) are sufficiently definite. Section 110(5)(A) is defined by the equipment limitations, and the subsequent case law which has consistently enforced square footage limitations. Section 110(5)(B) is clearly defined in the statute by square footage and equipment limitations. Furthermore, to the extent that the purpose of the exception is relevant, it is only required that the exception have a specific policy objective. TRIPS does not impose any requirements on the policy objectives that a particular country might consider special in light of its own history and national priorities. In this case, both exceptions rest upon sound public policy objectives related to the social benefits of fostering small businesses and preventing abusive tactics by the collecting societies.

C. Neither Section 110(5)(A) or (B) Conflicts with Normal Exploitation

30. Neither Section 110(5)(A) nor Section 110(5)(B) conflict with the normal exploitation of a work. Section 110(5)(A), almost by definition, cannot conflict with normal exploitation, as it was intended precisely to exempt those establishments which would not have otherwise justified a commercial license.[25]

---

24 EC Response to Panel Question 8 to both parties.

25 The EC appears to find a contradiction in the fact that the PROs did not generally license small business establishments, and that there were many complaints about their licensing practices being abusive with regard to such establishments. No such contradiction exists. The PROs did not attempt to license the vast majority of small businesses. Nevertheless, there were complaints that when the PROs did attempt to obtain licenses from any business, they often did so in an arbitrary and abusive manner, without regard for existing law or good faith business practices. Small business, generally being the least sophisticated and having the fewest resources, are the least able to respond to such tactics or defend their rights.

31. In evaluating normal exploitation, the Panel must look at the scope of the exception with respect to the panoply of exclusive rights, as well as with respect to the specific right which it exempts. As more fully explained in US Response to Panel Question 18 to the U.S., both perspectives are relevant. While the impact on the particular right affected is relevant, the proportion of that right to the rest of the exclusive rights is equally so. Notably, the TRIPS Article 13 test does not say "conflict with the normal exploitation of an exclusive right", but refers to the exploitation of the "work" as a whole.

D. Neither Section 110(5)(A) or (B) Causes Unreasonable Prejudice

32. Section 110(5)(A) and (B) do not cause right holders unreasonable prejudice, as the economic impact of the exceptions is minimal. The discussion below focuses primarily on Section 110(5)(B), since the EC aims most of its criticism, and the minimal empirical analysis it has conducted, at this subsection. It can be assumed, however, that the impact of subsection (A), the homestyle exemption, is a mere fraction of the numbers discussed below, as it affects fewer and smaller establishments than subsection (B). The United States also observes that, despite the more than 20 year history of the homestyle exemption, the EC has not provided any facts or data showing any prejudice to EC right holders as a result of the old homestyle exemption or amended Section 110(5)(A).[26]

1. Section 110(5)(B) Does Not Cause Unreasonable Prejudice Because Any Actual Harm to EC Right Holders is Minimal

33. The amount of prejudice resulting from Section 110(5)(B) is not unreasonable. In our first submission, the United States noted the irrelevance of the figures provided by the EC, and discussed the factors by which those figures must be reduced to yield a reasonable approximation of losses to EC right holders. The following empirical analysis supplements that already provided by the United States,[27] and is based on additional information recently received. It is designed to rebut the EC's assertions, particularly those made in its responses to the Panel's questions, that Section 110(5) is likely to cost EC right holders "millions" of dollars. The analysis demonstrates that the maximum loss to EC right holders of distributions from the largest U.S. collecting society, ASCAP, as a result of the Section 110(5) exemption is in the range of $294,113 to $586,332 - far less than the "millions" of dollars claimed by the EC. Especially in light of the size of the U.S. and EC markets, this figure is truly a minimal one, and does not establish any unreasonable degree of prejudice.

---

26 See EC Response to Question 3 asked by the Panel.

27 The data provided in the following analysis reflects that provided in the U.S. Responses to the Panel's Questions 9-11 to the United States. The empirical calculations above, however, replace those estimates provided in the U.S. Response to Panel Questions 11.b and 11.d.

(a) Starting-Point in the Analysis: Total Royalties Paid to EC Right Holders: $19.6 Million - $39 Million

34. To determine the degree of prejudice to EC right holders from the exemption, the logical starting-point is the total amount paid to EC right holders by the collecting societies. The EC has recently provided figures from ASCAP purporting to show that EC right holders received an average of $39,045,833 from ASCAP for the years 1996, 1997 and 1998.[28] According to the EC data, this figure of 39 million dollars represents an average of 13.7% of ASCAP's total distributions of domestic income for those three years. It must be noted here that in an earlier analysis conducted by the EC to determine the harm to EC right holders from Section 110(5) before it was amended in 1998, the EC used a figure of "less than 5%" for 1996, and noted that ASCAP's distributions to *all* foreign collecting societies were just 6.2%.[29] The EC estimate of "less than 5%" appears to be based on the figure "total domestic distributions for EU societies" (19,586,000)[30] as a percentage of total ASCAP distributions for 1996 (397,379,000)[31] Given the inconsistency in the EC methodology, the United States' analysis below will proceed based on a range for ASCAP's total payments to EC right holders of 19.6 million to 39 million.

(b) After Reducing for Amount Attributable to General Licensing - Losses to EC Right Holders: $3.7 - $7.4 Million

35. To determine the potential impact of Section 110(5) on total payments to EC right holders, the figure for such total payments must be reduced to account for the fact that a relatively small proportion of licensing revenue collected in the United States is attributable to music played in restaurants, bars and retail establishments. As discussed in the U.S. responses to the Panel's questions, ASCAP's annual reports demonstrate that the majority - approximately 58% - of collecting society revenue comes from radio and TV broadcasters.[32] Another quarter of ASCAP's revenue comes from foreign collecting societies (25-26%). Interest, member dues and revenues from symphonies and concerts account for approximately 2%. All other licensing revenues account for only 14% of ASCAP total revenues from domestic and foreign sources. This 14% figure includes fees from commercial background music services, and a wide variety of licensees, including conventions and sports arenas, as well as all restaurants, bars and retail establishments. It represents average collections of $65,581,000 from general licensees[33] for 1995-97. The average amount collected from such general licensees ($65,581,000) in turn represents 18.9% of ASCAP's average total *domestic* receipts for 1995-97 ($346,981,000).[34]

---

28 Exhibit EC-15 (average of three figures in line 4).

29 European Commission, Examination Procedure Regarding the Licensing of Music Works in the United States of America, 27 (23 Feb. 1998).

30 Exhibit EC-15 (line 2 for 1996).

31 ASCAP Annual Report (1996) (Exhibit US-19).

32 ASCAP Annual Reports 1995, 1996, 1997 (Exhibit US-19).

33 Ibid. (average of figures for 1995, $63,227,000, 1996, $66,192,000, and 1997, $67,324,000).

34 Ibid. (average of figures for 1995, $326,482,000, 1996, $356,035,000, and 1997, $358,428,000).

36. Thus, the first step in determining the losses to EC right holders is to reduce the total payments to EC right holders to 18.9% of that total. This accounts for the fact that at least 81.1% of EC income from ASCAP is unaffected by Section 110(5). This analysis yields a potential range of loss to EC right holders from Section 110(5) of only 3,701,754 (18.9% of 19,586,000) to 7,379,662 (18.9% of $39,045,833).[35]

(c) After Reducing to Account for Licensing Revenue from General Licensees that Do Not Meet the Statutory Definition of an "Establishment" - Losses to EC Right Holders: $1.85 - $3.69 Million

37. These estimates of losses to EC right holders must also be reduced to account for the fact that many general licensees are not eligible to take advantage of Section 110(5), regardless of whether they meet the square footage and equipment criteria or not. Section 110(5)(B) applies to "establishments", which are defined in the same statute as "a store, shop or any similar place of business open to the general public for the primary purpose of selling goods or services in which the majority of the gross square feet of space that is nonresidential is used for that purpose". Many types of general licensees, for example, background music services, sporting events and conventions would seem not to fit this definition, and thus the royalties paid by these licensees must be excluded from the analysis of losses resulting from Section 110(5).

38. No data are available to the United States regarding the percentage of general licensees that might qualify as "establishments" under Section 110(5). It seems reasonable to assume, however, that the percentage of revenue from such "non-establishment" licensees is significant given their prevalence and size. For that reason, the United States will assume that 50% of general licensing revenue is attributable to such licensees. After reducing the potential losses to EC right holders to 50%, the resulting range of potential loss is: 1,850,877 (50% of 3,701,754) to 3,689,831 (50% of $7,379,662).

(d) After Reducing to Account for Licensing Revenue from General Licensees that Do Not Play the Radio - Losses to EC Right Holders: $.56 Million - $1.13 Million

39. In addition, it is obviously important to take into account the fact that much of the revenue from general licensees that qualify as establishments is not attributable to the playing of radio or TV music, but rather to public performances of music from media other than radio or TV broadcasts, such as tapes/CDs, live bands, and jukeboxes. According to the National Restaurant Association, approximately x% of all restaurants play the radio[36], but not necessarily exclusively (they may also sometimes use live bands or CDs, etc.). According to the National Licensed Beverage Associa-

[35] This analysis assumes that distributions paid to EC right holders are attributable to the same sources of revenue in the same proportion as overall revenues. It is entirely possible, however, that distributions to EC right holders might by attributable to television and radio broadcasters or symphonies to a greater extent than general licensing.

[36] Confidential Exhibit US-18.

tion, 28% of its members play the radio, but again not necessarily exclusively. Taking an average of these two roughly comparable estimates, the United States assumes that 30.5% of establishments play radio music.

40. It is important to note that, given that establishments often play music from more than one source, this estimate - 30.5% of establishments that play the radio - does not correspond with the percentage of licensing revenue attributable to the playing of radio music, and indeed would significantly overstate such revenue. Nevertheless, for the purpose of deriving a conservative estimate and in light of the limited data available, the United States assumes for the sake of only this analysis that 30.5% of licensing revenue is attributable to the playing of radio music. Correspondingly, the losses to EC right holders from the Section 110(5) exemption for radio music must be reduced to this amount, and would range from $564,517 (30.5% of 1,850,877) to $1,125,398 (30.5% of 3,689,831).

(e) After Reducing to Account for Licensing Revenue from General Licensee Establishments that Play the Radio and Meet Size Limitations of Section 110(5): Losses to EC Right Holders: $294,113 to $586,332

41. Certainly the calculation of losses to EC right holders must also take into account that many eating, drinking and retail establishments that play radio music do not meet the square footage limits of Section 110(5)(B). Based on figures provided by the National Restaurant Association, 65.5% of restaurants meet the square footage criteria of the statute.[37] The United States has no data regarding the percentage of retail establishments that would meet the square footage criteria; however, the EC has presented a Dun & Bradstreet study commissioned by ASCAP purporting to demonstrate that 45% of retail establishments are exempt under Section 110(5)(B).[38]

42. According to the EC's own exhibit EC-16, Dun & Bradstreet estimated that there were 683,783 retail establishments in the United States, and 364,404 eating and drinking establishments.

43. Applying 45% to the total number of retail establishments (683,783) results in a total of 307,702 retail establishments that meet the square footage criteria of Section 110(5). Applying 65.5% to the total number of eating and drinking establishments (364,404) results in a total of 238,685 such establishments that meet the square footage criteria of Section 110(5). The total number of establishments (both retail and eating and drinking) meeting the square footage criteria of the statute is thus 546,387, which is 52.1% of all establishments. The loss to EC right holders is further reduced to $294,113 (52.1% of $564,517) to $586,332 (52.1% of $1,125,398).

(f) The U.S. Methodology is Conservative

44. The above figure is a conservative one, based on available information. For a number of reasons, the true amount of economic prejudice to EC right holders is

[37] The EC has presented a different figure, and estimates that 70% of eating and drinking establishments fall within the square footage limitations of the statute.

[38] EC first submission, para. 51; Exhibit EC-16.

likely to be even less than $294,113 to $586,332. For example, the United States has assumed that where 30.5% of establishments play the radio, 30.5% of licensing revenue is attributable to radio-playing. This figure is obviously too high, given the large proportion of establishments that play music from more than one type of media. In addition, the United States assumed that the 65.5% of restaurants (and 45% of retail establishments) that fit within the square footage limits of the exception accounted for a 65.5% (and 45%) loss of revenue. In fact, the exempt restaurants and retail establishments are necessarily smaller establishments, and almost certainly represent a smaller proportion of licensing revenue.

45. In addition, the above analysis does not take into account steps that ASCAP and BMI might take to minimize any impact of Section 110(5), for example by focusing licensing resources exclusively on larger stores that generally pay larger fees, or by charging more for the playing of music from CDs and tapes. Similarly, the analysis does not take into account the establishments that could take advantage of the private agreement concluded by the PROs with the NLBA. Given the significant membership of the NLBA, and the fact that membership is open to any establishment that is licensed to serve alcoholic beverages, the NLBA Agreement should result in another significant reduction in any estimate of potential losses to EC right holders resulting from Section 110(5). Because the United States currently has no precise data on this factor, and is trying to keep estimates as conservative as possible, this element has not been figured into the loss calculation above.

46. The United States recognizes that the above estimates are losses from ASCAP distributions only. Little data has been available to the United States regarding revenues or distributions of the smaller of the two major U.S. collecting societies, BMI. While the total loss to EC right holders would obviously have to take into account the BMI figures, these figures will certainly be even less than those calculated for ASCAP. As indicated above in Section IV.1.B, average domestic revenue for ASCAP for the years 1995-97 was approximately $347 million. BMI's average domestic revenue in 1995 and 1996 was $260.5 million.[39] Thus, including the BMI figures will not dramatically increase the any loss to EC right holders.

47. The United States also recognizes that the analysis also does not take into account music played from the television. Given that few establishments rely exclusively on television for music, and that the proportion of restaurants using television sets is even lower than the proportion playing the radio,[40] these figures appear unlikely to significantly increase the loss to EC right holders. Finally, the United States notes that Section 110(5)(B) exempts establishments above the square footage limits if they meet certain equipment limits. No information, however, is currently available on this factor.

48. The United States has endeavored here to present the Panel with the best estimates possible from the limited data available. The resulting figures are well-founded in fact and logic, and indicate the insignificant amount of prejudice that EC right holders might actually suffer as a result of Section 110(5). The EC has not to date offered any concrete facts which rebut any of the assumptions made above. The

---

[39] Exhibit US-23.

[40] Exhibit US-18.

only data offered thus far to support the EC's claim that its right holders have suffered unreasonable prejudice comes from a self-serving press release by the U.S. PROs asserting that their right holders will lose "tens of millions" of dollars. On the basis of this press release, the EC asks the Panel to conclude that EC right holders will suffer losses "in the sphere of millions of dollars".[41] The more rigorous analysis presented by the United States refutes this exaggerated and speculative claim, and establishes the minimal prejudice actually likely to occur.

2. *Right Holders Themselves Have Viewed Size Limits Comparable to Section 110(5)(B) as Reasonable and Voluntarily Supported Them*

49. In considering whether the passage of Section 110(5)(B) has caused right holders any unreasonable prejudice, the private agreement between the PROs and the NLBA is also highly relevant. Notably, the PROs voluntarily agreed to a blanket exemption of 3500 square foot in the context of their private agreement with the NLBA. The fact that they were willing, voluntarily, to forego the collection of any revenue from such establishments must indicate that the administrative costs of doing so did not justify the likely returns, and that it was preferable from the right holders' perspective to seek a higher degree of compliance from non-exempt restaurants.

50. Indeed, throughout the legislative debate regarding Section 110(5)(B), the PROs were willing to conclude a private agreement with the National Restaurant Association that, like the NLBA deal, would exempt all restaurants under 3500 square feet from paying royalties for radio music. In addition, during legislative consideration of Section 110(5)(B), the "ASCAP and BMI proposal" revolved around an exemption for establishments smaller than 3500 square feet.

V. CONCLUSION

51. In conclusion, the applicable standard for determining the TRIPS consistency of Section 110(5) of the U.S. Copyright Act is TRIPS Article 13. Section 110(5) is a permissible exception to the public performance right based on the criteria articulated in Article 13. Therefore, the United States respectfully requests that the Panel find that both Section 110(5)(A) and (B) are consistent with the TRIPS Agreement.

---

41 EC Response to Panel Question 4 to the EC.

ATTACHMENT 2.6

ORAL STATEMENT OF THE UNITED STATES AT THE SECOND MEETING WITH THE PANEL

(7 December 1999)

I. INTRODUCTION

1. The exceptions permissible to exclusive rights, and the standard by which they will be governed are issues of tremendous importance under TRIPS. Article 13 of TRIPS is a key provision that limits WTO Members' ability to restrict exclusive rights, but also provides them with vital flexibility in implementing their TRIPS obligations. The proper application of this standard to Section 110(5)(A) and (B) of the U.S. Copyright Law results in a conclusion that these provisions are fully consistent with the TRIPS Agreement.

II. FACTUAL ISSUES

2. In our second submission, the United States addressed several factual inaccuracies put forward by the EC. We won't repeat those explanations here, except to note that where the parties are in agreement as to the facts, the Panel should not engage in speculation regarding alternative factual scenarios that do not in fact exist. The parties agree that Section 110(5)(A) does not apply to nondramatic musical works. The parties agree that the square footage limitations of Section 110(5)(B) do not apply to Section 110(5)(A). This is the plain language of the statutes; no U.S. court has ruled otherwise, and these are the only facts before the Panel.

III. TRIPS ARTICLE 13 IS THE APPLICABLE STANDARD FOR EVALUATING EXCEPTIONS

3. We start with Article 13. The plain language of Article 13 indicates that it is the appropriate standard by which to judge exceptions to exclusive rights such as Section 110(5). This interpretation of Article 13 is confirmed by the recently-concluded WIPO Copyright Treaty ("WCT"), as well as the negotiating history of the TRIPS Agreement.

4. The text of Article 13 is straight-forward and applies to "limitations or exceptions to exclusive rights". Not *some* limitations, not limitations to *some* exclusive rights. Just limitations or exceptions to exclusive rights. In light of the clear direction from the Appellate Body regarding the importance of the plain language of the text in the interpretation of WTO agreements, the EC should face a high hurdle to convince this Panel to disregard it.

5. The WCT represents further evidence of the applicability of the Article 13 standard to exclusive rights provided under Berne. The EC's submission indicates that the EC "does not understand" the relevance of this agreement. We submit, however, that where 99 Berne Members get together and adopt by consensus a document stating that the same standard of TRIPS Article 13 applies to Berne rights, it is highly

relevant and extremely important. Under the Vienna Convention, subsequent agreements and subsequent practice are important tools in treaty interpretation. In the *Japan taxes* case, the WTO Appellate Body emphasized that subsequent practice can be established by concordant pronouncements that establish a pattern implying the agreement of the parties regarding a treaty's interpretation.[1]

6. Like TRIPS, the WCT is an agreement explicitly designed to provide a higher level of protection than Berne. It says explicitly that it is a "Special Agreement" within the meaning of Berne Article 20, that it does not derogate from existing obligations under Berne, and it specifically requires compliance with Articles 1-21 and the Appendix of the Berne Convention.

7. Article 10(2) of the WCT specifically states that "when applying the Berne Convention" Contracting Parties shall confine limitations to those that meet the same test set out in TRIPS Article 13. The preparatory materials of the WCT are also enlightening, as the Basic Proposal for the '96 Diplomatic Conference specifically discusses the application of the 3-step TRIPS test to minor reservations under Berne.

8. The U.S. view that Article 13 provides the standard governing all exceptions or limitations to exclusive rights is consistent with the context of Article 13, including TRIPS Article 2.2. It does not imply that TRIPS reduced the level of protection below the level permissible under Berne. The Berne Convention permits minor exceptions to exclusive rights.

9. As described at some length in the U.S. Answers to the Panel's Questions and the U.S. rebuttal submission, the subsequent practice of Berne members indicates widespread acceptance of the notion that exceptions to Article 11 and 11*bis* rights are permissible. Furthermore, the negotiating history of Berne, in particular from the Brussels and Stockholm conferences, confirms that Berne members intended that exceptions be allowed to the exclusive rights provided in Articles 11 and 11*bis*.

10. Commercial uses are not excluded *per se* from the scope of the minor reservations doctrine. The uses discussed in the General Reports may themselves be commercial in certain circumstances. The specific examples of minor reservations given were never intended to be an exhaustive list. To quote Ricketson: "The examples of uses given in the records of the Brussels and Stockholm Conferences are in no way an exhaustive list or determinative or which particular exceptions will be justified." (p. 536) The discussion of the minor reservations doctrine in the General Reports actually precludes the notion that the doctrine was limited to the exceptions specifically cited. The General Reports only list several traditional exceptions to the public performance right of Article 11. However, the Reports also make certain to note that the minor reservation doctrine is *also* applicable to Article 11*bis*, 13 and 14. It must have been intended that the doctrine apply to exceptions not specifically listed in the Reports, otherwise that language would have no meaning.

11. Nor is the applicability of the minor reservations doctrine frozen in 1967. Again, the WCT provides useful guidance on this issue. The Agreed Statement concerning Article 10 of the WCT states that Contracting Parties can "carry forward and

---

[1] Appellate Body Report, Japan - Taxes on Alcoholic Beverages ("Japan – Alcoholic Beverages II"), WT/DS8/AB/R, WT/DS10/AB/R, WT/DS11/AB/R, adopted 1 November 1996, DSR 1996:I, 97, at 106. 25.

appropriately extend into the digital environment limitations and exceptions in their national laws" that have been considered acceptable under Berne. We note that the EC was a signatory of both the WCT and the Agreed Statement.

12. Construing the minor reservation doctrine to apply only to exceptions in existence in 1967 also creates inequitable results, and renders Berne less relevant to the modern world. Many developing countries that are now members of Berne had no copyright law, or only a rudimentary one, in 1967. If the EC's argument is accepted, then most developing countries will not be allowed to have any exceptions. In addition, the flexibility of the principles of copyright protection represented in Berne would be drastically undermined were they not allowed to respond to changes and developments in technology as well as practice.

13. For the sake of completeness, I'll now briefly address Article 11*bis*(2). This is a compulsory licensing provision. Compulsory licenses are characterized by the requirement of equitable remuneration. It is not a wholly separate standard governing exceptions. It does not apply in lieu of TRIPS Article 13 and it doesn't affect the applicability of TRIPS Article 13 to this case. Article 11*bis*(2) can, and should, be read consistently with TRIPS Article 13.

14. Article 11*bis*(2) applies to "conditions" on 11*bis* rights. Ricketson writes that "the reference to 'conditions' in article 11*bis*(2) is usually taken to refer to the imposition of compulsory licenses". (p.525). The WIPO Guide to the Berne Convention (p. 70), the WIPO Glossary of Terms of the Law of Copyright and Neighboring Rights (pp. 50, 248), and even the title of 11*bis*(2) assigned by WIPO also refer to that provision as a compulsory licensing provision. It is highly significant that the World Intellectual Property Organization - the entity that administers the Berne Convention - has expressed this clear and consistent view.

15. Article 11*bis*(2) simply has no bearing on Section 110(5). Neither the negotiating history of Berne, nor the subsequent writings of commentators support the view that 11*bis*(2) represents a standard against which to judge exceptions to exclusive rights. If Article 11*bis*(2) had permitted and governed exceptions, there would have been no need for the negotiators at the Brussels and Stockholm conferences to reference Article 11*bis* in discussions about the minor reservations doctrine at all. Article 11*bis*(2) is not related to the minor reservations doctrine, and does not bear upon the scope of exceptions permissible under that doctrine.

IV. SECTION 110(5) MEETS THE ARTICLE 13 CRITERIA

16. I'll turn now to the applicability of Article 13 to Sections 110(5)(A) and (B). These sections apply to different works and have a different scope. Thus, they must be examined separately. Both provisions apply to certain special cases, do not conflict with the normal exploitation of the work and do not unreasonably prejudice the legitimate interests of the right holder.

A. *Interpreting the Article 13 Criteria*

17. Interpretation of the TRIPS Article 13 criteria requires a fact-intensive analysis by the Panel. Article 13 is intended to be a flexible mechanism to evaluate numerous different exceptions in many different contexts and legal systems. It demands a 'rule of reason' approach. The permissibility of exceptions under TRIPS Article 13

must necessarily be determined on a case-by-case basis, taking into account all the circumstances of an individual case.

18. In such an analysis, the market of the country imposing the exception is the most relevant. The United States and the EC agree on this issue. Moreover, while both actual losses and potential losses may be relevant to the analysis under Article 13, the key is *a realistic appraisal of the conditions that prevail in the market*. An analysis based on unrealistic and counter-factual assumptions is not reliable, is speculative, and basically unfair. The only way to avoid the danger of arbitrariness is to base the analysis on realistic market conditions.

B. Section 110(5)(A) and (B) Apply to Certain, Special Cases

19. Both Section 110(5)(A) and (B) represent exceptions that apply in certain special cases. The essence of this requirement is that exceptions be well-defined and of limited application. Both sub-sections (A) and (B) are sufficiently definite. Section 110(5)(A) is defined by the equipment limitations, and the subsequent case law. Section 110(5)(B) is clearly defined in the statute by square footage and equipment limitations.

20. Furthermore, to the extent that the purpose of the exception is relevant, it is only required that the exception have *a* specific policy objective. TRIPS does not impose any limitations on the policy objectives that a particular country might consider special in light of its own history and national priorities, and a Panel should be loathe to imply them. In this case, both U.S. exceptions rest upon sound public policy objectives related to the social benefits of fostering small businesses and preventing abusive tactics by the collecting societies.

C. Neither Section 110(5)(A) or (B) Conflicts with Normal Exploitation

21. Neither Section 110(5)(A) nor Section 110(5)(B) conflict with the normal exploitation of a work. The Panel's analysis of the issue of normal exploitation should be a broad one. There is no textual support in TRIPS for confining the analysis concerning normal exploitation to one exclusive right. The impact of an exception on a particular exclusive right is relevant, but no more relevant than the effect of the exception on the exploitation of the work as a whole. When considered in context, neither Section 110(5)(A) nor Section 110(5)(B) conflict with the normal exploitation of the works that they cover.

22. Section 110(5)(A) does not conflict with normal exploitation, as it was intended precisely to exempt those establishments which would not have otherwise justified a commercial license. More generally, the market to which Section 110(5) applies was never significantly exploited by the PROs. During Congressional consideration of Section 110(5)(B), ASCAP and BMI themselves advocated an exemption for establishments under 3500 square feet. (*Exhibit US - 16, CRS study comparing Aiken standard to "ASCAP/BMI proposal"*). In addition, they voluntarily signed a private agreement with the NLBA with the same square footage limitations. And they offered the same deal to the NRA. These actions by the PROs constitute important evidence that Section 110(5)(B) does not conflict with a *normal* exploitation of a work in the United States market.

D. *Neither Section 110(5)(A) or (B) Causes Unreasonable Prejudice*

23. Finally, we turn to the last prong of the TRIPS Article 13 standard: unreasonable prejudice. The economic effects of Section 110(5)(A) and (B) are minimal. Neither of these provisions cause EC right holders unreasonable prejudice. In fact, the EC has yet to provide a shred of evidence that Section 110(5)(A) causes its right holders *any* prejudice whatsoever. Given this situation, our empirical analysis will focus, as has the EC, on Section 110(5)(B).

24. In our first submission, the United States noted the irrelevance of the figures provided by the EC, and discussed the factors by which those figures must be reduced to yield a reasonable approximation of possible losses to EC right holders. The EC responded by asserting generally that the exception was costing its right holders millions of dollars. Thus, in our second submission, the United States has provided rebuttal evidence that Section 110(5)(B) is not costing EC right holders millions, but rather an amount that is insignificant. The analysis demonstrated that the maximum loss to EC right holders of distributions from the largest U.S. collecting society, ASCAP, as a result of the Section 110(5) exemption is in the range of 294 to 586 thousand dollars. This is in the range of 1%.

25. The United States has presented the Panel with the most precise estimates possible regarding the economic prejudice caused by Section 110(5). We've used data from ASCAP, from the NRA, from the NLBA, and even from the EC. Our analysis is based on the best information available, and has a firm factual and logical basis.

26. The EC has not to date offered any facts that rebut in any meaningful way any of the assumptions on which the U.S. analysis is based. The only "data" on losses offered by the EC thus far is a statement from a self-serving press release issued by ASCAP and BMI. In its answers to the Panel's questions, the EC makes some assertions regarding the music licensing market in Ireland. We do not believe that Ireland is a comparable market to the United States. And even if it was, actual data from the United States is certainly more relevant to the issue at hand.

27. The Panel's job is to weigh the facts presented. It must weigh the detailed evidence presented by the United States, which indicates prejudice in the range of a few hundred thousand dollars, against the assertions of the EC about Ireland. We respectfully submit that the U.S. analysis is the more credible one, and that it demonstrates that the amount of prejudice suffered by the EC is not unreasonable - in fact, it is barely measurable.

28. Our analysis is laid out in our Second Submission in significant detail. With the aid of US-exhibit 24, I will review it here briefly. Exhibit 24 has two pages - one for ASCAP and one for BMI. We've prepared these exhibits as an aid to this oral presentation, and you'll note that most of the numbers are rounded off. The precise figures are cited in the U.S. Second Submission. To simplify the presentation, I'll focus on the ASCAP analysis. As we noted in our brief, however, the numbers for BMI are even smaller. BMI collects less in annual revenues and collects for a lower percentage of EC right holders.

1. *Starting-Point: Royalties Paid to EC Right Holders: $19.6 Million - $39 Million*

29. The logical starting-point is the total amount paid to EC right holders by the collecting societies. In conducting an internal analysis of the effect of Section 110(5) on EC right holders in 1998, the EC based its calculations on distributions from the U.S. PROs to EC collecting societies. In 1996, such distributions were a bit under 19.6 million dollars. [2]

30. In its response to the Panel's questions, however, the EC argues that the relevant number is far higher, and cites figures from ASCAP purporting to show that EC right holders received an average of $39 million from ASCAP for the years 1996 - 98. Given the inconsistency in the EC methodology, the United States' analysis proceeds based on a range of 19.6 million to 39 million. (*line 1 of Exhibit US-24*).

31. Now these total figures - 19.6 - 39 million - represent payments from all licensees, including those that are not affected at all by Section 110(5)(B). So obviously it does not represent a realistic number for the potential loss to EC right holders. The only loss could come from establishments that meet the size and equipment limitations and play the radio. So we will take it step by step to reduce that total figure to exclude revenues that are unaffected by Section 110(5).

2. *Reduce to Amount Attributable to General Licensing - $3.7 - $7.4 Million*

32. Step One - You've got to exclude revenues from TV and radio broadcasting. Nothing in Section 110(5)(B) touches these revenues. And in fact license fees paid by TV and radio broadcasters are by far the largest portion of ASCAP's revenues. Licensing fees from establishments covered by Section110(5)(B) are considered general licensing fees. We know from ASCAP's Annual Reports that general licensing fees make up only 14% of ASCAP's total revenues. That's 18.9% of ASCAP's domestic revenues. So as you can see under Line 1 of the exhibit, right away you have to reduce the total amount paid to EC right holders to just 18.9% of that total, or 3.7 - 7.4 million dollars.

3. *Reduce to Account for Licensing Revenue from General Licensees that Do Not Meet the Statutory Definition of an "Establishment" - Losses to EC Right Holders: $1.85 - $3.69 Million*

33. Step Two - Section 110(5)(B) does not apply to all general licensing. General licensing is a very broad category. It essentially applies to anyone that is not a radio or television station. ASCAP's A-Z list of general licensees is Exhibit US-25. As you can see, this category includes everything from background music services, colleges

[2] The starting figure for BMI was taken from the EC's 1998 Trade Barriers Regulation Investigation Report, which indicated that of BMI's total distributions to rightholders of 217.3 million in 1996, 5.6% went to foreign collecting societies. We've made the realistic assumption that two-thirds of these foreign distributions are paid to EC right holders (217.3 * .056 * .67 = 8.15), and then followed the same calculations as described for ASCAP.

and universities, conventions, football teams, music-on-hold, private clubs, theme parks, trade shows, training seminars and tractor pulls. Restaurants are certainly included on the list, but so are many other types of licensees. The royalties paid by these licensees must be excluded from the analysis of losses resulting from Section 110(5)(B).

34. In accounting for this factor, the United States has made an assumption that 50% of general licensing revenue is attributable to such licensees. Given the variety of exclusive licensees and significance of some of the excluded ones, this figure is a conservative one. In Step Two on the exhibit, you can see that after reducing the potential losses to EC right holders to 50%, the resulting range of potential loss is about 1.8 million to 3.7 million.

4. *Reduce to Account for Licensing Revenue from General Licensees that Do Not Play the Radio - Losses to EC Right Holders: $.56 Million - $1.13 Million*

35. Now we go to step three. Obviously many restaurants, bars and retail stores do not play radio music. For most establishments, radio programming - with all of its advertisements, talk and interruptions - is an unattractive option. Who wants their customers to hear advertisements for their competitors? Much of the revenue from general licensees that qualify as establishments is not attributable to the playing of radio or TV music, but rather to public performances of music from media such as tapes/CDs, live bands, and jukeboxes.

36. The National Restaurant Association and the National Licensed Beverage Association estimate that approximately 33% and 28% of their members, respectively, play the radio. Such radio use is often not exclusive. Many establishments that play the radio will often play music from other sources as well. Taking an average of these two roughly comparable estimates, we have assumed that 30.5% of establishments play radio music.

37. It is important to note that, given that establishments often play music from more than one source, this estimate - 30.5% of establishments that play the radio - does not correspond with the *percentage of licensing revenue* attributable to the playing of radio music. Revenue from radio music is going to be much less. Nevertheless, we are being very conservative in these calculations, and have assumed for the sake of this analysis that 30.5% of licensing revenue is attributable to the playing of radio music. Correspondingly, the losses to EC right holders from the Section 110(5) exemption for radio music must be reduced to this amount. In line 3, you can see that this would range from about half a million to 1.1 million dollars.

5. *Reduce to Account for Licensing Revenue from General Licensee Establishments that Play the Radio and Meet Size Limitations of Section 110(5): Losses to EC Right Holders: $294,113 to $586,332*

38. In Step Four, we take a final reduction to take into account the fact that many eating, drinking and retail establishments that play radio music do not meet the square footage limits of Section 110(5)(B). According to figures provided by the National Restaurant Association, 65.5% of restaurants meet the square footage crite-

ria of the statute. According to the EC, there are 364,404 eating and drinking establishments in the United States. That means that about 239 thousand meet the square footage requirements of the statute.

39. On the retail side, the EC has presented a study commissioned by ASCAP purporting to demonstrate that about 45% of retail stores meet the square footage limits of the statute. The EC also alleges that there are 683,783 retail establishments in the United States. 45% of 684 thousand is about 307 thousand.

40. So, even using EC figures for the sake of today's analysis, we have about 239 thousand exempt restaurants and 307 thousand exempt retail stores. That's a total of 546 thousand exempt establishments, which is 52.1% of all establishments. In line 4, we've reduced the possible losses to EC right holders to 52.1%, which is about 294 - 586 thousand dollars.

41. If you follow the same four-step analysis for BMI, the result is a paltry 122 thousand dollars.

6. *The U.S. Methodology is Conservative*

42. As explained in the U.S. submission, these calculations are conservative and - if anything - overstate the true amount of economic prejudice to EC right holders. Some of the reasons these figures are conservative include:

- The United States has assumed that where 30.5% of establishments play the radio, 30.5% of licensing revenue is attributable to radio-playing. This figure is obviously too high, given the large proportion of establishments that play music from more than one type of media.
- Similarly, the United States assumed that the 65.5% of restaurants (and 45% of retail establishments) that fit within the square footage limits of the exception accounted for a 65.5% (and 45%) loss of revenue. In fact, the exempt restaurants and retail establishments are necessarily smaller establishments, and almost certainly represent a smaller proportion of licensing revenue.
- The analysis also does not take into account steps that ASCAP and BMI might take to minimize any impact of Section 110(5).
- Similarly, the analysis does not take into account the establishments that could take advantage of the private agreement concluded by the PROs with the NLBA.

7. *Any Minimal Prejudice from Section 110(5)(B) is Reasonable in Light of ASCAP and BMI's Advocacy of an Exemption of Almost Identical Scope*

43. Finally, in considering whether the passage of Section 110(5)(B) has caused right holders any unreasonable prejudice, the private agreement between the PROs and the NLBA is again relevant. The PROs voluntarily agreed to a blanket exemption of 3500 square feet. They offered the same deal to the NRA. Perhaps most significantly, during Congress' consideration of Section 110(5)(B), the "ASCAP and BMI proposal" also revolved around an exemption for establishments smaller than 3500 square feet. Presumably, ASCAP and BMI would not have proposed an exemption of 3500 square feet if they felt that such an exemption would cause their members any real prejudice.

V. CONCLUSION

44. To sum up, the applicable standard for determining the TRIPS consistency of Section 110(5) of the U.S. Copyright Act is TRIPS Article 13. Section 110(5) is a permissible exception to the public performance right based on the criteria articulated in Article 13. Therefore, the United States respectfully requests that the Panel find that both Section 110(5)(A) and (B) are consistent with the TRIPS Agreement.

45. Furthermore, the United States requests that the Panel clearly delineate its findings regarding sub-section (A) and sub-section(B) of Section 110(5), in order to provide maximum guidance to WTO members regarding the interpretation of the TRIPS provisions at issue.

ATTACHMENT 2.7

COMMENTS ON THE LETTER FROM THE DIRECTOR GENERAL OF WIPO TO THE CHAIR OF THE PANEL

(12 January 2000)

1. The United States appreciates this opportunity to comment on the material provided to the Panel by the International Bureau of the World Intellectual Property Organization (WIPO). The United States further appreciates the Panel's communication of January 10, 2000, regarding the deadline for submitting comments on these materials.

2. In the view of the United States, the extensive material provided by WIPO does not raise issues not already addressed by the Parties and discussed in the two Panel meetings in this case. The material further confirms the importance that Berne negotiators attached to the permissibility of exceptions under Articles 11 and 11*bis*, and the existence of the minor reservations doctrine. *See, e.g.*, Annexes X, XII and XIII. For this reason, the United States considers that these documents support the U.S. position in this case.

3.1 AUSTRALIA

3.1.1 WRITTEN SUBMISSION OF AUSTRALIA

(1 November 1999)

SYNOPSIS

- Exceptions or limitations to the right of authorising public communication of broadcast copyright works under the TRIPS Agreement must conform with:
  - the general conditions set by TRIPS Article 13, and
  - the specific conditions set by Article 11*bis* of the Berne Convention as incorporated in TRIPS,

  consistent with the general objectives and principles of TRIPS, in particular Article 7.
- It would be valuable to clarify the relationship between TRIPS and Berne as they apply to this specific right:
  - there is no hierarchy of authority between TRIPS Article 13 and Berne Article 11*bis*(2), but the latter provision provides more direct guidance as to the present case;
  - any exception or limitation would still need to conform with each of the two provisions;
  - this right is to be considered differently from other rights - such as the general reproduction right - in the light of the specific guidance provided by Berne 11*bis*(2);
  - 11*bis*2 specifies that conditions on this right shall in no circumstances be prejudicial to the author's entitlement to equitable remuneration.
- The diplomatic history of the Berne Convention provides further guidance as to how the "conditions" allowable under Berne 11*bis*(2) should be interpreted:
  - the right of equitable remuneration was strongly emphasised;
  - the only apparent exceptions considered were "minor reservations" relating to use of the work in a private setting or associated with public interest objectives, such as in educational or religious contexts.
- Consistent application of these two provisions to the right of public communication of broadcast works would entail giving due weight to Berne 11*bis*(2):
  - hence, the test established under TRIPS Article 13, applied to this right, should be coloured by the specific requirement for equitable remuneration;

- by setting conditions on the exercise of this right, and establishing a minimum standard involving equitable remuneration, 11*bis*(2) prescribes how rights and obligations are balanced, and exceptions and limitations are set, that is a specific instance of the general balance of interests that is required in TRIPS Article 7 and also expressed in Article 13;
- Article 9(2) of Berne, by contrast, has only limited and indirect relevance to the determination of the scope of allowable exceptions and limitations to this right.

• Equitable remuneration in relation to the right of public communication of broadcast works should entail recognition of any specific commercial benefits that are intended to result from public communication made for commercial objectives:
  - the confinement of this right to an entitlement to equitable remuneration represents a significant constraint on the exercise of the right, allowing exclusion of the right to prohibit public communication and to seek inordinate remuneration, and allowing for it to be implemented through compulsory licensing;
  - equitable remuneration in this context maintains the balance of rights and objectives called for in TRIPS Article 7;
  - it also clarifies the nature of "unreasonable prejudice" in the application of TRIPS Article 13 to the right of public communication of broadcast works.

TABLE OF CONTENTS

I. POLICY BACKGROUND

1.1 Historically, at a national level, copyright and related rights have been developed, enforced, and subject to limitations and exceptions with the overall goal of serving the broader public interest through the provision of effective and appropriate private rights. The WTO Agreement on Trade-Related Aspect of Intellectual Property Rights ("TRIPS") articulates this balance, already present in the established copyright norms of the Berne Convention for the Protection of Literary and Artistic Works

("Berne"),[1] sets it explicitly into an international trade context, and obliges WTO Members to observe it in a number of specific contexts in their implementation of intellectual property law. TRIPS is founded on the understanding that distortions and impediments to trade, and other forms of detriment to legitimate interests, are the consequence of disturbances to this balance.

1.2 Hence TRIPS affirms that a "balance of rights and obligations" is a key objective of the "protection and enforcement of intellectual property rights" (Article 7), and it provides for exceptions and limitations to be imposed on intellectual property rights, including copyright and related rights (Article 13). Any exceptions to the basic framework established by TRIPS should be aimed at sustaining this mutually beneficial balance, and should also be consistent with the specific provisions of TRIPS (including those provisions of other instruments incorporated within TRIPS by reference).

1.3 The present case concerns an exemption from the requirement to pay royalties to music composers and songwriters for the playing of radio and television broadcasts of their compositions in certain public places - exceptions to the right of communication to the public of broadcast copyright works, a right which has, in the Berne Convention, been clearly distinguished from the broadcast right itself. On the basis of the two first submissions, there appears to be no issue as to the initial scope of the rights, and the present case is more concerned with the legitimate scope of certain statutory exceptions to that right: hence it has less to do with the underlying nature of the right than with the degree to which that right can be limited or qualified, with reference to the questions of normal exploitation of a copyright work, unreasonable prejudice to the right holder's interests, and the right holder's entitlement to equitable remuneration.

1.4 The case therefore raises questions about the interaction of private intellectual property rights (IPR) and broader public policy goals, the way in which the broad objectives of TRIPS are to be reflected in national intellectual property systems, and how certain key provisions are to be implemented in individual jurisdictions. Since the case relates to key provisions of Berne, it also raises the question of how the diplomatic and interpretative history of relevant provisions of that Convention should be taken into account when interpreting obligations under TRIPS.

1.5 The General Report of the Rome Conference, in discussing the introduction of the new right of communication to the public through broadcasting (the "most important result" of that Conference[2]), notes that the text adopted by the Conference "had the characteristic of a compromise between two opposing tendencies": that of "entirely assimilating the broadcasting right into the other exclusive rights of the author", and that of considering the right "as the subject for intervention by the public authorities to protect the cultural and social interests linked to this new and special form of popular dissemination of intellectual works, especially musical works".'[3] This is a clear instance of the broader "balance of interests" noted in TRIPS 7, with

---

[1] For convenience and brevity, this submission generally cites provisions of TRIPS in the format "TRIPS 13", for "Article 13 of TRIPS", and "Berne 11*bis*(2)", for "para. 11*bis*(2) of Berne".

[2] Proceedings of the Conference Convened at Rome, BIRPI, Berne, 1929, p. 210.

[3] loc. cit.

specific bearing on the particular right at issue in the present case. The Report of the Sub-committee on Broadcasting at Rome notes that this provision reconciles "the general public interest of the State with the interests of authors",[4] the public interests under consideration being the potential use of the new medium of broadcasting for the dissemination of cultural works.

1.6 Australia's involvement as a third party in this case reflects:

- an immediate trade interest in ensuring that Australian composers and songwriters can obtain equitable remuneration in relation to the public communication of broadcasts of their musical works in the important US market;[5] and
- the need to preserve the integrity of the rules relating to trade-related IPRs: that is, ensuring that TRIPS (and, in this case, specifically the Berne provisions it incorporates) is interpreted and applied in national law in a manner that ensures that the common standards are fully respected, while maintaining a legitimate scope for public policy exceptions to IPRs, in a way that preserves the balance of interests enshrined in TRIPS and promotes its objectives.

Australia's approach is accordingly governed by the concern that there should be no unreasonable diminution of the legitimate interests of copyright owners, including the right to equitable remuneration where this is explicitly provided for; and that governments should have sufficient latitude to maintain the underlying balance of rights and obligations while giving full effect to specific TRIPS obligations.

1.7 In June 1998, the Australian House of Representatives Standing Committee on Legal and Constitutional Affairs tabled a report on the public performance and broadcast rights in relation to small business.[6] A key issue considered by the Committee was the international legal obligations concerning public performance and broadcast rights set out in TRIPS and Berne. As elements of this Committee's work may be of use in the present Panel's deliberations, a synopsis of this report is attached (Annex A). Australia continues to place strong emphasis on the continuing consistency of its own domestic intellectual property system with international obligations, and welcomes the opportunity that the present case provides to clarify and confirm those obligations as they apply to the right of public communication of broadcast works.

II. LEGAL ISSUES

2.1 The question before the Panel is whether the recently amended S.110(5) of the US Copyright Act ("S.110(5)") is in breach of TRIPS 9(1), which requires WTO Members to comply with Berne Articles 1 through 21 (save for 6*bis*), and the Berne

[4] op. cit. p.184.

[5] According to one industry estimate, the potential annual loss from the introduction of S.110(5) of the US Copyright Act would exceed AUD 1 million, a sum likely to rise given current market trends.

[6] *Don't Stop the Music*, http://www.aph.gov.au/house/committee/laca/Inquiryincopy.htm.

Appendix. This obligation is potentially affected by TRIPS Article 13 which sets bounds within which any limitations and exceptions to copyright and related rights under TRIPS must be confined. This submission sets out an approach to dealing with the legal issues of this case in a manner that should preserve both the legitimate interests of copyright holders and the public interest, as well as maintaining the integrity of the composite TRIPS-Berne system. Given that this is the first case before the WTO DSB to consider substantive TRIPS provisions on copyright, and in particular the linkages between specific Berne provisions and broader TRIPS provisions, this submission offers some considerations on interpretative questions.

The Scope and Objective of Berne Article 11*bis*: the Right of Public Communication of Broadcast Works, and Conditions on that Right

2.2 S.110(5) provides that certain forms of public communication of broadcast works shall not infringe copyright. This creates a clear exception to the right established in accordance with Berne 11*bis*(1) which provides to authors of literary and artistic works (including musical works) the exclusive right of authorizing *inter alia* "the public communication by loudspeaker or any other analogous instrument transmitting, by signs, sounds or images, the broadcast of the work".[7] This is subject to the provision (Article 11*bis*(2)) that it "shall be a matter for legislation in the countries of the [Berne] Union to determine the conditions under which [this right] may be exercised... [These conditions] shall not in any circumstances be prejudicial to the moral rights of the author, nor to his right to obtain equitable remuneration which, in the absence of agreement, shall be fixed by competent authority". This last provision bears the facilitative heading "Compulsory Licences". The context of the 11*bis*(2) suggests that it is intended in particular to ensure that arrangements for compulsory licensing of broadcast works do not deprive the right holder of equitable remuneration. This particular focus was confirmed at the Stockholm Conference. In addition, the scope of Berne 11*bis* is potentially affected by the so-called "minor reservations", discussed below (from 3.4), that form part of its negotiating history.

The Scope and Objective of TRIPS Article 13: General Limitations and Exceptions on Copyright

2.3 TRIPS 13 covers limitations and exceptions to exclusive rights pertaining to copyright works in general. Its immediate objective is to "confine" such limitations or exceptions. It has some important differences from parallel provisions in relation to trade marks (Article 17), designs (Article 26.2) and patents (Article 30) - these only cover exceptions, and not limitations, to exclusive rights. The need to confine limitations in TRIPS 13 as well as exceptions may be a consequence of the different nature of copyright compared with industrial property rights, entailing the broader range of legitimate non-commercial usages of copyright material, and the widespread use of compulsory and mechanical licensing in the exploitation of copyright works. Such measures limit the operation of the right rather than necessarily create excep-

---

7 Berne 11 is also relevant, in that it covers any public communication of the work, but Berne 11*bis* provides more specific guidance on the context at issue in this case.

tions. TRIPS 13 recognises the need to govern the way in which legislative restrictions on such rights operate, so as to maintain an appropriate balance of interests.

2.4 The notion of "limitation", in contrast to an "exception", accords with the operation of Berne 11*bis*(2), which sets bounds on the "conditions" which national legislation may set for the exercise of the specific rights provided in Berne 11*bis*(1).

Berne Convention Obligations in a TRIPS Context

2.5 How, and to what extent, do the history and accumulated interpretative material concerning the Berne Convention apply to Berne provisions within TRIPS when considered under the WTO DSU? This is not raised specifically as an issue by either party, but is implicit in the use made of background material about Berne in both first submissions. In interpreting the provisions at issue, the EC submission has drawn on the diplomatic history of Berne; the US submission (para 22) refers to the objective of TRIPS (Article 7), draws on scholarly commentary on Berne 9(2) in its detailed elucidation of TRIPS 13, and invokes the Berne doctrine of "minor reservations" that is not a specific Berne provision but was established in diplomatic conferences on Berne (para 18).

2.6 On the face of it, the Berne provisions at issue should be assessed as obligations arising through the effect of TRIPS, and not as Berne obligations in their own right. TRIPS binds WTO Members to certain provisions of a distinct international instrument, the Berne Convention. TRIPS 2.2 provides that TRIPS does not derogate from existing obligations under Berne: this suggests that any rights or exceptions permitted under TRIPS should be consistent with Berne in its own right. TRIPS was negotiated with a background understanding of the scope of the provisions of Berne, and, while there is not necessarily a direct linkage with the interpretative history of Berne, it is unquestionable that the Berne negotiations form part of customary international law in this area. Moreover, the inclusion of Berne provisions in TRIPS indicates that the object and purpose of TRIPS extend to the promotion of the full and effective implementation of those provisions.

2.7 It is submitted that both the interpretative history of Berne and the specific objectives of TRIPS are relevant to the application of overlapping TRIPS and Berne provisions, in the absence of any contradiction between the two. There are in fact certain instances where the background of Berne helps elucidate the way interests are balanced in TRIPS. In dealing with the complex issues at stake in this case, it would be useful to articulate more clearly how this linkage should operate.

Berne Article 11*bis*(2) and TRIPS Article 13: Reconciling the General and Specific Provisions

2.8 There are compelling policy and legal reasons to maintain consistency between Berne 11*bis* and TRIPS 13 when they are applied to the same right. This question has not been explicitly raised by either party, but is implicit in the interpretations made in their submissions. There is a need for clarity and consistency of application, particularly given that overlapping Berne and TRIPS provisions have not before been considered in a WTO DSU context.

2.9 The first question relates to their respective scope - does TRIPS 13 encompass Berne 11*bis*(2), or are they co-extensive in relation to broadcast works? A

WIPO commentary on the relationship between TRIPS 13 and exceptions and limitations in Berne remarks that:

> None of the limitations and exceptions permitted by the Berne Convention should, if correctly applied, conflict with the normal exploitation of the work and none of them should, if correctly applied, prejudice unreasonably the legitimate interests of the right holder. Thus, generally and normally, there is no conflict between the Berne Convention and TRIPS Agreement as far as exceptions and limitations to the exclusive rights are concerned.[8]

2.10 This suggests that no fundamental conflict need exist, and that all limitations and exceptions already allowed under Berne would also comply with TRIPS 13; but that does not mean that the exceptions or limitations ("conditions") afforded by one are coextensive with those allowed under the other. Ricketson[9] has suggested that TRIPS 13 is broader in scope than specific exceptions allowable under Berne. However, even if an exception to the right of public communication of broadcast works were found to be consistent with TRIPS 13, then the more specific Berne 11*bis*(2) would still apply and maintain the requirement for equitable remuneration. In effect, this would either add an additional step to the "three step" test of Article 13 when it is applied to public communication of broadcast works, or would more precisely determine the way that test is applied in this context.

2.11 There is no hierarchy of authority between TRIPS 13 and Berne 11*bis*(2). In the context of the conclusion of TRIPS, both provisions were adopted at once and have simultaneous effect as TRIPS obligations. However, Berne 11*bis*(2) has not been addressed so far in the submissions put to the panel, and the focus appears to be on TRIPS 13 only.[10]

2.12 Further, TRIPS 13, as a general provision, cannot override the more specific Berne 11*bis*(2): it is more likely that the latter provision indicates how the parties considered the general principle would apply in these circumstances, and there is no evidence to suggest that the general was intended to override the specific in this particular case; hence the specific provision should prevail in the event of any unclarity. This legal principle - *generalia specialibus non derogant* - is well established in common law and can be drawn on in the international context.[11] Further, TRIPS 13 provides that limitations and exceptions are to be *confined* in a certain way: this does not rule out further, more focussed constraints, based on specific Berne provisions. Since the two provisions are equally binding on WTO Members, and can be interpreted without conflict between them, an exception or limitation to the right of public

---

8 *Implications of the TRIPS Agreement on Treaties Administered by WIPO* (1996) Geneva, page 22-23.

9 Ricketson, Staniforth, *The Law of Intellectual Property*, LBC, Sydney, 1999, 16.560.

10 See for instance para. 17 of the first submission of the US.

11 The authority for relying on the principle of *generalias specialibus non derogant* is Article 38 of the Statute of the International Court of Justice which is generally regarded as a complete statement of the sources of international law. Article 38(1)(c) indicates that a valid source of international law is "the general principles of law recognised by civilized nations".

performance of broadcast works should comply with both TRIPS 13 and Berne 11*bis*(2).

2.13 The incorporation of Berne 11*bis* establishes this right under TRIPS; it would follow that any provision allowing limitations to that right (such as 11*bis*(2)) would also be significant in determining related TRIPS obligations. The General Report of the Brussels Conference states that Berne 11*bis*(1), "with its three separate items, is inseparable from paragraph 2".[12]

2.14 It is submitted that the preferable approach would be to acknowledge that Berne 11*bis*(2) influences the application of TRIPS 13 to rights established under Berne 11*bis* (but not its application to other rights). This would promote consistency of interpretation between the key provisions of TRIPS and of Berne incorporated within TRIPS. Berne 11*bis*(2) provides the clearest, most authoritative guidance as to how acceptable limitations and exceptions under TRIPS 13 apply to the right of public communication of broadcast works; at the same time, it establishes a direct test for TRIPS-consistency of any exception or limitation on that right.

III. ANALYSIS OF BERNE ARTICLE 11*BIS*

Scope of the Specific Limitations in Berne Article 11*bis*: Interpretative Background

3.1 The right of public communication of broadcast works was incorporated into the Berne Convention at the Brussels Conference (1948) with no significant opposition,[13] confirming that a distinct right existed over and above the broadcast right itself.

> The rationale for this is that the author thinks of his licence to broadcast as covering only the direct audience receiving the signal within the family circle. Once this reception is done in order to entertain a wider circle, often for profit, an additional section of the public is enabled to enjoy the work and it ceases to be merely a matter of broadcasting.[14]

3.2 The Brussels Conference considered the limitations that national legislation may place on this right, leading to the adoption of Article 11*bis*(2). Three delegations had made drafting proposals seeking to clarify that the right did not apply when the communication to the public was not in a commercial context, was made in a family or domestic circle, or was in a scholastic context.[15] These were withdrawn on the understanding that such reservations could be accommodated within the proposed text of Article 11*bis*(2), but subject to the understanding in the Broadcasting Sub-

---

[12] *Records of the Conference Convened in Brussels*, quoted in Berne Convention Centenary, WIPO, Geneva, 1986, p. 181.

[13] Ricketson, Staniforth (1987), *The Berne Convention for the protection of literary and artistic works: 1886-1986,* London: Eastern Press Ltd, page 453.

[14] WIPO Guide, Para. 11*bis* .12.

[15] *Records of the Conference Convened in Brussels*, BIRPI, Berne, 1951: proposal of the Netherlands on p.279; proposal of Monaco, p.278; proposal of Hungary, p. 278.

committee's report that exercise of the prerogative "will in no circumstances be prejudicial to the author's ... right to receive equitable remuneration".

3.3 Inasmuch as this provides guidance as to the nature of the TRIPS (and Berne within TRIPS) obligation, it is clear that no exception was contemplated that would allow public communication of broadcast works in the pursuit of commercial objectives without the possibility of securing equitable remuneration. The Brussels Conference General Report mentioned "free-of-charge exceptions made for religious, patriotic or cultural purposes"[16] as related to allowable conditions. The Stockholm Conference[17] clarified that this provision referred to "the compulsory licence which national legislations may impose, subject to just remuneration". The provision does not appear to extend to the effective extinguishment of the right in circumstances when equitable remuneration could be expected. As Ricketson notes, "the power to impose conditions on the exercise of rights set out in Article 11*bis*(1) does not carry with it the power to deny those rights".[18]

Minor Reservations under Berne Article 11*bis*

3.4 Since the first submissions by both parties refer to "minor reservations" under Berne,[19] it may be useful to clarify how such "reservations" would apply in a TRIPS context. It was in relation to Berne 11 - Right of Public Performance - that the issue of minor reservations first arose. During the Brussels Conference (1948) it was proposed that a general provision be inserted into the Berne Convention under which it would be permissible for State Parties to retain minor reservations that already existed in their national laws (e.g. religious ceremonies and performances by military bands at public fetes). The drafters of the Brussels Revision rejected this proposal on the basis that the adoption of such a general provision would encourage those nations which had not recognised such exceptions to incorporate them into their laws.[20] It was agreed that rather than dealing with this matter in the Convention itself, it would be dealt with in the General Report of the meeting as follows:

> Your rapporteur general has been entrusted with making an express mention of the possibility available to national legislation to make what are commonly called minor reservations. The Delegates of Norway, Sweden, Denmark, and Finland, the Delegate of Switzerland and the Delegate of Hungary, have all mentioned these limited exceptions allowed for religious ceremonies, military bands and the needs of the child and adult education. These exceptional measures apply to articles 11*bis*, 11*ter*, 13 and 14. You will understand that these references are

[16] *Records of the Conference Convened in Brussels*, quoted in Berne Convention Centenary, WIPO, Geneva, 1986, p. 181.

[17] *Records of the Stockholm Conference*, WIPO, Geneva, 1971, Main Committee I Report, p.1167.

[18] Ricketson (1987), page 525.

[19] EU submission, para 73; US submission, para 18.

[20] Ricketson (1987), page 533.

> just lightly pencilled in here, in order to avoid damaging the principles of the right.[21]

The last sentence underscores the *de minimis* nature of the types of exceptions that could fall under the minor reservations doctrine in relation to this particular right.

3.5 At the Stockholm Conference (1967) it was again agreed that the Berne Convention did not prevent State Parties from maintaining existing exceptions in their law on the basis that they qualified as minor reservations.[22] The Nordic countries proposed inserting into the General Report a sentence to the effect that the possibility allowed for in the Brussels Conference General Report for the making of minor reservations was still valid. The Record of the Stockholm Conference accordingly reads:

> In the General Report of the Brussels Conference, the Rapporteur was instructed to refer explicitly, in connection with Article 11, to the possibility of what it had been agreed to call 'the minor reservations' of national legislation. Some delegates had referred to the exceptions permitted in respect of religious ceremonies, performances by military bands, and the requirements of education and popularization. The exceptions also apply to articles 11*bis,* 11*ter,* 13 and 14. The Rapporteur ended by saying that these allusions were given lightly without invalidating the principle in the right.
>
> It seems that it was not the intention of the Committee to prevent States from maintaining in their national legislation provisions based on the declaration contained in the General Report of the Brussels Conference.[23]

3.6 Both the Brussels and Stockholm Conferences considered the minor reservation doctrine as applying to Article 11*bis* among other provisions. The legal status of the minor reservations is not entirely clear: are they strictly "reservations" to the application of the treaty to the countries expressing them, or are they implicit interpretations of the treaty language? Given that TRIPS does not permit formal reservations (Article 72), it is possible that TRIPS 13 was intended to provide the same degree of latitude that these minor reservations permitted under Berne; alternatively, the minor reservations could be seen as casting light on the practical interpretation of Berne 11*bis*(2). For instance, a "reserved" use could be deemed to be one for which the appropriate remuneration can be deemed equitably to be nil - given their non-commercial nature, and their private setting or their use in relation to a common public interest, it could be deemed inequitable to charge for such communications.

"Equitable Remuneration" under Article 11*bis*(2)

3.7 Article 11*bis*(2) provides that, whatever conditions are imposed on the exercise of the right of public communication of broadcast works, "in any circumstances" two clear entitlements should be preserved - moral rights (which appear not to apply

[21] *The Berne Convention for the Protection of Literary and Artistic Works from 1886 to 1986*,WIPO, Geneva, 1986, page 181.

[22] *WIPO Guide to the Berne Convention.* (1978) WIPO, Geneva, page 65.

[23] *Records of the Intellectual Property Conference of Stockholm* WIPO, Geneva, 1971, page 1166.

in the TRIPS context, owing to their exclusion from TRIPS 9(1)), and the right to obtain equitable remuneration. Neither first submission directly addresses the question of equitable remuneration. It merits consideration, firstly because exceptions and limitations to the right of public communication of broadcast works need to be assessed against Article 11*bis*(2), and secondly because Article 11*bis*(2) should inform the application of TRIPS 13 to that right.

3.8 The distinct nature of the public communication of a broadcast work creates an expectation of a distinct reward for the creator of the work. This was summarised in a submission to the recent Australian Parliamentary inquiry as follows:

> [the law gives] recognition that there are two levels of benefit. The radio station is gaining a benefit from broadcasting into people's homes. If someone at the point of reception chooses to gain a second commercial benefit by playing the music through the use of reception, then that is something that should attract some return for the author or composer.[24]

Hence the notion of 'equitable remuneration' should be informed by this expectation of a separate reward. The same inquiry report observed:

> Many composers emphasised the importance of their public performance royalties in allowing them to continue to compose music. ... There was a strong feeling that the value of the royalty was not just in its quantum, but in the knowledge that they were receiving some sort of financial reward for their work. In many cases, the principle of reward was considered to be as important as the money.[25]

3.9 Given the clear direction of Berne 11*bis*(2), equitable remuneration, either by agreement or the determination of an appropriate authority, is required for the public communication of broadcasts even in connection with relatively modest commercial objectives. The appropriate fee may also be very modest for individual small businesses seeking to secure commercial benefits from the broadcast works.[26] The level of equitable remuneration may be linked in a general way to the commercial benefits achieved by the business user - for instance, in attracting and retaining additional clientele, in creating a particular ambience, and in drawing on the popular appeal of a musical work. Representing a major group of users of copyright works, the US National Licensed Beverage Association (NBLA) has acknowledged the commercial benefits of music:

> The use of music in your business establishment is one way you can enhance your business, influence your customers' eating and drinking habits, and increase your profits.[27]

---

[24] Submission of APRA, cited in *Don't Stop the Music*, pp 67-68.

[25] *Don't Stop the Music*, p.68.

[26] The license fee charged by the collecting society ASCAP in the US for the small business exempted by the recent revision to S.110(5) was $30, for instance (see Annex US-7 to the First Submission of the US, 26 October).

[27] NLBA News, April 1997, p.2, supplied as Annex US-6 to the First Submission of the US, 26 October 1999.

3.10 Equitable remuneration is not simply the level of return that the right holder (or its agent) wants - Berne 11*bis*(2) notes that a competent authority can adjudicate on this point in the absence of agreement, and the right holder is not in a monopolistic bargaining position. Some objective assessment of the value of the use of the work to the business enterprise may be called for. At the same time, it is well recognised that enforcement of intellectual property rights should not be burdensome. The need for administrative efficiency has accordingly led to the creation of collective or "blanket" licensing arrangements.

3.11 It is inconsistent with the requirement for equitable remuneration to remove any legal possibility for securing appropriate returns for the public communication of broadcast works in contexts which are clearly and substantially commercial in nature, and when commercial benefits arise from use of the music, often as a conscious commercial judgement (such as the contexts noted by the NBLA, 3.9 above). For example, broadcast musical works are communicated to members of the public for their entertainment and for commercial gain, such as through increased patronage (even if no direct or distinct charge is levied for the communication of the broadcast as such), as an alternative to commercial music services or licenses for other forms of commercially-motivated public communication of works.

3.12 It would be consistent with the notion of "equitable remuneration" for the revenue to be scaled, within practical bounds, according to the overall commercial interests engaged. As discussed in para 3.6, equitable remuneration may even be determined to be nil for certain public-interest or *de minimis* public communications (such as those cited at the Brussels Conference). The matter is less clear in relation to incidental use of broadcast works, and in particular in the context of so-called "homestyle" reception of broadcasts on the premises of small businesses, especially when the public communication is incidental or unintended, and is not specifically directed at clientele in the course of pursuing commercial activities. In certain such limited contexts, "equitable remuneration" may also be effectively nil.[28] Nonetheless, the situation is clearer for significant and unambiguous commercial use of the copyright work. It would be difficult to maintain that, in the present case, the effective elimination of the public communication of broadcast right in a wide range of commercial settings amounts to a determination by the authorities, in the absence of agreement, that nil remuneration is the most equitable outcome in all those commercial settings. There was no consent to the removal of the public communication right or the entitlement to obtain equitable remuneration on the part of the right holders' representatives in the present case:

> ASCAP is totally committed to overturning the "Music Licensing Amendment" which allows for-profit restaurants, bars, grills and retailers to avoid paying for music performed over

[28] For instance, the Australian collecting society APRA has agreed to issue complimentary licenses in relation to small businesses when broadcasts are received on standard receivers and are not intended to be heard by the public.

> radio and television speakers. Very simply, it is not fair that any of us should be forced to work for free.[29]

3.13 The right in question is "to obtain" remuneration, and does not entail an obligation on the part of the user to pay remuneration when it is not as a matter of fact sought in any way (including through collective mechanisms) by the right holder. The first submission of the US points to situations in which right holders, or the collecting societies representing them, elect not, for practical or other reasons, to pursue their entitlement to equitable remuneration; but that should be distinguished from an outright abrogation of that right through legislation. The practical possibilities for collecting revenues, and the consequent degree to which right holders may choose to seek remuneration, are contingent matters which may change in the light of technological and commercial developments. The fact that it may be inconvenient to exercise a right in a particular commercial context does not in itself justify the removal of that right. Such exceptions need to be justified on public policy grounds in line with established principles.

3.14 In addition, there is a question as to how national treatment is observed in the situation where the right to obtain remuneration is denied in a foreign market, especially given the voluntary nature of collecting societies as a means of exercising the right of public communication of broadcast works.

The Nature of Public Communication

3.15 Article 11*bis* provides no further definition of the nature of "public communication": it is a matter that is still determined according to national legislation and judicial interpretation. Some of the "minor reservations" cited at the Brussels Conference in the context of 11*bis* (especially those relating to use in the family or domestic circle) may in fact have bearing on the way "public communication" is defined. This matter is apparently not at issue (paragraph 17 of the US submission), but Annex B of this submission sets out some background considerations on this issue should it be considered by the Panel.

IV. TRIPS ARTICLE 13 AND THE PUBLIC COMMUNICATION OF BROADCASTS

4.1 TRIPS 13 applies in general to limitations and exceptions to rights under Section 1 of Part II of TRIPS, and accordingly provides a test for the TRIPS consistency of limitations and exceptions to the right of public performance of broadcast works. When TRIPS 13 was drafted, the terms used closely followed Berne 9(2). Because of this textual linkage, the two provisions are often compared, and, on the face of it, the test established in TRIPS 13 does not appear to differ materially from the three-step test contained in Berne 9(2).[30] For instance, the first submission of the

[29] Marilyn Bergman, ASCAP President and Chairman of the Board, *http://www.ascap.com/meeting99/audiobackup.html.*

[30] Blakeney, Michael (1996) Trade-Related *Aspects of Intellectual Property Rights: A Concise Guide to the TRIPS Agreement.* London: Sweet and Maxwell, page 49.

US draws on material relating to Berne Article 9(2) in its interpretation of TRIPS Article 13.

4.2 There are nonetheless clear differences between the two provisions, especially when TRIPS 13 is applied to the right of public performance of broadcast works. In this context, therefore, Berne 9(2) refers to a different right, a different form of exploitation of a work and a different set of interests; it also refers to outright exceptions to the reproduction right, rather than to conditions or limitations on the right. The nature of the normal exploitation of works and of unreasonable prejudice to legitimate interests may significantly differ between the reproduction right and the right of public communication of broadcast works. The matter would be different if the case concerned an exception to the reproduction right.

4.3 Berne 9(2) may nonetheless give general or indirect guidance as to the application of TRIPS 13 to the public communication of broadcasts, especially in any endeavour to interpret the exact terms used. As far as the legal effect of TRIPS 13 and its object and purpose are concerned in relation to the right of public communication of broadcast works, then Berne 11*bis*(2) provides more direct and authoritative guidance. Berne 11*bis*(2) governs this specific right directly, and a coherent application of TRIPS would require consistency between TRIPS 13 and Berne 11*bis*(2).

4.4 In adopting Berne 9(2), the Stockholm Conference commented:

> If it is considered that reproduction conflicts with the normal exploitation of the work, reproduction is not permitted at all. If it is considered that reproduction does not conflict with the normal exploitation of the work, the next step would be to consider whether it does not unreasonably prejudice the legitimate interests of the author. Only if such is not the case would it be possible in certain special cases to introduce a compulsory license, or to provide for use without payment. A practical example might be photocopying for various purposes. If it consists of producing a very large number of copies, it may not be permitted, as it conflicts with a normal exploitation of the work. If it implies a rather large number of copies for use in industrial undertakings, it may not conflict with a normal exploitation of the work, but it may not unreasonably prejudice the legitimate interests of the author, provided that , according to national legislation, an equitable remuneration is paid. If a small number of copies is made, photocopying may be permitted without payment, particularly for individual or scientific use.[31]

In relation to the first criterion of a "special case" in the three-step test, Ricketson notes:

> The words 'in certain special cases' embody a general criterion, and this can be seen as possessing two distinct aspects. First,

[31] *Records of the Intellectual Property Conference of Stockholm,* Report on the Work of Main Committee I, WIPO, Geneva, 1971, p.1145.

> the use in question must be for a quite specific purpose: a broad kind of exemption would not be justified. Secondly, there must be something special about this purpose, 'special' here meaning that it is justified by some clear reason of public policy or some other exceptional circumstance.[32]

4.5 The second and third criteria were placed in that order to aid in the application of the rule. In other words, it is first necessary to decide whether there is a "conflict with a normal exploitation of the work". Only if this is answered in the negative is it necessary to consider whether there is "unreasonable prejudice to the legitimate interests of the author".[33]

4.6 Little guidance is provided on the meaning of the expression "normal exploitation of the work", although the Stockholm Conference records cited above in 4.4 indicate that making a very large number of copies may conflict with the "normal exploitation of a work".[34] In relation to this second criterion, Ricketson makes the following useful comment:

> Common sense would indicate that the expression normal exploitation refers simply to the ways in which an author might reasonably be expected to exploit his work in the normal course of events. Accordingly, there will be certain kinds of use which do not form part of his normal mode of exploiting his work - that is, uses for which he would not ordinarily expect to receive a fee - even though they fall strictly within the scope of his reproduction rights.[35]

4.7 Turning to the last criterion of "unreasonable prejudice", the question is not whether there is prejudice or not. It is a question of degree as to whether the use in the particular circumstances, is reasonable or not. The WIPO Guide on the Berne Convention provides the following examples:

> All copying is damaging in some degree: a single photocopy may mean one copy of the journal remaining unsold and, if the author had a share in the proceeds of publication he lost it. But was this prejudice unreasonable? Here scarcely. It might be otherwise if a monograph, printed in limited numbers, were copied by a large firm and the copies distributed in their thousands to its correspondents throughout the world. Another example is that of a lecturer who, to support his theme, photocopies a short article from a specialist journal and reads it to his audience: clearly this scarcely prejudices the circulation of the review. It would be different if he had run off large number of copies and handed them out, for this might seriously cut in on its sales.

---

32 Ricketson (1987), page 482.

33 *WIPO Guide to the Berne Convention.* WIPO, Geneva, 1978, page 55.

34 *Records of the Intellectual Property Conference of Stockholm* (1971) Geneva, page 1146.

35 Ricketson (1987), page 483.

Berne Article 11*bis*(2) as a Guide to the Application of TRIPS Article 13

4.8 As discussed above (2.14, 4.3), Berne 11*bis*(2) has more direct bearing on how TRIPS 13 should be applied in the present case. It stipulates that "conditions" applying to the public communication of broadcast works "shall not be prejudicial to the moral rights of the author, nor to his right to obtain equitable remuneration which, in the absence of agreement, shall be fixed by competent authority". This sheds light on how "normal exploitation", "unreasonable prejudice" and "legitimate interests" should be interpreted in relation to this particular right. For instance, it suggests that compulsory licenses may be consistent with normal exploitation. It lays emphasis on the author's moral rights and right to obtain equitable remuneration as legitimate interests in this context, and it implies that "unreasonable prejudice" would occur if those interests were impaired through the legislative application of any condition on the exercise of an Article 11*bis*(1) right.

TRIPS Article 13 in Relation to the Objectives of TRIPS

4.9 Ultimately, the interpretation of TRIPS Article 13 must be consistent with the objectives of TRIPS itself, as the first submission of the US notes (para 22). The key provisions in this context are Article 7 ("Objectives") and Article 8 ("Principles"); elements of the preamble may also be relevant. Article 7 focusses particularly on technological innovation, the transfer and dissemination of technology, and the interests of producers and users of technological knowledge, which are not directly at issue in this case. It also points to the need for protection and enforcement of intellectual property rights to be "conducive to social and economic welfare, and to a balance of rights and obligations". Concerns were expressed at the Rome Conference that the development of the then new technology of radiodiffusion as a means of promoting social and cultural welfare should not be impaired by a restrictive application of the new broadcasting right.

4.10 While not in the foreground of the TRIPS negotiations, the history of Berne suggests that the specific balance of interests involved in relation to the public performance of broadcast works appears to be between the right of the author to remuneration,[36] and the need for broadcasting media to develop and contribute to social and economic well-being. What factors should be considered in maintaining this balance? Clearly, it was not intended to give the author the right to prohibit the public communication of the broadcast of the work, as this would be an unreasonable constraint on the use of broadcast material. Some *de minimis* or public interest exceptions to the right were also entertained in relation to some jurisdictions at least - use within the family or domestic circle, in religious or educational contexts. The author, also, did not have an unlimited right to obtain remuneration - in effect, the author was not given monopoly bargaining power, and it was acknowledged that an independent authority may establish the level of remuneration that would be equitable.

[36] As well as the author's moral rights, if they are not excluded in this context - however, the reference to moral rights in Berne 11*bis*(2) is likely caught by the exclusion of "rights derived" from Berne Article 6*bis* in TRIPS Article 9(2).

4.11 Hence the balance struck was for an undiminished right of equitable remuneration in relation to use of works that did not fall within the "minor exception" or *de minimis* category. When, at the Rome Conference, Article 11*bis* was introduced in its initial form, the Sub-Committee on Broadcasting reported that the Article was intended "to bring the author's rights into harmony with the general public interests of the State, the only ones to which specific interests are subordinate,'[37] while it 'emphatically confirms the author's right".

4.12 It is submitted that this approach is wholly consistent with the broader objectives of the TRIPS agreement, and is in fact an exemplary application of the "balance" required by Article 7.

V. S.110(5) OF THE US COPYRIGHT ACT IN RELATION TO TRIPS

5.1 General considerations are now offered in relation to the TRIPS consistency of the legislative provision at issue. As suggested earlier, S.110(5) needs to be assessed against Berne 11*bis*(2) as well as TRIPS 13, and in particular against a reading of TRIPS 13 that gives full weight to the equal authority of Berne 11*bis*(2). If an exception to the right of public performance of broadcast works is considered inconsistent with Berne 11*bis*(2), then it would be ineffectual to claim that it was nonetheless consistent with TRIPS 13.

S.110(5) and Berne 11*bis*(2): the Need to Maintain Equitable Remuneration

5.2 The detailed commentary already provided suggests that it would be inconsistent with Berne 11*bis*(2) effectively to remove the right of authorising public communication of broadcast works when this is for specifically commercial objectives, given that no condition or reservation to this right has been contemplated which would amount to the denial of equitable remuneration in such a context. This may hinge on how "equitable remuneration" is to be determined, but it is difficult to envisage how no entitlement to remuneration for the author can be reconciled with intentional and direct use of copyright works for specifically commercial purposes.

Application of the Minor Reservations Doctrine

5.3 The present case relates to an exception to the Berne 11*bis*(1)(iii) right which precludes right holders from seeking equitable remuneration in connection with public communication of the broadcast musical work in a wide range of commercial settings - according to the US Congressional Research Service, some 70% of bars and restaurants in the United States.[38] Whatever the precise proportion, this exception clearly covers a substantial portion of the market for communication to the public of broadcast musical works; nor does it relate to communications essentially unrelated to commercial objectives. The "minor reservations" cited in the development of the Berne Convention (discussed from para 3.4) are distinct from this form of commercial usage in a portion of the market which is neither commercially negligible nor legally *de minimis*.

---

[37] *Proceedings of the Conference Convened at Rome*, BIRPI, Berne, 1929, p.183.

[38] Cited at www.ascap.com/legislative/legis_qa.html.

S.110(5) and the Three-Step Test of TRIPS 13

5.4 If it is considered relevant or necessary to consider consistency with TRIPS 13, the following analysis seeks to apply the above interpretation of that Article to the present case.

Special Case

5.5 S.110(5) provides an outright exemption for a wide range of establishments including food service, drinking and other establishments. There is no indication that the criteria chosen to define this exception were driven by public policy objectives, comparable to use in a research, educational or religious context. Equally, S.110(5) appears to provide a blanket exemption for such establishments rather than dealing with certain special cases: no special quality is conferred upon an establishment, and the nature of the use of a copyright work is not rendered less directly commercial, by the floorspace of the establishment. There does not appear to be any identification of "special use" or "exceptional circumstances" behind the S.110(5) exemption as is called for in the analysis above (4.4). Rather, the threshold applied is justified by contingent considerations about the practicalities of collecting royalties.

Conflict with a Normal Exploitation of the Work

5.6 S. 110(5) allows food service, drinking and other establishments to communicate broadcasts of musical work to the public in the direct pursuit of commercial gain. Broadcasts of musical work are often used by such establishments to attract, entertain and create an ambience for patrons. The right to equitable remuneration from the public communication of broadcasts in such commercial settings is a normal exploitation of musical work, distinct form other forms of exploitation. It is possible that right holders may, for practical reasons, elect not to seek such remuneration in certain commercial circumstances, but it is consistent with normal exploitation for them to have that choice, provided the principle of equitable remuneration is not denied. The US submission (para. 34) suggests that licensing fees for the establishments excluded under s.110(5)(A) "would likely be the lowest in the range"; this is arguably more consistent with equitable remuneration in the context of normal exploitation than there being no right to obtain fees at all. "Equitable remuneration" may be at an appropriately low level, but should also recognise the direct commercial gain made from public communication of broadcast works when this is applicable.

5.7 S.110(5) only conflicts with the rightholder's right to authorise the public communication of a broadcast of musical work and derive equitable remuneration from public communications, and does not interfere with the rightholder's other exclusive rights such as the right to reproduce, publish, broadcast or make an adaptation of the work. In this regard s.110(5) could be said to interfere only in a limited way with the rightholder's overall ability to exploit the work. However, Article 13(2) refers to conflict with *a* (in the sense of 'any') normal exploitation of the work - rather than to conflict with the overall commercialisation of the work. The right of public communication of a broadcast work has been explicitly recognised in the Berne Convention as a distinct right, giving rise to a distinct right of remuneration which forms one of the normal exploitations of the work.

Unreasonable Prejudice to the Legitimate Interest

5.8 We have suggested that in this context, Berne 11*bis*(2) clearly sets out considerations that apply to determination of unreasonable prejudice to the legitimate interests of right holders. A compulsory licensing system, a denial of monopolistic bargaining power, a *de minimis* or public interest educational exception are all forms of prejudice to legitimate interests that would be reasonable: Berne 11*bis*(2) suggests that denial of the right of *equitable* remuneration and of moral rights would be unreasonable.

5.9 It may be argued that any prejudice to rightholders is only minimal because they would receive royalties from broadcasting stations. S.110(5) allows many food service, drinking and other establishments to obtain commercial benefit through the broadcast of musical works by attracting and entertaining their patrons without any compensation to the right holders form whom they derive this commercial benefit. There is a strong argument that, just as for other inputs into a business, such as electricity and water, establishments should pay for the public communication of broadcasts of musical work when that communication is for commercial purposes, consistent with the principle of equitable remuneration. In this context, a "reasonable prejudice" to the interests of the rightholder would be a denial of the rightholders capacity to prohibit, or charge excessive fees for, public communication of their broadcast works. Given these more limited forms of conditions on this right, and for the reasons cited above, Article 11*bis*(2) suggests that the denial of equitable remuneration for such public communication is a more serious prejudice to legitimate interests.

5.10 If a provision entitles a wide range of establishments to communicate the broadcast of musical work to the public for immediate commercial objectives without paying any royalties to the authors, then some form of unreasonable prejudice could be established. The "unreasonableness" of s.110(5) may hinge on the magnitude of the directly commercial usage of copyright works to which the US hospitality and retail industry would be able to apply this exemption. Since this provision provides an absolute exemption for copyright infringement in a wide range of commercial contexts, it rules out any possibility for obtaining the equitable remuneration consistent with reasonable prejudice to their interests.

ANNEX A

"Don't stop the music!"
A report of the inquiry into copyright, music and small business

In June 1998 the Australian House of Representatives Standing Committee on Legal and Constitutional Matters tabled a report on the public performance and broadcast rights in relation to small business. This report was titled "Don't Stop the Music". The Committee's role was to inquire into and report on the collection of copyright royalties for licensing the playing of music in public by small business. Apart from considering the role played by copyright collection societies, the Committee considered the desirability of amending the Australian Copyright Act in relation to public performance and broadcast rights in a small business context. The Committee made a number of recommendations the following of which are of relevance to the matters before this Panel.

The Committee considered a number of submissions on the royalty scheme for the use of background music. The Committee noted that many small businesses felt that they should be exempt from having to pay a fee for the playing of music in their business. While the Committee was sympathetic to some of their arguments, the Committee did *not* consider that small businesses should be exempt from paying copyright royalty fee for the public performance of music.

The Committee noted that in some circumstances the use of music in a small business was only intended to be heard by one member of staff and there was a strong case in favour of exempting such businesses from paying licence fees. In this regard, the Committee recommended that the relevant collecting society consider granting a complimentary licence when:

- the means of performance is by the use of a radio or television set; and
- the business employs fewer than 20 people; and
- the music is not intended to be heard by customers or the business or by the general public. That is, neither the radio or television set nor any speakers are located in an area that is accessible to customers or the general public and any performance inadvertently heard by customers or the general public is manifestly unintentional.

However, the Committee found that for most small businesses, music is used to attract, entertain and create ambience for customers. Creating a blanket exemption for small businesses would mean that those businesses using music in a manifestly commercial manner would be exempt from paying licence fees. The Committee considered that this would not be an inequitable outcome and recommended against this course of action.

ANNEX B

Definition of "in public"

The rights contained in article 11*bis*(1)(iii) of the Berne Convention refer to the *public* communication of a broadcast of work. The question arises as to whether the circumstances envisaged by s.110(5) would amount to a *public* communication of a broadcast of work.

The Berne Convention does not provide a definition as to what is meant by the term *public* communication. The Brussels Conference (1948) provided some guidance in defining the *public* for broadcasting and communication rights:

> above all, where people meet: in the cinema, in restaurants, in tea rooms, railway carriages....It also appears from the programme that perhaps the most important of these "public places" were those where people worked and conducted their business, such as factories, shops and offices.[39]

On this point the WIPO Guide to the Berne Convention notes:

> In places where people gather (cafes, restaurants, tea-rooms, hotels, large shops, trains, aircraft etc) the practice is growing of providing broadcast programmes.... The question is whether the licence given by the author to the broadcasting station covers, in addition, all the use made of the broadcast, which may or may not be for commercial ends.
>
> The Convention's answer is "no". Just as in the case of a relay of a broadcast by wire, an additional audience is created (paragraph (10 (ii)) so, in this case too, the work is made perceptible to listeners (and perhaps viewers) other than those contemplated by the author when his permission was given. Although, by definition, the number of people receiving a broadcast cannot be ascertained with any certainty, the author thinks of his licence to broadcast as covering only the direct audience receiving the signal within the family circle. Once this reception is done in order to entertain a wider circle, often for profit, an additional section of the public is enabled to enjoy the work and it ceases to be merely a matter of broadcasting. The author is given control over this new public performance of his work.[40]

The Australian Copyright Act, like the Berne Convention, does not provide a definition of the term *in public*. However, the expression has been considered by the Australian courts over many years.[41] Under existing Australian case law, it is clear that

---

[39] Ricketson (1987), page 453.

[40] *WIPO Guide to the Berne Convention*, WIPO, Geneva, 1978, page 68.

[41] The most recent judicial comment on the meaning of their term 'in public' has been by the High Court in the 1997 case of APRA v Telstra. Justices Dawson and Gaudron in their joint judgement

the Australian courts will take into account the following factors in determining whether a performance is in public:

- First, a performance is "public" unless it takes place in a "domestic and private" setting;
- Secondly, where the performance occurs as an adjunct to a commercial activity, it will be in public;
- Thirdly, the audience in question clearly forms part of the copyright owner's public.

concluded: "Lying behind the concept of the copyright owner's public is recognition of the fact that where a work is performed in a commercial setting, the occasion is unlikely to be private or domestic and the audience is more appropriately to be seen as a section of the public. It is in a commercial setting that an unauthorised performance will ordinarily be to the financial disadvantage of the owner's copyright in a work because it is in such a setting that that owner is entitled to expect payment for the work's authorised performance."

3.1.2 ORAL STATEMENT BY AUSTRALIA AT THE THIRD PARTY HEARING

(9 November 1999)

Australia welcomes the opportunity to put its views on this case to the panel and the two parties.

Our submission is motivated by the direct trade interests related to equitable remuneration for public communication of broadcast musical works of Australian composers and songwriters. It is also intended to promote the integrity of the TRIPS Agreement, including the balance of rights and obligations that should serve the interests of producers and users of intellectual property.

Exceptions or limitations to the right of authorising public communication of broadcast works should conform with the general conditions set by TRIPS Article 13, and the specific conditions set by Article 11*bis* of the Berne Convention. They should also be consistent with the general objectives and principles of TRIPS, in particular Article 7.

We submit that it would be valuable to clarify the relationship between TRIPS and Berne as they apply to this specific right. There is no hierarchy of authority between TRIPS Article 13 and Berne Article 11*bis*, as the two provisions are on an equal footing as TRIPS obligations and both apply to this case. However, Berne 11*bis* does provide more direct guidance on the present case, which relates to a right which is defined and regulated distinctly from other rights such as the general reproduction right. 11*bis*(2) specifies that conditions on this right shall in no circumstances be prejudicial to the author's entitlement to equitable remuneration.

The diplomatic history of the Berne Convention provides further guidance as to how the "conditions" allowable under Berne 11*bis*(2) should be interpreted. The undiminished right of equitable remuneration has been strongly emphasised, and the only apparent exceptions considered were "minor reservations" relating to use of the work in a private setting or associated with public interest objectives, such as in educational or religious contexts.

The two tests - TRIPS 13 and Berne 11 *bis*(2) - could be applied in parallel to the right of public communication of broadcast works. However, the most consistent and systemically sound approach would be to give due weight to Berne 11 *bis*(2) in applying TRIPS 13 in this specific context. Accordingly, the TRIPS 13 test, applied to this right, should be subject to the specific requirement for equitable remuneration. Berne 11 *bis*(2) also suggests how the objectives of TRIPS 7 can be maintained in this context.

- By setting conditions on the exercise of this right, and establishing a minimum standard involving equitable remuneration, 11*bis*(2) prescribes how rights and obligations are balanced, and exceptions and limitations are set. This is a specific instance of the general balance of interests that is required in TRIPS 7 and expressed in TRIPS 13;
- Article 9(2) of Berne, by contrast, has only limited and indirect relevance to the determination of the scope of allowable exceptions and limitations to this right.

Equitable remuneration in relation to the right of public communication of broadcast works should entail recognition of any specific commercial benefits that are intended to result from public communication made for commercial objectives

- equitable remuneration in this context is consistent with the balancing of rights and obligations called for in TRIPS 7;
- it also clarifies the nature of "unreasonable prejudice" in the application of TRIPS Article 13 to the right of public communication of broadcast works.

3.1.3 RESPONSES OF AUSTRALIA TO WRITTEN QUESTIONS FROM THE PANEL

(19 November 1999)

Australia welcomes the opportunity to provide further background information on this case in response to the Panel's questions. It notes, however, that the copyright law and practice in Australia and in countries other than the US are not at issue in this case, and submits that TRIPS obligations should not be determined by the approach taken in any one national system, practice or tradition.

Q.1 Please give examples of exceptions in the copyright laws of your country or of other countries based on the "minor reservations" doctrine.

It is not evident in general which exceptions within copyright laws are based expressly on the minor reservations doctrine, as exceptions may be implicit in the definition of the right or may be justified in other ways. The clearest examples of the application of this doctrine can be found in the diplomatic records which acknowledge and confirm the existence of minor reservations, for instance:

> The Delegates of Norway, Sweden, Denmark and Finland, the Delegate of Switzerland and the Delegate of Hungary have all mentioned these limited exemptions allowed for religious ceremonies, military bands and the needs of child and adult education. These exceptional measures apply to Articles 11*bis*, 11ter, 13 and 14.[42]

Q.2. Is the communication to the public of music contained in broadcasts or played from sound recordings or live subject to exclusive rights or right of remuneration in your legislation, and are the rights in respect of such uses of music exercised by the right holders or by their collective management organizations?

This response is limited to this question as it relates to the communication to the public of musical works contained in broadcasts (as this is the subject matter of the case directly before the Panel), and does not consider the separate instances of playing music live or from sound recordings (which may be subject to different considerations.)

2(i) Existence of the right

The communication to the public of music contained in broadcasts is subject to exclusive rights in Australia, essentially through the operation of Sections 27 and 31 of the Copyright Act (1968). Section 27 provides, in part:

---

[42] General Report, Conference in Brussels, 1948, in *The Berne Convention for the Protection of Literary and Artistic Works from 1886 to 1986, WIPO*, 1986, page 181.

> (1) Subject to this section, a reference in this Act to performance shall:
>
> (a) be read as including a reference to any mode of visual or aural presentation, whether the presentation is by the operation of wireless telegraphy apparatus, by the exhibition of a cinematograph film, by the use of a record or by any other means ...
>
> ...
>
> (3) Where visual images or sounds are displayed or emitted by any receiving apparatus to which they are conveyed by the transmission of electromagnetic signals (whether over paths provided by a material substance or not), the operation of any apparatus by which the signals are transmitted, directly or indirectly, to the receiving apparatus shall be deemed not to constitute performance or to constitute causing visual images to be seen or sounds to be heard but, in so far as the display or emission of the images or sounds constitutes a performance, or causes the images to be seen or the sounds to be heard, the performance, or the causing of the images to be seen or sounds to be heard, as the case may be, shall be deemed to be effected by the operation of the r0eceiving apparatus.
>
> (4) Without prejudice to the last two preceding subsections, where a work or an adaptation of a work is performed or visual images are caused to be seen or sounds to be heard by the operation of any apparatus referred to in the last preceding subsection or of any apparatus for reproducing sounds by the use of a record, being apparatus provided by or with the consent of the occupier of the premises where the apparatus is situated, the occupier of those premises shall, for the purposes of this Act, be deemed to be the person giving the performance or causing the images to be seen or the sounds to be heard, whether he or she is the person operating the apparatus or not.

Section 31 of the same Act provides, in part:

> (1) For the purposes of this Act, unless the contrary intention appears, copyright, in relation to a work, is the exclusive right:
>
> (a) in the case of a literary, dramatic or musical work, to do all or any of the following acts:
>
> (i) to reproduce the work in a material form;
>
> (ii) to publish the work;
>
> (iii) to perform the work in public;
>
> (iv) to broadcast the work;
>
> (v) to cause the work to be transmitted to subscribers to a diffusion service;
>
> (vi) to make an adaptation of the work;
>
> (vii) to do, in relation to a work that is an adaptation of the first-mentioned work, any of the acts specified in relation to the first-mentioned work in subparagraphs (i) to (v), inclusive; ...

2(ii) Exercise of the right

The current domestic arrangement in Australia is that the rights in respect of public performance of broadcast musical works are exercised by a collective management organization. The right to authorise public performance of broadcast musical works is in practice exercised by the Australasian Performing Right Association Limited (APRA).[43] In exercising these rights, APRA provides for licenses for broadcast musical works on a scale linked with the extent of the public performance, as determined by the number of TV or radio sets and additional loudspeakers. To authorise musical performances at the premises by radio or TV sets, including TV sets used to show videos, free to air TV, satellite TV broadcasts and cable TV, for background and listening purposes only, the annual license fee for each radio set is $37.62 (and each additional speaker $0.94); and for each television set $37.62 (and each additional speaker $0.94). A distinct license is available to authorise performances of music in the workplace for the benefit of employees, at the annual rate of 56 cents per full-time employee, with a minimum annual fee of $37.62.

APRA issues a complimentary licence in instances where:

(a) the means of performance is by the use of a radio or television set; and

(b) the business employs fewer than 20 people; and

(c) the music is not intended to be heard by customers of the business or by the general public. That is, neither the radio or television set nor any speakers are located in an area that is accessible to customers or the general public and any performance inadvertently heard by customers or the general public is manifestly unintentional.

The following are illustrative examples of situations in which APRA would grant a complimentary licence in the exercise of this right:[44]

- A family run milk bar or corner store which has a radio or television behind the counter or in the back room of a composite shop/dwelling. The volume is such that customers may hear some music in the public access areas but the intention is to entertain staff during quiet trading periods.
- A chemist employing five staff with a radio located in the secure dispensing area for the benefit of the pharmacist. Some sound may be audible to customers.
- A service station with 12 employees playing the radio in a workshop and/or with a television behind the counter near the cash register. Customers fuelling cars, leaving vehicles for repair or paying for purchases may overhear music.
- A small hairdresser with a radio in the backroom of the salon which may at times be overheard by clients. The location of the radio shows that this is unintentional.

---

[43] The following information is drawn from the APRA website, www.apra.com.au.

[44] Quoted from the 1998 report of the Australian House of Representatives Standing Committee on Legal and Constitutional Affairs *Don't Stop the Music*, http://www.aph.gov.au/house/committee/laca/ Inquiryincopy.htm.

- A real estate agent where the receptionist has a radio on the desk. While the performance is audible to customers, the radio is for the receptionist's own enjoyment.
- A café playing a radio in the staff-only food preparation areas. The location of the radio and the volume indicate that, while music may sometimes be overheard by customers, it is not played for their benefit.
- A small hardware store with three employees where a radio is located in the storage/supply area behind the counter for the benefit of employees.
- A laundromat with five staff playing a radio in an open work area behind the counter. There are no additional speakers and the performance is intended for the benefit of employees.
- An owner/operator tailor with a television in the working area behind the counter. Performance is for the benefit of the owner.
- A doctor's surgery. The receptionist plays a radio at low volume. Music is not clearly audible to patients in the waiting room.

Q.3. Please explain which individual exclusive rights under which specific provisions of Articles 11(1) and 11 *bis*(1) of the Berne Convention are affected to what extent by which specific provision of Subsection (A) and/or (B) or Section 110(5).

Section 110(5) creates exceptions to the right of communication to the public of certain broadcast musical works, by providing that certain use made of the works is not infringement of copyright. It is apparently not in contention that this use is communication to the public.

Communication to the public is covered in general terms under Article 11(1) of Berne, and this would, on the face of it, include the forms of communication excepted under Section 110(5). Broadcasting itself could be viewed as a particular form of public communication of a work.

Article 11*bis* was introduced at the 1928 Rome Conference to provide international rules governing the broadcasting of literary and artistic works. It is therefore submitted that this is the more directly relevant provision. The WIPO *Guide to the Berne Convention* (p.65) comments:

> The second leg of this right [Article 11(1)] is the communication to the public of a performance of the work. It covers all public communication except broadcasting which is dealt with in Article 11*bis*. For example, a broadcasting organisation broadcasts a chamber concert. Article 11*bis* applies. But if it or some other body diffuses the music by landline to subscribers, this is a matter for Article 11.

Subsections A and B relate to the public communication of broadcast musical works, so that Article 11*bis* applies to both subsections. In particular, while Subsection A relates to potentially more limited forms of public communication, it was explicitly intended to cover intentional and direct communication to the public, and in particular to allow business proprietors to communicate broadcasts "for their customers' enjoyment"[45]

Q.4. In your view, what is the relationship between Article 13 of the TRIPS Agreement and Article 11*bis*(2) of the Berne Convention?

Please see section 2 of the Australian submission, in particular paras 2.11-2.12.

Does Article 13 of the TRIPS Agreement prevail over the exception in Article 11*bis*(2) with respect to the exclusive rights conferred by Article 11*bis*(1)(i-iii) of the Berne Convention in the sense that when the three conditions of Article 13 are met, no requirement to pay equitable remuneration arises?

No. There is no basis for ascribing greater authority to TRIPS Article 13 and for overruling or nullifying the effect of Berne Article 11*bis*(2), which was adopted upon the conclusion of the TRIPS Agreement in parallel with TRIPS Article 13.

Do the requirements of Article 11*bis*(2) of the Berne Convention prevail as a *lex specialis* over the requirements of Article 13 of the TRIPS Agreement, in the sense that if equitable remuneration is paid, there is no need to comply with the three-conditions test under Article 13?

This interpretation is possible, given that the two provisions appear to overlap and that Article 11*bis*(2) applies more specifically to the situation at issue (see paragraph 2.12 of Australia's third party submission). However, such an interpretation would only be necessary if it were concluded that there is conflict or contradiction between the two provisions. It is submitted that the test established by Article 11*bis*(2) could be viewed as a special application of the broader factors under consideration in the Article 13 test: in effect, the requirement for equitable remuneration (as opposed to unlimited or unconditional exercise of the right) provides a safeguard that limitations on the right are in accordance with the general requirements of Article 13.

Do the requirements of Article 13 and Article 11*bis*(2) apply on a cumulative basis in the sense that, on the one hand, even if the three-condition test of Article 13 is fulfilled, there is an additional, fourth requirement to pay equitable remuneration, and on the other hand, even if equitable remuneration is paid consistently with Article 11*bis*(2), it is necessary to comply in addition with the three conditions of Article 13? Please explain.

The preferred interpretation of the two provisions operating in conjunction should be that:

- both tests need to be fulfilled, independently if necessary; but that, if at all possible;

---

[45] Report of the House Committee on the Judiciary, H.R. Rep. No. 94-1476, 94th Cong., 2d Sess. 87 (1976), cited.

- Berne 11*bis*(2) should be seen as defining, in relation to the rights provided under 11*bis*(1), those limitations or exceptions that would - in the terms of TRIPS 13 - not be an unreasonable prejudice to the legitimate interests of the right holder in this context; that is, that the denial of equitable remuneration would automatically amount to an unreasonable prejudice to those interests in relation to this form of exploitation of the right to public communication of a broadcast musical work.

Q.5. In your view, to what extent has the Berne Convention become part of customary international law, and, if so, in particular which part of the Articles 1-21 of the Berne Convention?

No direct answer to this question is provided in this response. The rights and obligations currently at issue, including the relevant paragraphs of Berne, are direct treaty obligations, namely Article 9 of the TRIPS, and by reference Article 11*bis*(iii), Article 11*bis*(2) of the Berne Convention and Article 13 of TRIPS.

Q.6. Has the "minor exceptions" doctrine under the Berne Convention, and especially in the context of Article 11*bis*(1) and 11(1), acquired the status of customary international law? What is the legal significance of the "minor exceptions" doctrine under the Berne Convention in the light of subparagraphs (3)(a-c) or paragraph (4) of Article 31 of the VCLT or in the light of Article 32 of the VCLT? Has the "minor exceptions" doctrine or any other implied exception been incorporated, by virtue of Article 9.1 of the TRIPS Agreement, together with Articles 1-21 of the Berne Convention into the TRIPS Agreement? Please explain.

This response does not venture a conclusion on whether the minor reservations doctrine is part of customary international law. On the facts of this case, S. 110(5) of the US Copyright Act is unlikely to come within the scope of what was intended to be covered by the minor reservations doctrine. A clear sense of the limited scope of the minor reservations principle is provided by the General Report of the Conference in Brussels thus:

> Your Rapporteur-General has been entrusted with making an express mention of the possibility available to national legislation to make what are commonly called minor reservations. The Delegates of Norway, Sweden, Denmark and Finland, the Delegate of Switzerland and the Delegate of Hungary have all mentioned these limited exemptions allowed for religious ceremonies, military bands and the needs of child and adult education. These exceptional measures apply to Articles 11*bis*, 11ter, 13 and 14. You will understand that these references are just lightly pencilled in here, in order to avoid damaging the principle of the right.[46]

This was confirmed at the Stockholm Conference in the following terms:

[46] General Report, Conference in Brussels, 1948.

In the General Report of the Brussels Conference, the Rapporteur was instructed to refer explicitly, in connection with Article 11, to the possibility of what it had been agreed to call 'the minor reservations' of national legislation. Some delegates had referred to the exceptions permitted in respect of religious ceremonies, performances by military bands, and the requirements of education and popularization. The exceptions also apply to articles 11*bis,* 11*ter,* 13 and 14. The Rapporteur ended by saying that these allusions were given lightly without invalidating the principle in the right.

It seems that it was not the intention of the Committee to prevent States from maintaining in their national legislation provisions based on the declaration contained in the General Report of the Brussels Conference.[47]

[47] *Records of the Intellectual Property Conference of Stockholm* WIPO, Geneva, 1971, page 1166.

3.2 BRAZIL

3.2.1 ORAL STATEMENT AT THE THIRD PARTY HEARING

(9 November 1999)

On behalf of the Government of Brazil I thank you for your attention to this matter. Brazil welcomes the opportunity to participate in this Panel as a third party. What motivates Brazil to intervene in this dispute is essentially a systemic interest on the implications to the interpretation on the scope of exceptions contained in the WTO Agreement on Trade-Related Aspects of Intellectual Property Rights (the TRIPS Agreement). At the same time, our participation stems from concrete interests, since the portion of the market in the United States for Brazilian music has increased substantially over the last few years. Brazilian composers have complained that the US "Fairness in Music Licensing Act" is hurting their legitimate interests in that market.

As argued by the European Communities / Member States (EC/MS) in its first submission, the exemptions for commercial establishments provided by Section 110(5) of the US Copyright Act are, in Brazil's view, incompatible with multilateral obligations that stem from the TRIPS Agreement, insofar as this Agreement incorporates articles 1 through 21 of the Berne Convention for the Protection for the Literary and Artistic Works (1971).

By means of **Article 9 (1) of TRIPS**, these obligations have become an integral part of WTO rules, being fully subject to the dispute settlement mechanism of the Organization. **Article 11*bis*(1)(iii) of the Berne Convention** states that "*authors of literary and artistic works shall enjoy the exclusive right of authorizing (...) the public communication by loudspeaker or any other analogous instrument transmitting, by signs, sounds or images, the broadcast of the work*". **Article 11(1)(ii) of the Berne Convention** provides that "*Authors of dramatic, dramatico-musical and musical works shall enjoy the exclusive right of authorizing any communication to the public of the performance of their works*". Finally, **Article 11*bis*(2) of the Berne Convention** establishes that "*it shall be a matter of legislation in the countries of the Union to determine the conditions under which the rights mentioned in the preceeding paragraph may be exercised, but these conditions shall apply only in the countries where they have been prescribed. They shall not in any circumstances be prejudicial to the moral rights of the author, nor to his right to obtain equitable remuneration which, in the absence of agreement, shall be fixed by competent authority.*"

The United States claims that the point in question here is that Section 110(5) of the US Copyright Act creates a "minor" exception to the exclusive right over public performance. In this context, the US submission attempts to justify that those exceptions would be covered by Article 13 of the TRIPS Agreement on limitations and exceptions to copyrights and related rights. Brazil, however, is of the opinion that **this panel should consider Section 110(5) in light of the most specific provisions, which are those covered by Articles 11*bis*(1)(iii), 11(1)(ii) and 11*bis*(2) of the Berne Convention**. The US submission fails to explain how Section 110 (5) could be compatible with its commitments under those specific provisions.

The submissions by the European Communities and Australia provide some valuable contribution for this panel to understand the conflict between the exceptions to copyrights in the US legislation and the existing provisions under TRIPS and the Berne Convention.

Brazil concurs with the European Communities that the situations covered by Section 110 (5) refer (explicitly, in the case of Subsection (A), or implicitly, in the case of Subsection 7(B)) to "public communication" in the sense of Article 11*bis*(1)(iii) and Article 11(1)(ii) of the Berne Convention. Consequently, by denying protection under those provisions, the US is violating its commitments related to TRIPS Article 9 (1).

Most importantly, Brazil endorses the legal argumentation provided by the Australian submission that Article 11*bis*(2) of the Bern Convention provides more specific guidance to the panel on the application of Section 110(5). Bearing the burden of proof to invoke the exception, the US fails to explains the consistency (if any) between Section 110(5) and that provision.

Section 110(5) is admittedly a circumstance that is prejudicial to the author's right to obtain equitable remuneration. The denial of that right is recognized in paragraph 29 of the US submission.[1] When the US Copyright Act, as amended by the "Fairness in Music Licensing Act", permits the broadcasting of radio and television music in public places without the payment of a royalty fee, it is actually exempting owners from the application of a mandatory rule whose exceptions are not applicable to this case. Article 11*bis*(2) of the Berne Convention, however, defines that "in any circumstances" the conditions to the right of public communication should be prejudicial to the author's right to obtain equitable remuneration. In doing so, the US is violating of a mandatory rule on clear prerogatives of right holders.

As noted in the Australian submission, the scope of the exception provided by Section 110(5) is much larger than envisaged in the negotiating history of the Berne Convention. The Brussels Conference of 1948 emphasized the limitations of the concept of "minor reservations" as exceptional measures. Such reservations, later confirmed by the Stockholm Conference of 1967, aimed at situations such as, for instance, religious ceremonies, performances by military bands and the requirements of education and popularization - mostly characterized by their non-commercial nature. Such is not the case of Section 110(5), where establishments that benefit from the "homestyle exemption" are essentially commercial. The size of the establishment or the number of loudspeakers in a limited area, as defined by Section 110(5), does not characterize the nature of the use of the broadcasted work as non-commercial. To the contrary, such use is admittedly aimed at attracting customers and consequently improving the profits of the owners of the establishment.

The EC also notes that Since Section 110(5) entitles 70% of all drinking and eating establishments and 45% of all retail establishments in the US to play music from the radio and TV for the enjoyment of their customers without any limitation of

---

[1] "Section 110(5) does not affect a copyright owner's right to be compensated for these types of exploitation [i.e., primary performance]. Rather, it affects only secondary uses of broadcasts. Moreover, it does not exempt all secondary performance, but only those in establishments that use homestyle receiving equipment, or meet the square footage and other criteria in the statute".

any kind, it is more than reasonable to argue that the normal exploitation of the works is at risk and that the legitimate interests of the right holders can be prejudiced. In its submission, the US were unable to produce statistics that prove that the impact on right holder's revenues of the "Fairness in Music Licensing Act" is negligible. Brazil considers, however, that even if such statistics were available, the task of examining Section 110 (5) would still be unrelated to quantitative limitations on the size of the area of the establishments or the number of loudspeakers. Brazil considers that the most important task of this panel is to judge the legitimacy of the exception provided by Section 110 (5) in light of its essentially commercial nature.

3.2.2 RESPONSES OF BRAZIL TO WRITTEN QUESTIONS FROM THE PANEL

(17 November 1999)

Q.1 Please give examples of exceptions in the copyright laws of your country or of other countries based on the "minor reservations" doctrine.

In the Brazilian legislation there are a few examples of exceptions in the sense of the "minor reservations" doctrine mentioned in this question. Those are cases where there would be no violation of copyright, such as: (a) the reproduction in the daily or periodical press of news or informative articles, from newspapers or magazines, with a mention of the name of the author, if they are signed, and of the publication from which they have been taken; (b) the reproduction in newspapers or magazines of speeches given at public meetings of any kind; (c) the reproduction of literary, artistic or scientific works for the exclusive use of the visually challenged, provided that the reproduction is done without gainful intent, either in braille or by means of other process using a medium designed for such users; (d) the use of literary, artistic or scientific works, phonograms and radio and television broadcasts in commercial establishments for the sole purpose of demonstration to customers, provided that the said establishments market the materials or equipment that make such use possible.

Q.2 Is the communication to the public contained in broadcasts or played from sound recordings or live subject to exclusive rights or right of remuneration in your legislation, and are the rights in respect of such uses of music exercised by the right holders or by their collective management organizations?

According to the new Brazilian Law on Copyrights and Related Rights (Law 9.610, dated 19 February 1999), authors have the exclusive right to use their literary, artistic and scientific works, to derive benefit from them and to dispose of them. Authors and the owners of related rights may form non-profit-making associations for the exercise and defense of their rights. These associations of authors and of the owners of related rights shall jointly maintain a single central office ("Escritório Nacional de Arrecadação de Direitos - ECAD") for the collection and distribution of the royalties generated by the public performance of musical works with or without words and phonograms, including performance by broadcasting and transmissions by any means and by the presentation of audiovisual works. This central office shall not have any profit-making purpose and shall be directed and managed by the associations of which it is composed.

3.3 CANADA

3.3.1 WRITTEN SUBMISSION

(1 November 1999)

This dispute raises important issues of copyright protection, including the role of limited exceptions. Canada remains highly interested in these issues and looks forward to the outcome of the panel's deliberations.

3.4 JAPAN

3.4.1 WRITTEN SUBMISSION

(1 November 1999)

1. The European Communities and their member States claim that Section 110(5) of the United States Copyright Act is not in conformity with the US' obligations under the TRIPS Agreement, particularly with its Article 9(1), under which WTO Members must comply with Articles 11*bis*(1)(iii) and 11(1)(ii) of the Berne Convention.

2. Japan hereby submits its views on compatibility of Subsection (A) of Section 110(5) of the US Copyright Act with the US' obligations stemming from Article 9(1) of the TRIPS Agreement.

3. In considering the compatibility, it is necessary to examine relevant provisions of the Berne Convention and the TRIPS Agreement.

(i) Articles 11*bis* and 11 of the Berne Convention

As is stated in the "Guide to the Berne Convention for the Protection of Literary and Artistic Works (Paris Act, 1971)" published by the World Intellectual Property Organization (WIPO) in 1978, it has been agreed that the Berne Convention did not stop member countries from preserving their law on exceptions which come under the heading of "minor reservations" with regard to Articles 11*bis* and 11 of the Convention. However, to examine the relevant provision of the TRIPS Agreement will be helpful to clarify the meaning of "minor reservations".

(ii) Article 13 of the TRIPS Agreement

Article 13 of the TRIPS Agreement (Limitations and Exceptions) stipulates that WTO members can contain in their legislation limitations or exceptions to exclusive rights, provided that these limitations or exceptions are confined to certain special cases which do not conflict with a normal exploitation of the work and do not unreasonably prejudice the legitimate interests of the right holder (three-step test).

4. Although relationship between "minor reservations" and Article 13 of the TRIPS Agreement is not perfectly clear, there is persuasive authority that three-step test can be used in determining whether particular exception is in the boundary of "minor reservations." For example, Chairman Liedes of the Committee of Experts of WIPO once stated to the effect that all limitations and exceptions which were permissible under the Berne Convention would survive if they were in conformity with Article 13 of the TRIPS Agreement (Diplomatic Conference on Certain Copyright and Neighboring Rights Questions on December 10, 1996). Japan, therefore, considers that if Subsection A of Section 110(5) US Copyright Act covers only certain special cases which do not conflict with a normal exploitation of the work and do not unreasonably prejudice the legitimate interests of the right holder, the Subsection in question can be regarded as compatible with Article 13, and thus with Article 9(1), of the TRIPS Agreement.

5. In applying three-step test to the Subsection in question, Japan concurs with the United States on the conclusion that it is in conformity with Article 13 of the TRIPS Agreement.

6. For the reasons stated, Japan is convinced that Subsection (A) of Section 110(5) US Copyright Act is fully consistent with Article 9(1) of the TRIPS Agreement.

3.4.2 RESPONSES BY JAPAN TO WRITTEN QUESTIONS FROM THE PANEL

(19 November 1999)

Q.1 Please give examples of exceptions in the copyright laws of your country or of other countries based on the "minor reservations" doctrine.

In general, various conditions are complicatedly combined in provisions for limitations of and exceptions to copyright, and how copyrighted works are used under such provisions considerably differs from nation to nation. This makes it difficult to determine applicability of "minor reservations" doctrine to the related provisions of each domestic law and requires careful consideration thereupon.

Under these circumstances, Japan has so far examined only Subsection A of Section 110(5) of the United States Copyright Act which is under discussion in this Panel, and has no further adequate examples to present.

Q.2 Is the communication to the public of music contained in broadcasts or played from sound recordings or live subject to exclusive rights or right of remuneration in your legislation, and are the rights in respect of such uses of music exercised by the right holders or by their collective management organizations?

In Copyright Law of Japan, such uses of music are subject to exclusive rights, and such rights are exercised either by the right holders or by their collective management organizations. The latter generally exercise such rights as trustees of the former under trust agreements.

3.5 SWITZERLAND

3.5.1 ORAL STATEMENT AT THE THIRD PARTY HEARING

(9 November 1999)

I. INTRODUCTION

1. The complaint brought by the European Communities and their member States against the United States of America is based on the consideration that certain aspects of the US legislation relating to the protection of copyrighted works are incompatible with the WTO Agreement on Trade-Related Aspects of Intellectual Property Rights (TRIPS Agreement). The provision which is the subject matter of contention is Section 110(5) of Title 17 of the US Copyright Act, as amended by the "Fairness in Music Licensing Act of 1998". The contended provisions allow for the so-called "homestyle exemption", lately extended to use in wider public places without the authorization of the copyright owner, an exception sometimes also referred to as the "business exemption". Both types of exemptions are summarized in the first submission made by the European Communities and their member States on 5 October 1999 in a very comprehensive manner. Instead of citing the contended provisions, I refer to the summary made by the European Communities and their Member States to avoid repetition. Under the Sections of the US Copyright Act subject matter of this panel procedure, the copyright owner cannot exercise his exclusive right of public communication of broadcast works in the case of establishments which are open to the public and play radio or TV on their premises for the enjoyment of their customers in accordance with certain conditions set out by the Law. In other words, if these conditions are met, the rightholder cannot claim royalty fees.

2. Switzerland has notified under Article 10(2) of the Dispute Settlement Understanding (DSU) its interests in the matter before the panel requested by the European Communities and their member States as established on 26 May 1999. Switzerland holds the view that the above-mentioned measures are in violation of US's obligations under Article 9(1) of WTO TRIPS Agreement in conjunction with Articles 11(1) and 11*bis* of the Berne Convention and cannot be justified under Article 13 of the TRIPS Agreement. Switzerland takes great interest in this case, not only desiring to safeguard the claims of Swiss rightholders of musical works to obtain equitable remuneration for the communication of their works to the public in the important US market, but also to ensure that the TRIPS provisions, and by reference and incorporation also the relevant provisions of the Berne Convention, are construed and implemented in national laws consistently with the international obligations as agreed in the multilateral framework of WTO.

II. GENERAL REMARKS ON THE CASE BEFORE THE PANEL AND ON THE SUBMISSION OF THE EUROPEAN COMMUNITIES AND THEIR MEMBER STATES

3. Switzerland concurs with the content of the comprehensive submission made by the European Communities and their member States regarding the historical back-

ground, case law developments, legal and economic analysis regarding Section 110(5) A and B of the US Copyright Act.

4. The WTO Members agreed in the negotiations of the Uruguay Round to incorporate the Berne Convention (Articles 1 to 21) into the TRIPS Agreement by way of reference. Therefore, protection must be provided in accordance with the Berne Convention, unless the TRIPS Agreement provides explicitly for a different level of protection. The whole TRIPS Agreement has been, and is, commonly referred to as a "major advance" in the field of intellectual property law at the international level. The Berne Convention - compared to other international treaties in the field of copyright - was deemed at that time to be the international treaty which offered a relatively satisfactory level of protection. The only "Berne Minus" provision in the TRIPS Agreement is Article 9.1, sentence 2, which excludes *expressis verbis* Article 6*bis* (moral rights) of the Berne Convention. All other TRIPS provisions on Copyright were introduced in the Agreement for purposes of clarification or improving the corresponding provisions of the Berne Convention, not of diminishing the level of protection.

III. ARTICLE 13 TRIPS; RELATIONSHIP WITH ARTICLES 9(2) AND 11*BIS* BERNE CONVENTION

5. Article 13 of the TRIPS Agreement has to be understood as a Berne-plus element. It contains safe-guard-rails for all kind of limitations and exceptions by extending the three-steps impairment test of Article 9(2) Berne Convention from the reproduction right to all the exclusive rights covered by Section 1 of Part II of the TRIPS Agreement. Consequently, Article 13 of the TRIPS Agreement limits also the scope of "minor reservations" with regard to Articles 11*bis* and 11 of the Berne Convention. This is also confirmed by the fact that the WIPO Copyright Treaty explicitly clarifies that the three-step-test applies to all limitations and exceptions of the Berne Convention and those under WCT. Therefore in the case submitted to the panel, exceptions are only permitted:

- in certain special cases,
- if there is no conflict with the normal exploitation, and
- if there is no unreasonable prejudice to the legitimate interests of the right holder.

Referring to the detailed and in-depth analysis of the three-step-test by Australia, the Swiss delegation submits that none of the steps of the impairment test are fulfilled.

6. Furthermore, limitations and exceptions concerning Article 11*bis*(1) of the Berne Convention have to be consistent with Article 11*bis*(2) of the Convention. It stipulates that conditions regarding the exercise of the broadcasting and related rights "shall not be prejudicial to the moral rights of the author, *nor to his right to obtain equitable remuneration...*". To be consistent with the protection guaranteed by Article 9 (1) TRIPS Agreement containing explicitly only one Berne-minus-element in respect of Article 6*bis* of the Berne Convention, Article 13 of the TRIPS Agreement cannot allow limitations of Article 11*bis*(1) of the Berne Convention going beyond the limits fixed in Article 11*bis*(2).

7. In other words, limitations as in the case submitted to the panel are prejudicial to the legitimate interests of the right holders, because they do not respect the authors' right to obtain equitable remuneration.

IV. OTHER CONSIDERATIONS

8. As far as Article 7 of the TRIPS Agreement (Objectives) is concerned, it would be useful to remind that this provision is a "*lex generalis*", Article 13 TRIPS being a "*lex specialis*". Careful balance is already struck in the latter provision. One should first analyze whether the conditions set out by this Article are fulfilled or not. If they are not, it seems that there would be no need to refer to Article 7 TRIPS.

9. Furthermore, Switzerland wishes to point out that, after ratification of the WTO Agreement (and the TRIPS Agreement), the "homestyle exemption", which had previously posed problems, should not have been further extended in such an unjustifiable way as through Section 110(5) and the so-called "business exemption".

V. CONCLUDING REMARK

10. Switzerland concurs with the position of the European Communities and their member States and supports the pertinent arguments put forward by Australia.

3.5.2 RESPONSES OF SWITZERLAND TO WRITTEN QUESTIONS FROM THE PANEL

(19 November 1999)

Q.1 Please give examples of exceptions in the copyright laws of your country or of other countries based on the "minor reservations" doctrine.

Art. 22 Par. 1 of the Swiss Copyright Law (CRL[1]) provides an exception with regard to cable distribution and to communication to the public of broadcast works. These limitations comply with Art. 11*bis*(2) of the Berne Convention (BC) in the sense that they do not abolish or diminish the right of the author to obtain equitable remuneration for the exploitation of his work.

Q.2 Is the communication to the public of music contained in broadcasts or played from sound recordings or live subject to exclusive rights or right of remuneration in your legislation, and are the rights in respect of such uses of music exercised by the right holders or by their collective management organizations?

According to Art. 22 Par. 1 CRL, the right of communication to the public of broadcast works (all categories of works, not only musical works) is an exclusive right, but it is subject to compulsory collective management by collecting societies. It should be underlined that this legal construction is not a legal licence.

The right of communication to the public of music played from sound recordings or live is an exclusive right as well and is also exercised by the collecting societies. For works other than musical works, this right of communication is exercised individually by the author.

The collecting societies collect the copyright remuneration based on tariffs, which have to be approved by the Federal Arbitration Board for the Exploitation of Authors' Rights and Neighbouring Rights.

Q.3 Please explain which individual exclusive rights under which specific provisions of Articles 11(1) and 11*bis*(1) of the Berne Convention are affected to what extent by which specific provision of Subsection (A) and/or (B) of Section 110(5)?

Subsection (A) and (B) of Section 110(5) both affect the exclusive right of public communication of broadcast works as provided by Art. 11*bis*(1)(iii) BC be-

---

[1] Text of Art. 22 CRL (Translation by the International Bureau of WIPO):

The right to make broadcast works perceivable simultaneously and unaltered or to rebroadcast them within the framework of the rebroadcast of a transmitted program may only be asserted through the approved collecting societies.

The rebroadcasting of works over technical installations that are intended to serve a small number of receivers, such as installations in houses with more than one occupier or in a private building, shall be permitted.

This Article shall not apply to the rebroadcasting of subscription television programs or of programs that cannot be received in Switzerland.

cause both provisions do not comply with the conditions under which Art. 11*bis*(2) BC allows exceptions to the exclusive right of public communication of broadcast works.

Q.4 In your view, what is the relationship between Article 13 of the TRIPS Agreement and Article 11*bis*(2) of the Berne Convention? Does Article 13 of the TRIPS Agreement prevail over the exception in Article 11*bis*(2) with respect to the exclusive rights conferred by Article 11*bis*(1)(i-iii) of the Berne Convention in the sense that when the three conditions of Article 13 are met, no requirement to pay equitable remuneration arises? Do the requirements of Article 11*bis*(2) of the Berne Convention prevail as a *lex specialis* over the requirements of Article 13 of the TRIPS Agreement, in the sense that if equitable remuneration is paid, there is no need to comply with the three-conditions test under Article 13? Do the requirements of Article 13 and Article 11*bis*(2) apply on a cumulative basis in the sense that, on the one hand, even if the three-condition test of Article 13 is fulfilled, there is an additional, fourth requirement to pay equitable remuneration, and on the other hand, even if equitable remuneration is paid consistently with Article 11*bis*(2), is it necessary to comply in addition with the three conditions of Article 13? Please explain.

Switzerland is of the opinion that Art. 13 TRIPS and Art. 11 *bis*(2) BC apply on a cumulative basis in the sense that Art. 13 TRIPS makes the limitations that were acceptable under Art. 11*bis*(2) BC even narrower. When a remuneration is paid, it can usually be admitted that the third condition of the "3 steps-test" is fulfilled (it does not unreasonably prejudice the legitimate interests of the right holder). Nevertheless one of the two remaining conditions of the "3 steps-test" could not be fulfilled, in particular the first one providing that the limitations should be confined to "certain special cases".

Q.5 In your view, to what extent has the Berne Convention become part of customary international law, and if so, in particular which part of the Articles 1-21 of the Berne Convention?

We think the question whether the Berne Convention has become customary international law is irrelevant because Art. 1-21[2] of this Convention have been incorporated into the TRIPS Agreement and, as such, make fully part of the Agreement and are applicable between the Parties to the Agreement (Art. 9 Par. 1 TRIPS).

Q.6 Has the "minor exceptions" doctrine under the Berne Convention, and especially in the context of Articles 11*bis*(1) and 11(1) of the Berne Convention, acquired the status of customary international law? What is the legal significance of the "minor exceptions" doctrine under the Berne Convention in the light of subparagraphs (3)(a-c) or paragraph (4) of Article 31 of the VCLT or in the light of Article 32 of the VCLT? Has the "minor exceptions" doctrine or any other implied exceptions been incorporated, by virtue of Article 9.1 of the

[2] Except Art. 6*bis* BC.

TRIPS Agreement, together with Articles 1-21 of the Berne Convention into the TRIPS Agreement? Please explain.

Neither the legal status nor the scope of the "minor exceptions doctrine" are very clear. In the past, this doctrine has served - in the context of the successive revisions of the BC - to justify the maintaining of exceptions that already existed in national laws and that might have been problematic with regard to the improvements of the level of protection. Those "minor exceptions" are usually exceptions justified by a public interest and they are limited to very specific cases, reflecting national particularisms. However the "minor exceptions doctrine" cannot be based upon in order to justify the introduction of new exceptions which do not comply with Art. 11 *bis*(2) BC and 13 TRIPS.

4.1 LETTER FROM THE CHAIR OF THE PANEL TO THE DIRECTOR GENERAL OF WIPO

(15 November 1999)

At its meeting on 26 May 1999, the WTO Dispute Settlement Body established a panel pursuant to the request by the European Communities and its member States (please see the attached document WT/DS160/5), in accordance with Article 6 of the Dispute Settlement Understanding. On 6 August 1999, a Panel was composed to examine this complaint (please see the attached document WT/DS160/6).

The EC complaint relates to Section 110(5) of the United States Copyright Act, as amended by the "Fairness in Music Licensing Act" enacted on 27 October 1998, which exempts, under certain conditions, the communication or transmission embodying a performance or display of a work by the public reception of the transmission on a single receiving apparatus of a kind commonly used in private homes (subparagraph A) and, also under certain conditions, communication by an establishment of a transmission or retransmission embodying a performance or display of a non-dramatic musical work intended to be received by the general public (subparagraph B) from obtaining an authorization to do so by the respective right holder. The EC claims that Section 110(5) of the US Copyright Act appears to be inconsistent with the United States' obligations under the TRIPS Agreement, including, but not limited to, Article 9.1 of the TRIPS Agreement.

The Parties to the dispute refer to the provisions of the Paris Act 1971 of the Berne Convention for the Protection of Literary and Artistic Works, the substantive provisions of which (with the exception of Article 6*bis* on moral rights and the rights derived therefrom) have been incorporated into the TRIPS Agreement by Article 9.1. These provisions include, in particular, Articles 11 and 11*bis*, as well as the limitations applicable thereto. Given that the International Bureau of WIPO is responsible for the administration of that Convention, the Panel would appreciate any factual information available to the International Bureau on the provisions of the Berne Convention (1971) relevant to the matter, in particular the negotiating history and subsequent developments and practice concerning those provisions referred to by the Parties to the dispute.

The Parties have also referred to the so-called "minor reservations" doctrine (in particular in relation to Articles 11 and 11*bis*). The Panel would be interested in any factual information relevant to the status of this doctrine within the Berne Convention as reflected in the materials of Diplomatic Conferences as well as any other documentation relating to the Berne Union or work under the auspices of WIPO on copyright matters, as well as the state practice of the Berne Union members in this regard.

Furthermore, the Parties have referred to Article 13 of the TRIPS Agreement, which uses much of the language of Article 9(2) of the Berne Convention (1971). Even though the latter provision applies to the reproduction right, which is not at issue in this dispute, given the similarity of the language used in the two provisions, the Panel would appreciate any background information on the negotiating history of Article 9(2) and subsequent developments and practice concerning the provision.

It would facilitate the work of the Panel if such factual information could be made available by Wednesday 24 November 1999.

4.2 LETTER FROM THE DIRECTOR GENERAL OF WIPO TO THE CHAIR OF THE PANEL

(22 December 1999)

I have the honour to refer to your letter of November 15, 1999, relating to an ongoing dispute which is being dealt with by a panel under the Dispute Settlement Body of the World Trade Organization (WTO).

Please find attached a Note and Annexes, prepared by the International Bureau of the World Intellectual Property Organization (WIPO) in response to your questions. As indicated in paragraphs 18, 20 and 23 of the Note, the International Bureau of WIPO is prepared to furnish additional information, at your request.

NOTE

on Certain Questions Regarding the Berne Convention
raised by the World Trade Organization

1. This Note contains the observations of the International Bureau of the World Intellectual Property Organization (WIPO) in response to a request made by H.E. Mrs. Carmen Luz Guarda, Chair, Panel on United States - Section 110(5) of US Copyright Act, World Trade Organization (WTO), in a letter of November 15, 1999, addressed to Dr. Kamil Idris, Director General of WIPO.

2. The requested information, related to the dispute in the above-mentioned Panel under the WTO Dispute Settlement Body, is the following:

> (1) regarding Articles 11 and 11*bis* of the Berne Convention, as well as the limitations applicable thereon: "any factual information available to the International Bureau on the provisions of the Berne Convention (1971) relevant to the matter, in particular the negotiating history and subsequent developments and practice concerning those provisions referred to by the Parties to the dispute;"
>
> (2) regarding the so-called "minor reservations" doctrine (in particular in relation to Articles 11 and 11*bis*): "any factual information relevant to the status of this doctrine within the Berne Convention as reflected in the materials of Diplomatic Conferences as well as any other documentation relating to the Berne Union members in this regard;"
>
> (3) regarding Article 9(2) of the Berne Convention, given the similarity of the language used in that provision and in Article 13 of the Agreement on Trade-Related Aspects of Intellectual Property Rights (the TRIPS Agreement): "any background information on the negotiation history of Article 9(2) and subsequent developments and practice concerning the provision."

Question 1: Articles 11 and 11*bis* and the limitations applicable thereon

3. The origin of Article 11 of the Berne Convention (1971) is, as regards non-dramatic musical works, Article 9(3) of the Berne Convention (1886) which granted national treatment to authors of such unpublished works—and published works if a prohibition of performance was indicated on the title page. The Draft Convention, adopted at a conference organized by the International Literary Association in Berne in 1883, contained the following provision:

> "Article 5: Authors who are nationals of one of the Contracting States shall, in all the other States of the Union, enjoy the exclusive right of translation throughout the duration of the rights in their original works.

"That right shall include the rights of publication or performance."[1,2]

4. The Program proposed by the Swiss Federal Council for the International Conference for the Protection of Authors' Rights which was held from September 8 to 19, 1884, in Berne, contained in its Article 7 an identical provision, apart from an added alternative proposal regarding the right of translation.[3] Discussions of that proposal have been identified in the minutes of the Third Meeting of the Conference, where the Conference discussed a questionnaire of the German Delegation. An excerpt is attached to this Note as Annex I.[4] The Records of the Conference do not contain minutes or other records of the work of the Committee to which references are made in the text in Annex I, other than the report from that Committee which was presented at the fifth Meeting of the Conference. In the Committee's proposal, the reference to performance in Article 7 of the program had been taken out of the context of translation and placed separately in the draft Article 11. The relevant part of the Minutes of that meeting, dealing with that Article and with draft Article 2, to which reference is made in draft Article 11, are attached to this Note as Annex II.[5] (The reservation made by a Delegate in relation to draft Article 6 is not included, as it relates only to the question of formalities for protection.)

5. At the Second International Conference for the Protection of Literary and Artistic Works, in Berne, from September 7 to 18, 1885, discussions were based on the draft prepared by the 1884 Conference.[6] The opening discussion at the Conference of Articles 2 and 11 is attached to this Note as Annex III.[7] Excerpts of the Report of the Committee of the Conference as regards these Articles (Article 11 of the 1884 draft was renumbered to become Article 9 in the Committee's proposal) and as regards the Recommended Principles for Subsequent Unification are attached to this Note as Annex IV.[8] The Conference adopted Articles 2 and 9 without discussion, as proposed by the Committee.[9]

6. The Records of the Third International Conference for the Protection of Literary and Artistic Works, in Berne, from September 6 to 9, 1886, reflect that the Conference discussed a declaration from France regarding, *inter alia,* Article 9 of the Convention. An excerpt of the minutes of the Conference rendering the declaration and the discussion is attached to this Note as Annex V.[10]

---

1 The English translations used in the following, except for the Records of the 1967 Stockholm Conference which were published in English, are WIPO translations from: "1886—Berne Convention Centenary—1986," WIPO Publication No. 877 (E), in the following referred to as "Berne Centenary"

2 Berne Centenary, pp. 83f.

3 Berne Centenary, p. 85.

4 Source: Berne Centenary, p. 91.

5 Source: Berne Centenary, pp. 94f and 100.

6 Rule 2, Rules of Procedure, Berne Centenary, p. 110.

7 Source: Berne Centenary, pp. 111, 113 and 116.

8 Source: Berne Centenary, pp. 118f, 121 and 125.

9 Berne Centenary, p. 127.

10 Source: Berne Centenary, p. 132.

7. The official Records of the Berne Conferences do not contain indexes, and the preceding selection of negotiation history is based on a review of the records. As regards the following Conferences, the selections are partly based on the indexes of the official Records, partly on a review of the Records. As regards the 1967 Stockholm Conference, the selection is solely based on the indexes.

8. The Diplomatic Conference in Paris, from April 15 to May 4, 1896, adopted the Paris Additional Act and Interpretative Declaration, 1896. That Act and Declaration did not amend Article 9 of the Berne Act, but it amended Article 2, to which Article 9 refers, and it discussed certain amendments of Article 9 which were not adopted, and a proposal for a new Article 4*bis* which would have ruled out non-voluntary licenses for public performances. Annex VI to this Note contains excerpts of the Report on the work of the Committee of the Diplomatic Conference, prepared by Mr. Louis Renault, dealing with those Articles and proposal.[11] Annex VII to this Note contains the following excerpts of the Records of the Conference relevant to the proposed amendments of Article 9 and the proposed new Article 4*bis*:[12]

(1) proposals made by the French authorities and the International Bureau, regarding Articles 5 and 9;[13]

(2) wishes (vœux) expressed by various congresses and meetings since the adoption of the Convention;[14]

(3) the proposal for a new Article 4*bis* made by the Delegate of Germany;[15]

(4) summary minutes of the general discussion, regarding Article 9;[16]

(5) analytic table of the proposals, made at the Conference, regarding Article 9;[17]

(6) discussion and adaptation of the wishes of the Conference.[18]

9. The Berlin Act of the Convention, adopted at a Diplomatic Conference from October 14 to November 14, 1908, included a partial renumbering of the Articles, whereby the previous Article 9 became Article 11, in which paragraphs (1) and (3) related to performance of musical works. Those paragraphs had the following wording:

> "(1) The provisions of this Convention shall apply to the public performance of dramatic or dramatico-musical works, and of musical works, whether such works are published or not.

11 Source: Berne Centenary, pp. 136ff, 140, and 142.

12 Excerpts of the Records regarding the discussions on Article 2 are not included here, but can be provided at request.

13 Source: Actes de la conférence réunie à Paris du 15 avril au 4 mai 1896 (in the following referred to as "Actes 1896"), pp. 39f and 42f.

14 Source: Actes 1896, pp. 60ff.

15 Source: Actes 1896, p. 114.

16 Source: Actes 1896, p. 116.

17 Source: Actes 1896, p. 124.

18 Source: Actes 1896, p. 145.

"(3) In order to enjoy the protection of this Article, authors shall not be bound in publishing their works to forbid the public performance thereof."

10. Annex VIII to this Note contains excerpts from the General Report Presented to the Conference on Behalf of its Committee by Mr. Louis Renault dealing with this Article.[19] Annex IX to this Note contains the following excerpts from the Records of the Conference relevant to Article 11 of the 1908 Berlin Act of the Convention:

(1) proposal by the Government of Germany and the International Bureau, with notes[20] and Annex regarding the "vœux" expressed by the 1896 Paris Conference;[21]

(2) wishes (vœux) expressed by various congresses and meetings since the adoption of the 1896 Act of the Convention;[22]

(3) excerpts of the Minutes of the Conference regarding a presentation of the proposal of the Government of Germany, made by Professor, Dr. Osterrieth;[23]

(4) excerpts of the Minutes of the Conference regarding an oral proposal by the Delegation of Switzerland;[24]

(5) excerpts of the Minutes of the Conference containing an observation by the Delegation of Great Britain in connection with the adoption of Article 11, as proposed by the Commission.[25]

11. The 1914 Additional Protocol to the Convention was signed in Berne without a conference of revision. It did not amend Article 11 of the Convention.

12. The Rome Act of the Convention, adopted at a Diplomatic Conference from May 7 to June 2, 1928, did not amend Article 11, but it added Article 11*bis*, dealing with the right of broadcasting, which had the following wording:

"(1) Authors of literary and artistic works shall enjoy the exclusive right of authorizing the communication of their works to the public by radio-diffusion.

"(2) The legislations of the countries of the Union shall determine the conditions under which the right mentioned in the preceding paragraph may be exercised, but the effect of those conditions shall apply only in the countries where they have been prescribed. This shall not in any circumstances be prejudicial to the moral rights of the author, nor to his right to obtain an equitable remuneration which, in the absence of agreement, shall be fixed by the competent authority."

---

19 Source: Berne Centenary, pp. 154f.

20 Source: Actes de la conference féunie à Berlin du 14 octobre au 14 novembre 1908 (in the following referred to as "Actes 1908"), p. 46.

21 Source: Actes 1908, p. 53.

22 Source: Actes 1908, pp. 88f.

23 Source: Actes 1908, pp. 162 and 167.

24 Source: Actes 1908, p. 180.

25 Source: Actes 1908, p. 216.

13. Annex X to this Note contains the Report of the Sub-committee on Broadcasting[26] and excerpts of the General Report of the Drafting Committee (Rapporteur Mr. Edoardo Piola Caselli) relating to Article 11*bis*[27]. Annex XI to this Note contains the following excerpts from the Records of the Conference relevant to Article 11*bis* of the 1928 Rome Act of the Convention:

(1) excerpts from the Program of the Conference, containing the proposal of the Government of Italy and the International Bureau, regarding Articles 11 (for which no amendment was proposed) and 11*bis*;[28]

(2) observations of the Government of Germany;[29]

(3) proposed Article 11*bis* of the Government of Austria;[30]

(4) proposal for amendment of Article 11 of the Government of Great Britain;[31]

(5) proposed Article 11*bis* of the Government of France;[32]

(6) proposal for amendment of Article 11*bis* of the Government of Hungary[33]

(7) general observations and observations regarding Articles 11 and 11*bis* of the Government of the Netherlands;[34]

(8) proposal for amendment of Article 11*bis* of the Government of Norway;[35]

(9) observations of the Government of Sweden;[36]

(10) excerpts of the summary of the proposals and the discussion, prepared by the Berne Bureau, relating to Articles 11 and 11*bis*;[37]

(11) excerpts of the Minutes of the Conference regarding discussion and adoption of Articles 11 and 11*bis*.[38]

14. The Brussels Act of the Convention, adopted at a Diplomatic Conference from June 5 to 26, 1948, amended Article 11 in which paragraphs (1) and (3) related to performance of musical works. Those paragraphs had the following wording:

> "(1) Authors of dramatic, dramatico-musical and musical works shall enjoy the exclusive right of authorizing: (i) the public performance of their works; (ii) any communication to the public of the performance of their works. The application

[26] Source: Berne Centenary, p. 165.
[27] Source: Berne Centenary, pp. 173f.
[28] Source: Actes de la conférence réunie à Rome du 7 mai au 2 juin 1928 (in the following referred to as "Actes 1928"), pp. 75 and 76f.
[29] Source: Actes 1928, p. 88.
[30] Source: Actes 1928, p. 89.
[31] Source: Actes 1928, p. 93.
[32] Source: Actes 1928, p. 100.
[33] Source: Actes 1928, p. 105.
[34] Source: Actes 1928, pp. 108 and 109.
[35] Source: Actes 1928, pp. 111f.
[36] Source: Actes 1928, pp. 123f.
[37] Source: Actes 1928, pp. 254ff.
[38] Source: Actes 1928, p. 294.

of the provisions of Articles 11*bis* and 13 is, however, reserved.

"(3) In order to enjoy the protection of this Article, authors shall not be bound, when publishing their works, to forbid the public performance thereof."

The Brussels Act also amended Article 11*bis* of the Convention. Paragraphs (1) and (2) which relate to the right of broadcasting, were given the following wording:

"(1) Authors of literary and artistic works shall have the exclusive right of authorizing: (i) the broadcasting of their works or the communication thereof to the public by any other means of wireless diffusion of signs, sounds or images; (ii) any communication to the public, by wire or by rebroadcasting of the broadcast of the work, when this communication is made by an organization other than the original one; (iii) the public communication by loudspeaker or any other analogous instrument transmitting, by signs, sounds or images, the broadcast of the work.

"(2) It shall be a matter for legislation in the countries of the Union to determine the conditions under which the rights mentioned in the preceding paragraph may be exercised, but these conditions shall apply only in the countries where they have been prescribed. They shall not in any circumstances be prejudicial to the moral rights of the author, nor to his right to obtain equitable remuneration which, in the absence of agreement, shall be fixed by competent authority."

15. Annex XII to this Note contains:

(1) excerpts from the General Report on the Work of the Brussels Diplomatic Conference for the Revision of the Berne Convention, presented by Mr. Marcel Plaisant, Rapporteur-General, relating to Articles 11 and 11*bis*, and discussing in this connection also the so-called "minor reserves";[39]

(2) Report by the Sub-Committee on Broadcasting and Mechanical Instruments;[40]

(3) Report by the Sub-Committee on Articles 11 and 11*ter*.[41]

Annex XIII to this Note contains the following excerpts from the Records of the Conference relevant to Articles 11 and 11*bis* of the 1948 Brussels Act of the Convention, including the discussions regarding the so-called "minor reserves":

(1) excerpts from the Minutes of the Conference containing statements made at the adoption of Articles 11 and 11*bis*;[42]

---

39 Source: Berne Centenary, p. 181.

40 Source: Berne Centenary, pp. 185ff.

41 Source: Berne Centenary, p. 191.

42 Source: Documents de la conférence réunie à Bruxelles du 5 au 26 juin 1948 (in the following referred to as "Documents 1948"), p. 82.

(2) excerpts from the Records of the Conference, containing, under A, the proposals of the Government of Belgium and the Berne Bureau, under B, proposals, counter-proposals and observations made by Governments of countries, member of the Berne Union, and, under C, summary of the discussions and the outcome of the Conference, relating to Articles 11, including the so-called "minor reserves," and Article 11*bis* of the Convention;[43]

(3) wishes (vœux) expressed by various congresses and meetings between 1927 and 1935, relating to the right of public performance and the right of broadcasting;[44]

(4) wishes expressed by various congresses and meetings between 1936 and 1948;[45]

(5) Memorandum of "l'Organisation internationale de radiodiffusion".[46]

16. The Stockholm Act of the Convention, adopted at the Intellectual Property Conference of Stockholm, June 11 to July 14, 1967, adopted Articles 11 and 11*bis* in the same wording as that which appears in the Paris Act (1971). Annex XIV to this Note contains the following excerpts from the Records of that Conference (references relating solely to Article 11*bis*(3) have been omitted):

(1) excerpts from Proposals for Revision of the Substantive Copyright Provisions (Articles 1 to 20), Proposal by the Government of Sweden with the Assistance of BIRPI (the Basic Proposal), relating to Articles 11 and 11*bis*;[47]

(2) comments from the Government of the Federal Republic of Germany concerning Article 11 of the Basic Proposal;[48]

(3) comments from the Government of Israel concerning Article 11 and 11*bis* of the Basic Proposal;[49]

(4) comments from the Government of Portugal concerning Article 11 of the Basic Proposal;[50]

(5) comments from the Government of the United Kingdom concerning Article 11*bis* of the Basic Proposal;[51]

(6) comments from the Government of Switzerland concerning Article 11*ter* of the Basic Proposal, containing a reference to Article 11;[52]

(7) excerpts of summary of observations of governments, prepared by the BIRPI Bureau, as regards Articles 11 and 11*bis*;[53]

---

43 Source: Documents 1948, pp. 252 to 304.
44 Source: Documents 1948, pp. 448 to 454.
45 Source: Documents 1948, pp. 492f.
46 Source: Documents 1948, pp. 522 to 527.
47 Source: Records of the Intellectual Property Conference of Stockholm, June 11 to July 14, 1967 (in the following referred to as "Records 1967"), pp. 120 to 122.
48 Source: Records 1967, p. 618.
49 Source: Records 1967, p. 622.
50 Source: Records 1967, pp. 627f.
51 Source: Records 1967, p. 630.
52 Source: Records 1967, p. 664.

(8) proposal from the Government of Greece concerning Article 11(1);[54]

(9) comments from the Government of India concerning Article 11*bis* of the Basic Proposal;[55]

(10) proposal regarding the regime of cinematographic works, submitted by the Working Group of Main Committee I to Main Committee I;[56]

(11) proposals from the Government of Brazil concerning Article 11*bis* of the Basic Proposal;[57]

(12) proposals from the Secretariat to the Drafting Committee, concerning Articles 11 and 11*bis*;[58]

(13) Report of the Drafting Committee to Main Committee I;[59]

(14) Additional Report of the Drafting Committee to Main Committee I;[60]

(15) Draft Report of the Rapporteur of Main Committee II to the Committee with addendum, revision and a correction of the revision, relating to preferential rules for developing countries, and Draft Report (final version);[61]

(16) excerpts from the Report of the Work of Main Committee I (Rapporteur Svante Bergström) relating to Articles 11 and 11*bis*, including the general Introduction,[62] and excerpts from the Records showing the corrections made in the Draft Report of the Committee;[63]

(17) excerpts of the Summary Minutes of Main Committee I;[64]

---

[53] Source: Records 1967, pp. 670f.

[54] Source: Records 1967, p. 689.

[55] Source: Records 1967, pp. 690f.

[56] Source: Records 1967, p. 710.

[57] Source: Records 1967, p. 715.

[58] Source: Records 1967, pp. 721f.

[59] Source: Records 1967, p. 726.

[60] Source: Records 1967, p. 735.

[61] Source: Records 1967, pp. 735 to 739 and 760 to 762.

[62] Source: Records 1967, pp. 1131 to 1134, 1146, 1165 to 1168 and 1181f.

[63] Source: Records 1967, pp. 739, 740, 742f and 744.

[64] Source: Records 1967, pp. 851f (in the context of discussions regarding the right of reproduction, reference to Article 11*bis*(2) is made in para. 653.2), 856 (in the context of discussions regarding the right of reproduction, reference to Article 11 is made in para. 711.4), 865f (in the context of discussions regarding cinematographic works), 883 to 885 (in the context of discussions regarding the right of reproduction, reference to Article 11(3) is made in para. 1069.1 and to Article 11*bis* in para. 1063.1), 893, 902, 902 to 904, 904 to 905 (in the context of discussions regarding the right of public recitation, reference to Article 11 is made in paras. 1323.3, 1332, 1335 and 1336), 916 to 917 (in the context of discussions regarding reproduction of lectures, addresses and similar works, references to Article 11*bis* are made in paras. 1498.2, 1499.3 to 1500 and 1501.2), 921f (in the context of discussions on exceptions to translation rights, references to Article 11*bis* are made in paras. 1565.3 to 1567.3), 923 to 924 (in the context of discussions regarding the principle of equivalent protection in regard to the right of translation, reference to Article 11 is made in para. 1607), 926f (in the context of discussions regarding exceptions to the exclusive right of translation, references to Article 11*bis* is made in paras. 1652.1 to 1652.2, 1653.2 and 1658.1 to 1658.2), 928, 930 (in the context of the adoption of the Report of the Work of Main Committee I, reference to Article 11 is made in para. 1749), 936f (in the context of the adoption of the adoption of the Report of Main Committee I).

(18) excerpts of the Summary Minutes of the Plenary of the Berne Union.[65]

17. The Diplomatic Conference for the Revision of the Berne Convention which took place in Paris from July 5 to 24, 1971, did not amend the Articles discussed above, and the Records of that Conference have therefore not been analyzed for this Note. Such an analysis can be provided if requested.

18. The request made by H.E. Mrs. Carmen Luz Guarda regarding Articles 11 and 11*bis* of the Berne Convention, as well as the limitations applicable thereon, concerns also other "factual information available to the International Bureau," and "subsequent developments and practice concerning those provisions referred to by the Parties to the dispute." This request covers a vast amount of material which is not available in a systematic and detailed indexed form. Any selection of material considered relevant for the dispute will invariably imply risks of interpretations of the material which would be incompatible with the neutral status of WIPO in relation to the dispute. In order to fulfill the request neutrally, it would be necessary to carry through a complete review of major parts of the copyright and related rights activities of WIPO during the period of so-called "guided development"[66] from 1967 to 1991 and a general review of the implementation of the treaty provisions in all national laws of Berne Union Member States. Such research would take a long time, and it has therefore not been undertaken. The International Bureau is, however, prepared to furnish any non-confidential material in its possession which is specified in such a way that it can be identified without the need for the International Bureau to make any interpretations of the substantive provisions of the Berne Convention.

Question 2: The so-called "minor reservations" doctrine

19. The discussions regarding the so-called "minor reservations" doctrine apparently all took place in the context of the discussions regarding Article 11 of the Berne Convention. As regards this question reference can therefore be made to the materials referred to under Question 1.

20. The request made by H.E. Mrs. Carmen Luz Guarda regarding the "minor reservations" doctrine pertains to "any factual information relevant to the status of this doctrine within the Berne Convention as reflected in the materials of Diplomatic Conferences as well as any other documentation relating to the Berne Union members in this regard." As regards material other than what is referred to in the preceding paragraph, reference is made to the remarks made in paragraph 18, above.

Question 3: Article 9(2) of the Berne Convention

21. Article 9 of the Paris Act of the Berne Convention, granting the right of reproduction and regulating exceptions and limitations to that right was introduced at the Stockholm Conference. Annex XV to this Note contains the following excerpts from the Records of that Conference:

[65] Source: Records 1967, p. 805.

[66] A term used by Sam Ricketson in: "The Berne Convention, for the Protection of Literary and Artistic Works, Centre for Commercial Law Studies, Kluwer, 1987, p. 919.

(1) excerpts from Proposals for Revision of the Substantive Copyright Provisions (Articles 1 to 20), Proposal by the Government of Sweden with the Assistance of BIRPI (the Basic Proposal);[67]

(2) comments from the Government of Austria to the Basic Proposal;[68]

(3) comments from the Government of Belgium to the Basic Proposal;[69]

(4) comments from the Government of Czechoslovakia to the Basic Proposal;[70]

(5) comments from the Government of Denmark to the Basic Proposal;[71]

(6) comments from the Government of France to the Basic Proposal;[72]

(7) comments from the Government of the Federal Republic of Germany to the Basic Proposal;[73]

(8) comments from the Government of Ireland to the Basic Proposal;[74]

(9) comments from the Government of Israel to the Basic Proposal;[75]

(10) comments from the Government of Italy to the Basic Proposal;[76]

(11) comments from the Government of Japan to the Basic Proposal;[77]

(12) comments from the Government of Portugal to the Basic Proposal;[78]

(13) comments from the Government of South Africa to the Basic Proposal;[79]

(14) comments from the Government of United Kingdom to the Basic Proposal;[80]

(15) comments from the Government of Luxembourg to the Basic Proposal;[81]

(16) excerpts of summary of observations of governments, prepared by the BIRPI Bureau, as regards Article 9;[82]

(17) amendment to the Basic Proposal, proposed by the Government of Austria;[83]

---

67 Source: Records 1967, pp. 111 to 116.
68 Source: Records 1967, p. 611.
69 Source: Records 1967, p. 612.
70 Source: Records 1967, p. 613.
71 Source: Records 1967, p. 615.
72 Source: Records 1967, p. 615.
73 Source: Records 1967, p. 618.
74 Source: Records 1967, p. 620.
75 Source: Records 1967, p. 622.
76 Source: Records 1967, p. 623.
77 Source: Records 1967, p. 624.
78 Source: Records 1967, p. 627.
79 Source: Records 1967, p. 629.
80 Source: Records 1967, p. 630.
81 Source: Records 1967, p. 663.
82 Source: Records 1967, pp. 669f.
83 Source: Records 1967, p. 683.

(18) amendment to the Basic Proposal, proposed by the Government of the United Kingdom;[84]

(19) amendment to the Basic Proposal, proposed by the Governments of Czechoslovakia, Hungary and Poland;[85]

(20) amendment to the Basic Proposal, proposed by the Government of Greece;[86]

(21) amendment to the Basic Proposal, proposed by the Government of Monaco;[87]

(22) amendment to the Basic Proposal, proposed by the Government of the Federal Republic of Germany;[88]

(23) amendment to the Basic Proposal, proposed by the Government of France;[89]

(24) amendment to the Basic Proposal, proposed by the Governments of Austria, Italy and Morocco;[90]

(25) amendment to the Basic Proposal, proposed by the Government of India;[91]

(26) amendment to the Basic Proposal, proposed by the Government of Rumania;[92]

(27) amendment to the Basic Proposal, proposed by the Government of Japan;[93]

(28) amendment to the Basic Proposal, proposed by the Government of the Netherlands;[94]

(29) amendment to the Basic Proposal, proposed by the Government of India;[95]

(30) amendment to the Basic Proposal, proposed by the Working Group of Main Committee I;[96]

(31) text given to the Drafting Committee;[97]

(32) new text prepared for the Drafting Committee by the Secretariat;[98]

(33) Report of the Drafting Committee to Main Committee I;[99]

---

84 Source: Records 1967, p. 687.
85 Source: Records 1967, p. 688.
86 Source: Records 1967, p. 689.
87 Source: Records 1967, p. 690.
88 Source: Records 1967, p. 690.
89 Source: Records 1967, p. 690.
90 Source: Records 1967, p. 690.
91 Source: Records 1967, pp. 690f.
92 Source: Records 1967, p. 691.
93 Source: Records 1967, p. 691.
94 Source: Records 1967, p. 691.
95 Source: Records 1967, p. 692.
96 Source: Records 1967, p. 696.
97 Source: Records 1967, p. 709.
98 Source: Records 1967, p. 720.

(34) final text submitted by the Drafting Committee to Main Committee I;[100]

(35) Additional Report of the Drafting Committee to Main Committee I;[101]

(36) additional text proposed by the Secretariat to the Drafting Committee;[102]

(37) additional text submitted by the Drafting Committee to Main Committee I;[103]

(38) excerpts from the Report of the Work of Main Committee I (Rapporteur Svante Bergström) relating to Article 9, including the general introduction,[104] and excerpts from the Records showing the corrections made in the Draft Report of the Committee;[105]

(39) excerpts of the Summary Minutes of Main Committee I;[106]

(40) excerpts of the Summary Minutes of the Plenary of the Berne Union.[107]

22. The Diplomatic Conference for the Revision of the Berne Convention which took place in Paris from July 5 to 24, 1971, did not amend Article 9, and the Records of that Conference have therefore not been analyzed for this Note. Such an analysis can be provided if requested.

23. The request made by H.E. Mrs. Carmen Luz Guarda regarding Article 9(2) of the Berne Convention pertains to "any background information on the negotiation history of Article 9(2) and subsequent developments and practice concerning the provision." As regards material other than what is referred to in the preceding paragraphs, reference is made to the remarks made in paragraph 18, above.

---

99 Source: Records 1967, p. 726.

100 Source: Records 1967, p. 734.

101 Source: Records 1967, p. 735.

102 Source: Records 1967, p. 757.

103 Source: Records 1967, p. 758.

104 Source: Records 1967, pp. 1131 to 1134, 1142 to 1146, 1147 to 1149, 1164f.

105 Source: Records 1967, pp. 739, 740, 740f, 742f.

106 Source: Records 1967, pp. 837f, 851 to 855, 856 to 860, 860f (in the context of discussions regarding lawful quotations, reference is made to Article 9 in para. 776), 862, 881f (in the context of discussions regarding protection of official texts, reference is made to Article 9 in para. 1031), 883 to 885, 892 (in the context of discussions regarding reproduction of lectures, sermons, etc., reference is made to Article 9 in paras. 1145 and 1152.1), 901f (in the context of discussions regarding the right of translation, reference is made to Article 9 in para. 1275), 905 to 907 (in the context of discussions regarding mechanical reproduction rights, several references are made to Article 9), 922f (discussion of Article 9 in the context of its application on translations), 926 to 928, 931.

107 Source: Records 1967, pp. 804f.

BRAZIL - EXPORT FINANCING PROGRAMME FOR AIRCRAFT RECOURSE BY CANADA TO ARTICLE 21.5 OF THE DSU

Report of the Appellate Body

WT/DS46/AB/RW

Adopted by the Dispute Settlement Body on 4 August 2000

Brazil, *Appellant*	Present:
Canada, *Appellee*	Bacchus, Presiding Member
European Communities, *Third Participant*	Ehlermann, Member
United States, *Third Participant*	Lacarte-Muró, Member

TABLE OF CONTENTS

I. INTRODUCTION

1. Brazil appeals from certain issues of law and legal interpretation in the Panel Report, *Brazil - Export Financing Programme for Aircraft, Recourse by Canada to Article 21.5 of the DSU* (the "Article 21.5 Panel Report").[1] The Article 21.5 Panel was established pursuant to Article 21.5 of the *Understanding on Rules and Procedures Governing the Settlement of Disputes* (the "DSU") to consider a complaint by Canada with respect to the existence or consistency with the *Agreement on Subsidies and Countervailing Measures* (the "*SCM Agreement*") of measures taken by Brazil to comply with the recommendations and rulings of the Dispute Settlement Body (the "DSB") in *Brazil - Export Financing Programme for Aircraft* ("*Brazil - Aircraft*").[2]

2. The original panel found as follows: "... we find that payments on exports of regional aircraft under the PROEX interest rate equalization scheme are export subsidies inconsistent with Article 3 of the SCM Agreement."[3] The original panel then recommended "that Brazil withdraw the subsidies identified above without delay"[4], which in this dispute was found to be within 90 days.[5] On appeal, the Appellate Body upheld this recommendation.[6]

3. Brazil took steps to implement the recommendations and rulings of the DSB. Taking the view that the measures adopted by Brazil to comply with the recommen-

---

[1] Panel Report, *Brazil - Export Financing Programme for Aircraft - Recourse by Canada to Article 21.5 of the DSU* ("*Brazil – Aircraft (Article 21.5 – Canada)*"), WT/DS46/RW, adopted 4 August 2000.

[2] The recommendations and rulings of the DSB resulted from the adoption, by the DSB, of the Appellate Body Report in *Brazil - Export Financing Programme for Aircraft* ("*Brazil – Aircraft*"), WT/DS46/AB/R, adopted 20 August 1999, DSR 1999:III, 1161 and the original panel report in that dispute, *Brazil - Export Financing Programme for Aircraft* ("*Brazil – Aircraft*"), WT/DS46/R, adopted 20 August 1999, as modified by the Appellate Body Report, DSR 1999:III, 1221. The DSB recommended that Brazil "withdraw" its prohibited export subsidies within 90 days, that is, by 18 November 1999.

[3] Original panel report, *Brazil - Aircraft, supra*, footnote 2, para. 8.2.

[4] Original panel report, *Brazil - Aircraft, supra*, footnote 2, para. 8.4.

[5] *Ibid.*, para. 8.5.

[6] Appellate Body Report, *Brazil - Aircraft, supra*, footnote 2, para. 197.

dations and rulings of the DSB were not consistent with Article 3.1(a) of the *SCM Agreement*, Canada requested that the matter be referred to the original panel, pursuant to Article 21.5 of the DSU.[7] On 9 December 1999, the DSB referred the matter to the original panel.

4. The Article 21.5 Panel considered claims by Canada that Brazil had failed to comply with the recommendations and rulings of the DSB. Canada argued that Brazil continued to issue NTN-I bonds pursuant to letters of commitment issued before 18 November 1999 under the terms and conditions of PROEX before its modification; and that the modifications to PROEX adopted by Brazil did not constitute the withdrawal of the subsidies, as PROEX was still inconsistent with the prohibition on export subsidies under Article 3.1(a) of the *SCM Agreement*.

5. The Article 21.5 Panel Report was circulated to the Members of the World Trade Organization (the "WTO") on 9 May 2000. The Article 21.5 Panel concluded that, as a result of the continued issuance of NTN-I bonds pursuant to letters of commitment issued before 18 November 1999, and as a result of the inconsistency of PROEX as modified with Article 3.1(a) of the *SCM Agreement*, Brazil's measures to comply with the DSB's recommendation either do not exist or are not consistent with the *SCM Agreement*. Accordingly, the Article 21.5 Panel concluded that Brazil has failed to implement the DSB's recommendation that it withdraw the export subsidies for regional aircraft under PROEX within 90 days.[8]

6. On 22 May 2000, Brazil notified the DSB of its intention to appeal certain issues of law covered in the Article 21.5 Panel Report and legal interpretations developed by the Article 21.5 Panel, pursuant to Article 4.8 of the *SCM Agreement* and paragraph 4 of Article 16 of the DSU, and filed a Notice of Appeal pursuant to Rules 20 and 31(1) of the *Working Procedures for Appellate Review* (the "*Working Procedures*"). On 29 May 2000, Brazil filed its appellant's submission.[9] On 5 June 2000, Canada filed an appellee's submission.[10] On the same day, the European Communities and the United States each filed a third participant's submission.[11]

7. The oral hearing in the appeal was held on 19 June 2000. The participants and third participants presented oral arguments and responded to questions put to them by the Members of the Division hearing the appeal.

II. BACKGROUND

8. Before the original panel, the measures at issue were certain export subsidies granted under Brazil's *Programa de Financiamento às Exportações* ("PROEX") on sales of aircraft to foreign purchasers of Empresa Brasileira de Aeronáutica S.A. ("Embraer"), a Brazilian manufacturer of regional aircraft. The original panel described certain factual aspects of PROEX[12] as PROEX existed at that time. We provided a

---

7 WT/DS46/13 (26 November 1999).

8 Panel Report, *Brazil – Aircraft (Article 21.5 – Canada)*, *supra*, footnote 1, para. 7.1.

9 Pursuant to Rule 21(1) of the *Working Procedures*.

10 Pursuant to Rule 22 of the *Working Procedures*.

11 Pursuant to Rule 24 of the *Working Procedures*.

12 Original panel report, *Brazil - Aircraft*, *supra*, footnote 2, paras. 2.1-2.6.

summary of these aspects.[13] The Article 21.5 Panel described the factual aspects of PROEX as revised by Brazil (the "revised PROEX "), in light of the recommendations and rulings of the DSB.[14] Below we provide a summary of the factual aspects of the revised PROEX, based on the summary set out in the Article 21.5 Panel Report.

9. PROEX is administered by the Comitê de Crédito às Exportações (the "Committee"), an inter-agency group within the Ministry of Finance in Brazil. Day-to-day operations of PROEX are conducted by the Bank of Brazil.[15] Under PROEX, the Government of Brazil provides interest rate equalization subsidies for sales by Brazilian exporters, including Embraer, as described below.

10. The financing conditions for which interest rate equalization payments are made are set by Ministerial Decrees. The length of the financing term, which is determined by the product to be exported, varies normally from one year to ten years. In the case of regional aircraft, however, this term has often been extended to 15 years, by waiver of the relevant PROEX guidelines. The length of the financing term, in turn, determines the spread to be equalised: the payment ranges from 0.5 percentage points per annum, for a term of up to six months, to 2.5 percentage points per annum, for a term of nine years or more. Resolution No. 2667 of 19 November 1999 provides that, in respect of regional aircraft financing, "equalisation rates shall be established on a case by case basis and at levels that may be differential, preferably based on the United States Treasury Bond 10-year rate, plus an additional spread of 0.2% per annum, to be reviewed periodically in accordance with market practices."[16] The lending bank charges its normal interest rate for the transaction and receives payment from two sources: the purchaser and the Government of Brazil. In this way, PROEX reduces the financing costs of the purchaser and, thus, reduces the overall cost to the purchaser of purchasing an Embraer aircraft.

11. The involvement of PROEX in aircraft financing transactions begins when the manufacturer - Embraer - requests approval for PROEX interest rate equalization subsidies before the conclusion of a formal contract with a buyer. If the Committee approves the request, it then issues a letter of commitment to the manufacturer, committing the Government of Brazil to PROEX support, provided that the buyer and the manufacturer conclude a contract for the transaction within a specified period of time, usually 90 days (subject to renewal), and in accordance with the terms and

---

[13] Appellate Body Report, *Brazil - Aircraft*, *supra*, footnote 2, paras. 3-6.

[14] Panel Report, *Brazil - Aircraft (Article 21.5 - Canada)*, *supra*, footnote 1, paras. 2.1-2.6. Brazil informed the DSB that it had implemented the recommendations of the DSB through, in addition to Resolution 2667, Newsletter 2881. Newsletter 2881 establishes "the maximum percentages that may be applied under tax rate equalisation systems used for PROEX operations." These maximum percentages cover financing for up to ten years, with the highest interest rate equalization rate set at 2.5 per cent for financing of "over 9 years and up to 10 years". In the First Submission of Brazil to the Panel, however, Brazil indicated that Newsletter 2881 represents "an additional action that does not directly affect the question before this Panel". From this statement, the Article 21.5 Panel concluded that Brazil does not assert that Newsletter 2881 is relevant to its consideration of whether the revised PROEX is consistent with the *SCM Agreement*. Article 21.5 Panel Report, footnote 25. This conclusion was not appealed.

[15] *Ibid.*, para. 2.4.

[16] Panel Report, *Brazil - Aircraft (Article 21.5 - Canada)*, *supra*, footnote 1, para. 2.3.

conditions set forth in the original request.[17] The letter of commitment usually provides that PROEX payments will be made in 30 equal and consecutive semi-annual instalments during a financing period of 15 years. The first instalment payment is typically due six months after the delivery date of each aircraft.[18]

12. PROEX interest rate equalization payments begin after the aircraft is exported. The payments are made in the form of bonds issued by PROEX to the financing institution. After each export transaction is confirmed, the Bank of Brazil applies to the National Treasury of Brazil for the issuance of bonds designated as National Treasury Note - Series I ("NTN-I") bonds. The National Treasury issues these bonds and transfers them to the Bank of Brazil, which in turn passes the bonds to the lending bank (or its agent bank). The lending bank can redeem the bonds on a semi-annual basis for the duration of the financing, or can sell them on the market at a discount immediately upon receipt.[19] NTN-I bonds are denominated in Brazilian currency, indexed to the dollar as of the date the bonds are issued. The bonds can only be redeemed in Brazil, and only in Brazilian currency.[20]

III. ARGUMENTS OF THE PARTICIPANTS AND THE THIRD PARTICIPANTS

A. *Claims of Error by Appellant - Brazil*

1. *Issuance of NTN-I Bonds Pursuant to Letters of Commitment Issued before 18 November 1999*

13. Brazil argues that, contrary to the Article 21.5 Panel's findings, the continued issuance of NTN-I bonds pursuant to commitments made prior to the modification of PROEX is consistent with the *SCM Agreement*. In particular, Brazil submits that the subsidies in question have already been "granted" within the meaning of Article 3.2 of the *SCM Agreement*, and therefore no remedy is available under Article 3 for these subsidies. Brazil contends that the Article 21.5 Panel erred in concluding that PROEX interest equalization payments for regional aircraft are "granted" upon the issuance of NTN-I bonds, regardless of *when* the aircraft were sold. The Article 21.5 Panel improperly found that the timing of the "grant" of an export subsidy for the purpose of Article 3.2 of the *SCM Agreement* is legally distinct from the timing of when a subsidy is "conferred" under Article 1 of that Agreement.

14. In Brazil's view, the Article 21.5 Panel should have determined that a subsidy is "granted" when Brazil makes a "financial contribution" and a benefit is thereby "conferred". This occurs when a letter of commitment is issued and the transaction is finalized by a contract made pursuant to that commitment. Thus, for contracts that were signed before 18 November 1999, the subsidy has already been "granted" within the meaning of Article 3.2. Therefore, these subsidies are not subject to the DSB's recommendation to "withdraw" the prohibited export subsidies.

---

17 *Ibid.*, para. 2.5.

18 *Ibid.*, para. 2.6.

19 *Ibid.*

20 Panel Report, *Brazil - Aircraft (Article 21.5 - Canada), supra*, footnote 1, para. 2.6.

2. *Are Export Subsidies under PROEX "Permitted" under Item (k) of the Illustrative List?*

15. Brazil argues that subsidies under the revised PROEX are "permitted" under item (k) of the Illustrative List of Export Subsidies in Annex I of the *SCM Agreement* (the "Illustrative List"). Brazil argues that the Article 21.5 Panel erred in concluding that the first paragraph of item (k) may not be interpreted "*a contrario*" to establish that a subsidy is "permitted". According to Brazil, if subsidies of the type defined in the first paragraph of item (k) are "used to secure a material advantage in the field of export credit terms", they constitute prohibited export subsidies. If, by contrast, they are not "used to secure a material advantage in the field of export credit terms", then they do not constitute prohibited export subsidies under the *SCM Agreement*.

16. Brazil considers that the Article 21.5 Panel erred in concluding that the "material advantage" clause in the first paragraph of item (k) cannot be used to establish that an export subsidy is "permitted". The Article 21.5 Panel's reliance on footnote 5 of the *SCM Agreement* ignores the ordinary meaning of the text of item (k). The Article 21.5 Panel should have interpreted the "material advantage" clause "*a contrario*" and concluded that a payment that is *not* "used to secure a material advantage" is *not prohibited* under the *SCM Agreement*; in other words, that such a subsidy is "permitted".

17. Brazil notes that the first paragraph of item (k) applies, *inter alia*, to the "payment [by governments] of all or part of the costs incurred by exporters or financial institutions in obtaining credits". Brazil contends that the Article 21.5 Panel erred in concluding that PROEX payments are not "payments" within the meaning of the first paragraph of item (k). According to Brazil, the Article 21.5 Panel made two errors on this issue. The terms of the first paragraph of item (k) should not be interpreted narrowly so that financial institutions are not considered to incur costs in obtaining export credits. The fact that an exporter or a financial institution *provides* credits does not mean that it does not *obtain* them at a cost. Furthermore, the Article 21.5 Panel failed to distinguish between situations in which the lender is a financial institution *outside* Brazil and situations in which the lender is a financial institution *inside* Brazil.

18. According to Brazil, the Article 21.5 Panel erred in its conclusion that Brazil failed to demonstrate that PROEX subsidies are not "used to secure a material advantage in the field of export credit terms." In particular, the Article 21.5 Panel incorrectly held that an interest rate that results from a government guarantee, which Brazil submitted as evidence of the market for export credits, can never be a "commercial" rate. This conclusion is contradicted by the undisputed evidence in the Article 21.5 Panel record that rates supported by government guarantees are very much a part of the market. Neither the Article 21.5 Panel nor Canada pointed to any evidence of any commercial aircraft export financing not supported in some way by a government. The Article 21.5 Panel should have found that the term "commercial" for the purposes of assessing material advantage means any market rate that is not inconsistent with the *SCM Agreement*. The Article 21.5 Panel also erred by concluding that floating rate transactions were not relevant to an evaluation of the question of whether PROEX was "used to secure a material advantage in the field of export credit terms."

19. Furthermore, Brazil states, the Article 21.5 Panel erred in placing on Brazil the burden of proving that its measure implements the recommendations and rulings of the DSB, rather than placing on Canada the burden of proving that the measure does not implement them. The Article 21.5 Panel's reversal of the burden of proof was contrary to the holding of the Appellate Body in *Chile - Taxes on Alcoholic Beverages* ("*Chile - Alcoholic Beverages*")[21], which attaches a presumption of compliance to the measures taken by Members to implement DSB recommendations and rulings. Finally, Brazil argues that the Article 21.5 Panel applied an erroneous presumption of correctness to unsupported statements made by Canada regarding interest rates actually applied by Canada.

B. Arguments by Appellee - Canada

1. Issuance of NTN-I Bonds Pursuant to Letters of Commitment Issued before 18 November 1999

20. According to Canada, it is undisputed that Brazil took no steps to modify pre-existing PROEX letters of commitment pertaining to aircraft exported after 18 November 1999, and that Brazil continues to issue NTN-I bonds to provide interest equalization payments on aircraft exported after 18 November 1999 pursuant to the terms and conditions in letters of commitment issued before that date. The Article 21.5 Panel was consequently correct in finding that Brazil has failed to "withdraw" the prohibited export subsidies, as it continues to "grant" these subsidies. Whatever else "withdraw" may mean, at a minimum it must encompass ceasing to "grant or maintain" prohibited subsidies under Article 3.2 of the *SCM Agreement*, as Brazil continues to do.

21. Contrary to Brazil's assertion, Canada argues that the plain language and the structure of the *SCM Agreement* supports the Article 21.5 Panel's conclusion that the issue of whether a subsidy "exists" is legally distinct from the issue of when a subsidy is "granted" for the purpose of Article 3.2, and that PROEX subsidies are "granted" at the time the NTN-I bonds are issued. Moreover, as the Article 21.5 Panel observed, acceptance of Brazil's claim would permit a WTO Member, up to the final day of the implementation period, to contract to "grant" prohibited subsidies for years into the future and be insulated from any meaningful remedy under the WTO dispute settlement system.

2. Are Export Subsidies under PROEX "Permitted" under Item (k) of the Illustrative List?

22. Canada argues that the Article 21.5 Panel was correct in its finding that PROEX subsidies are not "permitted" under item (k) of the Illustrative List. Canada refers to Brazil's argument that the Article 21.5 Panel erred in concluding that the language in the first paragraph of item (k) cannot be used to establish that a subsidy which is contingent upon export performance within the meaning of Article 3.1(a) is

---

[21] Appellate Body Report, *Chile - Taxes on Alcoholic Beverages* ("*Chile - Alcoholic Beverages*"), WT/DS87/AB/R, WT/DS110/AB/R, adopted 12 January 2000, DSR 2000:I, 281, para. 74.

"permitted". Canada notes that this argument is at the core of Brazil's claim that the revised PROEX is in compliance with the *SCM Agreement*.

23. Canada submits that the Article 21.5 Panel correctly determined that the first paragraph of item (k) does not create such an "*a contrario*" exception. While Brazil urges that the Article 21.5 Panel should have looked only to the language of item (k) itself, Canada argues that the Article 21.5 Panel rightly began by interpreting the text of Article 3 and footnote 5 of the *SCM Agreement*, which contain the prohibition on, and the parameters of any exception to, the prohibition on export subsidies. In particular, the Article 21.5 Panel determined that, in its ordinary meaning, footnote 5 provides a textual basis for deciding when the Illustrative List can be used to demonstrate that a practice included in the Illustrative List is not a prohibited export subsidy. The Article 21.5 Panel correctly determined that only the provisions of the Illustrative List that affirmatively state that a practice is not an export subsidy fall within the scope of footnote 5, when read in conformity with its ordinary meaning. The first paragraph of item (k) does not contain such an affirmative statement. Therefore, in Canada's view, it does not create an exception to the prohibition in Article 3.

24. Canada notes that Brazil alleges the Article 21.5 Panel erred in concluding that PROEX payments are not "payments" within the meaning of the first paragraph of item (k) of the Illustrative List. Brazil disagrees with the Article 21.5 Panel's factual conclusion that financing institutions involved in financing PROEX-supported transactions that provide export credits cannot be seen as *obtaining* such credits. According to Canada, however, the Article 21.5 Panel's conclusion follows from the ordinary meaning of the text of item (k) as applied to PROEX payments, which, as found in the original proceedings, are made to reduce interest rates below market rates rather than to reimburse borrowing costs.

25. Canada also submits that the Article 21.5 Panel was not convinced, as argued by Brazil, that PROEX payments serve to reimburse costs incurred by financing institutions in obtaining credits. It found as an undisputed fact that the financial institutions receiving PROEX payments are in many cases leading international institutions which do not incur the additional costs faced by Brazilian financial institutions. Moreover, both the Article 21.5 Panel and the Appellate Body in the original proceedings had concluded that PROEX payments are payments to reduce the interest rate paid by purchasers of the aircraft. Canada argues that PROEX payments, in this context, do nothing to reduce the cost of obtaining credits for Brazilian financing institutions.

26. According to Canada, Brazil's claim, that the Article 21.5 Panel erred in several respects in finding that payments under the revised PROEX are "used to secure a material advantage to the field of export credit terms" is unfounded. In light of the Appellate Body's earlier analysis of "material advantage", the Article 21.5 Panel's task was to measure PROEX supported interest rates in relation to *commercial* rates that might be available in the marketplace. The Article 21.5 Panel's refusal to consider a transaction supported by a loan guarantee provided by the Export-Import Bank of the United States as evidence of such commercial interest rates was correct because, by its very nature, a government-guaranteed loan cannot be considered to be made at a commercial rate.

27. In addition, the Article 21.5 Panel correctly determined that, in the circumstances of this case, floating rate transactions were not relevant as evidence of the market for fixed interest rates. According to Canada, Brazil could not explain what

minimum rate it would apply if it provided PROEX payments in support of floating interest rates. In these circumstances, the Article 21.5 Panel had no choice but to disregard the floating rate transaction example provided by Brazil.

28. Furthermore, contrary to Brazil's allegation, the Article 21.5 Panel appropriately allocated the burden of proof at every stage of the proceeding. Brazil's argument completely mischaracterizes the finding of the Appellate Body in *Chile - Alcoholic Beverages*. The issue here has nothing to do with Brazil's previous measures or with presuming that Brazil is acting in bad faith, but rather with its failure to meet the burden of proof on an "affirmative defence". It was for Brazil to demonstrate that the market provided interest rates at the level of those resulting from the application of PROEX payments. Brazil did not prove that such rates exist.

C. Arguments of the Third Participants

1. European Communities

29. The European Communities begins its submission with comments on the agreement reached between Brazil and Canada, in this dispute, on, *inter alia*, the conduct of the procedure under Article 21.5 of the DSU. Although the European Communities accepts that parties may make agreements relating to procedural issues in dispute settlement proceedings, such agreements may not, in its view, affect the rights of third parties. The European Communities is concerned that, in certain disputes under Article 21.5, parties have agreed bilaterally to dispense with formal consultations under Article 4 of the DSU. The European Communities considers this to be inconsistent with the DSU and to prejudice third party rights. The European Communities recognizes that this issue was not raised before the Article 21.5 Panel and is not the subject of an appeal. However, the European Communities considers that it would be useful to all Members to have a ruling on this issue and would appreciate a statement from the Appellate Body to the effect that "the parties to a dispute may not enter into agreements regarding the conduct of dispute settlement proceedings that prejudice the rights and interests of other Members, in particular to participate as third parties." [22]

(a) Issuance of NTN-I Bonds Pursuant to Letters of Commitment Issued before 18 November 1999

30. According to the European Communities, the Article 21.5 Panel's finding that Brazil has not withdrawn PROEX subsidies made pursuant to letters of commitment issued before 18 November 1999 was correct, as Brazil continues to "grant" those subsidies within the meaning of Article 3.2 of the *SCM Agreement*. The subsidies are "granted" for the purposes of Article 3.2 when the NTN-I bonds are issued, rather than when the letters of commitment are issued. When the subsidy "exists" under Article 1 is not relevant to this issue.

[22] European Communities' third participant's submission, para. 15.

(c) Are Export Subsidies under PROEX "Permitted" under Item (k) of the Illustrative List?

31. The European Communities agrees with the Article 21.5 Panel's finding that the relationship between the prohibition contained in Article 3.1(a) of the *SCM Agreement* and the Illustrative List is governed exclusively by footnote 5. The interpretation "*a contrario*" of items in the Illustrative List, even in the qualified manner proposed by the United States, would read footnote 5 out of the *SCM Agreement*. Moreover, Brazil does not explain why the drafters would have restricted the scope of footnote 5 to only some of the measures in the Illustrative List.

32. The European Communities agrees with the Article 21.5 Panel's finding that a Member may demonstrate through positive evidence that a net interest rate below the relevant Commercial Interest Reference Rate ("CIRR") established by the *Arrangement on Guidelines for Officially Supported Export Credits* (the "*OECD Arrangement*") is not "used to secure a material advantage in the field of export credit terms". The European Communities considers, nevertheless, that the Article 21.5 Panel failed to formulate and apply the appropriate benchmark in order to assess whether an interest rate below the CIRR secures a "material advantage". According to the Article 21.5 Panel, the relevant benchmark would be the "minimum commercial interest rate" available in the marketplace, which the Article 21.5 Panel considered to exclude any officially supported rates. In the European Communities' view, the appropriate benchmarks are the interest rates available in the marketplace, irrespective of whether those interest rates are officially supported.

33. However, the European Communities agrees with the Article 21.5 Panel's conclusion that Brazil did not meet its burden of proving that the benchmark that it established, the 10-year United States Treasury Bond rate plus a spread of 20 basis points, is appropriate. The example provided by Brazil of a floating rate transaction guaranteed by the Export-Import Bank of the United States did not constitute, as rightly concluded by the Article 21.5 Panel, relevant evidence, since floating rates are not directly comparable to fixed rates.

2. *United States*

(a) Issuance of NTN-I Bonds Pursuant to Letters of Commitment Issued before 18 November 1999

34. The United States submits that in the context of this case, the Article 21.5 Panel's conclusion, that the continued issuance of NTN-I bonds pursuant to letters of commitment issued before 18 November 1999 is not consistent with the recommendation of the DSB to "withdraw" the subsidies pursuant to Article 4.7 of the *SCM Agreement*, was correct. Therefore, the United States believes that the Appellate Body should affirm the Article 21.5 Panel's ultimate conclusion. The United States notes, however, that it considers that the issue of when the subsidy "exists" under Article I of the *SCM Agreement* is not relevant to the question of Brazil's obligation to "withdraw" the subsidies found to be prohibited and to refrain from "granting" or "maintaining" such subsidies.

(b) Are Export Subsidies under PROEX "Permitted" under Item (k) of the Illustrative List?

35. As argued during previous stages of this dispute, the United States considers that the Appellate Body should reverse the Article 21.5 Panel's interpretation regarding the "*a contrario*" issue. The United States refers to its prior arguments on this issue. In addition, the United States disagrees with the following statement of the Article 21.5 Panel: "We agree with Brazil that the *SCM Agreement* should not be interpreted in a manner that provides special and *less* favourable treatment for developing country Members in the field of export credit terms if the text of the Agreement permits of an alternative interpretation."[23] The United States submits that there is no basis for employing this consideration as a method of interpretation.

36. The United States then argues that Brazil is incorrect when it argues that any rate offered by a commercial bank which is supported by a government-supplied loan guarantee that is consistent with the *SCM Agreement* is a "commercial" rate. In the view of the United States, the fact that a government-supplied loan guarantee is consistent with item (j) of the Illustrative List does not mean that the financing that is being guaranteed is "commercial". It simply means that the transaction does not constitute a prohibited export subsidy.

37. Furthermore, the Article 21.5 Panel erred by imposing on Brazil the burden of proving that PROEX, as revised, is not "used to secure a material advantage in the field of export credit terms." The United States considers that neither item (k) nor any other of the items in the Illustrative List constitutes an "affirmative defence." Instead, item (k) describes the legal standard that Canada, as the complainant, must demonstrate that Brazil has violated.

IV. ISSUES RAISED IN THIS APPEAL

38. The following issues are raised in this appeal:

(a) whether the continued issuance of NTN-I bonds, pursuant to letters of commitment issued before 18 November 1999, under the terms and conditions of PROEX as it existed before it was revised, is consistent with the recommendation of the DSB, made pursuant to Article 4.7 of the *SCM Agreement*, to withdraw the measures found to be prohibited export subsidies inconsistent with Article 3.1(a) of the *SCM Agreement*; and

(b) whether payments made under PROEX, as revised by Brazil, are "permitted" under Item (k) of the Illustrative List of Export Subsidies in Annex I of the *SCM Agreement* (the "Illustrative List").

[23] Panel Report, *Brazil - Aircraft (Article 21.5 - Canada), supra*, footnote 1, para. 6.47.

V. ISSUANCE OF NTN-I BONDS PURSUANT TO LETTERS OF COMMITMENT ISSUED BEFORE 18 NOVEMBER 1999

39. Canada's complaint, on this issue, is limited to the claim that Brazil has failed to "withdraw" the prohibited export subsidies under PROEX that were found by the original panel to be inconsistent with Article 3.1(a) of the *SCM Agreement*. Canada alleges that Brazil has continued, *after* the 90-day period of implementation which ended on 18 November 1999, to issue NTN-I bonds, pursuant to letters of commitment issued *before* 18 November 1999, on the basis of the terms and conditions of PROEX as that programme existed before Brazil revised it.

40. The Article 21.5 Panel found that the continued issuance of NTN-I bonds, pursuant to letters of commitment issued *before* 18 November 1999, represents the "grant" of subsidies contingent upon export performance inconsistent with the provisions of Article 3.2 of the *SCM Agreement*. The Article 21.5 Panel noted the finding by the original panel that export subsidies under PROEX are "granted", within the meaning of Article 27.4 of the *SCM Agreement*, when the NTN-I bonds are issued, and also noted that the Appellate Body had confirmed this finding.[24] In the Article 21.5 Panel's view, there was no basis on which to attribute a different meaning to the term "grant" in Article 3.2 of the *SCM Agreement* than that attributed to the word "grant" in Article 27.4 of that Agreement. Therefore, the Article 21.5 Panel reasoned that the issuance of NTN-I bonds by Brazil constitutes the "grant" of prohibited export subsidies within the meaning of Article 3.2.[25] Accordingly, the Article 21.5 Panel concluded that by continuing to "grant" prohibited export subsidies through the continued issuance of NTN-I bonds, Brazil has failed to implement the recommendation of the DSB that it "withdraw" these export subsidies for regional aircraft under PROEX within 90 days, that is, by 18 November 1999.[26]

41. On appeal, Brazil argues that the Article 21.5 Panel erred in finding that the continued issuance of NTN-I bonds, pursuant to letters of commitment issued *before* 18 November 1999, represents the "grant" of subsidies contingent upon export performance. Brazil argues that the *issuance* of the NTN-I bonds does not involve the "grant" of "PROEX subsidies", because "PROEX subsidies" are "granted" at an earlier stage. Brazil contends that "PROEX subsidies are granted when the Government of Brazil makes a financial contribution 'and a benefit is thereby conferred'"[27]; that is, the subsidies are "granted" when they are deemed to "exist" under Article 1. According to Brazil, "this occurs when a letter of commitment is issued and the transaction is finalized by a contract made pursuant to that commitment."[28] As a result, Brazil maintains that the continued issuance of NTN-I bonds after 18 November 1999, pursuant to these "previous PROEX commitments"[29], does not involve the "granting" of prohibited export subsidies which it is obliged to "withdraw".

---

24 Panel Report, *Brazil - Aircraft (Article 21.5 - Canada)*, *supra*, footnote 1, para. 6.10.
25 *Ibid.*, para. 6.11.
26 Panel Report, *Brazil - Aircraft (Article 21.5 - Canada)*, *supra*, footnote 1, para. 6.17.
27 Brazil's appellant's submission, para. 18.
28 *Ibid.*
29 *Ibid.*, p. 4, Heading III.

42. We recall the conclusion of the original panel that "payments on exports of regional aircraft under the PROEX interest rate equalization scheme are export subsidies inconsistent with Article 3 of the SCM Agreement".[30] On appeal, we upheld this conclusion of the original panel.[31] As a result, the DSB recommended that Brazil withdraw the prohibited export subsidies under PROEX within 90 days, that is, by 18 November 1999.

43. With respect to letters of commitment issued before 18 November 1999, Canada's complaint is limited to its allegation that Brazil has failed to "withdraw" the measure found to involve prohibited export subsidies because Brazil has continued to issue NTN-I bonds, *after* 18 November 1999.[32] We are not asked, in our examination of this issue, to address any other aspect of Brazil's obligation to "withdraw" the measures found to be prohibited export subsidies pursuant to the recommendation of the DSB.

44. We do not believe that Brazil's arguments about when a subsidy is deemed to "exist" under Article 1.1 of the *SCM Agreement*, and when it is "granted" under Article 3.2 of that Agreement, are relevant to our inquiry into the issue before us. The export subsidies under PROEX that are at issue in this appeal were found, by the original panel and by us, to be prohibited export subsidies inconsistent with Article 3.1(a) of the *SCM Agreement*. The existence of a "subsidy" was not contested by Brazil in the proceedings before the original panel[33]; and Brazil also conceded before the original panel that subsidies under PROEX were export contingent.[34] The only issue before us now is whether the continued issuance of NTN-I bonds by Brazil *after* 18 November 1999, pursuant to letters of commitment issued *before* 18 November 1999, is consistent with the recommendation of the DSB to "withdraw" the prohibited export subsidies within 90 days.

45. Turning to the ordinary meaning of "withdraw", we observe first that this word has been defined as "remove" or "take away"[35], and as "to take away what has been enjoyed; to take from."[36] This definition suggests that "withdrawal" of a subsidy, under Article 4.7 of the *SCM Agreement*, refers to the "removal" or "taking away" of that subsidy. We observe also that Brazil concedes that it has taken *no action* to implement the recommendation of the DSB with respect to transactions relating to NTN-I bonds issued pursuant to letters of commitment issued before 18 November 1999.[37] In this respect, the Article 21.5 Panel stated that "Brazil does not deny that it continues to issue NTN-I bonds in respect of commitments made prior to 18 November 1999."[38] Thus, NTN-I bonds continue to be issued, after 18 November 1999, on precisely the same terms and conditions as they were before. These bonds, in essence, represent disbursements made under PROEX. The financing institution

[30] Original panel report, *Brazil - Aircraft, supra*, footnote 2, para. 8.2.

[31] Appellate Body Report, *Brazil - Aircraft, supra*, footnote 2, para. 197.

[32] *Supra*, para. 39.

[33] Original panel report, *Brazil - Aircraft, supra*, footnote 2, para. 7.12.

[34] *Ibid.*

[35] *Concise Oxford English Dictionary* (Clarendon Press, 1995), p. 1609.

[36] *Black's Law Dictionary* (West Publishing, 1990), p. 1602.

[37] Panel Report, *Brazil - Aircraft (Article 21.5 - Canada), supra*, footnote 1, para. 6.7.

[38] *Ibid.*

can choose either to sell the bonds in the market or simply receive payments as they become due.[39] Thus, Brazil is continuing to make payments, after 18 November 1999, under a subsidy programme found to involve prohibited export subsidies inconsistent with Article 3.1(a) of the *SCM Agreement*, namely the PROEX programme as previously constituted. In our view, to continue to make payments under an export subsidy measure found to be prohibited is not consistent with the obligation to "withdraw" prohibited export subsidies, in the sense of "removing" or "taking away". Thus, we find that the recommendation of the DSB requires Brazil to stop issuing NTN-I bonds as from 18 November 1999 pursuant to letters of commitment issued before 18 November 1999.[40]

46. We note Brazil's argument before the Article 21.5 Panel that Brazil has a contractual obligation under domestic law to issue PROEX bonds pursuant to commitments that have already been made, and that Brazil could be liable for damages for breach of contract under Brazilian law if it failed to respect its contractual obligations.[41] In response to a question from us at the oral hearing, however, Brazil conceded that a WTO Member's domestic law does not excuse that Member from fulfilling its international obligations. Like the Article 21.5 Panel,[42] we do not consider that any private contractual obligations, which Brazil may have under its domestic law, are relevant to the issue of whether the DSB's recommendation to "withdraw" the prohibited export subsidies permits the continued issuance of NTN-I bonds under letters of commitment issued before 18 November 1999.

47. For all these reasons, we uphold the Article 21.5 Panel's conclusion that Brazil has failed to implement the recommendation of the DSB that it withdraw the export subsidies on sales of regional aircraft under PROEX pursuant to letters of commitment issued before 18 November 1999.

VI. ARE EXPORT SUBSIDIES UNDER PROEX "PERMITTED" UNDER ITEM (K) OF THE ILLUSTRATIVE LIST?

A. *Introduction*

48. The original panel found that export subsidies under PROEX are prohibited under Article 3.1(a) of the *SCM Agreement*, and we upheld this finding. The DSB recommended that Brazil "withdraw" these prohibited subsidies, pursuant to Article 4.7 of the *SCM Agreement*, by 18 November 1999. Brazil elected to implement the recommendation of the DSB by revising PROEX. Canada claims, in this aspect of these Article 21.5 proceedings, that Brazil has not "withdrawn" the prohibited export subsidies, as recommended by the DSB, because the revised PROEX is not consis-

39 See, *supra*, para. 12.

40 We recall that, in para. 18 of its appellant's submission, Brazil referred to the "finalization" of the contract made pursuant to a letter of commitment, as well as to the issuance of the letter of commitment itself (see, *supra*, para. 41). We note that our conclusion, in para. 45, is based on the date when the NTN-I bonds are issued, and not on the date when the letter of commitment is issued or when the contract is "finalized". For our reasoning, it is not relevant whether the letter of commitment was or was not "finalized" by a contract signed before 18 November 1999.

41 Panel Report, *Brazil - Aircraft (Article 21.5 - Canada)*, *supra*, footnote 1, para. 6.16.

42 *Ibid*.

tent with Brazil's obligations under Article 3.1(a) of the *SCM Agreement.*[43] Brazil maintains, in response, that the revised PROEX is justified by item (k) of the Illustrative List.[44]

49. The original panel found, and Brazil did not contest, that PROEX involves "subsidies" within the meaning of Article 1 of the *SCM Agreement* that are "contingent upon export performance" within the meaning of Article 3.1(a) of that Agreement.[45] The Article 21.5 Panel noted that Brazil did not suggest that the modifications Brazil has since made to PROEX mean that the revised PROEX does not involve export subsidies under Article 3.1(a).[46] Rather, Brazil maintains in these Article 21.5 proceedings that the export subsidies under the revised PROEX are justified by item (k) of the Illustrative List.[47] In this respect, the Article 21.5 Panel also stated that Brazil acknowledged that it is asserting, through its reliance on item (k), an alleged "affirmative defence", and that, therefore, the burden of establishing entitlement to that "defence" is on Brazil.[48]

50. To determine whether Brazil was entitled to the benefit of such a "defence", the Article 21.5 Panel considered the following issues. First, the Article 21.5 Panel stated that Brazil's "defence" depends upon the proposition that the first paragraph of item (k) may be used to establish that an export subsidy within the meaning of item (k) is "permitted" by the *SCM Agreement.* Then, the Article 21.5 Panel stated that Brazil's "defence" depends upon Brazil establishing: (a) that PROEX payments are "the payment by [governments] of all or part of the costs incurred by exporters or financial institutions in obtaining credits" within the meaning of the first paragraph of item (k); and (b) that PROEX payments are not "used to secure a material advantage in the field of export credit terms."[49]

51. The Article 21.5 Panel stated that Brazil's argument "depends upon" Brazil succeeding in its legal and factual arguments on *all three of these issues.*[50] Thus, if Brazil had failed to meet its burden of proof on *any one* of these issues, the Article 21.5 Panel could have rejected Brazil's argument on that basis alone. The Article 21.5 Panel stated that "[i]n this Article 21.5 dispute, however, we have decided to address all three elements of Brazil's defence. In our view, this more comprehensive approach will provide a greater degree of clarity and guidance to the parties in respect of implementation."[51] The Article 21.5 Panel, therefore, examined each of these three issues, and subsequently found that Brazil had not met its burden of proof on any of them. Consequently, the Panel concluded that the revised PROEX was not justified by item (k), and that, therefore, Brazil had not implemented the recommendation of the DSB that it "withdraw" its export subsidies under PROEX within 90 days.

---

43 Panel Report, *Brazil - Aircraft (Article 21.5 - Canada), supra,* footnote 1, para. 6.3.
44 *Ibid.*
45 Original Panel Report, *Brazil - Aircraft, supra,* footnote 2, paras. 7.12 and 7.15.
46 Panel Report, Brazil - Aircraft *(Article 21.5 - Canada), supra,* footnote 1, para. 6.21.
47 *Ibid.*, para. 6.22.
48 *Ibid.*
49 *Ibid.*
50 *Ibid.*
51 Panel Report, *Brazil - Aircraft (Article 21.5 - Canada), supra,* footnote 1, para. 6.23.

52. Having stated the Article 21.5 Panel's conclusions, we think it useful to summarize the Article 21.5 Panel's reasoning on each of these three issues.

53. As we have noted, the first issue is whether the first paragraph of item (k) of the Illustrative List may be interpreted such that payments *not* "used to secure a material advantage in the field of export credit terms" are "permitted" under the *SCM Agreement.* In examining this issue, the Article 21.5 Panel emphasized the importance of footnote 5 to Article 3.1(a). Footnote 5 provides that: "Measures *referred to in Annex I as not constituting export subsidies* shall not be prohibited under this or any other provision of this Agreement." (emphasis added) The Article 21.5 Panel said that: "In its ordinary meaning, footnote 5 relates to situations where a measure is referred to as *not* constituting an export subsidy."[52] The Article 21.5 Panel found that:

> The first paragraph of item (k) ... does not contain any affirmative statement that a measure is *not* an export subsidy nor that measures not satisfying the conditions of that item are *not* prohibited. To the contrary, the first paragraph of item (k) on its face simply identifies measures that *are* prohibited export subsidies. Thus, the first paragraph of item (k) on its face does not in our view fall within the scope of footnote 5 read in conformity with its ordinary meaning.[53]

The Article 21.5 Panel concluded that the first paragraph of item (k) cannot be used to establish that a subsidy which is contingent upon export performance within the meaning of Article 3.1(a) is "permitted".[54]

54. The second issue considered by the Article 21.5 Panel was whether export subsidies under the revised PROEX constitute the "payment" by Brazil "of all or part of the costs incurred by exporters or financial institutions in obtaining credits" within the meaning of the first paragraph of item (k). The Article 21.5 Panel found as follows:

> While the financial institutions involved in financing PROEX-supported transactions certainly *provide* export credits, they cannot be seen as *obtaining* such credits. ... In short, we do not agree that payments to a lender that amount to interest rate support can reasonably be understood to be payments of all or part of the costs of obtaining export credits.[55]

55. The third issue considered by the Article 21.5 Panel was whether export subsidies under the revised PROEX are "used to secure a material advantage in the field of export credit terms" within the meaning of the first paragraph of item (k) of the Illustrative List. The Article 21.5 Panel said that:

> ... a Member may under the first paragraph of item (k) as interpreted by the Appellate Body establish that a payment was not used to secure a material advantage in the field of export credit terms, even if it resulted in a below-CIRR interest rate, if it could establish that the net

---

52 *Ibid.*, para. 6.36.

53 *Ibid.*, para. 6.37.

54 *Ibid.*, para. 6.67. The Article 21.5 Panel repeated this conclusion in para. 6.106(ii).

55 Panel Report, *Brazil - Aircraft (Article 21.5 - Canada), supra*, footnote 1, para. 6.72.

interest rate resulting from the payment was not lower than the minimum *commercial* interest rate in respect of that currency.[56]

56. In its reasoning on this third issue, the Article 21.5 Panel considered evidence presented by Brazil in support of its argument.[57] The Panel examined the evidence and concluded "that Brazil has failed to demonstrate that PROEX payments are not 'used to secure a material advantage in the field of export credit terms' within the meaning of the first paragraph of item (k)."[58]

57. On appeal, Brazil argues that the Article 21.5 Panel erred in its findings on all three of these issues, and erred also in its finding that the burden of proof under item (k) is on Brazil. First, with regard to whether the first paragraph of item (k) may be used as a basis for arguing that certain export subsidies are "permitted", Brazil submits that the Article 21.5 Panel's reliance on footnote 5 was misplaced. Brazil emphasizes, first of all, that its argument that subsidies under the revised PROEX are "permitted" was not based on footnote 5 but rather on an "*a contrario*" interpretation of the text of the first paragraph of item (k).[59] Second, Brazil argues that the Article 21.5 Panel erred in its finding that Brazil failed to demonstrate that subsidies under the revised PROEX are the "payment" by governments "of all or part of the costs incurred by exporters or financial institutions in obtaining credits" within the meaning of the first paragraph of item (k).[60] And, third, Brazil argues that the Article 21.5 Panel erred in finding that Brazil failed to demonstrate that subsidies under the revised PROEX are *not* "used to secure a material advantage in the field of export credit terms." On this third issue, Brazil asserts that the Article 21.5 Panel erred in concluding that a net interest rate that "results from a government guarantee" is not a "commercial" rate.[61] On this issue, in addition, Brazil argues that the Article 21.5 Panel erred in rejecting evidence of a floating rate transaction as irrelevant to a fixed rate transaction.[62] Furthermore, Brazil submits that the Article 21.5 Panel reversed the burden of proof by requiring Brazil to demonstrate that subsidies under the revised PROEX are *not* "used to secure a material advantage in the field of export credit terms."[63]

58. Having stated the Article 21.5 Panel's conclusions, having summarized the Article 21.5 Panel's reasoning in reaching those conclusions, and having summarized Brazil's arguments on appeal with respect to those conclusions, we turn now to our own analysis of these three issues. We note at the outset that we agree with the Article 21.5 Panel that in order for Brazil to establish its alleged "affirmative defence", Brazil must succeed in its legal and factual arguments on *each* of the three issues examined by the Article 21.5 Panel. Thus, if Brazil is unsuccessful in proving *any one* of these three issues, Brazil's alleged "affirmative defence" under item (k) fails. With this in mind, we begin our analysis by addressing the last issue dealt with by the

56 *Ibid.*, para. 6.92.
57 *Ibid.*, paras. 6.94-6.105.
58 *Ibid.*, para. 6.106.
59 Brazil's appellant's submission, para. 26.
60 *Ibid.*, paras. 35-48.
61 Brazil's appellant's submission, para. 51.
62 *Ibid.*, para. 58.
63 *Ibid.*, paras. 60-61.

Article 21.5 Panel, that is, whether subsidies under the revised PROEX are "used to secure a material advantage in the field of export credit terms."

B. Are Export Subsidies under PROEX "Used to Secure a Material Advantage in the Field Of Export Credit Terms"?

59. In addressing this issue, we begin by recalling that, in this aspect of its complaint, Canada claims that Brazil has not "withdrawn" the prohibited export subsidies, as required by the DSB recommendation made pursuant to Article 4.7 of the *SCM Agreement*, because the revised PROEX is not consistent with Brazil's obligations under Article 3.1(a) of the *SCM Agreement*. Thus, it follows that this aspect of these Article 21.5 proceedings covers only the measures taken by Brazil for the purpose of "withdrawing" the prohibited export subsidy measure through revising the PROEX programme.

60. The first paragraph of item (k) of the Illustrative List reads as follows:

> The grant by governments (or special institutions controlled by and/or acting under the authority of governments) of export credits at rates below those which they actually have to pay for the funds so employed (or would have to pay if they borrowed on international capital markets in order to obtain funds of the same maturity and other credit terms and denominated in the same currency as the export credit), or *the payment by them of all or part of the costs incurred by exporters or financial institutions in obtaining credits, in so far as they are used to secure a material advantage in the field of export credit terms.* (emphasis added)

61. The first paragraph of item (k) contains examples - illustrations - of certain kinds of export credit practices that constitute prohibited export subsidies under Article 3.1(a) of the *SCM Agreement*. One of these examples, or illustrations, relates to the "payment by [governments] of all or part of the costs incurred by exporters or financial institutions in obtaining credits". Such "payments" are considered to be export subsidies under item (k) "in so far as they are used to secure a material advantage in the field of export credit terms." In our Report in *Brazil - Aircraft*, we examined the meaning of this "material advantage" clause in item (k). We ruled in that Report that the determination of whether a payment is "used to secure a material advantage" calls for a comparison between the export credit terms available under the measure at issue and some other "market benchmark".[64] We stated that "we see the second paragraph of item (k) as useful context for interpreting the 'material advantage' clause in the text of the first paragraph".[65] And, in this respect, we identified the Commercial Interest Reference Rate (the "CIRR"), defined in the *Arrangement on Guidelines for Officially Supported Export Credits* (the "*OECD Arrangement*"), as an "appropriate" "market benchmark" for assessing whether a payment "is used to secure a material advantage".[66] We explained:

---

64 Appellate Body Report, *Brazil - Aircraft*, *supra*, footnote 2, para. 181.

65 *Ibid.*

66 *Ibid.*

> ... the *OECD Arrangement* can be appropriately viewed as *one example* of an international undertaking providing a *specific market benchmark* by which to assess whether payments by governments, coming within the provisions of item (k), are 'used to secure a material advantage in the field of export credit terms'.[67] (emphasis added)

62. We also indicated, in that Report, that the CIRR represents the *minimum* authorized interest rate that can be offered to borrowers in officially-supported export credit transactions under the *OECD Arrangement.*[68] We then noted that:

> The fact that a particular *net* interest rate is below the relevant CIRR is a *positive indication* that the government payment in that case has been 'used to secure a material advantage in the field of export credit terms'.[69] (emphasis added)

63. The Article 21.5 Panel correctly concluded from our Report in *Brazil - Aircraft* that "the CIRR was not intended as the exclusive and immutable benchmark applicable in all cases."[70] The Article 21.5 Panel then stated that:

> ... we consider that a Member may under the first paragraph of item (k) as interpreted by the Appellate Body establish that a payment was not used to secure a material advantage in the field of export credit terms, *even if it resulted in a below-CIRR interest rate, ...*[71] (emphasis added)

64. We agree with this legal interpretation by the Article 21.5 Panel of the "material advantage" clause in item (k). Again, as we said in our Report in *Brazil - Aircraft*, the CIRR is "*one example*" of a "market benchmark" that may be used to determine whether a "payment" is used to "secure a material advantage". (emphasis added) The CIRR is a constructed interest rate for a particular currency, at a particular time, that does not always necessarily reflect the actual state of the credit markets.[72] Where the CIRR does not, in fact, reflect the rates available in the marketplace, we believe that a Member should be able, in principle, to rely on evidence from the marketplace itself in order to establish an alternative "market benchmark", on which it might rely in one or more transactions.[73] Thus, the CIRR is not, necessarily, the *sole* "market benchmark" that may be used to determine whether a payment "is used to secure a material advantage in the field of export credit terms", within the meaning of item (k) of the Illustrative List.

---

[67] *Ibid.*

[68] We note that a participant in the *OECD Arrangement* can always offer borrowers officially-supported export credits if, besides respecting the CIRR, it also respects the other "repayment terms and conditions" of the *OECD Arrangement* (see Introduction, *OECD Arrangement*).

[69] Appellate Body Report, *Brazil - Aircraft, supra*, footnote 2, para. 182.

[70] Panel Report, *Brazil - Aircraft (Article 21.5 - Canada), supra*, footnote 1, para. 6.84.

[71] *Ibid.*, para. 6.92.

[72] The CIRR is constructed on the basis of the rules and principles set out in Articles 15 and 16 of the *OECD Arrangement*.

[73] See, further, *infra*, para. 73. We note that it is not necessary for us to address, in these proceedings, whether transactions involving government intervention, such as government loan guarantees, can provide evidence of an appropriate "market benchmark", *below* the CIRR, to determine whether "payments", under item (k), are "used to secure a material advantage in the field of export credit terms."

65. Before addressing the issue of the application of the "material advantage" clause in this case, though, we must first examine the issue of burden of proof under item (k). The Article 21.5 Panel found that Brazil's argument under item (k) constituted an alleged "affirmative defence" for which Brazil bore the burden of proof.[74] Brazil appeals this finding.[75]

66. We recall that, before the original panel in *Brazil - Aircraft*, Brazil conceded that it had the burden of proof in demonstrating its alleged "defence" under item (k).[76] However, in these Article 21.5 proceedings, Brazil argues that this burden of proof, under item (k), is on Canada.[77] In our view, the fact that the measure at issue was "taken to comply" with the "recommendations and rulings" of the DSB does not alter the allocation of the burden of proving Brazil's "defence" under item (k). In this respect, we note that Brazil concedes that the revised PROEX measure is, in principle, prohibited under Article 3.1(a) of the *SCM Agreement*; yet Brazil asserts nonetheless that the PROEX measure is justified, under the first paragraph of item (k). Thus, in our view, Brazil is, clearly, using item (k) to make an affirmative claim in its defence. In *United States - Measure Affecting Imports of Woven Wool Shirts and Blouses from India*, we said: "It is only reasonable that the burden of establishing [an affirmative] defence should rest on the party asserting it."[78] As it is Brazil that is asserting this "defence" using item (k) in these proceedings, we agree with the Article 21.5 Panel that Brazil has the burden of proving that the revised PROEX is justified under the first paragraph of item (k), including the burden of proving that payments under the revised PROEX are *not* "used to secure a material advantage in the field of export credit terms."

67. To establish that subsidies under the revised PROEX are not "used to secure a material advantage in the field of export credit terms", Brazil must prove *either*: that the net interest rates under the revised PROEX are at or above the relevant CIRR, the specific "market benchmark" we identified in the original dispute as an "appropriate"[79] basis for comparison; *or*, that an alternative "market benchmark", other than the CIRR, is appropriate, and that the net interest rates under the revised PROEX are at or above this alternative "market benchmark".

68. Brazil does not argue that the net interest rates under the revised PROEX are at or above the relevant CIRR. Indeed, Brazil does not contest that the net interest rates under the revised PROEX are normally *below* the relevant CIRR.[80] Instead, Brazil argues that there is an alternative "market benchmark" that is "appropriate", and that the net interest rates under the revised PROEX are at or above this alternative "market benchmark". In Resolution 2667, Brazil identifies the United States Treasury

---

[74] Panel Report, *Brazil - Aircraft (Article 21.5 - Canada), supra*, footnote 1, para. 6.22.

[75] Brazil's appellant's submission, paras. 60-61. Brazil's arguments are summarized, *supra*, at para. 19.

[76] Original panel report, *Brazil - Aircraft, supra*, footnote 2, para. 7.17.

[77] Brazil's appellant's submission, paras. 60-61.

[78] Appellate Body Report, *United States – Measures Affecting Imports of Woven Wool Shirts and Blouses from India*, WT/DS33/AB/R, adopted 23 May 1997, DSR 1997:I, 323 at 335.

[79] Appellate Body Report, *Brazil - Aircraft, supra*, footnote 2, para. 181.

[80] Response of Brazil to Question 1 of the Article 21.5 Panel (Article 21.5 Panel Report, p. 133). We note that on 12 July 2000, the CIRR for export credit transactions of greater than eight and one half years involving U.S. dollars was 7.69 per cent, whereas the 10-year United States Treasury Bond rate plus 20 basis points was 6.29 per cent.

Bond rate plus 20 basis points (0.2 per cent) as the "appropriate" "market benchmark".[81] Before the Article 21.5 Panel, Brazil argued that the enactment of Resolution 2667:

> ... means, effectively ... that no application for PROEX interest equalization support for regional aircraft will be favorably considered unless it reflects a net interest rate to the borrower equal to or more than the 10-year United States Treasury Bond ("T-Bill") plus 0.2 per cent per annum.[82]

Brazil contends, on this basis, that the revised PROEX is *not* "used to secure a material advantage in the field of export credit terms" within the meaning of the first paragraph of item (k) of the Illustrative List.

69. To prove this argument, Brazil must establish *both* of two elements: first, Brazil must prove that it has identified an appropriate "market benchmark"; and, second, Brazil must prove that the net interest rates under the revised PROEX are at or above that benchmark.

70. We consider, first, whether Brazil has established an appropriate "market benchmark", other than the CIRR. In an effort to do so, before the Article 21.5 Panel, Brazil submitted evidence relating to two examples.

71. As its first example, Brazil submitted documentation relating to the terms of an export financing transaction, at a floating interest rate, for large civil aircraft supported by an export credit guarantee from the Export-Import Bank of the United States. Brazil argued before the Article 21.5 Panel that the interest rate for this transaction[83], plus an amount to reflect a one-time guarantee fee Brazil estimated would have been charged by the lender, should be compared to the "minimum" net interest rate for export credits benefiting from payments under the revised PROEX, that is, the 10-year United States Treasury Bond rate plus 20 basis points (or 0.2 per cent). In Brazil's view, the "minimum" net interest rate for PROEX-supported export credits is higher than the net interest rate of that particular Export-Import Bank transaction.[84] In addition, as its second example, Brazil argued that Canada, through the Canadian Export Development Corporation (the "EDC"), has provided export credits for regional aircraft at rates which are below the relevant CIRR.[85]

72. Brazil submitted to the Article 21.5 Panel that, given these two examples, Brazil should also be entitled to support export credits at net interest rates below CIRR, in particular the 10-year United States Treasury Bond rate plus 20 basis points. In this appeal, Brazil contends that the Article 21.5 Panel erred in finding that the evidence of these two examples did not establish an appropriate "market benchmark" for the revised PROEX. It becomes incumbent upon us, therefore, to examine both these examples cited by Brazil.

73. With regard to the first example - the guarantee contract concluded with the Export-Import Bank of the United States - we note that Brazil has presented evidence

---

[81] Panel Report, *Brazil - Aircraft (Article 21.5 - Canada), supra*, footnote 1, para. 6.19.

[82] Brazil's first submission to the Article 21.5 Panel, para. 6 (Article 21.5 Panel Report, p. 102).

[83] LIBOR plus 3 basis points, or 0.03 per cent.

[84] Panel Report, *Brazil - Aircraft (Article 21.5 - Canada), supra*, footnote 1, para. 6.94.

[85] *Ibid.*, para. 6.97; see Response of Canada to Question 4(a) of the Article 21.5 Panel (Panel Report, *Brazil - Aircraft (Article 21.5 - Canada)), supra*, footnote 1, at 82.

relating to one actual export credit transaction of this kind. On the basis of this *single* transaction, Brazil attempted to establish a *generalized* "market benchmark", applicable to *all* export credit transactions, this benchmark being the 10-year United States Treasury Bond rate plus 20 basis points. We note that the terms and conditions of export credit transactions in the marketplace vary considerably, depending on the circumstances of a particular export credit transaction, such as the product involved[86], the size or volume of the transaction, the type of export credit practice, the duration of the repayment term, the type of interest rate (fixed or floating) used, and when the transaction is concluded. In our view, Brazil has not demonstrated that the evidence it submitted, relating to a *single* Export-Import Bank export credit transaction, is sufficient, on its own, to justify the *generalized* "market benchmark" relied on by Brazil in *all* transactions relating to regional aircraft under the revised PROEX.

74. In addition, we also note that there would, in any event, be other difficulties in relying on the Export-Import Bank transaction to establish a "market benchmark" for PROEX. As we have noted, the terms and conditions of export credit transactions in the marketplace vary considerably. In identifying an "appropriate" "market benchmark" below the CIRR, a WTO Member must show that the "benchmark" on which it relies is based on evidence from relevant, comparable transactions in the marketplace. In this respect, we observe that the Export-Import Bank transaction relates to *large civil aircraft*, whereas PROEX payments involve *regional jet aircraft*. Further, the Export-Import Bank transaction involves *floating* interest rate financing, whereas PROEX involves *fixed* interest rate financing. Finally, the Export-Import Bank transaction involves a government *loan guarantee*, rather than the *interest rate equalization payments* made under PROEX.[87] We, therefore, have reservations - on which we need not opine - as to the relevance of the Export-Import Bank transaction, relied upon by Brazil, in attempting to establish a "market benchmark" for PROEX.

75. With respect to the second example - Brazil's assertions relating to EDC financing at below the relevant CIRR - we note that Canada has admitted that EDC financing has sometimes been offered at some, unspecified, interest rate below the relevant CIRR.[88] However, Brazil has provided *no evidence* of any specific transaction in which the EDC has offered financing at rates below the relevant CIRR, nor has Brazil offered any evidence of the specific rate actually offered by the EDC in these transactions. In our view, the admission by Canada that EDC has offered, in certain transactions, an unspecified interest rate *somewhere* below the applicable

---

86 We note that, in these proceedings, we are dealing with regional aircraft. Of course, item (k) applies in the context of export credit transactions involving other goods.

87 We recall that it is not necessary for us to decide, in this case, whether transactions involving government loan guarantees can provide an appropriate "market benchmark", below the CIRR, to determine whether a "payment", under item (k), is "used to secure a material advantage in the field of export credit terms." (*Supra*, para. 64, footnote 73).

88 Canada concedes that there were "instances where certain of EDC's financing transactions were at a rate less than the CIRR applicable on the date the transaction closed." However, Canada claims that with the exception of one Canada Account transaction, the interest rate charged in respect of regional aircraft has been "market-based". According to Canada, this is because the CIRR "lags" behind the market due to the fact that the CIRR is set once a month whereas market rates fluctuate more regularly. (See Response of Canada to Question 4(a) of the Article 21.5 Panel (Panel Report, *Brazil - Aircraft (Article 21.5 - Canada)*, *supra*, footnote 1, at 82-83).)

CIRR does not, in any way, identify an alternative *generalized* "market benchmark" below the CIRR. In short, Canada's admission does not explain why the specific interest rate chosen for the revised PROEX - the United States Treasury Bond 10-year rate, plus 20 basis points (or 0.2 per cent) - should be seen as an appropriate "market benchmark".

76. We, therefore, find that Brazil has not established an appropriate "market benchmark" for the revised PROEX under the "material advantage" clause of the first paragraph of item (k) of the Illustrative List. We said Brazil had to prove *both* that it had identified an appropriate "market benchmark" below the CIRR and that its net interest rates under the revised PROEX are at or above that benchmark.[89] As Brazil has not identified an "appropriate" "market benchmark" below the CIRR, it is not possible to determine whether the net interest rates under the revised PROEX are at or above such a "market benchmark".

77. For these reasons, we agree with the Article 21.5 Panel's conclusion that "Brazil has failed to demonstrate that PROEX payments are not 'used to secure a material advantage in the field of export credit terms' within the meaning of the first paragraph of item (k)" of the Illustrative List.[90]

C. Are Export Subsidies under PROEX "Payments" within the Meaning of the First Paragraph of item (k)?

78. Brazil also appeals the Article 21.5 Panel's finding that export subsidies under the revised PROEX are not "payments" within the meaning of the first paragraph of item (k). We have found that Brazil has failed to establish that export subsidies under the revised PROEX are not "used to secure a material advantage in the field of export credit terms" within the meaning of the first paragraph of item (k). As we noted earlier, in order to establish a justification under item (k), Brazil was required to prove each of the three issues it argued before the Article 21.5 Panel.[91] As Brazil has failed to prove one of the elements necessary to prove that payments made under the revised PROEX are justified by item (k), we do not believe it is necessary to examine the issue of whether export subsidies under the revised PROEX are "the payment [by governments] of all or part of the costs incurred by exporters or financial institutions in obtaining credits" within the meaning of the first paragraph of item (k). Therefore, we do not address the Article 21.5 Panel's findings[92] on this issue. These findings of the Article 21.5 Panel are moot, and, thus, of no legal effect.

---

89 See, *supra*, para 69.

90 Panel Report, *Brazil - Aircraft (Article 21.5 - Canada), supra*, footnote 1, para. 6.106.

91 See, *supra*, para. 58.

92 Panel Report, *Brazil - Aircraft (Article 21.5 - Canada), supra*, footnote 1, para. 6.72.

D. *May the First Paragraph of Item (k) be Interpreted to Establish that an Export Subsidy is "Permitted"?*

79. Brazil also appeals the Article 21.5 Panel's finding that "the first paragraph of item (k) cannot be used to establish that a subsidy which is contingent upon export performance within the meaning of Article 3.1(a) is 'permitted'".[93]

80. If Brazil had demonstrated that the payments made under the revised PROEX were not "used to secure a material advantage in the field of export credit terms", and that such payments were "payments" by Brazil of "all or part of the costs incurred by exporters or financial institutions in obtaining credits", then we would have been prepared to find that the payments made under the revised PROEX are justified under item (k) of the Illustrative List. However, Brazil has not demonstrated that those conditions of item (k) are met in this case. In making this observation, we wish to emphasize that we are not interpreting footnote 5 of the *SCM Agreement*, and we do not opine on the scope of footnote 5, or on the meaning of any other items in the Illustrative List.

81. However, we do not believe it is necessary for us to rule on these general questions in order to resolve this dispute. We, therefore, hold that the Article 21.5 Panel's finding that "the first paragraph of item (k) cannot be used to establish that a subsidy which is contingent upon export performance within the meaning of Article 3.1(a) is 'permitted'"[94] is moot, and, thus, is of no legal effect.

VII. FINDINGS AND CONCLUSIONS

82. For the reasons set out in this Report, the Appellate Body:

(a) upholds the conclusion of the Article 21.5 Panel that as a result of the continued issuance by Brazil of NTN-I bonds, after 18 November 1999, pursuant to letters of commitment issued before 18 November 1999, Brazil has failed to implement the recommendation of the DSB that it withdraw the prohibited export subsidies under PROEX within 90 days; and

(b) upholds the Article 21.5 Panel's findings that payments made under the revised PROEX are prohibited by Article 3 of the *SCM Agreement*, and are not justified under item (k) of the Illustrative List, and therefore upholds the Article 21.5 Panel's conclusion that Brazil has failed to implement the recommendation of the DSB that it withdraw the export subsidies for regional aircraft under PROEX within 90 days.

---

[93] *Ibid.*, para. 6.67. See also, Panel Report, *Brazil - Aircraft (Article 21.5 - Canada)*, *supra*, footnote 1, para. 6.106(ii).

[94] Panel Report, *Brazil - Aircraft (Article 21.5 - Canada)*, *supra*, footnote 1, para. 6.67. See also, Panel Report, *Brazil - Aircraft (Article 21.5 - Canada)*, *supra*, footnote 1, para. 6.106(ii).

9 780521 828543